TREES AND SHRUBS FOR NORTHERN GARDENS

BY DR. LEON C. SNYDER

New and Revised Edition

By Richard T. Isaacson

Bibliographer and Head Librarian

ANDERSEN HORTICULTURAL LIBRARY
UNIVERSITY OF MINNESOTA LIBRARIES
MINNESOTA LANDSCAPE ARBORETUM

The Library has received permission from Mrs. Margaret Nemerov
to quote from her husband's work including the poem *Trees.*

Permission has been granted from the University of Minnesota Press
for use of the drawings from the 1955 edition of
Rosendahl, Carl O. *Trees and Shrubs of the Upper Midwest.*

Cover illus.: *Rhododendron* 'Orchid Lights' & *Cercis canadensis* ' Northern Strain';
'Orchid Lights' azalea and 'Northern Strain' redbud, two Minnesota Landscape Arboretum
introductions. Photo by John Gregor.

Published by Andersen Horticultural Library
Minnesota Landscape Arboretum
3675 Arboretum Drive
Chanhassen MN 55317-0039

Printed in the United States of America on acid-free paper.

ISBN 0-915679-07-8 (paperback)
ISBN 0-915679-08-6 (hardcover)

TREES AND SHRUBS FOR NORTHERN GARDENS

A Minnesota Landscape Arboretum

Guide to Northern Gardening

PHOTOGRAPHS BY JOHN GREGOR

PREFACE

D r. Leon C. Snyder's *Trees and Shrubs for Northern Gardens*, first published in 1980, has become a standard reference to the trees, shrubs and vines that will thrive in North America's horticultural zones of 2 through 4. Gardeners, horticultural students and professional horticulturists have relied on its listings for study, selection and enjoyment.

Dr. Snyder had a distinguished career as educator, Head of the University of Minnesota's Department of Horticultural Science, and was founder and first Director of The Minnesota Landscape Arboretum.

Leon Snyder was born in Shepherd, Michigan in 1908, receiving a B.S. and Ph.D from the University of Washington in Seattle. He joined the University of Minnesota staff as extension horticulturist in 1945. He became Head of the Department of Horticultural Science in 1953 and became the first Director of the Minnesota Landscape Arboretum in 1958. He retired as Head of the Horticultural Science Department in 1970 and as The Arboretum's Director in 1976. He died in 1987.

Dr. Snyder wrote a weekly gardening column for the *Minneapolis Tribune* from 1966 to his death. He wrote five other gardening books: *Gardening in the Upper Midwest* (U. of Minnesota Press, 1978, revised 1985); co-authored *A Minnesota Gardener's Companion* (Minneapolis Tribune, 1981); *How Does Your Garden Grow?* (WCCO, 1982); *Flowers for Northern Gardens* (U. of Minnesota Press, 1983); and *Native Plants for Northern Gardens* (Andersen Horticultural Library/Minnesota Landscape Arboretum, 1991).

He was a true and generous educator, teaching, writing and answering the most trivial to complex horticultural questions over a long career. He and his wife, Vera, counselled and supported many horticultural students at the University. His influence and legacy indeed survive him.

Direct and important assistance has been made in preparing this new edition. Former Governor Elmer L. Andersen and Peter Olin, Director, The Minnesota Landscape Arboretum, helped shepherd this project to fruition. Grants were obtained from the revolving publication fund of Andersen Horticultural Library and The Minnesota Landscape Arboretum.

Maria Klein did the final editing and design of the manuscript. Fred Klein designed the cover and center photographic section. Their work has been done with style and professionalism.

A major contribution has been made by the photographer, John Gregor. Jerry and Lee Shannon generously allowed photographs to be taken of their beautiful landscape.

Peter Moe, Director of Operations at the Minnesota Landscape Arboretum, gave generously of his time and expertise. Mr. Douglas Armato, Director of the University of Minnesota Press, also gave generously of his expertise.

Andersen Horticultural Library staff and volunteers Nancy Allison, Lana Gayevski, Renee Jensen, Shauna Moore, Amy Owen, Evy Sand and Judy Spiegel spent many hours proofing and checking the manuscript. Shauna Moore, of the Andersen Horticultural Library's staff, executed the drawings found in the first chapters. Mark Funk, Ted Pew, Nancy Rose, David Stevenson and Mike Zins of the Minnesota Landscape Arboretum's staff also should be mentioned.

Final acknowledgement is made to the many individuals who established and worked to build the Minnesota Landscape Arborteum and the Andersen Horticultural Library into the renowned and respected institutions that they have become, without which this work would not have been possible.

Richard T. Isaacson, editor

January 2000

CONTENTS

Preface *v*

Introduction **3**

Planning The Landscape **9**

Planting Woody Plants **15**

Maintaining Woody Plants **21**

The Plants **27**

Plant Selection Guide and Photographs **137**

Basic Woody Plant Information **281**

Glossary **287**

Works Cited **293**

Illustration Credits **295**

Bibliography **297**

Index **299**

QUERCUS rubra.

Quercus rubra, red oak. Michaux, André. *Histoire des Chênes de l'Amérique.*
Paris: Crapelet Press, 1801. Engraving after original of P. J. Redouté.

INTRODUCTION

The new and expanded edition of *Trees and Shrubs for Northern Gardens* introduces many new plants to all gardeners looking to add woody plants to their landscape.

A primary objective of this new edition is to make the text easier to read and woody plant information easier to find. The editor developed the special features of this new book from many years of observing readers as they used the first edition. The new edition emphasizes common names, "user-friendly" terminology, and a practical approach. It also features quotations and illustrations from classic horticultural works dating from the 16th century to our own time.

The Character of Woody Plants

Woody plants provide long-term structure to our landscapes. While other plants (bedding plants, annuals, herbaceous perennials) can provide seasonal interest, woody plants offer year-round texture, mass, height, and form. Of course, woody plants also provide seasonal interest with color, fragrance, shade, and the like.

Value-Added Landscapes

At the dawn of the 21st century, it is well-established that woody plants add value to our landscapes. Homeowners seeking to sell their house, or buy a new one, understand that outdoor plantings add greatly to the aesthetic and monetary value of a property. A research update, published in *Grounds Maintenance* of July 1996, cited a U.S. Forest Service study in Chicago which found that there was a return of $2.38 for every dollar spent on trees and their maintenance.

Woody plants help filter the air to produce oxygen and in the process eliminate air-borne pollutants. A 50-percent tree canopy can reduce wind velocity in urban areas by half, compared to areas without trees, saving much on winter fuel bills. Another study conducted in Sacramento, California, found that urban trees could reduce the average summer temperature by 10 percent. Woody plants also intercept enough precipitation from runoff to significantly reduce the need for storm sewers and the possibility of flooding.

The natural world that we appreciate around us—birds, animals, and other plants—relies on woody plants to provide shelter, food and safe habitation.

Sample Plant Entry

Gardeners and plant lovers generally know plants by their common names. Unfortunately, this often creates problems as common names are quixotic, varying dramatically from one person to another and from one region to another. The plants in this book are arranged by scientific name, with common names prominently listed. Readers unfamiliar with scientific plant nomenclature can consult "How Plants Get Their Names" in the chapter on Basic Woody Plant Information.

All parts of the scientific name are given: family, genus, species, subspecies (or variety and form), and cultivars. Hardiness, mature specimen size, plant characteristics (habit, leaves, flower, fruit), landscape use, and plant culture are also featured. Further references include number of species found in a genus and the native habitat of a species.

For genera of plants important in northern landscapes (maples, ash, spiraea, viburnum, etc.), an introductory passage describes a plant's history or culture and its place in the landscape.

Cultivars

Cultivars have become ever more important for landscaping purposes as they are developed for specific site requirements and usages and for particular aesthetic reasons. For this reason, cultivars are emphasized in this second edition; these new crosses are often discussed first in the text.

To cite an example, maples have always been important ornamental and shade trees in the North. Recently, cultivars have been selected from crosses of red, silver and Norway maples. Desired characteristics such as rapid, sturdy growth, good fall color, hardiness, and adaptability to differing site conditions now are found in some of the new maple cultivars, listed on page 32 *before* the species. Additionally, readers will find many attractive, dependable woody plants among the species listed in this text, along with many desirable native plants.

Definitions of Common Terms

Some basic terms must be understood and kept in mind while using this text, among them **hardiness.** Broad hardiness indications—referring primarily to cold hardiness—are given in this text. However, many knowledgable plant people also rely on microclimates which they can develop in their own landscapes. The photographs in this text show hardy woody plants providing protection for many desirable but less hardy specimens. Lee & Jerry Shannon's garden in St. Paul is an excellent example of what can be accomplished. Not only do the evergreen borders provide excellent background and screening from their neighbors, but they also help create more benign microclimates so that less hardy plants can be grown. Further, the evergreen borders help maintain reliable winter snow cover. This

garden's boxwood, wisteria, and perennial gardens can rely on shelter from winds and harsher elements.

Protected location is another term used regularly in this book. It too has to do with microclimates. Exposure to drying winter winds stresses many conifers. Excessive heat and drought prevent many plants from thriving. A protected location provides basic protection from winds and other harsh weather-related factors.

Woody plants grown in containers are an extreme example of an unprotected site and generally do not flourish in the far North. Because of the extreme range of temperatures in the North, container planting is not recommended. Further discussion of hardiness and microclimates can be found in "Planning the Landscape".

Mature growing size should be considered as *average* mature size when grown in a landscape. For example, the Minnesota state tree, *Pinus resinosa* or red pine, can be found towering majestically over our heads in Itasca State Park. However, in most landscape situations it grows to the height we have indicated in this text.

The Minnesota Landscape Arboretum and Andersen Horticultural Library

The Minnesota Landscape Arboretum was established in 1958 as a unit of the University of Minnesota's Department of Horticultural Science. A nationally renowned gardening resource, the Arboretum presents more than 5,000 species and cultivars of plants in natural and landscaped settings throughout its 995 acres. Visitors can see many of the plants described in this book planted in landscape settings. The Arboretum presents a varied education program, from children's to university-level classes. Its research department has introduced many of the ornamental plants discussed in this book.

Andersen Horticultural Library, part of the University of Minnesota Library System, is housed at the Arboretum. One of the most eminent United States horticultural research libraries, it has varied research collections including a special collection of classics of horticulture, botany and natural history. The works cited in this new edition can be found in these collections. In addition, the Library produces many research and horticultural publications, which are used by individuals and institutions throughout the world.

Cited Authors and Illustrations

A feature of this new edition are the many quotations from contemporary horticultural and natural history writers and from classics of the past. The history of plant literature is reflected in quotes ranging from herbals of the sixteenth century to writings of our own time. Be they Henry David Thoreau, Donald Peattie, Charles Sprague Sargent, or Vita Sackville-West, they all shed light on the nature of woody plants.

Ann Zwinger, in her essay "What's a Nice Girl Like Me Doing in a Place Like This?" from *The Nearsighted Naturalist* (1998, 283-85), explains a shared perspective.

> "Natural history writing deals with the basic issues of our existence, reminds us of our vulnerability, freshens our outlook, and never allows us to rest on our laurels because, as every naturalist knows, laurels are prickly to rest on... We write natural history with a deep devotion to this earth and, more than in any other discipline, tend to hang our lives on it... Classical natural history writing is based on three main principles: detailed and precise fieldwork; absolute scientific accuracy; and a graceful literary style that combines both."

Quotations are identified for quick reference. An example of a writer and work quoted in this text is Marion Fry, author of *A Space of One's Own* (1992, 5). 1992 refers to the date of publication, and 5 is the cited page.

The text pages are illustrated with drawings, woodcuts, paintings, and engravings from books in the collections of Andersen Horticultural Library. Many of these volumes are treasured editions housed in the Special Collections of the Library.

They are listed in the "Illustration Credits" at the end of this text. The drawings are used mainly for interest and ornamentation and should not be considered identification tools for specific plants.

Finally, those who love and live with poetry, understand that poets combine disparate associations and can change the way we look at the world. The poem *TREES* by Howard Nemerov, former Poet Laureate of the United States, reflects the way many horticulturists, amateur and professional, regard woody plants. We talk of many practical concerns in this text, but we must also remember that we share our world with these fellow living beings.

> *To be a giant and keep quiet about it,*
> *To stay in one's own place;*
> *To stand for the constant presence of process*
> *And always to seem the same;*
> *To be steady as a rock and always trembling,*
> *Having the hard appearance of death*
> *With the soft, fluent nature of growth,*
> *One's Being deceptively armored,*
> *One's Becoming deceptively vulnerable;*
> *To be so tough, and take the light so well,*
> *Freely providing forbidden knowledge*
> *Of so many things about heaven and earth*
> *For which we should otherwise have no word—*
> *Poems or people are rarely so lovely,*
> *And even when they have great qualities*
> *They tend to tell you rather than exemplify*
> *What they believe themselves to be about,*
> *While from the moving silence of trees,*
> *Whether in storm or calm, in leaf and naked,*
> *Night or day, we draw conclusions of our own,*
> *Sustaining and unnoticed as our breath,*
> *And perilous also—though there has never been*
> *A critical tree—about the nature of things.*

Dessiné par P. J. Redouté.

Gravé par Sellier.

VIBURNUM acerifolium.

Viburnum acerifolium, mapleleaf viburnum. Ventenat, Etienne P. *Choix de Plantes ....*
Paris: Crapelet, 1803-1808. Engraving after drawing of P. J. Redouté.

PLANNING THE LANDSCAPE

Selecting, planting and maintaining woody plants for the landscape are among the most important landscaping decisions facing homeowners. If one chooses the wrong bedding plants or perennials to beautify a landscape, one can easily make improvements in the next year's plans. But woody plants are less easy to move or change. Also, the investment the homeowner makes when choosing a single shade tree can be daunting. Essentially, the planning process should entail detailed evaluations of both the existing or improved site and an evaluation of what the owners of the property want and expect from the landscape. While this process often involves much effort and investment, homeowners can gain great satisfaction in selecting and planting woody plants.

Everyone is aware of the potential of plants to beautify one's property. However, woody plants can also help define architecture and the various use areas of the landscape, provide emphasis, seasonal interest and privacy. Plants do much to condition our surroundings. A single shade tree can moderate the temperature at least 15 degrees in summer heat. They also help produce environments or microclimates to enable other plants to do well. Plants add the third dimension to our landscapes.

Early in the planning process homeowners need to decide whether they want to invest their time and effort in evaluating their landscapes and researching which woody plants to choose for their sites, or whether they want to consult with and rely on those that have expertise in this process. Landscape architects, landscape designers, arborists and knowledgeable plant personnel are some who have expertise that the property owner might want to bring into the evaluation, selection and maintenance process. Using texts such as this one, visits to

an arboretum where one can see how plants really look in mature plantings, visits to nurseries and garden centers, and critical looks at other landscapes are also helpful in the planning process. As with interior design for our homes, one can haphazardly choose furnishings or invest much study and monies in achieving a desired, pleasing environment.

It is always important to keep in mind during the design, planting and maintenance processes that the plants we are focusing on are living organisms and have diverse characteristics. We cannot guarantee a successful use of woody plants without keeping in mind their requirements and needs. One may "want" to plant flowering dogwoods or Japanese maples in zone 4 landscapes but this book will advise you not to. Moreover, those in warmer areas also may want to plant some of the evergreens, trees, shrubs and vines found in this text but would be well advised not to.

Evaluation of Site

Many factors should be carefully examined in the existing and future landscape. This evaluation and the process briefly described below should be completed before one thinks of plant material. Marion Fry, in her excellent handbook *A Space of One's Own* (1992, 5) states it this way: "How people will use and maintain the space, share the space and feel in the space are at the core of the design process." Although a thorough discussion of the landscape design process and its principles is outside of the purpose of this text, some practical advice can be given.

Perhaps a first step is to draw a rough sketch of your property and the existing features. It is easiest to do this on graph paper to allow one to mark relative measurement and scale, roughly measuring by stepping off features and marking them on your plan. All under and above ground utilities should be clearly marked. House, garage and other structures should be placed. If the walkways, driveways, fencing, garden areas and other landscape features will remain the same, they can be marked. Another useful tool during these early stages is the use of a camera to take photographs of areas needing improvement. One can easily mark photos with pens or use cut-outs of trees etc. to help evaluate possible improvements.

Now is the chance for the homeowner to consider major improvements in the landscape. Drainage problems, privacy issues, problems with topography and the like are best addressed before getting further into the design process. Consultation with a landscape architect or designer in these early planning stages could help solve some of these problems.

Now also is the time to consider how you want to utilize your landscape. Do you need children's play areas, are you a nature lover and want to attract wildlife to your yard, or are you a gardener and want protected areas where you can intensively garden? Is maintenance a primary concern? Are there views you want to frame or is privacy more important? Questions like these and others need to be addressed.

Evaluating Your Soil Type and Drainage

It is important to know the type of soil on your property so you can select the best trees and shrubs for your landscape. Some plants, like the sugar maple, grow best on moisture-retentive clay loam soil. Others, like the native red maple, grow well in slightly acid sandy soils provided they receive sufficient moisture. Although most plants require well-aerated soil, some will grow where the soil is periodically saturated with water. Some will survive spring floods so long as the flooding occurs while the plants are still dormant. Most trees and shrubs grow best on soils that are neutral or slightly acid. Some plants like azaleas and blueberries require acid soil, and a few like green ash and lilac tolerate soils that are slightly alkaline. Consulting the plant selection lists concerning existing soil conditions

Sample plans show existing features and proposed modifications.

may be necessary. Many times it is far easier and more successful to fit woody plants to soil conditions than trying to change soil conditions.

Soils are classified as mineral or organic depending on their origin. Mineral soils are made up of rock particles, whereas organic soils are derived from decomposed organic matter. The size of the rock particles in mineral soils varies greatly. Sand is made up chiefly of rock particles ranging in size from 0.002 to 0.08 inch, silt is composed of particles from 0.0001 to 0.002 inch; and clay is made up of particles smaller than 0.0001 inch. Sand particles are visible with the unaided eye, silt particles under an ordinary microscope, and clay particles with the aid of an electron microscope.

A loam soil is a mixture of various sizes of rock particles plus varying amounts of organic matter. A sandy loam contains a high percentage of sand particles, a silt loam a high percentage of silt, and a clay loam a high percentage of clay. Sandy loams are

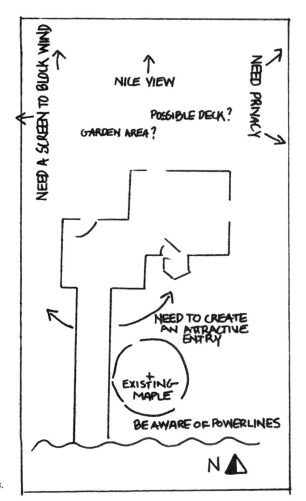

generally droughty and low in plant nutrients. Clay loams, on the other hand, are moisture-retentive and high in plant nutrients. Silt loams fall somewhere between the two. Owing to their small size, there is a tendency for the soil particles in clay loams to run together and form hard lumps if such soils are worked when they are wet. General soil improvement will be covered in the next chapter on planting.

Careful evaluation of existing drainage should be made realizing water travels following the avenue of least resistance. If you have a desired soil type, water will naturally percolate down through the soil into the existing water table. Evaluations such as whether drainage can be improved by such changes as slowing down water movement on steep slopes or changing drainage patterns to move excess water prudently off your property (not onto the neighbors!) can best be made now. Again, professional consultations can be an important consideration when trying to solve drainage problems.

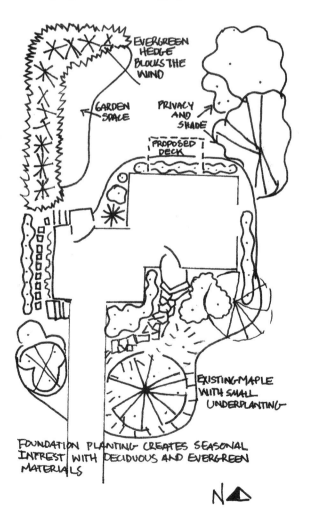

EVERGREEN HEDGE BLOCKS THE WIND

GARDEN SPACE

PRIVACY AND SHADE

PROPOSED DECK

EXISTING MAPLE WITH SMALL UNDERPLANTING

FOUNDATION PLANTING CREATES SEASONAL INTREST WITH DECIDUOUS AND EVERGREEN MATERIALS

N

Evaluating Plant Hardiness

Plants differ greatly in their hardiness, or ability to grow and thrive in a given area. This hardiness is genetically determined. Much plant research centers on the hardiness of individual plants including valuable research done at institutions such as The Minnesota Landscape Arboretum, and cross institutional organizations such as the Landscape Plant Development Center.

For plants that are propagated from seed it is generally true that the more southern the seed source, the less hardy the plants. Take for example, the red maple, *Acer rubrum*, a tree native from Florida to Canada. Maples grown from a southern seed source will be less hardy than those grown from a northern source. However, seed source may not always be a predictor of hardiness.

Several plant hardiness zone maps (or predicting macroclimates) have been produced. The ones consulted for this text are: the *USDA Plant Hardiness Zone Map* (1990), and the *Canadian Plant Hardiness Zone Map*. Based on minimum winter temperatures, these zones do not take into account variations in rainfall and types of soil. These zones should be considered only broadly accurate. In this book, comments on plant hardiness are keyed to zones 2, 3 and 4. The zone given is the most northern zone in which the plant can be generally recommended; it should do equally well in zones immediately to the south. Sometimes a plant can be grown in sheltered locations in the zone north of the one recommended. For instance, in large metropolitan areas such as the Twin Cities in Minnesota, a more favorable climate certainly exists close to its center compared to outlying districts in its suburbs even to the south. If a plant is recommended for trial in a zone, it should be hardy in the next zone to the south.

Evaluating the Microclimate

Microclimates in the landscape are very important to the successful placement of woody plants. What are microclimates? They are the actual climatic conditions in your landscape and can vary greatly throughout even a small area. Factors that determine microclimates include how much sunlight, how much wind, how much water is naturally or artificially present. Prevailing winds can help cool an area in the summer but generally make a site in the North a less desirable area for marginally hardy plants.

It is of prime importance that each area's microclimate is honestly evaluated. It also can vary with the season of the year; for instance, a location protected from wind in the growing season can become more windswept after leaves fall in the autumn. Some of our plant growing areas can be greatly improved. A landscape enhanced and protected by evergreen plantings can reduce winds and cause winter snows to settle and cover plantings. This one design element can determine relative failure or success of one's plans. There are many other practical steps that can be taken to enhance one's plant growing capabilities.

Further Considerations

In the planning process many basic questions need to be asked and answered. How much shade do I already have in my landscape? Is salt from roadways a problem I should plan for? How much privacy do I have or want? Is the level of future maintenance needs important to me—do I relish spending weekends doing basic maintenance chores or are these tasks I'd rather skip? Is what I am planning/thinking about what my family or household really wants, or needs?

Perhaps these evaluation and planning steps have all been made previously. Whatever, now is the time to place existing trees, shrub borders and landscaped areas on your plan. This will allow the homeowner to evaluate placement of new woody plants.

Selecting Woody Plants

Only now after the described planning process has been completed, should one begin thinking which woody plants should be planted. Too many times homeowners select handsome specimens in the nursery, and after they bring them home attempt to fit them into their landscape.

As stated before, many find this selection

process one of the most fulfilling parts of gardening and landscaping. However, one can easily be seduced by this planning process. The garden writer, Josephine Nuese (1970, 3), in *The Country Garden* describes this well:

> For this is the gardener's cocktail hour. And just as in the candle-lit dusk of the cocktail hour all men are brilliant and all women beautiful so, in the catalogues, all plants are enchanting, all bloom unceasingly, all are easy to grow, all suited to your area. It is one of the happiest of all delusions, putting stars into the eyes and mush into the mental processes.

This text with its detailed descriptions of plants and where they grow best will hopefully help make more informed choices.

Utilizing your plan you can now start planning for new plants. Your scaled plan can help in the proper placement of plants, avoiding overplanting and crowding. It is tempting to place young, immature woody plants closer than they should be and to attempt the achievement of an immediate landscape effect. Overplanting causes plants to become crowded, necessitating at the minimum more pruning than usual. Many times it results in the need for landscape renovation just as plantings start reaching maturity. Crowded plants do not allow appreciation of their natural growth characteristics, can be less healthy than properly spaced plants, and will need more maintenance.

Look carefully at written descriptions of the mature size of plants. Selecting a tree, shrub or evergreen in correct scale is as important as selecting beautiful color and form. The successful selection of correctly sized woody plants will become most evident years later as they approach mature size.

Considerations of growth habit, size, texture, mass, foliage color, silhouette and form now become important. Taste in selection of woody plants include such considerations as avoiding too many contrasting colors, textures and varieties. A danger for plant lovers is trying to fit all our favorite plants into our landscape giving too much variety and contrast.

These are some of the planning considerations that should be made for using the diverse world of woody plants in the landscape.

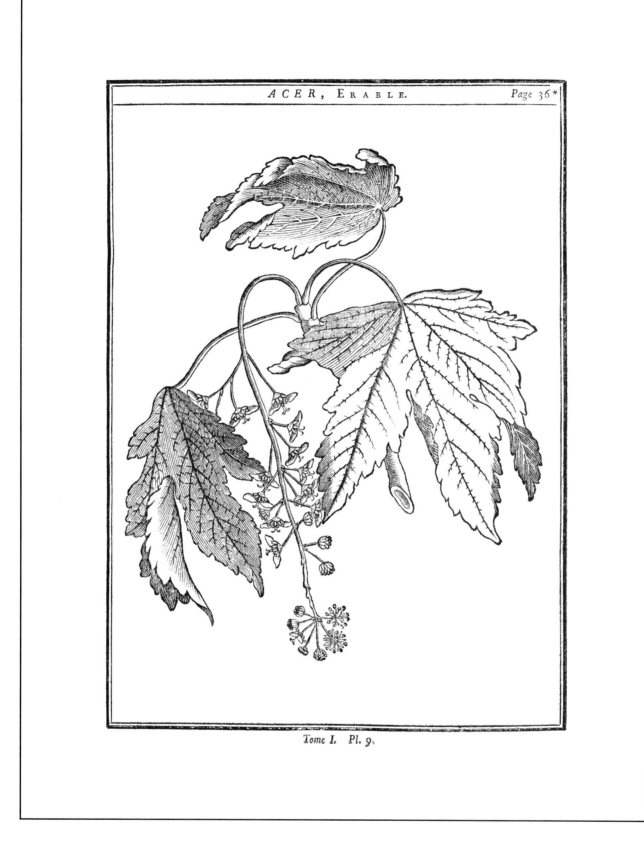

Acer tataricum, Tatarian maple. Duchamel du Monceau, Henri Louis.

Traité des Arbres et Arbustes. 2 vol. Paris: Guérin & Delatour, 1755.

PLANTING WOODY PLANTS

Success in establishing trees, shrubs, and vines depends largely on the care taken in planting. Although homeowners may have many years in which to care properly for woody plants, they have only the single moment of planting to give a plant's roots the necessary conditions and environment.

Much of a woody plant's life-sustaining activity takes place out of sight where it cannot be essentially changed or improved. Wade Harris, writing in the *American Conifer Society Bulletin* (1997, 83), reports that while the trunk of a tree makes up 60% of its weight, interestingly the feeder roots and the leaves make up the same percentage of 5% each, and the weight of the transport roots equals that of branches. Planting woody plants requires extra care so that the root environment can properly function. Protecting the plants before they are set in the ground, spacing and planting them properly, and employing proper pruning techniques and staking (if needed) should further improve your chances of success.

Container and Balled-and-Burlapped Plants

Today, many woody plants are purchased as container stock. You will need to exercise special care when transporting container or balled-and-burlapped plants in open vehicles: such plants are usually purchased in full leaf, so their tops are susceptible to wind damage. Wrap them with plastic before transporting.

Keep in mind that container-grown stock has been growing in a very artificially restrained environment. To grow properly these plants have been pampered. When moved into your landscape, these plants, and especially their roots, have to adapt to more average growing conditions. Failure to give these plants either a proper environment for growing roots, or careful maintenance until an adequate root system has developed, will likely lead to disappointment. However, with care, you can easily create conditions for success.

Bare Root Plants

Before you purchase bare root plants, make certain that they are still dormant. Take care at all times to protect the roots of dormant plants against drying out. The nursery usually wraps the roots in moist sphagnum moss or shingle tow, or uses a moisture-proof paper. When you get the plants home, unwrap them and examine the roots. If they are at all dry, soak them in cool water for a few hours before planting. Do not leave them in water for more than 12 hours.

Spacing

When spacing trees and shrubs, consider their mature size and form. Many homeowners tend to plant trees and shrubs too close together. While this does produce an immediate landscape effect, after a few years the plants become tall and leggy and lose their natural beauty. Before planting, closely observe the mature height and width of the woody plants described in this text. Check with your utility company before you site trees to avoid overhead and underground utilities. In general, large shrubs should be spaced 6 to 9 feet apart; medium shrubs, 4 to 6 feet apart; and small shrubs, 2 to 4 feet apart.

Soil Improvement

Regardless of the type of soil in your landscape, it will probably need improvement. Adding organic matter to soil improves the texture and aeration of clay soils and increases the moisture and nutrient retention of sandy soils. Organic matter is constantly being oxidized and used up, so you will need to replenish it at frequent intervals. Ideally, you should make soil improvements for an area larger than the hole you dug for planting. These improvements will reduce soil compaction around plantings.

The soil is a reservoir of chemical elements, present in both insoluble and soluble forms. Only those elements that are in solution in soil water can enter the plant through root hairs that penetrate between soil particles. At least 16 elements are believed to be essential to plant growth.

• Carbon, hydrogen, and oxygen are used in photosynthesis, a process that occurs in green plants in the presence of light. Carbon dioxide is a gas that makes up 0.03 percent of the atmosphere; it enters the plant through tiny openings in the leaves called stomates. The carbon dioxide used in photosynthesis is replenished by a reverse process, called respiration, which occurs in living organisms and by the decay and the burning of fossil fuels. Water (hydrogen and oxygen) enters through the root hairs from the soil.

• Nitrogen is a constituent of plant proteins and chlorophyll. It is associated with vegetative growth and a healthy green color in plants.

• Phosphorus is needed for flowering and fruiting and is an essential constituent of certain plant proteins. It also hastens the maturation of plant cells and aids in carbohydrate movement within a plant.

• Potassium plays a catalytic role in the movement of carbohydrates within a plant. It is also associated with strong root development and sturdy stems.

• Calcium, magnesium, iron, sulfur and molybdenum also are associated with necessary plant functions and development.

Other elements are also essential for proper plant growth, but only nitrogen, phosphorus, and potassium are used in such quantities that they must be replaced (see *Fertilizing the Soil* in the chapter on plant maintenance).

Best Times to Plant

With the growth of containerized woody plant material, planting dates are not as crucial as with bare-root stock. Bare-root stock should be attempted only during periods of natural dormancy. Early spring in the

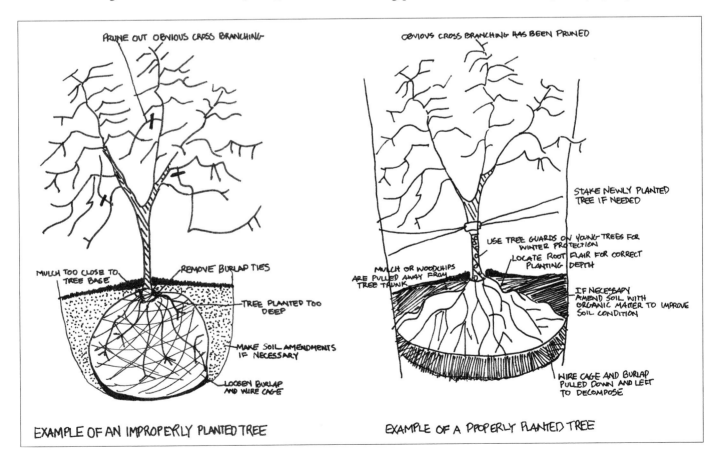

EXAMPLE OF AN IMPROPERLY PLANTED TREE

EXAMPLE OF A PROPERLY PLANTED TREE

North is recommended. Fall planting of bare-root stock is less successful in the North.

Container grown stock can be successfully planted up through mid-summer if adequate care is provided, especially supplemental watering. (Container stock has ususally been carefully watered and fertilized to insure good growth.) Woody plant material planted from containers needs only to be somewhat established before it goes into dormancy in the fall. As a general cut-off date for planting container stock, perhaps the first of August can be suggested.

General Planting Tips

Make a planting hole for woody plants that is deep and wide enough to accommodate the roots without crowding. If the soil in your garden is poor, separate the topsoil from the subsoil as you dig. Discard the subsoil, which is low in organic matter and plant nutrients. If necessary, amend the topsoil with better soil and organic matter at this time.

In good soil, let the root ball rest on solid undisturbed soil at the bottom of the hole. In poor soil, make the hole much deeper and larger than the root ball; put good topsoil in the bottom and firm carefully before putting the plant in place.

Homeowners with poorly drained soils need to make an extra effort in planting. Improving only pockets of poorly drained soils in planting woody plants often causes these pockets to become reservoirs into which water will drain. After heavy rains or watering these improved areas can become waterlogged.

Planting Container and Balled-and-Burlapped Stock

Few people realize the importance of correct planting depth. In fact, one of the most common failures with woody plants is incorrect planting depth. It is discouraging, to say the least, to see a tree reaching maturity suddenly die because it was planted too deeply and rotted, or its roots girdled the tree beneath the soil surface.

For either container or balled-and-burlapped stock, check the depth of the plant before filling in the soil. With the plant held in place in the planting hole, lay a lath or shovel handle across the top of the hole. The root flare (i.e., the place where roots emerge from the trunk) should be positioned right at the surface (see drawing).

In planting container and balled-and-burlapped stock, be sure to handle the root ball carefully. With container-grown plants, remember to remove the container before planting. Use snips to cut away the container rather than trying to pry a root-bound plant out of its container. You can wait to remove the container until you've set the plant in its prepared planting hole.

When planting balled-and-burlapped stock, loosen the burlap around the top of the ball and fold it back into the planting hole when the hole is about half-filled. With balled-and-burlapped roots covered with specially treated or artificial materials or wrapped in a wire basket, remove all such materials within the planting hole, carefully jockeying the plant to minimize root disturbance. Also remove all wire and twine, which could girdle stems or roots in the future.

Carefully examine the surface root structure at this time looking for impacted or encircled roots. If these are present, spread and disentangle them to prevent future girdling. You may cut off these roots if you cannot disentangle them.

Planting Bare Root Stock

Plant bare root stock with the same care. Spread out the roots over a small pyramid of good topsoil and fill in around the roots with topsoil. For very poor soils, fill in with a mixture of topsoil and peat or well-rotted manure. If your soil is acceptable, you can backfill with the original soil. Firm this soil by tamping with your feet.

Watering

It is a good practice to soak the roots and new soil *as you plant* to help eliminate air pockets and make certain newly planted roots are in good contact with the soil. As you water, make sure you do not completely destroy the structure of the soil by tamping or tramping too heavily on wet soils. A popular, effective method is to fill the planting hole with soil to approximately one-half, firming and tamping as you fill, then soak well. After the water has disappeared, continue filling soil to proper depth. Whatever planting method you use make certain you carefully soak the area after planting.

Following planting you will need to ensure adequate water supply until the roots are fully established. Container-grown stock is often watered daily at the nursery, so transplanted woody plant material needs special care to prevent it suffering from water stress. Unless sufficiently watered, container-grown plants may fail because root growth does not occur beyond its container-sized root ball. If rainfall is not adequate, water at least once a week, applying at the very least an inch of water each time. Take care to note your soil type, however: overwatering in a heavy clay soil can exclude air and kill developing roots. In general, once woody plants are established, they should not require watering except during dry periods.

Pruning at Planting

After planting, the tree or shrub may need some pruning. When you prune, consider the plant material's natural form. This is a good time to thin the branches and correct the juvenile shape of the plant and trim any damaged, inward growing branches. Recent research has shown that trees can more quickly regenerate their root systems when they have more foliage, so avoid heavy pruning.

Support for New Plants

A few newly planted trees need support to prevent wind from swaying the trees and loosening the soil around the roots. Usually, trees planted in very exposed situations or on slopes are candidates for staking. Other less exposed locations usually do not warrant staking.

To ensure adequate support, drive sturdy stakes into the ground about 1 to 2 feet away from the trunk, avoiding the root ball. Use a strip of soft cloth or broad, flat straps to anchor the stakes to the tree. Never use wire or heavy cord. For larger trees, you may need to arrange several stakes around the trunk. Remove all supports after the first winter before the support device harms the tree. Remem-

ber to give newly planted trees winter protection (as described in the chapter on maintenance).

Mulching

Young trees and shrubs grow better if they do not have to compete with grass or emerging weeds. This competition can be eliminated by cultivation (which can harm surface feeder roots) or mulching, which can be more effective. Mulching also conserves moisture and keeps the growing roots cooler. Wood chips are most popular, but straw, hay, coarse compost or grass clippings can also be used. Mulching also prevents damage from lawn mowers and weeders, a major problem in many landscapes.

Shrub borders should be entirely mulched. Around a tree or large shrub, lay a circle of mulch 3–6 feet out from the trunk depending on the size of the specimen. Avoid piling mulching material against the trunk or stem. Layer it just deep enough to discourage weed growth, approximately 3 inches. More is not better as too deep a layer of mulch can be detrimental. Excessive mulch or the use of black plastic can cut off essential oxygen to the roots and cause injury. It's amazing how tough woody plants really are when they manage to survive heavy plastic mulch covered by crushed rock, typical of many commercial plantings. However, it is acceptable to use organic mulches over landscape fabric to help cut down on weeds. As part of your yearly maintenance, check the depth of mulch and supplement broken-down organic mulch with new material.

Propagation

Most woody plants are propagated by seeds, cuttings, or grafting. The complex science of plant propagation is best managed by professionals at a commercial facility, so it is generally recommended that most amateurs purchase woody plants from a reliable nursery or garden center. Readers who might enjoy exploring the world of woody plant propagation can consult the many detailed texts which give specifics on propagation for each type of plant. In the discussion of plants in this text, a few brief guidelines on propagation are given.

USDA Cold Hardiness Zone Map—United States

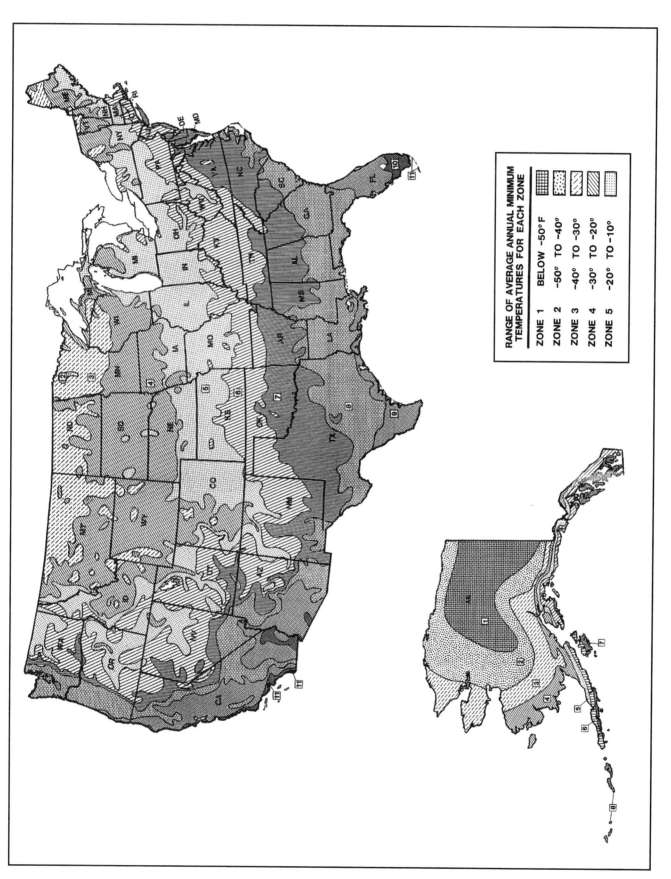

RANGE OF AVERAGE ANNUAL MINIMUM
TEMPERATURES FOR EACH ZONE

ZONE 1   BELOW −50°F
ZONE 2   −50° TO −40°
ZONE 3   −40° TO −30°
ZONE 4   −30° TO −20°
ZONE 5   −20° TO −10°

COLD HARDINESS ZONE MAP — CANADA

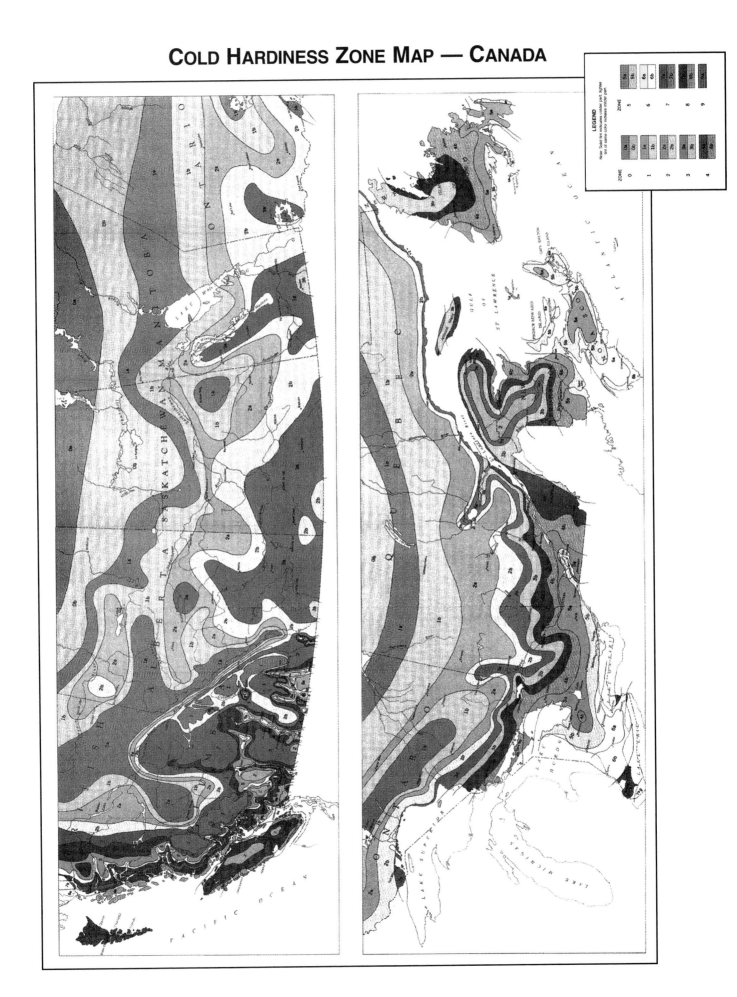

Maintaining Woody Plants

Fertilizing the Soil

Trees and shrubs grow quite well in nature. Leaves fall to the ground, decay, and return essential elements to the soil. Decaying branches, logs, and tree stumps also replenish the soil. When trees and shrubs are planted in our landscapes, they may grow in sod where their roots must compete with grass for moisture and nutrients. Moreover, fallen leaves are not allowed to decay; they are raked and removed (and, hopefully, composted).

It is essential, therefore, to improve our soils. Adding organic matter and commercial fertilizers results in faster-growing plants with more colorful foliage and greater production of flowers and fruit. Organic matter can be added in the form of farm manures, composts, or by plowing under cover crops (such as nitrogen-fixing legumes) before plants are planted. Compost used as mulch also replenishes the soil.

Types of Fertilizers

For trees and shrubs, a fertilizer relatively high in nitrogen is best. A 10-8-6 or a 10-6-4 mix are good woody plant fertilizers. The first number in a fertilizer refers to the percentage of nitrogen, the second to the percentage of phosphorus pentaoxide (P_2O5), and the third to that of potassium oxide (K_2O).

The form of the nitrogen in fertilizer should be considered. Nitrogen derived from organic sources like cottonseed or soybean meal or dried blood is made available to plants slowly, whereas nitrogen from inorganic sources such as ammonium nitrate, ammonium sulfate, and synthetic urea is made available quickly. Organic nitrogen produces visible results over a longer period of time than does inor-

ganic nitrogen, but these results are not noticeable until the soil warms up and soil organisms become active in the spring. A relatively new development in fertilizers is pelletized (or coated) inorganic fertilizers, which can act more like organic fertilizers. If the cost of nitrogen is a consideration, note that inorganic sources of nitrogen are much cheaper than the organic sources.

For acid-loving plants like evergreens, azaleas, and blueberries, it is best to use fertilizers that produce an acid reaction when added to the soil. Such fertilizers are specifically formulated for acid-loving plants.

When to Fertilize

Apply fertilizer either late in the fall after the plants have stopped growing or early in the spring before the leaves come out. For most plants, fertilizing just as the leaves are expanding in the spring is the optimum time to apply fertilizer. If you have a problem with runoff in the fertilized area, it is definitely best to fertilize at this time. Avoid fertilizing woody plants after the mid-point in their growing season to allow time for wood to mature properly in the fall.

You can best judge how often to fertilize by the growth and appearance of the tree or shrub. The plant itself is the best guide for determining whether fertilizer is required. Short terminal growth and pale green leaves often indicate the need for fertilizer.

On some soils an annual feeding may be necessary, but remember that fertilizing more, and more often, is not necessarily the best for landscape plants. Furthermore, fertilizing poorly growing plants may not be a good idea except in nutrient-starved soils. (There are many other reasons for plants to grow poorly besides poor fertility of soils.)

How to Fertilize

Apply fertilizer where it will produce optimal results. In most trees and shrubs the bulk of the feeding roots grow in a circular band. They reach just beyond the spread of the branches and extend inwards about two-thirds of the distance from the outer circumference to the trunk or main stems of the woody plant. (Greedy feeders such as silver maple can extend this distance an unbelievable distance.) Apply fertilizer within this circular band of roots, but do not place it closer than 12 inches from the base of large plants to avoid any danger of fertilizer injury to the trunk.

The amount of fertilizer to be used is determined by analyzing the fertilizer. Generally it is safe to follow recommendations on the fertilizer packaging *conservatively*. Shrubs or vines are fed by broadcasting the specific fertilizer's recommended application rates around the specimen's base. Again, a conservative amount is best.

There are several methods of applying fertilizer. In cultivated soil, you can broadcast fertilizer and cultivate it into the soil. Note that continuous surface applications encourage shallow roots; this is especially true in grassy areas where the lawn is heavily fertilized.

In grassy areas, apply the fertilizer in the root area of the plant. Use a punch bar or soil auger to open holes within the circular band of roots. Space the holes about 2 feet apart and approximately 18 inches deep. Make three to five holes for each 0.4 inch in diameter of the tree measured at the 2-foot level (a tree that is 10 inches in diameter will need 75 to 125 holes). Next, apply the required amount of fertilizer equally to the all holes, then fill the holes with peat moss or good topsoil. Slanting the holes toward the base of the plants will expose more roots to the fertilizer.

Commercial applicators often use a compressed air auger to make holes. They also employ root feeders that use water under pressure to open the holes and inject the fertilizer in solution. Liquid fertilizers have the advantage of being quickly absorbed by plants, but the effect does not last as long as that of dry fertilizers.

Still another method of applying fertilizers is to use foliar sprays containing soluble fertilizers in weak concentration. When foliar-feeding, use fertilizers recommended for this method of application and follow instructions closely. Foliar-feeding is especially beneficial in dry seasons.

Winter Protection

Plants grown in northern gardens are susceptible to the ravages of winter. Each winter brings new and diverse problems. An early freeze in the fall, before plants are fully hardened for winter, can injure plants. Late freezes in the spring or sudden, extreme drops in temperatures in the spring also can damage plant material. Other plants can be killed by extremely low temperatures in mid-winter. Certain evergreens, such as yews, hemlocks, and arborvitae, are susceptible to winter burn. Winter burn develops when the sun, reflected from a snowy surface, causes a temperature buildup in leaves, followed by a sudden temperature drop when the sun disappears behind a cloud or building. This sudden drop in temperature causes the formation of ice crystals within living plant cells, resulting in their death. Sunscald on thin-barked trees like the Norway maple is caused by the same phenomenon.

There are many effective ways to protect woody plants against winter injury, some of which are labor-intensive. Tender plants like garden roses, tender grapes, and blackberries, which would be killed if left exposed to our winter temperatures, can weather the winter successfully if you cover them. (Tie the stems into a tight bundle. Dig a trench up to the base of the plant, loosen the soil around the base, bend the plant over into the trench, and cover with soil. Do this about October 20th, then cover with heavy mulch when the weather turns cold.) However, most gardeners rely on hardier, specially bred varieties of plants that do not require these extreme measures.

Other protective measures include stretching burlap around a wooden frame to shade broadleafed woody plants like many of the rhododendrons. This can also safeguard evergreens from winter burn, but it may be safer to choose burn-resistant varieties or choose a site that has natural winter shade. You can prevent sunscald on tree bark by using commerically available plastic cylinders or wrapping materials around susceptible trunks.

Rodent and Deer Control

Rodents can be very destructive to all woody plants; for instance, members of the rose family are very susceptible to rodent damage. Field mice usually feed under the protective cover of tall weeds or grass or under snow. Damage by mice is usually confined to the base of plant stems, but it is not uncommon for mice to completely girdle young fruit trees. Rabbits feed above the snow and are most active during the winter. They cut off small branches and strip the bark from larger stems and also can girdle small trees. Pocket gophers are most active during the growing season. They feed on roots and can completely kill young trees and shrubs.

Deer are also destructive when browsing. They are especially fond of young apple and crabapple trees. In winter they feed on evergreens like arborvitae. Male deer also can strip the bark off young trees by polishing their antlers on the trunks.

The best way to control these pests—although it may be difficult for many homeowners—is to reduce the numbers of the animals causing the damage. This can be done by hunting, trapping, or by using poison baits where allowed by ordinance. If these methods are unacceptable, the only option is to protect individual plants or plantings. A cylinder of hardware cloth placed around the plant and pushed into the soil protects a shrub or tree from mouse injury. The mesh of the screen must be fine, no more than 0.4 inch wide, and the top of the screen must project above the snow. Cylinders of chicken wire, used similarly, can protect plants from rabbits. You can also try repellents such as moth balls or blood meal, but you'll have to replenish them at frequent intervals, and they are seldom effective during long northern winters.

Little can be done about a plant injury once it has occurred. Corrective pruning is the only way of improving the appearance of a plant damaged by

rabbits. A tree girdled by mice can be saved only by bridge grafting or, if the affected plant is too small for this, by cutting it off right below the girdled section.

Insect and Disease Control

Few plants are completely immune to insect and disease problems, but in many plants these problems are minor. Try to select plants least likely to develop problems. For example, since the Bechtel flowering crabapple will probably develop cedar-apple rust, the Hopa crabapple apple scab, and the Van Eseltine crabapple fire blight, it's simpler to avoid these varieties and plant the many more resistant crabapples instead. Or, the paper birch and the European white-barked birches are very susceptible to the bronze birch borer, an insect which is likely to kill these trees at an early age. You can sidestep such a fate by selecting a river birch that is more resistant to this insect, and plant in areas where this birch will not experience environmental stresses.

Learn to recognize plant symptoms associated with insects and diseases. If you can detect insects and diseases in their earliest stages, you have a better chance of preventing serious losses by using a protective spray. Your County Extension Office can help diagnose plant problems, evaluate whether control measures are needed, and recommend specific chemicals. For large trees you will need to call upon a trained tree specialist who has the proper spray equipment. Use sprays only for those insects and diseases that cause serious injury.

Pruning

Pruning of trees and shrubs is an art and a science that continues to baffle most amateurs. Well executed pruning can make woody plants not only more attractive but healthier. No simple guidelines for becoming a good pruner exist. You can only learn by experience. Prune for the following reasons:

• To improve the health and appearance of the plant. Removing any dead or diseased wood improves the appearance and checks the spread of disease.

• To reduce breakage. Narrow-angled crotches are weak and apt to split. Wide-angled branches are strong and resist breakage. Removing narrow-angled crotches when the branches are small will reduce future breakage.

• To remove branches that interfere with foot traffic or power lines. Remove lower branches as the tree grows if they interfere with the use of an area. You will damage the tree less if you remove branches when they are still small.

• To limit the size of the plant. Ideally, homeowners should select plants that will not outgrow their space, but they seldom do. They often plant trees and shrubs where space is limited, then pruning becomes the only way of limiting the size of the plant. Use tip pruning methods (see description below).

• To improve flowering and fruiting. The largest and showiest flowers and fruits are produced on vigorous young stems 2 to 4 years old. You can renovate old shrubs by removing the oldest stems at the ground. Pruning out some of the older wood in a fruit tree will encourage the growth of vigorous young branches.

Pruning Tools

Use tools of high-quality steel. Such tools cost more, but they enable you to do a better job of pruning and they last longer than inexpensive tools. Keep tools sharp, since a clean cut heals faster than a jagged cut. If you plan to prune, you should acquire the following basic tools:

• A pair of hand pruning shears is your most important pruning tool. The type with a shearing action works much better than the anvil type in which a single blade cuts against a flat surface. If you time it correctly, you can accomplish most of your pruning with a single pair of hand shears.

• A pair of long-handled shears, called loppers, is useful for larger branches up to 1.5 inches in diameter. Loppers are also handy for pruning raspberries and shrubs where cuts are made near the ground.

• For hedges, you will need a pair of hedge shears.

• For large branches, you should have a

pruning saw. There are many types of saws on the market. The type with a removable blade, similar to a hacksaw but with coarser teeth, is excellent for all but very large branches.

When to Prune

When to prune depends on a number of factors like time of bloom, disease, and sap flow. A few guidelines will help you prune at the optimal time.

• Shrubs and flowering trees that bloom on old wood—Prune as soon as they finish blooming.

• Shrubs that bloom in the summer on new wood—Prune in early spring.

• Trees susceptible to diseases that might spread on pruning tools, such as oaks with oak wilt or trees and shrubs possibly affected with fire blight—Prune in winter when there is less danger of spreading the disease.

• Trees, shrubs and vines that have a heavy sap flow in the early spring, such as maples, ironwood, and grapes—Prune either in winter or after the leaves are fully open. Pruning in late winter is best since this shortens the time that wounds are exposed to desiccation before callus [healing tissue] starts to grow. Further, pruning plants when dormant allows you to study the structure of the plant uninhibited by covering foliage.

For specific recommendations on pruning, consult the section on plants that require special consideration (see clematis, for example).

As stated earlier, knowing how to prune requires skill and experience. Each plant has a different habit of growth and requires special pruning. Except where you must limit size because of a space shortage, your goal in pruning is to preserve and enhance the natural form of the plant.

Tip Pruning

Two general types of pruning are practiced, tip pruning and renewal pruning. Tip pruning (pruning out of new outer growth) is suitable for formal hedges and wherever size must be limited. This type of pruning usually requires hedge shears or a power trimmer. On evergreens you can use a pruning knife. When pruning hedges, start soon after the hedge is planted to train the plants gradually into their desired mature shape. Prune so the base of the hedge is wider than the top. This permits light to reach the bottom and keeps dense growth down to the ground. Hedges may need pruning several times during the growing season.

Renewal Pruning

Renewal pruning means removing entire stems or branches. With most shrubs, you should cut the oldest stems near the ground. Do not take out more than a third of the older stems at one time (thus, in three years a shrub can be completely renewed). After removing the old stems, you might need to do a little tip pruning to balance the shape of the shrub.

General pruning of trees thins out branches, which allows light to enter and favors vigorous new growth. It also entails removing narrow crotches and branches that cross or grow toward the center of the tree. As with shrubs, some tip pruning may be needed. Make all cuts close to the main stem or branches. Never leave excess wood as large stubs. Wound dressings are not required; it is best to leave clean wounds to callus over naturally.

Common sense should rule in the care of woody plants, and the care and maintenance described in this chapter should not demand too much of you. In general, woody plants require less annual care than plantings of perennials or bedding plants. For a relatively small investment of time, woody plants can enhance your landscape and bring you pleasure over a long period of time.

THE
PLANTS

Fraxinus sp., ash. Kennion, Edward. *An Essay on Trees in Landscape.*
London: T. Bensley for C. J. Kennion, 1815.

ABELIALEAF

ABELIALEAF, WHITE FORSYTHIA
Abeliophyllum distichum Nakai.
FAMILY: OLEACEAE, OLIVE FAMILY
HARDY IN ZONE 4
5 feet tall, 5 feet wide

HABIT. Deciduous shrub; there is one species in this genus.
BRANCHES. Arching, angular, brownish gray; pith chambered.
BUDS. Small, superposed, with 2 to 4 outer scales.
LEAVES. Opposite, simple, ovate to elliptic-ovate, acuminate, broadly wedge-shaped or rounded at the base, less than 1 to 2 in. long, entire, pinnately veined.
FLOWERS. White, in short axillary racemes, in April; corollas tubular, with spreading lobes, 0.5 in. across.
FRUIT. Flattened, wafer-like up to 1 in. wide, in early summer.

LANDSCAPE USE

Abeliophyllum is useful in protected foundation and border plantings where the early and showy white spring bloom is welcome. This shrub is often described as white forsythia because of its similar spring bloom. However, its flower buds are generally more hardy than most forsythias. Research at The Minnesota Landscape Arboretum showed little flower bud damage on this species at -32º F. *Abeliophyllum* has generally an undistinguished summer habit. Native to central Korea, it was introduced into North America at the Arnold Arboretum in 1924.

CULTURE

Plant in well-drained soil in full sun or partial shade. It has no serious insect or disease problems. This shrub should be planted in a protected location. Easily propagated by softwood or hardwood cuttings.

The FIRS

Abies Mill.
FAMILY: PINACEAE, THE PINE FAMILY

Conifers add seasonal interest and bold form to the landscape. Concolor fir, *Abies concolor*, is one of our most ornamental conifers, although it needs the right location in the North.

The balsam fir, *A. balsamea*, is slower growing which is actually a plus as this species looks best in the landscape when young. There are also a number of dwarf fir cultivars that can be tried in the North. Other firs are less hardy and should be only considered for protected locations or perhaps southern zone 4.

BALSAM FIR
Abies balsamea (L.) Mill.
HARDY IN ZONES 2 TO 4
50 feet tall, 25 feet wide

HABIT. Upright tree with narrow, pyramidal form; there are 50 species of fir in the northern temperate zones worldwide.
BRANCHES. Covered with fine, soft, grayish hairs.
BARK. Smooth on young stems, becoming grooved with irregular, reddish brown scaly plates on mature trees.
LEAVES. Blunt or slightly bifid at apex, about 0.5 to 1 in. long.
FRUIT. Male cones are yellow; female cones violet when young, becoming grayish brown and resinous at maturity, 2 to 2.5 inches long.

LANDSCAPE USE

Balsam fir is a good specimen tree when young, but it is likely to be sparse in foliage at maturity. This fir can be grown for its fragrance; it is one of the most popular conifers used for Christmas trees. Unlike many conifers, balsam fir is tolerant of both shade and wet conditions. It is slow to moderate in growth (6 inches or less per year).

One of our hardiest conifers, this fir is an important and useful tree for the far North (zones 2-3). It should also be considered for native or wildlife areas, especially with moist conditions. It is one of the first trees to reappear after a forest fire in the northwoods.

As the American naturalist, Henry Beston, states in *Especially Maine* (1970, 132): "The dark of the returning evergreens is to be seen on every side, young pines, spruces, and fir balsams rising up in power from the floors of fallen leaves." Native from Labrador to West Virginia and west to Minnesota, it has been in cultivation since 1698.

Charles Sprague Sargent in his magnificent *Silva of North America*, vol 12 (1898, 110) describes balsam "Hardy..., of a cheerful color and in early years of vigorous and rapid growth, it was at one time popular in the northern states for the decoration of country door-yards. But, too often prematurely old, the naked trunks of these planted trees, surmounted with crowns of scanty half-dead foliage, show that the beauty of the Balsam Fir cannot long survive its removal from the cold moist northern forests which are its home, and in which, even under the most favorable conditions, it rarely outlives a century." However, balsam fir certainly is welcome in our homes for decoration at holiday time. *See photograph pages 166-67.*

CULTURE

Trees prefer slightly acid soil but will grow on neutral soil. A cool, moist site such as a north slope is ideal. It will not grow well in dry situations. Propagated by stratified seeds or from cuttings taken in March.

CULTIVAR:

Numerous cultivars have been named, but few of them are commercially available.

'Nana'   balsam fir
HARDY ZONE 4; HARDY WITH SNOW COVER IN ZONE 3
A low-spreading form about 1.5 to 2 feet tall.

CONCOLOR FIR, WHITE FIR
Abies concolor (Gord. & Glend.) Lindl.
HARDY IN ZONE 4 IN PROTECTED LOCATIONS
50 feet tall, 26 feet wide

HABIT. Dense, conical tree with needles that are smooth or minutely downy and yellowish green.
BARK. On mature trees deeply fissured and scaly, gray.
BUDS. Globose to broadly conic, light brown.
LEAVES. Bluish green with pale bands beneath, 1.5 to 2.25 in. long, and spreading outward and upward.
FRUIT. Male cones red to reddish purple; female cones 2 to 5 in. long.

LANDSCAPE USE

Use this fir as a specimen tree where it can be viewed from indoors during the winter months. Its long, bluish green needles are unique in the landscape. Some selections of concolor fir seem to have a bluer foliage; some rival the bluest specimens of blue spruce. Faster growing than other firs. Concolor refers to the needles having the same bluish green color on top and bottom.

One of Minnesota's earliest horticultural authors, Samuel B. Green, over one hundred years ago in his *Forestry in Minnesota* (1898, 161) wrote "The White Fir is justly gaining in popularity as an ornamental evergreen...It has stood for more than ten years on the grounds of the Minnesota Experiment Station without serious injury and has made pretty specimens about six feet high and nearly as broad."

Several cultivars have been named, but are not grown in the North. Native from Colorado to New Mexico and California, it has been in cultivation since 1872.

CULTURE

Plant in moist, well-drained soil, preferably in full sun. Concolor fir seems to withstand problem soils but does not like heavy, clay soils. It does have more drought tolerance than other firs. Protection from winter wind is necessary. In a well chosen site, this fir can be one of the most ornamentally useful conifers. Unfortunately, not for every location.

Other firs to try:

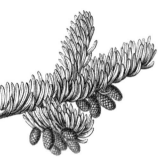

FRASER FIR
A. fraseri (Pursh) Poir.
TRIAL IN PROTECTED LOCATIONS OF ZONE 4
30 feet tall, 20 feet wide in favorable conditions

Recently this fir has become an important Christmas tree. Imported from the South for the holiday season, its dark, shining needles and its tolerance of dryer conditions make it a good holiday tree. Trial in only the most protected locations of zone 4.

NIKKO FIR
A. homolepis Sieb. & Zucc.
TRIAL IN PROTECTED LOCATIONS OF ZONE 4
40 feet tall, 30 feet wide in cultivation

A pyramidal tree with horizontal branching. It needs a moist, well-drained soil and protection in the winter as it readily develops winter burn in our climate. Perhaps best for zone 4 areas outside of the midwest where winter burn is not as much of a problem because winters are not as sunny.

KOREAN FIR
A. koreana Wils.
TRIAL IN PROTECTED LOCATIONS OF ZONE 4
25 feet tall, 18 feet wide in favorable conditions.

It has done poorly at the Arboretum in a site that should be suited for its growth.

ARIZONA CORKBARK FIR

A. lasiocarpa ssp. arizonica (Merriam) Murr.

TRIAL IN PROTECTED LOCATIONS OF ZONE 4

Seldom reaches 40 feet tall in zone 4

This attractive fir can be used in protected locations. The dwarf conifer, *Abies lasiocarpa* 'Green Globe', has done well at the Arboretum in a protected site.

NORDMANN FIR

A. nordmanniana (Steven) Spach.

FOR PROTECTED LOCATIONS IN ZONE 4

40 feet tall, 30 feet wide in cultivation

This fir is available in seed form in the nursery trade; otherwise it is difficult to find. In its native Asia and more temperate climates it can be one of the most handsome conifers, often growing over 100 feet tall. Only for plant collectors and protected sites in zone 4.

VEITCH FIR

A. veitchii Lindl.

HARDY IN ZONE 4; FOR PROTECTED LOCATIONS IN ZONE 3

Seldom reaches mature height of 60 feet in cultivation

Rarely found, mostly propagated from seed. This fir features dark green foliage.

The MAPLES

Acer L.

FAMILY: ACERACEAE, MAPLE FAMILY

Maples are among the most versatile and useful of the North's trees. Maples have a wide range in sizes and shapes from Amur maple, *A. tataricum ginnala*, which is often grown as a large shrub, to sugar maple, *A. saccharum*, and silver maple, *A. saccharinum*, which are among North America's largest growing deciduous trees.

They can offer dense shade and screening (Norway maple, *A. platanoides*) or add decorative features to the landscape. *A. pensylvanicum* has striped bark. Many such as the Amur maple, *A. tatarium ginnala*, cultivars feature colorful samaras (fruit), and others feature glorious fall color (*A. saccharum* and *A. rubrum* cultivars). When considering maples you should carefully look at the many cultivars available as they have been selected or bred for specific features.

Travelers coming back to zone 4 climatic conditions from more temperate climates often wish to plant the many cultivars of Japanese maple (*A. palmatum*). This species and its cultivars are not hardy. The Arboretum has a number of Japanese maples growing in large containers in its Home Demonstration Garden; these are wintered indoors. They are stored in proper conditions to allow these maples to experience a period of dormancy. For most home owners, moving and winter storing such large landscape plants is a daunting prospect.

John Gerard, in his famous *Herball or Generall Historie of Plants* (1597-98, 1299) describes the maple in his beautiful Elizabethan prose: "The great Maple is a beautifull and high tree, with a barke of a meane smoothnes: the substance of the woode is tender and easie to worke on; it sendeth foorth on every side very many goodly boughes and branches, which make an excellent shadow against the heate of the sunne."

The relatively newer cultivars that are crosses between mainly silver maple, *A. saccharinum*, and red maple, *A. rubrum*, (sometimes given the hybrid species designation of *A. x freemanii*) often have tolerance of the more alkaline soils of the western plains.

CULTIVARS:

(Of interspecific parentage)

Autumn Blaze™   maple

A. 'Jeffersred'
ZONE 4
50 feet tall, 35 feet wide

This rapidly growing selection is a hybrid of red and silver maple. It has orange to red fall color, an oval canopy and an adaptability for most soils. Selected by Glenn Jeffers of Fostoria, Ohio. Dr. Ed Hasselkus of Wisconsin rates this highly for fall color.

Celebration®

A. 'Celzam'
ZONE 4
45 feet tall, 20 feet wide

A more compact grower, this selection is another hybrid between red and silver maple. It features golden fall color and an upright growth habit. This cultivar seems to combine desirable characteristics of its parents in that it grows fast when young and shows tolerance of droughty soils. It is seedless. The leaves resemble *A. saccharinum*.

'Marmo'   maple

ZONE 4
65 feet tall, 40 feet wide

A hybrid between *A. rubrum* and *A. saccharinum* from a tree located at The Morton Arboretum in Chicago. Of upright, oval form it has a strong central leader. It has not been extensively tested in our area, but is reported to be hardy in zone 4. Specimens tested at the Arboretum have not had good fall color.

Norwegian Sunset®   maple

A. 'Keithsform'
TRIAL IN ZONE 4
35 feet tall, 25 feet wide

This maple is a cross between *A. truncatum* and *A. platanoides*, but it most closely resembles *A. platanoides*, although smaller in size and having a smaller leaf. It is more of an upright

grower but has not proven too hardy, so consider protected locations in zone 4. An introduction of J. Frank Schmidt Nursery in Oregon.

Pacific Sunset™   maple

A. 'Warrenred'
ZONE 4?
30 feet tall, 25 feet wide

Another introduction of J. Frank Schmidt Nursery. It is a cross between *A. truncatum* and *A. platanoides*. Similar to Norwegian Sunset®, it is of unproven hardiness so should be considered only for protected locations. A spreading, rounded canopy with dark green foliage.

Scarlet Sentinel™   maple

A. 'Scarsen'
TRIAL IN ZONE 4
40 feet tall; 20 feet wide

An upright vase forming cultivar that was also selected for its outstanding orange-red fall color. It has not been evaluated at The Minnesota Landscape Arboretum.

HEDGE MAPLE

Acer campestre L.

FOR PROTECTED LOCATIONS IN ZONE 4
30 to 50 feet tall, 30 to 50 feet wide

HABIT. Roundheaded tree; there are 150 species of maple distributed worldwide.
BRANCHES. Light brown, smooth or hairy, becoming corky.
BUDS. Small and woolly.
LEAVES. Simple, dark green above, palmately veined and lobed with 3 to 5 rounded lobes, 2 to 4 in. long, heart-shaped or square at the base, entire; fall color yellow or rust; petioles 2 to 4 in. long.
FLOWERS. Green, in upright, hairy corymbs, in early May.
FRUIT. Wings spread horizontally, 1 to 1.5 in. long.

LANDSCAPE USE

Where hardy, plant hedge maple as a specimen tree or use for an informal hedge or screen as it is tolerant of pruning. Native to Europe and western Asia, it was introduced into North America by early settlers.

In Sowerby's *English Botany* vol 2 (1790-1820, 233) he states: "Pliny mentions the curious knobs and excrescences of this tree, which in their contortions often represent the heads or figures of birds, beasts, or odd creatures of the imagination, and we have recently seen a collection of walking-sticks the handles of which were formed into all sorts of curious devices from the natural growths of the Maple."

CULTURE

In protected sites it is tolerant of varied growing conditions (sun or part shade, dry to wet, and acidic to alkaline soils). It grows best in clay loam soils. The species is propagated by seeds. It is suited only for protected sites. At the Arboretum this species has survived but not thrived.

BOXELDER
Acer negundo L.
HARDY IN ZONES 2 TO 4
50 feet tall, 40 feet wide

HABIT. Medium-sized tree of irregular form.
BRANCHES. Green or occasionally reddish brown; leaf scars encircle the stem and meet at an acute angle.
LEAVES. Pinnately compound with 3 to 5, rarely 7 to 9 leaflets; leaflets pinnately veined, 2 to 2.5 in. long, ovate to lance-oblong, coarsely serrate, acuminate at tips and wedge-shaped at base, bright green above, and turning slightly yellow in fall.
FLOWERS. Yellowish green, in May; male flowers in corymbs on slender pedicels; female flowers in drooping racemes.
FRUIT. Wings spread at an acute angle and are incurved, 1 to 1.2 in. long.

LANDSCAPE USE

Boxelder is often planted in shelterbelts and used as a shade tree in drier parts of the Dakotas and Nebraska. It is not recommended where rainfall is adequate or soils are not alkaline. Native in Eastern United States and Canada to the Great Plains it has been cultivated since 1688. A brittle tree, it often loses branches in winds and ice storms.

Hal Borland in his book, *A Countryman's Woods* (1983, 162), can find reason to praise this weed tree: "One of th[e] virtues is its seeds, which ripen in the usual maple form as samaras, or keys, each containing a fat nut-like seed with a broad, flat wing. These seeds are borne in bunches that hang in light tan tassels after the leaves have fallen. Each autumn they festoon the trees, and there they are all winter, providing nutritious handouts to hungry birds and squirrels. Even the gluttonous evening grosbeaks will eat them after they have eaten all the free-lunch sunflower seeds in sight."

CULTURE

Boxelder is a very drought-resistant species and it also tolerates a wide range of soils. Propagated by seeds. Harbors the ubiquitous boxelder bug, which can be quite annoying.

CULTIVARS:

'Sensation'   boxelder
HARDY IN ZONES 3 AND 4
30 feet tall, 25 feet wide

A new, improved cultivar which features slower growth and good red fall color. Especially valuable in zone 3 for alkaline soils. Grows about the same size as the species. This cultivar is still being evaluated at the Arboretum, with only variable performance.

'Variegatum'   boxelder
TRIAL IN PROTECTED LOCATIONS OF ZONE 4
40 feet tall, 30 feet wide

Leaves are variegated. This cultivar has not been hardy in Arboretum trials.

NORWAY MAPLE
Acer platanoides L.
HARDY IN FAVORABLE SITES IN ZONE 4
55 feet tall, 45 feet wide

HABIT. Tree with rounded crown.
BRANCHES. Smooth, brownish to olive-brown; leaf scars meet, forming a sharp angle.
LEAVES. Simple, with 5 palmate, pointed lobes, 4 to 7 in. across, nearly round in outline, bright green above, lustrous below with hairs in axils of veins; milky juice exudes when petioles or leaf blades are broken; fall color yellow.
FLOWERS. Greenish yellow, 0.32 in. across, in erect, many flowered stalked corymbs, in May.
FRUIT. Wings nearly horizontal, 1 to 2 in. long; fruits ripen in September and October.

LANDSCAPE USE

The Norway maple is widely used as a street or specimen tree wherever dense shade is desired. In maturity, the species is about as broad as it is tall. However, cultivars have been selected to give other forms in the landscape. The Norway maple's large, 5-pointed leaves retain their dark green foliage through the summer until late into the fall. Its yellow fall color can be pleasing but often the leaves drop green in early frosts.

This maple's canopy is good for summer screening and its dense texture adds visual weight to a landscape. Its yellow spring blossoms are attractive but are seldom noticed. This maple is one of the first native European trees to be introduced into North America. William Hamilton brought this maple to the Colonies in the 18th century for his Philadelphia estate.

CULTURE

This maple is adapted to a wide range of soils. Some dieback can occur in zone 4 following a severe winter, so in exposed sites or farther north, consider red or sugar maples. Norway maple prefers full sun, but sunscald can be a problem on the trunks of young trees. It is recommended to wrap the trunk for the winter.

Norway maple is one of our most pollution tolerant shade (not boulevard) trees for urban conditions. Its dense shade and prolific surface roots make use in lawns a problem. Consider using mulch or shade tolerant ground covers (ground covers are more of a challenge) under these trees at maturity. Farther south this species can be invasive, but in the North it generally has not been a problem. The species is propagated by seeds and its cultivars are budded on seedlings.

CULTIVARS:

'Columnare'
HARDY IN PROTECTED SITES
OF ZONE 4
45 feet tall, 15 feet wide

Introduced in France in the 19th century, this cultivar has a narrow, columnar shape.

'Crimson King'   Norway maple
ZONE 4
40 feet tall, 35 feet wide

The blood-red leaf color of this popular cultivar persists through the growing season. Young bark certainly needs wrapping in the winter in the North. 'Royal Red' might be a better cultivar for exposed zone 4 locations. Originally from Belgium, this cultivar has been grown in the U.S. since 1947.

'Crimson Sentry'   Norway maple
ZONE 4
30 feet tall, 20 feet wide

A sport of 'Crimson King' featuring more upright branching, smaller leaves. Introduced by A. McGill & Son Nursery in 1972.

'Deborah'   Norway maple
ZONE 4
45 feet tall, 40 feet wide

Similar to the 'Schwedleri' cultivar, but hardier and of more vigorous growth. Introduced by Holmlund Nursery in 1978. Leaves are somewhat crinkled but leathery.

Emerald Lustre®   Norway maple
A. p. 'Pond'
ZONE 4
50 feet tall, 50 feet wide

Introduction of Bailey Nursery in 1979. Features glossy foliage and vigorous oval growth habit. Good hardiness in zone 4.

'Emerald Queen'   Norway maple
ZONE 4
50 feet tall, 45 feet wide

An upright growing tree introduced in Canada in 1962 by A. McGill Nursery. Ascending branching with leaves deep green.

'Fairview'   Norway maple
ZONE 4
45 feet tall, 35 feet wide

Another A. McGill Nursery introduction with branching similar to 'Emerald Queen'.

'Globosum'   Norway maple
ZONE 4
15 feet tall, 15 feet wide

Grafted on a standard at desired height, it forms a dense globe. This cultivar was introduced in Belgium in 1873.

Parkway®   Norway maple
A. p. 'Columnarbroad'
FOR PROTECTED LOCATIONS IN ZONE 4
35 feet tall, 25 feet wide

Oval, upright grower with good foliage. Has been variable in hardiness. Introduced by J. Frank Schmidt Nursery in 1970.

'Princeton Gold'   Norway maple
ZONE 4
45 feet tall, 40 feet wide

Golden yellow foliage throughout the summer. Introduced in 1987, it can provide an accent in the landscape.

'Royal Red'   Norway maple
HARDY IN ZONE 4, FOR PROTECTED LOCATIONS IN ZONE 3
35 feet tall, 25 feet wide

'Royal Red' has proven to be hardier than 'Crimson King' with reddish purple leaves throughout the season. Selected by Martin Holmason in 1962. *See photograph pages 182-83.*

'Schwedleri'   Norway maple
ZONE 4
50 feet tall, 45 feet wide

Named after its German selector in 1869. Leaves are red in early spring but slowly turn dull green. Form and size is similar to the species.

'Superform'   Norway maple
ZONE 4
50 feet tall, 40 feet wide

Fast growing, with dark green foliage. Introduced by
Milton Nursery in 1963.

'Variegatum'   Norway maple
ZONE 4
50 feet tall, 40 feet wide

Less hardy form featuring green leaves with white edging.
Has a shimmering aspect in the landscape.

RED MAPLE, SCARLET MAPLE
Acer rubrum L.
HARDY IN ZONES 3 AND 4
50 feet tall, 45 feet wide

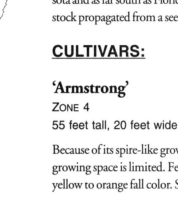

HABIT. Medium-sized tree.
BRANCHES. Upright when young,
becoming spreading at maturity, smooth,
green in summer, reddish brown in winter.
BARK. On mature trees becoming dark gray and rough.
BUDS. Reddish in winter, blunt with several overlapping scales.
LEAVES. Simple, 3- to 5-lobed, 2.2 to 4 in. long with crenate-
serrate margins, short-acuminate lobes, and somewhat heart-
shaped bases; fall color yellow to red.
FLOWERS. Mostly red, in dense clusters, in April; male and
female flowers usually on separate trees.
FRUIT. Wings, 0.5 to less than 1 in. long, often red, turning
brown in May and June, borne on pedicels 2.2 to 4 in. long.

LANDSCAPE USE
Red maple and its many cultivars are among the best selections for street and ornamental plantings if their soils are not
too alkaline. These large-sized trees are very colorful in spring
with prominent red buds followed by red fruits. Against its
light gray younger bark, the buds and flowers of red maples
can be a feature of the early spring landscape.

Donald Peattie in his *A Natural History of Trees* (1950,
466) states: "At all seasons of the year the Red Maple has
something red about it. In winter the buds are red, growing
a brilliant scarlet as winter ends, the snow begins to creep
away, and the ponds to brim with chill water and trilling
frog music. So bright, in fact, that if one takes an airplane
flight anywhere across the immense natural range of this tree
(the most widespread of all our Maples), one can pick out —
as far below as the color can be detected – the Red Maples,
by the promise of spring in their tops."

This tree has been cultivated in North America since
1656. About the same time, John Tradescant the younger
was introducing this native into England. For best fall color,
cultivars should be selected giving desired fall foliage. *See
photo p. 138-39.*

CULTURE
Tolerant of wet conditions, it prefers slightly acid, sandy loam
soil. As red maple survives in wet native soils low in oxygen, it
has proved to be a tree useful for the generally poorer and compacted soils of street or parking lots. Because of its relative adaptability, this species and its cultivars can be useful in many differing landscape conditions. It does not grow on alkaline soils
where it may develop chlorosis from a manganese deficiency.

As with many maples, sunscald can be a problem, so
younger tree trunks should be wrapped for the winter. Red
maple can suffer from drought. The species is propagated
from seed, while the cultivars are budded on seedling stock.
Because the geographic range of this species is wide, from
eastern United States and Canada as far west as central Minnesota and as far south as Florida and Texas, it is important to plant
stock propagated from a seed source from its northern range.

CULTIVARS:

'Armstrong'   red maple
ZONE 4
55 feet tall, 20 feet wide

Because of its spire-like growth, this cultivar is suitable where
growing space is limited. Features rapid growth with good
yellow to orange fall color. Selected in Ohio in 1947.

Autumn Flame®
ZONE 4
45 feet tall, 35 feet wide

Introduced in 1964 by A. McGill Nursery, this
cultivar features a dense, rounded crown.
Good red fall color.

'Autumn Spire'
ZONES 3 AND 4
50 feet tall, 25 feet wide

Introduced by Dr. Harold Pellett of The
Minnesota Landscape Arboretum in 1992. It was selected from
a red maple population near Grand Rapids, Minnesota. Its
broadly columnar form makes it a great selection for narrow lots
or tight spaces. This cultivar also has bright red fall color.

Karpick®   red maple
ZONE 4
40 feet tall; 20 feet wide

A narrow, upright cultivar that makes a good street tree. It
broadens out somewhat with age.

Northfire®   red maple

A. 'Olson'
ZONE 3 AND 4
45 feet tall; 30 feet wide

An upright, but broadly growing cultivar selected in the Brainerd, Minnesota area by Roger Landsburg. Good fall color.

'Northwood'   red maple

HARDY IN ZONES 3 AND 4
70 feet tall, 50 feet wide

Introduced by The Minnesota Landscape Arboretum in 1980 from a selection made in northern Minnesota. Oval-shaped, open canopy with dark green foliage turning to a good red in the fall. Fast growing. *See photograph page 183.*

October Glory®   red maple

FOR PROTECTED LOCATIONS OF ZONE 4
50 feet tall, 35 feet wide

A typical red maple with bright red fall color. Less hardy, so used in the South. Bark splitting can be a problem in the winter in our area. Arboretum trials have not been successful.

Red Sunset®   red maple

A. r. 'Franksred'
FOR PROTECTED LOCATIONS OF ZONE 4
50 feet tall, 40 feet wide

Fall color on trees in the Arboretum has been more yellow than red. Also, it has not performed very successfully in Arboretum trials. Bark splitting is occasionally a problem in winter. Introduced by J. Frank Schmidt, Jr. of Oregon in 1966.

SILVER MAPLE
Acer saccharinum L.

HARDY IN ZONES 3 AND 4
80 feet tall, 50 feet wide

HABIT. Very large, spreading tree.
BRANCHES. Smooth, green in summer becoming reddish brown in winter, with a disagreeable odor when crushed.
BUDS. Pointed, sometimes reddish.
BARK. Gray and quite smooth on young trees, becoming rough and darker as trees mature.
LEAVES. Hairy when young, 3 to 5.5 in. across, with 5 deeply cleft-pointed lobes and coarse, doubly serrate margins and square bases; leaf color bright green above and silvery-white beneath; fall color yellow; petioles slender, 3 to 4.75 in. long.
FLOWERS. Short-stalked and green to red, in April.

FRUIT. Wings divergent, 1.2 to 2.2 in. long; hairy when young, on pendulous pedicels, 1 to 2 in. long, in May and June.

LANDSCAPE USE

Silver maple is often planted as a fast growing lawn specimen, although it should be considered only for large yards and parks as its mature size is too large. It is used extensively in western regions of zones 3 and 4 where other maples do not do as well. Silver maples have a very invasive root system which can prevent one from gardening within its long reach. Branches on mature trees are brittle and sometimes break in storms. Those considering silver maple might alternatively consider one of the interspecific cultivars discussed above.

Charles Sprague Sargent in *Garden and Forest*, vol 3 (1891, 133) astutely comments on silver maple's growth rate: "It is this rapidity of growth that has made the Silver Maple a favorite with people who are in a hurry to obtain immediate effects and do not care to look very far ahead...[or] without much regard being paid to the fitness of the position selected for it."

CULTURE

Silver maple is tolerant of a wide range of soils and moisture levels. Optimum growth occurs in moist soils. Propagated from seeds (as anyone who has one in their yard finds out too readily) and by budding. It can suffer from chlorosis in alkaline conditions.

CULTIVARS:

'McKay's Seedless'

ZONE 4
60 feet tall, 50 feet wide

An introduction of McKay Nursery from Waterloo, Wisconsin. A seedless variety with rapid growth.

'Silver Queen'   silver maple

HARDY IN ZONE 4, FOR PROTECTED LOCATIONS IN ZONE 3
50 feet tall, 45 feet wide

Somewhat smaller than the species, it also has an oval canopy.

'Skinneri'   silver maple

ZONE 4
60 feet tall, 45 feet wide

Features a cutleaf and more upright growth. Introduced in 1938 by Skinner Nursery in Canada.

SUGAR MAPLE, HARD MAPLE
Acer saccharum Marsh.
HARDY IN ZONES 3 AND 4
65 feet tall, 50 feet wide

HABIT. Large tree with oval or rounded crown.
BRANCHES. Brown with small lenticels.
BARK. Gray, becoming furrowed on mature trees.
BUDS. Sharp pointed, with overlapping scales.
LEAVES. 3- to 5-lobed, 3 to 5.5 in. across, with narrow and deep sinuses, acuminate lobes, and heart-shaped bases; leaf margins coarsely toothed; fall color yellow to red.
FLOWERS. Greenish yellow, 0.2 in. across, borne on corymbs on slender, nodding pedicels, 1 to 2.75 in. long, in May.
FRUIT. Wings slightly spreading, 1 to 1.5 in. long; ripens in September and October.

LANDSCAPE USE
One of North America's prized native trees, sugar maple is found throughout eastern North America to western Minnesota. This large growing tree can be a traffic stopper with its fall color. It is often used as a street or lawn tree on moisture-retentive soils, but suffers from salt damage so care should be used in using this maple as a boulevard tree. Also, sugar maple does not do well where its roots are restricted or disturbed. It is somewhat shade tolerant.

As its common name indicates it is the tree most often used for maple syrup, although other maples are used (even boxelders in the far North!). Humphrey Marshall in one of the first books published in North America on trees, *Arbustrum Americanum* (1785, 4) in the collection of Andersen Horticultural Library noted this: "The back inhabitants make a pretty good sugar, and in considerable quantity, of the sap of this and the Silver-leaved Maple; and though these have generally been preferred, yet all our Maples yield a sap which affords a pretty good sugar." This book has been called the first truly indigenous botanical essay published in the western hemisphere. *See photographs pages 142-43, 158.*

CULTURE
Grows best on north-facing slopes in cool, moist, clay loam soils. Conversely, sugar maples can be short-lived in sandy soils. It is also intolerant of compacted soils. Although you often see sugar maple planted as a boulevard tree, it is intolerant of salt. Propagated from seeds or by budding.

One of the sugar maple's most serious problems is tattering of its leaves in windy summer weather. Many newer cultivars have been bred to help alleviate this problem. To ensure hardiness, it is important that sugar maples be propagated from a northern seed source.

CULTIVARS:

'Commemoration'   sugar maple
ZONE 4
50 feet tall, 35 feet wide

Vigorous, with distinctive glossy, dark green leaves.

Fall Fiesta™   sugar maple
A. s. 'Bailsta'
ZONE 4
50 to 75 feet tall, 50 feet wide

A recent Bailey Nurseries of Minnesota introduction described as having dark green leaves resistant to leaf tatter with good fall color. An upright, rounded canopy.

'Flax Mill Majesty'   sugar maple
ZONE 4
60 feet tall, 50 feet wide

A selection of Flax Mill Nursery of New York. This vigorous tree is noted for its symmetrical ovate form.

'Globosum'   sugar maple
ZONE 4
20 feet tall, 15 feet wide

A compact rounded head suitable for a protected location. This cultivar generates a lot of comment at the Arboretum, although it is difficult to find in the nursery trade.

Green Mountain®   sugar maple
ZONE 4, FOR PROTECTED LOCATIONS IN ZONE 3
55 feet tall, 40 feet wide

A 1964 introduction of the Princeton Nurserymen's Research Association. Resistant to summer scorching with dark green foliage, it also features an oval crown with red-orange fall color.

'Legacy'   sugar maple
ZONE 4
50 feet tall, 35 feet wide

Introduced by Willet Wandell in 1983. It resists foliage tatter. Fall color red with orange and yellow. Noted for its abundance of foliage providing dense shade.

Whitebark maple
ssp. *leucoderme* (Sm.) Desm.

Specimens have survived but not thrived at the Arboretum. Farther south this is a very attractive tree.

MOUNTAIN MAPLE
Acer spicatum Lam.
HARDY IN ZONES 2 TO 4
20 to 25 feet tall, 15 to 20 feet wide

HABIT. Large shrub or small tree.
BRANCHES. Purplish red and hairy when young.
BUDS. Stalked, pointed, 0.20 to 0.28 in. long.
LEAVES. 3- to 5-lobed, 2.2 to 4 in. long, with coarsely serrate leaf margins, acuminate lobes, and heart-shaped bases; upper leaf surface yellowish green and undersurface hairy; fall color red; petioles as long as blades.
FLOWERS. Small, perfect, greenish yellow, in erect racemes 3 to 5.5 in. long, in June after the leaves are open.
FRUIT. Wings spreading at nearly right angles, 0.5 in. long; ripens in September.

LANDSCAPE USE
Use for naturalizing in partial shade. It has been cultivated since 1750 and is native in northeastern North America, as far south as Georgia, and as far west as Minnesota.

J.C. Loudon, an early 19th century English author, in his *Arboretum et Fruticetum Britannicum*, vol 1 (1838, 407) writes "In British gardens it forms a low tree, 8 ft. or 10 ft. high, very ornamental in autumn" and goes on to give its costs at that time "Price, in London, 1s. 6d. a plant...at New York, 25 cents, and seeds 1 dollar per quart".

CULTURE
Propagate from seeds obtained from a seed source in the north of its wide range. In cultivated areas, only does well in moist, acidic soils in shady locations.

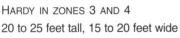

TATARIAN MAPLE
Acer tataricum L.
HARDY IN ZONES 3 AND 4
20 to 25 feet tall, 15 to 20 feet wide

HABIT. A shrub or small tree.
BRANCHES. Slender, brown, with prominent lenticels.
BUDS. Small, 0.20 to 0.32 in. long, brownish black, often hairy.
LEAVES. Simple, broadly ovate to ovate-oblong, 2 to 4 in. long, with 2 inconspicuous basal lobes, doubly serrate leaf margins, acuminate tips, and rounded or heart-shaped bases; upper leaf surface bright green and glabrous, veins on undersurface pubescent when young; fall color yellow to red; pedicels of flowers 0.5 to 2 in. long.
FLOWERS. Greenish white, in upright panicles, in May.
FRUIT. Wings nearly parallel, often red in July, 0.7 to 1 in. long; ripens in September.

LANDSCAPE USE
Used for screen planting or as an attractive clump specimen. Although it is most often grown in clump form, there is a ma-

ture single trunk specimen in the Home Demonstration Garden at the Arboretum that is very striking. It is very similar to the closely related Amur maple. Native to southeastern Europe and western Asia, it was introduced into North America in 1759.

CULTURE
Propagated from seeds. Prefers sandy loam soil but grows in any well-drained soil that is not alkaline.

AMUR MAPLE
Acer tataricum ssp. ginnala (Maxim.) Wesm.
HARDY IN ZONES 3 AND 4
20 feet tall, 20 feet wide

HABIT. Large, multi-stemmed shrub or small tree.
BRANCHES. Gray, slender, smooth.
BUDS. Small reddish brown, 0.12 to 0.2 in. long.
LEAVES. Simple, elongate, with two basal lobes, 1.5 to 3 in. long; lateral lobes pointed and terminal lobes acuminate; leaf margin doubly serrate; upper leaf surface dark green and undersurface light green and smooth; foliage turns an attractive orange to red in the fall; petioles slender, 0.5 to 1.5 in. long.
FLOWERS. Light yellow, fragrant, in long peduncled panicles, in early May.
FRUIT. Wings nearly parallel, 1 in. long including nutlets, usually turning from green to brown but in selected forms to bright red.

LANDSCAPE USE
A versatile small tree that can be grown as a small single trunk tree, clump specimen, large shrub or large hedge. Native to central and northern China, Manchuria, and Japan, it was introduced into North America in 1860. Its leaves are clean and attractive all summer long and depending on the selection of this maple can feature outstanding fall color. Some of Amur maple's cultivars with their brighter samaras can be stunning.

CULTURE
Prefers slightly acid, sandy loam soil but it is adaptable to a wide range of soil types and pH levels, although it needs a well drained soil. In truly alkaline soils it can develop chlorosis. Propagated by seeds or by softwood cuttings. Tolerates heavy pruning so this maple can be used as a hedge or screen. Amur maple can withstand partial shade. This maple in some areas can be a problem weed tree, but in the North it does not often spread.

CULTIVARS:

'Bailey Compact'   Amur maple
ZONES 3 AND 4
8 feet tall, 6 feet wide

Grows 8 feet at maturity in comparison to the 20 feet of the subspecies. Finer textured. Also sometimes sold as 'Compacta'.

'Embers'   Amur maple
ZONES 3 AND 4
15 feet tall, 20 feet wide

Bailey Nursery selected this variety for its red samaras and red fall color. It can be featured as a small, upright specimen tree as it is somewhat broader than the subspecies.

'Emerald Elf'   Amur maple
ZONES 3 AND 4
6 feet tall, 6 feet wide

Dark red fall color.

'Flame'
ZONES 3 AND 4
20 feet tall, 20 feet wide

The United States Department of Agriculture selected this Amur maple for its brilliant red fall color. Full-sized.

Other maples to try:

Those who enjoy trying unusual, hard-to-obtain varieties can try the following maples in favorable locations in zone 4.

ROCKY MOUNTAIN MAPLE
A. glabrum Torr.
TRIAL IN PROTECTED PARTS OF ZONE 4
30 feet tall, 20 feet wide in native habitat

Native in the Rocky Mountains from South Dakota to Montana and south to California and New Mexico. Try planting this maple in sheltered locations in cool, moist soil. One of the maples that has not done well in our area but it should be tested further.

PAPERBARK MAPLE
A. griseum (Franch.) Pax.
TRIAL IN ZONE 4
25 feet tall, 12 feet wide

Of variable hardiness, some authorities list this as a zone 4 maple, so it is worth a try in protected locations. A majestic maple growing up to 25 feet tall, its exfoliating bark is memorable.

MANCHURIAN MAPLE
A. mandschuricum Maxim.
TRIAL IN ZONE 4
30 feet tall, 25 feet wide

This maple is worth trying in zone 4. It is a small-sized maple reaching 30 feet. Native to Manchuria and Korea.

MIYABE MAPLE
A. miyabei Maxim.
TRIAL IN ZONE 4
30 feet tall, 20 feet wide

Has survived at the Arboretum. In its native Japan grows to 40 feet and features a small, rounded form. Needs moist, slightly acidic soils.

STRIPED MAPLE
A. pensylvanicum L.
TRIAL IN ZONE 4 IN PROTECTED LOCATIONS
15 feet tall, 10 feet tall

One of the most ornamental small maples, it features attractive, striped bark. Needs a very protected location. Best when planted in sheltered, shady areas where the soil is moist. Subject to winter sunscald when planted in the open. Propagated by seeds. Worth a trial for the right location. At The Minnesota Landscape Arboretum, there is a cultivar 'Erythrocladum' in its collection.

SYCAMORE MAPLE
A. pseudoplatanus L.
TRIAL IN ZONE 4
55 feet tall, 40 feet wide under good growing conditions

Very large growing under more temperate growing conditions, this maple can be tried in zone 4.

THREE-LEAVED MAPLE
A. triflorum Komar.
ZONE 4
20 feet tall, 20 feet wide

This small tree has bark similar to the paper bark maple (*A. griseum*) and has survived for many years at The Minnesota Landscape Arboretum. Considered the hardiest of the trifoliate maples.

SHANTUNG MAPLE, PURPLEBLOW MAPLE
A. truncatum Bunge.
HARDY IN ZONE 3 AND 4
20 feet tall, 20 feet wide

Native to northern China, it was introduced into North America in 1881. Prefers well-drained clay loam soil. Plant in full sun as a lawn specimen in a protected location. Arboretum specimens have done reasonably well.

THE KIWI

ARCTIC KIWI

Actinidia arguta (Sieb. & Zucc.)
Planch. & Miq.
FAMILY: ACTINIDIACEAE, KIWI FAMILY
FOR PROTECTED LOCATIONS IN ZONE 4
20 to 25 feet long

HABIT: Vigorous, high-climbing, twining vine; there are 30 species mainly from Asia.
BRANCHES. Brown with prominent vertical lenticels; pith brown and chambered; axillary.
BUDS. Small, enclosed by leaf bases; no terminal buds.
LEAVES. Alternate, simple, broad-ovate to elliptic, 3 to 4.5 in. long, with sharply serrate margins, acuminate tips, and rounded to somewhat heart-shaped or square bases; upper leaf surface dark green; stiff hairs on midrib of undersurface; petioles 1.2 to 3.2 in. long, sometimes with stiff hairs.
FLOWERS. Usually polygamo-dioecious, whitish or greenish, 3 or more in clusters, less than 1 in. wide, in June and July.
FRUIT. Edible, ellipsoid berries, 1 in. long, greenish yellow, in September and October.

LANDSCAPE USE

A native of Japan, Korea and Manchuria, this vine was introduced as an ornamental into North America in 1874. A prolific grower where hardy, this vine can be used for screening purposes. Although northern hardy kiwis produce small fruit (when male and female forms are grown in proximity), this species is grown for its vining habit. (Most often even this species' flowers/fruits are killed by winter temperatures). Many gardeners are tempted to try the more temperate-growing kiwis that are grown for their fruit.

CULTURE

Both male and female plants need to be planted in proximity for flowering/fruiting. Best grown in slightly acidic, well-drained soil in full sun, it needs stout support. Propagated from seeds or by hardwood or softwood cuttings. Not for exposed locations.

CULTIVARS:

'Ananasnaja'   kiwi
HARDY IN ZONE 4
15 feet long

A female cultivar that has fruited at the Arboretum in good years. It needs a male pollinator.

'Issai'   kiwi
HARDY IN ZONE 4
15 feet long

A self-fertile selection although fruiting is more assured if a male form is also planted. Without a male the fruit is seedless, although smaller. This cultivar is less often damaged by spring frosts in the North than is the species. Fruit are 1 to 1.5 in. in diameter and smooth skinned.

KOLOMITKA KIWI

Actinidia kolomitka. (Rupr. & Maxim.) Maxim.
VARIABLY HARDY TO ZONE 3 (DEPENDING ON SEED SOURCE)
20 to 30 feet long

HABIT. Ornamental vine.
BRANCHES. Brown with prominent lenticels; pith brown with fine chambers.
BUDS. Enclosed by leaf bases.
LEAVES. Alternate, simple, broad-ovate, 3 to 5 in. long, with sharply serrate margins; purple when young, gradually changing to green with prominent white and pink blotches taking up a good portion of the leaf surface; petioles 1.5 in. long, glabrous.
FLOWERS. White, up to 5 to a cluster, 0.5 in. across, often hidden by leaves.
FRUIT. Variably-sized from a small grape to 1 in.; smooth skinned, green pulp, in August and September.

LANDSCAPE USE

An attractive vine when used in the proper location where its white and pink leaf coloration can blend with its surroundings, or alternately, it can be used as a visual accent. The species can be grown for its fruit if both male and female forms are grown.

This kiwi was introduced into Europe in the 1870s from its native Asia. It is described as being a very vigorous grower in its native habitat growing up to 50 feet. The Arnold Arboretum introduced it into North America in the 1880s. The cultivar 'Arctic Beauty' is most often available in the trade (some authorities do not recognize 'Arctic Beauty' as a cultivar, but consider it a common name of the species).

CULTURE

Seems variably hardy from zone 3 southward. Grows well in full sun in the North in acid soils with pH between 7.0 and 5.0. Less vigorous than other kiwi. There are many other kiwi cultivars from Russia which need evaluation.

CULTIVAR:

'Arctic Beauty'   kiwi
HARDY IN ZONE 4; TRIAL IN ZONE 3
20 feet long

'Arctic Beauty' is often listed as being hardy in zone 3. This cultivar is a male form (non-fruiting) whose foliage is quite large and purple when young. Mature leaves are white and pink variegated.

THE BUCKEYES & HORSECHESTNUTS

Aesculus L.

FAMILY: HIPPOCASTANACEAE; HORSECHESTNUT

Generally, buckeyes are trees with bold character. Their large, coarse textured leaves and large panicled flowers are unusual in the landscape. However, they are not without problems including summer leaf scorch (browning of leaf margins and possible defoliation) and variable hardiness. The cultivar, 'Autumn Splendor', a Minnesota Landscape Arboretum introduction, is an improved variety for the North. There are a number of less hardy species and varieties that can be tried by those who like to experiment.

A. 'Autumn Splendor'   buckeye

ZONE 4

35 feet tall, 30 feet wide

A strain introduced in 1980 at The Minnesota Landscape Arboretum. Its dark green foliage color is outstanding and features good resistance to leaf scorch. It also has brilliant orange-red fall color and forms a dense, rounded canopy. Flowers are greenish yellow on terminal spikes. An outstanding ornamental useful as a specimen tree. *See photos p 140,178.*

OHIO BUCKEYE
Aesculus glabra Willd.

HARDY IN ZONES 3 AND 4

30 to 40 feet tall, 20 to 25 feet wide

HABIT. Upright tree of oval form; there are 15 species distributed worldwide.
BRANCHES. Stout, reddish brown to ashy gray, hairy at first becoming smooth, emitting a disagreeable odor when crushed.
BARK. Thick, ashy gray, deeply furrowed and plated.
BUDS. Large, 0.5 in. long, smooth with prominent brown scales.

LEAVES. 5 to 7 leaflets; leaflets elliptic to obovate, 3.2 to 4.5 in. long, with acuminate tips and wedge-shaped bases; fall color golden yellow, rarely reddish yellow.
FLOWERS. Greenish yellow, 0.5 to 1.2 long, in upright panicles, 4 to 5.5 in. long, in May.
FRUIT. Obovoid, 1.2 to 2 in. long, spiny, in September.

LANDSCAPE USE

Although smaller than other *Aesculus* species, its texture makes this buckeye seem even larger than it is in the landscape. Use as a specimen. Its attractive spring flowers and extreme hardiness make this a tree to consider for the North.

Native from Pennsylvania to Nebraska and south to Alabama, it has been in cultivation since 1901. Its shiny, dark brown nut, often called buckeyes, may be objectionable, but children find them irresistible when they fall off the trees in fall. Its fruit and bark should be considered toxic, however.

CULTURE

Buckeyes are not for dry soils; a well-watered landscape is ideal. Leaf scorch is a common problem on this buckeye. They relish full sun, will withstand part shade.

VARIETY:

Texas buckeye

var. *arguta* (Buckl.) B.L. Robinson.
ZONE 4
18 feet tall, 15 feet wide

This variety is sometimes given a species rank. Trees are smaller and leaflets are narrower than in the species.

COMMON HORSECHESTNUT

Aesculus hippocastanum L.
FOR PROTECTED LOCATIONS IN ZONE 4
40 to 50 feet tall, 25 to 32 feet wide

HABIT. Upright, oval trees.
BRANCHES. Stout, reddish yellow to grayish brown.
BUDS. Large, 1 in. long, reddish brown, varnished with a sticky gum.
LEAVES. 5 to 7 leaflets; leaflets obovate, 4 to 9.5 in. long, with doubly serrate margins, acuminate tips, and wedge-shaped bases; upper leaf surface dark green; undersurface hairy when young, with rusty hairs at base.
FLOWERS. White, tinged with red, 0.5 in. long, in panicles 7.5 to 12 in. long.
FRUIT. Spiny, 2.2 in. across, with 1 or 2 seeds.

LANDSCAPE USE

Native to northern Greece and Bulgaria. There is no definitive answer how this species got its common name, but this tree probably was used as a folk medicine for horses in pre-Linnaen Europe. John Rea, a gardener of Shropshire, published a book which has been called the most important English book on gardening published in the later seventeenth century. In this book, *Flora: Seu de Florum Cultura* (1676, 224) he states "The name was imposed from the property of the Nuts, which in Turky are given to Horses in their Provender, to cure such as have coughs, or are broken winded".

Introduced in North America by a shipment of seeds that Peter Collinson sent to John Bartram of Philadelphia in 1741. It features outstanding flowers in late spring. Horsechestnut can be used as a specimen tree where its coarse and bold texture can make an impact.

CULTURE

A sheltered location is best in the North because sunscald has been a problem on trees in the Arboretum. A moisture retentive but well-drained soil helps prevent leaf scorch in the summer. Propagated by seeds and budding.

CULTIVARS:

Most of the following are of unproven hardiness in zone 4.

| **'Alba'** | Ohio buckeye |

Flowers are pure white.

| **'Baumannii'** | Ohio buckeye |

Flowers are white, double.

| **'Umbraculifera'** | Ohio buckeye |

Dwarf shrubby form.

Other buckeyes and horsechestnuts to try:

The following members of this genus can be tried in our area. Most are not often grown in the home landscape.

RED HORSECHESNUT

A. x carnea Hayne.
FOR PROTECTED LOCATIONS IN ZONE 4
30 feet tall, 25 feet wide

Plant in well-drained soil in a sheltered location. A specimen tree needing a very protected location in the North. 'Briotii' and 'Rosea' are also found in the trade and with the same limited hardiness.

YELLOW BUCKEYE, SWEET BUCKEYE

A. flava Sol.
ZONES 3 AND 4
50 feet tall, 40 feet wide

Formerly *A. octandra*. Native from Pennsylvania to southern Illinois and south to Georgia. Similar to *A. glabra* for culture and landscape use.

BOTTLEBRUSH BUCKEYE

A. parviflora Walt.
CAN BE TRIED IN PROTECTED LOCATIONS OF ZONE 4
8 feet tall, 12 feet wide

Where hardy, this clump-forming shrub needs space to expand.

PAINTED BUCKEYE

A. sylvatica Bartr.
ZONE 4
12 feet tall, 15 feet wide

This buckeye can be used as an ornamental lawn specimen. It has been of variable hardiness.

TREE OF HEAVEN

Tree of heaven
Ailanthus altissima (Mill.) Swingle.

(Hardy in only southern parts of zone 4. A weed tree which is not recommended for planting even where it is hardy as it soon becomes a pest.)

AKEBIA

FIVELEAF AKEBIA
Akebia quinata (Houtt.) Decne.
FAMILY: LARDIZABALACEAE
FOR PROTECTED LOCATIONS IN ZONE 4
25 feet long

HABIT. Twining vine; there are 4 species from Asia.
BRANCHES. Slender, at first green, becoming brown at maturity.
BUDS. Small with 10 to 12 overlapping, sharp-pointed scales.
LEAVES. Deciduous, alternate, palmately compound with 5 leaflets; leaflets obovate or elliptic to oblong-obovate, 1.2 to 2.2 in. long, with notched tips and rounded to broadly wedge-shaped bases; petioles 1.5 to 3 in. long.
FLOWERS. Polygamo-monoecious; pistillate flowers purplish brown, 1 to 1.2 in. across; staminate flowers rosy purple, smaller in May.
FRUIT. Sausage-like pods, 2.2 to 3.2 in. long, purplish violet, in September and October.

LANDSCAPE USE
Native to Central China, Japan and Korea, it was introduced into North America in 1845. Use on a trellis or pergola for screening. In the Pacific Northwest and other less severe climates this vine becomes a pest and is sometimes called the kudzu of the North. The leaves often darken and persist on the vine into winter.

CULTURE
This vigorous vine prefers good soil and full sun. It is such a vigorous grower that it can be cut to the ground in the spring, yet it still can cover an amazing amount of vertical space. Propagated from seeds or cuttings. Fruit and seeds are seldom produced under cultivation unless the flowers are hand-pollinated.

The ALDERS

EUROPEAN ALDER, BLACK ALDER
Alnus glutinosa (L.) Gaertn.
FAMILY: BETULACEAE, BIRCH FAMILY
HARDY IN ZONE 4
50 feet tall, 32 feet wide

HABIT. Upright tree of oval form, becoming open with age; there are 35 species distributed worldwide.
BRANCHES. Glabrous, greenish brown.
BARK. Grayish brown.
BUDS. Prominent, stalked, reddish purple, 0.5 in. long.
LEAVES. Oval or obovate to suborbicular, 1.5 to 4 in. long, with coarsely and doubly serrate margins, rounded or notched tips, and broad, wedge-shaped bases, nearly smooth except for tufts of hairs beneath; petioles short, with ovate to lanceolate stipules.
FLOWERS. Staminate catkins 2 to 4 in. long and pistillate catkins 1.2 to 2 in. long, egg-shaped, in April.
FRUIT. Nutlets mature in October and persist in pistillate catkins over winter.

LANDSCAPE USE AND CULTURE
Because it is found mostly on wet sites in its native habitat, this tree can be a welcome addition for problem sites in the northern landscape. As with other alders, European alder fixes its own nitrogen from the atmosphere so consequently will tolerate poorer soils. This alder features handsome glossy foliage and catkins which persist into the winter. It can be short-lived in dry sites. Native to Europe, the Caucasian Mountains and Siberia, it was introduced into North America by early settlers. Propagated by seeds and budding.

As John Evelyn in his famous *Silva* (1706, 98) in the collection of Andersen Horticultural Library at the Arboretum states, alder is "the most faithful lover of water and boggy places." Henry David Thoreau was an admirer of alder. In his *Journal*, vol. 1 (1841, 216-217) he whimsically states: "With cheerful heart I could be a soujourner in the wilderness if I were sure to find there the catkins of the alder. When I read of them in the accounts of Northern adventurers, by Baffin's bay or Mackenzie's river, I see how even there too I could dwell. They are my little vegetable redeemer. Methinks my virtue will not flag ere they come again."

CULTIVARS:

The following cultivars are available and can be tried in zone 4.

'Aurea'
European alder
TRIAL IN PROTECTED LOCATIONS IN ZONE 4
30 feet tall, 20 feet wide

Leaves golden yellow.

'Imperialis'   European alder
Hardy in zone 4
30 feet tall, 20 feet wide.

Deeply divided leaves.

'Laciniata'   European alder
HARDY IN ZONE 4
30 feet tall, 20 feet wide

Leaves finely cut.

'Pyramidalis'   European alder
HARDY ZONE 4
35 feet tall, 12 feet wide

Narrow, upright form.

WHITE ALDER, GRAY ALDER
Alnus incana (L.) Moench.
HARDY IN ZONES 2 TO 4
50 feet tall, 25 feet wide

HABIT. Large growing, somewhat pyramidal tree.
BRANCHES. Glabrous, gray-brown.
BARK. Gray.
LEAVES. Alternate, broad-ovate to oval; base rounded or cuneate; doubly serrate; upper leaf surface dullish green, grayish underneath; petiole pubescent, 0.5 to 1 in. long.

LANDSCAPE USE AND CULTURE
Again, tolerates wet or even dry soils so is useful in problem sites. Hardy.

CULTIVAR:

'Laciniata'   white alder
HARDY ZONE 3
40 feet tall, 30 feet wide

Leaves light green and finely divided into 6 or 8 pairs of lobes.

SPECKLED ALDER, SMOOTH ALDER
Alnus rugosa (Du Roi) Spreng.
HARDY IN ZONES 2 TO 4
20 feet tall, 16 feet wide

HABIT. Large shrub or small tree.
BRANCHES. Smooth with horizontally striped lenticels.
LEAVES. Deciduous, alternate, simple, pinnately-veined, elliptic to obovate, with serrulate margins, acute or obtuse tips, and wedge-shaped bases; upper leaf surface dark green; undersurface light green and smooth or with hairs on veins.

LANDSCAPE USE
Prefers a wet soil high in organic matter; therefore like other alders it can be a useful plant for problem locations. It is native from Maine to Minnesota and south to Florida. Readily identified by its distinctive speckled bark and twigs.

CULTURE
This native is hard to obtain in the nursery trade. It is readily propagated from seed collected from the wild or from specialty seed houses.

OTHER ALDERS TO TRY:

HAZEL ALDER
A. serrulata (Ait.) Willd.
FOR PROTECTED LOCATIONS IN ZONE 4
Height variable to 18 feet

A native of eastern North America it is found often in wet sites in more southern locations. For the North, *A. rugosa* is very similar and is hardier. Hard to find in the nursery trade.

SITKA ALDER
A. sinuata (Reg.) Rydb.
HARDY IN ZONE 2 TO 4
30 feet tall, 18 feet wide

Native in Western North America, it is listed as being hardy to zone 2. It grows over a wide range, so it probably is important to find a source from its northern range. Shrub or small tree.

MOUNTAIN ALDER
A. tenuifolia Nutt.
HARDY ZONE 2 TO 4
25 feet tall, 18 feet wide

Another native of western North America listed as being hardy to zone 2. Small tree.

The SERVICEBERRIES
Amelanchier Medik.
FAMILY: ROSACEAE, ROSE FAMILY

These useful small trees and large shrubs can serve many functions in the home landscape; they should be used more. Some are grown for their fruit which also attracts wildlife. All are of informal habit with soft texture. They have many common names; in the east they are called shad, shadbush, sarviceberry, in the midwest serviceberry and Juneberry. They are also called sugar pear, Indian pear, May cherry and more (from these common names one senses their useful character). Native Americans used them both fresh and dried. Pemmican, a food staple, was made combining dried and pulverized deer meat with berries from this genus along with melted fat.

Most species of this genus are drought tolerant, some can be grown in wet soils. There are other *Amelanchier* that can be grown in shelterbelts or for screening where they can be spaced 5 feet apart. If growing them as shrubs, older trunks can be removed (as one treats lilacs) to keep the planting vigorous. *See photograph page 170-71.*

SASKATOON SERVICEBERRY
Amelanchier alnifolia (Nutt.) Nutt.
HARDY IN ZONES 2 TO 4

3 to 12 feet tall, 6 to 9 feet wide

HABIT. Suckering shrub; there are 25 species distributed worldwide.
BUDS. 0.3 in. long, chestnut brown.
LEAVES. Pinnately veined with 8 to 10 pair of lateral veins curving upward and forking, 1 to 2 in. long, elliptic to quadrate-rounded, broadly obovate, sometimes serrate-dentate, mostly above middle, with rounded or square tips and rounded bases; young leaves at first yellowish-pubescent, soon becoming smooth.
FLOWERS. Erect racemes 0.5 to 1.2 in. long, in early May.
FRUIT. Globose to reverse pear-shaped, purplish blue, sweet and juicy, in July.

LANDSCAPE USE
Native in the Great Plains from Manitoba and Saskatchewan to Nebraska. Over this wide range these plants can range in size from 12 feet tall to colonies of shrubs only half as tall. Its fragrant May flowers, blooming before the leaves, are one of the most welcome spring sights in the plains.

Professor Charles S. Sargent in his *Silva of North America*, vol 4 (1892, 132) states this plant "was noticed early in this century by the party of explorers who, under the leadership of Lewis and Clark, first crossed North America; and it was introduced into cultivation by David Douglas who, in 1826, sent seeds to the London Horticultural Society."

It is often planted as an ornamental shrub and for its edible fruit that is prized for making Juneberry pies. Birds also love the fruit, so some means of protection (such as bird netting) is necessary in order to enjoy the fruit. If growing for fruit consider some of the varieties listed below that were developed in Canada. Although somewhat self-fertile, planting two or more varieties insure more productive fruiting.

CULTURE
Grow in full sun as Juneberry becomes leggy in part shade. Requires little pruning and has no disease or pest problems. The species is propagated by seeds and cuttings.

CULTIVARS:
A number of cultivars have been selected for the size and quality of the fruit. All are hardy in zones 2 to 4.

'Northline'   Saskatoon serviceberry

Developed in Canada in 1960. One of the biggest producers of fruit.

'Pembina'   Saskatoon serviceberry

Developed in Canada in 1956. More suckering.

'Regent'   Saskatoon serviceberry

Shrub growing 4 to 6 feet with excellent foliage.

'Smokey'   Saskatoon serviceberry

A very productive cultivar originating in Canada in 1956.

'Thiessen'   Saskatoon serviceberry

Described as a heavy producer of large fruit.

DOWNY SERVICEBERRY
Amelanchier arborea

(Michx.f.) Fern.
HARDY IN ZONES 2 TO 4
25 feet tall (rarely taller), 15 to 20 fe

HABIT. Narrow upright shrub or small tree.
BUDS. Broadly ovate, 0.2 to 0.5 in. long, greenish yellow or cinnamon brown.
LEAVES. Ovate to slightly obovate, 1.5 to 3.2 in. long, with sharply and often doubly serrate margins nearly to base, acuminate tips, and heart-shaped bases.
FLOWERS. In short, moderately dense racemes, 2 to 3 in. long, ascending to nodding, in early May.
FRUIT. Globose, reddish purple, dry, and tasteless, in late June and early July.

LANDSCAPE USE AND CULTURE

Native in eastern North America from Canada to Florida, it is often found naturalized at the edge of woods. Occasionally planted as a small clump tree. Often it has a brilliant red fall color, while the bluish gray bark and twigs can provide winter interest. Culture is the same as *A. alnifolia*.

SHADBLOW, SHADBLOW SERVICEBERRY
Amelanchier canadensis (L.) Medik.

HARDY IN ZONES 2 TO 4
15 feet tall, 13 feet wide

HABIT. Upright shrub.
LEAVES. Similar to *A. arborea*, but with young leaves hairy on both sides.
FLOWERS. In erect, compact racemes, 1.2 to 2 in. long, in early May.
FRUIT. Nearly black and juicy, in early July.

LANDSCAPE USE AND CULTURE

Native in swamps from Maine to South Carolina, it has been in cultivation since 1623. Useful for naturalizing in low, wet soils. Most often grown in multi-stemmed clumps in the shrub border. Often confused with *A. arborea* in the trade.

Samuel Green in his *Forestry in Minnesota* (1898, 243) states "The Indians of Minnesota and Dakota gather the berries in rather large quantities and sell small quantities in some of the remote towns." *See photograph pages 180-81.*

CULTIVAR:

'Prince William'   downy serviceberry
HARDY IN ZONE 4; TRIAL ZONE 3
10 feet tall, 6 feet wide

This cultivar fruits heavily. An upright growing multi-stemmed shrub.

APPLE SERVICEBERRY
Amelanchier x grandiflora Rehd.

HARDY IN ZONES 2 TO 4
25 feet tall, 20 feet wide

HABIT. A small, clump tree.
LEAVES. Purplish when unfolding and woolly-hairy, soon becoming smooth.
FLOWERS. Rather large with obtuse petals, occasionally tinged with purple in bud, in early May.

LANDSCAPE USE

A naturally occurring hybrid between *A. arborea* and *A. laevis*, it has been cultivated since 1870. Often grown as an ornamental clump specimen. The cultivars are most often planted.

CULTURE

Suckers produced by this clump forming specimen can be a problem in the landscape.

CULTIVARS:

Autumn Brilliance®   apple serviceberry
HARDY ZONE 4, FOR PROTECTED LOCATIONS IN ZONE 3
25 feet tall, 15 feet wide

Introduced in 1986 by Willet Wandell. Has resistance to leaf spot. An upright growing small tree. The long-lasting autumn foliage lives up to its name.

'Ballerina'   apple serviceberry
ZONE 4
15 feet tall, 15 feet wide

Introduced from the Netherlands. Upright growing with white flowers.

'Coles Select'   apple serviceberry
ZONE 4
20 feet tall, 15 feet wide

Good red fall color. This small tree is more spreading than other *A. x grandiflora* cultivars. Noted for its thicker, glossy foliage.

'Princess Diana' apple serviceberry
ZONE 4
20 feet tall, 18 feet wide

Described as having the most brilliant red fall color of all the serviceberries. A spreading, small tree.

'Robin Hill' apple serviceberry
TRIAL IN ZONE 4
20 feet tall, 15 feet wide

Buds tinged with pink, but flowers white when open. Introduced in 1932.

'Strata' apple serviceberry
ZONE 4
20 feet tall, 25 feet wide

An introduction of Dr. Ed Hasselkus of Wisconsin. It is broadly spreading with white flowers, dark fruit and good fall color.

ALLEGHANY SERVICEBERRY
Amelanchier laevis Wieg.
HARDY IN ZONES 2 TO 4
25 to 30 feet tall, 20 to 25 feet wide

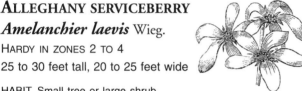

HABIT. Small tree or large shrub.
BRANCHES. Spreading, slender, smooth, at first reddish brown, becoming grayish brown by second year.
BUDS. Up to 0.5 in. long, green, tinged with red, with overlapping scales.
LEAVES. Elliptic-ovate to ovate-oblong, 1.2 to 2.5 in. long, with serrate margins nearly to the base, acuminate tips, and somewhat heart-shaped or rounded bases, quite smooth and purplish when young.
FLOWERS. In slender, many flowered, nodding racemes, in early May; petals linear-oblong, up to 0.5 in. long; top of ovary smooth.
FRUIT. Purple or nearly black, sweet, in late June or early July.

LANDSCAPE USE
Native from Newfoundland to Georgia and west to Minnesota and Kansas, it has been in cultivation since 1870. Many consider this the most attractive and useful species.

The Alleghany serviceberry is often found as a slender growing clump specimen which suckers very little. It has clean, attractive foliage and good dark red fall color. This useful ornamental probably has the largest flowers of all serviceberry species. Use as a featured specimen or in a shrub border. *See photograph page 168.*

CULTURE
If grown on a *Sorbus* understock, as is sometimes the case, this selection suckers too readily. Propagated by seeds.

CULTIVARS:

'Cumulus'
Alleghany serviceberry
ZONE 4
25 feet tall, 20 feet wide

Introduced in 1972 by the Princeton Nurserymen's Research Association.

'Snowcloud' Alleghany serviceberry
ZONE 4
30 feet tall, 20 feet wide

Introduced in 1992 by the Princeton Nurserymen's Research Association. Selected for its upright growth habit. Often grown as a smaller growing boulevard tree.

RUNNING SERVICEBERRY
Amelanchier stolonifera Wieg.
HARDY IN ZONES 2 TO 4
3 to 6 feet tall, 6 feet wide

HABIT. Upright, suckering shrub, often forming thickets.
LEAVES. Elliptic, rarely elliptic-oblong or suborbicular, rounded at base or occasionally somewhat heart-shaped, 0.5 to 2 in. long, finely serrate, usually quite or nearly entire along lower third of leaves, densely white tomentose beneath when young.
FLOWERS. In short, upright racemes; petals obovate-oblong, about 0.30 in. long, white, in early May.
FRUIT. Purplish black, sweet, in July.

LANDSCAPE USE AND CULTURE
The same as for *A. alnifolia.*

OTHER SERVICEBERRIES TO TRY:
There are many other serviceberries that could be tried. *A. lamarckii* zone 4, 25 feet tall with limited suckering; and *A. ovalis* zone 4 are two.

LEAD PLANT AND INDIGOS

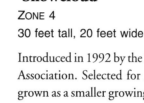

LEAD PLANT
Amorpha canescens Pursh.
FAMILY: LEGUMINOSAE, PEA FAMILY
HARDY IN ZONES 2 TO 4
3 feet tall, 3 feet wide

HABIT. Low shrub; there are 15 North American species.
BRANCHES Angled, densely grayish hairy.
LEAVES. Spreading, 2 to 4.5 in. long, with 15 to 45 leaflets;

leaflets elliptic to oblong-lanceolate, 0.3 to 0.8 in. long, acute or obtuse, rounded at base, hairy and gray on both sides.
FLOWERS. Blue, in dense, clustered spikes 1.2 to 5.5 in. long, in June and July; calyx villous, standards wedge-shaped to obovate.
FRUIT. Straight-backed pods, 0.16 in. long, ripen in September.

LANDSCAPE USE

Many do not recognize *Amorpha* as woody plants because they are most often used as an herbaceous perennial for a flower border or as a prairie plant. Cultivated since 1883, it is native from Michigan to Saskatchewan and south to Indiana. It is drought tolerant.

It is pictured and described in *Curtis's Botanical Magazine* (1882, plate 6618), a magazine started in 1787 and still being issued. It states "This, the 'Lead Plant' of the United States, is said to be so called from a belief that its presence indicates the presence of that ore in the soil-a superstition probably due to the leaden hue of the plant; a better name is that of the genus, 'Bastard Indigo'."

CULTURE

Needs well-drained soil and full sun. Propagated by cuttings, division, or by seeds planted as soon as they are ripe or in the spring following stratification. It can be rejuvenated in the spring by pruning out older wood.

INDIGO BUSH, FALSE INDIGO
Amorpha fruticosa L.
HARDY IN ZONES 3 TO 4
12 feet tall, 12 feet wide

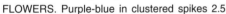

HABIT. Tall shrub.
BRANCHES. Sparingly hairy, becoming smooth.
LEAVES. Green, with 11 to 25 leaflets; leaflets oval or elliptic, 0.5 to 1.5 in. long, rounded at both ends, sharp-pointed, finely hairy to smooth.
FLOWERS. Purple-blue in clustered spikes 2.5 to 5.5 in. long, in May and June; calyx sparingly hairy to smooth, with lobes shorter than tubes; standards orbicular-obovate, 0.24 in. long.
FRUIT. Curved pods 0.3 in. long, ripens in August.

LANDSCAPE USE

Native from Connecticut to Minnesota and south to Louisiana and Florida. It makes a good lakeshore or pond edge plant. Cultivated since 1724.

CULTURE

Needs a moist soil and full sun. Propagated by seeds that require acid treatment and cold stratification.

FRAGRANT FALSE INDIGO
Amorpha nana Nutt.
HARDY IN ZONES 2 TO 4
2 feet tall, 2 feet wide

HABIT. Very low shrub.
BRANCHES. Smooth.
LEAVES. Crowded on the stem, 1.2 to 4 in. long, rounded or sharp-pointed at apex, wedge-shaped or rounded at base, smooth.
FLOWERS. Purple, in usually solitary racemes, 2 to 4 in. long, in May and June; calyx smooth with lobes half as long as tube; standards wedge-shaped to obovate, 0.16 in. long.
FRUIT. Straight-backed pods, 0.2 in. long, ripens in September.

LANDSCAPE USE

An interesting shrub for naturalizing or in prairie plantings. Cultivated since 1811, it is native from Manitoba and Saskatchewan to Iowa and New Mexico.

CULTURE

Full sun. Propagated by seeds or cuttings.

PORCELAIN BERRY

PORCELAIN BERRY
Ampelopsis brevipedunculata (Maxim.) Trautv.
FAMILY: VITACEAE, GRAPE FAMILY
FOR PROTECTED LOCATIONS IN ZONE 4
15 feet long

HABIT. Vigorous deciduous vine that climbs by tendrils; there are 25 species distributed in North America and Asia.
BRANCHES. Hairy when young.
LEAVES. Alternate, simple, broad-ovate, 2.2 to 4.5 in. long, acuminate, heart-shaped, 3-lobed with lateral lobes broadly triangular-ovate, spreading, coarsely serrate, dark green above, lighter beneath and with spreading hairs; petioles as long as blade or shorter, hairy.
FLOWERS. Perfect, small, greenish, 5-merous, in July and August; inflorescence a cyme on hairy stalks 0.5 to 1.5 in. long.
FRUIT. Attractive 1- to 4-seeded berries, 0.25 to 0.30 in. across, changing from pale lilac to bright blue in September and October.

LANDSCAPE USE

For those looking for a prolific vine for summer screening, porcelain berries should be considered. This grape relative grows 15 feet in a season so a sturdy trellis or support is needed. As it clings by tendrils it needs a support it can grasp. The fruit are bead-like with green, turquoise, red and purplish blue berries appearing in the same cluster. Berries do not persist into the winter, or last in dried bouquets. It is a native of northeast Asia.

CULTURE

Needs full or part sun with well-drained soil. Annual pruning of dead wood in the spring is necessary. If a less vigorous grower is wanted, consider the cultivar 'Elegans'. Easily grown from cuttings.

CULTIVAR:

'Elegans'
porcelain berry
TRIAL IN PROTECTED
LOCATION IN ZONE 4
Rarely 15 feet

This cultivar features smaller leaves than the species. It is also less vigorous and not as hardy in zone 4. With a reasonable location 'Elegans' should still be root hardy and grow 10 to 12 feet annually. Nancy Rose, of the Arboretum's research staff, has had excellent luck with this cultivar. She considers it to be hardy in most locations of zone 4. In severe winters or winters without snowcover it probably will suffer dieback to the ground. This cultivar has variegated leaves that include some pink pigmentation when the leaves first appear in the spring.

BOG ROSEMARY

BOG ROSEMARY
Andromeda polifolia L.
FAMILY: ERICACEAE, HEATH FAMILY
HARDY IN ZONES 2 TO 4
1 foot tall, 1 foot wide

HABIT. Low evergreen shrub with creeping rootstocks; there are 2 species distributed in the northern hemisphere.
STEMS. Upright with few side branches.
BUDS. Small with 2 outer scales in winter.
LEAVES. Oblong to linear, 0.5 to 1.5 in. long, usually acute, with edges rolled backward, glaucous beneath, entire.
FLOWERS. In terminal, nodding umbels, in May and June; calyx small, 5-lobed, usually reddish, corolla globose to urn-shaped with 5 short, recurved lobes, 0.25 in. long, white to pink; stamens 10.
FRUIT. Are 5-valved capsules, subglobose to obovoid.

LANDSCAPE USE

This bog plant is native over a large area in cooler areas of the world including North America, northern Europe and Asia. It could make a good ground cover or ornamental plant if its growing requirements are met.

CULTURE

To grow this plant you must duplicate its native ecology which is bog-like and cool. A soil that is moisture retentive with a lower pH level would be ideal.

CULTIVAR:

There are many compact growing cultivars of this species that would be worth exploring if you have the correct growing conditions. Among them:

'Nana'   bog rosemary
ZONES 2 TO 4
12 inches tall, 2 feet wide

A vigorous, small plant suitable for bog gardens with usually pink flowers.

JAPANESE ANGELICA & OTHERS

JAPANESE ANGELICA
Aralia elata (Miq.) Seem.
FAMILY: ARALIACEAE, ARALIA FAMILY
FOR PROTECTED LOCATIONS IN ZONE 4
32 feet tall, 20 feet wide

HABIT. Large shrub or small tree; there are 40 species distributed worldwide.
LEAVES. Very large, sometimes 3 feet long, bipinnate; leaflets ovate to elliptic-ovate, 2.2 to 4.5 in. long, acuminate, serrate with rather broad teeth, dark green above, glaucous beneath.
FLOWERS. In broad corymbose inflorescences consisting of a short main axis with several subumbellate spreading branches 12 to 17 in. long, terminating in umbels, creamy white in August.
FRUIT. Ripens in September and October.

LANDSCAPE USE

In a protected location this small tree could be a feature in a landscape. If relatively protected, it would make a good choice for a tree in a parking area. Its flowers in August are quite showy (it has a tropical look). There are cultivars available including a variegated form, but these would be less hardy.

CULTURE

Needs full sun but tolerates diverse soil conditions. Only for protected locations of zone 4.

BRISTLY SARSAPARILLA
Aralia hispida Vent.
HARDY IN ZONES 2 TO 4
3 feet tall, 3 feet wide

HABIT. A subshrub.
STEMS. Woody at base with creeping rootstocks.
LEAVES. Bipinnate, leaflets ovate to elliptic-oblong, 0.5 to 2.5 in.

long, acute, rounded or broadly wedge-shaped at base, sharply and irregularly serrate, smooth or hairy on veins beneath.
FLOWERS. White, in June and July; umbels on slender pedicels, 3 or more in loose terminal corymbs.
FRUIT. Subglobose, 0.2 to 0.3 in. across, purple-black, in August and September.

LANDSCAPE USE

Useful for naturalized areas or shady wildflower gardens. Native in northeastern United States and Canada as far west as Minnesota. Hard to obtain in the nursery trade.

Curtis's Botanical Magazine (1808, plate 1085) dismisses it: "This plant, first detected by Michaux in the steep rocky mountains between Canada and Hudson's Bay...[has] no beauty or other pleasing qualities to recommend them..."

CULTURE

Needs well-drained soils and tolerates some shade. Propagation is by seed which have dormant embryos and impermeable seed coats. Mechanical or chemical scarification may be required for germination.

HERCULES CLUB, DEVIL'S WALKING STICK
Aralia spinosa L.
FOR PROTECTED LOCATIONS IN ZONE 4
20 feet tall, 20 feet wide

HABIT. Small tree or large shrub.
STEMS. Stout, little-branched, very prickly.
LEAVES. Bipinnate, 15 to 30 in. long, usually prickly above; leaflets ovate, 2 to 3 in. long, acuminate, serrate with small teeth, glaucous and nearly smooth beneath.
FLOWERS. Small, white, in large, hairy panicles 7.5 to 14 in. long, in August.
FRUIT. Globose, black, 0.25 in. across, in September and October.

LANDSCAPE USE

Not completely hardy, this exotic looking shrub often dies back to the ground at the Arboretum. Native from southern Pennsylvania to eastern Iowa and south to Florida and eastern Texas, it has been in cultivation since 1688. Its dramatic form makes it worth trying. Both in mid-summer flowering and fall fruit it is a feature plant at the back of a shrub or perennial border. Its common names are applied from the thickly armored canes which are often dried and used as canes or clubs for curiosities. This woody plant has more merit than being a curiosity.

CULTURE

Plant in protected location in full sun. Propagated from seeds and its suckers. Dr. Snyder in his first edition wished for hardier strains of this genus; gardeners are still looking for a hardier strain.

BEARBERRY

BEARBERRY
Arctostaphylos uva-ursi (L.) A. Gray.
FAMILY: ERICACEAE, HEATH FAMILY
HARDY IN ZONES 2 TO 4
6 inches tall, 3 feet wide

HABIT. Prostrate, evergreen shrub with rooting branches; there are 50 species distributed in North America.
BRANCHES. Smooth or slightly woolly when young.
BUDS. Small, ovoid with few outer scales in winter.
LEAVES. Alternate, simple, entire, obovate or obovate-oblong, up to 1 in. long, wedge-shaped, with edges folded backward; upper leaf surface bright green, undersurface lighter.
FLOWERS. Few, in nodding racemes, in May and June; calyx persistent, with 4 to 5 parts; corolla urn-shaped, 0.15 to 0.25 in. long, white, tinged with pink; stamens 8 to 10.
FRUIT. Red, drupe-like, with 4 to 10 nutlets, in August and September.

LANDSCAPE USE

Bearberry makes an excellent ground cover in a well-drained, sandy and acid soil. In favorable sites mats spreading to 15 feet are not unknown and can be used for erosion control. Seed source is important with this plant, so purchase only plants from northern strains.

It is native over a wide range including northern Europe, Asia, and North America. In North America it is found as far south as Virginia and New Mexico. It also has many other common names including fox plum, whortleberry, and barren myrtle. Kinnikinick was the name Native Americans gave to this plant. Cultivated since 1800.

CULTURE

Requires an acidic soil of between 5.0 to 7.0 pH and also good drainage. It grows best in full sun but will withstand light shade. It has drought tolerance. Where used as a ground cover, it can be maintained with a yearly high mowing. Winter snow cover is probably not necessary but certainly a plus. Propagated by seeds and cuttings.

CULTIVAR:

'Massachusetts'   bearberry
ZONES 3 AND 4
12 inches tall, 3 feet wide

Features smaller leaves than the species. Introduced by Mr. Robert Tichner of Oregon.

DUTCHMAN'S PIPE

DUTCHMAN'S PIPE
Aristolochia macrophylla Lam.
FAMILY: ARISTOLOCHIACEAE
BIRTHWORT FAMILY
HARDY IN ZONE 4
32 feet long

HABIT. Twining vine; there are 300 species distributed worldwide.
BRANCHES. Smooth.
LEAVES. Deciduous, alternate, kidney-shaped, 4 to 12 in. long, pointed or obtuse, dark green and smooth above, pale green beneath; petioles 1.2 to 2.5 in. long.
FLOWERS. 1 or 2, axillary, on pedicels 1.2 to 2 in. long with a bract below center, in May; perianth U-shaped, tubular, yellowish green, and smooth outside, constricted at the mouth and spreading into a 3-lobed, smooth, brownish purple limb up to 0.5 in. across, shaped like a meerschaum pipe.
FRUIT. Capsules 2.2 to 3.2 in. long and 6-ribbed, in September.

LANDSCAPE USE
A vine that can provide screening because of its dense foliage and vigorous growth habit. It is also grown for its handsome large leaves and attractive pipe-like flowers (the flowers are somewhat hidden by the leaves). Native in mountains of eastern North America from Pennsylvania to Georgia, it has been in cultivation since 1783. It was formerly named *A. durior*.

CULTURE
Propagated by seeds, division or cuttings. An aggressive grower that needs space and sturdy support. Grows best in full sun although it tolerates part shade. A well-drained, good garden soil is best.

The CHOKEBERRY
Aronia *Medik.*
FAMILY: ROSACEAE, ROSE FAMILY

There has been recent interest and research on chokeberry as a very suitable ornamental shrub and fruit producer for extreme northern climates. In Russia and Europe there has been much success in cultivating these shrubs for their fruit. Closely related to *Sorbus* (mountain ash) these shrubs are sometimes grafted on *Sorbus* rootstocks.

RED CHOKEBERRY
Aronia arbutifolia (L.) Pers.
FOR PROTECTED LOCATIONS IN ZONE 4
9 feet tall, 3 feet wide

HABIT. Upright shrub; there are only 2 recognized species in North America.
BRANCHES. Slender, woolly.
LEAVES. Elliptic to oblong or obovate, acute or abruptly acuminate, smooth above, except the midrib, grayish woolly beneath.
FLOWERS. Woolly inflorescences, 1.2 to 1.5 in. across, white or reddish, in May; calyx lobes glandular.
FRUIT. Subglobose or pear-shaped, 0.2 in. across, bright or dull red, in September and October.

LANDSCAPE USE
Used for the back of the shrub border or naturalistic plantings. Colorful fruit and outstanding fall red color are its chief landscape assets. The fruit often remains on the plant over winter. At the Arboretum it has not been as hardy as *A. melanocarpa* or *A. prunifolia*. Cultivated since 1700, it is native from Massachusetts to Florida west to Texas mainly in wetlands.

CULTURE
Plant in more protected areas. Propagated by seeds, divisions and cuttings. Seemingly tolerates wet or dry conditions. It suckers in favorable conditions forming a dense thicket. Its leggy growth habit in the landscape can be overcome by planting smaller shrubs or perennials at its base.

CULTIVAR:

'Brilliantissima'   red chokeberry

FOR PROTECTED LOCATIONS IN ZONE 4
4 feet tall, 5 feet wide

Selected for its rich crimson foliage in the fall and for its larger and showier flowers. Trial in only the most protected areas of zone 4.

BLACK CHOKEBERRY
Aronia melanocarpa (Michx.) Elliott.

HARDY IN ZONES 3 AND 4; FOR
PROTECTED LOCATIONS IN ZONE 2
6 feet tall, 5 feet wide

HABIT. Low shrub.
BRANCHES. Nearly smooth.
LEAVES. Elliptic or obovate to oblong-oblanceolate, abruptly acuminate or obtusish, 0.5 to 2.2 in. long, bright green and smooth or nearly so beneath, turning striking red in the fall.
FLOWERS. White on flat-topped corymbs, smooth or nearly so, in May.
FRUIT. Globose, 0.25 to 0.50 in. across, shiny black or black-purple, in August and September.

LANDSCAPE USE

Although less showy than *A. arbutifolia*, this species is fully hardy. Grown for its glossy green foliage and quite showy spring flowers. Useful for shrub borders and naturalistic plantings. Stunning in the fall with its glossy red fall color. The fruit usually drops by mid-winter. Native from Nova Scotia to Florida and West to Minnesota, it has been in cultivation since 1700. It has been cultivated in Europe for its fruit. *See photograph page 169.*

CULTURE

Tolerates both wet and droughty conditions. It prefers a slightly acidic soil. Propagated by seeds, divisions and cuttings. It spreads through suckers, but these can be easily controlled if desired.

CULTIVAR & VARIETY:

var. elata Rehd.   black chokeberry

ZONES 3 AND 4
5 feet tall, 5 feet wide

Grown for its glossier green leaves and showier flowers.

'Autumn Magic'   black chokeberry

ZONES 3 AND 4
3 to 5 feet tall, 3 to 4 feet wide

Introduction of the University of British Columbia. An upright grower with good flower and fruit production. Outstanding fall color.

PURPLE CHOKEBERRY
Aronia x prunifolia (Schneid.) Graebn.

HARDY IN ZONE 4
9 feet tall, 6 feet wide

HABIT. Tall shrub similar to *A. arbutifolia* except for color of fruit.
FRUIT. Subglobose, 0.30 to 0.40 in. across, purplish black, lustrous.

LANDSCAPE USE AND CULTURE

Native from Nova Scotia to Florida and west to Indiana, it has been in cultivation since 1800. Intermediate in hardiness between *A. arbutifolia* and *A. melanocarpa*. Plant towards the back of the shrub border. Available in the trade only from seed.

SOUTHERNWOOD & SAGEBRUSH

SOUTHERNWOOD
Artemisia abrotanum L.

FAMILY: COMPOSITAE, DAISY FAMILY
HARDY IN ZONES 3 AND 4
3 feet tall, 3 feet wide

HABIT. Subshrub with upright smooth or slightly hairy branches; there are 300 species distributed worldwide, mostly non-shrubby.
LEAVES. 0.5 to 2.2 in. long, simple to thrice pinnate, with narrow obtuse lobes, smooth or slightly hairy.
FLOWERS. Yellow, perfect, and female, all fertile, in August; heads numerous, several flowered, 0.20 in. across.

LANDSCAPE USE

Seldom used as a shrub. It is strongly scented with finely divided leaves. Native to southern Europe this plant has a long history as an herb.

    Gerard in his famous herbal, *The Herball* (1597-98, 1107), found in the collection of Andersen Horticultural Library, lists many "virtues" of southernwood including, "the tops, floures or seed boyled, and stamped raw with water and drunke, helpeth them that cannot take their breaths without holding their neckes straight up." Has upright growth.

CULTURE

Needs well-drained soil and full sun. A spring pruning will help keep this subshrub handsome. Easily propagated by layering.

FRINGED SAGEBRUSH, MOUNTAIN SAGE

Artemisia frigida Willd.

HARDY IN ZONES 2 TO 4

7.5 to 20 inches tall, 20 inches wide

HABIT. Subshrub with procumbent stems and ascending branches, silky-hairy.
LEAVES. 0.5 to 1.5 in. long, with 3 to 5 linear lobes, silky-hairy.
FLOWERS. Yellow, small, 0.16 in. across, numerous, in racemes or raceme-like panicles, in August.

LANDSCAPE USE

Native from the Yukon and Minnesota to Idaho and western Texas, Siberia and northern Europe. Attractive in a sunny rock garden. Can be mat forming with numerous spreading stems from a woody base. Seeds can remain viable in the soil for many years, so it is a good plant to select for disturbed areas.

CULTURE

For a sunny location. It can grow a 6 to 8 foot deep taproot, so a well-drained soil is a must. Withstands a slightly alkaline soil. Propagated from seed, division and layering.

The
BARBERRIES
Berberis L.
FAMILY: BERBERIDACEAE, BARBERRY FAMILY

Although there are nearly 500 species of this diverse genus, few are suited for the North. However, those that are hardy can be valuable for many purposes. The common Japanese barberry, *B. thunbergii,* used as a hedge or in a shrub border makes an indelible impression when one tries to take a shortcut through them. Their prickly small thorns can deter even the most determined trespasser.

As Henry Mitchell in *One Man's Garden* (1992, 41) puts it: "almost all are, alas, severely thorny. Of course you don't have to run out and pat them every day, but they are annoying in a minor way when it is necessary to get among the shrubs to pull up poison ivy, seedling maples, dogwood, oaks, and so on." Many new cultivars (some hardy) have been recently introduced. *See photograph page 182-83.*

CULTIVARS:

(Of interspecific parentage)

Emerald Carousel®   barberry
B. 'Tara'
ZONE 4
4 feet tall, 4 feet wide

An introduction from Bailey Nurseries of Minnesota. A selection from a cross between *B. thunbergii* and *B. koreana.* Bailey's states it "combines the hardiness and better flowering and fruiting characteristics of Korean with the better plant habit of Japanese." Has good red fall color which persists for a long time in the fall. It also has attractive red fruit in the fall.

Golden Carousel®   barberry
B. 'Bailsel'
ZONE 4
4 feet tall, 4 feet wide

Golden Carousel® has unique yellow foliage which can fade

during the growing season. Like many other lighter foliaged plants, if planted in part shade it will retain its coloration. A hybrid of *B. koreana* and a cultivar of *B. thunbergii*.

KOREAN BARBERRY
Berberis koreana Palib.
HARDY IN ZONES 3 AND 4
8 feet tall, 6 feet wide

HABIT. Suckering shrub; there are 450 species distributed worldwide.
BRANCHES. Grooved, reddish, and spiny, with flat 3-lobed spines.
LEAVES. Obovate or elliptic, 1 to 2.5 in. long, rounded at apex, wedge-shaped at base, rather densely spinulose-serrulate, paler and netted beneath.
FLOWERS. Racemes 0.5 to 1.2 in. long, in late May or early June, very showy.
FRUIT. Bright red, retaining their color well into winter.

LANDSCAPE USE
This Korean native was introduced into North America in 1905. Planted for its showy yellow flowers, red fruit, and brilliant red fall color. A suckering shrub, it can be used in a shrub border if suckers are kept under control. Perhaps better planted by itself or where you want a mass planting. An outstanding large shrub for the right location. *See photograph page 165.*

CULTURE
Does well in full sun, withstands part shade. Propagated from seed and suckers.

JAPANESE BARBERRY
Berberis thunbergii DC.
HARDY IN ZONE 4
6 feet tall, 6 feet wide (smaller in the North)

HABIT. Compact, branched shrub.
BRANCHES. Strongly grooved, at first yellowish or purplish red, becoming purple-brown the second year.
STEMS. Spines that are usually simple, 0.2 to 0.7 in. long.
LEAVES. Obovate to spatulate-oblong, ½ to 1-¼ in. long, obtuse or rarely acute at apex, narrowed at base to a petiole 0.08 to 0.40 in. long; leaf margin entire; upper leaf surface bright green and undersurface glaucescent.
FLOWERS. Yellow, 0.32 to 0.40 in. across, solitary or in clusters of 2 to 4, in late May and early June; pedicels 0.24 to 0.40 in. long.
FRUIT. Ellipsoid, up to ½ in. long, bright red, in September and October.

LANDSCAPE USE
As the common name suggests this species is native to Japan. It was introduced into North America in 1864. It makes a good barrier shrub because of its prickles, so is often used for hedges. There are many cultivars selected for fruit, growth habit, leaf color, and fall color.

Again, Henry Mitchell in his *One Man's Garden* (1992, 186) deftly describes this shrub: "Its sharp spines discourage dogs and mail carriers (both of whom are much given to arranging thoroughfares through small treasures)...Its little leaves, half an inch or so long and nicely oval, are good steady green and somewhat leathery or firm, turning in the fall to orange-crimson and scarlet - a display not sufficiently exclaimed over by garden writers, if I may say so, who commonly tend to be snobs themselves...it will grow in dry, barren, hostile ground with no fertilizer, no spraying, no care. As a result, it was soon to be seen in all manner of dismal places, holding on for dear life on bleak, cold, windy December days in Pittsburgh and Chicago."

CULTURE
Some dieback occurs in severe winters, so protected locations are best although one sees Japanese barberry almost everywhere. Prefers a moist, well-drained soil. Propagated from seed and cuttings.

CULTIVARS:
The following cultivars are about as hardy as the species.

'Atropurpurea'   Japanese barberry
ZONE 4
4 feet tall, 5 feet wide

Leaves are purplish throughout the season if grown in full sun. Ninety-five percent have purple leaves when grown from seed.

'Atropurpurea Nana'   Japanese barberry
ZONE 4
1.5 feet tall, 3 feet wide

Commonly known as Crimson Pygmy Japanese barberry. A dwarf form with purple leaves. Some dieback can be expected in most winters.

'Aurea'   Japanese barberry
TRIAL IN ZONE 4 (PROBABLY MUCH LESS HARDY THAN THE SPECIES)
Leaves golden yellow in full sun. An accent plant.

Burgundy Carousel®   Japanese barberry

B.t. 'Bailtwo'

ZONE 4

3 feet tall, 5 feet wide

Features larger leaves in a burgundy-purple summer color.

Jade Carousel™   Japanese barberry

B. t. 'Bailgreen'

ZONE 4

3 feet tall, 4 feet wide

A particularly dense, compact grower.

'Kobold'   Japanese barberry

ZONE 4

20 inches tall, 3 feet wide

Similar in dwarf habit to 'Atropurpurea Nana', this dwarf cultivar features glossy green foliage. Many authorities compare the growth habit of this cultivar to a mounded dwarf boxwood.

'Rose Glow'   Japanese barberry

ZONE 4

3 feet tall, 3 feet wide

Originated in Europe, this cultivar features foliage that starts red and matures to a deep purplish red. The yellow flowers are striking against its red foliage. Often sold as 'Rosey Glow'.

Ruby Carousel®   Japanese barberry

B.t. 'Bailone'

ZONE 4

3 feet tall, 3 feet wide

Dark red foliage. This like other dark foliaged cultivars can be used as accents.

'Sparkle'   Japanese barberry

TRIAL IN ZONE 4

3 feet tall, 4 feet wide

Dark green foliage that is displayed on arching branches. Its glossy foliage and arching habit are what differentiates this cultivar from the species.

'Thornless'   Japanese barberry

ZONE 4

4 feet tall, 4 feet wide

As its name suggests, for those looking for a friendlier shrub.

The BIRCHES

Betula L.
FAMILY: BETULACEAE, BIRCH FAMILY

When one thinks of a northern landscape, one of the smaller trees one thinks of is paper birch. Birch adds interest to the landscape especially in winter. Paper birch needs the right location; one with cooler, moister soil is ideal. To be successful, one should try to duplicate their native habitat, where most birch are woodland trees protected from drying winds and exposure. There are problems with birch, such as bronze birch borer, that are aggrevated by being planted in stress situations. Some species are also resistant to diseases and pests. Perhaps the most pertinent consideration is where to use birch as these ornamental trees can be short-lived or unsuccessful under stressful conditions.

Charles S. Sargent in volume nine of his *Silva of North America* (1894, 48) lists the commerical uses of birch: "The compact straight-grained wood of several species of Betula is valued by the cabinet-maker or is employed in the manufacture of spools, shoe-lasts, and other small articles...From the bark, which separates from the young stems and from the branches of several species in thin layers and is impervious to water, light canoes, shoes, boxes, cords, and a covering for buildings are made. The bark contains an astringent principle and a resinous balsamic oil sometimes used in tanning leather. In North America the bark and leaves of the different species of Betula are esteemed as domestic remedies for chronic diseases of the skin and for rheumatism and gout...The sweet sap of many of the species is used as a beverage, and is sometimes made into wine."

CULTIVAR:

(Of interspecific parentage)

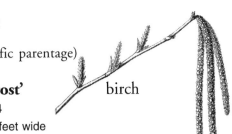

'Crimson Frost'
TRIAL IN ZONE 4
35 feet tall, 20 feet wide

A cross between *B. szechuanica* and *B. pendula 'Purpurea'*, this birch features reddish purple foliage. Of borderline hardiness, it needs the perfect location with cool, moist conditions to do well. Of bold character it also needs a special site so it fits in with most landscapes. Introduced by Evergreen Nursery in 1987.

YELLOW BIRCH
Betula alleghaniensis Britt.
HARDY IN ZONES 2 TO 4
70 feet tall (more often 45 feet), 50 feet wide

HABIT. Large tree; there are 60 species distributed in the northern hemisphere.
BRANCHES. Slender, hairy.
BARK. Yellowish or silvery gray, separating into thin flakes, becoming reddish brown on old trunks.
LEAVES. Ovate to oblong-ovate, 3.2 to 4.5 in. long, with pale hairs on the veins, becoming nearly smooth at maturity; leaf margin serrate; petioles slender, 0.5 to 1 in. long.
FRUIT. Female catkins short stalked or subsessile, 0.5 to 1.2 in. long; and less than 1 in. thick; bracts 0.2 to 0.3 in. long with 3 narrow, ascending lobes; wings of fruit slightly narrower than the nutlets.

LANDSCAPE USE

Because it is so large growing, this species needs space to do well or fit in with the landscape. Yellow birch is a valued forestry tree, with a fine grained wood used specially for veneers. Native from Newfoundland to Manitoba and south to Georgia and Tennessee, it has been cultivated since 1800. It was formerly known as *B. lutea*. The seeds of this birch are a unique heart shape.

CULTURE

This species is somewhat resistant to the bronze birch borer, a major problem of birch. It needs cool, moist soils.

WATER BIRCH, RED BIRCH
Betula fontinalis Sarg.
ZONE 4
40 feet tall, 25 feet wide

HABIT. Shrubby tree.
BRANCHES. Slender, upright, covered with numerous glands.
BARK. Smooth, black when young turning reddish brown at maturity.

LEAVES. Broad ovate, doubly serrate except entire near base, 1 to 1.5 in. long; heart-shaped or wedge-shaped at the base, blunt to sharp pointed apex; dark green above, lighter green underneath; petiole hairy, later glabrous, 0.5 in.
FLOWERS. Catkins; male and female catkins on same tree; 2 to 2.5 in. long.
FRUIT. Pendulous cones, 1 to 1.5 in. long, scaled enclosing a winged seed.

LANDSCAPE USE

Was known as *B. occidentalis*. Water birch has a more shrubby habit and features reddish bark. Native from Alaska to Oregon east to Colorado.

CULTURE

Needs a moist, protected site.

CHERRY BIRCH, SWEET BIRCH
Betula lenta L.
HARDY IN ZONE 4, FOR PROTECTED
LOCATIONS IN ZONE 3
Usually much smaller than its native 80 feet tall, 50 feet wide

HABIT. Large tree.
BRANCHES. Slightly hairy when young, coming smooth and red-brown at maturity, with aromatic, wintergreen flavor when crushed.
BARK. Dark reddish brown, fissured into thick plates on old trunks.
LEAVES. Oblong-ovate, 2.2 to 4.5 in. long, acuminate at apex, usually heart-shaped at base, sharply and doubly serrate, silky-hairy below when young, with 9 to 12 pairs of veins; fall color golden yellow; petioles 0.5 to 1 in. long.
FRUIT. Female catkins nearly sessile, ovoid-oblong, 0.5 to 1.2 in. long, and less than 0.5 in. thick; bracts about 0.16 in. long, smooth with short lobes; wings of fruit as broad as nutlets.

LANDSCAPE USE

Cherry birch should be considered for landscape situations where a larger growing birch is needed. This birch has dark hued bark and has the graceful nature of all birch. It gets its common name, cherry birch, from its cherry-like bark. The common name, sweet birch, comes from the wintergreen-like flavor of young branches inner bark.

A handsome tree with pyramidal form when young, becoming open and roundheaded at maturity. Its yellow fall color is an outstanding feature. Native from Maine to Alabama and west to Ohio, it has been in cultivation since 1759.

CULTURE

Does best in moist but well-drained soil. It will tolerate heavier soils and dryer conditions (but not dry soils) than other birches. It doesn't seem to get chlorotic in alkaline soils. This species seems resistant to the bronze birch borer and also birch leaf miner. Propagated by seed. Difficult to find in the landscape trade.

RIVER BIRCH
Betula nigra L.
HARDY IN ZONE 4, FOR PROTECTED LOCATIONS IN ZONE 3
65 feet tall, 50 feet wide

HABIT. Medium-sized tree.
BRANCHES. Hairy.
BARK. Reddish brown, peeling in papery strips, becoming black with age.
LEAVES. Rhombic-ovate, acute, doubly serrate, 1.2 to 3.2 in. long, dark green above, whitish below, and hairy when young; fall color golden.
FRUIT. Female catkins oblong-cylindric, 1 to 3 in. long; bracts hairy, with upright, linear-oblong, nearly equal lobes; wings of fruit half as wide to nearly as wide as nutlets.

LANDSCAPE USE
This highly ornamental tree is native from Massachusetts to Florida and west to Minnesota and Kansas. It has been cultivated since 1736. Although native in wet sites, this species does well on upland soils that are moisture retentive. River birch is especially handsome used as a clump tree specimen. *See photographs pages 159 and 172-73.*

CULTURE
Select landscape plants from local or more northern seed sources; avoid plants from southern seed sources. Resistant to the bronze birch borer, but birch leaf miner can be a problem. Longer-lived on drier soils than paper birch. This birch may develop chlorosis in soils that are alkaline. Will withstand heat but not dry soils.

CULTIVAR:

Heritage®   river birch
B. 'Cully'
ZONE 4
45 feet tall, 35 feet wide

Features a lighter hued exfoliating bark than the species. The leaves are slightly larger than the species. Introduced by Earl Cully of Illinois in 1979. Very resistant to bronze birch borer.

PAPER BIRCH, CANOE BIRCH
Betula papyrifera Marsh.
HARDY IN ZONES 2 TO 4
80 feet tall (usually smaller)
50 feet wide

HABIT. Roundheaded tree.
BRANCHES. Hairy when young and often slightly glandular.
BARK. White, exfoliating in papery strips.
LEAVES. Ovate to narrow-ovate, 1.5 to 4 in. long, acuminate, wedge-shaped or rounded at base, coarsely and usually doubly serrate, smooth above, hairy on the veins beneath or nearly smooth; petioles stout, 0.2 to 1 in. long, hairy.
FRUIT. Female catkins cylindric, 1 to 2 in. long, slender-stalked, usually pendulous; bracts hairy with sub-erect or spreading lateral lobes slightly shorter than the middle lobe.

LANDSCAPE USE
A feature of landscapes from Labrador to British Columbia and south to Pennsylvania, Nebraska and Montana, it has been in cultivation since 1750. Most often planted in clump form. Cooler summertime climates can feature this tree in their landscapes; others should use paper birch carefully. Those wanting birch in their landscape often plant river birch instead.

Donald Peattie in his *A Natural History of Trees* (1950, 166) writes: "Wherever it grows the Paper Birch delights in the company of Conifers and in the presence of water; it loves a white and rushing stream; it loves a cold clear lake where its white limbs are reflected."

Paper birch was used by Native Americans to make their canoes using tamarack for sewing the seams. The canoe's frame was made commonly of arborvitae and everything was made water-tight with pine resin.

CULTURE
Needs cool, moist soil. It is often short-lived if planted as a specimen tree in landscape conditions. Under stress, it is very susceptible to the bronze birch borer. If used in the landscape, keep watered and mulch in a wide circle around each specimen. Even in good planting conditions, paper birch is short-lived (40 to 60 years).

EUROPEAN BIRCH
Betula pendula Roth.
HARDY IN ZONES 2 TO 4
65 feet tall (usually smaller), 50 feet wide

HABIT. Medium-sized tree.
BRANCHES. Pendulous, especially on older trees.
BARK. White, flaking.
LEAVES. Rhombic-ovate, 1 to 2.7 in. long, acuminate, usually wedge-shaped at base but sometimes square, doubly ser-

rate, smooth; petioles slender, 0.7 to 1 in. long.
FRUIT. Female catkins cylindric, 0.7 to 1 in. long, slender-stalked; bracts minutely hairy or smooth.

LANDSCAPE USE

The cultivars of this species are more often planted as small ornamental specimens. Like most birch, they are most effective in multi-stemmed groupings. Native to Europe and Asia Minor, it was introduced into North America during colonial times. The bark resembles paper birch.

CULTURE

Needs a site similar to paper birch (cool and moist). Propagated by seeds and cuttings. Susceptible to the bronze birch borer which usually kills the tree in landscape conditions before it reaches maturity.

CULTIVARS:

Several cultivars have been named and are commonly planted.

'Dalecarlica' European birch

HARDY IN ZONES 2 TO 4
35 feet tall, 25 feet wide

A distinctive tree with pendulous branches and leaves; leaves are deeply lobed with long, tapering points to each lobe. Also sold as 'Laciniata' and 'Lanceolata'.

'Fastigiata' European birch

Dense and pyramidal when young. This cultivar has not done well at the Arboretum.

'Gracilis' European birch

ZONES 3 AND 4
15 feet tall, 12 feet wide

Leaves of this weeping tree are finely divided and cut nearly to the midrib.

'Purpurea' European birch

FOR PROTECTED LOCATIONS IN ZONE 4
15 feet tall, 12 feet wide

Leaves are deep purple in the spring, gradually losing their purple color as the summer progresses. Arboretum trees have not been long-lived. Introduced in France in 1870. Probably a zone 5 plant.

'Youngii' European birch

ZONES 3 AND 4
15 feet tall, 12 feet wide

An irregular tree with drooping branches lacking a central leader. A novelty that is short-lived in our area. Introduced in England in 1873.

JAPANESE WHITE BIRCH
Betula platyphylla var. japonica (Miq.)
Hara.

HARDY IN ZONE 4
50 feet tall, 30 feet wide

HABIT. Medium-sized tree.
BRANCHES. Glandular.
BARK. White, exfoliating in papery strips.
LEAVES. Broadly ovate-triangular with square to subcordate bases.

LANDSCAPE USE

Native to Japan and northern China, it was introduced into North America in 1902. Has a more pyramidal habit than other birches, but is not as stiff as many pyramidal trees. Often confused with the variety *B. mandshurica* var. *japonica*.

CULTURE

Of variable resistance to the bronze birch borer. Probably less susceptible than *B. pendula*, a tree it resembles. It also is more resistant to the birch leaf miner than other species. A good specimen tree for cool, moist conditions. Not as hardy as other birch species.

CULTIVAR:

'Whitespire'

Japanese white birch
ZONE 4
35 feet tall, 25 feet wide

Dr. Ed Hasselkus of the University of Wisconsin selected this variety for its whiter bark and greater resistance to the bronze birch borer. It was introduced in 1983. While it is more resistant to the borer it still should be grown in a location where it is not subjected to heat and water stress. Dr. Hasselkus indicates there are many trees sold under the name 'Whitespire' that do not have the resistance his introduction enjoys. Care should be taken to find the true 'Whitespire' birch. There is also a cultivar called 'Whitespire Senior' in the trade.

GRAY BIRCH
Betula populifolia Marsh.
HARDY IN ZONE 4
30 feet tall, 25 feet wide

HABIT. Small tree.
BRANCHES. Densely glandular, ascending.
BARK. Chalky or ashy white.
LEAVES. Triangular-ovate or deltoid, 2 to 3 in. long, long-acuminate, square at base, coarsely and doubly serrate, glutinous when young, shiny on upper surface; petioles slender, 0.2 to 1 in. long.
FRUIT. Female catkins cylindric, 0.2 to 1 in. long, on slender stalks; bracts spreading, minutely hairy.

LANDSCAPE USE
A rather short-lived tree adapted to poor soils. Native from Nova Scotia to Ontario and south to Delaware. Cultivated since 1750. Can be considered for sites that will support few other trees. It often is confused with quaking aspen.

CULTURE
Tolerates both wet and dry soils. Plant in spring just as buds are starting to open and use balled and burlapped trees. Suckers from the roots. More resistant to the bronze birch borer than *B. papyrifera* and *B. pendula*. Is susceptible to birch leaf miner.

SWAMP BIRCH, BOG BIRCH
Betula pumila L.
HARDY IN ZONES 2 TO 4
16 feet tall, 10 feet wide

HABIT. Tall shrub.
BRANCHES. Densely hairy when young.
LEAVES. Suborbicular to broad-elliptic or obovate, 0.2 to 1 in. long, obtuse or acutish, rounded or wedge-shaped at base, coarsely crenate-dentate, usually densely hairy beneath when young and grayish white and net-veined, often becoming quite smooth at maturity, with 4 to 6 pairs of veins.
FRUIT. Female catkins cylindric-oblong, upright, stalked, 0.2 to 1 in. long; bracts hairy with lateral lobes spreading, shorter than middle lobe; wings of fruit about half as broad as nutlets.

LANDSCAPE USE
Useful for naturalistic plantings and wet sites. Native from Newfoundland to Alberta and south to New Jersey and Minnesota, it has been in cultivation since 1762.

CULTURE
Propagated and usually available from mail order nurseries by seed.

Other birches to try:

DWARF BIRCH
B. nana L.
ZONES 2 TO 4
3 to 4 feet tall

Grows over a wide range, so try to get specimens from northern seed.

SANDBERG BIRCH
B. x sandbergii Britt.
HARDY IN ZONES 2 TO 4
30 feet tall, 18 feet wide

Not readily available in the landscape trade. A naturally occurring hybrid found along Lake Superior and in the West in spruce bogs. A cross between *B. papyrifera* and *B. pumila glandulifera*.

WHITEBARK HIMALAYAN BIRCH
B. utilis var. jacquemontii (Spach) Winkl.

For trial only in favorable, very protected sites in zone 4. Originated in Asia, sometimes listed as a cultivar. Probably zone 5.

BOXWOOD

KOREAN BOXWOOD
Buxus microphylla var. koreana Nakai.
FAMILY: BUXACEAE, BOXWOOD FAMILY
HARDY IN ZONE 4
5 feet tall, 3 feet wide

HABIT. Upright, evergreen shrub; 70 species are distributed worldwide.
BRANCHES. Short-hairy when young.
LEAVES. Opposite, green, obovate or elliptic to oblong-elliptic, 0.2 to 0.5 in. long, notched at apex, wedge-shaped at base, hairy on midrib above; fall color purplish brown; petioles short-hairy.
FLOWERS. Small, without petals, in axillary and terminal clusters, monoecious, in May.
FRUIT. Subglobose or obovoid, 3-horned capsules, in September.

LANDSCAPE USE
The best boxwood to try in the North. Native to Korea, it was introduced into North America in 1919. Boxwood can

be used for specimen plants, topiary and edging to formal beds. It can be formally sheared or left more natural. The evergreen leaves of boxwood in the North routinely turn a brownish yellow in the winter. There are other boxwood selections that have been hardy for individuals in the North, but this boxwood seems the most reliable.

John Parkinson in his *Paradisi in Sole* (1629, 606-07) writes: "The lowe or dwarfe Boxe is of excellent use to border up a knot, or the long beds in a Garden, being a marvuailous fine ornament thereunto, in regard it both groweth lowe, is ever greene, and by cutting may bee kept in what maner every one please…"

CULTURE

Grows dense in full sun, less dense in part shade. Boxwood is tolerant of soil pH as long as the soil is neither too wet nor too dry. Winter burn is a problem, so exposed winter conditions should be avoided. Some northern gardeners cover boxwood with evergreen boughs for the winter. A good snow cover is very beneficial. Propagated by seeds and cuttings.

CULTIVAR:

'Wintergreen' boxwood
TRIAL IN ZONE 4
2 feet tall, 3 feet wide

A variable selection in both hardiness and habit. Purchase only from a northern grower. It is generally more dwarf than the species.

Other boxwood to try:

AMERICAN BOX
B. sempervirens L.
FOR VERY PROTECTED LOCATIONS OF ZONE 4
5 feet tall, 5 feet wide (grows much larger in the south)

Protected from winter winds, this box can be tried. There are some successful plantings in protected locations in the Twin Cities area.

SCOTCH HEATHER

SCOTCH HEATHER
Calluna vulgaris (L.) Hull.
FAMILY: ERICACEAE, HEATH FAMILY
FOR PROTECTED LOCATIONS IN EASTERN PARTS OF ZONE 4
1.5 feet tall, 3 feet wide

HABIT. Small, evergreen shrub; it has only 1 species distributed in the northern hemisphere.
BUDS. Small in winter with few scales.
LEAVES. Opposite, scale-like, 4 ranked, oblong-ovate, less than 0.1 in. long, sagittate at base.
FLOWERS. Dense racemes, 3 to 6 in. long, from July to September; individual flowers nodding, campanulate, usually rosy pink, persistent.
FRUIT. 4-valved capsules, in October.

LANDSCAPE USE

Those choosing this plant or its numerous cultivars in zone 4 relish challenges. Heather needs specific cultural requirements which are difficult to meet in most of zone 4; heather will not thrive unless these requirements are strictly met. Native to Europe and Asia Minor, it was introduced into North America by early settlers. The numerous cultivars are planted more often.

CULTURE

Requires an acidic, well-drained soil, preferably sand with ample organic matter. Avoid overly rich soil and use a summer mulch to keep the soil cool and moist. Some winter protection is needed to shade the evergreen foliage. Propagated by seed or softwood cuttings.

SWEETSHRUB

SWEETSHRUB, CAROLINA
ALLSPICE
Calycanthus floridus L.
FAMILY: CALYCANTHACEAE
FOR PROTECTED LOCATIONS IN ZONE 4
6 feet tall, 6 feet wide

HABIT. Coarse, deciduous shrub; there are 6 species distributed in Asia and North America.
BARK. Aromatic.
BUDS. Hidden by petiole bases.
LEAVES. Opposite, simple, ovate or elliptic to narrow-elliptic, 2 to 4.7 in. long, acute or acuminate, wedge-shaped or rounded at base, grayish green and densely hairy on undersurface; petioles short, stout, 0.20 in. long.
FLOWERS. Perfect, perigynous, dark reddish brown, 2 in. across, fragrant, in June and July; parts of perianth numerous, spirally arranged, not differentiated into sepals and petals; stamens 10 to 30.
FRUIT. Obovoid, 2.2 to 2.7 in. long, usually contracted at the mouth.

LANDSCAPE USE

An ornamental shrub which needs a protected location in zone 4. Those finding this shrub in flower for the first time quickly understand why this shrub is a feature in the early to mid-summer landscape. Its fragrance is unique and hard to describe (strawberries? pineapple?). Its brownish red flowers are unusual. It is best planted in a shrub border where its habit of overwinter dieback is not as objectionable (even where dieback is not a problem, this shrub can have an ungainly habit). Sweetshrub's dried wood also has a camphor-like fragrance. Native from Virginia to Florida, it has been cultivated since 1726.

CULTURE

Sweetshrub grows in shade or full sun, preferably in moist, loamy soil. It is best planted in the North in groups of 3 or more so its fragrance and flowering makes a sufficient impact. It is difficult to transplant when mature, so start with smaller specimens. It is a slow starter in the North's springs and leafs out late. Propagated by seed and cuttings.

TRUMPET VINE

TRUMPET VINE
Campsis radicans (L.) Seem.
FAMILY: BIGNONIACEAE, BIGNONIA FAMILY
FOR PROTECTED LOCATIONS IN ZONE 4
30 feet long

HABIT. Vigorous clinging vine (technically a shrub that climbs) with aerial rootlets that cling to walls; there are 2 species distributed in North America and Asia.
LEAVES. Opposite, odd pinnate with 9 to 11 leaflets; leaflets short-stalked, elliptic to ovate-oblong, 1 to 3 in. long, acuminate, wedge-shaped at base, serrate.
FLOWERS. Large, showy, trumpet-shaped, from July to September, usually orange outside, scarlet inside, 2.2 to 3.5 in. long and 1.5 to 2 in. wide.
FRUIT. Cylindric-oblong capsules, 3 to 4 in. long, beaked.

LANDSCAPE USE

In the right location in the North, this vine can be a rampant grower (when grown farther south it is often too rampant a grower). The showy orange and red flowers are striking in mid-summer. It is native from Pennsylvania to Missouri and south to Florida and Texas. Attractive to hummingbirds. *See photograph page 152.*

CULTURE

Needs a protected location such as a south facing wall. It will not grow well in zone 4 in anything but a protected location. A south facing wall is also recommended because this vine likes full sun. Although the vine clings by aerial roots, additional support may be required because of the weight of the stems and foliage. Propagated by seed and cuttings.

The
PEASHRUBS
Caragana Fabr.
FAMILY: LEGUMINOSAE, PEA FAMILY

Those from more temperate climates wonder about anyone choosing these shrubs, but because of their tolerance of adverse conditions they can be valuable in zones 2 to 4. They are used where winter winds are a problem (as in shelterbelts), for alkaline soil conditions, and generally where hardiness is a test. They vary in their ornamental value.

SIBERIAN PEASHRUB
Caragana arborescens Lam.
HARDY IN ZONES 2 TO 4
16 feet tall, 10 feet wide

HABIT. Large, upright shrub; there are 80 species distributed in Europe and Asia.
BRANCHES. Hairy when young.
LEAFLETS. 8 to 12, bright green, obovate to elliptic-oblong, 0.4 to 1 in. long, rounded at apex and mucronate, hairy when young, later smooth.
FLOWERS. 1 to 4 in fascicles, yellow, 0.2 to 1 in. long, on pedicels 0.2 to 1 in. long, in May; calyx with very short teeth.
FRUIT. Pods 1.2 to 2 in. long, in August.

LANDSCAPE USE

Native to Siberia and Manchuria, this shrub was introduced into North America in 1752. This peashrub is often used in shelterbelts in the Northern Plains. It can be used in the landscape as a background shrub or as a large hedge in more naturalistic plantings. It can be pruned for use as a small tree.

David Fairchild in his *The World was My Garden* (1938, 439) remarks on its use in shelterbelts "It branches close to the ground and, when planted around small fields, serves to lift the winter winds." We think of Mr. Fairchild as an explorer of the tropics, but he did travel through Canada. *See photograph on page 157.*

CULTURE

Needs full sun. It grows best in well-drained soils, but is touted as being tolerant of heavy clay soils. The species is propagated by seed; cultivars by cuttings and grafting. Drought resistant and tolerant of alkaline soils and salt.

CULTIVARS:

'Lorbergii' Siberian peashrub
ZONES 2 TO 4

A selection with narrow leaflets and light yellow flowers.

'Pendula' Siberian peashrub
ZONES 2 TO 4
Usually budded on to a standard

A weeping form that must be grafted on a standard. An interesting novelty. Height depends upon how grafted.

'Walker' Siberian peashrub
ZONES 2 TO 4
5 feet tall, 5 feet wide

A trailing plant with finely cut leaves. An introduction from Morden, Manitoba. Can be effectively used as a grafted specimen, weeping small tree.

SHORTLEAF PEASHRUB
Caragana brevifolia Komar.
HARDY IN ZONES 2 TO 4
3 feet tall, 3 feet wide

HABIT. Low, rare shrub.
LEAVES. Having spiny rachis and stipules; leaflets narrow-obovate to obovate-lanceolate, less than 0.2 in. long, acute.
FLOWERS. 0.2 to 0.7 in. long on pedicels less than 0.2 in. long, in May; calyx with spinulose lobes.

LANDSCAPE USE AND CULTURE

Makes an attractive low hedge that requires little pruning. Native in northwestern China and Kashmir. Hard to obtain in the nursery trade but it is sometimes available in seed form.

RUSSIAN PEASHRUB
Caragana frutex (L.) K. Koch.
HARDY IN ZONES 2 TO 4
6 to 9 feet tall, 3 feet wide

HABIT. Upright, suckering shrub.
BRANCHES. Slender, yellowish.
LEAFLETS. 4, obovate to oblong-obovate, 0.2 to 1 in. long, rounded or notched at apex, wedge-shaped at base, membranous, dull green.
FLOWERS. 1 to 3, bright yellow, 0.7 to 1 in. long, on pedicels nearly as long as the flowers, in May and June.
FRUIT. Pods, cylindric, 1 to 1.2 in. long, smooth.

LANDSCAPE USE

Useful for erosion control as this is a shrub that suckers freely. Hard to control for use in a shrub border unless this peashrub can be controlled by mowing. Smaller than *C. arborescens*. Flowers are larger than most peashrubs. Native from southern Russia to Turkestan and Siberia, it was introduced into North America in 1752. Attractive to hummingbirds.

CULTURE

Resistant to leaf diseases and insect problems that can be bothersome in other peashrubs. If the shrub planting needs to be renewed, older branches can be pruned to the ground during dormancy. Propagated by seed. Tolerates drought.

CULTIVAR:

'Globosa' Russian peashrub
ZONES 2 TO 4
2 feet tall, 2 feet wide

A compact globe-shaped form that does not sucker. Height depends upon how grafted. Excellent as a formal hedge.

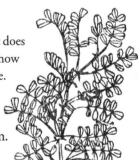

LITTLELEAF PEASHRUB
Caragana microphylla Lam.
HARDY IN ZONES 2 TO 4
9 feet tall, 8 feet wide

HABIT. Small leaved shrub.
BRANCHES. Long, spreading; young branches finely silky.
LEAFLETS. 12 to 18, grayish green, oval to obovate, less than 0.3 in. long, rounded or notched at apex, silky-hairy at first, becoming smooth.

FLOWERS. 1 to 2, yellow, about 0.7 in. long on pedicels less than 0.1 in. long, in May and June; calyx finely hairy, tubular, with short teeth.
FRUIT. Pods to 1 in. long.

LANDSCAPE USE AND CULTURE

Large growing shrub for the back of a shrub border. Native to Siberia and Manchuria, it was introduced into North America in 1789. Propagated by seed.

PYGMY PEASHRUB
Caragana pygmaea (L.) DC.
HARDY IN ZONES 3 AND 4, FOR PROTECTED LOCATIONS IN ZONE 2
3 feet tall, 3 feet wide

HABIT. Spreading shrub.
BRANCHES. Slender, smooth.
LEAFLETS. 4, linear-oblanceolate, 0.3 to 0.5 in. long, acuminate and spine-pointed; stipules spiny, short.
FLOWERS. Solitary, about 0.7 in. long on pedicels 0.4 in. long, in May and June; calyx narrow-campanulate with triangular teeth.
FRUIT. Pods 0.7 to 1 in. long, cylindric, smooth.

LANDSCAPE USE AND CULTURE

Widely planted in western Minnesota and the Dakotas as it is resistant to alkali chlorosis. It is also drought tolerant. It can be used in foundation plantings, shrub borders and for hedges. Native in northwest China and Siberia, it was introduced into North America in 1751.

HORNBEAMS

EUROPEAN HORNBEAM
Carpinus betulus L.
FAMILY: BETULACEAE, BIRCH FAMILY
TRIAL IN PROTECTED LOCATIONS OF ZONE 4
50 feet tall, 30 feet wide

HABIT. Small tree; there are 35 species distributed throught the northern hemisphere.
BRANCHES. Smooth and olive-brown, with prominent lenticels.
BARK. At first smooth, grayish, becoming rough and scaly at maturity.
BUDS. About less than 0.2 in. long, smooth.
LEAVES. Ovate to ovate-oblong, heart-shaped or rounded at base, 2.2 to 4.7 in. long; fall color yellow to yellowish green.
FRUIT. Female catkins 2.7 to 5.5 in. long; bracts of female catkins 1.1 to 2 in. long with ovate-lanceolate middle lobe and ovate lateral lobes, entire or remotely toothed on margins, 3- to 5-veined at base.

LANDSCAPE USE

Useful as a specimen tree either with a single trunk or in clumps. One of the shrubby trees used in hedge rows, especially in England and Europe. It tolerates clipping more than most trees and its young branches can be intertwined to form an impenetrable barrier for hedge rows. Native to Europe and the Middle East, it was introduced into North America by early settlers.

CULTURE

Needs a moist soil to do its best. Propagated by seed.

CULTIVARS:

'Columnaris'   European hornbeam
A dense, upright tree with an egg-shaped form. Of borderline hardiness, it should only be tried in protected sites in zone 4.

'Fastigiata'   European hornbeam
TRIAL IN ZONE 4
35 feet tall, 20 feet wide

Similar to 'Columnaris' but becoming vase-shaped. Of borderline hardiness, it should only be tried in protected sites in zone 4. Introduced in Europe in the 1880s.

AMERICAN HORNBEAM, BLUE BEECH, MUSCLEWOOD, WATER BEECH, IRONWOOD
Carpinus caroliniana T. Walt.
HARDY IN ZONES 3 AND 4, FOR PROTECTED LOCATIONS IN ZONE 2
30 feet tall (seldom much larger)
25 feet wide

HABIT. Small understory tree or large shrub.
BRANCHES. Slender, reddish brown, shining, smooth or slightly hairy.
BARK. Smooth, bluish gray, fluted, giving a muscular appearance.
BUDS. About 0.2 in. long, hairy at first.
LEAVES. Ovate-oblong, 2.2 to 4.7 in. long, 1 to 2.2 in. wide, acuminate, rounded or subcordate at base, sharply and doubly serrate, smooth except on veins beneath and with axillary tufts of hairs; fall color orange to red.
FRUIT. Female catkins on slender stalks, 2 to 4 in. long; bracts ovate to ovate-lanceolate, 0.7 to 1 in. long, 5- to 7-veined at base, with short and broad lateral lobes usually with 1- to 5-pointed teeth.

LANDSCAPE USE

Native from Nova Scotia to Minnesota and south to Florida and Texas, it has been in cultivation since 1812. Selected for its slate gray, interestingly textured bark and variable fall color. It can be used as a specimen tree or grown in clumps. One of the more interesting uses of this tree is in the curved allée at Dumbarton Oaks in Washington DC.

CULTURE

Prefers moist, slightly acidic soil. Withstands some shade (it is an understory tree) and also periodic wet soils. Suckers freely, so mowing around the base can help to keep this under control. Somewhat difficult to transplant. Propagated by seed.

THE HICKORIES

BITTERNUT HICKORY
Carya cordiformis
(Wangenh.) K. Koch.
FAMILY: JUGLANDACEAE,
WALNUT FAMILY
HARDY IN ZONE 4, FOR PROTECTED
LOCATIONS IN ZONE 3
80 feet tall, 50 feet wide

HABIT. Large, deciduous tree; there are 25 species distributed in Asia and North America.
BRANCHES. Rusty-hairy at first, finally smooth, shiny, and reddish brown.
BARK. Broken into thin scales, light brown; pith brown.
BUDS. With valvate scales, sulfur yellow.
LEAFLETS. 5 to 9, ovate-lanceolate, acuminate, serrate, 3 to 5.7 in. long; light green and hairy on undersurface, particularly along the midrib, becoming nearly smooth at maturity.
FRUIT. Obovoid to subglobose, 4-winged above center, less than 0.1 in. long; husks thin, splitting below the middle, nuts subglobose to broadly ovoid, slightly compressed, abruptly contracted into a sharp point, nearly smooth, gray, thin-shelled, bitter.

LANDSCAPE USE

This tree is seldom planted or found in the nursery trade but is worth preserving if native in the landscape. Native from Quebec to Minnesota and south to Florida and Louisiana. This tree's nuts lives up to its common name, so it is not a good tree to attract wildlife.

CULTURE

An insect gall can mar the beauty of the tree and affect its health.

PIGNUT HICKORY
Carya glabra (Mill.) Sweet.
HARDY IN ZONE 4
95 feet tall, 50 feet wide

HABIT. Tall tree.
BRANCHES. Slender, smooth or nearly so

BARK. Dark gray, fissured.
BUDS. With outer scales smooth, inner scales hairy.
LEAFLETS. 3 to 7 (usually 5), oblong to oblong-lanceolate, acuminate, sharply serrate, 3 to 5.7 in. long, nearly smooth; petioles and rachis smooth, green.
FRUIT. Obovoid, slightly winged near the apex, about 1 in. long, smooth; husks split only to center; nuts usually brownish, not angled; kernels bitter.

LANDSCAPE USE AND CULTURE

This handsome shade tree tolerates drier soils than do the other hickories. It is slower growing on dry soils. This tree has beautiful yellow color in the fall. Cultivated since 1750, it is native from Maine to Ontario and south to Florida, Alabama and Mississippi. Best transplanted as a small seedling or plant the nuts where you would like the tree to grow.

SHELLBARK HICKORY
Carya laciniosa (Michx.f.) Loud.
HARDY IN ZONE 4
95 feet tall, 50 feet wide

HABIT. Large tree.
BRANCHES. Hairy when young, later becoming smooth.
BARK. Becoming rough and shaggy at maturity.
BUDS. Large, 1 in. long.
LEAFLETS. Typically 7, rarely 5 or 9, oblong-lanceolate, 4 to 8 in. long, acuminate, serrate, hairy or smooth and often persistent during winter.
FRUIT. Ellipsoid to subglobose, 1.5 to 2.7 in. long, 4-ribbed above the middle; nuts ellipsoid or subglobose, compressed and obscurely 4-angled, pointed at ends, yellow or reddish, thick shelled; kernels sweet.

LANDSCAPE USE

A handsome lawn tree with large, bright green, bold foliage. Its interesting shaggy bark is similar to *C. ovata*. Native from New York to Iowa and south to Tennessee and Oklahoma, it has been in cultivation since 1800. Trees were planted by Peter Gideon near Excelsior, Minnesota about 1870 from seed collected in Illinois. These trees are still living and seedlings from them are growing well in the Arboretum.

CULTURE

Plant in moist, well-drained soil.

SHAGBARK HICKORY
Carya ovata (Mill.) K. Koch.
HARDY IN ZONE 4
95 feet tall (usually smaller), 50 feet wide

HABIT. Large tree.
BRANCHES. Scurfy-hairy at first, smooth and bright reddish brown at maturity.

BARK. Light gray, becoming shaggy with long plates that separate from the trunk at the base.

BUDS. Large, with the inner bud scales expanding and quite conspicuous when unfolding.

LEAFLETS. 5, rarely 7, elliptic to oblong-lanceolate, 4 to 5.7 in. long, acuminate, serrate, densely ciliate, hairy and glandular when young, becoming smooth at maturity; fall color yellow.

FRUIT. Subglobose, 1.2 to 2.2 in. long, with thick husk that splits to base, nuts ellipsoid to broad-obovoid, slightly flattened and angled, white, rather thin-shelled; kernels sweet.

LANDSCAPE USE

An excellent specimen tree, it is also grown for its edible nuts and attractive fall color. Native from Quebec to Minnesota and south to Florida and Texas, it has been cultivated since 1629.

CULTURE

Plant in moist, fertile soil. Difficult to transplant when larger because of its deep growing taproot.

CARYOPTERIS

CARYOPTERIS, BLUE SPIREA

Caryopteris x clandonensis Simmonds & Rehd.
FAMILY: VERBENACEAE, VERVAIN FAMILY
FOR PROTECTED LOCATIONS OF ZONE 4
3 feet tall, 3 feet wide

HABIT. Low, spreading shrub; there are 6 species native to Asia.

LEAVES. Opposite, short-petioled, ovate-lanceolate to lanceolate, broadly wedge-shaped at base, entire or with a few triangular teeth.

FLOWERS. Bright blue, in many flowered cymes, in August and September.

LANDSCAPE USE

A hybrid between *C. incana* and *C. mongholica*. Of borderline hardiness, it is best thought of as a short-lived dieback shrub that must be pruned back to live wood or replaced each spring. It blooms on new wood in late summer or fall. Introduced in 1933.

CULTURE

For protected sites of zone 4. It has not done well at the Arboretum. In the North it sometimes is treated as an annual, being replanted every spring. Needs a well-drained soil. Propagated by cuttings.

CULTIVARS:

These have the same questionable hardiness.

'Blue Mist'   Caryopteris

A selection with light blue flowers.

'Dark Knight'   Caryopteris

Similar to 'Blue Mist' but with darker flowers.

CHESTNUTS

AMERICAN CHESTNUT

Castanea dentata (Marsh.) Borkh.
FAMILY: FAGACEAE, BEECH FAMILY
HARDY IN ZONE 4
80 feet tall, 50 feet wide

HABIT. Large tree; there are 12 species distributed throughout the northern hemisphere.

BRANCHES. Smooth or nearly so.

LEAVES. Oblong-lanceolate, acuminate, wedge-shaped at base, coarsely serrate, 4.7 to 9 in. long, smooth.

FRUIT. 0.2 to 1 in. across; husk usually contains 2 to 3 nuts, and is 2 in. across.

LANDSCAPE USE

This tree has all but disappeared within its natural range owing to the ravages of the chestnut blight, a disease caused by the fungus *Endothia parasitica*. The chestnut blight has spared more isolated plantings.

Chestnuts have been sparingly planted from the Twin Cities southward in Minnesota, Wisconsin, Iowa and Nebraska. Because the species is susceptible to the chestnut blight disease, widespread planting is not advised. The American Chestnut Foundation is an organization that furthers research and trials of this tree.

One can only wonder what it was like before the blight, seeing these magnificent trees in their native habitat. Thoreau, in his *Journal* vol 5 (1852, 407) describes gathering the nuts: "The chestnuts are about as plenty as ever-both in the fallen burrs & out of them. There are more this year than the squirrels can consume. I picked 3 pints this afternoon...I love to gather them if only for the sense of the bountifulness of nature they give me."

CHINESE CHESTNUT

Castanea mollissima Blume.
FOR PROTECTED LOCATIONS IN ZONE 4
50 feet tall, 40 feet wide

HABIT. Shrubby tree.

BRANCHES. Short-hairy and on vigorous shoots with long, spreading hairs.

LEAVES. Elliptic-oblong to oblong-lanceolate, 3 to 6 in. long, acuminate, rounded or square at base, coarsely serrate, whitish hairy or green and soft-hairy on undersurface, at least on the veins; petioles short-hairy beneath.
FRUIT. 1 in. across, with usually 2 to 3 nuts in each husk; spines of husk hairy.

LANDSCAPE USE AND CULTURE

In the trials at the Arboretum's Horticultural Research Center, these trees have been short-lived and showed considerable dieback. Native in China and Korea, they were introduced into North America in 1853. Planted for its edible nuts. Propagated by cuttings or grafting.

CATALPAS

COMMON CATALPA, SOUTHERN CATALPA
Catalpa bignonioides Walt.
FAMILY: BIGNONIACEAE, BIGNONIA FAMILY
FOR PROTECTED LOCATIONS IN ZONE 4
65 feet tall, 50 feet wide

HABIT. Medium-sized tree with a broad, roundish crown; there are 11 species distributed in Asia and North America.
BRANCHES. Wide-spreading.
BARK. Light brown with thin scales.
LEAVES. Often in whorls of 3, ovate, 4 to 8 in. long, abruptly acuminate, square to subcordate at base, sometimes with a pair of small lobes; upper leaf surface light green and nearly smooth; undersurface light green and hairy, especially on the veins; unpleasant odor when crushed; petioles 3 to 6.2 in. long; panicles broad-pyramidal, 5.7 to 8 in. high.
FLOWERS. 1.5 to 2 in. across, white, with 2 yellow stripes and thickly spotted purple-brown color inside; oblique limb and entire lower lobes; in late June and early July.
FRUIT. 7.7 to 12 in. long, slender, with thin walls.

LANDSCAPE USE

This handsome tree is rather large for the average home landscape, but is very attractive in parks. Native in Georgia, Florida and Mississippi, it has been cultivated since 1726.

CULTURE
Propagated by seed.

NORTHERN CATALPA, WESTERN CATALPA, INDIAN BEAN TREE
Catalpa speciosa (Warder & Barney) Engelm.
HARDY IN ZONE 4, FOR PROTECTED LOCATIONS IN ZONE 3
80 feet tall (usually smaller), 50 feet wide

HABIT. Large pyramidal tree.
BARK. Dark reddish brown, broken into thick scales.
LEAVES. Ovate to ovate-oblong, 6 to 12 in. long, long-acuminate, square to heart-shaped at base, bright green and smooth above, densely hairy beneath, scentless; petioles 4 to 6 in. long.
FLOWERS. Few, white, in 6 in. long panicles in mid- to late-June; about 2.2 in. across, with slightly oblique limb, emarginate lower lobe, and 2 yellow stripes and inconspicuous purple-brown spots inside.
FRUIT. Capsules 8 to 17 in. long, slender, with thick walls.

LANDSCAPE USE

As with other catalpas, best used in large scale landscapes. Although it is a fast growing tree, its wood is very durable. Native from southern Illinois and Indiana to western Tennessee and northern Arkansas, it has been cultivated since 1754.

In flower in late June it is very showy and its long pods in late summer and fall are unique. Some consider it a messy tree for the landscape. Slow to leaf out in the spring and of a rather coarse texture. One of the more interesting stories in American horticulture, this tree was widely touted for timber and planted in plantations throughout much of the Midwest in the late 1800's.

CULTURE

Will withstand some drought in poor, sandy soils. It will also withstand soils that have limited spring flooding. Propagated by seed.

CEANOTHUS

NEW JERSEY TEA
Ceanothus americanus L.
FAMILY: RHAMNACEAE, BUCKTHORN FAMILY
HARDY IN ZONE 4
3 feet tall, 3 feet wide

HABIT. Low spreading shrub; there are 50 species distributed throughout North America.
BRANCHES. Slender, upright, hairy when young.
LEAVES. Ovate to ovate-oblong, 1 to 3 in. long, acute or acuminate, irregularly serrulate, dull green above, light green and hairy or nearly smooth beneath, petioles 0.2 to 0.5 in. long.
FLOWERS. White, in terminal and axillary, slender-peduncled panicles, from June to September.
FRUIT. Less than 0.2 in. across, in September and October.

LANDSCAPE USE

An attractive native which is suitable for shrub borders or foundation planting. The blue flowered western species are very showy but are not hardy in zone 4. This species is native across eastern Canada and south to South Carolina and Texas. It has been cultivated since 1713.

CULTURE

Grows in sandy and acidic soils. Withstands droughty conditions. Good for poor soils as it fixes nitrogen from the atmosphere. Difficult to transplant.

INLAND CEANOTHUS
Ceanothus ovatus Desf.
HARDY IN ZONE 4
2 feet tall, less than 2 feet wide

HABIT. Upright shrub.
BRANCHES. Slightly hairy and often slightly glandular.
LEAVES. Elliptic to elliptic-lanceolate, 0.7 to 2.2 in. long, obtuse to acute, to crenate-serrulate, shiny above, nearly smooth below; petioles less than 0.2 in. long.
FLOWERS. Inflorescences similar to those on *C. americanus* but smaller.
FRUIT. Less than 0.2 in. across.

LANDSCAPE USE AND CULTURE

Culture same as for *C. americanus*. Native from New England to Nebraska, Colorado and Texas, it has been in cultivation since 1830. Good for naturalizing.

BITTERSWEETS

ORIENTAL BITTERSWEET
Celastrus orbiculatus Thunb.
FAMILY: CELASTRACEAE, BITTERSWEET FAMILY
FOR PROTECTED LOCATIONS IN ZONE 4
30 feet long

HABIT. Vigorous twining vine; there are 30 species distributed worldwide.
BRANCHES. Pith solid, white.
LEAVES. Suborbicular to obovate or oblong-obovate, 2 to 4 in. long, acute or abruptly acuminate, wedge-shaped at base, crenate-serrate.
FLOWERS. In small axillary cymes, in June.
FRUIT. Orange-yellow, less than 0.3 in. across, with scarlet aril, ripening in October.

LANDSCAPE USE AND CULTURE

The plants at the Arboretum have lacked hardiness. Native to Japan and China, it was introduced into North America in 1860. All members of this genus are polygamo-dioecious, so one needs to have both female and male plants in proximity. It has often become a nuisance plant farther south of zone 4.

CHINESE BITTERSWEET
Celastrus rosthornianus Loes.
HARDY IN ZONE 4
20 feet long

HABIT. Vigorous, twining vine.
BRANCHES. Reddish brown, slightly lenticellate; pith chambered.
LEAVES. Elliptic or elliptic-ovate to elliptic-lanceolate, 2 to 4.2 in. long, acuminate, rounded or broadly wedge-shaped at base, crenate-serrate, dark green above, pale green beneath; petioles 0.2 to 0.6 in. long.
FLOWERS. In short-stalked or subsessile axillary cymes, in June, often forming racemes, to 2 in. long, on short lateral branches.
FRUIT. Abundant, yellow with red arils, ripening in October.

LANDSCAPE USE

A vigorous vine that grows on most well-drained soils. Native in China, it was introduced into North America in 1907. Attractive in fruit, its arils soon shatter so it is not suitable for dried arrangements. Often confused with *C. loeseneri* (zone 5) in the trade. It is difficult to obtain in the nursery trade.

CULTURE

Propagated by seed and cuttings. Needs both male and female plants.

AMERICAN BITTERSWEET
Celastrus scandens L.
HARDY IN ZONES 2 TO 4
20 feet long

HABIT. Vigorous, climbing vine.
BRANCHES. Pith solid, white.
LEAVES. Ovate to oblong-ovate, 2 to 4 in. long, acuminate, broadly wedge-shaped at base, serrulate, smooth; petioles 2 to 8 in. long.
FLOWERS. In panicles 2 to 4 in. long, in June.
FRUIT. Subglobose, about 0.3 in. across, yellow, with crimson arils and seeds, ripening in October.

LANDSCAPE USE

This is the hardiest and most attractive of the bittersweet for the North. It needs a strong trellis or fence as it is a prolific grower. For dried arrangements the fruiting branches can be harvested as soon as they reach maturity. The fruit retains its orange and red color when dried. Native in Canada and northern United States south to New Mexico, it has been in cultivation since 1736.

E.H. Wilson, in his *If I Were to Make a Garden*, (1931, 94) calls it the native waxwork and states it can be "seen to best advantage as a tangle on and over large rocks. In the autumn, when laden with yellow fruit which opens and exposes the seeds with their brilliant orange-scarlet covering, there are few plants of equal beauty."

CULTURE

American Bittersweet needs male and female plants as for others in this genus. This is difficult to insure as most nurseries sell plants unlabelled as to sex. It thrives on most well-drained soils. It develops best fruit in full sun, but will withstand some shade. Propagated by seed or cuttings. Needs stout support. Although this species can become a nuisance outside of zone 4, in the North it has not needed special control measures.

HACKBERRY

HACKBERRY
Celtis occidentalis L.
FAMILY: ULMACEAE, ELM FAMILY
HARDY IN ZONES 3 AND 4
95 feet tall, 65 feet wide

HABIT. Large, deciduous tree with spreading crown; there are 70 species distributed worldwide.
BRANCHES. Smooth or slightly hairy.
BARK. Grayish brown with corky ridges that are very characteristic; winter buds rather small.
LEAVES. Alternate, simple, ovate to oblong-ovate, 2 to 2.7 in. long, acute to acuminate, oblique and rounded or broadly wedge-shaped at base; serrate except at base; upper leaf surface bright green and usually smooth and shiny; undersurface paler and smooth or slightly hairy veins; petioles 0.2 to 1 in. long.
FLOWERS. Polygamo-monoecious on young branches in May; male flowers in clusters below, perfect flowers above and solitary in leaf axils; calyx 4- to 5-lobed; stamens 4 to 5.
FRUIT. Orange-red to dark purple; subglobose or ovoid drupes 0.2 to 0.4 in. thick, on slender stalks, with firm outer coat, scanty pulp, and bony stone, in September; stones pitted.

LANDSCAPE USE

A hardy, drought resistant tree often used as a large shade tree or street tree. Native from Quebec to Manitoba south to North Carolina, Alabama and Kansas, it has been cultivated since 1636. Hackberry's mature shape is similar to American elm although it is not as vase-shaped. It can be too large for some landscapes. Hackberry is one of our premier midwestern trees. Hackberry has grandeur at maturity with a very distinctive bark. *See photograph page 139.*

CULTURE

Will grow in drier soils, alkaline soils and withstand exposed locations. Withstands city conditions and also stress conditions where other trees do not do well. Witches'-broom and a nipple gall on the leaves are two common problems that may mar the beauty of the tree but do little harm (usually the leaves are so far overhead, one cannot see any infestations even if there are any).

However, these problems cause many to dismiss hackberry as suitable for most cultivated areas. Dr. Donald Wyman in his *Trees for American Gardens* (1990, 184) says: "[hackberry] is susceptible to attacks from either a small mite or a mildew fungus or both, deforming the buds and resulting in a bunch of twigs growing from one place, often called 'witches broom' disease. A goodly proportion of these small twigs die each year, giving the tree a most unsightly appearance. It is well whenever possible to use species not so troubled..." Most Midwest gardeners ignore this tree's problems and use it for problem landscape areas. Seed propagated.

BUTTONBUSH

BUTTONBUSH
Cephalanthus occidentalis L.
FAMILY: RUBIACEAE, MADDER FAMILY
HARDY IN ZONE 4
10 feet tall, 8 feet wide

HABIT. Deciduous shrub; there are 10 species distributed worldwide.
BRANCHES. Slender, smooth, shiny, olive-green at first, becoming red in winter; terminal buds lacking, lateral ones small, conic in depressions above leaf scar, often superposed.
LEAVES. Opposite or whorled, simple, ovate to elliptic-lanceolate, 2.2 to 5.7 in. long, acuminate; upper leaf surface shiny bright green; undersurface lighter and smooth or somewhat hairy; petioles 0.2 to 0.7 in. long.
FLOWERS. Small, 4-merous, sessile, creamy white, in globose heads, in July and August; calyx lobes short, ovate, obtuse, corolla with long, slender tube and 4-lobed limb.
FRUIT. Capsules separating into two 1-seeded nutlets.

LANDSCAPE USE AND CULTURE

A shrub suited for problem wet sites. Native from New Brunswick to Ontario and south to Florida, Texas and California, one finds this shrub in swamps and other wet sites. It is rather coarse textured, especially during winter when devoid of leaves. Blooms in July and August when there are few shrubs blooming.

KATSURA TREE

KATSURA TREE
Cercidiphyllum japonicum Sieb. & Zucc.
FAMILY: CERCIDIPHYLLACEAE
FOR THE MOST PROTECTED SITES IN ZONE 4
30 feet tall, 25 feet wide

HABIT. Small deciduous tree (especially in our zone), usually dividing near the base into several upright stems; pyramidal when young, spreading with age; there is only one species found in Asia.
BUDS. None terminal, lateral buds with 2 scales.
LEAVES. Opposite or subopposite, suborbicular or broad-ovate, 2 to 4 in. long, obtuse, heart-shaped or subcordate at base, crenate-serrate, dark bluish green above, whitish beneath; petioles 0.7 to 1 in. long.
FLOWERS. Small, dioecious, developing from axillary buds or spurs before the leaves and lacking a perianth; male flowers nearly sessile, with slender filaments and red anthers; female flowers on pedicels, with 3 to 5 carpels and long purple styles.
FRUIT. Dehiscent pods to 0.7 in. long, in October.

LANDSCAPE USE
Used as a smaller, ornamental tree or clump shrub. Its heart-shaped leaves resemble redbud. The Katsura tree's petioles and leaf veins are red and distinctive early in the spring. Summer foliage is an unusual blue-green hue. Certainly worth trying in a protected site.

CULTURE
Of borderline hardiness in zone 4, Katsura trees should be considered only for protected locations. Prefers a moist soil; it will not tolerate dry soils.

EASTERN REDBUD

EASTERN REDBUD
Cercis canadensis L.
FAMILY: LEGUMINOSAE, PEA FAMILY
HARDY IN PROTECTED SITES IN ZONE 4
30 feet tall (usually 20 feet in the North), 20 feet wide

HABIT. Deciduous tree, usually quite spreading forming a broad round crown; there are 6 species distributed in the northern hemisphere.
BRANCHES. Slender, smooth.
BUDS. Small, superposed, with several outer scales.
LEAVES. Alternate, simple, broad-ovate to suborbicular, 2.7 to 4.7 in. long, usually heart-shaped at base, entire, hairy to smooth on undersurface.

FLOWERS. Pea-like, 4 to 8 in a fascicle, rosy pink, 0.2 in. long, in early May; calyx broad-campanulate, with short obtuse teeth; petals of unequal size (the 3 upper petals are smaller); stamens 10, all free.
FRUIT. Flat legumes, constricted between the seeds, in September.

LANDSCAPE USE
In the North, redbud can be used as an ornamental specimen tree or a clump shrub for protected locations. It flowers before the leaves appear with its flowers held tight to its branches. It is one of our most distinctive North American natives in bloom. Native from New Jersey to Missouri and south to Florida, Texas and New Mexico, this tree was introduced into cultivation in 1641. None of the other cultivars of redbud are reliably hardy.

CULTURE
Only redbud from seed sources selected in the North should be planted. One of these selections was from a tree growing at the Horticultural Research Center at the Arboretum (see below). Another is from a source selected in Wisconsin. Both seem hardy if planted in a protected location. They prefer good loam soils.

Although reasonably hardy, redbud might be considered a relatively short-lived tree for zone 4. The late J.C. Raulston (*Fine Gardening*, no. 19, 1991) speculates that even under optimum conditions, they have a normal life span of 20 to 30 years because they are pioneer plants of woodland margins.

CULTIVAR:

'Northern Strain'   redbud
HARDY IN ZONE 4 IN A PROTECTED LOCATION
30 feet tall, 20 feet wide

This strain originated from a seed source at the Horticultural Research Center of The Minnesota Landscape Arboretum. It was introduced in 1992. It combines the ornamental characteristics of redbud with good hardiness. Plant in a protected location. After seeing this tree in full bloom most gardeners covet one for their own landscapes. *See photographs on cover, p 137, 146-47, and 180-81.*

JAPANESE FLOWERING QUINCE
Chaenomeles speciosa (Sweet) Nakai.
TRIAL IN PROTECTED AREAS OF ZONE 4

While it is possible these could be vegetatively hardy in zone 4, the flower buds are most often killed during the winter even in zone 5. Since this shrub is grown for its attractive flowers (its growth habit is rather undistinguished), there are better shrubs to choose from for the North.

FERNBUSH

FERNBUSH, DESERT SWEET
Chamaebatiaria millefolium (Torr.) Maxim.
FAMILY: ROSACEAE, ROSE FAMILY

HARDY IN ZONE 4

8 feet tall, 8 feet wide

HABIT. Aromatic shrub; there are 2 species native to North America.
LEAVES. Pubescent and more or less glandular; oblong, 0.7 to 2 in. long, finely divided into 15-20 pair of primary leaves less than 0.3 in. long; 10-17 pair of secondary leaves less than 0.4 in. long.
FLOWERS. Terminal panicles, 1 to 4 in. long, in July; petals white, broadly obovate, 0.20 in. long; sepals lanceolate, acute.
FRUIT. Follicles, lanceolate, 0.20 in. long.

LANDSCAPE USE
This North American native's fern-like foliage is aromatic and essentially evergreen. In winter the foliage folds in upon itself. Fernbush can be considered for problem dry sites. It is native to dry rocky areas from Idaho to Arizona and California. Although not widely available, worth seeking out for problem sites. The flowers attract butterflies.

CULTURE
Needs full sun. It is tolerant of drought and poor soils. Fernbush is another native that is difficult to obtain in the nursery trade.

FALSE CYPRESS

FALSE CYPRESS
Chamaecyparis obtusa (Sieb. & Zucc.) Endl.
FAMILY: CUPRESSACEAE, CYPRESS FAMILY

FOR PROTECTED LOCATIONS IN ZONE 4

95 feet tall, 50 feet wide (in our region much smaller)

HABIT. Large broad-pyramidal tree; there are 8 species in North America and Asia.
BRANCHES. Arranged in horizontal tiers.
BARK. Reddish brown, rather smooth, peeling in thin strips.
LEAVES. Closely appressed, obtuse, dark green above, with white bands below.
FRUIT. Cones, globose, orange-brown, 0.3 to less than 0.5 in. across; scales 8 to 10, depressed on back with a small mucro; seeds 2 to 5 per scale, narrowly winged.

LANDSCAPE USE
Being of borderline hardiness, unless it is sited in a protected location this evergreen often is unsuccessful in the North. Although the species gets very large in more temperate areas,

in the North this species remains much smaller.

The numerous cultivars of false cypress are more often planted than the species. The most successful of these are the dwarf cultivars which can be used in a rock garden where they receive snow cover. Native in Japan, this plant was introduced into North America in 1861. *See photograph of unidentified species pages 178-79.*

CULTURE
Only for protected or reliably snow covered sites.

<u>CULTIVARS:</u>
(Numerous cultivars have been named, but only dwarf false cypress should be used in protected locations in zone 4)

'Nana'   Hinoki false cypress
A dwarf form that might be planted in a sheltered spot. Winter shade is required to prevent winter burn.

SAWARA FALSE CYPRESS
Chamaecyparis pisifera (Sieb. & Zucc.) Endl.
FOR PROTECTED LOCATIONS IN ZONE 4

95 feet tall, 50 feet wide (in our region much smaller)

HABIT. Large, pyramidal tree.
BRANCHES. Spreading, flattened, 2-ranked, and arranged in horizontal whorls.
BARK. Red-brown, rather smooth, peeling in thin strips.
LEAVES. Appressed, acuminate, ovate-lanceolate with slightly spreading tips, dark green above, with whitish hands beneath.
FRUIT. Cones 0.2 in. across, dark brown; scales 10 to 12, with a small mucro in center; seeds 1 to 2 per scale, broadly winged.

LANDSCAPE USE
Again, in the North this species does not reach its native, large-sized height. Consider only the dwarf conifers that can be protected or enjoy snow cover. The species has the general appearance of arborvitae and is inferior as a landscape plant in our area.

CULTURE
Protected sites.

<u>CULTIVARS :</u>
Numerous cultivars have been named. The following can be tried in zone 4. Dwarf forms should be more successful.

'Boulevard'
A narrow pyramidal form which at maturity can reach 10 feet. Silvery blue foliage.

'Filifera' sawara false cypress

A dwarf form about 6 or more feet tall with stringy, drooping branches. This cultivar is growing very well in the Arboretum and is one of the most attractive of all the dwarf conifers. Slow growing.

'Filifera Aurea' sawara false cypress

A golden form of doubtful hardiness.

'Filifera Nana' sawara false cypress
ZONE 4
2 feet tall, 3 feet wide

A dwarf form which stands a better chance of survival because of its dwarf size.

'Squarrosa' sawara false cypress

A cultivar with juvenile foliage and needle-like leaves. Subject to winter burn.

WHITE CEDAR FALSE CYPRESS
Chamaecyparis thyoides (L.) BSP.
FOR PROTECTED LOCATIONS IN ZONE 4
65 feet tall, 30 feet wide (in our region much smaller)

HABIT. Upright tree.
BRANCHES. Upright-spreading to horizontal, forming a narrow, spire-like crown.
BARK. Reddish brown, fissured into flat, connected ridges.
LEAVES. Closely appressed, dark bluish or light green.
FRUIT. Cones bluish purple; seeds 1 or 2 on each scale with wings as broad as the seed.

LANDSCAPE USE

Some authorities rate this as being the hardiest of all false cypress species, although specimens at the Arboretum have not proven so. Native from Maine to Florida and Mississippi, it has been cultivated since 1727.

CULTURE

Seek your specimens from northernmost strains. Again, plant only in protected locations in moist sites.

HAIRY BROOM

HAIRY BROOM
Chamaecytisus hirsutus (L.) Link.
FAMILY: LEGUMINOSAE, PEA FAMILY
FOR PROTECTED LOCATIONS IN ZONE 4
3 feet tall, 3 feet wide

HABIT. Deciduous shrub; there are 30 species native to Europe.
BRANCHES. Hairy.
LEAVES. 3-foliate, alternate; leaflets obovate or elliptic to obovate-oblong, 0.2 to 0.7 in. long, acute to obtuse, hairy beneath, slightly hairy or nearly smooth above.
FLOWERS. Yellow, pea-like, about 1 in. long, in axillary clusters of 2 to 4, in early May; standards stained with brown in center; calyx hairy.
FRUIT. Dry legumes about 1 in. long.

LANDSCAPE USE

This is the hardiest of the broom species. It is used as a ground cover in more temperate climates. Some dieback can be expected in most winters in zone 4, but the basal portion of the upright stems usually bloom profusely. Native to southeastern Europe, it was introduced into North America in 1739. It was previously named *Cytisus hirsutus*.

CULTURE

Tolerates poor soils. Authorities generally list this plant as being short-lived even under better conditions. Easily propagated from seed.

LEATHERLEAF

LEATHERLEAF
Chamaedaphne calyculata (L.) Moench.
FAMILY: ERICACEAE, HEATH FAMILY
HARDY IN ZONES 2 TO 4
3 to 4 feet tall, 3 feet wide

HABIT. Upright evergreen shrub; there is 1 species distributed throughout the northern hemisphere.
BRANCHES. Spreading
BUDS. Small with several outer scales.
LEAVES. Alternate, elliptic or obovate to oblong or lanceolate, 0.4 to 1 in. long, obtuse or acute, revolute, dull green and slightly scaly above, densely scaly beneath, entire, more or less appressed to the stem.
FLOWERS. Nodding, on short pedicels, in terminal leafy racemes 1.5 to 4.7 in. long, in May; corolla white, 0.2 in. long.
FRUIT. Globose, 10-valved capsules; seeds small, wingless.

LANDSCAPE USE

Another site specific plant to use in problem wet sites. Native in northern Europe, northern Asia, and in North America in Canada south to Georgia, it has been in cultivation since 1748. Could be used in naturalistic plantings.

CULTURE

Requires a moist site. Does best in acid, peaty soils.

WHITE FRINGE TREE

WHITE FRINGE TREE
Chionanthus virginicus L.
FAMILY: OLEACEAE, OLIVE FAMILY
HARDY IN ZONE 4
15 feet tall (usually 8 feet in the North),
10 feet wide

HABIT. Large deciduous shrub or
small tree; there are 100 species distributed in North
America and Asia.
BRANCHES. Stout, hairy when young; winter buds with several outer acute scales.
LEAVES. Simple, opposite, narrow-elliptic to oblong or obovate-oblong, 3 to 8 in. long, acute or acuminate, wedge-shaped at base, dark green and shiny above, paler and hairy at least on the veins beneath, becoming smooth at maturity; fall color golden yellow; petioles 0.4 to 1 in. long, hairy.
FLOWERS. White, fragrant, dioecious, in panicles 4 to 8 in. long, usually with leafy bracts at the base, in June; 4-cleft calyx with triangular lobes; petals 4, 0.5 to 1 in. long, and about 0.08 in. broad; staminate flowers have a sterile pistil.
FRUIT. Ellipsoid drupes, 0.5 to 0.7 in. long, dark blue, ripening in September.

LANDSCAPE USE

A very ornamental small tree or large growing shrub that needs a protected site in zone 4. It has done reasonably well in a protected spot at the Arboretum growing to about 6 feet. Native from New Jersey to Florida and west to Texas, it has been cultivated since 1736. Panicles on male plants are large and showier than those on female plants, but only the female plants produce the fruit. The botanical name can be translated loosely as the snow flowering tree of Virginia.

Donald Peattie in his *A Natural History of Trees* (1950, 556) describes it aptly: "[it] is as gracile and feminine-seeming as any...[and] is a raving beauty when in mid-spring it is loaded from top to bottom with the airest, most ethereal yet showy flowers boasted by any member of our northern sylva."

CULTURE

Needs moist slightly acid soils to do best. It grows best in full sun, but will grow well in part shade. It will tolerate less than perfect conditions, but it needs a protected site in the North. Propagated by seed.

YELLOWWOOD

YELLOWWOOD
Cladrastis lutea (Michx.f.) K. Koch.
FAMILY: LEGUMINOSAE, PEA FAMILY
FOR PROTECTED LOCATIONS IN ZONE 4
30 feet tall, 25 feet wide

HABIT. Small, deciduous tree of spreading habit; there are 5 species distributed in North America and Asia.
BARK. Smooth and wood yellow.
BUDS. Naked, superposed, and protected by persistent bases of petioles.
LEAVES. Compound, odd-pinnate; leaflets 7 to 11, elliptic or ovate, 2.7 to 4 in. long, abruptly short-acuminate, broadly wedge-shaped at base, smooth, bright green; fall color golden yellow.
FLOWERS. White, perfect, 1 in. long, fragrant, in long drooping panicles 10 to 15 in. long, in June; calyx campanulate, 5-toothed; stamens 10, nearly free.
FRUIT. Narrow to oblong pods to 3 in. long, constricted between the 3 to 6 seeds.

LANDSCAPE USE

This small tree has flowered in the Twin Cities area; the Arboretum's plantings seem of variable hardiness. The showy flowers and attractive fall color makes this a good ornamental lawn tree if grown in a rather protected location. Native from North Carolina to Kentucky and Tennessee, it has been cultivated since 1812. It was previously known as *C. kentukea*. *See photograph page 169.*

CULTURE

Needs full sun, a well-drained moist soil and of course a protected spot. It should not be pruned in the spring as it will bleed profusely. It should be protected from sunscald in the winter by wrapping the major branches and trunk. Propagated by seed.

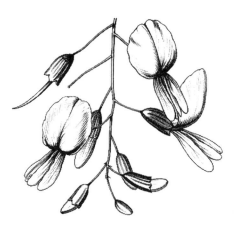

The CLEMATIS

Clematis L.

FAMILY: RANUNCULACEAE; BUTTERCUP FAMILY

Certainly one of the most ornamental vines, clematis can become one of the features of many landscapes. This genus contains over 300 species native throughout the world and hundreds of cultivars. If chosen carefully for hardiness, it can be a long-lived spot of color. Colors range from blue and red to white and yellow in all shades and blends. Clematis flowers are generally sepals masquerading as petals. The fluffy seed heads also can be very ornamental. The name, clematis, is derived from an ancient Greek word for climbing plant.

Vining clematis climb by twisting their leafstalks around their supports. At the Arboretum, all the vine type of clematis are grown on chicken wire supported on wooden trellises. In November the chicken wire and plants are removed from the trellises, laid on the ground, and covered with marsh hay or straw. In the spring the wire is re-attached to the trellises, and when growth starts the vines are pruned back to live wood and the dead portions are pulled from the wire.

As a group, clematis likes neutral soil. On very acid soils, lime must be used. A cool root zone is required, so use a summer mulch, other plantings, or a ground cover at the base of the vines to keep the soil cool. However, do not plant where the roots will have to compete for water and nutrients. Plant only from pot-grown specimens as they are difficult to transplant from open ground. Care should be taken in planting as their tender stems are easily damaged. Plant where the vines will receive a minimum of 6 to 8 hours of sunlight. It is sometimes recommended to plant clematis crowns below the surface of the soil to protect them from mechanical damage and rodents.

A little dappled shade in the heat of noonday is appreciated. As at the Arboretum, there is something pleasing about combining clematis and roses. Propagation of hybrids is by cuttings, grafting and layering; species are also propagated by seed. There are also smaller shrubby, non-vining clematis which are usually grown in herbaceous borders.

Correct timing for pruning clematis is complex. The large flowered hybrids fall into 3 groups; those flowering on old wood in spring (they can be lightly pruned and shaped only right after flowering); those flowering on short new wood in the spring (again, they can be pruned and shaped directly after flowering); and those flowering on new wood during summer and autumn (they can be pruned and shaped early in the spring, or they can routinely be cut back to 2 feet early in the spring). Pruning at other times will reduce amount of bloom.

CULTIVARS:

There are hundreds of named hybrids to choose from. The first clematis hybrid was recorded in England in 1835. The hybrids can be assumed to be zone 4 unless otherwise noted. Light pruning indicates little pruning desired. The following have done especially well at the Arboretum.

'Ascotiensis'   clematis
A lavender-blue hybrid developed in 1871 with large, 5 to 6 in. nodding flowers, in July and August. Should grow to 10 feet. Tolerates hard spring pruning.

'Barbara Dibley'   clematis
An unusual flower color, a combination of purple and red with darker midribs. June flowering. Developed by the George Jackman firm in England. 6 feet. Light late winter pruning.

'Bees Jubilee'   clematis

It was hybridized in England in the 1950's. Often thought of as a darker 'Nelly Moser' (pink). Very large flowers up to 7 in. are flat and solitary in June with some repeat bloom. More exacting culture. Light late winter pruning.

'Belle of Woking'   clematis

Double-flowering hybrid with a unique silvery pink color. Hybridized by the Jackman firm in England in 1875. A slow grower to 6 feet. Midsummer bloom. Light late winter pruning.

'Blue Bird'   clematis

ZONES 2 TO 4

A hybrid between *C. macropetala* and *C. alpina*. Introduced by Dr. Skinner of Manitoba. Light blue flowers in June repeat through the season. Prolific grower to 10 feet. Light late winter pruning.

'Comtesse de Bouchaud'   clematis

ZONES 2 TO 4

A rose pink hybrid of the *jackmanii* type. Profuse bloomer. Developed in 1903, it has long been one of the most popular of all clematis. 6 feet and midsummer bloom. Tolerates hard spring pruning.

'Daniel Deronda'   clematis

Single to semi-double blue-purple flowers with lighter midrib. 6 feet. June bloom and some repeat. Light late winter pruning.

'Dr Ruppel'   clematis

Large 8 in. flowering hybrid. Pink with a reddish bar down the petal with prominent stamens. 6 to 8 feet. A Fisk hybrid obtained from Argentina in 1975. Light late winter pruning. Hardy in zone 4, for protected locations in zone 3. *See photograph page 162.*

C. texensis 'Duchess of Albany'

Introduced in 1890 by Jackman. Pink, upright, bell-shaped flowers are 1 to 1.5 in. across, from late June to early October. 6 feet. Tolerates hard pruning in the spring.

'Duchess of Edinburgh'   clematis

ZONES 2 TO 4

Hybridized by Jackman in England in 1875. Open double white blooms, 4 in. across in June. 4 to 5 feet. Slow growing. Light late winter pruning.

'Elsa Spaeth'   clematis

A prolific bloomer with lavender-purple, open 8 in. blooms. Blooms in late June with repeat fall blooms. 6 feet. Also known as 'Xerxes'. Light late winter pruning.

'Ernest Markham'   clematis

ZONES 2 TO 4

Bright magenta flowers, 3 to 6 in. across, in July and August. Prolific grower to 12 feet. Tolerates hard spring pruning.

C. viticella 'Etoile Violette'

Flowers are medium-sized, 3 to 4 in. across, dark purple, and very prolific. Plant blooms from late June to September, with peak in early July. 12 feet. Tolerates hard spring pruning.

'Gipsy Queen'   clematis

ZONES 2 TO 4

Also spelled Gypsy in the trade, this is an 1871 introduction. A rich plum color, with unique tapering petal shape. 10 feet. Tolerates hard spring pruning.

'Hagley Hybrid'   clematis

ZONES 2 TO 4

A beautiful lavender-pink hybrid with 6 in. blooms. Blooms from late June to September, with peak in mid-July. Tolerates hard spring pruning.

'Henryi'   clematis

HARDY IN ZONE 4, FOR PROTECTED LOCATIONS IN ZONE 3

Very large white flowers with a dark center, 4 to 6 in. across. Often found as *C. henryi*, but hybridized in 1858. Flowers June and later repeat. 8 feet. Can take some spring pruning.

'Huldine'   clematis

A pearly white hybrid with a touch of mauve-pink on the reverse side of sepals. Flowers 3 to 5 in. across. Blooms from late June until September, with peak in early July. One of the best of the white clematis. 12 feet. Tolerates hard spring pruning. *See photograph pages 152-53.*

'Jan Pawl II/John Paul II'   clematis

A Fisk introduction. White with some pink, 6 to 8 in. across. 6 feet. Light late winter pruning.

'Lady Betty Balfour'   clematis

Dark purple and blues, 5 in. across. Fall blooming. 12 feet. Tolerates hard spring pruning.

'Lady Northcliffe'   clematis

Flowers dark purple, single 4 to 6 in. across, from late June to early October, with peak in mid-July. 4 to 5 feet. Light late winter pruning.

'Lasurstern'   clematis

Dark blue, large, 7 in. blooms. Contrasting cream stamens. Flowers in June with some repeat bloom in September. 7 feet. Light late winter pruning. *See photograph pages 174-75.*

'Lincoln Star'

Modern hybrid, originated in 1954. Clear pink, 4 to 5 in. bloom. June and repeat in August. 4 feet. Light late winter pruning.

'Madame Baron Veillard' clematis

Flowers lilac-rose, single, 4 to 5 in. across, from late July to October. 12 feet. Tolerates hard spring pruning. Introduced in 1885.

'Madame Edouard Andre' clematis

Flowers velvety red, 4 to 5 in. across, from mid-June to September, with peak bloom about July 1. 6 feet. Tolerates hard spring pruning.

Macropetala 'Markham's Pink' clematis

ZONES 2 TO 4

Vigorous grower to 10 feet. Similar to the species except for its color. Reddish purple with lighter margin. June flowering. Has one of the most attractive seed heads. Also known as 'Markhamii'. Light late winter pruning.

'Mrs Cholmondeley' clematis

ZONES 2 TO 4.

A sparse bloomer with very large, 6 in. blooms of light blue color in late June and early July. A few blooms as late as September. 18 feet. Light spring pruning.

'Multi Blue' clematis

Double dark blue with sepals tipped with white, 4 to 5 in. across. June and repeat in fall. 6 feet. Light spring pruning.

'Nelly Moser' clematis

HARDY IN ZONE 4, FOR PROTECTED LOCATIONS IN ZONE 3

A very popular hybrid introduced in 1897. Flowers a pale mauve-pink with a deep pink bar down center of every sepal, 6 to 8 in. across. June and repeat in September. 8 feet. Light spring pruning.

'Niobe' clematis

ZONES 2 TO 4

Ruby-red, contrasting cream stamens, 4 to 6 in. across. Flowering time depends upon pruning. 6 feet. Can be pruned heavily for fall bloom, or light pruning for early summer to fall bloom.

'Ramona' clematis

ZONES 3 AND 4

Also sold as 'Hybrida Sieboldiana'. Flowers light purple with white center, 4 to 5 in. across. 10 feet. Generally light pruning.

'Rouge Cardinal/Red Cardinal' clematis

A newer French hybrid. Crimson with other reds, 3 to 4 in. across. July and repeat September. 5 feet. Tolerates hard spring pruning.

'Star of India' clematis

An 1867 introduction. Reddish plum with red colorations. July to September. 10 feet. Tolerates hard spring pruning.

'The President' clematis

ZONES 3 AND 4

A fine variety introduced in 1876 with large, dark purple blooms 6 in. across. From early June until October; peak bloom in late June. 6 feet. Light spring pruning.

'Ville de Lyon' clematis

ZONES 2 TO 4

Flowers single, carmine-red, 4 in. across, from late June until frost; peak bloom in early July. Introduced in 1899. 8 feet. Tolerates hard spring pruning.

'Will Goodwin' clematis

HARDY IN ZONE 4, FOR PROTECTED LOCATIONS IN ZONE 3

Bluish lavender with dark stamens. 6 to 8 in. across. June to September. 8 feet. Light spring pruning.

CURLY CLEMATIS, LEATHER FLOWER
Clematis crispa L.

FOR PROTECTED LOCATIONS IN ZONE 4

10 feet long

HABIT. Vigorous, climbing vine; there are 200 species distributed worldwide.

FLOWERS. Bell-shaped, 2 to 4 in. long, and 0.7 to 1 in. across, dark purple from June to October, with peak bloom in mid-August.

FRUIT. Plumed achenes, in September.

LANDSCAPE USE AND CULTURE

Bell-shaped, dark purple, fragrant blossoms. Flowers over a long time in summer. The sepals curl back to give this clematis an open face. Native from Virginia to Missouri and south to Florida and Texas, it has been cultivated since 1726. Needs a stout trellis. Tolerates moist soil. Needs winter protection; however, this clematis is variously rated from zone 4 to 7 for hardiness by differing authorities.

FRAGRANT TUBE CLEMATIS
Clematis heracleifolia var. davidiana
(Verl.) Hemsl.

HARDY IN ZONES 2 TO 4

3 feet tall, 3 feet wide

HABIT. Semi-woody, nonclimbing plant.
LEAVES. With 3 leaflets; leaflets broad-ovate, 2.2 to 6 in. long, square or broadly wedge-shaped at base, coarsely dentate or slightly lobed, with pointed teeth.
FLOWERS. Fragrant, indigo-blue, tubular 1 in. across, from mid-August into September.
FRUIT. Achenes with plumose styles.

LANDSCAPE USE AND CULTURE

One of the herbaceous type perennials in this genus that is often used in a perennial border. Native to northern China, it was introduced into North America in 1868.

SOLITARY CLEMATIS
Clematis integrifolia L.
HARDY IN ZONE 4
3 feet tall, 18 inches wide

HABIT. Semi-woody, non-climbing plant.
LEAVES. Simple, ovate to oblong-ovate, 2.2 to 4 in. long, acute, entire, green on both sides.
FLOWERS. Blue, violet, or white, 1 to 1.5 in. across, in July and August.
FRUIT. Plumose styles, in September.

LANDSCAPE USE AND CULTURE

Used in perennial borders, this plant needs staking for support. Native to Europe and Asia, it was introduced into North America in 1573.

JACKMAN CLEMATIS
Clematis x jackmanii T. Moore.
HARDY WITH WINTER PROTECTION IN ZONE 3
10 feet long

HABIT. Vigorous, climbing vine.
LEAVES. Pinnately compound, the upper ones often simple; leaflets ovate, usually slightly hairy on undersurface.
FLOWERS. On slender pedicels, velvety dark purple, 4.7 to 5.5 in. across, in late June to October, with peak bloom in July.

LANDSCAPE USE AND CULTURE

This popular clematis was developed by crossing *C. lanuginosa* and *C. viticella*. One of the most commonly found landscape plants of North America, it was introduced c. 1860. Plant by a trellis where the clematis will receive at least 8 hours of sunlight each day. Some authorities consider this vine a cultivar.

CULTIVAR:

'Alba'   Jackman clematis
Large, single, 4.7 in. blooms from late June into August, with peak in early July. White sepals have a bluish tinge around the edges.

Clematis macropetala Ledeb.
HARDY IN ZONES 2 TO 4
6 feet long

HABIT. Climbing vine.
LEAVES. Biternate, to 5 in.; leaflets ovate to lanceolate, 1 in., acute, tapered sometimes cordate at base; serrate to lobed, subglabrous.
FLOWERS. Nodding bell, 2.5 to 3 in. across, solitary, on pedicels to 2.5 in.; pale blue with purple-blue shading, in June.

LANDSCAPE USE AND CULTURE

A favorite species of dependable habit. In the fall it features very attractive seedheads. 'Blue Bird' and 'Markham's Pink' are two common cultivars closely related to this species (treated with hybrid listing). Native of China, it was introduced by Reginald Farrer in 1910.

Clematis mandshurica Rupr.
HARDY IN ZONE 4
6 feet long

HABIT. Climbing vine.
LEAVES. 1- to 2-pinatisect, lanceolate-ovate, short acuminate or cordate at base, pubescent beneath.
FLOWERS. Terminal and axilliary inflorescences, pedicels braceate, sepals white, to 0.5 in long.

LANDSCAPE USE AND CULTURE

Has showy flowers and seems very hardy. Was classified *C. recta var. mandshurica*. Native to China and Japan.

ORIENTAL CLEMATIS
Clematis orientalis L.
HARDY WITH WINTER PROTECTION IN ZONE 4
20 feet long

HABIT. Vigorous, climbing vine.
LEAVES. Pinnately compound with 3 to 5 leaflets; leaflets ovate to oblong-ovate or lanceolate, 0.5 to 2 in. long, lobed or coarsely toothed.
FLOWERS. Yellow, 1 to 1.5 in. across, bell-shaped, from early August through September.
FRUIT. Having long, plumose styles, in September and October.

LANDSCAPE USE AND CULTURE

A prolific grower, this clematis is often used to cover fences in more temperate climates. Native from Persia to the Himalayas, it was introduced into North America in 1731.

GROUND CLEMATIS
Clematis recta L.
HARDY IN ZONES 3 AND 4
3 feet tall, 3 feet wide

HABIT. A variable species with a non-climbing habit.
LEAVES. With 5 to 7 leaflets; leaflets ovate to lanceolate, rounded or square at base.
FLOWERS. White, 0.7 to 1 in. across in terminal panicles, from mid-June through July.

LANDSCAPE USE AND CULTURE
Used as a background plant in perennial borders. Staking is required to keep stems from falling over. Native to Europe and northern Asia, it was introduced into North America in 1597. The variety *mandshurica* is now classified as a species.

GOLDEN CLEMATIS
Clematis tangutica (Maxim.) Korsh.
HARDY IN ZONE 4
10 feet long

HABIT. Vigorous climber with woody base.
LEAVES. Pinnate or bipinnate; leaflets oblong-lanceolate to lanceolate, 1 to 3 in. long, serrate, sometimes lobed, smooth, bright green.
FLOWERS. Bell-shaped, bright yellow, 1 to 2 in. long, usually solitary, in June and July.
FRUIT. Clusters showy, with plumose styles, in September.

LANDSCAPE USE AND CULTURE
A handsome yellow flowered clematis used for trellis, arbor or fence. Native to Mongolia and northern China, it was introduced into North America in 1890.

SWEET AUTUMN CLEMATIS
Clematis terniflora DC.
HARDY IN ZONE 4
30 feet long

HABIT. Vigorous, climbing vine.
LEAVES. Pinnate with 3 to 5 leaflets; leaflets ovate, 1 to 4 in. long, acute, subcordate or rounded at the base, entire or sometimes lobed, smooth.
FLOWERS. Small, white, fragrant, 0.7 to 1 in. across, produced in abundance from late August to October.
FRUIT. Plumose, in October.

LANDSCAPE USE AND CULTURE
A fast-growing climber grown for its late summer, fragrant, white flowers. Native to Japan, it was introduced into North America in 1864. E.H. Wilson, in his classic *If I Were to Make a Garden* (1931, 43), describes this clematis: "But *Clematis paniculata* in myriad fragrant stars is content to hang a bridal veil on fence and wall, pergola and porch." It has been a clematis that has been previously named *C. paniculata* and *C. maximowicziana*. Whatever its correct name, it is a useful large growing vine.

SCARLET CLEMATIS
Clematis texensis Buckl.
HARDY WITH WINTER PROTECTION IN ZONE 4
6 feet long

HABIT. Vigorous vine, woody at base.
LEAVES. With 4 to 8 leaflets; the terminal leaflet is replaced by a tendril; leaflets broad-ovate, 1 to 3 in. long, subcordate at base, sometimes lobed, dark green and leathery.
FLOWERS. Solitary, slender-stalked, urn-shaped, much narrowed at the mouth, 0.7 to 1 in. long, scarlet, from July to September.
FRUIT. With plumose styles, in September and October.

LANDSCAPE USE AND CULTURE
One of the most useful of the clematis species. Relatively difficult to obtain, but worth seeking out. Native in Texas, it has been cultivated since 1878. It has unique pitcher-shaped flowers. Its cultivar 'Duchess of Albany' (listed in the above cultivar listing) is more readily available.

VIRGIN'S BOWER
Clematis virginiana L.
HARDY IN ZONES 2 TO 4
20 feet long

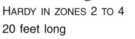

HABIT. Vigorous, climbing vine.
LEAVES. Pinnate; leaflets usually 5, ovate, 2 to 3.5 in. long, acuminate, rounded or subcordate at base, dentate.
FLOWERS. Dioecious, dull white, 0.7 to 1 in. across, in axillary leafy panicles, in June and July.
FRUIT. Clusters with plumose styles, in August and September.

LANDSCAPE USE AND CULTURE
This clematis is sometimes used as a ground cover for steep banks. A prolific grower, it can grow into nearby trees and shrubs. The seed heads provide winter interest. Available in the nursery trade in both seed and plant forms.

SUMMERSWEET

SUMMERSWEET
Clethra alnifolia L.
FAMILY: CLETHRACEAE
HARDY IN ZONE 4, FOR PROTECTED LOCATIONS IN ZONE 3
6 feet tall, 6 feet wide

HABIT. Deciduous shrub with star-shaped hairs; there are 30 species distributed worldwide.
BUDS. Small, hairy.
LEAVES. Alternate, simple, pinnately veined, obovate to obovate-oblong, 1.5 to 4 in. long, acute to short-acuminate, wedge-shaped at base, sharply serrate, smooth or nearly so.
FLOWERS. Perfect, white, fragrant, in upright panicled racemes 2 to 6 in. long; sepals 5, distinct; petals 5, distinct; stamens 10; anthers opening by a pore or slit; ovaries superior, 3-celled; styles cylindric, slender, 3-fid at apex.
FRUIT. 3-valved capsules.

LANDSCAPE USE

Another of the summer blooming shrubs that need specific cultural requirements to do well. Its spicy fragrance and blooms, however, are outstanding in the landscape. It blooms over a 3 to 5 week period in mid- to late-summer. The flower buds are also ornamental.

This shrub should be planted in groups of 3 or more to make an impact in the shrub border. It seldom reaches the size it grows to in its native habitat. If a special acidic bed is prepared for azaleas in the landscape, perhaps summersweet could be included. Cultivars have been selected for better form and fragrance. Native from Maine to Florida, perhaps some of this shrub's variability is due to where its parent plants were collected. *See photograph page 163.*

CULTURE

Summersweet requires an acidic soil; shrubs in neutral soil at the Arboretum have not done as well. It withstands some shade. It needs a late spring pruning to eliminate the dead wood and shape the shrub. This shrub is a variable performer withstanding some winters well and suffering in the next. Propagated by seed or cuttings.

CULTIVARS:

'Hummingbird'   summersweet
FOR PROTECTED LOCATIONS IN ZONE 4
Compact form to 4 feet.

Good glossy green foliage. Dieback in the North is common.

'Paniculata'   summersweet
FOR PROTECTED LOCATIONS IN ZONE 4
6 to 8 feet tall; 5 feet wide

A superior form, that has all the growing requirements and attributes of the species. Good rounded form.

'Rosea'   summersweet
ZONE 4
Selected for its flowers which are pink in bud fading to very light pink.

'Ruby Spice'   summersweet
ZONE 4, TRIAL IN ZONE 3
5 feet tall, 4 feet wide

A hardier cultivar to try. 'Ruby Spice' has pink flowers that retain their color in full sun.

SWEET FERN

SWEET FERN
Comptonia peregrina (L.) Coult.
FAMILY: MYRICACEAE, SWEET GALE FAMILY
HARDY IN ZONES 3 AND 4, IN PROTECTED LOCATIONS IN ZONE 2
3 feet tall, 3 feet wide

HABIT. Deciduous shrub; there is 1 species.
BRANCHES. Brown, covered with spreading hairs.
BUDS. Small, scaly.
LEAVES. Alternate, simple, linear-oblong, deeply pinnatifid with roundish, ovate, oblique, often mucronate lobes, 2 to 4.7 in. long and 0.5 in. wide, hairy, fragrant, dark green.
FLOWERS. Usually monoecious in cylindric catkins; no perianth; staminate flowers with 3 to 4 stamens, in catkins 0.5 in. long with acuminate brown ciliate bracts; female catkins globose-ovoid, 0.5 in. to 1 in. across, with 8 linear-subulate, persistent bracts at the base.
FRUIT. Nutlets subtended by elongated subulate bracts, in bur-like heads.

LANDSCAPE USE

Sweet fern is often used as a ground cover on exposed slopes. Native from Nova Scotia to Manitoba and south to North Carolina, it has been cultivated since 1714. One of the most aromatic of all woody plants, it is often planted for this reason alone. Curled, dried foliage often remains on the plant into the winter and catches early snows. Perhaps best grown where it can form a naturalized colony on its own.

CULTURE

Requires well-drained, acid soil. Although it will survive on gravely, poor soils it will also thrive in most garden soils as long as they are acidic. Should be purchased in potted form grown from root cuttings, since bare root stock or balled and burlapped stock is difficult to transplant. Sweet fern fixes its own nitrogen which helps it survive on poor soils. A planting can be kept vigorous by removing some of the older canes in the fall. Propagated by softwood cuttings and seed.

The
DOGWOODS
Cornus L.
FAMILY: CORNACEAE, DOGWOOD FAMILY

This genus ranges from the herbaceous bunch berry, *C. canadensis* (not treated here), which grows as a ground cover in northern areas to large trees and shrubs. The eastern flowering dogwood, *C. florida*, is not hardy along with others such as the kousa dogwood, *C. kousa* and the Cornelian cherry, *C. mas*. However, there are many useful hardy dogwoods to try. They can add interest to the landscape throughout dormant times of the year. One thinks of the red-twigged forms and the gray dogwood, *C. racemosa*.

Vita Sackville-West in *In Your Garden Again* (1953, 49) describes *C. alba* in winter: "The glory of this plant is the red bark of its bare stems throughout the winter. Caught by the light of the sinking sun...it is as warming to the heart as a log-fire on the hearth after a cold day." Variegated-leaved forms of Cornus add interest to the shrub border in the summer and are often used as an accent. *See photograph page 182-83.*

TATARIAN DOGWOOD
Cornus alba L.
HARDY IN ZONES 2 TO 4
10 feet tall, 10 feet wide

HABIT. Upright shrub; 45 species are distributed worldwide.
BRANCHES. Upright, usually bloodred, especially during late winter; pith ample, white.
LEAVES. Opposite, ovate to elliptic, 1.5 to 3 in. long, acute to acuminate, usually rounded at base; upper leaf surface dark green, rough, and often somewhat bullate; undersurface glaucous, with 5 to 6 pairs of veins; petioles 0.5 to 1 in. long.
FLOWERS. Yellowish white, in cymes 1 to 2 in. across, in May and June.
FRUIT. White or slightly bluish, in August and September; stone higher than broad, acute at ends, flattened.

LANDSCAPE USE
Used as a border shrub for its bright red stems in winter. Its cultivars are most often grown. Native to Siberia, Manchu-

ria and northern Korea, it was introduced into North America in 1906. Does not spread as quickly as *C. stolonifera*.

CULTURE
Tolerates many soil conditions, but it likes a moist, well-drained situation best. Propagated by seed and cuttings. Plantings need periodic rejuvenation in order to have the best twig color. Prune out older stems when dormant.

CULTIVARS:

These cultivars are planted more often than the species.

'Argenteo-marginata'   Tatarian dogwood
ZONES 3 AND 4
9 feet tall, 7 feet wide

A variegated selection with white leaf margins. Several selections are sold under this cultivar name or under the names 'Elegantissima' and 'Variegata'.

'Bud's Yellow'   Tatarian dogwood
ZONES 3 AND 4
6 feet tall, 6 feet wide

Introduced by Boughen Nurseries in Saskatchewan. More resistant to problems that trouble the similar looking *C. stolonifera* 'Flaviramea'.

'Gouchaultii'   Tatarian dogwood
ZONES 3 AND 4
6 feet tall, 6 feet wide

Similar to 'Argenteo-marginata' but with a yellow and rose leaf margin. Good red stem color in winter.

Ivory Halo®   Tatarian dogwood
C. 'Bailhalo'
ZONES 3 AND 4
5 feet tall, 8 feet wide

An introduction of Bailey Nurseries featuring cleaner variegated foliage than other cultivars. Compact growing.

'Sibirica'   Tatarian dogwood
ZONES 3 AND 4
9 feet tall, 7 feet wide

Similar to the species but winter stems coral-red. Confused in the trade.

'Spaethii'   Tatarian dogwood
ZONES 3 AND 4
Leaves with narrow yellow border.

Pagoda dogwood
Cornus alternifolia L.f.
HARDY IN ZONES 3 AND 4
25 feet tall, 20 feet wide

HABIT. Large shrub or small tree.
BRANCHES. Smooth, green, spread in irregular whorls forming horizontal tiers.
LEAVES. Alternate, slender-stalked, elliptic-ovate, 2 to 5 in. long, acuminate, wedge-shaped at base, with 5 to 6 pairs of veins; petioles 0.7 to 2 in. long.
FLOWERS. Creamy white, in cymes 1.5 to 2.2 in. across, in early June.
FRUIT. Less than 0.3 in. across, bluish black, on red pedicels in August.

LANDSCAPE USE
Excellent as a small specimen tree or can be planted toward the back of the shrub border. Its horizontal branching can make this a feature in the landscape. Its late summer fruit is also attractive. Can be trained as a single stemmed tree or used as a clump specimen. *See photograph pages 180-81.*

Native from New Brunswick to Minnesota and south to Georgia and Alabama, it has been cultivated since 1880. The only tree form of dogwood that is hardy in our area. This dogwood can be short-lived. Perhaps best in a shrub border.

CULTURE
Does best in a cool, moist soil. Needs a somewhat acidic soil to do well. Many times when used as a lawn specimen the conditions prove too hot and dry. Propagated by seed.

Silky dogwood
Cornus obliqua Raf.
HARDY IN ZONES 2 TO 4
10 feet tall, 10 feet wide

HABIT. Open, spreading shrub.
BRANCHES. Purple to yellowish red.
LEAVES. Elliptic-ovate to oblong, 2 to 3 in. long, acuminate, wedge-shaped at base, dark green and smooth above, glaucous beneath with grayish white or brownish hairs on veins.
FLOWERS. Cymes, creamy white, 1.5 to 2 in. wide, slightly villous, in June.
FRUIT. Blue or sometimes white, in September; stones furrowed.

LANDSCAPE USE AND CULTURE
Formerly named *C. purpusii*. Best used for naturalizing in soils that are too wet for other shrubs. It is native from Quebec to Minnesota and south from Pennsylvania to Kansas. Cultivated since 1888.

Gray dogwood
Cornus racemosa Lam.
HARDY IN ZONE 4, FOR PROTECTED LOCATIONS IN ZONE 3
12 feet tall, 10 feet wide

HABIT. Suckering shrub.
BRANCHES. Gray; pith white to light brown.
LEAVES. Narrow-elliptic to ovate-lanceolate, 1.5 to 4 in. long, long-acuminate, wedge-shaped at base, appressed-hairy or nearly smooth, glaucous beneath; fall color purple; petioles 0.3 to more than 0.5 in. long.
FLOWERS. White, 1 to 2 in. wide, in rather loose paniculate cymes, in June; petals oblong, obtuse.
FRUIT. White, less than 0.20 in. across, on red pedicels, in September; seeds broader than long, slightly ribbed.

LANDSCAPE USE
A native shrub that is widely used in naturalized plantings. Native from Maine to Minnesota and south to Georgia and Nebraska, it has been cultivated since 1827.

One of the most ornamental dogwoods, its clean bark is attractive year around and its rosy red pedicels can be a feature of the landscape in the fall and early winter against a backdrop of snow. It is also sometimes sold as a single stemmed, small tree. *See photograph page 180.*

CULTURE
It can withstand wet or dry conditions, but does best in moist, cooler soils. Plant in full sun, but it can withstand some shade. It suckers freely, so plant where this will not be a problem. Propagated by seed and cuttings.

This species has proven to be variably hardy. Many plants available in the trade have not proved to be hardy for zone 4. Use only plants that were selected from the northernmost reaches of its natural range.

Round-leaved dogwood
Cornus rugosa Lam.
HARDY IN ZONES 2 TO 4
10 feet tall, 6 feet wide

HABIT. Upright shrub.
BRANCHES. Green, spotted with purple when young, becoming purplish or yellowish at maturity; pith white.
LEAVES. Suborbicular to broad-ovate, 2 to 4.7 in. long, acute or short-acuminate, slightly hairy above, pale and densely hairy beneath, with 6 to 8 pairs of veins; petioles less than 0.5 in. long.
FLOWERS. Creamy white, in dense cymes 2 to 2.7 in. across, in June.
FRUIT. Light blue or greenish white, less than 0.2 in. across, in September; seeds subglobose.

LANDSCAPE USE AND CULTURE

This native grows in dense shade so it is useful in the woodland landscape. Hard to obtain in the nursery trade, but offered most often from seed. Propagated by seed and cuttings. Native from Nova Scotia to Manitoba and in the south from Virginia to Iowa, it has been cultivated since 1784.

REDOSIER DOGWOOD
Cornus stolonifera Michx.
HARDY IN ZONES 3 AND 4
10 feet tall, 12 feet wide

HABIT. Shrub with suckering habit.
BRANCHES. Stem color various, mostly bloodred, brightest in late winter; pith white, large.
LEAVES. Ovate to oblong-lanceolate, 2.2 to 4.7 in. long, acuminate, rounded at base, dark green above, glaucous beneath, with about 5 pairs of veins; petioles 0.5 to 1 in. long.
FLOWERS. Dull white, in cymes 1.2 to 2 in. across, in May.
FRUIT. White, globose, 0.2 in. across, in September.

LANDSCAPE USE

Incorrectly named and commonly found in the trade as *C. sericea* (botanists have moved this shrub back and forth between names). Widely planted for its brightly colored winter stems, especially the selected cultivars.

Allow plenty of room for the shrubs to naturally spread. Best used in the shrub border in conjunction with other shrubs. Native from Newfoundland to Alaska and south to Virginia and Nebraska, it has been cultivated since 1656. Often found in wet locations in its native habitat.

CULTURE

Widely adaptable to varying soil conditions, but prefers moist and cool sites. Propagated by seed and cuttings.

CULTIVARS AND VARIETIES:

A number of cultivars have been selected based on size and stem color.

'Baileyi'   redosier dogwood
ZONES 3 AND 4
8 feet tall, 8 feet wide

Nonsuckering plant, winter color duller than the species. Shade tolerant. Often listed as *C. baileyi*.

'Cardinal'   redosier dogwood
ZONES 3 AND 4
8 to 10 feet tall, 8 to 10 feet wide

Bright cherry-red stemmed cultivar introduced by Dr. Harold Pellett at The Minnesota Landscape Arboretum.

var. *coloradensis*   redosier dogwood
ZONES 3 AND 4
8 feet tall, 8 feet wide

Leaves smaller, plant more compact than in the species.

'Flaviramea'   redosier dogwood
ZONES 3 AND 4
8 feet tall, 8 feet wide

Selection with yellow stems. Introduced in Germany at the turn of the century. Also, yellow fall leaf color.

'Isanti'   redosier dogwood
ZONES 3 AND 4
6 feet tall, 9 feet wide

A compact selection. Introduced by The Minnesota Landscape Arboretum in 1971.

'Kelseyi'   redosier dogwood
A dwarf selection under 3 feet tall. Subject to leaf spot and not reliably winter hardy.

'Silver and Gold'   redosier dogwood
ZONES 3 AND 4
6 feet tall, 8 feet wide

Variegated foliage, yellow stems. Originated at the Mt. Cuba Center in Greenville, Delaware in 1987.

Other dogwoods to try:

FLOWERING DOGWOOD
C. florida L.
FOR PROTECTED LOCATIONS IN EASTERN PARTS OF ZONE 4, NOT SUCCESSFUL ELSEWHERE.
30 feet tall, 25 feet wide

Flowering dogwood needs an acid based soil and probably other special climatic or site requirements that are difficult to replicate in zone 4 in the Midwest.

CORNELIAN CHERRY
C. mas L.
FOR PROTECTED LOCATIONS IN EASTERN PARTS OF ZONE 4, NOT SUCCESSFUL ELSEWHERE
25 feet tall, 20 feet wide

As with the flowering dogwood, it is generally unsuitable for conditions in most of zone 4.

BLOODTWIG DOGWOOD

C. sanguinea L.

FOR PROTECTED LOCATIONS IN ZONE 4
12 feet tall, 10 feet wide

Plants at the Arboretum have not done well. A large, coarse textured shrub.

HAZELS

AMERICAN HAZEL

Corylus americana Marsh.

FAMILY: BETULACEAE; BIRCH FAMILY
HARDY IN ZONES 3 AND 4, FOR PROTECTED LOCATIONS IN ZONE 2
10 feet tall, 6 feet wide

HABIT. Large shrub; there are 15 species distributed throughout the northern hemisphere.
BRANCHES. Glandular-hairy when young.
LEAVES. Broad-ovate or oval, short-acuminate, rounded or subcordate at base, irregular and doubly serrate, 2.2 to 4.7 in. long, sparingly hairy above, soft-hairy beneath; petioles glandular-hairy, 0.3 to 0.6 in. long.
FRUIT. Male catkins 1.2 to 2.7 in. long; in clusters of 2 to 6; involucres about twice as long as nut, deeply and irregularly lobed, downy and often glandular-bristly; seeds are subglobose nuts, about 0.5 in. across.

LANDSCAPE USE AND CULTURE

Occasionally planted in naturalistic plantings or for larger growing shrub borders. Native from Maine to Saskatchewan and south to Georgia and Oklahoma, it has been cultivated since 1798. The edible nuts are sometimes gathered from native stands.

EUROPEAN HAZEL

Corylus avellana L.

FOR PROTECTED LOCATIONS IN ZONE 4
15 feet tall, 10 feet wide

HABIT. Large shrub.
BRANCHES. Glandular-hairy.
LEAVES. Suborbicular to broad-obovate, abruptly acuminate, heart-shaped at base, doubly serrate and often slightly lobed, 2 to 4 in. long; upperleaf surface slightly hairy or nearly smooth; undersurface hairy, particularly on veins; petioles 0.3 to 0.6 in. long.
FRUIT. Male catkins 1 to 2 in. long; in clusters of 1 to 4 nuts; involucres shorter or rarely slightly longer than nuts, deeply and irregularly divided into narrow lobes; seeds nuts globose to ovoid, 0.2 to 1 in. long.

LANDSCAPE USE AND CULTURE

The species is seldom planted in our region due to a lack of hardiness, although it has been cultivated for centuries in Europe for the edible nuts. Native to Europe.

CULTIVAR:

'Contorta'

Commonly referred to as Harry Lauder's walking stick it features very contorted growth. It unfortunately is not hardy in zone 4.

TURKISH HAZEL

Corylus colurna L.

FOR PROTECTED LOCATIONS IN ZONE 4
30 feet tall, 15 feet wide

HABIT. A small tree in our region.
BRANCHES. Glandular-hairy, older branches furrowed, corky.
BARK. Light yellowish gray.
LEAVES. Broadly ovate to obovate, acuminate, heart-shaped at base, doubly serrate or crenate-serrate and sometimes lobed, 3 to 4.7 in. long, nearly smooth above, hairy on veins beneath; petioles 0.2 to 1 in. long, glandular-hairy at first.
FRUIT. Male catkins 2 to 2.7 in. long; clustered, involucres deeply divided into linear, recurved glandular lobes; seeds nuts 0.2 to 0.7 in. across.

LANDSCAPE USE AND CULTURE

Less hardy than other species, the Turkish hazel has done less well at the Arboretum. This is unfortunate, as this species has its uses as a pyramidal, ornamental tree. Native to southeastern Europe and western Asia, it was introduced into North America in 1582. Difficult to grow from seed. It is worth more trial.

BEAKED HAZEL

Corylus cornuta Marsh.

HARDY IN ZONES 2 TO 4
9 feet tall, 6 feet wide

HABIT. Large shrub.
BRANCHES. Slightly hairy when young.
LEAVES. Ovate to obovate, rarely ovate-oblong, acuminate, subcordate at base, densely serrate and sometimes lobed, 1.5 to 4 in. long, nearly smooth above, downy beneath on veins; petioles 0.2 to 0.6 in. long.
FRUIT. Clusters of 1 to 2 nuts; involucres tubular, much constricted above the nut, 1 to 1.5 in. long, densely bristly; nuts are ovoid, less than 0.2 in. long, thin-shelled.

LANDSCAPE USE AND CULTURE

Used in naturalistic plantings. Similar to *C. americana* except for the longer beak on the fruit. Native from Quebec to Saskatchewan and south to Georgia and Missouri, it has been cultivated since 1745.

SMOKEBUSH

SMOKEBUSH
Cotinus coggygria Scop.
FAMILY: ANACARDIACEAE
CASHEW FAMILY
DIEBACK SHRUB IN ZONE 4
12 feet tall, 10 feet wide

HABIT. Large shrub; there are 3 species distributed throughout the northern hemisphere.
LEAVES. Oval to obovate, 1 to 3 in. long, rounded or slightly notched at apex, smooth; fall color yellow and purple; petioles 0.4 to 1.5 in. long.
FLOWERS. About 0.1 in. across, polygamous, borne in fruiting panicles 6 to 7.7 in. long with numerous sterile pedicels furnished with long-spreading purplish or greenish hairs with a few kidney-shaped, reticulate.
FRUIT. Less than 0.2 in. across.

LANDSCAPE USE

Although smokebush often dies back to the ground in zone 4, it is still a useful ornamental. When this shrub blossoms (not dependable in zone 4), it can be a feature of the landscape. The blooms form at the ends of the branches and as the flowers fade, the hairs elongate into feathery puffs that are very ornamental. The leaves are slow to develop their fall color.

The species is not planted as often as its cultivars. Native from southern Europe to central China, it has been cultivated since 1656 in North America.

CULTURE

Plant where a dieback shrub will not be a problem. Tolerant of differing soil types, it will take some drought. Heavy pruning is necessary in the spring when all deadwood should be removed. Grown essentially as an herbaceous perennial it should remain vigorous in the landscape (even further south it is often recommended all growth be removed in the spring to retain its vigor).

CULTIVARS:

Several cultivars with purplish summer foliage have been introduced.

'Nordine'   smokebush
FOR PROTECTED LOCATIONS IN ZONE 4
8 feet tall, 10 feet wide

A selection made at the Morton Arboretum near Chicago. Similar to 'Royal Purple'. Perhaps hardier than 'Royal Purple', but still dies back in most winters.

'Royal Purple'   smokebush
FOR PROTECTED LOCATIONS IN ZONE 4
8 feet tall, 8 feet wide

One of the best cultivars for summer leaf color. The leaves stay purplish red all season. The smoky flowers are outstanding against the almost black foliage. The shrub grows late into the fall and is subject to winter dieback. All dead wood should be pruned out as soon as growth starts in the spring. Plant in a shrub border for a color accent.

AMERICAN SMOKETREE
Cotinus obovatus Raf.
HARDY IN ZONE 4
30 feet tall, 12 feet wide

HABIT. Upright small tree.
LEAVES. Obovate to elliptic-obovate, 2.2 to 4.7 in. long, rounded at apex, silky-hairy on undersurface when young; fall color brilliant orange or scarlet; petioles 0.2 to 1.2 in. long.
FLOWERS. Dioecious; fruiting panicles 4 to 6 in. long, with rather inconspicuous pale purplish or brownish hairs on the sterile pedicels.
FRUIT. Sparingly produced, about 0.1 in. across.

LANDSCAPE USE

Plant toward the back of a shrub border or use as a specimen tree in the lawn. The flowers have more of a greenish hue than *C. coggygria*. Native from Alabama to Texas, it has been cultivated since 1882. Usually has good fall color in oranges and purples. Should be used more often.

CULTURE

It seems tolerant of a wide range of soil types. For use as a specimen tree avoid the pruning given to other smokebush varieties.

COTONEASTERS

CREEPING COTONEASTER
Cotoneaster adpressus Bois.
FAMILY: ROSACEAE; ROSE FAMILY
FOR PROTECTED LOCATIONS IN ZONE 4
1 foot tall, 3 feet wide

HABIT. Deciduous prostrate shrub; there are 70 species distributed throughout the northern hemisphere; irregularly branched, creeping.

LEAVES. Broad-oval or obovate, acutish or obtuse, mucronulate, 0.2 to 0.6 in. long, usually wavy at the margin; upper leaf surface dull green; undersurface ciliolate and sparingly hairy when young; petioles less than 0.1 in. long.

FLOWERS. 1 to 2, pinkish, subsessile in June; calyx slightly hairy.

FRUIT. Subglobose, less than 0.3 in. long, bright red, usually with 2 nutlets in August and September.

LANDSCAPE USE AND CULTURE

As this species often kills back to the snowline, plant in protected sites that will have dependable winter snow cover. It is notable for its showy fruit. Native to western China, it was introduced into North America in 1896.

CRANBERRY COTONEASTER

Cotoneaster apiculatus Rehd. & E.H. Wils.

FOR PROTECTED LOCATIONS IN ZONE 4

3 feet tall, 3 feet wide

HABIT. A low-spreading shrub; young stems greenish red-brown with appressed hairs, older stems gray-brown and ragged in appearance.

LEAVES. Suborbicular to orbicular-ovate, apiculate, smooth at maturity or only slightly ciliate, 0.2 in. long.

FLOWERS. Pink, solitary, with short-acuminate sepals, in early June.

FRUIT. Showy, subglobose, red, 0.3 in. long, in August and September.

LANDSCAPE USE

Useful as a rock garden plant with winter protection, although in more temperate locations it is used as a ground cover. This is the hardiest of the low-spreading cotoneasters but it will kill back to the snowline in a severe winter. Native to western China, it was introduced into North America in 1910.

CULTURE

An adaptable species, it tolerates a wide range of soil types and conditions. However, it doesn't like long term wet conditions.

EUROPEAN COTONEASTER

Cotoneaster integerrimus Medik.

HARDY IN ZONES 2 TO 4

6 feet tall, 6 feet wide

HABIT. Upright branched shrub.

BRANCHES. Appressed-woolly when young, becoming smooth and shiny at maturity.

LEAVES. Suborbicular to broad-ovate or oval, obtuse or acute, usually mucronate, rounded at base, 0.7 to 2 in. long; upper leaf surface dark green and smooth; undersurface whitish or grayish and hairy; petioles less than 0.2 in. long, pubescent.

FLOWERS. Pinkish, in nodding glabrous 2- to 4-flowered cymes, in late May; sepals rounded.

FRUIT. Subglobose, red, 0.2 in. across, in August.

LANDSCAPE USE

Use as a background shrub in a shrub border. Native to Europe and northern Asia, it was introduced into North America in 1656. It is difficult to find in the nursery trade.

CULTURE

Fire blight has been a serious problem in our area.

HEDGE COTONEASTER

Cotoneaster lucidus Schlecht.

HARDY IN ZONES 2 TO 4

10 feet tall, 6 feet wide

HABIT. Upright shrub.

BRANCHES. Hairy when young.

LEAVES. Elliptic to ovate, acute, broadly wedge-shaped, rarely rounded at base, 0.7 to 2 in. long, smooth and shiny above, hairy beneath when young, becoming nearly smooth at maturity; fall color red; petioles 0.2 in. long, nearly smooth.

FLOWERS. Pinkish, in 3- to 8-flowered cymes, in early June; calyx tubes smooth or slightly hairy.

FRUIT. Subglobose or obovoid, black, 0.3 to 0.4 in. long, with 3 to 4 nutlets, in September.

LANDSCAPE USE

The most widely planted of all the cotoneasters in the North. It is often used as a border shrub or for a formal hedge. Sometimes sold as the Peking cotoneaster. Native to the Altai Mountains of China and Mongolia, it was introduced into North America in 1840.

CULTURE

Oystershell scale (an insect) can be a pest on this species. Prefers well-drained soil with good moisture, but hedge cotoneaster will withstand some drought. Full sun or part shade.

MANY-FLOWERED COTONEASTER

Cotoneaster multiflorus Bunge.

HARDY IN ZONE 4

15 feet tall, 12 feet wide

HABIT. Large shrub.

BRANCHES. Arching, slender, hairy at first, soon becoming smooth, purplish.

LEAVES. Broad-ovate to ovate, acute or obtuse, rounded or broadly wedge-shaped at base, 0.7 to 2 in. long, at first hairy beneath, soon smooth; petioles 0.1 to 0.4 in. long.
FLOWERS. White, less than 0.5 in. across, in many flowered, usually loose smooth corymbs, in late May; calyx smooth.
FRUIT. Subglobose or obovoid, red, 0.3 in. across, with 1 to 2 nutlets, in August and September.

LANDSCAPE USE

This is a beautiful shrub either in bloom or in fruit. Birds are fond of the fruit and quickly devour them soon after they ripen. Although large growing, it could be featured in a conspicuous place towards the back of a shrub border. Native to western China, it was introduced into North America in 1854.

CULTURE

Fire blight can be a problem on this species. Needs full sun and well-drained soil.

Other cotoneasters to try:

SPREADING COTONEASTER
C. divaricatus Rehd. & E.H. Wils.
TRIAL IN PROTECTED LOCATIONS IN ZONE 4
Seldom reaches the mature height (6 feet) of more temperate climates. It has attractive fruit.

The
HAWTHORNS
Crataegus L.
FAMILY: ROSACEAE, ROSE FAMILY

The glossy green foliage of hawthorns are unique, especially in those that are resistant to the hawthorn rust disease. Many are small-scaled trees having horizontal branching. These often suit modern landscapes. During flowering and fruiting periods these small trees are outstanding. Hawthorns in general have a distinctive character that can be used as a feature in the northern landscape.

RUSSIAN HAWTHORN
Crataegus ambigua C.A. Mey.
HARDY IN ZONE 4
15 feet tall, 20 feet wide

HABIT. Small, spreading tree; there are 200 species distributed throughout the northern hemisphere.
BRANCHES. At first hairy, later smooth and more or less purplish.
THORNS. Few, less than 0.2 in. long.
LEAVES. Deeply and narrowly 4- to 7-lobed with few apical, sharp teeth, glabrate, 2 to 2.7 in. long.
FLOWERS. White, less than 0.2 in. across, in corymbs of 12 to 18 flowers, in mid-May; calyx and pedicels smooth; anthers red.
FRUIT. Red, small, usually with 2 nutlets, in September.

LANDSCAPE USE

This hawthorn's spreading habit, early bloom, fine-textured foliage, and bright colored fruit are valuable assets in the landscape. Although its branching is horizontal, it can be quite twisted.
It has done well at the Arboretum and should be used more. Native to southeastern Russia, it was introduced into North America in 1858. Few thorns.

CULTURE

Highly resistant to hawthorn rust. Prefers slightly alkaline soils. Propagated by seed.

COCKSPUR HAWTHORN
Crataegus crus-galli L.
HARDY IN ZONE 4, FOR PROTECTED
LOCATIONS IN ZONE 3
30 feet tall, 25 feet wide

HABIT. Large shrub or small tree.
BRANCHES. Wide-spreading and rigid.
THORNS. Slender, numerous, 1.5 to 2.7 in. long.
LEAVES. Obovate to oblong-obovate, usually rounded at apex, wedge-shaped at base, 0.7 to 3 in. long, sharply serrate above the base, quite smooth, dark green, and somewhat leathery; fall color orange to scarlet.
FLOWERS. 0.2 in. wide, in flat clusters 2 to 2.7 in. across, in late May; sepals entire or minutely glandular-serrate.
FRUIT. Subglobose, red, 0.4 in. across, with thin and dry flesh, in September; seeds nutlets, usually 2.

LANDCAPE USE

Cockspur hawthorn is showy in bloom and again in the fall in fruit. It has outstanding glossy, dark green foliage. It deserves to be used often. The species can be used for a barrier plant in the landscape because of its strong thorns; those wishing a thornless variety should try its thornless cultivars. Native from Quebec to North Carolina and Kansas, it has been cultivated since 1656.

Charles S. Sargent in volume 4 of his *Silva of North America* (1894, 93) writes: "it is particularly beautiful. It flowers later than most trees, and after its large and beautifully lustrous leaves are fully developed. Its habit is always good and often striking..." *See photograph page 165.*

CULTURE

This species is almost completely resistant to the hawthorn rust. It is one of our toughest smaller trees and will survive stress conditions better than many ornamentals. Cockspur hawthorn needs a well-drained soil and full sun.

CULTIVARS:

Crusader®   cockspur hawthorn
C.c. 'Cruzam'
ZONE 4
15 feet tall, 15 feet wide

It is resistant to hawthorn rust with some rust appearing on fruit. Thornless. Introduced by Lake County Nursery in 1980. There are some that consider this cultivar the same as 'Inermis'.

'Inermis'   cockspur hawthorn
ZONE 4
18 feet tall, 18 feet wide

The thornless form of the cockspur hawthorn has all the desirable features of the species. *See photograph page 151.*

ENGLISH HAWTHORN
Crataegus laevigata (Poir.) DC.
HARDY IN PROTECTED LOCATIONS IN ZONE 4
15 feet tall, 15 wide

HABIT. Shrubby spreading small tree.
THORNS. Stout, 1 in. long.
LEAVES. Simple, alternate, 1 to 2.5 in. long, broad-ovate; lobes rounded, glabrous, dark green.
FLOWERS. 0.7 in. across, in May, white with red anthers, in clusters of 5 to 12.
FRUIT. Deep red, 0.2 to 0.5 in. long; in September and October.

LANDSCAPE USE AND CULTURE

The species is native to Europe and northern Africa. The cultivar 'Superba' is more commonly grown than this species. The cultivar 'Paul's Scarlet' is susceptible to hawthorn rust and is seldom grown.

CULTIVAR:

'Superba'   English hawthorn
FOR PROTECTED LOCATIONS IN ZONE 4
15 feet tall, 12 feet wide

Introduced by the Princeton Nurserymen's Research Assoc. in 1966. It has large red flowers with white centers and its fruit persists into winter. It also has resistance to hawthorn rust. Sold in the trade as Crimson Cloud hawthorn. This cultivar's wavy branch habit is unique.

DOWNY HAWTHORN
Crataegus mollis
(Torr. & A. Gray) Scheele.
HARDY IN ZONE 4
30 feet tall, 35 feet wide

HABIT. Roundheaded tree.
THORNS. Stout, 2 in. long.
LEAVES. Broad-ovate, 2.2 to 4 in. long, sharply and doubly serrate, with 4 to 5 pairs of short and acute lobes, densely hairy beneath at first, later hairy chiefly on veins.
FLOWERS. 1 in. across, with a red disk, in May; inflorescences finely hairy.
FRUIT. Usually pear-shaped, scarlet, 0.5 in. across, with sweet mealy flesh, in September; seeds nutlets 4 to 5.

LANDSCAPE USE AND CULTURE

Susceptible to hawthorn rust. It is a handsome specimen but limited in use because of the rust. Native from southern Ontario to Virginia and west to South Dakota and Kansas.

Crataegus x mordenensis Boom
HARDY IN ZONES 2 TO 4
16 feet tall, 16 feet wide

HABIT. Small, upright tree.
THORNS. Short to 0.2 in. long.
LEAVES. 3-lobed, 2 to 2.7 in. long, acute, wedge-shaped at base, finely serrate, bright green above.
FLOWERS. In corymbs 2 in. across, in late May; individual flowers 0.7 in. across with 25 to 30 petals; stamens mostly transformed into petals; styles 2 to 3, often united.
FRUIT. Red, sparsely produced, in September.

LANDSCAPE USE AND CULTURE
Highly resistant to hawthorn rust this small tree was developed at the Morden Experiment Station in Manitoba from a cross between *C. laevigata* 'Pauls Scarlet' and a native species, probably *C. succulenta*. Graft incompatability has been a problem with some of the cultivars.

CULTIVARS:
Two cultivars have been named by the Morden Station.

'Snowbird'   hawthorn
ZONES 3 AND 4.
12 feet tall, 18 feet wide

A selection with double white flowers with glossy leaves. Considered to be hardier than 'Toba'. This is actually an open pollinated seedling of 'Toba'.

'Toba'   hawthorn
ZONES 3 AND 4
12 feet tall, 12 feet wide
Flowers double, opening white and turning pink.

WASHINGTON HAWTHORN
Crataegus phaenopyrum
(L.f.) Medik.
FOR PROTECTED LOCATIONS IN ZONE 4
30 feet tall, 20 feet wide

HABIT. Upright tree.
THORNS. Slender, to 2.7 in. long.
LEAVES. Broad- or triangular-ovate, acute, square or heart-shaped at base, 1 to 2.7 in. long, sharply serrate and 3- to 5-lobed, bright green and shiny above, paler beneath; fall color scarlet and orange; petioles slender, 0.2 to 1 in. long.
FLOWERS. 0.2 in. across, in many flowered corymbs, in early June; sepals entire, deltoid; stamens 20, with yellow anthers.
FRUIT. Globose, scarlet, 0.3 in. across, with deciduous sepals that leave a circular scar, in September and October; seeds nutlets 3 to 5.

LANDSCAPE USE
Noted for its heavy fruit production, it is native from Virginia to Alabama and Missouri and has been cultivated since 1738.

CULTURE
Although this species is not immune to hawthorn rust, the rust lesions remain small and seldom cause premature defoliation.

DOTTED HAWTHORN
Crataegus punctata Jacq.
HARDY IN ZONES 2 TO 4
30 feet tall, 30 feet wide

HABIT. Roundheaded tree.
BRANCHES. Hairy when young, spread horizontally.
THORNS. Short, stout, or sometimes wanting.
LEAVES. Obovate, 2 to 4 in. long, obtuse or acute, narrowed at the base into margined petioles 0.2 in. long, irregularly serrate, sometimes lobed above the middle.
FLOWERS. 0.2 to 0.7 in. across, in early June; inflorescences hairy, many flowered sepals nearly entire; stamens 20.
FRUIT. Subglobose or pear-shaped, dull red, dotted, 0.2 to 0.7 in. long, in October; seeds nutlets 5.

LANDSCAPE USE AND CULTURE
Susceptible to hawthorn rust. This is one of the most common native hawthorns, being conspicuous in pastures. Native from Quebec to Minnesota and south to Georgia, it has been cultivated since 1746. Not easily found in the nursery trade.

GREEN HAWTHORN
Crataegus viridis L.
HARDY IN ZONE 4
30 feet tall, 30 feet wide

HABIT. A mostly spineless small tree.
LEAVES. Variable, alternate, shallowly 3-lobed near the tip, dark green, smooth, glabrous below, 1 to 2.5 in. long.
FLOWERS. White, clustered, 0.5 to 1 in. across, in early June; stamens 20.
FRUIT. 0.1 to 0.3 in. in diameter, globe-shaped, in late August to October and persisting.

LANDSCAPE USE AND CULTURE
The species is native from Virginia to the Mississippi Valley. The commonly available cultivar 'Winter King' seems to be hardy in zone 4.

CULTIVAR:

'Winter King'   hawthorn

ZONE 4 IN PROTECTED LOCATIONS
35 feet tall, 20 feet wide

It was introduced by Simpson Nursery of Indiana in 1955. Noted for its persistant orange-red fruit. Silver-gray bark.

DAPHNES

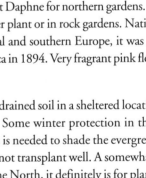

BURKWOOD DAPHNE
Daphne x burkwoodii
Turrill.
FAMILY: THYMELAEACEAE
HARDY IN PROTECTED LOCATIONS OF ZONE 4
3 feet tall, 5 feet wide

HABIT. Upright, deciduous to semi-evergreen shrub; there are 50 species distributed throughout the northern hemisphere.
BRANCHES. Very numerous, dark brown, covered with hairs when young; glabrous with age.
LEAVES. Partially evergreen, linear-oblanceolate to elliptic-oblanceoate, apiculate at tip, sessile, 1 in. long.
FLOWERS. 6 to 16 in umbels surrounded by foliage leaves, terminal on ultimate branches, fragrant, white tinged with pink, in May; pedicels less than 0.1 in. long.

LANDSCAPE USE

A hybrid between *D. caucasica* and *D. cneorum*. Very ornamental and grown for its fragrance. As with many offspring it combines features of both parents. It is most often grown in its two described cultivars.

CULTURE

Propagated by cuttings. This daphne needs well-drained soil, it will not tolerate wet conditions. Tolerates an acid soil, but does best in a neutral soil. Protection from winter sun is necessary in the North with evergreen boughs. Dislikes hot summer conditions in the Midwest, so best sited in locations that are cool and dry.

In Arboretum trials this daphne seems hardy, but very particular upon growing conditions. However, gardeners seeing a thriving daphne usually covet them for their own landscapes.

CULTIVARS:

'Carol Mackie'   daphne

FOR PROTECTED LOCATIONS IN ZONE 4
3 feet tall, 4 feet wide

A beautiful variegated form with pink blushed, fragrant flow-ers. Found in the garden of Carol Mackie of New Jersey in the 1960's. There is some confusion in the nursery trade on this cultivar.

'Somerset'   daphne

FOR PROTECTED LOCATIONS IN ZONE 4
2 feet tall, 4 feet wide

Pink, fragrant flowers. Not variegated, but otherwise similar to 'Carol Mackie'. An upright, somewhat vase-shaped shrub. More floriferous than the species.

Rose daphne, garlard flower
Daphne cneorum L.

FOR PROTECTED LOCATIONS IN ZONE 4
1.5 feet tall, 2.5 feet wide

HABIT. Procumbent shrub.
BRANCHES. Slender, trailing, and ascending; young branches hairy.
LEAVES. Evergreen, crowded, oblanceolate, 0.4 to 0.7 in. long, usually obtuse and mucronulate, wedge-shaped at base, dark green and shiny above, glaucescent beneath, smooth.
FLOWERS. Bright, rosy-pink, 0.4 in. across, fragrant, sessile, in 6- to 8-flowered heads, in early May; calyx tubes less than 0.3 in. long, grayish, slightly hairy outside; sepals ovate, obtuse; bracts spatulate, obtuse, leafy.
FRUIT. Yellowish brown, in August and September.

LANDSCAPE USE

This is the best Daphne for northern gardens. It can be used as a ground cover plant or in rock gardens. Native to the mountains of central and southern Europe, it was introduced into North America in 1894. Very fragrant pink flowers.

CULTURE

Plant in well-drained soil in a sheltered location that receives full sunlight. Some winter protection in the form of evergreen boughs is needed to shade the evergreen foliage. Rose daphne does not transplant well. A somewhat temperamental shrub in the North, it definitely is for plant connoisseurs.

FEBRUARY DAPHNE
Daphne mezereum L.

FOR PROTECTED LOCATIONS IN ZONE 4
3 feet tall, 3 feet wide

HABIT. Upright shrub.
BRANCHES. Stout, smooth.
LEAVES. Deciduous, oblong to oblanceolate, 1 to 3 in. long, obtuse to acute, wedge-shaped at base, grayish green beneath, smooth.
FLOWERS. Open in late April before the leaves in sessile

clusters of 3; lilac-purple or rosy-purple, 0.5 in. across, very fragrant.

FRUIT. Subglobose, scarlet, 0.3 in. across, in August and September.

LANDSCAPE USE

Grown for its early, fragrant flowers and brightly colored fruit. Native from Europe to the Caucus and Altai Mountains of Asia, it has been cultivated since 1561. Slow growing. Those who have this plant (and have enough of it!) to cut and bring into the house to enjoy its early spring fragrance, know one of the pleasures of the plant world.

CULTURE

Plant in well-drained soil and in a sheltered location. Relishes cool summer conditions. This shrub may be short-lived, but certainly is always a challenge. Grown from seed which takes two years to germinate.

DEUTZIAS

SLENDER DEUTZIA

Deutzia gracilis Sieb. & Zucc.

FAMILY: HYDRANGEACEAE; HYDRANGEA FAMILY
FOR PROTECTED LOCATIONS IN ZONE 4
3 feet tall, 3 feet wide

HABIT. Small shrub; there are 60 species distributed throughout the northern hemisphere.
BRANCHES. With yellowish gray bark.
LEAVES. Oblong-lanceolate, 1 to 2.2 in. long, long-acuminate, broadly wedge-shaped or rounded at base, unequally serrate; upper leaf surface with scattered star-shaped hairs; undersurface nearly smooth and green.
FLOWERS. White, 0.2 to 0.7 in. long, in upright panicles or racemes, 1.5 to 3.5 in. long, in early June; calyx slightly scaly, with short triangular, greenish white lobes; petals elliptic to oblong; filaments with short, spreading teeth.

LANDSCAPE USE

This species has not been very hardy in Arboretum plantings, frequently killing back to the snowline. Best used with other shrubs in a border as it is what is often called a leggy shrub. Native to Japan, it was introduced into North America in 1840.

CULTURE

Grows in most soils in either full sun or partial shade. A periodic heavy spring pruning might keep this shrub looking better. None of this species cultivars seem hardy for zone 4.

LEMOINE DEUTZIA

Deutzia x lemoinei Lemoine.

HARDY IN PROTECTED LOCATIONS
OF ZONE 4
6 feet tall; 6 feet wide

HABIT. Roundheaded shrub.
BRANCHES. Smooth or nearly so when young, older branches with brown exfoliating bark.
LEAVES. Elliptic-lanceolate to lanceolate, 1 to 2.2 in. long, long-acuminate, wedge-shaped at base, sharply serrulate, green on both sides, with scattered star-shaped hairs beneath; petioles less than 0.2 in. long.
FLOWERS. White, 0.2 to 0.7 in. high, in early June; pedicels slender, smooth; calyx teeth triangular, much shorter than tubes; petals obovate, partly valvate in bud; filaments toothed below the apex; styles 3, shorter than the longer stamens.

LANDSCAPE USE

Originated in 1891, this is a cross between *D. parviflora* and *D. gracilis*. This is one of the hardiest species of this genus, getting its hardiness from *D. parviflora*, a native of northern China. It blooms freely and makes an excellent spring flowering shrub for the shrub border.

CULTURE

Some dieback may occur in exposed sites so a reasonably protected site is best.

CULTIVAR:

'Compacta'   deutzia

ZONE 4
Similar to the species but more compact, to 4 feet tall.

DIERVILLAS

DIERVILLA,
BUSH HONEYSUCKLE
Diervilla lonicera Mill.

FAMILY: CAPRIFOLIACEAE;
HONEYSUCKLE FAMILY
HARDY IN ZONES 3 AND 4, FOR PROTECTED LOCATIONS
IN ZONE 2
3 feet tall, 3 feet wide

HABIT. Suckering shrub; there are 3 species native to North America.
BRANCHES. Nearly round.
LEAVES. Ovate to ovate-oblong, 1.5 to 4 in. long, acuminate, subcordate to broadly wedge-shaped at base, serrate and

ciliolate; fall color red; petioles less than 0.2 in. long.
FLOWERS. Yellow, 0.4 to 0.7 in. long, usually in 3-flowered cymes, in July; limb of corolla nearly as long as tube.
FRUIT. Capsules brown, about 0.3 in. long, in September.

LANDSCAPE USE AND CULTURE

This native shrub with attractive, glossy leaves and red fall color makes a good bank ground cover and grows well either in full sun or in partial shade. The species is variable and several unnamed strains are available in nurseries. Native from Newfoundland to Saskatchewan and south to North Carolina, it has been cultivated since 1720. As the old seed heads persist into the next year, cutting the entire shrub back to the ground every spring can improve its appearance.

DIERVILLA, SOUTHERN
BUSH HONEYSUCKLE
Diervilla sessilifolia Buckl.

HARDY IN ZONE 4
4 feet tall, 3 feet wide

HABIT. Suckering shrub.
BRANCHES. 4-angled.
LEAVES. Subsessile, ovate-lanceolate, 2 to 6 in long, acuminate, heart-shaped or rounded at base, sharply serrate.
FLOWERS. Sulphur-yellow, 0.4 to 0.7 in. long, in 3- to 7-flowered cymes often crowded into a dense terminal panicle, in July; limb of the corolla shorter than tube.
FRUIT. Capsules brown, 0.3 to 0.5 in. long, in September.

LANDSCAPE USE AND CULTURE

This southern species is surprisingly hardy and vigorous. Native from North Carolina to Georgia and west to Alabama, it has been in cultivation since 1844.

LEATHERWOOD

LEATHERWOOD
Dirca palustris L.
FAMILY: THYMELAEACEAE
HARDY IN ZONES 2 TO 4
6 feet tall, 6 feet wide

HABIT. Deciduous shrub; there are 2 species native in North America.
BRANCHES. Flexible with very tough bark, smooth.
BUDS. Small, conical, enclosed by petiole base before the leaves fall; terminal buds lacking.
LEAVES. Alternate, simple, short-petioled, elliptic to obovate, 1 to 2.7 in. long, obtuse, wedge-shaped at base, light green above, glaucous beneath and hairy when young; fall color golden yellow.

FLOWERS. Pale yellow, perfect, without petals, 0.2 to 0.3 in. long, in axillary clusters of 2 to 3, in April.
FRUIT. Ellipsoid drupes, 0.3 in. long, pale green or reddish, maturing and dropping in late May or early June.

LANDSCAPE USE

An excellent shrub for naturalizing or for a shrub border. Often used as a shade tolerant shrub. Native from New Brunswick to Ontario and south to Florida and Missouri, it has been cultivated since 1750. *See photograph page 168.*

CULTURE

In full sun this shrub becomes very dense and symmetrical, requiring little pruning; in shade it is quite irregular in shape, with sparse, spreading branches. Propagated by seed.

OLIVES

RUSSIAN OLIVE, OLEASTER
Elaeagnus angustifolia L.
FAMILY: ELAEAGNACEAE
HARDY IN ZONES 3 AND 4
22 feet tall, 16 feet wide

HABIT. Large shrub or small tree, sometimes thorny; there are 45 species distributed throughout the northern hemisphere.
LEAVES. Oblong-lanceolate to linear-lanceolate, 1.5 to 3 in. long, acute or obtuse, usually broadly wedge-shaped at base; upper leaf surface dull green and undersurface silvery; petioles 0.2 to 0.3 in. long.
FLOWERS. 1 to 3, yellow inside, silvery outside, short-stalked, 0.4 in. long, fragrant, in June; calyx tubes bell-shaped, about as long as the limbs; styles of perfect flowers enclosed at the base by a tubular disk.
FRUIT. Ellipsoid, yellow, coated with silvery scales, about 0.4 in. long, with sweet mealy flesh, in September and October.

LANDSCAPE USE

Best used as a background small tree or accent in a border. It is sometimes used as an ornamental, clump specimen. In many parts of North America it is considered an invasive tree. Russian olive is useful in the plains as it withstands alkaline soils and exposed locations. Native from southern Europe to western and central Asia. The fragrant flowers and silvery foliage add seasonal interest. Outside of alkaline areas it perhaps should be used sparingly.

CULTURE

Requires a well-drained soil and grows best in full sun, it also will withstand some drought. Verticillium wilt sometimes affects this tree in wet weather. Many times a short-lived tree.

SILVERBERRY
Elaeagnus commutata Bernh.
HARDY IN ZONES 3 AND 4, FOR
PROTECTED LOCATIONS IN ZONE 2
10 feet tall, 6 feet wide

HABIT. Upright, stoloniferous shrub.
BRANCHES. Reddish brown, thornless.
LEAVES. Short-petioled, ovate to oblong or ovate-lanceolate, 0.7 to 4 in. long, acute or obtuse, wedge-shaped at base, silvery on both surfaces, sometimes with scattered brown scales beneath.
FLOWERS. 1 to 3, yellow, silvery outside, short-stalked, less than 0.2 in. long, fragrant, in June.
FRUIT. Broad-ellipsoid, 0.4 in. long, silvery with dry mealy flesh, in September and October.

LANDSCAPE USE AND CULTURE
As it suckers freely, care should be taken where silverberry is planted. Native from eastern Canada to the Northwest Territory and south to Minnesota and Utah, it has been cultivated since 1813. Useful for naturalizing, its silvery foliage has an attractive sheen. As with other species in this genus, silverberry has nitrogen fixing properties, so is suitable for planting in poor soils. Propagated by seed.

AUTUMN OLIVE
Elaeagnus umbellata Thunb.
HARDY IN ZONES 3 & 4
10 feet tall, 10 feet wide

HABIT. Spreading spiny shrub.
BRANCHES. Yellowish brown, often partly silvery.
LEAVES. Elliptic to ovate-oblong, 1 to 2.7 in. long, obtuse to short-acuminate, rounded to broadly wedge-shaped at base, often with crisped margin; upper leaf surface usually with silvery scales when young; undersurface sometimes smooth and silvery, usually mixed with brown scales.
FLOWERS. Yellowish white, scaly outside, 0.2 in. long, fragrant, in June; tube much longer than the limb, gradually narrowed toward the base and slightly constricted; styles scaly.
FRUIT. Subglobose to ovoid, 0.2 to 0.3 in. long, silvery mixed with brown scales at first, red finally, on pedicels 0.3 to 0.5 in. long, in September and October.

LANDSCAPE USE AND CULTURE
The texture of this species is sometimes considered too coarse for landscape use, but autumn olive is widely grown in wildlife plantings. Needs a protected location in zone 4. Native to China, Korea and Japan, it was introduced into North America in 1830.

ARALIAS

TATARIAN ARALIA
Eleutherococcus sessiliflorus (Rupr. & Maxim.) S.Y. Hu.
FAMILY: ARALIACEAE; GINSENG FAMILY
HARDY IN ZONES 3 AND 4
9 feet tall, 9 feet wide

HABIT. Upright shrub; there are 30 species native to Asia.
BRANCHES. Spreading, stout, with a few short prickles.
BUDS. Ovoid with several outer scales.
LEAVES. With 3 to 5 leaflets; leaflets oblong-ovate to oblong, oblanceolate, dark green, 2.2 to 5.5 in. long.
FLOWERS. Inconspicuous, dull purple, borne in dense, globe-shaped heads in July and August.
FRUIT. Black, ellipsoid, 0.4 to 0.5 in. long, borne in dense globe-shaped heads, in September and October.

LANDSCAPE USE
Formerly known as *Acanthopanax sessiliflorus*. Use in shrub border in full sun or partial shade. Native to North China, Manchuria, and Korea.

CULTURE
Prefers rich, fertile soil. Propagated by seed. No special insect or disease problems.

FIVE-LEAVED ARALIA
Eleutherococcus sieboldianus (Mak.) Koidz.
HARDY IN ZONE 4, FOR PROTECTED LOCATIONS IN ZONE 3
7 feet tall, 7 feet wide

HABIT. Upright shrub.
BRANCHES. Arching, slender, smooth or with a few prickles, light brown.
BUDS. Conic-ovoid with 3 scales.
LEAVES. With 5 to 7 leaflets; leaflets bright green, pinnately veined, 1.5 to 2.5 in. long, serrate, with acute tips and wedge-shaped bases; petioles 1 to 3 in. long, often covered with short bristles.
FLOWERS. Dioecious, greenish white, in umbels 0.5 to 1 in. across and in a stalk 2 to 4 in. long, in June and July.
FRUIT. Black, globose 0.3 in. long.

LANDSCAPE USE
Formerly known as *Acanthopanax sieboldianus*. Can be used in foundation plantings or in shrub borders in full sun or partial shade. Grown for its foliage as its flowers and fruit are inconspicuous. Leaves persist into late fall. It has an arching mature habit, but it can be kept pruned to a more upright shape. Reportedly very tolerant of pollution, this shrub is native to Japan and was introduced into North America in 1859.

CULTURE

Prefers moist, fertile soil although it is tolerant of a wide range of conditions. Propagated by softwood cuttings. It suckers readily. A good shrub for difficult situations, it grows vigorously under many adverse conditions.

TRAILING ARBUTUS

TRAILING ARBUTUS
Epigaea repens L.
FAMILY: ERICACEAE; HEATH FAMILY
HARDY IN ZONES 2 TO 4
8 inches tall, 3 feet wide

HABIT. Prostrate evergreen shrub; there are 3 species native to North America and Asia.
STEMS. Stiff-hairy.
LEAVES. Alternate, simple, ovate or suborbicular to oblong-ovate, 0.7 to 3 in. long, rounded and mucronulate at apex, subcordate or rounded at base, ciliate, leathery, rough on both surfaces with stiff hairs, dark green above; petioles 0.2 to 1.2 in. long.
FLOWERS. Dioecious, white to pink, very fragrant, in short terminal and axillary bracted spikes, in May; sepals ovate to lanceolate, acuminate, 0.2 to 0.3 in. long; corolla tubes about 0.2 in. long; staminate flowers slightly larger than pistillate flowers.
FRUIT. Berry-like, whitish capsules, 0.3 in. across, dehiscing to shed seeds.

LANDSCAPE USE

In native areas, this plant forms large colonies and is prized for its fragrance. Although it is difficult to find in the nursery trade, it should not be dug from the wild. A native that needs a replication of its native ecology to survive.

CULTURE

Needs a specially prepared bed with acid, well-drained soil in most landscapes. It is difficult to transplant because it has a deep taproot. Potted nursery plants, grown from seed or cuttings, should be used.

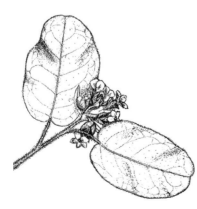

The EUONYMUS

Euonymus L.
FAMILY: CELASTRACEAE

Attractive, variable shrubs with many uses in the landscape. Winged euonymus, *E. alatus*, features winged branches, clean foliage and outstanding fall color; others such as *E. fortunei*, *E. nana* and *E. obovata* are useful as ground covers. Euonymus in general have attractive and unique fruit.

WINGED EUONYMUS
Euonymus alatus (Thunb.) Sieb.
HARDY IN ZONES 3 AND 4
16 feet tall, 12 feet wide

HABIT. Deciduous, spreading shrub; there are 170 species distributed worldwide.
BRANCHES. Spreading, usually with 2 or 4 broad corky wings.
LEAVES. Short-petioled, elliptic to obovate, 1 to 2 in. long, acute at apex and base, finely and sharply serrate, dark green; fall color bright crimson or rosy scarlet.
FLOWERS. Yellowish, about 0.2 in. across, usually 3, in short-stalked cymes, in June.
FRUIT. Usually 4 ovoid purplish red pods 0.2 to 0.3 in. long, in September and October; seeds brown with orange-red aril.

LANDSCAPE USE

This tall-growing, attractive species, with corky winged stems and vivid fall leaf color, makes an excellent specimen shrub. The fall color is a very striking pinkish red. It has a horizontal growth habit that can be useful in the landscape. It also can be used as a tall-growing hedge or screen. Native to northeastern Asia to central China, it was introduced into North America about 1860.

It was not described in *Curtis's Botanical Magazine* (1919, plate 8823) until much later: "[it has] long been valued in gardens for its great autumnal beauty, its leaves at that season turning to soft, rich shades of red. It may be described as one of the best hardy shrubs for autumnal colour..."

CULTURE

Needs full sun for full fall color. It tolerates different soil types but needs good drainage. For hedging and screening purposes, it tolerates heavy pruning (it can be kept in a range from 3 to 7 feet). When choosing plants for hedge purposes, select those with good lower branching.

CULTIVARS:

'Compactus' winged euonymus
FOR PROTECTED LOCATIONS IN ZONE 4

A compact form usually not more than 6 feet tall, with smaller leaves than on the species. Has not been fully hardy in plantings at the Arboretum.

'Nordine' winged euonymus
ZONE 4

9 feet tall, 9 feet wide

A selection made at the Morton Arboretum near Chicago from a Korean strain. Lower than the species and remains dense to the ground. It is hardier than 'Compactus' and more fruitful than the species. Deserves to be grown more than it is.

WAHOO
Euonymus atropurpureus Jacq.
HARDY IN ZONES 2 TO 4

25 feet tall, 16 feet wide

HABIT. Large shrub or small tree.
BRANCHES. 4-angled, greenish.
BUDS. Small, green with a tinge of red, appressed, with 5 to 6 scales.
LEAVES. Elliptic or ovate-elliptic, 1.5 to 4.7 in. long, acuminate, serrulate, hairy beneath; fall color usually golden; petioles 0.2 to 0.7 in. long.
FLOWERS. Purple, about 0.4 in. across, 7 to 15 borne on a slender stalk 0.7 to 1.7 in. long, in June.
FRUIT. Deeply 4-lobed, 0.2 in. across, crimson, in October; seeds brown with scarlet arils.

LANDSCAPE USE AND CULTURE
Useful as a naturalizing shrub. Attracts birds. Native from New York to Minnesota and south to Florida and Texas. Good fall color. Difficult to find in the nursery trade.

WINTERBERRY EUONYMUS
Euonymus bungeanus Maxim.
FOR PROTECTED LOCATIONS IN ZONE 4

16 feet tall, 10 feet wide

HABIT. Shrub or small tree.
BRANCHES. Slender, nearly round.
LEAVES. Elliptic-ovate to elliptic-lanceolate, 2 to 4 in. long, long-acuminate, broadly wedge-shaped at base; serrulate; petioles 0.3 to 0.9 in. long.
FLOWERS. Yellowish, in 3- to 7-flowered cymes on stalks 0.4 to 0.7 in. long, in June.
FRUIT. Deeply 4-lobed, about 0.4 in. across, yellowish to pinkish white, in October and November; seeds white or pinkish with orange arils.

LANDSCAPE USE AND CULTURE
Of variable hardiness, this euonymus can be used as a background in a shrub border. Native to northern China and Manchuria, it was introduced into North America about 1883. This euonymus is also difficult to obtain in the nursery trade. Scale insects can be a major problem on this euonymus.

EUROPEAN SPINDLE TREE
Euonymus europaeus L.
HARDY IN ZONE 4

20 feet tall, 12 feet wide

HABIT. Upright shrub or small tree.
LEAVES. Elliptic-ovate to lance-oblong, 1 to 3 in. long, acuminate, wedge-shaped at base, crenate-serrate; petioles 0.2 to 0.5 in. long.
FLOWERS. Yellowish green, about 0.4 in. across, usually 3 to 5 on a stalk 0.7 to 1.2 in. long, in late May.
FRUIT. Red to pink, 4-lobed, about 0.2 in. across, in September and October; seeds white with orange aril.

LANDSCAPE USE
A good background shrub grown mostly for its colorful fruit. The species is less commonly planted than its cultivar. Native from Europe to western Asia, it has been cultivated in North America since early colonial times.

CULTURE
Tolerant of a wide range of soils and light conditions.

CULTIVAR:

'Aldenhamensis' European euonymus
ZONE 4

The pink capsules are borne on slender pedicels. Has more fruit than the species. Can be used as a hedge.

WINTERCREEPER
Euonymus fortunei (Turcz.) Hand.-Mazz.
HARDY WITH SNOW COVER IN ZONE 4

1.5 feet tall, 3 feet wide

HABIT. Evergreen shrub that sometimes trails along the ground and roots along the stem, sometimes climbs and attaches itself by rootlets, and sometimes grows upright.
BRANCHES. Nearly round, minutely warty.
LEAVES. Elliptic or elliptic-ovate, rarely elliptic-obovate, 1 to 2.2 in. long, acute or short-acuminate, broadly wedge-shaped at base, serrulate.
FLOWERS. Greenish white, in 5- to 12-flowered dense cymes on stalks 0.7 to 2 in. long, in June and July.
FRUIT. Depressed-globose, about 0.3 in. across, pink with orange arils, in October.

LANDSCAPE USE

The hardiest of evergreen species of *Euonymus*; however, only the creeping types that are covered by snow survive in zone 4. Native to China, it was introduced into North America in 1907. There are many cultivars of variable hardiness. There are better plants to try in the North as a ground cover.

CULTURE

Plant these creeping shrubs where they will receive winter shade and dependable snow cover.

CULTIVARS:

The following cultivars have proved to be dependable with snow cover.

'Coloratus'   wintercreeper
ZONE 4

A vigorous selection with large leaves that turn purple in the fall.

'Gracilis'   wintercreeper

As sold in the nursery trade, this cultivar includes several forms with variegated leaves ranging in color from white to pink. Questionable hardiness.

'Minimus'   wintercreeper
ZONE 4

A low creeper with small leaves about 0.4 in. long sometimes sold as 'Kewensis'.

HAMILTON EUONYMUS, CHINESE SPINDLE TREE
Euonymus hamiltonianus Wallich.
HARDY IN ZONE 4
20 feet tall, 12 feet wide

HABIT. Large shrub or small tree.
BRANCHES. Stout, greenish red, smooth.
LEAVES. Elliptic, oblong, or ovate-elliptic, 2.2 to 4 in. long, abruptly acuminate, broadly wedge-shaped at base, finely serrate, dark green.
FLOWERS. 4-merous with purple anthers, in June.
FRUIT. Deeply 4-lobed, pink with orange arils, in October.

LANDSCAPE USE AND CULTURE

A large, coarse-textured shrub suitable for background shrub planting or with proper pruning use as a small tree. Native from Japan to the Himalayas, it was introduced into North America in 1825. Fall color is an attractive purple-red which along with the pink fruit make this species a feature in the fall landscape. Difficult to obtain in the nursery trade.

VARIETY:

Several geographic varieties have been named. The following is recommended for zone 4.

ssp. *maackii* (Rupr.) Komar.
Capsules pink to red that is native from North China to Korea. Advertised as an alternative, hardier choice to *E. alatus*.

DWARF EUONYMUS
Euonymus nanus Bieb.
HARDY IN ZONES 3 AND 4
3 feet tall, 3 feet wide

HABIT. Low, spreading shrub.
BRANCHES. Ascending, angled, smooth.
LEAVES. Alternate, whorled, or occasionally opposite, linear to linear-oblong, 0.2 to 1.2 in. long, obtuse or acute, entire or remotely denticulate and revolute, dark green; leaves green until late fall and sometimes remain on plants all winter.
FLOWERS. About 0.15 in. across, brownish purple, 1 to 3 on slender stalks 0.2 to 1 in. long, in June.
FRUIT. 4-lobed, pink, 0.7 to 1 in. across, very showy in August.

LANDSCAPE USE AND CULTURE

This species is sprawling in habit and often roots where the branches touch the ground. Use in front of the shrub border. Native from the Caucasian Mountains to western China, it was introduced into North America in 1883. The cultivar, 'Turkestanicus' is more often found.

CULTIVAR:

'Turkestanicus'   dwarf euonymus
ZONES 3 AND 4
3 feet tall, 4 feet wide

More upright and denser than the species and planted more often. Even this cultivar is too informal and sprawly for most landscapes.

RUNNING EUONYMUS
Euonymus obovatus Nutt.
HARDY IN ZONE 4
1 foot tall, 3 feet wide

HABIT. Procumbent deciduous shrub with rooting stems.
LEAVES. Obovate or elliptic-obovate, 1 to 2.2 in. long, acute to obtuse, wedge-shaped at base, crenate-serrate, light green and dull above.
FLOWERS. Greenish purple, 0.2 in. across, 1 to 3 on a stalk 0.2 to 1 in. long, in May.
FRUIT. Usually 3-lobed, about 0.2 in. across, crimson, warty, with scarlet arils, in August and September.

LANDSCAPE USE AND CULTURE

A coarse ground cover that might be used where the evergreen species such as *E. fortunei* winter kills. Native in eastern Canada and south to Kentucky and Indiana, it has been cultivated since 1820.

KOREAN PEARLBUSH

KOREAN PEARLBUSH
Exochorda serratifolia Moore.
FAMILY: ROSACEAE; ROSE FAMILY
HARDY IN ZONES 3 AND 4
8 feet tall; 6 feet wide

HABIT. Vigorous shrub; there are 4 species native to China.
LEAVES. Sharply serrate above middle; broadly obovate, 1 to 3 in. long, 2 in. wide; fall color yellow.
FLOWERS. Narrow oblong-obovate, 1 to 2 in. long petals, notched at the apex, white.
FRUIT. Turbinate capsule persists into the next spring.

LANDSCAPE USE AND CULTURE

Available as the attractive cultivar described below.

CULTIVAR:

'Northern Pearls'   Korean pearlbush
HARDY IN ZONE 4, FOR PROTECTED LOCATIONS IN ZONE 3
6 to 8 feet tall, 5 feet wide

In 1995, The Minnesota Landscape Arboretum introduced 'Northern Pearls' which has an upright-oval shape in the landscape. Flower buds are hardy to -35 degrees F. The fruit persists and is attractive through the winter.

Very floriferous and ornamental, 'Northern Pearls' is a welcome addition when looking for a large-growing ornamental shrub. Named for the pearl-like flower buds. Many authorities consider *Exochorda* a genus with much potential in the landscape. Northern gardeners are fortunate to have this introduction.

BEECHES

AMERICAN BEECH
Fagus grandifolia Ehrh.
FAMILY: FAGACEAE, BEECH FAMILY
FOR PROTECTED LOCATIONS IN COOL, MOIST SITES IN ZONE 4
80 feet tall, 60 feet wide (it seldom reaches this size in zone 4)

HABIT. Large tree; there are 10 species distributed throughout the northern hemisphere.
BARK. Light gray and usually quite smooth.
BUDS. Elongate, lustrous brown.
LEAVES. Ovate-oblong, acuminate, usually broadly wedge-shaped at base, coarsely serrate, 2.2 to 4.7 in. long; upper leaf surface dark bluish green; undersurface light green and silky when young, becoming smooth at maturity; petioles short, 0.1 to 0.3 in. long.
FRUIT. Involucre, brown, with slender straight or recurved prickles, about 0.7 in. long, on stalks 0.2 to 0.4 in. long.

LANDSCAPE USE

Native from New Brunswick to Ontario and south to Florida and Texas, it has been cultivated since about 1800. Although native in eastern Wisconsin, it has done poorly in western parts of zone 4. It apparently dislikes the cold, dry winters. Specimens planted in optimum conditions are growing slowly at the Arboretum. It is doubtful they will ever approach the size they attain in eastern North America.

CULTURE

Plant on a north-facing slope or in sheltered locations where they receive adequate moisture.

European beech
Fagus sylvatica L.
FOR PROTECTED LOCATIONS, EASTERN PARTS OF ZONE 4
95 feet tall, 65 feet wide (it seldom reaches this size in zone 4)

HABIT. Large tree.
BARK. Gray, smooth.
BUDS. Slight silky, dull.
LEAVES. Ovate or elliptic, acute, broadly wedge-shaped or rounded at base, remotely denticulate, 2 to 4 in. long; upper leaf surface shiny dark green; undersurface light green and usually smooth at maturity; petioles 0.2 to 0.4 in. long.
FRUIT. Involucres, brown, about 1 in. long, with usually upright prickles.

LANDSCAPE USE AND CULTURE

Not reliably hardy in most of zone 4. Native in southern and central Europe to the Crimea, it was introduced into North America by early settlers.

The FORSYTHIA
Forsythia L.
FAMILY: OLEACEAE, OLIVE FAMILY

Those tired of the long dormant season in the North look forward to early spring bloom. Forsythia was for many years a shrub which would only bloom in zones 3 and 4 after a mild winter, or where snow cover had protected flower buds over the winter. New cultivars now make forsythias more reliable for spring bloom.

Outside of their spring bloom, forsythias are coarse-textured shrubs that do not add much to the landscape. An ideal place for forsythia is one where spring bloom can be enjoyed, but where the shrub would not be noticeable the rest of the year.

CULTIVARS:

'Arnold Dwarf' forsythia
FOR PROTECTED LOCATIONS IN ZONE 4
3 feet tall, 6 feet wide

This cultivar can be a useful ground cover. Does not reliably blossom in zone 4.

x intermedia 'Beatrix Farrand' forsythia
ZONE 4
9 feet tall, 9 feet wide

An older cultivar which many times does not bloom in zone 4.

x intermedia 'Lynwood Gold' forsythia
ZONE 4
6 feet tall, 6 feet wide

Many times blooms only on portions of the shrub covered by winter snows. One of the better growth habits of the forsythia cultivars.

'Meadowlark' forsythia
HARDY IN ZONE 4, FOR PROTECTED LOCATIONS IN ZONE 3
9 feet tall, 7 feet wide

A collaborative effort of the Agricultural Experiment Stations in North and South Dakota and the Arnold Arboretum,

this is a reliable bloomer in zone 4. Flower bud hardiness is rated to -35 degrees F.

'Northern Gold'
HARDY IN ZONE 4, FOR PROTECTED LOCATIONS IN ZONE 3
8 feet tall, 6 feet wide

Upright shrub developed in Ottawa by D.R. Sampson. Reliable bloomer in zone 4.

'Northern Sun' forsythia
ZONE 4
8 feet tall, 8 feet wide

Introduced in 1982 by The Minnesota Landscape Arboretum. Features clear yellow bloom. Dependable bloomer in zone 4. Research at The Minnesota Landscape Arboretum showed little flower bud damage at -32 degrees F. *See photograph page 157.*

x intermedia 'Spring Glory' forsythia
FOR PROTECTED LOCATIONS IN ZONE 4
8 feet tall, 8 feet wide

Not reliable, as flower buds are killed in most winters. In more temperate zones, this is one of the most ornamental forsythias.

'Sunrise' forsythia
ZONE 4
5 feet tall, 5 feet wide

Flower buds are often killed in zone 4 winters. Hybridized at Iowa State University.

EARLY FORSYTHIA
Forsythia ovata Nakai.
HARDY IN ZONE 4, FOR PROTECTED LOCATIONS IN ZONE 3
6 feet tall, 6 feet wide

HABIT. Large shrub; 6 species are native to Europe and Asia.
BRANCHES. Spreading, grayish yellow at first, becoming gray when older.
LEAVES. Ovate or broad-ovate, 2 to 2.7 in. long, abruptly acuminate, square or sometimes subcordate or broadly wedge-shaped at base, serrate or sometimes nearly entire; petioles 0.3 to 0.5 in. long.
FLOWERS. Solitary, short-stalked, in early May; sepals broad-ovate, half as long as the corolla tube; corolla amber-yellow, 0.2 to 0.7 in. long, with broad lobes.

LANDSCAPE USE AND CULTURE
This is the hardiest of the forsythia species, although its hardiness remains quite variable. Best used in shrub borders.

The ASH

Fraxinus L.

FAMILY: OLEACEAE, OLIVE FAMILY

Ash are one of the featured shade, street or ornamental trees in the northern landscape. Many are native to northern North America. The newly developed cultivars are selected for their smaller growing height so are more suitable for smaller-scaled landscapes. Many of the ash species are very large for most landscapes. In the right location, ash are generally trouble-free with few insect and disease problems. In stress situations ash can develop disease problems which have been collectively called 'ash decline'.

Jonathan Carver in his *Travels Through the Interior Parts of North America* (1781, 497) in the collection of Andersen Horticultural Library is amazed at the size of what he calls the ash he saw: "which is only found near the head branches of the Mississippi. This tree grows to an amazing height, and the body of it is so firm and sound, that the French traders who go into that country from Louisiana to purchase furs make of them periguays; this they do by excavating them by fire, and when they are completed, convey in them the produce of their trade to New Orleans, where they find a good market both for the vessels and cargoes."

William Coles in his *Adam in Eden* (1657, 306) lists many of the medicinal uses of ash in seventeenth century England "There is scarce any part about the Ash but is good for the Dropsy...The said leaves and Bark, boiled in Wine and drunk, do likewise open and comfort the Liver and Spleene, and ease the paines and Stitches of the sides...".

CULTIVARS:

(Of interspecific parentage)

'Northern Gem'   ash
HARDY IN ZONES 3 & 4
45 feet tall, 45 feet wide

A by-specific hybrid between *F. mandshurica* and *F. nigra* developed at the Morden Research Station in Manitoba. It has a broad oval form and low seed production.

'Northern Treasure'   ash
HARDY IN ZONES 3 & 4
50 feet tall, 30 feet wide.

Another introduction from the Morden Research Station with an upright growing habit. Advertised as an excellent street tree.

WHITE ASH
Fraxinus americana L.
HARDY IN ZONES 4, AND SELECTIVELY IN PROTECTED LOCATIONS OF ZONE 3
95 feet tall, 50 feet wide

HABIT. Tall tree; 65 species are distributed worldwide.
BRANCHES. Dark green or brownish, smooth or shiny.
LEAVES. With 5 to 9, usually 7 leaflets; leaflets stalked, ovate to ovate-lanceolate, 2.2 to 6 in. long, acuminate, wedge-shaped or rounded at base, usually entire, or slightly dentate toward the apex, dark green above, glaucous and usually smooth beneath; fall color varies from yellow to deep purple; petioles 0.2 to 0.6 in. long.
FLOWERS. Anthers, oblong, pointed.
FRUIT. 1 to 2 in. long, with a round body and narrow-oblong to spatulate wing.

LANDSCAPE USE
Although this tree grows too large for many landscapes, it is one of the best of the ashes. It is a handsome tree if sited well.

Native from Nova Scotia to Minnesota and south to Florida and Texas, it has been cultivated since 1724. An important tree in American history, not the least because baseball bats have traditionally been made from white ash. *See photograph page 178.*

CULTURE

To do its best it needs a rich, moist soil, although it seems to be somewhat adaptable to other conditions. Full sun. It can suffer in drought.

CULTIVARS:

Autumn Applause®   American ash
FOR PROTECTED LOCATIONS IN ZONE 4
Not tested in our area, perhaps a zone 5 tree. Grows to 45 feet. Introduced by Willet Wandell in 1975.

'Autumn Blaze'   American ash
ZONES 3 AND 4
60 feet tall, 30 feet wide

An introduction of the Morden Research Station in Manitoba in 1982. Advertised as a good ash for the Great Plains area of North America.

Autumn Purple®
F.a. 'Junginger'
ZONE 4
60 feet tall, 40 feet wide

A male, seedless ash with deep purple fall color. Some winter injury has been observed at the Arboretum. Introduced by McKay Nurseries of Wisconsin in 1956.

Northern Blaze™   American ash
F.a. 'Jeffnor'
HARDY IN ZONE 3 & 4
50 feet tall, 30 feet wide

A newer introduction from Jeffries Nursery in Manitoba. It is an upright grower. It is reputed to be resistant to many problems of ash including winter trunk splitting.

'Rosehill'

Another seedless selection with bronze-red fall color. This cultivar has not been very winter hardy in Arboretum trials. Introduced in 1966 by Evert Asjes, Jr.

Skyline®   American ash
F.a. 'Skycole'
TRIAL IN ZONE 4
45 feet tall, 40 feet wide

A broad oval shaped American ash which has not been evaluated at The Minnesota Landscape Arboretum.

EUROPEAN ASH
Fraxinus excelsior L.
FOR PROTECTED LOCATIONS IN EASTERN PARTS OF ZONE 4
95 feet tall, 50 feet wide

HABIT. Large tree in areas where hardy.
BRANCHES. Smooth.
BUDS. Black or nearly so.
LEAVES. With 7 to 11 leaflets; leaflets sessile, ovate-oblong to ovate-lanceolate, 2 to 4 in. long, acuminate, wedge-shaped at base, serrate, dark green above, lighter green beneath, smooth except for hairs along the midrib beneath.
FLOWERS. Polygamous; anthers ovoid, apiculate, shorter than the filaments.
FRUIT. Lanceolate to narrow-oblong, 1 to 1.5 in. long, obtuse or emarginate to acute.

LANDSCAPE USE AND CULTURE

There are better ash for zone 4. For those wanting to attempt this ash, plant it in a protected location. It has not done well at the Arboretum. Native to Europe and Asia Minor. Prefers a good soil and reliable soil moisture. This species is very susceptible to ash borer.

MANCHURIAN ASH
Fraxinus mandshurica Rupr.
HARDY IN ZONES 3 AND 4
65 feet tall, 30 feet wide

HABIT. Upright tree.
BRANCHES. Obtusely quadrangular, smooth.
BUDS. Dark brown.
LEAVES. With 9 to 11 leaflets; leaflets sessile, oblong-ovate to oblong-lanceolate, 2.7 to 4.7 in. long, long-acuminate, wedge-shaped at base, sharply serrate, dull green above, and often sparingly hispid, usually pilose or hispid on the veins beneath, rufous-tomentose at base; rachis slightly winged.
FLOWERS. Dioecious.
FRUIT. Oblong-lanceolate, 1 to 1.2 in. long.

LANDSCAPE USE AND CULTURE

Native to northeastern Asia, the species was introduced into North America in 1882. Grown both as a species and the cultivar listed below.

CULTIVAR:

'Mancana'   ash
ZONES 3 AND 4
45 feet tall, 25 feet wide

Selection from the Morden Research Station in Manitoba in 1982. It is often grown where drought can be a problem. A male form so this cultivar is seedless. A very upright grower.

BLACK ASH
Fraxinus nigra Marsh.
HARDY IN ZONES 3 AND 4
80 feet tall, 50 feet wide

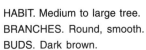

HABIT. Medium to large tree.
BRANCHES. Round, smooth.
BUDS. Dark brown.
LEAVES. With 7 to 11 leaflets; leaflets sessile, oblong to oblong-lanceolate, 2.7 to 4.7 in. long, long-acuminate, obliquely wedge-shaped or rounded at base, serrate with small incurved teeth, dark green above, lighter green beneath, smooth except for rusty hairs at base and along midrib beneath; fall color yellow.
FLOWERS. Dioecious; anthers oblong, apiculate, on short filaments.
FRUIT. Narrow-oblong to oblong-ovate, 1 to 1.2 in. long, rounded or emarginate with flat body and wing decurrent at base.

LANDSCAPE USE
Another large growing ash, suitable for locations needing a large-scaled shade tree. Native from Newfoundland to Lake Winnipeg and south to West Virginia, it has been in cultivation since 1800.

CULTURE
Tolerates wet soils, so good for problem sites. Hardy.

CULTIVAR:

'Fallgold'   black ash
ZONES 3 AND 4
50 feet tall, 25 feet wide

Turns yellow early in the fall. Selected in 1975 from a location near Portage la Prairie, Manitoba. It is seedless and adaptable to a wide range of soil types and conditions.

GREEN ASH, RED ASH
Fraxinus pennsylvanica Mar
HARDY IN ZONES 3 AND 4
65 feet tall, 50 feet wide

HABIT. Large tree.
BRANCHES. Densely hairy.
LEAVES. With 5 to 9 leaflets; leaflets stalked, ovate to oblong-lanceolate, 3 to 5.5 in. long; acuminate, broadly wedge-shaped at base, crenate-serrate or entire, hairy beneath; petioles 0.1 to 0.2 in. long.
FLOWERS. Panicles, rather compact, hairy; anthers linear-oblong, on short filaments.
FRUIT. 1 to 2.2 in. long with wings lanceolate to oblong-obovate, rounded or acuminate, rarely emarginate, and decurrent to below the middle.

LANDSCAPE USE
This is the most widely planted species of ash in our region. It also has many cultivars to consider. Very drought resistant and fast growing, green ash is an excellent large growing street tree. Native from Nova Scotia to Manitoba and south to Georgia and Mississippi, it has been cultivated since 1783. Variable yellow fall color. *See photograph page 159.*

CULTURE
Although it is native along moist river margins, this species and its many cultivars seem to tolerate a wide range of soil, moisture and stress conditions. It has tolerance of saline and alkaline soils. This is certainly one reason it is widely planted. This ash needs full sun and again tolerates differing soil types, drought and salt.

CULTIVARS:

Several cultivars have been named. Most of these are male trees selected for form and foliage color.

'Bergeson'
ZONES 2 TO 4
60 feet tall, 35 feet wide

Super hardy. A green ash introduced in 1982 by Melvin Bergeson of Bergeson Nursery in Fertile, Minnesota. More upright and rounded crown than some other green ash cultivars.

Centerpoint™   green ash
HARDY IN ZONE 4
45 feet tall, 35 feet wide

Centerpoint™ has a very symmetrical canopy and lustrous, green leaves. Originally found in Iowa by Mr. Al Ferguson. It is a Landscape Plant Development Center introduction.

Dakota Centennial™   green ash
F.p. 'Whapeton'
HARDY ZONES 3 AND 4
40 feet tall, 35 feet wide

Selected at North Dakota State University for its hardiness. It has an oval canopy. It has not been evaluated at The Minnesota Landscape Arboretum.

'Foothills'

HARDY IN ZONES 2 TO 4
40 feet tall, 30 feet wide

A newer cultivar selected in Calgary, Alberta that is reputed to withstand -40 degree F. It forms an upright, oval canopy. Not tested at the Minnesota Landscape Arboretum.

'Kindred' green ash

ZONES 3 AND 4
50 feet tall, 30 feet wide

A hardy selection from North Dakota with a central stem. Found by Ben Gilbertson of Kindred.

Leprechaun™ green ash

F.p. 'Johnson'
ZONE 4
15 feet tall, 15 wide

Has a compact upright growth pattern with very small leaves. It is grafted on a standard. Good street tree for under power lines.

'Marshall's Seedless' green ash

ZONES 3 AND 4
60 feet tall, 40 feet wide

A seedless variety with good green foliage color. Introduced in 1946 by Porter-Walton Co. of Salt Lake City. There is some controversy whether this truly is a seedless variety.

'Patmore' green ash

ZONES 2 TO 4
60 feet tall, 35 feet wide

Along with 'Bergeson', this cultivar seems to be the hardiest cultivars for extreme conditions. A compact, oval crown with outstanding dark green foliage. Seedless. Found by Richard Patmore growing near Edmonton, Alberta; introduced in 1981 in the U.S. It was planted on the White House grounds in 1989.

Prairie Dome®

F.p. 'Leeds'
ZONES 3 AND 4
40 feet tall, 35 feet wide

A seedless variety introduced by North Dakota State University in 1986. Globe-shaped crown.

Prairie Spire® green ash

F.p. 'Rugby'
ZONES 3 AND 4
55 feet tall, 30 feet wide

Selected for its hardiness and upright pyramidal shape. Introduced in 1986 by North Dakota State University. Seedless.

'Summit' green ash

ZONES 3 AND 4
60 feet tall, 30 feet wide

Has a central leader. Foliage is not as good as on 'Marshall's Seedless'. Introduced by Summit Nurseries of Stillwater, Minnesota in 1957.

BLUE ASH
Fraxinus quadrangulata Michx.

HARDY IN ZONE 4
50 feet tall, 30 feet wide

HABIT. Small tree in our area.
BRANCHES. 4-angled and slightly winged, smooth.
LEAVES. With 7 to 11 leaflets; leaflets short-stalked, ovate to lanceolate, 2.2 to 4.7 in. long, acuminate, broadly wedge-shaped or rounded at base, sharply serrate, dark green, smooth except along the midrib beneath; fall color golden yellow.
FLOWERS. Perfect, in short panicles; anthers short-oblong, obtuse, nearly sessile.
FRUIT. Oblong, 1 to 2 in. long, emarginate, winged at the base.

LANDSCAPE USE

Features a rounded crown and dark green foliage. Native from Michigan to Tennessee and Arkansas, it has been cultivated since 1823. It is called blue ash because it exudes a blue colored substance from wounded bark. *See photograph page 143.*

CULTURE

Grows in droughty soils and under alkaline conditions. Difficult to propagate.

GAULTHERIAS

CREEPING SNOWBERRY
Gaultheria hispidula (L.)
Muhlenb. & Bigelow.
FAMILY: ERICACEAE, HEATH FAMILY
HARDY IN ZONES 2 TO 4
Grows 18 in. wide

HABIT. Trailing evergreen shrub; there are 170 species distributed worldwide.
BRANCHES. With appressed, stiff hairs.
LEAVES. Orbicular-ovate to ovate, 0.1 to 0.4 in. long, narrowed at ends, folded backward, shiny and smooth above, paler beneath and rusty hairs on midrib.
FLOWERS. White, 4-merous, 0.1 in. long, in June.
FRUIT. Subglobose, white, about 0.2 in. across, usually minutely bristly, aromatic in August and September.

LANDSCAPE USE
Suitable for rock gardens, it produces a dense green carpet studded with larger than you would expect white berries in late summer. It is entirely prostrate with very small leaves. It perhaps can be grown at the base of other acid loving plants such as azaleas. The flowers are often hidden by the foliage.

Native from Newfoundland to British Columbia and south to North Carolina and Minnesota in coniferous forests and sphagnum bogs. It has been cultivated since 1880.

CULTURE
Requires a cool, evenly moist, well-drained, partly shaded area and acidic soil. It is exacting in its growing requirements and difficult to transplant. Propagate by seed or cuttings.

WINTERGREEN, CHECKERBERRY
Gaultheria procumbens L.
HARDY IN ZONES 2 TO 4
6 in. tall, 12 in. wide

HABIT. Low, evergreen shrub spreading by rhizomes.
BRANCHES. Upright, smooth or slightly hairy, leafy at the top.
LEAVES. Oval or obovate, rarely suborbicular, 0.2 to 1.5 in. long, obtuse and apiculate, crenate-serrate (often with bristly teeth), lustrous bright green above, often variegated, smooth; petioles about 0.1 in. long.
FLOWERS. Nodding, on pedicels 0.1 to 0.3 in. long, solitary from June to September; corolla ovoid, 0.2 to 0.3 in. long; filaments hairy.
FRUIT. Subglobose, 0.3 to 0.4 in. across, scarlet August to April.

LANDSCAPE USE
An interesting evergreen ground cover. Young leaves and berries have a wintergreen flavor and was the original source of oil of wintergreen which was found in many early American patent medicines. Its colorful, red fruit are edible. Native as an understory, small subshrub from Newfoundland to Manitoba and south to Georgia and Minnesota, it has been cultivated since 1762.

CULTURE
Again, needs an acid and sandy soil.

BOX HUCKLEBERRY

BOX HUCKLEBERRY
Gaylussacia brachycera
(Michx.) Torr. & A. Gray.
FAMILY: ERICACEAE, HEATH FAMILY
FOR PROTECTED LOCATIONS IN ZONE 4
18 in. tall, 18 in. wide

HABIT. Evergreen shrub; 40 species are distributed in the Americas.
STEMS. Creeping and ascending.
BRANCHES. Spreading, smooth-angled.
BUDS. Ovoid with 3 outer scales.
LEAVES. Alternate, elliptic, 0.2 to 1 in. long, entire, slightly folded backward, smooth.
FLOWERS. Few, in short axillary racemes with deciduous bracts and bractlets, in June; calyx 5-lobed; corolla tubular-campanulate, cylindric-ovoid, 0.15 in. long, white or pink.
FRUIT. Dark blue, berry-like drupes, in July and August, edible.

LANDSCAPE USE
An attractive, evergreen ground cover for acid soils. Native from Pennsylvania to Virginia and west to Tennessee and Kentucky, it has been cultivated since 1796.

CULTURE
Needs acidic conditions, well-drained soils, and partial shade. Requires winter snow cover to survive in zone 4. Propagated by seed or cuttings.

DYER'S GREENWEED

DYER'S GREENWEED, COMMON WOADWAXEN
Genista tinctoria L.
FAMILY: LEGUMINOSAE, PEA FAMILY
FOR PROTECTED LOCATIONS IN ZONE 4
3 feet tall, 3 feet wide

HABIT. Upright shrub with slender little-branched shoots; there are 90 species distributed throughout the northern hemisphere.
BRANCHES. Striped, smooth or hairy when young.
LEAVES. Simple, elliptic-oblong to oblong-lanceolate, 0.4 to 1

in. long, nearly smooth, ciliate, bright green.
FLOWERS. Yellow, pea-like, in many flowered racemes, in late June and July.
FRUIT. Narrow-oblong, compressed pods that are smooth or slightly hairy, 6- to 10-seeded.

LANDSCAPE USE

When pruned, this species makes an attractive shrub in zone 4. It adds a unique shape to the landscape with numerous thin, upright stems (resembling brooms). Plants stay green into the winter. Native to Europe and western Asia, it was introduced into North America in 1789.

CULTURE

Needs well-drained, sandy or infertile soils in full sun. Will grow in either acidic or alkaline soils (they are nitrogen fixing plants so do well in poor soils). Drought tolerant.

Reported as very hardy, but plants in the Arboretum kill back nearly to the ground each winter. Needs heavy pruning each spring. Difficult to transplant, so established plants should not be moved. Propagated by seed.

CULTIVAR:

'Royal Gold'   woadwaxen
FOR PROTECTED LOCATIONS IN ZONE 4
1.5 feet tall, 2 feet wide

A floriferous variety with golden yellow bloom. Treat as for the species.

GINKGO

GINKGO,
MAIDENHAIR TREE
Ginkgo biloba L.
FAMILY: GINKGOACEAE
HARDY IN ZONE 4
65 feet tall, 30 feet wide

HABIT. Deciduous tree; there is 1 species.
LEAVES. Fan-shaped, parallel-veined, alternate, partly in clusters of 3 to 5 on short spurs, slender-stalked, more or less notched or divided at the broad summit, 2 to 3 in. across.
FLOWERS. Dioecious, in late May; staminate flowers in catkins; pistillate flowers on long pedicels; ovaries with 2 ovules.
FRUIT. Yellow, fleshy, drupe-like, with fleshy outer and bony inner coat, in October; pulpy outer layer ill-smelling and acrid; seeds sweet, edible.

LANDSCAPE USE

Widely planted as a street or ornamental tree. Some consider this tree to be slow growing, but in good sites it seems to produce moderate growth when young. Outstanding yellow fall color with the unique feature that the fan-shaped leaves often seem to fall all together overnight. This is captured by Howard Nemerov in his poem, *The Consent* (1977, 476).

> "...The ginkgo trees
> That stand along the walk drop all their leaves
> In one consent... "

Native to eastern China, it was introduced into North America in 1784. There are specimens growing in China which are over one thousand years old. Fossil remains dating back 200 million years are found in various parts of the world including North America. Ginkgo are gymnosperms so they are more closely related to pines than to deciduous trees. The rarely grown females produce fruit that are prized in oriental cuisine. There are also reputed to be many medicinal uses of the leaves and fruit of ginkgo. E.H. Wilson, in his *Aristocrats of the Garden* (1926, 136), states "This noble tree is unlike any other and none exceeds it in beauty or dignity." He saw many of the ancient specimens of ginkgo on his treks in the orient. *See photograph pages 178-79.*

CULTURE

One of the trees most resistant to insect or disease problems, ginkgo also tolerates city conditions. Full sun is best but they will withstand some shade. These trees will grow in any soil that is not too alkaline or in a soil having poor drainage.

Small trees are easier to establish than larger trees. Propagated by seed or grafting. Because the female produces objectionable smelling fruit, ginkgos are most often vegetatively reproduced from male trees. Nurseries rely on grafting scions of cultivars onto seedling root stocks.

CULTIVARS:

Numerous cultivars have been selected. These are male trees.

Autumn Gold™   ginkgo
ZONE 4
45 feet tall, 30 feet wide

An upright growing tree with golden yellow fall coloration. A cultivar introduced in California by the Saratoga Horticultural Foundation.

'Fairmount'   ginkgo
ZONE 4
A conical selection. Difficult to find in the nursery trade.

'Fastigiata' ginkgo
ZONE 4
A narrow upright selection.

'Magyar' ginkgo
ZONE 4
65 feet tall, 40 feet wide

Upright branching with uniform growth habit.

Princeton Sentry® ginkgo
ZONE 4
40 feet tall, 18 feet wide

Narrowly pyramidal form introduced in 1967 by the
Princeton Nurserymen's Research Association.

Shangri-la® ginkgo
ZONE 4
45 feet tall, 25 feet wide

An upright, pyramidal grower. An introduction of Willet
Wandell in 1984.

The HONEYLOCUST
Gleditsia L.
FAMILY: LEGUMINOSAE, PEA FAMILY

These useful ornamental trees offer a fine textured,
open structured tree for the landscape. They are
generally medium sized and can offer color interest if
a color foliaged cultivar is chosen. They can suffer from
disease problems if placed in stress situations (lack of
water, over fertilization, compacted soils). One attractive feature is that the leaflets shatter as they fall in
the autumn meaning minimal fall maintenance.

J.C. Loudon in his *Encyclopaedia of Trees and
Shrubs* (1842, 251) describes them, "[they] can only
be considered as ornmental trees; but in that character they hold the first rank; their delicate acacia-like
foliage, and the singularly varied, graceful, and picturesque forms assumed by the tree...will always recommend it in ornamental plantations." *See photograph
page 138.*

HONEYLOCUST
Gleditsia triacanthos L.
HARDY IN ZONE 4, FOR PROTECTED LOCATIONS IN ZONE 3
65 feet tall, 50 feet wide

HABIT. Deciduous tree; 14 species are distributed worldwide.
BRANCHES. Armed with stout simple or branched spines 2.2
to 4.7 in. long.
BUDS. Very small, superposed, the upper ones larger and
scaly, the lower ones covered by the base of the petiole.
LEAVES. Alternate, pinnately or bipinnately compound, 5.5 to
7.7 in. long, with 20 to 30 leaflets; leaflets on pinnate leaves
are oblong-lanceolate, 0.7 to 1.2 in. long, remotely crenate-
serrulate, hairy on midrib beneath; leaflets smaller on the bipinnate leaves, 0.3 to 0.8 in. long.
FLOWERS. Polygamo-dioecious with perfect and pistillate flowers on the same tree, greenish, in axillary racemes, in June.
FRUIT. Brown, elongated pods 12 to 18 in. long, become sickle-
shaped and twisted, many-seeded, remain on trees into winter.

LANDSCAPE USE
A fast growing, fine-textured shade and street tree. The small
compound leaflets allow enough light to reach the ground
so plantings can grow under mature specimens.

Native from Pennsylvania to Nebraska and south to Mississippi and Texas, it has been cultivated since 1700. The species is not often planted because of its thorns. There are many cultivars developed from the form *inermis* that are thornless.

CULTURE

Transplants easily. Tolerant of drought, acidic soils and salt (which makes it a good urban tree). Grows best in rich, moist, loam soils and in full sun. Propagated largely by grafting on seedling roots. Susceptable to Nectria canker if planted in stress situations or if the tree is wounded during wet summer periods.

CULTIVARS AND VARIETIES:

There are many other cultivars, but the following seem to be grown in zone 4.

f. inermis (L.) Zab. thornless honeylocust

Numerous cultivars of this variety, mostly male selections have been named. The following are considered to be the best that are commercially available:

Imperial® honeylocust

G.t. 'Impcole'
ZONE 4
35 feet tall, 30 feet wide

A cultivar with wide-angled branches. More compact than other honeylocusts. Produces a few seed pods. Some dieback occurs following a severe winter. Introduced by Cole Nursery in 1957.

Shademaster® honeylocust

ZONE 4
45 feet tall, 40 feet wide

Upright tree with ascending branches and dark green foliage. Introduced by the Princeton Nurserymen's Research Association in 1956.

Skyline®

G.t. 'Skycole'
ZONE 4
45 feet tall, 35 feet wide

Pyramidal shape with ascending branches and dark green foliage. Introduced by Cole Nursery in 1957.

Sunburst®

G.t. 'Suncole'
ZONE 4
40 feet tall, 35 feet wide

A wide-spreading tree with golden yellow leaves that turn green as they mature. Some dieback occurs following a severe winter. Introduced by Cole Nursery in 1954.

The KENTUCKY COFFEE TREE
Gymnocladus Lam.
FAMILY: LEGUMINOSAE, PEA FAMILY

Of the five species of *Gymnocladus*, only *G. dioica* is grown in the North. It should be considered only where a large growing shade tree is desired. Charles S. Sargent in his *Silva of North America* (1894, 67-78) lists its other uses (other than as a coffee substitute): "[it] is slightly astringent and purgative...a decoction of the fresh green pulp of the unripe fruit is used in homoepathic practice, and the bruised leaves are said to destropy insects feeding on them".

KENTUCKY COFFEE TREE
Gymnocladus dioica (L.)
K. Koch.

HARDY IN ZONE 4, FOR PROTECTED LOCATIONS IN ZONE 3
80 feet tall, 50 feet wide

HABIT. Deciduous tree; there are 5 species found in China and North America.
BRANCHES. Stout, hairy at first.
BUDS. Small, superposed, indistinctly scaly; terminal buds lacking.
LEAVES. Bipinnate, 6 to 14 in. long; leaflets ovate or elliptic-ovate, 2 to 3 in. long, acute, rounded or wedge-shaped at base, hairy beneath when young, entire; petioles 1.5 to 2.2 in. long.
FLOWERS. Terminal panicles, dioecious or polygamous, regular, greenish white, hairy, in June; female inflorescence to 10 in. long, male inflorescence smaller and denser; calyx tubular, 5-lobed; petals 5, oblong, slightly longer than the sepals; stamens 10; ovaries with 4 to 8 ovules; styles short.
FRUIT. Pods, broad-oblong (becoming thick, flat, and pulpy), brown, 6 to 10 in. long, in October, often staying on plants until spring; seeds large, 0.7 to 1 in. long.

LANDSCAPE USE

This native tree of bold character makes an excellent shade tree and deserves to be planted much more than it is. It is also good for cites, as it withstands pollution. The large, bipinnate leaves, coarse branching and large seed pods are distinctive. Also its ridged bark makes this tree notable in the winter landscape.

Native from New York to Minnesota and south to Tennessee and Oklahoma, it has been cultivated since 1748. It gets its common name from early settlers who used the seeds as a coffee substitute (unroasted seeds and also the leaves should be considered toxic).

The natural history writer, Donald Culross Peattie in *A Natural History of Trees of Eastern and Central North America* (1950, 400) again aptly describes this tree: "Lovely though the broad fronds of its foliage are in summer, they turn yellow at the first touch of autumn and promptly drop. After the leaflets are gone, the naked axis of the branches of the compound leaf drops too, so that the tree seems to be shedding its very twigs. Only the Great pods cling on, like open purses, their contents scattered in a spendthrift's gesture." The newly introduced cultivar listed below was introduced by The Minnesota Landscape Arboretum and is especially worth seeking out.

CULTURE

The Kentucky coffee tree is particularly free of insect and disease problems. It grows best in evenly moist, rich soil. It is, however, tolerant of alkaline soils, and withstands drought. It needs full sun. Like many of the larger members of the pea family, it is relatively difficult to transplant when it becomes larger. There are those who object to this tree's propensity to drop fruiting pods, leaves and rachis, but most will value its bold character and trouble-free growing habit. Propagated from seed and grafting.

CULTIVAR:

'Stately Manor'   Kentucky coffee tree
ZONE 4
40 to 60 feet tall, 35 feet wide

This cultivar has a more upright growth habit and a narrower crown. It is a male selection so it does not produce seed pods. Introduced by The Minnesota Landscape Arboretum in 1996. One of the most handsome shade trees available. *See photograph page 145.*

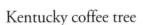

SILVERBELLS

MOUNTAIN SILVERBELL
Halesia monticola (Rehd.) Sarg.
FOR PROTECTED LOCATIONS IN EASTERN PARTS OF ZONE 4
30 feet tall, 20 feet wide

CAROLINA SILVERBELL
Halesia tetraptera Ellis.
FOR PROTECTED LOCATIONS IN EASTERN PARTS OF ZONE 4
30 feet tall, 20 feet wide

Hardiness for most of zone 4 has not been good for this genus. Since there are reports of varying hardiness, perhaps trial in the eastern part of zone 4 might be warranted. The Carolina silverbell (formally named *H. carolina*) is native from West Virginia to Florida and west to eastern Texas and the mountain silverbell from North Carolina to Tennessee and south to Georgia. A seed source from the northern part of the species ranges would be necessary.

SIBERIAN SALT TREE

SIBERIAN SALT TREE
Halimodendron halodendron (Pall.) Voss.
FAMILY: LEGUMINOSAE, PEA FAMILY
HARDY IN ZONES 2 TO 4
6 feet tall, 6 feet wide

HABIT. Deciduous shrub; there is 1 species native to Asia.
BRANCHES. Spreading, spiny; silky-hairy when young.
BUDS. Ovoid with several outer scales.
LEAVES. Pinnate with 2 or 4 leaflets and spinescent rachis; stipules subulate, spinescent; leaflets oblanceolate, 0.2 to 1 in. long, rounded or mucronate at apex, wedge-shaped at base. grayish or bluish green, minutely silky to smooth.
FLOWERS. Pale purple or lilac, in lateral, slender-stalked, 2- to 3-flowered racemes in June and July; calyx cup-shaped, with 5 short teeth, hairy, and persistent; corolla with petals of nearly equal length with an orbicular standard, reflexed side petals, and an obtuse, curved keel; stamens 10, fused except for uppermost which is free; ovaries stipitate, with many ovules; styles curved, with small terminal stigmas.
FRUIT. Legumes, obovoid to oblong, inflated with thick leathery walls, 0.2 to 1 in. long, brownish yellow.

LANDSCAPE USE

A shrub that can be useful in problem sites. It has an attractive bloom. It was early described and beautifully pictured in *Curtis's Botanical Magazine* (1807, Pl. 1016), in the collection of Andersen Horticultural Library at the Arboretum: "This beautiful shrub thrives well with us in the open air, but is said to be in general very shy of flowering, which has been attributed to the want of salt in the soil, as its native place is in the dry barren salt fields on the borders of the river Irtis, in Siberia. Introduced by the late Dr. William Pitcairn, in 1779...Flowers in June and July. Propagated by seed, also by layers and grafting." Native from Transcaucasia to Turkestan and Altai, it was introduced into North America before 1876.

CULTURE

The Siberian saltree is tolerant of alkaline soils. Propagated by seed. It is difficult to find in the landscape trade.

WITCHHAZELS

VERNAL WITCHHAZEL
Hamamelis vernalis Sarg.
FAMILY: HAMAMELIDACEAE
FOR PROTECTED LOCATIONS IN ZONE 4
8 feet tall, 8 feet wide

HABIT. Upright, suckering shrub; there are 5 species distributed throughout the northern hemisphere.
LEAVES. Obovate to oblong-obovate, obtusely pointed, narrowed toward the broadly wedge-shaped or square base, 2 to 4 in. long, hairy.
FLOWERS. Fragrant in late March to early May; sepals dark red inside; petals 0.2 in. long, light yellow, often reddish toward the base.
FRUIT. Broad-obovoid, 0.2 to 0.5 in. long, maturing in the fall.

LANDSCAPE USE

This shrub has little to recommend it except its early bloom (such as forsythia). Because of its early bloom, the flower petals have the unique feature of rolling up in inclement weather. Cut branches also are often forced. It forms a mounded, multi-stemmed shrub. Often holds dead foliage over winter. Native from Missouri to Oklahoma and Louisiana, it has been cultivated since 1908. For protected sites.

The witch in its common name probably came into usage because of its method of seed dispersal. When the fruit capsules ripen, the seeds fly through the air, hence suggesting witchcraft.

CULTURE

Some dieback occurs following a severe winter. Grows in most any condition, sun or part shade, poorly drained soils, different pH levels, but needs moist soil to do well.

COMMON WITCHHAZEL
Hamamelis virginiana L.
HARDY IN PROTECTED SITES OF ZONE 4
12 feet tall, 10 feet wide

HABIT. Large shrub with rather coarse texture.
LEAVES. Bright green, obovate or elliptic, obtusely short-acuminate or obtusish, narrowed toward the base and sub-cordate, rarely broadly wedge-shaped, 3 to 6 in. long, coarsely crenate-dentate, nearly smooth or hairy on veins beneath, with 5 to 7 pairs of veins; petioles 0.2 to 0.6 in. long, hairy.
FLOWERS. In late September and October, petals bright yellow, 0.2 to 0.7 in. long.
FRUIT. Broad-obovoid, 0.2 to 0.5 in. long, maturing in the fall of the next year.

LANDSCAPE USE

Provides interest in the landscape in the fall with its attractive yellow leaf color and its October bloom. Its flowers often go unnoticed as flowering competes with the drying fall leaves. Plant toward the back of a shrub border or prune into a small specimen tree. Native from Canada to Georgia and west to Nebraska, it has been cultivated since 1736.

In an interesting article in the Fall 1995 issue of *Arnoldia*, Sheila Connor gives an account of how it was gathered and distilled in Connecticut for its healing properties; how it was used by Native Americans; and why it is given the common name, witchhazel. Vita Sackville-West, one of the 20th centuries most famous garden writers, in *Country Notes* (1940, 15) aptly describes the startling flowering habit "The dark brown twigs look as though some child had amused itself by tying them up with bunches of yellow ribbons, and then snipping the ends short."

CULTURE

Will grow in sun or part shade. Prefers a uniformly moist soil, but is somewhat tolerant of other conditions.

Ivy

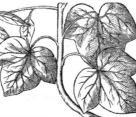

English ivy
Hedera helix L.
FAMILY: ARALIACEAE,
GINSENG FAMILY
TRIAL IN SHELTERED LOCATIONS WITH
GOOD SNOW COVER IN ZONE 4
4 inches tall

HABIT. Climbing or creeping evergreen vine; there are 11 species distributed worldwide.
LEAVES. On juvenile branches alternate, 3- to 5-lobed, entire, 1.5 to 4 in. long, dark green above, often with whitish veins, pale or yellowish green beneath.
FLOWERS AND FRUIT. Produced rarely in our region.

LANDSCAPE USE

Ivy is a popular ground cover and vine in more temperate locations. In zone 4 it needs a protected site with reliable snow cover. Selected varieties can be successfully used as ground covers, but specimens used as vines generally winter kill to the ground. Native from Europe to the Caucasus, it has been in cultivation since ancient times.

CULTURE

After selecting a hardier cultivar, a site should be chosen that gives good protection in the winter. They all winter kill when grown in the open or when exposed to the sun during the winter. With adequate snow cover or with a covering of straw or hay, they will withstand the winter and resume growth in the spring. *Hedera* grows best in part shade.

CULTIVARS:

There are hundreds of named cultivars, mostly grown as houseplants. The following have shown the greatest amount of hardiness.

'Baltica'   ivy

One of the hardiest clones with small leaves.

'Bulgaria'   ivy

A selection made by the Missouri Botanic Garden.

Sea Buckthorn

Sea buckthorn
Hippophae rhamnoides L.
FAMILY: ELAEAGNACEAE
HARDY IN ZONE 4, FOR PROTECTED LOCATIONS IN ZONE 3
10 feet tall, 10 feet wide

HABIT. Deciduous shrub or small tree; there are 3 species native to Asia.
BRANCHES. Spiny, covered with silvery scales or star-shaped hairs.
BUDS. Small, round, with few outer scales.
LEAVES. Silvery, willow-like, alternate, short-petioled, linear to linear-lanceolate, 0.7 to 2.2 in. long, acute, covered on both surfaces with silvery-white scales, becoming glabrescent above at maturity.
FLOWERS. Dioecious, borne in short axillary racemes, in late April; male flowers sessile, small, yellowish, with 2 valvate sepals and 4 stamens; female flowers yellow, on short pedicels.
FRUIT. Drupe-like, subglobose to ovoid, 0.2 to 0.3 in. long, orange yellow, in October.

LANDSCAPE USE

Sea buckthorn can be grown either as a small tree or shrub. It can also be used for hedging and screening. The female plants bear astringent berries which persist throughout the winter. It can add interesting, silvery gray foliage and texture to the landscape. Native from Europe to the Altai Mountains, western and northern China, and the northwestern Himalayan Mountains, it was introduced into North America in 1923.

CULTURE

Tolerates salt and poor soil but requires a well-drained soil. It does sucker and this can be objectionable. Propagated by seed.

CULTIVAR:

'Sprite'   sea buckthorn
ZONE 4
5 feet tall, 5 feet wide

A more compact plant that makes an interesting silver-gray hedge. More upright growing than the species. A male, non-fruiting selection (although the fruit is very attractive on this plant).

The
HYDRANGEAS
Hydrangea L.
FAMILY: HYDRANGEACEAE

Although relatively coarse-textured, these shrubs are very popular in home landscapes. They are generally trouble-free and need low maintenance. They do best when kept well-watered. Their blooms are showy. Many are not hardy for zone 4, so choice of species and cultivars is important. Most hydrangeas need rejuvenation through spring pruning, when it is best to remove some of the older stems to the ground. Hydrangeas propagate readily from cuttings. One of the most attractive hydrangeas, *H. quercifolia* (oakleaf hydrangea), has not been hardy in zone 4.

HILLS-OF-SNOW HYDRANGEA
Hydrangea arborescens L.
HARDY IN ZONES 3 AND 4
3 feet tall, 6 feet wide

HABIT. Informal, upright shrub; there are 23 species distributed in Asia and North America;
BRANCHES. Sparingly hairy when young.
LEAVES. Ovate to elliptic, acute or acuminate, rounded or heart-shaped at base, 2 to 8 in. long, serrate, smooth or sometimes minutely hairy beneath; petioles 0.7 to 2 in. long.
FLOWERS. In terminal corymbs 2 to 6 in. across, mostly fertile in the species in June and July; sterile flowers few in the species, 0.2 to 0.7 in. across, turning from green to white to brown.
FRUIT. Brown, 0.1 in. in diameter, prominently 10-ribbed, in September.

LANDSCAPE USE
This hydrangea can be used in foundation plantings, a shrub border, or as an informally grown hedge. It is very coarse textured and the flowers can bend the stems down to the ground, giving a very unkept appearance. Attractive downy foliage. Native from New York to Iowa and south to Florida and Louisiana, it has been cultivated since about 1800. The spent blooms, as in most of the hydrangeas, are often dried for dried arrangements.

CULTURE
Tolerates some shade but blooms best in full sun in moisture-retentive soils. This shrub blooms on new wood, so it is best to prune it nearly to the ground either in the fall or in the early spring.

CULTIVARS AND VARIETIES:

The following cultivars are planted more often than the species.

'Annabelle'   hydrangea
ZONES 3 AND 4
5 feet tall, 4 feet wide

Flowers are sterile in large, terminal corymbs up to 10 in. across. A selection of the U. of Illinois. Better habit with stiffer stems than the species. *See photographs pages 148-49, 162.*

'Grandiflora'   hills-of-snow hydrangea
HARDY IN ZONE 4, PROTECTED LOCATIONS IN ZONE 3
6 feet tall, 5 feet wide.

An older cultivar commonly called the hills-of-snow hydrangea. It has all sterile flowers and smaller corymbs. Developed in the late 19th century.

ssp. *radiata* (Walter) E. McClintock
HARDY IN ZONE 4
4 feet tall, 4 feet wide

An older unusual appearing shrub in the landscape. Because of the white, downy hairs of the underleaf, it appears to shimmer in the wind.

FRENCH HYDRANGEA, BIGLEAF HYDRANGEA
Hydrangea macrophylla (Thunb.) Ser.
FOR PROTECTED LOCATIONS WITH WINTER PROTECTION IN ZONE 4
3 feet tall, 3 feet wide

HABIT. Upright shrub.
BRANCHES. Stout, smooth.
LEAVES. Thick, obovate to elliptic or broad-ovate, short-acuminate, broadly wedge-shaped at base, 2.7 to 6 in. long, coarsely serrate with triangular obtusish teeth, bright green and shiny above, light green and smooth or minutely hairy beneath; petioles stout, 0.4 to 1 in. long, leaving large scars, the opposite ones contiguous around the stem.
FLOWERS. Blue or pink, rarely white, in June and July; corymbs peduncled, sparingly appressed-hairy, in the sterile form globose and 6 to 8 in. or more across, in the fertile form flattened; petals ovate-oblong soon deciduous, styles 3 to 4; sterile ray flowers large, with entire or dentate sepals.
FRUIT. Brown capsules, one-third to one-fourth superior, ovoid, with the short styles 0.2 to 0.3 in. long in September.

LANDSCAPE USE
This species and its numerous cultivars are commonly grown in the spring in greenhouses and featured for Mother's Day. Some of the hardier cultivars are sometimes tried in zone 4 outdoors but seldom survive our winters. Native in Japan, it was introduced into North America in 1850.

CULTURE
Not successful in zone 4. If outdoor planting is attempted, position cultivars near a house foundation or similar location and mulch heavily with straw or marsh hay for the winter. Plants are, of course, often grown in greenhouses or wintered in a cool, frostfree room. The color of the flowers is affected by soil acidity; e.g. it is blue on very acid soils.

CULTIVAR:

Many cultivars have been named, but most are not hardy in the North.

'Nikko Blue'
FOR PROTECTED LOCATIONS IN ZONE 4

Reported to be one of the hardiest but has not survived in Arboretum plantings.

PANICLE HYDRANGEA
Hydrangea paniculata Sieb.

HARDY IN ZONE 4, FOR PROTECTED LOCATIONS IN ZONE 3
12 feet tall, 10 feet wide

HABIT. Large shrub or small tree.
BRANCHES. Stout, hairy.
LEAVES. Elliptic or ovate, acuminate, rounded or wedge-shaped at base, 2 to 4.7 in. long, serrate, sparingly hairy or nearly smooth above, stiff-hairy beneath, particularly on the veins.
FLOWERS. In large panicles 6 to 10 in. long, in August and September; styles 2 to 3; sterile flowers with 4 entire, elliptic sepals, white, changing later to purplish.
FRUIT. Brown capsules, with the calyx-limb about the middle, in September and October.

LANDSCAPE USE
The late summer-flowering habit is welcome because few woody plants bloom at this time. Can be grown as a specimen tree, but most often as a shrub for the back of a shrub border. Native to Japan and China, it was introduced into North America in 1862. Our grandparents often grew this trouble-free plant and we can too if we want a coarse, bold shrub for the landscape. Despite its many faults it can be useful in the North.

CULTURE
Since flowering is on new wood, pruning back the lateral branches in the spring produces larger flower clusters. Pruning is essential to keep this shrub's appearance acceptable in the landscape.

CULTIVARS:

The following cultivars are usually planted in preference to the species.

'Compacta'   P.G. hydrangea
ZONE 4
6 feet tall, 6 feet wide

Sold as the compact PeeGee hydrangea.

'Grandiflora'   P.G. hydrangea
ZONE 4
8 feet tall, 12 feet wide

Known as the PeeGee (or P.G.) hydrangea. The flowers are all sterile and the panicles can reach a length of 16 in. and a width of 12 in. If wanted to be kept more compact, prune back every year. It can also be pruned into a small growing tree.

Vita Sackville-West in *In Your Garden* (1951, 129) wrote of her appreciation of this old-fashioned shrub as its flowers turned from white, pink to greenish "you never know where you are with it, as you never know where you are with some human personalities."

'Kyushu'   hydrangea
ZONE 4

6 feet tall, 6 feet wide

Good foliage.

'Praecox'   hydrangea
ZONE 4

Contains a mixture of sterile and fertile flowers, with most of the sterile flowers at the base. Blooms in July.

'Tardiva'   hydrangea
ZONE 4

6 feet tall, 8 feet wide

Blooms later in August. Like the P.G. hydrangea, this cultivar can also be pruned into a small growing tree.

'Unique'   P.G. hydrangea
ZONE 4

8 feet tall, 8 feet wide

Larger flower panicles than PeeGee hydrangea.

CLIMBING HYDRANGEA
Hydrangea petiolaris
Sieb. & Zucc.

TRIAL IN SHELTERED AREAS IN ZONE 4

80 feet long

HABIT. Climbing vine.
STEMS. Climb by aerial rootlets.
BRANCHES. Flaky brown bark when older.
LEAVES. Broad-ovate or oval, acute or acuminate, heart-shaped or rounded at base, 2 to 4 in. long, serrate, nearly smooth dark green and shiny above; petioles 0.7 to 3 in. long.
FLOWERS. White, in rather loose corymbs, 6 to 10 in. across, in June and July; stamens 15 to 20; styles usually 2; sterile flowers about 1 in. across, with entire sepals.

LANDSCAPE USE
The vine can be tried in a protected location, but it never gets as large in the North. Native to Japan and China, it was introduced into North America in 1865. Also listed as *H. anomala* var. *petiolaris*.

CULTURE
It has not proven to be hardy at Arboretum trials, but has been grown in protected locations in the Twin City area.

ST. JOHN'S-WORT

KALM'S ST. JOHN'S-WORT
Hypericum kalmianum L.
FAMILY: GUTTIFERAE

HARDY IN ZONE 4

18 inches tall, 3 feet wide

HABIT. Low shrub; 400 species are distributed worldwide.
STEMS. 2- to 4-angled.
LEAVES. Linear-oblong to oblanceolate, 1 to 2 in. long, bluish green above, glaucous beneath.
FLOWERS. 0.2 to 1 in. across, bright yellow, in few flowered cymes, in August; sepals foliaceous, oblong, acute; stamens about half as long as petals; styles 5, united below, slightly longer than stamens.
FRUIT. Ovoid capsules, 0.2 to 0.4 in. across, beaked.

LANDSCAPE USE
An interesting low plant for foundation or border plantings where a symmetrical mound-shaped shrub is desired. Native from Quebec to Ontario and south to Illinois, it has been cultivated since 1760. Propagate by early summer cuttings or seed.

CULTURE
The old seed heads should be sheared off each spring. Tolerant of dry soils. Bloom is on new wood and is showy in summer.

SHRUBBY ST. JOHN'S-WORT
Hypericum prolificum L.
HARDY IN ZONE 4

5 feet tall, 3 feet wide

HABIT. Upright shrub.
BRANCHES. Rather stout with exfoliating bark, 2-angled.
LEAVES. Short-petioled, narrow-oblong to oblanceolate, 1 to 3 in. long, obtuse, dark shiny green above and pellucid-punctate.
FLOWERS. About 0.7 in. across, bright yellow, in terminal or axillary, few flowered cymes, in July and August; styles 3, united at base.
FRUIT. Oblong capsules, to 0.4 in. long, not furrowed.

LANDSCAPE USE AND CULTURE
More vigorous than *H. kalmianum* but otherwise quite similar. Tolerant of dry soils. Native from New Jersey to Iowa and south to Georgia, it has been cultivated since 1750. There are probably others in this genus that can be grown in the North.

WINTERBERRIES

Ilex 'Sparkleberry'
FAMILY: AQUIFOLIACEAE, HOLLY FAMILY
ZONE 4, FOR PROTECTED LOCATIONS
IN ZONE 3
12 feet tall, 10 feet wide

Introduced by the National Arboretum in Washington D.C. Usually grows to a somewhat leggy 8 feet in the North. Grows well in moist locations. In order to fruit it needs a late type male cultivar for pollination. 'Sparkleberry' lives up to its name in the fall and early winter when the red berries are a feature in the landscape. Berries persist into the winter. A cross between *I. verticillata* and *I. serrata*.

WINTERBERRY, BLACK ALDER
Ilex verticillata (L.) A. Gray.
HARDY IN ZONES 3 AND 4
10 feet tall, 10 feet wide

HABIT. Deciduous shrub with much branching; there are 400 species distributed worldwide.
BRANCHES. Spreading.
BUDS. Small, ovoid, with 3 outer scales.
LEAVES. Alternate, simple, elliptic or obovate to oblanceolate or oblong-lanceolate, 1.2 to 2.7 in. long, acute or acuminate, wedge-shaped, serrate or doubly serrate, usually hairy beneath, at least on veins.
FLOWERS. Dioecious, axillary, solitary or fascicled or in cymes, short-stalked, in June and July; staminate, inflorescences with 2 to 10 flowers.
FRUIT. Globose, bright red, about 0.2 in. across, berry-like, in October.

LANDSCAPE USE
Use as a background shrub in a shrub border as it becomes a feature in the fall and early winter with its brilliant red fruit. Native from Canada to Florida and west to Minnesota and Missouri, it has been cultivated since 1736.

CULTURE
Both sexes need to be planted for fruiting. Cultivars are usually female (fruiting) selections so male selections have to be planted at the same time. Chlorosis can be a problem on alkaline soils.

CULTIVARS:

There are many cultivars. Most are named female fruiting selections needing a male pollinator to fruit.

'Afterglow'　　　　　　　winterberry
ZONE 4
4 feet tall

Features fall orange fruit. It needs an early male pollinator. Introduced by Simpson Nursery of Indiana in 1976.

'Red Sprite'　　　　　　　winterberry
ZONE 4
2 to 3 feet tall

More compact. Has persistant red fruit. Needs an early type male pollinator.

'Shaver'　　　　　　　　winterberry
ZONE 4

Large clusters of red berries make this an outstanding variety. It grows to 6 feet. This upright growing cultivar has performed well in Arboretum trials.

'Winter Red'　　　　　　　winterberry
ZONE 4
6 to 8 feet

Needs a late male pollinator. Another Simpson Nursery introduction.

BUTTERNUTS & WALNUTS

BUTTERNUT
Juglans cinerea L.
FAMILY: JUGLANDACEAE
HARDY IN ZONES 3 AND 4
65 feet tall; 50 feet wide

HABIT. Roundheaded tree; there are 15 species distributed throughout the northern hemisphere.
BRANCHES. Hairy, glandular when young.
BARK. Gray, deeply fissured; upper margin of leaf scars straight or rounded.
LEAVES. 11 to 19 leaflets; leaflets oblong-lanceolate, acuminate, appressed-serrate, 2.2 to 4.7 in. long, finely hairy above, hairy and glandular beneath; petioles and rachis glandular-hairy.
FLOWERS. Male, in catkins 2 to 3 in. long; female flowers in 5- to 8-flowered spikes.
FRUIT. Clusters of 2 to 5, ovoid-oblong, 1.5 to 2.2 in. long, viscid-hairy; nuts ovoid-oblong, with 4 prominent and 4 less prominent, sharp irregular ridges and many broken ridges between, thick-shelled.

LANDSCAPE USE
If found growing naturally, it can be a feature of a landscape. Butternut does make a good shade tree while it also can be

grown for its edible nuts. Native from New Brunswick to Georgia and west to the Dakotas and Arkansas, it has been cultivated since 1633. The lumber is less valuable than that of *J. nigra*.

CULTURE

Prefers a rich, well-drained soil, although it will grow slowly on more alkaline, drier soils. A major disease, the butternut canker, is decimating the native populations of this species in the wild.

BLACK WALNUT

Juglans nigra L.

HARDY IN ZONE 4, FOR PROTECTED LOCATIONS IN ZONE 3
80 feet tall, 50 feet wide

HABIT. Tall, roundheaded tree.
BRANCHES. Hairy.
BARK. Deeply furrowed, brown, upper margins of leaf scars notched.
LEAVES. 15 to 23 leaflets ovate-oblong, to ovate-lanceolate, acuminate, rounded at base, irregularly serrate, 2.2 to 4.7 in. long; upper leaf surface at first minutely hairy, finally nearly smooth and somewhat shiny; undersurface hairy and glandular.
FLOWERS. Male catkins 2 to 4.7 in. long, stamens 20 to 30; female flowers in clusters of 2 to 5.
FRUIT. Globose or slightly pear-shaped, 1.2 to 2 in. across, hairy; nuts ovoid and pointed or subglobose and somewhat broader than high, slightly compressed, strongly and irregularly ridged, 1 to 1.5 in. across.

LANDSCAPE USE

This is the most commonly planted nut tree in the North. It is many times too large for small properties but is suitable for parks and other large areas. Native from Massachusetts to Florida and west to Minnesota and Texas, it has been cultivated since 1686.

CULTURE

Black walnut has a natural toxicity to many other plants so one should check to see if a plant selected for a location close to black walnut suffers from this toxin. Prefers a rich, well-drained soil. Because this species has taproots and is difficult to transplant, it is advisable to start with small trees or plant the nuts where trees are desired.

CULTIVARS:

Numerous cultivars have been selected based on the quality of the nuts and the thickness of the shells. Many of these do not produce mature nuts in our climate.

'**Thomas**'   black walnut

One of the best of the named cultivars for our region.

'**Weschcke**'   black walnut

Another good selection for the North.

ENGLISH WALNUT, PERSIAN WALNUT

Juglans regia L.

FOR PROTECTED LOCATIONS IN ZONE 4
65 feet tall, 30 feet wide

HABIT. Broadheaded tree.
BRANCHES. Smooth.
BARK. Silvery gray, remaining smooth for a long time.
LEAVES. 5 to 9, rarely 13 leaflets; leaflets elliptic to obovate or oblong-ovate, acute or acuminate, entire, rarely and chiefly on young plants obscurely serrate, 2.2 to 4.7 in. long, smooth except small axillary tufts of hairs beneath.
FLOWERS. Male catkins 2 to 4 in. long; female flowers few, in terminal racemes.
FRUIT. Subglobose, smooth, green, 1.5 to 2 in. across; nuts usually ovoid or ellipsoid, pointed, more or less wrinkled, usually thick-shelled.

LANDSCAPE USE AND CULTURE

Commonly grown for its edible nuts in warmer parts of the country, especially in California. A strain from the Carpathian Mountains has proved to be hardier than the species, but it has not proved hardy on the St. Paul Campus of the University or at the Arboretum. Prefers a deep, well-drained soil. This species is native from southeastern Europe to the Himalayan Mountains and China.

The JUNIPERS

Juniperus L.
FAMILY: CUPRESSACEAE, CYPRESS FAMILY

Junipers are among the most widely planted small-growing evergreens in the North. The ground-hugging cultivars make good ground covers for full sun and well-drained locations. Even Pfitzer-like junipers are often used as ground covers. Junipers of all shapes and sizes are used for foundation plantings. Specimens of various sizes and shapes can be used in rock gardens and as accents in flower borders. Many upright-growing selections are not hardy in the North. However, if you are looking for an upright-growing juniper, consider some of the cultivars of *J. scopulorum* and *J. chinensis.*

A major problem with junipers in the North is winter burn on susceptible varieties. It occurs even on the most hardy junipers in very exposed sites. Careful selection of varieties and care in siting normally prevents this problem. If the site is completely exposed to winter winds and sun, choose the hardiest varieties. It is important that juniper go into the winter in a well-watered state.

John Gerard in his *Herball* (1597, 1190) lists 11 paragraphs of medicinal and other uses for juniper, including helps for liver, kidneys, stomach, chest, for coughs, poisons, fevers, and even to drive away serpents. *See photograph on pages 156 and 178-79.*

CHINESE JUNIPER
Juniperus chinensis L.

TREE FORMS GENERALLY NOT HARDY; SHRUB FORMS USUALLY HARDY IN ZONE 4; MAY BE HARDY IN ZONE 3
1 to 50 feet tall, 3 to 10 feet wide

HABIT. Variable species ranging from low, spreading shrubs to upright pyramidal trees; there are 60 species distributed worldwide.

BRANCHES. Slender.
LEAVES. Often scale-like and needle-like; scale-like leaves narrowly rhombic, closely appressed, obtuse, less than 0.1 in. long; needle-like leaves usually in 3's, spiny pointed, with 2 white bands above.
FLOWERS. Dioecious.
FRUIT. Subglobose, 0.2 to 0.3 in. across, brown with a thick mealy bloom, ripening the second year; seeds 2 to 3.

LANDSCAPE USE
Useful in foundation and border plantings. Native to China, Mongolia, and Japan, it was introduced into North America before 1767.

CULTURE
Plant in full sun in well-drained soil. Winter burn can be a variable problem determined by the susceptability of the cultivar and its planting location.

CULTIVARS:
There are many named cultivars. The following have been tested at the Arboretum and are suitable for planting in zone 4. New cultivars appear each year and some of these may be hardy.

'Ames'   juniper
ZONE 4
10 feet tall, 8 feet wide

A broad-pyramid shrub; leaves needle-like, bluish green, turning green at maturity. Introduced in 1935 from Iowa State University by Prof. T.J. Maney.

'Blaauw'　　　　　　juniper

ZONE 4

3 feet tall, 4 feet wide

A vase-shaped shrub, with blue-green foliage; leaves scale-like except in center where needle-like leaves can be found. Has a bold appearance in the landscape. Introduced from Japan in 1924.

'Hetzii'　　　　　　juniper

ZONE 4

10 feet tall, 9 feet wide

A spreading selection with bluish green foliage. Introduced by the Fairview Evergreen Nursery of Pennsylvania in 1920.

'Iowa'　　　　　　juniper

ZONE 4

10 feet tall, 10 feet wide

Similar to 'Ames' but a little more spreading. Introduced in 1930.

'Maney'　　　　　　juniper

ZONES 3 AND 4

6 feet tall, 5 feet wide

A hardy, semi-erect shrub; leaves acicular, bluish green. Quite resistant to winter burn. Snow breakage sometimes a problem when planted where deep snow accumulates. One of the best cultivars introduced from Ames, Iowa.

'Mountbatten'　　　　　　juniper

ZONE 4

12 feet tall, 8 feet wide

An upright shrub; leaves mostly needle-like, grayish green. Originated as a seedling in Sheridan Nurseries in Ontario in 1940's.

'Robusta Green'　　　　　　juniper

ZONE 4

1 to 2 feet tall, 4 feet wide

An irregular, upright form with bright green foliage. Slow growing. Introduced by Monrovia Nurseries of California in 1973.

'San Jose'　　　　　　juniper

ZONE 4

1 foot tall, 3 feet wide

Low, creeping form; leaves mostly acicular, grayish green. Introduced by Clarke's Nursery of San Jose, California in the 1930's.

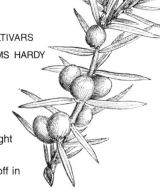

COMMON JUNIPER
Juniperus communis L.

TREE FORMS NOT HARDY; CULTIVARS AND VARIETIES OF SHRUB FORMS HARDY IN ZONES 2 TO 4

12 inches to 30 feet tall, 3 to 10 feet wide

HABIT. Spreading shrub or upright tree.
BARK. Reddish brown, peeling off in papery shreds.
LEAVES. Needle-like, tapering from the base to a spiny point, about 0.2 in. long, concave above and with a broad white band, bluntly keeled below.
FLOWERS. Rarely monoecious.
FRUIT. Globose or broadly ovoid, 0.2 in. across, short-stalked, bluish or black, ripening the 2nd or 3rd year; seeds usually 3.

LANDSCAPE USE

Useful in mass plantings for naturalizing or as a ground cover. Native in North America from Canada to Pennsylvania, New Mexico, and California, in Europe, in the western Himalayan Mountains; and in northeastern Asia. Cultivated since 1560.

CULTURE

Plant in full sun or in light shade. Propagated by cuttings.

CULTIVARS AND VARIETIES:

Blueberry Delight™　　　　　　juniper

J.c. 'AmiDak'

ZONES 3 AND 4

1 foot tall, 4 feet wide

A low, spreading variety with dark green needles. Named for its prolific production of blue fruit. Introduced by North Dakota State University.

'Depressa Aurea'　　　　　　juniper

ZONE 4

3 feet tall, 8 feet wide

A spreading form, with new growth that is golden yellow. A selected cultivar of the variety depressa introduced in the 1930's.

'Effusa'　　　　　　juniper

ZONE 4

1 foot tall, 4 feet wide

A dwarf, spreading shrub; leaves 0.2 to 0.4 in. long, with a silvery white band and 2 green bands above, convex and green below. Introduced from the Netherlands in 1944.

'Repanda' juniper
ZONES 3 AND 4
1 foot tall, 6 feet wide

A dwarf, rounded shrub; leaves 0.2 to 0.3 in. long, slightly curved inward, with a broad silvery band above, convex and green below. It seems to be quite resistant to winter burn. Introduced from Holland in the 1940's.

var. *saxatilis* mountain juniper
Native in the Arctic and in mountains of Europe and North America. A dwarf, prostrate shrub to 1.5 feet tall and 6 feet wide; leaves upturned, dense, 0.4 to 0.6 in. long, mucronate, with broad, glaucous band above. Probably confused in the trade.

CREEPING JUNIPER
Juniperus horizontalis Moench.
HARDY IN ZONES 2 TO 4
4 to 8 inches tall, 3 to 6 feet wide

HABIT. Creeping shrub.
BRANCHES. Long and trailing, with numerous short branchlets.
LEAVES. Mostly scale-like, acute or cuspidate, glandular on the back, bluish green or steel blue; needle-like leaves, when present, 0.2 in. long, mucronulate, slightly spreading.
FLOWERS. Dioecious.
FRUIT. 0.2 to 0.3 in. across, on recurved pedicels, light blue, 1- to 4-seeded.

LANDSCAPE USE
The species and its numerous cultivars are valued as ground covers, especially on sandy soils. Also used in rock gardens. Native from Nova Scotia to Alberta and south to New Jersey and Montana, it has been cultivated since 1836.

CULTURE
Tolerates drier conditions and sandy soils. Cultivars are propagated by cuttings.

CULTIVARS:

Numerous cultivars have been named, and more appear on the market each year. Many are similar.

'Andorra Compact' juniper
ZONES 3 AND 4
18 inches tall, 5 feet wide

More compact than 'Plumosa' (Andorra juniper). Spreading and dense turning dark in the winter. Also called 'Plumosa Compacta' and 'Compacta' in the trade.

'Bar Harbor' juniper
ZONES 3 AND 4
1 foot tall, 10 feet wide

An older, low, spreading form with leaves mostly acicular, bluish green, turning plum-purple in the fall. Introduced from Mount Desert Island, Maine in the 1930's.

'Blue Chip' juniper
ZONES 3 AND 4
6 to 10 inches tall, 4 feet wide

Selected for its low, compact shape and blue foliage throughout the year.

'Blue Prince' juniper
ZONES 3 AND 4
6 inches tall, 4 feet wide

A very prostrate growing juniper introduced by Van Vloten Nursery in Alberta, Canada. Bright blue-green foliage.

'Douglasii' Waukegan juniper
ZONE 4
1 foot tall, 10 feet wide

Often called the Waukegan juniper because it was discovered near the Douglas Nursery in Waukegan, Illinois in the nineteenth century. This older cultivar has leaves both scale-like and acicular, steel-blue, turning purple in the fall.

'Dunvegan Blue' juniper
ZONES 3 AND 4
1 foot tall, 4 feet wide

An older, low, spreading selection with a bright bluish green color.

'Hughes' juniper
ZONES 3 AND 4
1 foot tall, 10 feet wide

A low growing cultivar with distinct radial branching; leaves silvery blue. Introduced from Cedar Rapids, Iowa in 1970.

'Plumosa' juniper
ZONES 3 AND 4
1 foot tall, 10 feet wide

Commonly sold as Andorra juniper. A dense, wide-spreading juniper with leaves both scale-like and acicular, grayish green, turning purple in the fall. Arboretum specimens have sustained severe winter injury some years. Introduced from Andorra Nurseries in Pennsylvania in 1907.

Prairie Elegance™   juniper

J.h. 'BowDak'
ZONES 3 AND 4
6 to 12 inches tall, 5 feet wide

A 1991 introduction of North Dakota State University. A male variety with good summer green color.

'Prince of Wales'   juniper

ZONES 3 AND 4
6 inches tall, 4 feet wide

Very low, dense, bright green selection from High River, Alberta. Introduced by the Morden Experiment Station of Manitoba in 1967.

'Webberi'   juniper

ZONES 3 AND 4
6 inches tall, 3 feet wide

A mat-like, spreading form with a fine texture and bluish green color. Introduced by Sherwood Nursery in Oregon in 1971.

'Wiltonii'   juniper

ZONES 3 AND 4
3 inches tall, 4 feet wide

Sometimes sold as 'Blue Rug', 'Blue Vase' and 'Wilton Carpet'. Very low, creeping form with leaves silver-blue, turning purplish in fall. Introduced in 1914 by South Wilton Nurseries.

Juniperus x media Van Melle.

HARDY IN ZONE 4, FOR PROTECTED LOCATIONS
IN ZONE 3
5 to 8 feet tall, 4 to 5 feet wide

HABIT. Wide spreading, upright shrub.
BARK. Scaly, reddish brown.
LEAVES. In pairs, sometimes in 3's; grayish green, glaucous.
FRUIT. Bluish black; ovoid to 0.5 inch long.

LANDSCAPE USE AND CULTURE

A cross between *J. chinensis* and *J. sabina* (not accepted by some authorities who still treat these cultivars under *J. chinensis*). Some of the most ornamental cultivars belong to this classification. Used for specimen shrubs and mass plantings.

CULTIVARS:

Gold Star®   juniper

ZONE 4
3 feet tall, 6 feet wide

A golden tipped variety on light green branches. A mutation from 'Pfitzeriana Aurea' made by Bakker Nursery in Ontario in 1961.

'Mint Julep'   juniper

ZONE 4
3 feet tall, 6 feet wide

A spreading female cultivar with arching branches and foliage a rich green color. Sometimes sold as 'Sea Green'. Introduced by Monrovia Nursery in California in 1960.

'Old Gold'   juniper

ZONE 4
2 feet tall, 4 feet wide

Golden hued foliage. Another mutation from 'Pfitzeriana Aurea' introduced from Holland in 1958. Has done well in the North.

'Pfitzeriana'   juniper

ZONES 3 AND 4
6 feet tall, 10 feet wide

A widely planted conifer of spreading habit with leaves both scale-like and needle-like, bright green. The taxonomists do not accept this name as a cultivar believing it should be termed just a Pfitzer Group. Winter burn of Arboretum plants have been a problem.

'Pfitzeriana Aurea'   juniper

ZONE 4
6 feet tall, 8 feet wide

Similar to 'Pfitzeriana' except the leaves are tinged with golden yellow in summer. Introduced by D. Hill Nursery of Dundee, Illinois in 1923.

'Pfitzeriana Glauca'   juniper

ZONE 4
6 feet tall, 8 feet wide

Similar to 'Pfitzeriana' except the leaves are mostly acicular and bluish green. Plants in the Arboretum have shown considerable winter burn. Introduced by Texas Nursery, Sherman, Texas in 1940.

'Ramlosa'   juniper

ZONE 4
4 feet tall, 6 feet wide

Dark green foliage on a Pfitzer-like plant.

JAPANESE GARDEN JUNIPER
Juniperus procumbens (Endl.) Miq.
HARDY IN ZONE 4
1 foot tall, 6 feet wide

HABIT. Low, spreading shrub.
BRANCHES. Glaucous.
LEAVES. Needle-like and in 3's, linear-lanceolate, 0.2 to 0.3 in. long, spiny-pointed, concave above and smooth, bluish below.
FRUIT. Subglobose, 0.3 in. across, 2- to 3-seeded.

LANDSCAPE USE
Can make a handsome ground cover. Native to Japan, it was introduced into North America in 1843. Incorrectly listed as a variety of *J. chinensis*.

CULTURE
Adapted to a wide variety of soils but does best in full sun and in well-drained sites. Slight winter burning occurs in a winter with little snow cover.

CULTIVAR:

'Nana'   dwarf Japanese garden juniper
ZONE 4
6 inches tall, 4 feet wide

Similar to the species but slower growing and suitable for rock gardens. Brought back from Japan in 1904 by Arthur Hill of D. Hill Nursery in Dundee, Illinois.

SAVIN JUNIPER
Juniperus sabina L.
MOST CULTIVARS HARDY IN ZONE 4; A FEW HARDY IN ZONE 3
10 to 16 feet tall (more commonly 6 feet), 6 feet wide

HABIT. Variable species ranging from upright to low, spreading shrubs.
BRANCHES. Rather slender, with a strong disagreeable odor when bruised.
LEAVES. Mostly scale-like, rhombic-ovate, appressed, obtuse or acutish, less than 0.1 in. long, glandular on the back, dark green; needle-like leaves, which are often present, are slightly spreading, 0.15 in. long, concave and glaucous above, with a prominent midrib.
FLOWERS. Monoecious or dioecious.
FRUIT. On scaly recurved pedicels, subglobose or ovoid, 0.2 in. across, brownish blue, with usually 2 seeds.

LANDSCAPE USE
Used in mass plantings or as specimen conifers. The cultivars are most often planted. Native from the mountains of southwestern and central Europe to Siberia, it has been cultivated since before 1580.

CULTURE
This species and its cultivars grow on a variety of soils that are tolerant of limestone.

CULTIVARS:

'Arcadia'   juniper
ZONES 3 AND 4
1 to 2 feet tall, 6 feet wide

A compact cultivar with horizontal branching with leaves mostly scale-like, dark green. Said to be resistant to juniper blight, but Arboretum plants have been killed by the blight. Occasionally some winter burn occurs. Selected from seedlings grown by Dundee-Hill Nursery, Dundee, Illinois, from seed obtained from Russia in 1933.

'Blaue Donau/Blue Danube' juniper
ZONE 4
3 feet tall, 10 feet wide

Introduced from Austria in 1956. A spreading shrub with upcurved branches and leaves mostly scale-like. Coarse textured with blue-gray foliage.

'Blue Forest'   juniper
HARDY IN ZONE 4
1 foot tall, 3 feet wide.

A ground hugging cultivar that does well in rock gardens or trailing over a wall. The needles have a bright bluish cast.

'Broadmoor'   juniper
HARDY IN ZONE 4, FOR PROTECTED LOCATIONS IN ZONE 3
1 foot tall, 4 feet wide

Another selection made by the Dundee-Hill Nursery. A low, spreading male selection with horizontal branching with leaves grayish green. Arboretum plants have shown no winter injury.

'Buffalo'   juniper
HARDY IN ZONE 4, FOR PROTECTED LOCATIONS IN ZONE 3
1 foot tall, 4 feet wide

Similar to 'Tamariscifolia' but with feathery branches with leaves bright green. This cultivar has shown no winter injury in Arboretum trials.

Calgary Carpet™   juniper
ZONES 3 AND 4
18 inches tall, 4 feet wide

A selection from Arcadia juniper. It has a very low spreading habit with good green color.

'Mini Arcade'   juniper
ZONES 3 AND 4
1 foot tall, 4 feet wide

A shorter cultivar selected from the cultivar 'Arcadia' with good green foliage.

'Pepin'   juniper
ZONE 4
3 feet tall, 4 feet wide

Blue-green foliage with good disease resistance.

'Skandia'   juniper
ZONES 3 AND 4
1 foot tall, 4 feet wide

Another selection from the Dundee-Hill Nursery. Introduced in the early 1950's. Similar to 'Arcadia' but not as tall. Excellent as a ground cover under low windows. Also spelled incorrectly as 'Scandia' in the trade. Softer texture.

'Tamariscifolia'   juniper
FOR PROTECTED LOCATIONS IN ZONE 4
2 feet tall, 9 feet wide

A selection from southern Europe with a spreading, mounded form and leaves mostly needle-like, short, and bluish green. Some winter burn has been observed in Arboretum plantings. Dates from 1839.

'Von Ehren'   juniper
ZONE 4
4 feet tall, 6 feet wide

A vase-shaped shrub with leaves mostly needle-like, 0.2 in. long, light green.

SARGENT JUNIPER
Juniperus sargentii (Henry) Tak.
HARDY IN ZONE 4
2 feet tall, 2 feet wide

HABIT. Low, spreading shrub.
BRANCHES. 4-angled.
LEAVES. Mostly scale-like in pairs, sometimes whorled in 3; dark bluish green.
FRUIT. Black; 0.2 in. long; seeds in 3.

LANDSCAPE USE AND CULTURE
Used in mass plantings and as specimens. Native to China and Japan, it was discovered by C.S. Sargent in 1892. Resistant to the juniper rusts.

CULTIVARS:

'Glauca'   Sargent juniper
ZONE 4
1.5 feet tall, 6 feet wide

Dwarf compact growth. Blue-green foliage.

'Viridis'   Sargent juniper
ZONE 4
2 feet tall, 8 feet wide

Light green foliage.

ROCKY MOUNTAIN JUNIPER
Juniperus scopulorum Sarg.
HARDY IN ZONES 3 AND 4
30 feet tall, 15 feet wide

HABIT. Tree with short trunk and irregular round-topped crown.
BRANCHES. Ascending, slender.
BARK. Reddish brown, shreddy.
LEAVES. Rhombic-ovate, acute or acuminate, closely appressed, dark or yellowish green or glaucous.
FLOWERS. Monoecious or dioecious.
FRUIT. Subglobose, 0.2 to 0.3 in. across, bright blue, bloomy, ripening the second season; seeds 1 or 2.

LANDSCAPE USE
Frequently planted for screens, background groupings, and in foundation plantings. Most often planted in cultivar form, some of which have been selected for resistance to juniper rusts. Native from Alberta to British Columbia and south to northern Arizona and western Texas, it has been cultivated since 1836.

CULTURE
Propagated from seed and by grafting. The species serves as alternate host for cedar-apple rust, so select resistant cultivars. These junipers are more drought tolerant than other species and cultivars.

CULTIVARS:

'Blue Haven'   juniper
ZONE 4
18 feet tall, 6 feet wide

A pyramidal form with bright blue color. Also sold as 'Blue Heaven'. With good blue color, it was introduced by

Plumfield Nursery in Fremont, Nebraska in 1963.

'Blue Trail' juniper
ZONES 3 AND 4
18 feet tall, 6 feet wide

A columnar form blue-silver foliage.

'Medora' juniper
ZONES 3 AND 4
12 feet tall, 5 feet wide

A narrow, columnar tree selected in the badlands of North Dakota in the 1940s. The one of the most upright of all junipers tested at the Arboretum. Needs little pruning.

'Moonglow' juniper
ZONE 4
18 feet tall, 8 feet wide

A dense, globe-shaped selection. From Hillside Gardens in Leighton, Pennsylvania. Introduced in 1970.

'Sutherland' juniper
ZONES 3 AND 4
18 feet tall, 5 feet wide

A narrow, pyramidal tree with bright green foliage. Introduced by Sutherland Nurseries, Boulder, Colorado in the 1940s.

'Welchii' juniper
ZONES 3 AND 4
9 feet tall, 5 feet wide

A pyramidal tree of compact form and silvery green color.

'Wichita Blue' juniper
ZONE 4
18 feet tall, 6 feet wide

A dense, pyramidal tree of bright bluish green color. Introduced by Monrovia Nursery of California in 1976.

'Winter Blue' juniper
ZONES 3 AND 4
2 feet tall, 5 feet wide

Introduced by C.V. Berg of Helena, Montana in 1977. Has silvery blue foliage and a spreading form.

SINGLE SEED JUNIPER
Juniperus squamata Buch.-Ham. & D. Don.
HARDY IN ZONE 4
Variable growing size

HABIT. Variable growing shrub.
LEAVES. In whorls of 3, gray-green with 2 white bands on upper surface, green undersurface.
FRUIT. Ovoid, to 0.5 in. long; scales 3 to 6; seeds single.

LANDSCAPE USE AND CULTURE
Species rarely planted, with the cultivars selected for specific purposes. Many feature blue hued foliage. Tolerates dry soils.

CULTIVAR:

'Blue Star' juniper
ZONE 4
2 feet tall, 4 feet wide

Introduced in 1965 this cultivar is often used as a ground cover.

RED CEDAR
Juniperus virginiana L.
HARDY IN ZONES 3 AND 4
65 feet tall, 40 feet wide

HABIT. Large tree.
BRANCHES. Upright, spreading, forming broad-pyramidal heads; branches very slender.
BARK. Reddish brown, shredding in long strips.
LEAVES. Both scale-like and acicular; scale-like leaves rhombic-ovate, acute or acuminate, less than 0.1 in. long; needle-like leaves 0.2 in. long, spiny-pointed, concave and glaucous above, opposite or in whorls of 3.
FLOWERS. Male usually dioecious.
FRUIT. Subglobose or ovoid, 0.2 in. long, bloomy, ripening the first season; seeds 1 or 2.

LANDSCAPE USE
The species is frequently planted in shelterbelts and for screen plantings. The cultivars are used for more ornamental purposes. Native from Canada to Florida and west to the Rocky Mountains, it has been cultivated since 1664.

CULTURE
The species is susceptible to the cedar-apple rust. Tolerant of drier, exposed conditions.

CULTIVARS:

'Canaertii' juniper
ZONE 4
20 feet tall, 8 feet wide

A dense, pyramidal form with stout, spreading branches and dark green color. Found by Canaert d'Hamale at Mechelen, Belgium in 1868.

Emerald Sentinel™   juniper

J.v. 'Corcorcor'
ZONE 4
25 feet tall, 12 feet wide

A columnar growing selection suitable for screening purposes. Bright green foliage.

'Grey Owl'   juniper

ZONE 4
4 feet tall, 5 feet wide

A spreading form with silvery gray foliage. Introduced in Holland in 1949.

'Manhattan Blue'   juniper

ZONE 4
18 feet tall, 8 feet wide

A broad-pyramidal tree with bluish green foliage.

BOG LAUREL

BOG LAUREL
Kalmia polifolia Wangenh.
FAMILY: ERICACEAE, HEATH FAMILY
HARDY IN ZONES 2 TO 4
2 feet tall, 2 feet wide

HABIT. Low evergreen shrub; there are 7 species native to North America.
BRANCHES. 2-edged, smooth or minutely hairy.
BUDS. With 2 outer scales.
LEAVES. Opposite or in 3's, sessile or nearly so, oblong, 0.7 to 1.2 in. long, obtuse revolute, glaucous-white beneath, smooth.
FLOWERS. In several flowered terminal umbels, in June; pedicels slender, 0.7 to 1 in. long, smooth; calyx lobes ovate-oblong, obtuse; corolla 0.5 in. across, saucer-shaped, rose-purple; stamens 10, with slender filaments; anthers open by apical pores; ovaries 5-celled, becoming subglobose dry capsules.

LANDSCAPE USE

Bog laurel can be used as a ground cover if its exact growing conditions are met. Native in acid bogs from Labrador to the Hudson Bay and south to Pennsylvania and Minnesota, and from Alaska to Washington.

Although *K. latifolia* or mountain laurel is often listed as being hardy in zone 4, it has not proved hardy in the western regions of North America. It needs cultural requirements similar to most azaleas and rhododendrons (generally acidic, moist soils and protection from winter sun). Conditions must be met before attempting this plant. It might be worth trial in eastern parts of zone 4 in locations meeting these conditions.

CULTURE

Bog laurel is seldom cultivated owing to its specific cultural requirements: it must be planted in acid soil in a moist site. Propagated by seed.

JAPANESE KERRIA

JAPANESE KERRIA
Kerria japonica (L.) DC.
FAMILY: ROSACEAE, ROSE FAMILY
FOR PROTECTED LOCATIONS IN ZONE 4
3 feet tall, 3 feet wide

HABIT. Deciduous shrub; there is 1 species native to China.
BRANCHES. Green, striped, smooth.
BUDS. Small, with several scales.
LEAVES. Alternate, simple, with stipules, oblong-ovate, acuminate, 0.7 to 2 in. long, doubly serrate, bright green and smooth above, paler and slightly hairy beneath; petioles 0.2 to 0.6 in. long.
FLOWERS. Yellow, solitary, perfect 1 to 1.7 in. across, on lateral branches, in May; sepals short, entire; petals 5, oval; stamens numerous, about half as long as petals; styles as long as stamens; carpels 5 to 8.
FRUIT. Brownish black achenes formed from carpels.

LANDSCAPE USE

Plant in a shrub border under protected locations where it will receive good snow cover. Its attractive yellow flowers are showy over a long period and its bright green branches add interest. It grows double the size in more favorable climates. Although it has experienced dieback in plantings at the Arboretum, it still is worth trial in a protected location. Native to central and western China, it was introduced into North America in 1834.

CULTURE

Needs a very protected location in zone 4 with good soil conditions. Tolerates shade. It blooms on old wood, so prune to shape the plant after blooming. It also needs pruning of dead wood in the spring. Propagated largely by softwood cuttings. The cultivars of this plant are probably less hardy than the species.

BEAUTY BUSH

BEAUTY BUSH
Kolkwitzia amabilis Graebn.
FAMILY: CAPRIFOLIACEAE, HONEYSUCKLE FAMILY
FOR PROTECTED LOCATIONS IN ZONE 4
9 feet tall, 9 feet wide

HABIT. Large upright deciduous shrub; there is 1 species native to China.
BRANCHES. Hairy when young, older branches covered with brown flaky bark.
BUDS. With several pairs of pointed hairy scales.
LEAVES. Opposite, simple, broad-ovate, 1 to 2.7 in. long, acuminate, rounded at base, remotely and shallowly toothed or nearly entire, ciliate, dull green above and sparingly hairy, pilose on veins beneath; petioles pilose, 0.1 in. long.
FLOWERS. In pairs, forming terminal corymbs 2 to 2.7 in. across on short lateral branches, in June; sepals 5, narrow, long-hairy, pilose, spreading; corolla bell-shaped, 5-lobed, about 0.2 in. long, pink, yellow in throat, minutely hairy; stamens 4, about as long as corolla tube.
FRUIT. Dry capsules.

LANDSCAPE USE

The common name describes this attractive shrub which unfortunately is not completely hardy in zone 4. It can be attractive in the shrub border especially in flower as its foliage is rather coarse. Plants at the Arboretum have been short-lived; they grow for several years and may bloom, but they usually die before reaching full maturity. They will not grow to their native 9 feet in the North. Native in central China, it was introduced into North America in 1901.

CULTURE

Plant in a sheltered location with good soil in full sun. Flowers on old wood. Propagated by seed or softwood cuttings.

LARCH & TAMARACK

EUROPEAN LARCH
Larix decidua Mill.
FAMILY: PINACEAE, PINE FAMILY
HARDY IN ZONES 3 AND 4
80 feet tall, 50 feet wide

HABIT. Large deciduous tree; at first pyramidal but becoming open and irregular with age; there are 14 species distributed throughout the northern hemisphere.
BRANCHES. Slender, smooth, yellowish.
BARK. Dark grayish brown.
LEAVES. Flattened, 0.7 to 1 in. long, keeled below, soft bright green.
FLOWERS. Female, purple.
FRUIT. Cones, ovoid, 0.7 to 1.2 in. long, with 40 or 50 suborbicular scales, loosely appressed at maturity, the uppermost scales closing the apex; wings of the seeds extend to the upper margins of the scales.

LANDSCAPE USE AND CULTURE

European larch needs a large scaled landscape or park to function well as it grows very large. Native to northern and central Europe, it was introduced into North America by early settlers. It transplants well when dormant and tolerates adverse conditions.

CULTIVAR:

'Pendula'   European larch
HARDY IN ZONE 4
Variable growing size

Branches pendulous. An excellent weeping tree. It is usually grown in the form that is grafted on a standard, so the height varies. *See photograph page 154.*

JAPANESE LARCH
Larix kaempferi (Lam.) Carriere.
HARDY IN ZONE 4
65 feet tall, 30 feet wide

HABIT. Upright tree.
BRANCHES. Short, horizontal; yellowish or reddish brown and usually bloomy, smooth or slightly hairy.
BARK. Scales off in narrow strips, leaving red scars.
LEAVES. Flattened, 0.2 to 1.2 in. long, rather broad, obtuse, light or bluish green; white bands, each with 5 rows of stomata, on undersurface of leaves.
FRUIT. Cones, ovoid, 0.2 to 1.2 in. long, with numerous square or slightly notched scales; bracts concealed.

LANDSCAPE USE

A very handsome conifer, it is fast growing when young. It can grow to 12 feet in five to six years. Although somewhat smaller than European larch, it needs space to fit in the landscape. Its reddish younger branches are attractive in the winter. Native to Japan, it was introduced into North America in 1861. Incorrectly found as *L. leptolepis. See photograph page 159.*

CULTURE

It transplants well when dormant. Japanese larch needs a moist, good garden soil to do well. Doesn't tolerate drought or shade.

TAMARACK, AMERICAN LARCH
Larix laricina (Du Roi) K. Koch.
HARDY IN ZONES 2 TO 4
65 feet tall, 40 feet wide

HABIT. Tree with narrow-pyramidal head and short horizontal branches.
BRANCHES. Smooth, reddish yellow.
BARK. Reddish brown.
LEAVES. 1 to 1.2 in. long, obtuse, light bluish green.
FRUIT. Cones, globose-ovoid, 0.2 to 0.7 in. long, with 12 to 15

suborbicular scales that are smooth and striate outside, minutely crenulate and bevelled at the margin and with bracts that are one-fourth as long as scales.

LANDSCAPE USE

This native species of our swamps is surprisingly tolerant of drought. It can be used for shelterbelts. Its yellow fall color (it is a deciduous conifer) is attractive. Native in bogs from Alaska and Canada to Minnesota and Pennsylvania, it has been cultivated since 1737. A native that should be used more often.

Again, Donald Peattie *A Natural History of Trees* (1950, 34) captures tamarck in the Spring: "soon after the wild geese have gone over and the ice in the beaver ponds is melted, [the tamaracks]... put forth an unexpected, subtle bloom. The flowers are followed in a few weeks by the renewing foliage...And there is no more delicate charm in the North Woods than the moment when the soft, pale-green needles first begin to clothe the military sternness of the Larch. So fine is that foliage, and so oddly clustered in sparse tufts, that Tamarck has the distinction among our trees of giving the least shade. The northern sunlight reaches right to the bottom of a Tamarck grove."

CULTURE

Relishes moist soils though drought tolerant. Does not tolerate pollution or shade.

LABRADOR TEA

LABRADOR TEA
Ledum groenlandicum Oedr.
FAMILY: ERICACEAE, HEATH FAMILY
HARDY IN ZONES 2 TO 4
3 feet tall, 3 feet wide

HABIT. Evergreen shrub; there are 4 species distributed throughout the northern hemisphere.
BRANCHES. Rusty hairs when young.
BUDS. Ovoid, with several scales.
LEAVES. Alternate, short-petioled, entire, elliptic to oblong or narrow-oblong, 0.7 to 2 in. long, obtuse, densely rusty hairs beneath, revolute.
FLOWERS. Rather small, 0.2 in. across, white, on slender pedicels in umbel-like terminal clusters, in June; calyx lobes 5, acute or acutish; petals 5, spreading, oblong; stamens 5 to 8, with slender pedicels; anthers open by apical pores; ovaries 5-celled with elongated styles.
FRUIT. Oblong capsules 0.2 in. long; capsules open from the base upward into 5 valves.

LANDSCAPE USE

Labrador tea can be used for natural landscapes or can be planted near pools and in rock gardens. Although this attractive plant is found growing in acid bogs and other wet places, it is seldom cultivated. It resembles an azalea in appearance.

Ann Zwinger in her classic *Land Above the Trees* (1972, 366) describes it as bearing "feathery white flowers in clusters that light the banks of dark leaves...The leaves have a peculiar rusty covering beneath, like a rusted steel-wool pad."

Native from Greenland to Alberta and Washington south to Pennsylvania and Minnesota, it has been cultivated since 1763. Its foliage was used by pioneers for making a strong tea. One of our regions most attractive native shrubs.

CULTURE

Needs acid, moist soils. Will decline to grow in any other conditions. It tolerates some shade and is easily transplanted. Propagated by seed and softwood cuttings.

SHRUB BUSH CLOVER

SHRUB BUSH CLOVER
Lespedeza bicolor Turcz.
FAMILY: LEGUMINOSAE, PEA FAMILY
FOR PROTECTED LOCATIONS IN ZONE 4
6 feet tall, 3 feet wide

HABIT. Deciduous shrub; there are 40 species distributed worldwide.
BRANCHES. Angular or flat, sparingly hairy at first.
BUDS. With several outer scales.
LEAVES. Alternate, with 3 leaflets; leaflets broad-ovate to obovate, 0.7 to 2 in. long, rounded at apex and bristle-tipped; upper leaf surface dark green; undersurface grayish green and sparingly appressed-hairy; middle leaflet long-stalked; petioles glabrous or sparingly hairy.
FLOWERS. Pea-like, rosy purple, about 0.4 in. long, in axillary racemes, in August and September; calyx silky with short, subequal teeth; petals clawed; standards obovate to oblong; wings free; keels obtuse, incurved.
FRUIT. Broad-elliptic, rostrate legumes or pods 0.2 to 0.3 in. long and slightly appressed-hairy.

LANDSCAPE USE

This shrub should be planted in the shrub border where its late summer, rosy pea-like bloom will be most welcome. It has an informal habit. It also could be included in a perennial border in the North because of its habit of dying back. Native from northern China to Manchuria and Japan, it was introduced into North America in 1856. It should be used more.

CULTURE

It should be treated as a dieback shrub; prune it back to live wood soon after growth starts in the spring. Since it blooms on new wood, the dieback is not serious. Propagated by seed.

PRIVETS

AMUR PRIVET

Ligustrum amurense Carriere.

FAMILY: OLEACEAE, OLIVE FAMILY
FOR PROTECTED LOCATIONS IN ZONE 4
9 feet tall, 6 feet wide

HABIT. Upright pyramidal shrub; there are 50 species distributed worldwide.
BRANCHES. Hairy.
LEAVES. Elliptic to oblong, 1 to 2.2 in. long, obtuse to acute, rounded or broadly wedge-shaped at base, ciliolate, sometimes shiny green above, smooth except for hairs on veins beneath; petioles 0.1 in. long, usually hairy.
FLOWERS. In hairy panicles 1 to 2 in. long, in June and July; calyx smooth or slightly hairy near the base; corolla 0.3 in. long; anthers slightly exserted, not reaching the middle of the lobes.
FRUIT. Globose-ovoid, 0.2 to 0.3 in. long, slightly bloomy, in September and October.

LANDSCAPE USE

This species is often planted for formal hedges or as a background shrub in the shrub border. Native to China, it was introduced into North America in 1860.

Generally privet should be used very carefully because of its lack of hardiness. Several golden-leaved privet are in the landscape trade. *L. x vicaryi* (golden Vicary privet), a cross between *L. ovalifolium* 'Aureum' and *L. vulgare*, is lacking in hardiness and usually winter kills.

CULTURE

This privet has a tendency to grow late in the fall, and this growth frequently kills back from the first severe cold of the winter. Needs pruning after flowering to keep attractive. It can be pruned heavily so does make a good hedging plant. Tolerant of a wide variety of conditions, although in the North needs a relatively protected location. Propagated by softwood cuttings.

REGEL PRIVET

Ligustrum obtusifolium var. regelianum

(Koehne) Rehd.
FOR PROTECTED LOCATIONS IN ZONE 4
4.5 feet tall, 6 feet wide

HABIT. Low shrub.
BRANCHES. Arching and hairy.
LEAVES. Oblong to obovate, 0.7 to 2.2 in. long, acute or obtuse, wedge-shaped at base, hairy beneath; petioles 0.1 in. long, hairy.
FLOWERS. In nodding panicles 0.7 to 1.2 in. long, in July; calyx hairy; corolla 0.3 to 0.4 in. long; anthers nearly as long as lobes.
FRUIT. Subglobose, about 0.2 in. long, black, slightly bloomy, in September and October.

LANDSCAPE USE AND CULTURE

Some dieback can be expected in most winters in the North. In a protected location it can be used for foundation and border plantings. Its horizontal branching makes it recognizable in the landscape. Native to Japan, it was introduced into North America in 1885.

COMMON PRIVET

Ligustrum vulgare L.

FOR PROTECTED LOCATIONS IN ZONE 4
9 feet tall, 6 feet wide

HABIT. Large shrub.
BRANCHES. Slender, spreading; young branches minutely hairy.
LEAVES. Oblong-ovate to lanceolate, 1 to 2.2 in. long, obtuse to acute, smooth; petioles 0.1 to 0.4 in. long.
FLOWERS. Pediceled, in rather dense panicles that are 1 to 2.2 in. long, in June and July; anthers longer than corolla tube but shorter than limb.
FRUIT. Subglobose or ovoid, 0.2 to 0.3 in. long black, shiny, in September and October.

LANDSCAPE USE

The species is of variable hardiness depending on the seed source. Native to Europe and northern Africa, it has been cultivated since early times. It is most often found in the landscape trade in the cultivars listed below.

CULTIVARS:

'Cheyenne'   privet

ZONE 4
4 feet tall, 5 feet wide

A selection made at Cheyenne, Wyoming. The hardiest cultivar of those tested at the Arboretum, but even this selection has killed back after severe winters.

'Lodense'   privet

TRIAL IN ZONE 4
3 feet tall, 3 feet wide

A low form 3 feet tall that is sometimes sold. Plants have not been hardy in Arboretum trials.

TWINFLOWER

TWINFLOWER
Linnaea borealis L.
FAMILY: CAPRIFOLIACEAE,
HONEYSUCKLE FAMILY
HARDY IN ZONES 2 TO 4
4 inches tall, 3 feet wide

HABIT. Evergreen, trailing subshrub; there is 1 species distributed worldwide.
STEMS. Slender, sparingly hairy.
LEAVES. Simple, opposite, roundish or obovate, 0.2 to 1 in. long, acute or obtuse, with few crenate teeth, usually ciliate and with scattered hairs above.
FLOWERS. In pairs on slender upright stalks, fragrant, from June to August; calyx with 5 lanceolate sepals, 0.1 in. long; corolla campanulate, 5-lobed, 0.2 to 0.3 in. long, white, tinged and striped with rose-purple; stamens 4.
FRUIT. Ovoid, dry, yellow, indehiscent, about 0.1 in. long, 1-seeded, in September and October.

LANDSCAPE USE
An attractive, small growing woody subshrub which is often thought of as an herbaceous perennial. It is an attractive plant for a rock garden or for naturalizing in partial shade.
It is especially attractive on a rock wall where one can see it at eye level. Native around the world in the northern hemisphere, it has been cultivated since 1762.

CULTURE
Requires an acid soil. Propagated by seed.

TULIP TREE

TULIP TREE
Liriodendron tulipifera L.
FAMILY: MAGNOLIACEAE, MAGNOLIA FAMILY
FOR PROTECTED LOCATIONS IN EASTERN PARTS OF ZONE 4
90 feet tall, 50 feet wide

One of the premier American native trees which is unfortunately not hardy in most of zone 4. It is worth a trial in eastern parts of zone 4.

The HONEYSUCKLES
Lonicera L.
FAMILY: CAPRIFOLIACEAE,
HONEYSUCKLE FAMILY

Because honeysuckles have diseases and pests that often make the leaves and growth unsightly, it has not been cultivated in the landscape as much as it once was. The Minnesota Landscape Arboretum has introduced varieties which are resistant to the honeysuckle witches'-broom aphid. This aphid causes abnormal growth, dieback, and often death. It is a major problem in the North. Some of the more widely grown honeysuckle are not hardy in the North (*L. fragrantissima, L. x heckrottii*). Those selecting honeysuckle in our area should choose carefully.

Lonicera 'Freedom' honeysuckle
HARDY IN ZONE 4, FOR PROTECTED AREAS OF ZONE 3
8 feet tall, 6 to 8 feet wide

This hybrid resembles the growth and scale of L. korolkowii. The leaves are blue-green, flowers white, tinged with pink, and fruit are small and red. This large growing shrub is most often used for screening or windbreak purposes. Its informal, open habit makes it less desirable for specimen plantings.

Resistant to the honeysuckle witches'-broom aphid, this shrub is of easy culture. It tolerates a wide variety of soil types. 'Freedom' was introduced by The Minnesota Landscape Arboretum in 1986. It does best in full sun. A fast grower. See also *L. tatarica* 'Honey Rose'.

SCARLET TRUMPET HONEYSUCKLE, BROWN'S HONEYSUCKLE
Lonicera x brownii (Regel) Carriere.
HARDY IN ZONES 2 TO 4
Vine, 30 or more feet

HABIT. Climbing vine; there are 180 species distributed throughout the northern hemisphere.
LEAVES. Similar to those of *L. sempervirens*.
FLOWERS. Scarlet-red with a 2-lipped corolla and a tube about 2 in. long that is lobed at the base.
FRUIT. Similar to those of *L. sempervirens*.

LANDSCAPE USE

A hybrid species developed by crossing *L. sempervirens* and *L. hirsuta*. The cultivar, 'Dropmore Scarlet' is most often grown. Blooms from June through September in usual clusters of six blooms. Attracts hummingbirds.

CULTURE

A vigorous growing vine well suited for the North. Will grow in full sun or partial shade in a good gardening soil, although it is tolerant of alkaline soils. It can be rejuvenated by a hard pruning.

CULTIVAR:

'Dropmore Scarlet'   honeysuckle
ZONES 3 AND 4

This cultivar was developed in 1950 by Dr. Frank Skinner of Dropmore, Manitoba. It blooms almost continuously from June until November. This is the hardiest vine honeysuckle that can be grown in the North. It is sterile, so does not produce fruit. Although aphids are sometimes a problem, it also features attractive, clean foliage. This cultivar most often is smaller in size in the North growing to 8 to 10 feet. *See photograph page 163.*

SWEETBERRY HONEYSUCKLE
Lonicera caerulea var. edulis Regel.
HARDY IN ZONES 3 AND 4
4.5 feet tall, 3 feet wide

HABIT. Spreading shrub with many branches.
BRANCHES. At first green and hairy, later turning yellowish or reddish brown, with flaky bark.
BUDS. Spreading, with 2 outer scales.
LEAVES. Oblong to lanceolate, 0.7 to 3 in. long, acute to obtusish, usually rounded at base, at least slightly hairy when young, rarely smooth, bright green.
FLOWERS. On short nodding stalks, in May; bracts subulate, exceeding the short-ciliate calyx; corolla tubular-funnelform, 0.2 to 0.5 in. long, yellowish white, usually hairy outside, with tubes usually longer than spreading lobes; stamens longer than limb; styles longer than stamens, smooth.
FRUIT. Oblong, 0.2 to 0.5 in. long, dark blue, bloomy, in June.

LANDSCAPE USE AND CULTURE

Native to eastern Siberia, it was introduced into North America in 1871. One of the lower growing honeysuckles more suitable for modern landscapes.

LIMBER HONEYSUCKLE
Lonicera dioica L.
HARDY IN ZONES 2 TO 4
9 feet tall, 9 feet wide

HABIT. Twining vine or bushy shrub.
LEAVES. Very short-petioled or sub-sessile, elliptic to oblong, 1.5 to 3 in. long, obtuse or acutish, wedge-shaped at base, with cartilaginous, transparent, often wavy margins, glaucous beneath; upper pair of leaves united at base.
FLOWERS. In sessile or short-stalked spikes of usually several whorls, in June; corolla about 0.2 in. long, greenish or whitish yellow, often tinged with purple, smooth outside; stamens as long as limb; styles longer than stamens, usually smooth.

LANDSCAPE USE AND CULTURE

Although hard to obtain, this unique native species should be planted more often. Native from Quebec to Saskatchewan and south to North Carolina and Iowa, it has been cultivated since 1636.

Seeing just a branch of this honeysuckle with its unique leaves that are joined around the stem in a disk-like habit, one could guess it was a eucalyptus or some more exotic plant. It is unique in the landscape. It is very informal in growth habit, best used where it can sprawl naturally against a support or in naturalistic plantings. Tolerates drought. As with most fruiting honeysuckles, the birds relish the tart berries.

In the *Botanical Register* (1816, Plate 138), a popular English periodical of its day, it states: "Although introduced by Mr. Peter Collinson as far back as 1766, by no means common in our gardens. A peculiarly glaucous hue distinguishes it from most others of the genus."

AMUR HONEYSUCKLE
Lonicera maackii (Rupr.) Maxim.
HARDY IN ZONES 2 TO 4
16 feet tall, 12 feet wide

HABIT. Large shrub.
BRANCHES. Short-hairy.
BUDS. Small, ovoid.
LEAVES. Ovate-elliptic to ovate-lanceolate, 2 to 3 in. long, acuminate, broadly wedge-shaped or rounded at base, dark green above, lighter beneath, usually hairy along the veins on both sides; petioles 0.1 to 0.2 in. long, glandular-hairy.
FLOWERS. White, changing to yellow in June; calyx limbs bell-shaped, divided to the middle into ovate or lanceolate teeth; corolla 0.7 in. long, usually smooth outside, fragrant; tubes thin, not swollen, one-third to one-half as long as limb; stamens and styles one-half to two-thirds as long as limb.
FRUIT. Dark red, in September and October.

LANDSCAPE USE AND CULTURE

Native to Manchuria and Korea, it was introduced into North America in 1860. A large growing, informal shrub it is generally too large for home landscapes. It has become invasive in Eastern North America from Illinois to West Virginia. It is one of the earliest shrubs to leaf out in the spring.

VARIETY:

f. *podocarpa* Rehd.
HARDY IN ZONE 4

Also native to Asia, this smaller-sized shrub features a more spreading habit than the species and darker green leaves. Usually planted in preference to the species, this variety is attractive in fruit.

SAKHALIN HONEYSUCKLE
Lonicera maximowiczii var. *sachalinensis* F. Schmidt.
HARDY IN ZONES 3 AND 4
8 feet tall, 9 feet wide

HABIT. Roundheaded shrub.
BRANCHES. Smooth, purplish.
LEAVES. Elliptic to ovate, 1 to 2 in. long, acute, wedge-shaped at base, ciliate, smooth or nearly so and glaucescent beneath, red when unfolding; fall color golden yellow.
FLOWERS. On peduncles 0.5 to 1 in. long, dark purple, in June; corolla about 0.4 in. long, smooth outside, shorter than limb; stamens about as long as limb, hairy to the apex; ovaries united.
FRUIT. Ovoid, red, in August.

LANDSCAPE USE AND CULTURE

This is an attractive shrub with clean foliage and attractive flowers and fruits. It is the only honeysuckle that turns golden yellow in the fall. Native to Manchuria and Korea, it was introduced into North America about 1855.

TATARIAN HONEYSUCKLE
Lonicera tatarica L.
HARDY IN ZONES 2 TO 4
12 feet tall, 9 feet wide

HABIT. Large upright shrub.
BRANCHES. Smooth, becoming gray with age.
LEAVES. Ovate to ovate-lanceolate, 1 to 2.2 in. long, acute to acuminate, rarely obtusish, rounded or somewhat heart-shaped at base, dark green above, light to bluish green beneath; petioles less than 0.2 in. long.
FLOWERS. Pink to white, in June; corolla 0.5 to 0.7 in. long, tube slightly swollen on one side at base, shorter than limb,

lateral lobes of upper lip divided to the base, spreading; stamens and style shorter than limb.
FRUIT. Globose, orange to red, in July and August.

LANDSCAPE USE AND CULTURE

The cultivars of this species have been widely planted in zone 4. Being susceptible to aphids they are no longer used as much in the landscape. They have been widely planted in shelterbelts, border plantings and in hedges. They are frequently planted by birds, and volunteer plants are common in woods and open fields. Native from southern Russia to Altai and Turkestan, it was introduced into North America in 1752.

CULTIVARS:

'Arnold Red'
ZONE 3 AND 4
8 feet tall, 8 feet wide

Flowers deep red.

'Honey Rose'
ZONES 3 AND 4
8 feet tall, 6 feet wide

Introduced by the Minnesota Landscape Arboretum in 1994, this selection features attractive rosy red flowers and resistance to the witches'-broom aphid. Useful for screening and for windbreaks. An improvement on the species and its other cultivars.

'Rosea'   honeysuckle
HARDY IN ZONE 3 & 4
8 feet tall, 6 feet wide

Flowers pink outside, lighter pink inside.

'Zabelii'   honeysuckle
HARDY IN ZONE 3 & 4
8 feet tall, 6 feet wide

Flowers red. Plants quite upright. Frequently planted for hedges or screens. Some experts consider this to be a variety of the species *L. korolkowii*.

VIENNA HONEYSUCKLE
Lonicera x xylosteoides Tausch.
HARDY IN ZONES 3 AND 4
6 feet tall, 6 feet wide

HABIT. Shrub.
LEAVES. Usually rhombic-ovate, broadly wedge-shaped at base, bluish green, slightly hairy.
FLOWERS. Small, pink to yellow, in late May.
FRUIT. Small, dark red, in July and August.

LANDSCAPE USE AND CULTURE

A variable hybrid species resulting from a cross between *L. tatarica* and *L. xylosteum*. The cultivars are widely available and planted.

CULTIVARS:

'Clavey's Dwarf' honeysuckle

A compact hedge plant 4.5 feet tall, with bluish green foliage and light yellow flowers. Requires little pruning. Also sold under L. xylosteum 'Clavey's Dwarf'.

'Miniglobe' honeysuckle

A 1981 introduction from the Morden Research Station, it is the same size as 'Emerald Mound' but is hardier for the North. Grows 4 feet wide and tall.

EUROPEAN FLY HONEYSUCKLE
Lonicera xylosteum L.

HARDY IN ZONES 3 AND 4
6 feet tall, 6 feet wide

HABIT. Rounded shrub.
BRANCHES. Smooth or hairy.
LEAVES. Broad-ovate or elliptic-ovate or obovate, 1 to 2.2 in. long, acute, broadly wedge-shaped to rounded at base; upper leaf surface dark or grayish green and sparingly hairy or smooth; undersurface paler and hairy, rarely smooth; petioles 0.1 to 0.3 in. long.
FLOWERS. 0.4 in. long, white to yellowish white, in early June.
FRUIT. Small, dark red, in August.

LANDSCAPE USE AND CULTURE

Native from Europe to Altai, the species is seldom planted in the North.

CULTIVAR:

'Emerald Mound' honeysuckle

ZONE 4
A dwarf mound-shaped shrub 3 feet tall and up to 6 feet across with dark green foliage.

Other honeysuckles to try:

ALPS HONEYSUCKLE
L. alpigena L.

HARDY IN ZONE 4
6 feet tall, 3 feet wide

Most often cultivated in its 'Nana' form which can be grown as a 3 foot hedge. Green, crinkly leaves. Not readily available.

BELLE HONEYSUCKLE
L. x bella Zab.

HARDY IN ZONES 2 TO 4
9 feet tall, 9 feet wide

This hybrid species of rounded shrubs was developed by crossing *L. morrowii* and *L. tatarica*. A yellowish white flowering cultivar 'Albida' is sometimes found.

DONALD HONEYSUCKLE
L. glaucescens (Rydb.) Rydb.

HARDY IN ZONES 2 TO 4
9 feet tall, 9 feet wide

Similar to *L. dioica* and considered by some authors to be a variety of it.

HAIRY HONEYSUCKLE
L. hirsuta Eaton.

HARDY IN ZONES 2 TO 4
Twining vine 9 feet long

This native North American vine is difficult to obtain.

MORROW HONEYSUCKLE
L. morrowii A. Gray.

HARDY IN ZONES 3 AND 4
6 feet tall, 6 feet wide

Native to Japan, it was introduced into North America in 1875. This species is planted for formal hedges and can also be used in the shrub border for its broad, mass effect. Difficult to obtain.

TRUMPET HONEYSUCKLE
L. sempervirens L.

FOR PROTECTED LOCATIONS IN EASTERN PARTS OF ZONE 4
20 feet long

This species is not as hardy as the cultivar, L. x brownii 'Dropmore Scarlet'. Since the two are quite similar, there is little need to plant the species in western parts of zone 4. There are many cultivars of this species which are not reliably hardy in zone 4.

MATRIMONY VINES

COMMON MATRIMONY VINE
Lycium barbarum L.

FAMILY: SOLANACEAE, NIGHTSHADE FAMILY
HARDY IN ZONE 4, FOR PROTECTED LOCATIONS IN ZONE 3
10 feet long

HABIT. Upright or spreading shrub; there are 100 species distributed worldwide.

BRANCHES. Arching or recurving, light gray, usually spiny.

LEAVES. Oblong-lanceolate, rarely elliptic-lanceolate, 0.7 to 2.2 in. long, acute or obtuse, narrowed into a slender petiole 0.2 to 0.8 in. long, grayish green, thick.

FLOWERS. 1 to 4 in leaf axils, from June to September; calyx usually 1- to 3-lobed, divided, with obtuse lobes; corolla dull lilac-purple.

FRUIT. Ovoid or short-oblong, 0.4 to 0.7 in. long, scarlet to orange-red, from August to October.

LANDSCAPE USE AND CULTURE

Incorrectly listed as *L. halimiifolium*. Frequently escaped from cultivation. This sprawling shrub is seldom planted, but often volunteers. Although flowers and fruits are colorful, plants can become a nuisance when seedlings appear in flower borders or among other shrubs. Native to southeastern Europe and western Asia. Probably has the same uses as the more commonly available Chinese matrimony vine.

CHINESE MATRIMONY VINE
Lycium chinense Mill.
HARDY IN ZONE 4, FOR PROTECTED LOCATIONS IN ZONE 3

12 feet long

HABIT. Rambling shrub.

BRANCHES. Arching and often prostrate, usually unarmed, light yellowish gray.

LEAVES. Rhombic-ovate to ovate-lanceolate, 1 to 3 in. long, acute or obtusish, broadly to narrowly wedge-shaped at base, bright green; petioles 0.4 in. long.

FLOWERS. 1 to 4 in leaf axils, from June to September; calyx 3- to 5-toothed, with acute lobes; corolla purple, about 0.4 in. long.

FRUIT. Ovoid to oblong, 0.5 to 1 in. long, scarlet to orange-red, from August to October.

LANDSCAPE USE AND CULTURE

A useful trailing shrub for bank covers and for planting above walls. Leaves stay green late in the fall; fruits are very colorful. Native to eastern Asia, it was introduced into North America before 1709. Known as *gouqizi* in China, the juice from its leaves are used as a treatment for insect bites and in a juvenile state, commonly available as a vegetable in Chinese markets. Of easy culture but best used for naturalistic plantings.

MAACKIA

AMUR MAACKIA
Maackia amurensis Rupr. & Maxim.
FAMILY: LEGUMINOSAE, PEA FAMILY
HARDY IN ZONES 3 AND 4
30 feet tall, 20 feet wide

HABIT. Small tree; there are 8 species native is Asia.

LEAVES. 7 to 11 leaflets; leaflets elliptic to oblong-ovate, 2 to 3 in. long, short-acuminate, rounded at base, smooth.

FLOWERS. About 0.3 in. long, in panicled racemes 4 to 8 in. long, in July and August.

FRUIT. 1.2 to 2 in. long, in September.

LANDSCAPE USE

An interesting mid-summer flowering tree with very attractive, clean foliage. Native to Manchuria it was introduced into North America in 1864. It can be grown as a single or multiple trunked specimen. Slow growing. *See photograph page 147.*

CULTURE

It is well-suited for poor soils (being in the pea family, it fixes nitrogen in the soil) and is also drought tolerant. It will do better on reasonable soils with adequate water.

CHINESE MAACKIA
Maackia chinensis Takeda.
FOR PROTECTED LOCATIONS IN ZONE 4

30 feet tall, 30 feet wide

HABIT. Small to medium tree.

LEAVES. 11 to 13 leaflets; leaflets ovate to elliptic, 0.7 to 2.2 in. long, obtuse, hairy beneath.

FLOWERS. Less than 0.5 in. long, in panicled racemes, in July and August.

LANDSCAPE USE AND CULTURE

Not as hardy as *M. amurensis*. Introduced from its native China in 1908. Hard to find in the nursery trade. E.H. Wilson, in his *China Mother of Gardens*, (1929, 47) notes native specimens 65 feet tall and trunk circumference of 7 feet.

OSAGE ORANGE

OSAGE ORANGE
Maclura pomifera (Raf.) Schneid.
FAMILY: MORACEAE; MULBERRY FAMILY
FOR PROTECTED LOCATIONS IN EASTERN PART OF ZONE 4
30 feet tall, 30 feet wide

LANDSCAPE USE AND CULTURE

This species has not been hardy in plantings at The Minnesota Landscape Arboretum. For the adventurous, it might be worth a trial in eastern parts of zone 4. Native from Arkansas to Oklahoma and Texas.

The MAGNOLIAS
Magnolia L.
FAMILY: MAGNOLIACEAE

This is one genus which almost everyone wishes would do better in the North. Even the hardiest magnolias such as *M. stellata* and its cultivars should be placed carefully in the landscape. Others including the saucer magnolia and the many hybrids are of doubtful hardiness. Choose your magnolia carefully and search out microclimates in your yard where they might flourish.

CUCUMBERTREE
Magnolia acuminata (L.) L.
HARDY IN ZONE 4
65 feet tall, 50 feet wide

HABIT. Pyramidal tree; 125 species are distributed worldwide.
BRANCHES. Smooth or slightly hairy, red-brown, shiny.
BARK. Dark brown, becoming furrowed.
BUDS. Hairy.
LEAVES. Elliptic or ovate to oblong-ovate, 4 to 9.2 in. long, short-acuminate, rounded or acute at base, soft-hairy and light green beneath; petioles 1 to 1.2 in. long.
FLOWERS. Campanulate, 2.2 to 3 in. long, in May; petals obovate-oblong, greenish yellow, bloomy; sepals lanceolate, much smaller than petals, soon reflexed.
FRUIT. Ovoid to oblong, 2 to 3 in. long, in August and September.

LANDSCAPE USE

The cucumbertree is hardy in zone 4, but this magnolia is one of the least showy in bloom. It also is one of the largest magnolias so should be placed carefully. As in most magnolia, the fruit with its dangling seeds are also an attractive feature. Use as a specimen or shade tree for large areas.
It is native from New York to Georgia and west to Illinois and Arkansas and has been cultivated since 1736.

Humphry Marshall in one of the first books on North American trees, *Arbustrum Americanum* (1785) remarks on its common name "The seed-vessels are about three inches long, somewhat resembling a small Cucumber; from whence the inhabitants where it grows natural, call it the Cucumber-tree."

CULTURE
It should be placed in a protected location, one not being windswept in the winter. It needs a good garden soil with adequate moisture. Trouble-free otherwise.

LOEBNER MAGNOLIA
Magnolia x loebneri Kache.
FOR PROTECTED LOCATIONS IN ZONE 4
25 feet tall, 20 feet wide

HABIT. Small tree in our area.
BRANCHES. Densely hairy when young.
BUDS. Densely hairy.
LEAVES. Obovate, 1.5 to 4 in. long, obtusely pointed, gradually tapering at base, smooth and dark green above, light green and netted beneath with hairs on veins; petioles 0.1 to 0.4 in. long.
FLOWERS. On short peduncles, about 4 in. across, white and fragrant, in May; petals 12 to 15, narrow-oblong, spreading and finally reflexed.
FRUIT. About 2 in. long, twisted, with few red carpels, in September.

LANDSCAPE USE

This hybrid species which originated before 1910 resulted from a cross between *M. kobus* and *M. stellata*. The cultivars listed below are most often grown.

CULTURE
Needs a very protected location to do well in zone 4.

CULTIVARS:

'Leonard Messel'
ZONE 4
20 feet tall, 15 feet wide

Introduced in England in 1955. Research published in 1994 from The Minnesota Landscape Arboretum showed little damage to flower buds at -32 degrees F.

'Merrill'   magnolia
ZONE 4
30 feet tall, 25 feet wide

A selection from the Arnold Arboretum in 1939 that flowers at an early age of about 5 years. Use as a specimen tree. Dr. Snyder reported an 8-year-old plant in his yard grew to about 15 feet tall and had shown no winter injury except for an occasional flower bud that failed to open. 'Merrill' is one of the best magnolias to try in zone 4. The same research evaluating flower bud hardiness noted this cultivar showed considerable flower bud damage at -32 degrees F. *See photograph page 161.*

STAR MAGNOLIA
Magnolia stellata (Sieb. & Zucc.) Maxim.
HARDY IN ZONE 4
20 feet tall, 9 feet wide

HABIT. Shrub or small tree.
BRANCHES. Densely hairy when young.
BUDS. Densely hairy.
LEAVES. Obovate or narrow-elliptic to oblong-obovate, 1.5 to 4 in. long, obtusely pointed or obtusish, gradually tapering at base, smooth and dark green above, light green and netted beneath and smooth or appressed-hairy on veins; petioles 0.1 to 0.4 in. long.
FLOWERS. Short-stalked, about 3 in. across, white, fragrant, in early May; petals and sepals alike, 12 to 18, narrow-oblong, spreading and finally reflexed.
FRUIT. About 2 in. long, twisted and with few fertile carpels, in September.

LANDSCAPE USE
This species and its cultivars are the magnolias to try in zone 4. They are as welcome as forsythia in the spring as they are among the earliest to bloom. One thinks of this magnolia when one reads Shakespeare's "Rough winds do shake the darling buds of May." We are often impatient to see the hairy bud scales drop to expose the dazzling white blossoms. The blooms are very showy as they bloom on bare twig; they are slightly fragrant.

The star magnolia can be used as a specimen tree or in the shrub border. Often they grow more shrub-like than tree-like in our zone. They are also attractive in leaf and their gray branches can be attractive in winter. They flower consistently the first week of May at The Minnesota Landscape Arboretum, although the flowers can be damaged by a late frost. They are native to Japan, and were introduced into North America in 1862. *See photograph page 146.*

CULTURE
Again, a protected location will help ensure that the star magnolia and its cultivars will do well in zone 4. It is also best to avoid an exposed southern exposure as this tends to make the flowers open earlier where they can be more susceptible to late spring frosts. If used as a specimen plant, careful pruning can be used to open up its structure to make the tree more ornamental. Although full sun is best, they will withstand partial shade.

Does well in slightly acidic soils; in alkaline soils the star magnolia needs acidic soil treatment.

CULTIVARS:

'Centennial'   magnolia
ZONE 4
12 feet tall, 12 feet wide

Originated at the Arnold Arboretum. Flowers are larger and petals wider than in the species. Plants at the Arboretum have not bloomed as well as 'Royal Star'.

'Royal Star'   magnolia
ZONE 4
15 feet tall, 12 feet wide

Introduced in 1947, this is a vigorous cultivar to try in the North. It has done well in diverse plantings.

'Waterlily'   magnolia
ZONE 4
12 feet tall, 12 feet wide

Buds are first pink, then white. This cultivar is confused in the trade as there seems to be a number of variant forms. Flowers are slightly larger and have more petals than in the species. The cultivar 'Water Lily' in England is white.

UMBRELLA MAGNOLIA
Magnolia tripetala L.
HARDY IN ZONE 4
30 feet tall, 20 feet wide

HABIT. Small, open-headed tree.
BRANCHES. Smooth.
BUDS. Smooth.
LEAVES. Oblong-obovate, 9.8 to 20 in. long, acute or short-acuminate, usually wedge-shaped at base, pale and hairy beneath (at least when young); petioles 0.5 to 1 in. long.
FLOWERS. 7 to 9.5 in. across, white, opening after the leaves in June; petals 6 to 9, oblong-obovate, 3 to 4.5 in. long; sepals shorter than petals; becoming reflexed, light green; filaments purple.
FRUIT. Ovoid-oblong, 2.7 to 4 in. long, rose-colored, in September.

LANDSCAPE USE
This magnolia has bold, very large leaves and an open spreading habit. Since the flowers open after the leaves are fully open, the flowers are less conspicuous than those on magnolias that bloom before the leaves open. The fruit on this magnolia is especially attractive.

Native from Pennsylvania to Alabama and west to Arkansas and Mississippi, it has been cultivated since 1752. The common name, umbrella magnolia, comes from its leaves which are similar to the rib arrangement of an umbrella.

CULTURE

It needs to be planted in a protected location.

Other magnolias to try:

KOBUS MAGNOLIA
M. kobus DC.
FOR PROTECTED LOCATIONS IN ZONE 4
40 feet tall, 20 feet wide

Trial in a protected location. Native to Japan, it was introduced into North America in 1892. Hard to obtain.

ANISE MAGNOLIA
M. salicifolia (Sieb. & Zucc.) Maxim.
FOR PROTECTED LOCATIONS IN ZONE 4
25 feet tall, 20 feet wide

Anise magnolia has done well at The Minnesota Landscape Arboretum, blooming quite reliably. Twigs have an anise scent when crushed.

SAUCER MAGNOLIA
M. x soulangiana Soul.-Bod.
TRIAL IN SHELTERED LOCATIONS IN ZONE 4
30 feet tall, 20 feet wide

As with the above magnolia, while it might grow vegetatively in a protected spot in zone 4, it does not blossom. Even in more southern zones, the flower buds are often killed in a difficult winter or blossoms are ruined in a spring frost.

CREEPING MAHONIA

CREEPING MAHONIA
Mahonia repens G. Don.
FAMILY: BERBERIDACEAE, BARBERRY FAMILY
FOR PROTECTED LOCATIONS IN ZONE 4
18 in. tall, 18 in. wide

HABIT. Evergreen, stoloniferous shrub; there are 70 species distributed in North America and Asia.
BUDS. With numerous pointed scales.
LEAVES. Alternate, odd-pinnate; leaflets 3 to 7, broad-ovate, 1 to 2.2 in. long, spinulose-dentate, dull bluish green above, petioles 0.7 to 1 in. long.
FLOWERS. Yellow, in many flowered racemes, in late May; sepals 9; petals 6.
FRUIT. Black berries 0.2 to 0.3 in. long, in August and September.

LANDSCAPE USE

A handsome broad-leaved evergreen ground cover in other parts of the country, in zone 4 mahonia becomes more problematical. It will do well where there is reliable snowcover, but in exposed sites usually browns out or dies back. It is native in the mountains from British Columbia to New Mexico and east to the Black Hills of South Dakota. It has been cultivated since 1822.

CULTURE

Best planted where there is good snow cover. Propagated by seed or from suckers of established plantings. The closely related *M. aquifolium* (Oregon grape) is not hardy.

The FLOWERING CRABS and APPLES

Malus Mill.
FAMILY: ROSACEAE, ROSE FAMILY

What would our northern landscapes be without this genus? Not only are the ornamental varieties widely grown, but the many apples and edible crabs make autumn a season gardeners look forward to. Apple trees are very ornamental whether in bloom or fruit. As apple trees mature they feature a distinctive character in the winter landscape. They also make wonderful specimens for espalier (*see photograph page 164.*) Whether old reliable apples such as 'Haralson', 'Beacon' or 'Chestnut Crab' or newer introductions such as 'Honeycrisp' and Zestar™ are planted, all can add much to our lives. The use of edible plants in the landscape can be accomplished without major commitments by gardeners. A minimal spraying program is all that can be required.

One of the busiest weekends at The Minnesota Landscape Arboretum is the spring weekend when the flowering crabs are in bloom. One thinks of Thoreau experiencing the overaboundance of spring bloom as quoted in his *Journal*, vol 3 (1850, 81) "Yesterday when I walked to Goodman's hill It seemed to me that the atmosphere was never so full of fragrance and spicy odors. There is a great variety in the fragrance of the apple blossoms as well as their tints...reminding us of Arabian gales & what mariners tell of the spice islands."

Ornamental crabapples are outstanding in bloom but also can have interesting summer leaf color and good bark characteristics. Also importantly they are a good size and scale for modern landscapes.

When choosing flowering crabs for the landscape, factors to keep in mind include disease resistance, size, form, flower color and fruiting characteristics. The following lists can help in selecting crabs. The disease resistance ratings reflect research done at The Minnesota Landscape Arboretum. Flowering crabs are often grown to enjoy the colorful fruit through the fall and winter months. However, one cultivar was selected because it has no fall fruit, the cultivar 'Spring Snow'. Under the listing of cultivars by fruit some also indicate they have few fruit. *See photographs pages 140-41, 164.*

FLOWERING CRAB SELECTION LISTS

Smaller-Growing Varieties
Camelot® (10 feet)
'Coral Cascade' (15 feet)
Coralburst® (15 feet)
'David' (12 feet)
'Doubloons' (15 feet)
Golden Raindrops® (15 feet)
Guinevere® (8 feet)
'Indian Magic' (15 feet)
'Jewelberry' (8 feet)
Lancelot® (8 feet)
'Liset' (15 feet)
'Louisa' (15 feet)
Madonna® (15 feet)
'Mary Potter' (12 feet)
Molten Lava® (15 feet)
'Oekonomierat Echtermeyer' (15 feet)
'Pink Spires' (15 feet)
'Radiant' (15 feet)
'Red Jade' (10 feet)

Red Jewel® (15 feet)
'Sinai Fire' (15 feet)
'Snowdrift' (15 feet)
'Sparkler' (15 feet)
'Strawberry Parfait' (15 feet)
'Thunderchild' (15 feet)
Weeping Candied Apple® (15 feet)
'White Cascade' (15 feet)
M. sargentii & cultivars (5 to 10 feet)

Flowering Crabs with Red Blossoms

(All have a pinkish cast)
'Cardinal'
Centurion®
'Indian Summer'
'Kelsey'
'Oekonomierat Echtermeyer'
'Prairifire'
'Profusion'
'Purple Prince'
'Radiant'
'Red Barron'
'Royalty'
'Selkirk'
'Sparkler'

Flowering Crabs with Pink Flowers

'Adams'
Brandywine®
Camelot®
Coralburst®
'Hopa'
'Indian Magic'
'Liset'
'Louisa'
'Pink Spires'
'Red Splendor'
'Robinson'
'Strawberry Parfait'
'Thunderchild'
'Van Eseltine'
'Vanguard'
Velvet Pillar®
Weeping Candied Apple®
M. coronaria & cultivar
M. ioensis and cultivars

Flowering Crabs with White Bloom

(Many are pink in bud)
'Adirondack'
'Beverly'
'Bob White'
'Callaway'
'Coral Cascade'
'David'
'Dolgo'

'Donald Wyman'
'Doubloons'
'Flame'
Golden Raindrops®
Guinevere®
Harvest Gold®
'Jewelberry'
Lancelot®
Madonna®
'Mary Potter'
Molten Lava®
'Ormiston Roy'
'Professor Sprenger'
'Red Jade'
Red Jewel®
'Sentinel'
'Sinai Fire'
'Snowcloud'
'Snowdrift'
'Spring Snow'
Sugar Tyme®
'White Cascade'
'Winter Gold'
M. baccata and cultivars
M. floribunda
M. prunifolia
M. sargentii and cultivars
M. x zumi and cultivar

Flowering Crabs with Colored Fruit

'Adams' (red)
'Adirondack' (red)
'Beverly' (red)
'Bob White' (yellow)
Brandywine® (yellow, non-persistent)
'Callaway' (red)
Camelot® (red)
'Cardinal' (red)
Centurion® (pink)
'Coral Cascade' (orange-red)
Coralburst® (red)
'David' (red)
'Dolgo' (red, non-persistent)
'Donald Wyman (red)
'Doubloons' (yellow)
'Flame' (red)
Golden Raindrops® (yellow)
Guinevere® ((red)
Harvet Gold® (golden)
'Hopa' (red)
'Indian Magic' (orange-red)
'Indian Summer' (red)
'Jewelberry' (red)
'Kelsey' (red)
Lancelot® (yellow)

Lists continued on next page

Lists continued from page 133

'Liset' (yellow)
'Louisa' (yellow)
Madonna® (red-orange)
'Mary Potter' (red)
Molten Lava® (red)
'Oekonomierat Echtermeyer' (red)
'Ormiston Roy' (red)
'Pink Spires' (red)
'Prairifire' (red)
'Professor Sprenger' (red-orange)
'Profusion' (red)
'Purple Prince' (red)
'Radiant' (red)
'Red Barron' (red)
'Red Jade' (red)
Red Jewel® (red)
'Red Splendor' (red)
'Robinson' (red)
'Royalty' (red, few)
'Selkirk' (red)
'Sentinel' (red)
'Sinai Fire' (red)
'Snowcloud' (orange-red)
'Snowdrift' (orange-red)
'Sparkler' (red)
'Strawberry Parfait' (yellow-red)
Sugar Tyme® (red)
'Thunderchild' (red)
'Van Eseltine' (yellow)
'Vanguard' (red)
Velvet Pillar® (red, few)
Weeping Candied Apple® (red)
'White Cascade' (yellow)
'Winter Gold' (yellow)
M. baccata 'Jackii' (red)
M. baccata 'Walters' (yellow)
M. floribunda (red)
M. sargentii & cultivars (red)

FLOWERING CRAB CULTIVARS:

'Adams'   flowering crab
ZONE 4
20 feet tall, 20 feet wide

Introduced by Adams Nursery in 1951. Pink bloom, with persistent red fruit. Good disease resistance. Round-shaped crown.

'Adirondack'   flowering crab
ZONE 4
18 feet tall, 10 feet wide

White bloom, red fruit. Good disease resistance. Very dense and upright. *See photograph page 160-61.*

'Beverly'   flowering crab
ZONE 4
20 feet tall, 20 feet wide

Introduced in Europe by Aire den Boer in 1940. Pink in bud, flowers open white, with persistent red fruit. One of the earliest fruiting varieties. Good disease resistance to apple scab, somewhat susceptible to fireblight. Upright growing spreading with age.

'Bob White'   flowering crab
ZONE 4
20 feet tall, 25 feet wide

Introduced in 1876 from the Arnold Arboretum. White bloom, yellow fruit. Reasonable disease resistance. Rounded crown, dense.

Brandywine®   flowering crab
M. 'Branzam'
ZONE 4
20 feet tall, 15 feet wide

Introduced by Lake County Nursery Exchange in 1979. Pink double bloom, yellow non-persistent fruit. Foliage has a dark red cast. Moderate disease resistance. It has been damaged by rust in Arboretum trials. Upright, spreading broadly with age.

'Callaway'   flowering crab
ZONE 4
20 feet tall, 20 feet wide.

A rounded shaped, small canopy. White flowers with dark red fruit. It has excellent resistance to apple scab, with slight susceptibility to fireblight and rust.

Camelot®   flowering crab
M. 'Camzam'
ZONE 4
10 feet tall, 8 feet wide

A very dwarf variety with double, pink bloom. It has good disease resistance.

'Cardinal'   flowering crab
ZONE 4
15 feet tall, 20 feet wide

This variety has a spreading habit and features good disease resistance. The flowers are bright red with a dark purplish red foliage which holds throughout the summer. It has dark red fruit.

Centurion®   flowering crab
M. 'Centzam'
ZONE 4
20 feet tall, 15 feet wide

Introduced by Lake County Nursery Exchange in 1979. Red blossoms, pinkish red persistent fruit. Good disease resistance. This cultivar is an upright grower that broadens with age.

'Coral Cascade' flowering crab
FOR PROTECTED LOCATIONS IN ZONE 4
15 feet tall, 12 feet wide

Introduced by Henry Ross in 1990. Red buds, turning to white blooms, orange-red fruit. Good disease resistance. Noted for its fall fruit. Semi-weeping in habit.

Coralburst® flowering crab
M. 'Coralcole'
HARDY IN ZONE 4, FOR PROTECTED LOCATIONS IN ZONE 3
15 feet tall, 15 feet wide

Pink, semi-double blooms, red fruit. Good disease resistance. Small leaves and compact growth give this cultivar a fine texture.

'David' flowering crab
HARDY IN ZONE 4
12 feet tall, 12 feet wide

Introduced by Mr. Arie den Boer in 1957. Pink bloom fading to white, red persistent fruit. Reasonable disease resistance. Rounded, compact form.

'Dolgo' flowering crab
ZONES 2 TO 4
35 feet tall, 30 feet wide

Introduced by Dr. N.E. Hansen of South Dakota State U. in 1917. White bloom, red, non-persistent fruit ripening early. Used for jelly. Moderate disease resistance in Arboretum trials. Spreading but upright.

'Donald Wyman' flowering crab
ZONE 4
20 feet tall, 25 feet wide

Introduced by the Arnold Arboretum. White bloom, red persistent fruit. Good disease resistance. Rounded form, but spreading with age.

'Doubloons' flowering crab
ZONE 4
15 feet tall, 15 feet wide

Features a dense, upright canopy with good disease resistance. It has double white flowers with yellow persistant fruit.

'Flame' flowering crab
ZONES 2 TO 4
24 feet tall, 20 feet wide

Introduced by the University of Minnesota in 1934. White bloom, red persistent fruit. Apple scab can be a problem. Roundheaded tree.

Golden Raindrops® flowering crab
M. 'Schmidtcutleaf'
ZONE 4
15 feet tall, 12 feet wide

Introduced by J. Frank Schmidt Nursery. White bloom, yellow fruit. Good disease resistance. Upright, cone-shaped. Has unique deeply cut green foliage. In Arboretum trials, this cultivar has suffered winter and fire blight damage.

Guinevere® flowering crab
M. 'Guinzam'
ZONE 4
8 feet tall, 10 feet wide

Off-white bloom, red fruit. Unique, rounded compact form.

Harvest Gold® flowering crab
M. 'Hargozam'
ZONE 4
20 feet tall, 15 feet wide

Introduced by Lake County Nursery Exchange in 1979. White bloom, golden, persistent fruit. Good disease resistance. Upright grower. Research at The Minnesota Landscape Arboretum showed no injury of stem tissue at an extreme minus 32 degrees F. on this cultivar.

'Hopa'
ZONES 2 TO 4
25 feet tall, 20 feet wide

Introduced by Dr. N.E. Hansen of South Dakota State U. in 1920. Rosy-pink bloom, red fruit often used for jelly. Withstands drought. Upright grower, spreading in maturity. It is very susceptible to apple scab, so is generally not recommended.

'Indian Magic'
ZONE 4
15 feet tall, 15 feet wide

Introduced by Simpson Nursery. Dark pink bloom, orangish red persistent fruit. This cultivar suffers from scab, which can cause defoliation in summer. Round, open canopy.

Flowering Crabs and Apples continued on page 185

USING THE PLANT SELECTION GUIDE

Selection of plant material is an art. As such, originality of selections and combinations of plant materials determine the artfulness of the completed landscape. It is important to remember that the lists on the following pages are selective, as there are many other desirable options that can be chosen. Consulting this and other texts and careful observation of plant materials will suggest many other possibilities.

Selection of plant material is made by evaluating desired colors, scale, form, and balance. The plant selection process is defined well by H. Stuart Ortloff and Henry B. Raymore in *The Book of Landscape Design* (1959, 114-115).

As used in the arts, composition is the placing together of objects in such a way that they seem united into a pleasing, balanced, harmonious whole. In creating plant compositions, therefore, the designer is not so much concerned with the worth, rarity or beauty of the individual plants as with how their form, height, texture and color of both foliage and bloom will blend with other plants in the group to create a harmonious whole serving a definite purpose in carrying out the basic landscape pattern.

The plant selection categories:

- Large Trees for Street Planting
- Smaller Trees for Street Planting
- Trees Providing Shade
- Small Ornamental Trees
- Shrubs for Foundation Plantings
- Woody Plants for Borders
- Woody Plants Used as Perennials
- Conifers
- Vines That Cling to Stone or Brick
- Vines That Cover Fences or Trellises
- Woody Plants Having Horizontal Habits
- Woody Plants Having Columnar or Pyramidal Habits
- Woody Plants Having Weeping Habits
- Woody Plants Having Globular Habits
- Woody Plants for Multi-trunked Specimens
- Woody Plants Used as Ground Covers
- Woody Plants Clipped for Formal Hedges
- Woody Plants for Screening
- Woody Plants for Shelterbelts
- Woody Plants with Good Fall Color
- Woody Plants with Interesting Bark
- Trees with Showy Flowers
- Shrubs and Vines with Showy Flowers
- Woody Plants Used for Edible Landscaping
- Woody Plants with Fragrance
- Woody Plants with Attractive Fruit
- Native Woody Plants of the Midwest Region
- Woody Plants for Acidic Soils
- Woody Plants for Dry Sandy Soils
- Woody Plants for Wet Locations
- Shade Tolerant Woody Plants
- Alkaline Tolerant Woody Plants
- Woody Plants for Parking Lots
- Woody Plants for Disturbed Sites
- Woody Plants for Soil Stabilization/Erosion Control
- Growing Height of Trees
     - 75 feet and over
     - 35 to 75 feet
     - 15 to 35 feet
- Growing Height of Shrubs
     - 15 feet and over
     - 10 to 15 feet
     - 6 to 9 feet
     - 3 to 5 feet
     - To 3 feet
- Woody Plants for Barriers
- Woody Plants Tolerant of Air Pollution
- Deer-Resistant Plants
- Woody Plants with Colored Summer Foliage
- Dioecious Plants
- University of Minnesota–Minnesota Landscape Arboretum Introductions

The PHOTO SELECTION GUIDE

Large Trees for Street Planting

Large trees are defined as being over 55 feet. One important factor to consider when choosing street trees is the degree of tolerance to salt. Damage from street salting can be a major problem. Those planting near power lines should consider smaller street trees.

Acer Autumn Blaze™ • Maple
Acer Celebration® • Maple
Acer platanoides & cultivars • Norway maple
Acer rubrum & cultivars • Red maple
Acer saccharum & cultivars • Sugar maple (not salt tolerant)
Celtis occidentalis • Hackberry
Fraxinus americana & cultivars • White ash
Fraxinus mandshurica & cultivars • Manchurian ash
Fraxinus nigra & cultivars • Black ash
Fraxinus pennsylvanica & cultivars • Green ash
Fraxinus quadrangulata • Blue ash
Ginkgo biloba & cultivars • Ginkgo
Gleditsia triacanthos & cultivars • Honeylocust
Gymnocladus dioica & 'Stately Manor' • Kentucky coffee tree
Phellodendron 'His Majesty' • Cork tree
Phellodendron species • Cork tree
Quercus bicolor • Swamp white oak
Quercus palustris • Pin oak
Tilia americana & cultivars • Basswood
Tilia cordata & cultivars • Linden

**Honeylocust (*Gleditsia triacanthos*)
shown as a boulevard tree
near Cedar Lake, Minneapolis.**

Hackberry (*Celtis occidentalis*) a large-growing shade tree. A view looking up into the crown.

Spring bloom on red maple (*Acer rubrum*) on the boulevard by Lake of the Isles, Minneapolis.

Smaller trees for Street Planting

Smaller street trees are defined as growing under 50 feet. Again, salt tolerance can be of major importance.

Acer tataricum • Tatarian maple
Acer tataricum ginnala • Amur maple
Acer triflorum • Three-flowered maple
Acer truncatum • Shantung maple
Aesculus 'Autumn Splendor' • Buckeye
Aesculus glabra • Ohio buckeye
Alnus species & cultivars • Alder
Amelanchier species & cultivars • Shadbush
Caragana arborescens • Siberian peashrub
Carpinus caroliniana • American hornbeam
Crataegus crus-galli & cultivars • Cockspur hawthorn
Crataegus viridis & cultivars • Green hawthorn
Fraxinus pennsylvanica Leprechaun™ • Green ash
Gleditsia Imperial® • Honeylocust
Maackia amurensis • Amur maackia
Magnolia stellata • Star magnolia
Malus cultivars • Crabapples (there are many upright growing cultivars)
Prunus maackii • Amur cherry
Prunus nigra 'Princess Kay' • Ornamental plum
Prunus tomentosa • Nanking cherry
Prunus virginiana 'Schubert' • Ornamental cherry
Pyrus Mountain Frost™ and Prairie Gem® • Ornamental pear
Sorbus alnifolia • Korean mountain ash
Sorbus aucuparia • European mountain ash
Staphylea trifolia • American bladdernut
Syringa pekinensis • Pekin lilac
Syringa reticulata & cultivars • Japanese tree lilac
Tilia 'Glenleven' and 'Harvest Gold' • Linden
Tilia mongolica • Mongolian linden

Spring at the Arboretum with flowering crabapples (*Malus*).

Aesculus 'Autumn Splendor' (buckeye) can be used as a lower-growing street tree.

Trees Providing Shade

Those considering selecting trees for shade purposes should evaluate what other activities will take place in the same area. Questions of whether the planner wants other landscape plants in the same area will determine degree of shade wanted. Those wanting a perfect lawn might not want full shade or want surface roots that will impact on mowing. Whether a tree has characteristics such as shedding fruit, or produces unusually large amounts of leaves in the fall should also be considered.

Acer Autumn Blaze™ and Celebration® • Maple
Acer platanoides & cultivars • Norway maple
Acer rubrum & cultivars • Red maple
Acer saccharum & cultivars • Sugar maple
Aesculus 'Autumn Splendor' • Buckeye
Aesculus glabra • Ohio buckeye
Aesculus hippocastanum • Horsechestnut
Betula alleghaniensis • Yellow birch
Betula lenta • Cherry birch
Betula nigra • River birch
Carya glabra • Pignut
Carya laciniosa • Shellbark hickory
Carya ovata • Shagbark hickory
Catalpa species • Catalpa
Celtis occidentalis • Hackberry
Fraxinus americana & cultivars • White ash
Fraxinus mandshurica & cultivars • Manchurian ash
Fraxinus nigra & cultivars • Black ash
Fraxinus pennsylvanica & cultivars • Green ash
Fraxinus quadrangulata • Blue ash
Ginkgo biloba & cultivars • Ginkgo
Gleditisia triacanthos & cultivars • Honeylocust
Gymnocladus dioica & 'Stately Manor' • Kentucky coffee tree

Sugar maples (*Acer saccharum*) are among the most commonly grown shade trees. Surface roots can be a problem in lawn areas.

Blue ash (*Fraxinus quadrangulata*).

Pin oak (*Quercus palustris*) is one of the most trouble free shade trees.

143

White oak (*Quercus alba*) is a handsome shade tree.

Juglans cinerea • Butternut
Juglans nigra • Black walnut
Magnolia acuminata • Cucumber tree
Ostrya virginiana • Ironwood
Phellodendron 'His Majesty' • Cork tree
Phellodendron amurense • Amur cork tree
Phellodendron sachalinense • Sakhalin cork tree
Quercus alba • White oak
Quercus bicolor • Swamp white oak
Quercus coccinea • Scarlet oak
Quercus ellipsoidalis • Northern pin oak
Quercus imbricaria • Shingle oak
Quercus macrocarpa • Bur oak
Quercus palustris • Pin oak
Quercus rubra • Red oak
Tilia 'Glenleven' • Linden
Tilia americana & cultivars • Basswood
Tilia cordata & cultivars • Littleleaf linden

Amur cork tree (*Phellodendron amurense*) is a good shade tree with distinctive bark.

Kentucky coffee tree (*Gymnocladus dioica*), here in the cultivar 'Stately Manor', is a Minnesota Landscape Arboretum introduction that makes a superior shade tree.

Small Ornamental Trees

Ornamental is defined as having a desired characteristic that adds color from flower, fruit or leaves, good texture from leaves or bark, or seasonal interest. They are usually smaller in scale than shade trees. They can also be large sized shrubs that are pruned and trained as small trees.

Acer tataricum • Tatarian maple
Acer tataricum ginnala & cultivars • Amur maple
Acer triflorum • Three-flowered maple
Acer truncatum • Shantung maple
Aesculus 'Autumn Splendor' • Buckeye
Amelanchier species & cultivars • Serviceberry
Aralia elata • Japanese angelica
Betula fontinalis • Water birch
Betula lenta • Cherry birch
Betula nigra & cultivars • River birch
Betula papyrifera • Paper birch
Betula pendula cultivars • European birch
Betula platyphylla var *japonica* & cultivars • Japanese white birch
Caragana arborescens • Siberian peashrub
Carpinus caroliniana • American Hornbeam
Cercis canadensis 'Northern Strain' • Redbud
Chionanthus virginicus • White fringe tree
Cladrastis lutea • Yellowwood
Cornus alternifolia • Pagoda dogwood
Cotinus obovatus • American smoketree
Crataegus crus-galli & cultivars • Cockspur hawthorn
Crataegus x mordenensis & cultivars • Hawthorn
Crataegus viridis & cultivars • Green hawthorn
Elaeagnus angustifolia • Russian olive
Hydrangea paniculata 'Grandiflora' • Peegee hydrangea
Maackia amurensis • Amur maackia
Magnolia x loebneri & cultivars • Loebner magnolia
Magnolia stellata & cultivars • Star magnolia
Magnolia tripetala • Umbrella magnolia
Malus species & cultivars • Flowering crabs

'Prairifire' crabapple (*Malus* 'Prairifire') is one of the most disease-resistant and best red flowering cultivars.

Star magnolia (*Magnolia stellata*) makes a handsome ornamental tree, especially when in bloom.

Small Ornamental Trees continued

Prunus 'Newport' • Ornamental plum
Prunus americana • Native wild plum
Prunus maackii • Amur cherry
Prunus nigra 'Princess Kay' • Ornamental plum
Prunus pensylvanica & cultivars • Pin cherry
Prunus triloba & cultivars • Flowering plum
Prunus virginiana 'Schubert' • Ornamental cherry
Ptelea trifoliata • Hop tree
Pyrus Mountain Frost™ and Prairie Gem® • Ornamental pear
Pyrus ussuriensis • Ussurian pear
Robinia pseudoacacia 'Purple Robe' • Black locust
Sorbus americana • American mountain ash
Sorbus decora • Showy mountain ash
Staphylea trifolia • American bladdernut
Syringa pekinensis • Pekin lilac
Syringa reticulata & cultivars • Japanese tree lilac
Viburnum lentago • Nannyberry viburnum
Xanthoceras sorbifolium • Yellowhorn

Amur maackia (*Maackia amurensis*) is grown for its very clean, attractive foliage.

'Princess Kay' ornamental plum (*Prunus nigra* 'Princess Kay') is stunning in bloom with its glistening white flowers against the almost black bark.

The 'Northern Strain' redbud (*Cercis canadensis* 'Northern Strain') is a welcome addition to zone 4 landscapes. It can be grown as a small ornamental tree or a multi-stemmed shrub.

Viburnum trilobum (American highbrush cranberry) is stunning in late summer through the fall. It is seen here beautifully contrasted with an ornamental grass at the Minnesota Landscape Arboretum.

Hydrangea arborescens 'Annabelle' is a very floriferous shrub.

HYDRANGEA ARB
'ANNABEL
65889

Shrubs for Foundation Plantings

Important characteristics in shrubs for foundation plantings include compact growth, those needing little maintenance and selected ornamental characteristics. Also a successful foundation planting usually limits the number of different shrubs to only a carefully selected few. Too much contrast or too many varieties can produce a dotted, busy effect.

Abeliophyllum distichum • Abelialeaf
Aronia melanocarpa • Black chokeberry
Berberis thunbergii & cultivars • Japanese barberry
Buxus microphylla koreana • Korean boxwood
Caragana frutex 'Globosa' • Globe Russian peashrub
Caragana pygmaea • Pygmy peashrub
Ceanothus americanus • New Jersey tea
Cornus alba cultivars • Tatarian dogwood
Cornus stolonifera cultivars • Redosier dogwood
Deutzia x lemoinei 'Compacta' • Compact Lemoine deutzia
Dirca palustris • Leatherwood
Eleutherococcus sieboldianus • Five-leaved aralia
Hydrangea species & cultivars • Hydrangea
Hypericum kalmianum • Kalm's St. John's-wort
Juniperus species & cultivars • Juniper
Lonicera x xylosteoides cultivars • Honeysuckle
Lonicera xylosteum 'Emerald Mound' • Honeysuckle
Microbiota decussata • Russian cypress
Philadelphus cultivars • Mockorange
Physocarpus opulifolius & cultivars • Ninebark
Pinus mugo cultivars • Mugo pine
Potentilla fruticosa cultivars • Potentilla
Prunus x cistena • Purpleleaf sandcherry
Rhododendron species & cultivars • Rhododendron and azalea
Rhus aromatica 'Gro-low' • Fragrant sumac
Ribes alpinum • Alpine currant
Rosa cultivars • Rose
Spiraea species & cultivars • Spirea
Stephanandra incisa & 'Crispa' • Stephanandra
Syringa meyeri • Meyer lilac
Syringa cultivars • Lilac (smaller varieties)
Taxus x media 'Taunton' • Yew
Thuja occidentalis cultivars • Arborvitae
Viburnum species & cultivars • Viburnum
Weigela cultivars • Weigela

The ninebark (*Physocarpus opulifolius*) – a very versatile shrub.

Woody Plants for Borders

Shrubs and small trees can be selected for their screening abilities in border plantings. Also ornamental characteristics of woody plants can give a pleasing, well designed finish to a property. They help define our space, provide privacy, prevent areas from being used as footpaths, provide seasonal interest and provide backgrounds for flower borders.

Abeliophyllum distichum • Abelialeaf
Acer tataricum ginnala & cultivars • Amur maple
Amelanchier species & cultivars • Serviceberry
Aralia elata • Japanese angelica
Aralia spinosa • Hercules club
Aronia species & cultivars • Chokeberry
Berberis koreana • Korean barberry
Berberis thunbergii & cultivars • Japanese barberry
Calycanthus floridus • Sweetshrub
Caragana species & cultivars • Peashrub
Ceanothus americanus • New Jersey tea
Chamaebatiaria millefolium • Fernbush
Chamaecyparis species & cultivars • False cypress
Chionanthus virginicus • White fringe tree
Clematis species • Herbaceous-type clematis
Clethra alnifolia • Summersweet
Cornus alba & cultivars • Tatarian dogwood
Cornus alternifolia • Pagoda dogwood
Cornus racemosa • Gray dogwood
Cornus stolonifera & cultivars • Redosier dogwood
Cotinus coggygria cultivars • Smokebush
Cotinus obovatus • American smoketree
Cotoneaster integerrimus • European cotoneaster
Cotoneaster lucidus • Hedge cotoneaster
Cotoneaster multiflorus • Many-flowered cotonester
Crataegus ambigua • Russian hawthorn
Crataegus crus-galli & cultivars • Cockspur hawthorn
Crataegus laevigata & cultivars • English hawthorn
Crataegus x mordenensis & cultivars • Hawthorn
Deutzia x lemoinei • Lemoine deutzia
Dirca palustris • Leatherwood
Eleutherococcus sessiliflorus • Tatarian aralia
Eleutherococcus sieboldianus • Five-leaved aralia
Euonymus alatus & cultivars • Winged euonymus
Euonymus europaeus 'Aldenhamensis' • Euonymus
Euonymus hamiltonianus • Hamilton euonymus
Euonymus nanus • Dwarf euonymus
Exochorda serratifolia 'Northern Pearls' • Pearlbush
Forsythia cultivars • Forsythia
Hamamelis virginiana • Common witchhazel
Hippophae rhamnoides • Sea buckthorn
Hydrangea arborescens & cultivars • Hills-of-snow hydrangea
Hydrangea paniculata & cultivars • Peegee hydrangea
Ilex verticillata & cultivars • Winterberry

'Carefree Wonder' rose. A good rose for landscape use.

Woody Plants for Borders continued

Juniperus species & cultivars • Juniper
Lespedeza bicolor • Shrub bush clover
Lonicera species & cultivars • Honeysuckle
Magnolia x loebneri & cultivars • Loebner magnolia
Magnolia stellata & cultivars • Star magnolia
Philadelphus species & cultivars • Mockorange
Physocarpus opulifolius & cultivars • Ninebark
Potentilla fruticosa cultivars • Potentilla
Prunus x cistena • Purpleleaf sandcherry
Prunus glandulosa & cultivars • Dwarf flowering almond
Prunus tomentosa • Nanking cherry
Prunus triloba & cultivars • Flowering plum
Ptelea trifoliata • Hop tree
Rhododendron species & cultivars • Rhododendron and azalea
Ribes species & cultivars • Alpine currant
Robinia hispida • Rose acacia
Rosa species & hybrids • Rose
Spiraea species & cultivars • Spirea
Staphylea trifolia • American bladdernut
Syringa species & cultivars • Lilac
Tamarix ramosissima cultivars • Tamarisk
Taxus species & cultivars • Yew
Thuja occidentalis & cultivars • Arborvitae
Viburnum species & cultivars • Viburnum
Weigela cultivars • Weigela

An effective use of various conifers in the Lee & Jerry Shannon garden, St. Paul.

Hawthorn (*Crataegus crus-galli 'Inermis'*). A trouble-free, smaller tree with disease-resistance.

Woody Plants Used as Perennials

Some of these plants are usually not viewed as woody plants. They can successfully be used in flower borders, and prairie or woodland plantings.

Amorpha canescens • Lead plant
Amorpha nana • Fragrant false indigo
Artemisia abrotanum • Southernwood
Artemisia frigida • Fringed sagebush
Caryopteris species & cultivars • Caryopteris
Clematis species & cultivars • Clematis
Cytisus hirsutus • Hairy broom
Epigaea repens • Trailing arbutus
Lespedeza bicolor • Shrub bush clover
Linnaea borealis • Twinflower
Paeonia suffruticosa & cultivars • Tree peony
Rosa species & cultivars • Rose
Yucca species & cultivars • Yucca

Conifers

Abies species & cultivars • Fir
Chamaecyparis species & cultivars • False cypress
Juniperus species & cultivars • Juniper
Larix species & cultivars • Larch (deciduous conifer)
Microbiota decussata • Russian cypress
Picea species & cultivars • Spruce
Pinus species & cultivars • Pine
Pseudotsuga menziesii glauca • Douglas fir
Taxodium distichum • Bald cypress (deciduous)
Taxus species & cultivars • Yew
Thuja occidentalis & cultivars • American arborvitae
Tsuga canadensis • Canadian hemlock

Vines That Cling to Stone or Brick

Campsis radicans • Trumpet creeper (still needs support)
Parthenocissus tricuspidata • Boston ivy

Vines that Cover Fences or Trellises

Actinidia species & cultivars • Arctic kiwi
Akebia quinata • Fiveleaf akebia
Ampelopsis brevipedunculata & cultivars • Porcelain berry
Aristolochia macrophylla • Dutchman's pipe
Campsis radicans • Trumpet vine
Celastrus species • Bittersweet
Clematis species & cultivars • Clematis
Lonicera x brownii & cultivars • Honeysuckle
Menispermum canadense • Common moonseed
Parthenocissus inserta • Thicket creeper
Parthenocissus quinquefolia & *engelmannii* • Virginia creeper
Smilax hispida • Bristly greenbrier
Vitis species & cultivars • Grape
Wisteria macrostachys & cultivar • Wisteria

Woody Plants Having Horizontal Habits

Cornus alternifolia • Pagoda dogwood
Crataegus species & cultivars • Hawthorn
Euonymus alatus • Winged euonymus

Woody Plants Having Columnar or Pyramidal Habits

Many woody plants are more naturally pyramidal in growth. One thinks of the spruce, pine and many of the lindens as having this characteristic. However, some woody plants are specifically selected for their columnar or pyramidal shape.

Abies balsamea • Balsam fir
Acer 'Armstrong' • Maple
Acer platanoides 'Columnare' • Norway maple
Acer rubrum 'Autumn Spire' • Red maple
Alnus glutinosa 'Pyramidalis' • European alder
Betula pendula 'Fastigiata' • European birch
Carpinus betulus 'Columnaris', 'Fastigiata' • European hornbeam
Fraxinus pennsylvanica Prairie Spire® • Green ash
Ginkgo biloba 'Fastigiata', Princeton Sentry®, Shangri-la® • Ginkgo
Gleditsia triacanthos Skyline® • Honeylocust
Juniperus scopulorum 'Blue Haven', 'Blue Trail', 'Medora', 'Sutherland', 'Welchii', 'Wichita Blue' • Juniper
Juniperus virginiana 'Canaertii', Emerald Sentinel™ • Juniper
Malus 'Pink Spires', 'Red Jewel' • Flowering crabs
Malus baccata 'Columnaris' • Flowering crab
Picea glauca 'Conica' • Dwarf Alberta spruce
Picea pungens 'Hoopsii' • Colorado spruce
Pinus sylvestris 'Fastigiata' • Scotch pine
Populus 'Tower' • Poplar
Populus alba 'Pyramidalis' • Bolleana poplar
Populus nigra 'Italica' • Lombardy poplar
Pyrus Mountain Frost™ • Ornamental pear
Rhamnus frangula 'Columnaris' • Tall Hedge buckthorn
Thuja occidentalis 'Brandon' & 'Pyramidalis' • Arborvitae
Tilia americana 'Boulevard', 'Fastigiata', Frontyard™, 'Redmond' • Linden

Above left: **Trumpet vine (*Campsis radicans*), a rampant-growing vine that is marginally hardy in zone 4.**

Above right: ***Parthenocissus tricuspidata* (Boston ivy) climbing on the Leon C. Snyder Education Building at The Minnesota Landscape Arboretum.**

***Clematis* 'Huldine', blooms from June to September.**

Woody Plants Having Weeping Habit

Betula pendula & cultivars • European birch
Caragana arborescens 'Pendula', 'Walker' • Siberian peashrub
Larix decidua 'Pendula' • European larch
Malus 'Louisa', 'Oekonmierat Echtermeyer', 'Red Jade', Weeping Candied Apple® • Flowering Crabs
Picea abies 'Pendula' • Norway spruce
Pinus banksiana 'Uncle Fogy' • Jack pine
Pinus strobus 'Pendula' • White pine
Salix 'Prairie Cascade' • Willow
Salix caprea 'Pendula' • Pussy willow
Salix x pendulina • Wisconsin weeping willow
Salix x sepulcralis chrysocoma • Niobe weeping willow
Tsuga canadensis 'Pendula' • Canada hemlock
Ulmus davidiana 'Camperdownii' • David elm

Woody Plants Having Globular Habit

Abies lasiocarpa 'Green Globe' • Arizona corkbark fir
Acer platanoides 'Globosum' • Norway maple
Acer saccharum 'Globosum' • Sugar maple
Caragana frutex 'Globosa' • Russian peashrub
Lonicera x xylosteoides 'Miniglobe' • Honeysuckle
Lonicera xylosteum 'Emerald Mound' • Honeysuckle
Picea abies 'Nidiformis', 'Pumila' • Norway spruce
Picea pungens 'Globosa' • Colorado spruce
Pinus mugo 'Compacta' • Swiss mountain pine
Pinus resinosa 'Wissota' • Norway pine
Thuja occidentalis 'Hetz Midget', 'Little Giant', 'Woodwardii' • American arborvitae

Woody Plants for Multi-trunked Specimens

Acer tataricum • Tatarian maple
Acer tataricum ginnala & cultivars • Amur maple
Alnus rugosa • Speckled alder
Amelanchier species & cultivars • Serviceberry
Betula species & cultivars • Birch
Carpinus species & cultivars • Hornbeam
Cercidiphyllum japonicum • Katsura tree
Cercis canadensis 'Northern Strain' • Redbud
Cornus alternifolia • Pagoda dogwood
Elaeagnus angustifolia • Russian olive
Ostrya virginiana • Ironwood
Prunus maackii • Amur cherry
Sorbus americana • American mountain ash
Staphlea trifolia • American bladdernut
Syringa species & cultivars • Lilac

Picea abies 'Acrocona' (Norway spruce) in winter garb.

A pendulous form of European larch (*Larix decidua*) in the Lee & Jerry Shannon garden, St. Paul.

Woody Plants Used as Ground Covers

The successful use of ground covers in the North is a challenge. More temperate regions have no difficulty selecting a wide range of plant material for use as ground covers. Northern gardeners have to be more selective. Determining factors in the North include how exposed the site is and whether it will receive reliable snowcover. Many are also very specific as to what soil types they need. Many of these ground covers are not dense enough to eliminate the necessity of periodic weeding. Especially in the North, smaller growing shrubs are often planted as ground covers.

Andromeda polifolia • Bog rosemary
Arctostaphylos uva-ursi • Bearberry
Caragana brevifolia • Shortleaf peashrub
Caragana frutex 'Globosa' • Russian peashrub
Caragana pygmaea • Pygmy peashrub
Comptonia peregrina • Sweet fern
Diervilla lonicera • Bush honeysuckle
Diervilla sessilifolia • Southern bush honeysuckle
Euonymus fortunei cultivars • Wintercreeper
Euonymus obovatus • Running euonymus
Gaultheria hispidula • Creeping snowberry
Gaultheria procumbens • Wintergreen
Gaylussacia brachycera • Box huckleberry
Juniperus species & cultivars • Juniper
Lycium species • Matrimony vine
Mahonia repens • Mahonia
Pachysandra species & cultivars • Pachysandra
Parthenocissus quinquefolia • Virginia creeper
Paxistima canbyi • Paxistima
Potentilla tridentata • Wineleaf potentilla
Rhus species & cultivars • Sumac
Robinia hispida • Rose acacia
Rosa cultivars • Rose
Sorbaria sorbifolia • False spirea
Spiraea cultivars • Spirea
Stephanandra incisa & cultivars • Cutleaf stephanandra
Symphoricarpos species & cultivars • Snowberry & coralberry
Vaccinium vitis-idaea • Cowberry
Vinca minor • Periwinkle
Xanthorhiza simplicissima • Yellowroot

Pachysandra (*Pachysandra terminalis*), an attractive ground cover, can be used wherever there is reliable snow cover in zone 4.

Amur cherry (*Prunus maackii*) as a clump specimen. Its distinctive bark makes it a landscape feature throughout the year.

155

Woody Plants Clipped for Formal Hedges

Characteristics to look for in woody plant hedging include how adaptable the plant material is to shearing or pruning, branching characteristics, rate of growth, and pest and disease resistance. What is acceptable or even desirable growth characteristics for a few plants, soon becomes an irritation if applied to the monoculture of hedges.

Acer tataricum ginnala & cultivars • Amur maple
Berberis thunbergii & cultivars • Japanese barberry
Buxus microphylla koreana • Korean boxwood
Caragana brevifolia • Shortleaf peashrub
Caragana frutex 'Globosa' • Globe Russian peashrub
Caragana pygmaea • Pygmy peashrub
Cotoneaster lucidus • Hedge cotoneaster
Ligustrum species & cultivars • Privet
Lonicera tatarica 'Zabelii' • Honeysuckle
Lonicera x xylosteoides 'Clavey's Dwarf' • Honeysuckle
Lonicera xylosteum 'Hedge King' • Honeysuckle
Physocarpus opulifolius 'Nanus' • Dwarf ninebark
Picea glauca • White spruce
Rhamnus frangula 'Columnaris' • Tall hedge buckthorn
Ribes alpinum & cultivars • Alpine currant
Thuja occidentalis & cultivars • Arborvitae
Tsuga canadensis • Hemlock
Viburnum opulus 'Nanum' • European highbush cranberry
Viburnum trilobum 'Alfredo', 'Compactum' • American
   highbush cranberry

Woody Plants for Screening

There are many other woody plants that can be used for screening purposes. Density, texture and seasonal characteristics become most important when choosing woody plants for screening.

Abies species • Fir
Acer campestre • Hedge maple
Acer platanoides & cultivars • Norway maple
Acer tataricum • Tatarian maple
Acer tataricum ginnala & cultivars • Amur maple
Caragana arborescens • Siberian peashrub
Carpinus species & cultivars • Hornbeam
Euonymus alatus • Winged euonymus
Hydrangea arborescens & cultivars • Hydrangea
Juniperus scopulorum & cultivars • Juniper
Juniperus virginiana & cultivars • Juniper
Larix species • Larch
Lonicera species & cultivars • Honeysuckle
Philadelphus species & cultivars • Mockorange
Picea species & cultivars • Spruce
Pinus species & cultivars • Pine
Rhus species & cultivars • Sumac
Ribes aureum • Golden currant
Salix purpurea 'Nana' • Dwarf arctic willow
Syringa species & cultivars • Lilac
Thuja occidentalis & cultivars • Arborvitae
Viburnum species & cultivars • Viburnum

Woody Plants for Shelterbelts

Hardiness, the capabilities of withstanding drought, a fast growth rate, and trouble-free culture are some of the characteristics of woody plants used for this purpose.

Acer negundo • Boxelder
Acer saccharinum • Silver maple
Acer tataricum ginnala • Amur maple
Caragana arborescens • Siberian peashrub
Caragana frutex • Russian peashrub
Caragana microphylla • Littleleaf peashrub
Celtis occidentalis • Hackberry
Cornus stolonifera 'Baileyi' • Dogwood
Cotoneaster lucidus • Hedge cotoneaster
Elaeagnus angustifolia • Russian olive
Fraxinus pennsylvanica • Green ash
Juniperus scopulorum • Rocky Mountain juniper
Juniperus virginiana • Red cedar
Larix decidua • European larch
Lonicera tatarica & cultivars • Honeysuckle
Malus baccata • Siberian crabapple
Picea glauca densata • Black Hills spruce
Picea pungens • Colorado spruce
Populus species & cultivars • Cottonwood, poplar
Prunus americana • Wild plum
Prunus virginiana 'Schubert' • Ornamental cherry
Rhus species • Sumac
Salix alba • White willow
Salix pentandra • Laurel willow
Salix purpurea & cultivars • Purple osier willow
Shepherdia species • Buffaloberry
Syringa x chinensis • Chinese lilac
Syringa vulgaris • Common lilac
Thuja occidentalis • Arborvitae
Viburnum dentatum • Arrowwood

Clockwise, top left:

Many different spirea can be used in mass plantings or as ground covers. Here, *Spiraea japonica* 'Froebelii'.

Caragana arborescens (Siberian peashrub) is often used in shelterbelt plantings.

Forsythia 'Northern Sun', another Arboretum introduction, can be used in a shrub border for screening.

Another photograph showing the effective use of conifers for screening at the Lee & Jerry Shannon garden in St. Paul. An additional benefit of these conifers is to help establish a very beneficial microclimate allowing the Shannons to grow a wide variety of plant material in their landscape.

The many forms of prostrate juniper (*Juniperus*) can be used for ground covers.

Alpine currant (*Ribes alpinum*), here combined effectively with the perennial, lady's mantle, near the Arboretum's herb garden. It is one of the most used shrubs for hedges.

Plants with Good Fall Color

Acer rubrum & cultivars • Red maple (red, yellow)
Acer saccharum & cultivars • Sugar maple (red, yellow)
Acer spicatum • Mountain maple (red)
Acer tataricum • Tatarian maple (red, yellow)
Acer tataricum ginnala & cultivars • Amur maple (orange, red)
Aesculus 'Autumn Splendor' • Buckeye (orange-red)
Amelanchier species & cultivars • Serviceberry (red, yellow)
Aronia species & cultivars • Chokeberry (red)
Berberis koreana • Korean barberry (red)
Berberis thunbergii & cultivars • Japanese barberry (red)
Betula species & cultivars • Birch (yellow)
Carpinus caroliniana • American hornbeam (orange, red)
Carya species • Hickory (yellow)
Celastrus species • Bittersweet (yellow)
Chionanthus virginicus • White fringe tree (yellow)
Cladrastis lutea • Yellowwood (yellow)
Cotinus obovatus • American smoke tree (orange)
Diervilla lonicera • Bush honeysuckle (red)
Dirca palustris • Leatherwood (yellow)
Euonymus species & cultivars • Euonymus (red, pink)
Fraxinus americana & cultivars • White ash (purple, yellow)
Fraxinus nigra & cultivars • Black ash (yellow)
Ginkgo biloba & cultivars • Ginkgo (yellow)
Hamamelis virginiana • Witchhazel (yellow)
Larix laricina • Tamarack (yellow)
Nyssa sylvatica • Sour gum (red)
Parthenocissus quinquefolia • Virginia creeper (red)
Parthenocissus tricuspidata • Boston ivy (red)
Populus species & cultivars • Poplar, aspen, cottonwood (yellow)
Potentilla tridentata • Wineleaf potentilla (wine-red)
Prunus pensylvanica • Pin cherry (red)
Pyrus ussuriensis • Ussurian pear (red)
Quercus alba • White oak (purple)
Quercus ellipsoidalis • Northern pin oak (red)
Quercus palustris • Pin oak (red)
Rhus species & cultivars • Sumac (red, yellow)
Sorbus species & cultivars • Mountain-ash (red, yellow)
Taxodium distichum • Bald cypress (yellow)
Vaccinium species & cultivars • Blueberry (red)
Viburnum species & cultivars • Viburnum (red)
Xanthorhiza simplicissima • Yellowroot (yellow)

Many woody plants are effective in the fall with colorful berries. Here the American highbush cranberry (*Viburnum trilobum*) combines colorful fruit with good fall foliage.

Sugar maples (*Acer saccharum*) are famed for their fall color. Colors range from reds, oranges, to yellow.

Woody Plants with Interesting Bark and Twigs

(very noticeable in winter)

Acer griseum • Paperbark maple (reddish brown)
Acer pensylvanicum • Striped maple (striped)
Acer rubrum & cultivars • Red maple (gray)
Alnus rugosa • Speckled alder (speckled)
Amelanchier arborea • Downy serviceberry (bluish gray)
Amelanchier canadensis • Shad (gray)
Betula fontinalis • Water birch (reddish brown)
Betula lenta • Cherry birch (reddish brown)
Betula nigra & cultivars • River birch (exfoliating reddish brown)
Betula papyrifera • Paper birch (exfoliating white)
Betula pendula & cultivars • European birch (white)
Betula platyphylla japonica & cultivars • Japanese white birch (white)
Carpinus caroliniana • American hornbeam (gray)
Carya ovata • Shagbark hickory (shaggy brown)
Cladrastis lutea • Yellowwood (gray)
Cornus alba & cultivars • Tatarian dogwood (red, yellow twigs)
Cornus racemosa • Gray dogwood (gray twigs)
Cornus stolonifera • Redosier dogwood (red, yellow twigs)
Euonymus alatus & cultivars • Winged euonymus (winged twigs)
Gymnocladus dioicus & cultivar • Kentucky coffee tree (ridged bark)
Kerria japonica • Kerria (bright green twigs)
Phellodendron amurense & cultivars • Amur cork tree (corky)
Pinus resinosa • Red pine (reddish brown)
Pinus sylvestris • Scotch pine (reddish brown)
Populus alba & cultivars • White poplar (greenish white)
Populus tremuloides • Quaking aspen (gray-green)
Prunus maackii • Amur cherry (reddish brown)
Quercus macrocarpa • Bur oak (ridged bark)
Rhus typhina • Staghorn sumac (velvety twigs)
Salix species & cultivars • Willow (yellow, red)
Tilia americana 'Redmond' • Linden (reddish twigs)

River birch (*Betula nigra*) features exfoliating brown bark.

Even trees not noted for good fall color, such as this green ash (*Fraxinus pennsylvanica*), can add much to the fall landscape.

Conifers are usually not thought of as providing fall color, but the deciduous evergreen, Japanese larch (*Larix kaempferi*) has good yellow fall color.

Trees with Showy Flowers

Acer rubrum & cultivars • Red maple
Aesculus species & cultivars • Buckeye and horse chestnut
Amelanchier x grandiflora • Apple serviceberry
Amelanchier laevis • Allegheny serviceberry
Aralia elata • Japanese angelica
Catalpa species • Catalpa
Cercis canadensis 'Northern Strain' • Redbud
Chionanthus virginicus • White fringe tree
Cladrastis lutea • Yellowwood
Cornus alternifolia • Pagoda dogwood
Crataegus species & cultivars • Hawthorn
Magnolia species & cultivars • Magnolia
Malus species & cultivars • Flowering crabs and apples
Prunus species & cultivars • Cherry, apricot, plum
Pyrus ussuriensis • Ussurian pear
Robinia pseudoacacia • Black locust
Sorbus species & cultivars • Mountain-ash
Syringa pekinensis • Pekin lilac
Syringa reticulata & cultivars • Japanese tree lilac
Xanthoceras sorbifolium • Yellowhorn

'Adirondack' crabapple (*Malus* 'Adirondack').

Merrill magnolia's (*Magnolia x loebneri* 'Merrill')
beautiful white spring blossoms.

Shrubs and Vines With Showy Flowers

Abeliophyllum distichum • Abelialeaf
Amelanchier species & cultivars • Serviceberry
Aronia species & cultivars • Chokeberry
Berberis koreana • Korean barberry
Calycanthus floridus • Sweetshrub
Campsis radicans • Trumpet vine
Caragana arborescens • Siberian peashrub
Caryopteris x clandonensis • Blue spirea
Cephalanthus occidentalis • Buttonbush
Chionanthus virginicus • White fringe tree
Clematis species & cultivars • Clematis
Clethra alnifolia & cultivars • Summersweet
Cotinus coggygria & cultivars • Smokebush
Cotoneaster multiflorus • Many-flowered cotoneaster
Daphne species & cultivars • Daphne
Deutzia x lemoinei • Lemoine deutzia
Epigaea repens • Trailing arbutus
Exochorda serratifolia 'Northern Pearls' • Pearlbush
Forsythia cultivars • Forsythia
Genista tinctoria • Dyer's greenweed
Hamamelis virginiana • Witchhazel
Hydrangea species & cultivars • Hydrangea
Hypericum species • St. John's-wort
Lonicera species & cultivars • Honeysuckle
Magnolia species & cultivars • Magnolia
Paeonia suffruticosa & cultivars • Tree peony
Philadelphus species & cultivars • Mockorange
Potentilla fruticosa & cultivars • Potentilla
Prunus species & cultivars • Cherry
Rhododendron species & cultivars • Rhododendron or azalea
Ribes odoratum • Clove currant
Robinia hispida • Rose acacia
Rosa species & cultivars • Rose
Rubus odoratus • Flowering raspberry
Spiraea species & cultivars • Spirea
Syringa species & cultivars • Lilac
Tamarix ramosissima & cultivars • Tamarisk
Viburnum species & cultivars • Viburnum
Vinca minor • Periwinkle
Weigela cultivars • Weigela
Yucca species • Yucca
Wisteria macrostachya & cultivar • Wisteria

Clematis 'Dr Ruppel', a showy clematis.

Hydrangea arborescens 'Annabelle' with daylilies.

Rosa 'Robusta', one of the many roses that can be used as shrubs.

Woody Plants Used for Fragrance

Abies balsamea • Balsam fir
Amelanchier alnifolia & cultivars • Saskatoon serviceberry
Artemisia abrotanum • Southernwood
Calycanthus floridus • Sweetshrub
Chamaebatiaria millefolium • Fernbush
Chionanthus virginicus • White fringe tree
Clematis heracleifolia var. davidiana • Fragrant tube clematis
Clethra alnifolia & cultivars • Summersweet
Comptonia peregrina • Sweet fern
Daphne species & cultivars • Daphne
Elaeagnus angustifolia • Russian olive
Epigaea repens • Trailing arbutus
Malus ionensis • Prairie crabapple
Philadelphus species & cultivars • Mockorange
Rhododendron species & cultivars • Selected azalea and rhododendron
Ribes odoratum • Clove currant
Robinia pseudoacacia • Black locust
Rosa species & cultivars • Selected rose
Syringa species & cultivars • Lilac
Tilia species & cultivars • Linden

Woody Plants Used for Edible Landscaping

Actinidia species & cultivars • Kiwi (very small fruit)
Amelanchier species & cultivars • Shadbush (small edible berries)
Aronia species & cultivars • Chokeberry (not much interest in North America)
Carya species • Hickories & pecans
Corylus species • Hazels
Ginkgo biloba • Ginkgo (odoriferous nuts on female tree)
Juglans species • Walnuts
Malus species & cultivars • Flowering crabs & apples
Morus species • Mulberry
Prunus species & cultivars • Cherries, plums, apricots
Pyrus cultivars • Pears
Ribes cultivars • Currants, gooseberries
Rubus cultivars • Raspberries, blackberries
Sambucus species & cultivars • Elderberries
Vaccinium cultivars • Blueberries
Vitis cultivars • Grapes

Summersweet (*Clethra alnifolia*) in bloom.

'Asessippi' lilac (*Syringa x hyacinthiflora* 'Asessippi').

'Dropmore Scarlet' honeysuckle (*Lonicera x brownii* 'Dropmore Scarlet'), an attractive vine.

163

Woody Plants with Attractive Fruit

Abies species & cultivars • Fir (cones)

Acer tataricum ginnala & cultivars • Amur maple (red samaras)

Aesculus glabra • Ohio buckeye (shiny brown nuts in spiny case)

Aesculus hippocastanum • Horsechestnut (shiny brown nuts in spiny case)

Amelanchier species & cultivars • Shadbush (red berries)

Ampelopsis brevipedunculata & cultivars • Porcelain berry (multicolor)

Aronia species & cultivars • Chokeberry (red, purple berries)

Berberis species & cultivars • Barberry (red berries)

Catalpa species • Catalpa (dark brown long pods)

Celastrus species • Bittersweet (orangish red fruit)

Clematis species & cultivars • Clematis (plumed achenes)

Cornus species & cultivars • Dogwood (red, purple, white berries)

Cotinus species & cultivars • Smokebush (plumed fruit)

Cotoneaster species & cultivars • Cotoneaster (red berries)

Crataegus species & cultivars • Hawthorn (red berries)

Euonymus species & cultivars • Euonymus (orange, red pods)

Exochorda serratifolia 'Northern Pearls' • Pearlbush (brown winter capsules)

Gaultheria procumbens • Wintergreen (red berries)

Gymnocladus dioica • Kentucky coffee tree (brown pods)

Hydrangea species & cultivars • Hydrangea (dried, spent blooms)

Ilex verticillata & cultivars • Winterberry (red berries)

Juniperus species & cultivars • Juniper (bluish silver berries)

Lonicera species & cultivars • Honeysuckle (red berries)

Magnolia acuminata • Cucumber tree (green conelike)

Magnolia tripetala • Umbrella magnolia (reddish pink fruit)

Malus species & cultivars • Crabapples

Mitchella repens • Partridgeberry (red berries)

Picea species & cultivars • Spruce (cones)

Pinus species & cultivars • Pine (cones)

Prunus species & cultivars • Cherry (red, purple berries with stones)

Ptelea trifoliata • Hoptree (winged samaras)

Rhus species & cultivars • Sumac (hairy red)

Robinia pseudoacacia • Black locust (dark brown pod)

Rosa species & cultivars • Rose (red, orange hip)

Sorbus species & cultivars • Mountain ash (red berries)

Staphylea trifolia • Bladdernut (brown capsule)

Symphoricarpos species & cultivars • Snowberry (white, red berries)

Viburnum species & cultivars • Viburnum (red, purple berries)

Clockwise, top left:

American highbush cranberry (*Viburnum trilobum*) in late summer fruit.

Korean barberry (*Berberis koreana*), a spreading shrub that has attractive bloom and fruit.

'Professor Sprenger' crabapple (*Malus*), one of our best flowering crabs. It is featured at the entrance of the Leon C. Snyder Education Building at the Arboretum.

Fruit on Cockspur hawthorn (*Crataegus crus-galli*).

Raspberries (*Rubus*) grown as a screen and property divider (almost a hedge) at the Lee & Jerry Shannon garden, St. Paul.

'McIntosh' apples (*Malus*) grown as an espalier in the Home Demonstration Garden at The Minnesota Landscape Arboretum.

Native Woody Plants of the Midwest Region

Dr. Snyder in his *Native Plants for Northern Gardens* (1991, 1) lists reasons for using native plants in landscapes: "One of the primary reasons is that native plants have the further advantage of being adapted, through centuries of growth, to our climatic conditions. They are also better able to resist the effects of our native insects and diseases. Another reason is maintained landscapes featuring native plants also blend into their natural surroundings better than those planted with introduced species."

Abies balsamea • Balsam fir
Abies concolor • Concolor fir
Acer negundo • Boxelder
Acer rubrum • Red maple
Acer saccharinum • Silver maple
Acer saccharum • Sugar maple
Acer spicatum • Mountain maple
Aesculus glabra • Ohio buckeye
Alnus rugosa • Speckled alder
Amelanchier species • Serviceberry
Amorpha species • Lead plant & false indigo
Arctostaphylos uva-ursi • Bearberry
Aristolochia macrophylla • Dutchman's pipe
Aronia species • Chokeberry
Betula alleghaniensis • Yellow birch
Betula nigra • River birch
Betula papyrifera • Paper birch
Carpinus caroliniana • American hornbeam
Carya cordiformis • Bitternut
Carya laciniosa • Shellbark hickory
Carya ovata • Shagbark hickory
Catalpa speciosa • Catalpa
Ceanothus americanus • New Jersey tea
Ceanothus ovatus • Inland ceanothus
Celastrus scandens • American bittersweet
Celtis occidentalis • Hackberry
Cephalanthus occidentalis • Buttonbush
Cercis canadensis • Redbud
Chamaedaphne calyculata • Leatherleaf
Chionanthus virginicus • White fringe tree
Cladrastis lutea • Yellowwood
Clematis virginiana • Virgin's bower
Comptonia peregrina • Sweet fern
Cornus alternifolia • Pagoda dogwood
Cornus racemosa • Gray dogwood
Cornus stolonifera • Redosier dogwood
Corylus americana • American hazel
Cotinus obovatus • American smoketree
Crataegus crus-galli • Cockspur hawthorn
Crataegus mollis • Downy hawthorn
Crataegus punctata • Dotted hawthorn
Diervilla lonicera • Bush honeysuckle
Dirca palustris • Leatherwood
Elaeagnus commutata • Silverberry
Epigaea repens • Trailing arbutus
Euonymus atropurpureus • Wahoo
Fraxinus americana • White ash
Fraxinus nigra • Black ash
Fraxinus pennsylvanica • Green ash
Fraxinus quadrangulata • Blue ash
Gaultheria hispidula • Creeping snowberry
Gaultheria procumbens • Wintergreen
Gaylussacia brachycera • Box huckleberry
Gleditsia triacanthos • Honeylocust
Gymnocladus dioica • Kentucky coffee tree

Native Woody Plants of the Midwest Region continued

Hamamelis virginiana • Common witchhazel
Hydrangea arborescens • Hills-of-snow hydrangea
Hypericum kalmianum • Kalm's St. John's-wort
Hypericum prolificum • Shrubby St. John's-wort
Ilex verticillata • Winterberry
Juglans cinerea • Butternut
Juglans nigra • Black walnut
Juniperus communis • Common juniper
Juniperus horizontalis • Creeping juniper
Juniperus scopulorum • Rocky Mountain juniper
Juniperus virginiana • Red cedar
Kalmia polifolia • Bog laurel
Larix laricina • Tamarack
Ledum groenlandicum • Labrador tea
Lonicera dioica • Limber honeysuckle
Magnolia acuminata • Cucumber tree
Magnolia tripetala • Umbrella magnolia
Mahonia repens • Creeping mahonia
Malus coronaria • Wild sweet crabapple
Malus ioensis • Prairie crabapple
Menispermum canadense • Common moonseed
Mitchellia repens • Partridgeberry
Morus rubra • Red mulberry
Nemopanthus mucronatus • Mountain holly
Ostrya virginiana • Ironwood
Parthenocissus inserta • Woodbine
Parthenocissus quinquefolia • Virginia creeper
Physocarpus opulifolius • Common ninebark
Picea glauca • White spruce
Picea mariana • Black spruce
Picea pungens • Colorado spruce
Pinus banksiana • Jack pine
Pinus ponderosa scopulorum • Ponderosa pine
Pinus resinosa • Red pine
Pinus strobus • White pine
Populus deltoides • Cottonwood
Populus tremuloides • Quaking aspen
Potentilla fruticosa • Potentilla
Potentilla tridentata • Wineleaf potentilla
Prunus americana • Wild plum
Prunus besseyi • Western sandcherry
Prunus nigra • Canada plum
Prunus pensylvanica • Pin cherry
Prunus serotina • Black cherry
Prunus virginiana • Chokecherry
Pseudotsuga menziesii glauca • Douglas fir
Ptelea trifoliata • Hop tree
Quercus alba • White oak
Quercus bicolor • Swamp white oak
Quercus coccinea • Scarlet oak
Quercus ellipsoidalis • Northern pin oak
Quercus macrocarpa • Bur oak
Quercus palustris • Pin oak
Quercus rubra • Red oak
Rhus aromatica • Fragrant sumac
Rhus glabra • Smooth sumac
Rhus trilobata • Skunkbush sumac
Rhus typhina • Staghorn sumac
Ribes odoratum • Clove currant
Robinia hispida • Rose acacia
Robinia pseudoacacia • Black locust
Rosa blanda • Smooth wild rose
Rubus parviflorus • Thimbleberry

Balsam fir (*Abies balsamea*) is a popular Christmas tree because of its fragrance and good needle retention.

Salix discolor • Pussy willow
Sambucus canadensis • American elder
Sambucus pubens • Scarlet elder
Shepherdia argentea • Silver buffaloberry
Shepherdia canadensis • Russet buffaloberry
Smilax hispida • Bristly greenbrier
Sorbus americana • American mountain ash
Sorbus decora • Showy mountain ash
Staphylea trifolia • American bladdernut
Symphoricarpos albus • Snowberry
Symphoricarpos orbiculatus • Coralberry
Taxus canadensis • Canadian yew
Thuja occidentalis • American arborvitae
Tilia americana • Basswood
Tsuga canadensis • Canadian hemlock
Vaccinium vitis-idaea • Cowberry
Viburnum species • Viburnums
Vitis riparia • Riverbank grap

Woody Plants for Acidic Soils

Those choosing plants from this list who do not have acidic soils must amend their soils so they become acidic. This can be a major task before and after planting.

Abies balsamea • Balsam fir
Acer rubrum & cultivars • Red maple
Acer spicatum • Mountain maple
Acer tataricum ginnala & cultivars • Amur maple
Andromeda polifolia • Bog rosemary
Arctostaphylos uva-ursi • Bearberry
Aronia melanocarpa • Black chokeberry
Calluna vulgaris & cultivars • Scotch heather
Carpinus caroliniana • American hornbeam
Ceanothus americanus • New Jersey tea
Chamaedaphne calyculata • Leatherleaf
Chionanthus virginicus • White fringe tree
Clethra alnifolia • Summersweet
Comptonia peregrina • Sweet fern
Cornus alternifolia • Pagoda dogwood
Daphne x burkwoodii • Burkwood daphne
Epigaea repens • Trailing arbutus
Gaultheria hispidula • Creeping snowberry
Gaultheria procumbens • Wintergreen
Gaylussacia brachycera • Box huckleberry
Ilex verticillata • Winterberry
Kalmia polifolia • Bog laurel
Ledum groenlandicum • Labrador tea
Linnaea borealis • Twinflower
Mitchella repens • Partridgeberry
Nyssa sylvatica • Sour gum
Potentilla tridentata • Wineleaf potentilla
Quercus coccinea • Scarlet oak
Quercus palustris • Pin oak
Rhododendron species & cultivars • Rhododendron or azalea
Vaccinium species & cultivars • Blueberry & others
Xanthoceras sorbifolium • Yellowhorn
Xanthorhiza simplicissima • Yellowroot

Woody Plants for Dry Sandy Soils

Xeroscape gardening (gardening using little supplemental watering) is very important in some regions of North America. Also, some landscape conditions will receive less care including less supplemental water in droughty periods. Woody plants again vary greatly in the degree to which they will thrive in or survive these conditions.

Acer negundo • Boxelder
Amorpha canescens • Lead plant
Arctostaphylos uva-ursi • Bearberry
Aronia melanocarpa • Black chokeberry
Artemisia abrotanum • Southernwood
Betula populifolia • Gray birch
Caragana species & cultivars • Peashrub
Catalpa speciosa • Catalpa
Ceanothus americanus • New Jersey tea
Celtis occidentalis • Hackberry
Chamaebatiaria millefolium • Fernbush
Comptonia peregrina • Sweet fern
Elaeagnus angustifolia • Russian olive
Epigaea repens • Trailing arbutus
Fraxinus pennsylvanica & cultivars • Green ash
Gaultheria procumbens • Wintergreen
Gleditisia triacanthos & cultivars • Honeylocust
Halimodendron halodendron • Siberian salt tree
Hippophae rhamnoides • Sea buckthorn
Hypericum species • St. John's-wort
Juniperus scopulorum, J. squamata, J. virginiana & cultivars • Juniper
Malus ioensis • Prairie crabapple
Phellodendron amurense • Amur cork tree
Picea glauca • White spruce
Pinus banksiana • Jack pine
Prunus besseyi • Western sandcherry
Quercus ellipsoidalis • Northern pin oak
Quercus imbricaria • Shingle oak
Quercus macrocarpa • Bur oak
Quercus muehlenbergii • Chinkapin oak
Rhus species & cultivars • Sumac
Shepherdia argentea • Silver buffaloberry
Staphylea trifolia • American bladdernut
Tamarix ramossisima & cultivars • Tamarisk
Yucca glauca • Soapweed

Clockwise, top left:

Leatherwood (*Dirca palustris*), a native shrub that should be used more.

Wild plum (*Prunus americana*) perfumes the midwest landscape early in the spring. It is a good pollinator for cultivated plums.

Yellowwood (*Cladrastis lutea*) needs a protected location in the North.

Black chokeberry (*Aronia melanocarpa*) is a small shrub that should be used more often.

Rhus typhina (Staghorn sumac) has very attractive foliage and velvety branching, here in cultivar 'Laciniata'.

A shad or Juneberry (*Amelanchier laevis*) at the Arboretum.

White oak (*Quercus alba*) is one of the best native oaks.

Woody Plants for Wet Locations

Wet locations are defined as having periodic (usually spring) excess water. Woody plants are not water plants, so none will grow in aquatic conditions. Some, however, are much more tolerant of excess water than others in this listing.

Abies balsamea • Balsam fir
Acer rubrum & cultivars • Red maple
Alnus glutinosa • European alder
Alnus incana • White alder
Alnus rugosa • Speckled alder
Andromeda polifolia • Bog rosemary
Betula nigra & cultivars • River birch
Betula pumila • Swamp birch
Cephalanthus occidentalis • Buttonbush
Chamaedaphne calyculata • Leatherleaf
Cornus olbiqua • Silky dogwood
Cornus stolonifera & cultivars • Redosier dogwood
Fraxinus nigra & cultivars • Black ash
Ilex verticillata & cultivars • Winterberry
Kalmia polifolia • Bog laurel
Larix laricina • Tamarack
Ledum groenlandicum • Labrador tea
Nyssa sylvatica • Sour gum
Picea mariana • Black spruce
Populus species & cultivars • Poplar, aspen, cottonwood
Quercus bicolor • Swamp white oak
Rhododendron canadense • Rhodora
Salix species & cultivars • Willow
Sambucus canadensis • American elder
Taxodium distichum • Bald cypress
Thuja occidentalis & cultivars • Arborvitae
Viburnum lentago • Nannyberry
Viburnum trilobum • American highbush cranberry
Xanthorhiza simplicissima • Yellowroot

Shadbush (*Amelanchier*) and other woody plants give a wash of color in early spring in a naturalistic setting at the Arboretum.

Shade Tolerant Woody Plants

Abeliophyllum disticum • Abelialeaf
Abies balsamea • Balsam fir
Acer pensylvanicum • Striped maple
Acer spicatum • Mountain Maple
Acer tataricum ginnala & cultivars • Amur maple
Amelanchier species & cultivars • Serviceberry
Aralia hispida • Bristly sarsaparilla
Berberis koreana • Korean barberry
Buxus microphylla koreana • Korean boxwood
Calycanthus floridus • Sweetshrub
Carpinus caroliniana • American hornbeam
Celastrus scandens • Bittersweet
Clethra alnifolia • Summersweet
Cornus species & cultivars • Dogwood
Diervilla lonicera • Bush honeysuckle
Dirca palustris • Leatherwood
Eleutherococcus sieboldianus • Five-leaved aralia
Epigaea repens • Trailing arbutus
Euonymus fortunei & cultivars • Wintercreeper
Gaultheria procumbens • Wintergreen
Hamamelis virginiana • Witchhazel
Linnaea borealis • Twinflower
Lonicera tatarica & cultivars • Tatarian honeysuckle
Mahonia repens • Mahonia
Menispermum canadensis • Common moonseed
Microbiota decussata • Russian cypress
Mitchella repens • Partridgeberry
Ostrya virginiana • Ironwood
Pachysandra terminalis • Pachysandra
Parthenocissus quinquefolia • Virginia creeper
Paxistima canbyi • Paxistima
Prunus pensylvanica • Pin cherry
Sambucus pubens • Scarlet elder
Sorbaria sorbifolia • False spirea
Stephanandra incisa & 'Crispa' • Stephanandra
Taxus species & cultivars • Yew
Thuja occidentalis & cultivars • American arborvitae
Tsuga canadensis • Canadian hemlock
Viburnum species & cultivars • Viburnum
Vinca minor • Periwinkle
Zanthoxylum americanum • Prickly ash

Betula nigra (river birch) can withstand moderately wet and also moderately dry soils.

Taxus x media 'Taunton' ('Taunton' yew) needs a protected location and will withstand partly shaded conditions.

Alkaline Tolerant Woody Plants

Acer negundo • Boxelder
Acer saccharinum • Silver maple
Alnus incana • White alder
Amorpha canescens • Lead plant
Artemisia frigida • Fringed sagebrush
Berberis koreana • Korean barberry
Caragana species & cultivars • Peashrub
Catalpa bignonioides • Catalpa
Celtis occidentalis • Hackberry
Clematis species & cultivars • Clematis
Cornus stolonifera • Redosier dogwood
Crataegus ambigua • Russian hawthorn
Elaeagnus angustifolia • Russian olive
Fraxinus pennsylvanica • Green ash
Fraxinus quadrangulata • Blue ash
Gymnocladus dioica • Kentucky coffee tree
Halimodendron halodendron • Siberian salt tree
Hippophae rhamnoides • Sea buckthorn
Hydrangea arborescens & cultivars • Hills-of-snow hydrangea
Hypericum kalmianum • Kalm's St. John's-wort
Juglans nigra • Black walnut
Juniperus virginiana & cultivars • Red cedar
Lonicera x brownii • Browns honeysuckle
Malus species & cultivars • Crabapple
Ostrya virginiana • Ironwood
Picea glauca & cultivars • White spruce
Potentilla fruticosa & cultivars • Potentilla
Quercus macrocarpa • Bur oak
Ribes odoratum • Clove currant
Robinia hispida • Rose acacia
Robinia pseudoacacia • Black locust
Rosa species & cultivars • Rose
Salix species & cultivars • Willow
Sambucus pubens • Scarlet elder
Shepherdia argentea • Silver buffaloberry
Spiraea species & cultivars • Spirea
Syringa species & cultivars • Lilac
Viburnum lantana • Wayfaringbush
Viburnum opulus • European highbush cranberry
Weigela cultivars • Weigela

Woody Plants for Parking Lots

Parking areas are often sites with specific problems for woody plants. Many are hot and dry where maintenance is a low priority. Root zones can be restricted, soil can be compacted and the sites are usually very exposed. Only the toughest plants and those with nonexacting root requirements will survive.

Acer platanoides & cultivars • Norway maple
Acer tataricum ginnala • Amur maple
Caragana species & cultivars • Peashrub
Celtis occidentalis • Hackberry
Crataegus species & cultivars • Hawthorn
Diervilla lonicera • Bush honeysuckle
Elaeagnus angustifolia • Russian olive
Fraxinus nigra 'Fallgold' • Black ash
Gymnocladus dioica • Kentucky coffee tree
Juniperus virginiana • Red cedar
Maackia amurensis • Amur maackia
Malus species & cultivars • Flowering Crabs

Woody Plants for Parking Lots continued

Phellodendron amurense • Amur cork tree
Populus tremuloides • Quaking aspen
Prunus americana • American plum
Quercus bicolor • Swamp white oak
Rhus aromatica 'Gro-low' • Fragrant sumac
Rosa cultivars • Selected rose cultivars
Sambucus canadensis • American elder
Sambucus pubens • Scarlet elder
Shepherdia argentea • Silver buffaloberry
Sorbus alnifolia • Korean mountain ash
Spiraea species & cultivars • Spirea
Syringa reticulata • Japanese tree lilac
Tilia species & cultivars • Linden

Woody Plants for Disturbed Sites

Whether it is after construction or in an area where the topsoil is depleted, plants often lead the way to reclaim problem areas. The soil can be just very poor, or compacted with problem drainage.

Abies balsamea • Balsam fir
Acer negundo • Boxelder
Alnus glutinosa • European alder
Betula alleghaniensis • Yellow birch
Betula populifolia • Gray birch
Caragana arborescens • Siberian peashrub
Celtis occidentalis • Hackberry
Elaeagnus angustifolia • Russian olive
Gymnocladus dioica • Kentucky coffee tree
Juniperus scopulorum • Rocky Mountain juniper
Juniperus virginiana • Red cedar
Pinus banksiana • Jack pine
Populus deltoides & cultivars • Cottonwood
Populus tremuloides • Quaking aspen
Rhus species • Sumac
Robinia pseudoacacia • Locust

Woody Plants for Soil Stabilization/Erosion Control

Artemisia frigida • Fringed sagebrush
Caragana frutex • Russian peashrub
Diervilla lonicera • Bush honeysuckle
Elaeagnus commutata • Silverberry
Lycium chinense • Chinese matrimony vine
Rhus species • Sumac
Shepherdia canadensis • Buffaloberry
Sorbaria sorbifolia • Ural false spirea
Symphoricarpos species & cultivars • Snowberry

Clematis tolerate alkaline soils, here
Clematis 'Lasurstern'.

Japanese white spirea (*Spiraea japonica* 'Albiflora') also tolerates alkaline soils.

Many roses withstand alkaline conditions, here *Rosa* 'William Baffin'.

175

Oak and pine in winter.

GROWING HEIGHT OF WOODY PLANTS

TREE HEIGHTS

75 feet and over

Acer saccharinum • Silver maple
Carya species • Bitternut, pecan
Celtis occidentalis • Hackberry
Fraxinus americana • White ash
Fraxinus excelsior • European ash
Fraxinus nigra • Black ash
Gymnocladus dioica • Kentucky coffee tree
Juglans nigra • Black walnut
Larix decidua • European larch
Picea abies • Norway spruce
Pinus resinosa • Red pine
Pinus strobus • White pine
Platanus x acerifolia • London plane
Platanus occidentalis • Buttonwood
Populus deltoides & 'Siouxland' • Cottonwood
Populus nigra • Black poplar
Prunus serotina • Black cherry
Quercus rubra • Red oak
Salix alba • White willow
Tilia americana • Basswood

White ash (*Fraxinus americana*), a tall-growing native.

35 to 75 feet

Abies balsamea • Balsam fir
Abies concolor • Concolor fir
Acer 'Autumn Blaze', Celebration®, 'Marmo' • Maple
Acer campestre • Hedge maple
Acer negundo • Boxelder
Acer platanoides & cultivars • Norway maple
Acer rubrum & cultivars • Red maple
Acer saccharinum cultivars • Silver maple
Acer saccharum & cultivars • Sugar maple
Aesculus 'Autumn Splendor' • Buckeye
Aesculus glabra • Ohio buckeye
Aesculus hippocastanum • Horsechestnut
Alnus glutinosa • European alder
Alnus incana • White alder
Betula alleghaniensis • Yellow birch
Betula fontinalis • Water birch
Betula lenta • Cherry birch
Betula nigra & Heritage® • River birch
Betula papyrifera • Paper birch
Betula pendula & cultivars • European birch
Betula platyphylla japonica & 'Whitespire' •
    Japanese white birch
Carpinus betulus & cultivars • European hornbeam
Catalpa bignonioides • Common catalpa
Catalpa speciosa • Northern catalpa
Fraxinus americana & cultivars • White ash
Fraxinus mandshurica & 'Mancana' • Manchurian ash
Fraxinus nigra 'Fallgold' • Black ash
Fraxinus pennsylvanica & cultivars • Green ash
Fraxinus quadrangulata • Blue ash
Ginkgo biloba & cultivars • Ginkgo
Gleditsia triacanthos inermis & cultivars • Honeylocust
Gymnocladus dioica 'Stately Manor' • Kentucky coffee tree
Juglans cinerea • Butternut
Juglans regia • English walnut
Juniperus virginiana • Red cedar
Larix kaempferi • Japanese larch
Larix laricina • Tamarack
Magnolia acuminata • Cucumber tree
Malus 'Dolgo' • Flowering crab

Aesculus 'Autumn Splendor'.

Flowers of *Sorbaria sorbifolia* (False spirea).

Morus rubra • Red mulberry
Ostrya virginiana • Ironwood
Phellodendron 'His Majesty' • Cork tree
Phellodendron amurense & 'Macho' • Amur cork tree
Phellodendron sachalinense • Sakhalin cork tree
Picea glauca & 'Densata' • White & Black Hills spruce
Picea mariana • Black spruce
Picea omorika • Serbian spruce
Picea pungens & glauca • Colorado & Colorado blue spruce
Pinus banksiana • Jack pine
Pinus cembra • Swiss stone pine
Pinus densiflora • Japanese red pine
Pinus flexilis • Limber pine
Pinus koraiensis • Korean pine
Pinus nigra • Austrian pine
Pinus ponderosa scopulorum • Ponderosa pine
Pinus sylvestris • Scotch pine
Pinus wallichiana • Himalayan pine
Populus 'Highland', 'Nor'easter', 'Prairie Sky', 'Robusta', 'Tower'
 • Poplar
Populus alba • White poplar
Populus nigra 'Afghanica', 'Italica' • Poplar
Populus tremuloides & 'Pikes Bay' • Quaking aspen
Pseudotsuga menziesii glauca • Douglas fir
Quercus alba • White oak
Quercus bicolor • Swamp white oak
Quercus coccinea • Scarlet oak
Quercus ellipsoidalis • Northern pin oak
Quercus imbricaria • Shingle oak
Quercus macrocarpa • Bur oak
Quercus muehlenbergii • Chinkapin oak
Quercus palustris • Pin oak
Quercus veluntina • Black oak
Robinia pseudoacacia & 'Frisia', 'Purple Robe' • Black locust
Salix 'Prairie Cascade' • Willow
Salix x pendulina • Wisconsin weeping willow
Salix pentandra • Laurel willow
Salix x sepulcralis chrysocoma • Niobe weeping willow
Sorbus alnifolia • Korean mountain ash
Sorbus aucuparia • European mountain ash
Taxodium distichum • Bald cypress
Thuja occidentalis • American arborvitae
Tilia 'Glenleven' • Linden
Tilia americana & cultivars • Basswood
Tilia cordata & cultivars • Littleleaf linden
Tsuga canadensis • Canadian hemlock

15 to 35 feet (duplicates some large shrubs)

Acer Norwegian Sunset®, & Pacific Sunset™ • Maple
Acer negundo 'Sensation' • Boxelder
Acer platanoides 'Crimson Sentry', 'Globosum', 'Parkway' •
 Norway maple
Acer saccharum 'Globosum' • Sugar maple
Acer spicatum • Mountain maple
Acer tataricum • Tatarian maple
Acer tataricum ginnala & 'Embers', 'Flame', Red Rhapsody™ •
 Amur maple
Alnus rugosa • Speckled alder
Amelanchier arborea • Downy serviceberry
Amelanchier x grandiflora & cultivars • Serviceberry
Amelanchier laevis & cultivars • Allegheny serviceberry
Aralia elata • Japanese angelica
Aralia spinosa • Hercules club
Betula pendula 'Dalecarlica', 'Gracilis', 'Youngii' • European
 birch
Betula populifolia • Gray birch
Carpinus caroliniana • American hornbeam
Cercidiphyllum japonicum • Katsura tree

Cercis canadensis 'Northern Strain' • Redbud
Cladrastis lutea • Yellowwood
Cornus alternifolia • Pagoda dogwood
Corylus colurna • Turkish hazel
Cotinus obovatus • American smoketree
Crataegus crus-galli • Cockspur hawthorn
Crataegus mollis • Downy hawthorn
Crataegus phaenopyrum • Washington hawthorn
Crataegus punctata • Dotted hawthorn
Crataegus viridis & 'Winter King' • Green hawthorn
Elaeagnus angustifolia • Russian olive
Euonymus atropurpureus • Wahoo
Euonymus bungeanus • Winterberry euonymus
Euonymus europaeus • European spindle tree
Euonymus hamiltonianus • Hamilton euonymus
Fraxinus pennsylvanica Leprechaun™ • Green ash
Juniperus scopulorum • Rocky Mountain juniper
Maackia amurensis • Amur maackia
Maackia chinensis • Chinese maackia
Magnolia x loebneri 'Leonard Messel', 'Merrill' • Magnolia
Magnolia stellata & 'Royal Star' • Star magnolia
Magnolia tripetala • Umbrella magnolia
Malus cultivars • Crabapple
Malus baccata & 'Columnaris', 'Jackii' • Crabapple
Malus coronaria • Wild sweet crabapple
Malus floribunda • Japanese flowering crabapple
Malus ioensis & 'Plena' • Prairie crabapple
Malus prunifolia • Plum-leaved crabapple
Morus alba tatarica • Russian mulberry
Picea pungens 'Bakeri', 'Hoopsii' • Colorado blue spruce
Pinus mugo • Swiss mountain pine
Pinus strobus 'Fastigiata' • White pine
Prunus 'Newport' • Ornamental plum
Prunus americana • Wild plum
Prunus maackii • Amur cherry
Prunus mandshurica • Manchurian apricot
Prunus nigra 'Princess Kay' • Ornamental plum
Prunus padus • European bird cherry
Prunus padus commutata • Mayday tree
Prunus pensylvanica • Pin cherry
Prunus sargentii • Sargent cherry
Prunus virginiana & 'Schubert' • Canada red chokecherry
Ptelea trifoliata • Hop tree
Pyrus ussuriensis & Mountain Frost™, Prairie Gem® •
 Ornamental pear
Quercus mongolica • Mongolian oak
Salix 'Flame', 'Golden Curls' • Hybrid willow
Salix matsudana & 'Tortulosa' • Peking willow
Sorbus americana • American mountain ash
Sorbus aucuparia Cardinal Royal® • Mountain ash
Sorbus decora • Showy mountain ash
Sorbus x hybrida • Oak-leaved mountain ash
Staphylea trifoliata • American bladdernut
Syringa pekinensis • Peking lilac
Syringa reticulata & cultivars • Japanese tree lilac
Tilia mongolica • Mongolian linden
Viburnum lentago • Nannyberry
Xanthoceras sorbifolium • Yellowhorn

Ginkgo (*Ginkgo biloba*).

**False cypress
(*Chamaecyparis*) with
spreading juniper.**

***Sorbus alnifolia* (Korean mountain ash).**

Cornus racemosa (Gray dogwood).

SHRUB HEIGHTS

15 feet and over (Duplicates some trees)

Aesculus glabra arguta • Texas buckeye
Acer tataricum ginnala • Amur maple
Amelanchier canadensis • Shadblow
Amelanchier x grandiflora 'Ballerina' • Apple serviceberry
Aralia elata • Japanese angelica
Betula pumila • Swamp birch
Caragana arborescens • Siberian peashrub
Cercis canadensis 'Northern Strain' • Redbud
Chamaecyparis species & cultivars • False cypress
Chionanthus virginicus • White fringe tree
Crataegus ambigua • Russian hawthorn
Crataegus crus-galli Crusader®, 'Inermis' • Hawthorn
Crataegus laevigata & 'Superba' • English hawthorn
Crataegus x mordenensis • Hawthorn
Hippophae rhamnoides • Sea buckthorn
Hydrangea paniculata • Panicle hydrangea
Juniperus scopulorum & cultivars • Juniper
Juniperus virginiana & cultivars • Juniper
Magnolia stellata 'Royal Star' • Star magnolia
Malus x zumi • Zumi crabapple
Picea abies 'Acrocona', 'Mucronata' • Norway spruce
Ptelea trifoliata • Hop tree
Rhamnus frangula • Glossy buckthorn
Rhus typhina • Staghorn sumac
Salix caprea • Pussy willow
Salix discolor • Pussy willow
Shepherdia argentea • Silver buffaloberry
Syringa pekinensis • Pekin lilac
Syringa vulgaris & cultivars • Common lilac
Taxus cuspidata • Japanese yew
Thuja occidentalis 'Brandon', 'Pyramidalis', 'Sherman', 'Techny' • American arborvitae
Viburnum lentago • Nannyberry
Xanthoceras sorbifolium • Yellowhorn
Zanthoxylum americanum • Northern prickly ash

10 to 15 feet

Amelanchier alnifolia & cultivars • Saskatoon serviceberry
Amorpha fruticosa • Indigo bush
Cephalanthus occidentalis • Buttonbush
Cornus alba • Tatarian dogwood
Cornus obliqua • Silky dogwood

'Miss Kim' lilac (*Syringa patula* 'Miss Kim') blooming with peonies.

Cornus racemosa • Gray dogwood
Cornus rugosa • Dogwood
Cornus stolonifera & 'Cardinal' • Redosier dogwood
Corylus americana • American hazel
Corylus avellana • European hazel
Cotinus coggygria • Smokebush
Cotoneaster lucidus • Hedge cotoneaster
Cotoneaster multiflorus • Many-flowered cotoneaster
Crataegus x mordenensis 'Snowbird' & 'Toba' • Hawthorn
Elaeagnus commutata • Silverberry
Elaeagnus umbellata • Autumn olive
Euonymus alatus • Winged euonymus
Hamamelis virginiana • Common witchhazel
Ilex verticillata • Winterberry
Juniperus chinensis 'Ames', 'Hetzii', 'Mountbatten' • Juniper
Juniperus sabina • Savin juniper
Juniperus scopulorum 'Medora' • Juniper
Lonicera maackii • Amur honeysuckle
Lonicera maximowiczii sachalinensis • Sakhalin honeysuckle
Lonicera tatarica & cultivars • Tatarian honeysuckle
Magnolia stellata 'Centennial' & 'Waterlily' • Star magnolia
Malus cultivars • Flowering crabs
Pinus mugo pumilio • Mugo pine
Pinus strobus 'Pendula' • White pine
Pinus sylvestris 'Watereri' • Scotch pine
Prunus triloba simplex • Flowering plum
Sambucus pubens • Scarlet elder
Sambucus racemosa & cultivars • European red elder
Staphylea trifolia • American bladdernut
Syringa x chinensis • Chinese lilac
Syringa oblata • Early lilac
Syringa villosa • Late lilac
Syringa vulgaris cultivars • Common lilac
Tamarix ramosissima • Fivestamen tamarisk
Thuja occidentalis 'Gold Cargo', 'Wareana' • American arborvitae
Viburnum lantana • Wayfaringbush
Viburnum opulus & 'Roseum' • European highbush cranberry
Viburnum prunifolium • Blackhaw
Viburnum sargentii • Sargent highbush cranberry
Viburnum trilobum • American highbush cranberry

6 to 9 feet

Acer tataricum ginnala 'Bailey Compact' • Amur maple
Aronia arbutifolia • Red chokeberry
Aronia melanocarpa • Black chokeberry
Aronia x prunifolia • Purple chokeberry
Berberis koreana • Korean barberry
Calycanthus floridus • Sweetshrub
Caragana frutex • Russian peashrub
Caragana microphylla • Littleleaf peashrub
Chamaebatiaria millefolium • Fernbush
Clethra alnifolia & 'Rosea' • Summersweet
Cornus alba & cultivars • Dogwood
Cornus stolonifera & cultivars • Redosier dogwood
Corylus cornuta • Beaked hazel
Cotinus coggygria & cultivars • Smokebush
Cotoneaster integerrimus • European cotoneaster
Deutzia x lemoinei • Lemoine deutzia
Dirca palustris • Leatherwood
Eleutherococcus sessiliflorus • Tatarian aralia
Eleutherococcus sieboldianus • Five-leaved aralia
Euonymus alatus cultivars • Dwarf winged euonymus
Exochorda serratifolia 'Northern Pearls' • Pearlbush
Forsythia species & cultivars • Forsythia
Halimodendron halodendron • Siberian salt tree
Hamamelis vernalis • Vernal witchhazel
Hydrangea paniculata & cultivars • Hydrangea

Douglas fir (*Pseudotsuga menziesii glauca*).

Pagoda dogwood (*Cornus alternifolia*).

Ilex 'Sparkleberry' • Holly
Ilex verticillata 'Winter Red' • Winterberry
Juniperus chinensis 'Iowa', 'Maney', 'Robusta Green' • Juniper
Juniperus scopulorum 'Welchii' • Juniper
Kolkwitzia amabilis • Beauty bush
Lespedeza bicolor • Shrub bush clover
Ligustrum amurense • Amur privet
Ligustrum vulgare • Common privet
Lonicera 'Freedom' • Honeysuckle
Lonicera dioica • Limber honeysuckle
Lonicera tatarica & cultivars • Honeysuckle
Malus sargentii & 'Tina' • Sargent flowering crabs
Nemopanthus mucronatus • Mountain holly
Philadelphus coronarius • Sweet mockorange
Philadelphus lewisii & 'Blizzard', 'Waterton' • Mockorange
Philadelphus x virginalis & cultivars • Mockorange
Physocarpus opulifolius & 'Luteus', 'Nugget', 'Snowfall' •
    Common ninebark
Pinus aristata • Bristle-cone pine
Pinus banksiana 'Uncle Fogy' • Jack pine
Pinus densiflora 'Umbraculifera' • Japanese umbrella pine
Prinsepia sinensis • Cherry prinsepia
Prunus besseyi • Western sandcherry
Prunus x cistena • Purpleleaf sandcherry
Prunus maritima • Beach plum
Prunus tomentosa • Nanking cherry
Rhododendron species & cultivars • Azalea and rhododendron
Rhus glabra & cultivars • Smooth sumac
Rhus trilobata • Skunkbush sumac
Rhus typhina 'Laciniata' • Cutleaf staghorn sumac
Ribes aureum • Golden currant
Ribes odoratum • Clove currant
Robinia hispida • Rose acacia
Rosa species & cultivars • Rose
Rubus odoratus • Flowering raspberry
Rubus parviflorus • Thimbleberry
Salix caprea 'Pendula' • Weeping pussy willow
Salix purpurea • Purple osier willow
Sambucus canadensis & cultivars • American elder
Shepherdia canadensis • Russet buffaloberry
Sorbaria sorbifolia • Ural false spirea
Spiraea species & cultivars • Spirea
Stephanandra incisa • Cutleaf stephanandra
Syringa x hyacinthiflora & cultivars • Lilac
Syringa patula & 'Miss Kim' • Lilac
Syringa x persica • Persian lilac
Syringa x prestoniae & cultivars • Lilac
Syringa vulgaris cultivars • Common lilac
Tamarix ramosissima 'Summer Glow' • Tamarisk
Taxus canadensis • Canadian yew
Thuja occidentalis 'Aurea', 'Little Giant', 'Woodwardii' •
    American arborvitae
Viburnum 'Emerald Triumph' • Viburnum
Viburnum acerifolium • Mapleleaf viburnum
Viburnum cassinoides • Witherod
Viburnum dentatum & cultivar • Arrowwood
Viburnum lantana 'Mohican' • Viburnum
Viburnum lantanoides • Hobblebush
Viburnum opulus 'Compactum', 'Xanthocarpum' • Viburnum
Viburnum rafinesquianum • Downy arrowwood
Viburnum sargentii 'Onondaga' • Viburnum
Viburnum trilobum cultivars • American highbush cranberry
Weigela florida & 'Centennial' & 'Red Prince' • Weigela
Yucca filamentosa • Spanish bayonette

'Pocahontas' lilac
(*Syringa x hyacinthiflora*
'Pocahontas').

Shadbush
(*Amelanchier canadensis*).

(*Cercis
canadensis*
'Northern
Strain').

3 to 5 feet

Abeliophyllum distichum • Abelialeaf
Amelanchier stolonifera • Running serviceberry
Aronia arbutifolia 'Brilliantissima' • Chokeberry
Aronia melanocarpa elata & 'Autumn Magic' • Black chokeberry
Artemisia abrotanum • Southernwood
Berberis Emerald Carousel® • Barberry
Berberis thunbergii & cultivars • Japanese barberry
Betula nana • Dwarf birch
Buxus species & cultivars • Boxwood
Caragana arborescens 'Walker' • Siberian peashrub
Caragana brevifolia • Shortleaf peashrub
Caragana pygmaea • Pygmy peashrub
Caryopteris x clandonensis & cultivars • Caryopteris
Ceanothus americanus • New Jersey tea
Chamaecytisus hirsutus • Hairy bloom
Chamaedaphne calyculata • Leatherleaf
Clethra alnifolia 'Hummingbird' • Summersweet
Cornus alba Ivory Halo® • Dogwood
Deutzia x lemoinei 'Compacta' • Lemoine deutzia
Diervilla sessilifolia • Southern bush honeysuckle
Forsythia 'Sunrise' • Forsythia
Genista tinctoria • Dyer's greenweed
Hippophae rhamnoides 'Sprite' • Sea buckthorn
Hydrangea arborescens & 'Annabelle', 'Grandiflora' • Hydrangea
Hypericum prolificum • Shrubby St. John's-wort
Ilex verticillata 'Afterglow', 'Red Sprite' • Winterberry
Juniperus chinensis 'Blaauw' • Juniper
Juniperus communis 'Depressa Aurea' • Juniper
Juniperus x media cultivars • Juniper
Juniperus sabina 'Blue Danube', 'Pepin', 'Von Ehren' • Juniper
Juniperus virginiana 'Grey Owl' • Juniper
Kerria japonica • Japanese kerria
Ligustrum obtusifolium regelianum • Regel privet
Ligustrum vulgare 'Cheyenne' • Privet
Lonicera caerulea edulis • Sweetberry honeysuckle
Lonicera x xylosteoides 'Clavey's Dwarf', 'Miniglobe' • Honeysuckle
Lonicera xylosteum 'Emerald Mound' • Honeysuckle
Philadelphus 'Buckley's Quill', 'Miniature Snowflake',
'Snowgoose' • Mockorange
Philadelphus coronarius 'Aureus' • Golden mockorange
Physocarpus monogynus • Mountain ninebark
Physocarpus opulifolius 'Dart's Gold', 'Nanus' • Ninebark
Picea abies 'Clanbrassiliana', 'Nidiformis', 'Pumila' • Norway
    spruce
Picea glauca 'Conica' • Dwarf Alberta spruce
Picea omorika 'Nana' • Dwarf Serbian spruce
Picea pungens 'Globosa', 'Montgomery' • Colorado blue spruce
Pinus mugo 'Compacta' • Mugo pine
Pinus resinosa 'Wissota' • Red pine
Pinus strobus 'Nana' • White pine
Prunus fruticosa • European dwarf cherry
Prunus glandulosa & cultivars • Dwarf flowering almond
Prunus tenella • Russian almond
Rhododendron cultivars • Azalea and rhododendron
Rhus aromatica • Fragrant sumac
Ribes alpinum & 'Green Mound' • Alpine currant
Rosa species & cultivars • Rose
Salix purpurea 'Gracilis', 'Nana' • Willow
Spiraea species & cultivars • Spirea
Symphoricarpos albus • Snowberry
Symphoricarpos orbiculatus • Coralberry
Syringa meyeri & 'Palibin' • Meyer lilac
Taxus x media & cultivars • Yew
Thuja occidentalis 'Holmstrup' • Arborvitae
Vaccinium cultivars • Blueberries
Viburnum opulus 'Nanum' • Viburnum
Weigela 'Java Red', 'Pink Delight', 'Pink Princess', 'Polka' • Weigela
Yucca glauca • Soapweed

To 3 feet

Abies balsamea 'Nana' • Dwarf balsam fir
Amorpha canescens • Lead plant
Amorpha nana • Fragrant False Indigo
Andromeda polifolia & 'Nana' • Bog rosemary
Aralia hispida • Bristly sarsaparilla
Arctostaphylos uva-ursi & 'Massachusetts' • Bearberry
Artemisia frigida • Fringed sagebrush
Buxus species & cultivars • Boxwood
Calluna vulgaris & cultivars • Scotch heather
Caragana frutex 'Globosa' • Globe Russian peashrub
Ceanothus ovatus • Inland ceanothus
Clematis heracleifolia var. davidiana • Clematis
Clematis integrifolia • Clematis
Clematis recta • Clematis
Comptonia peregrina • Sweet fern
Cotoneaster adpressus • Creeping cotoneaster
Cotoneaster apiculatus • Cranberry cotoneaster
Daphne x burkwoodii & 'Carol Mackie', 'Somerset' • Burkwood daphne
Daphne mezereum • February daphne
Deutzia gracilis • Slender deutzia
Deutzia lonicera • Bush honeysuckle
Epigaea repens • Trailing arbutus
Euonymus fortunei & cultivars • Euonymus
Euonymus nanus • Dwarf euonymus
Euonymus obovatus • Running euonymus
Forsythia 'Arnold Dwarf' • Forsythia
Gaultheria hispidula • Creeping snowberry
Gaultheria procumbens • Wintergreen
Gaylussacia brachycera • Box huckleberry
Genista tinctoria 'Royal Gold' • Greenweed
Hypericum kalmianum • Kalm's St. John's-wort
Juniperus chinensis 'San Jose' • Juniper
Juniperus communis Blueberry Delight™, 'Depressa Aurea', 'Effusa', 'Repanda' • Juniper
Juniperus horizontalis & cultivars • Juniper
Juniperus x media 'Old Gold' • Juniper
Juniperus procumbens & 'Nana' • Japanese garden juniper
Juniperus sabina cultivars • Juniper
Juniperus sargentii & 'Glauca', 'Viridis' • Juniper
Juniperus scopulorum 'Winter Blue' • Juniper
Juniperus squamata 'Blue Star' • Juniper
Kalmia polifolia • Bog laurel
Ledum groenlandicum • Labrador tea
Linnaea borealis • Twinflower
Microbiota decussata • Russian cypress
Mitchella repens • Partridgeberry
Pachysandra procumbens • Allegheny spurge
Pachysandra terminalis & cultivars • Pachysandra
Paxistima canbyi • Cliff green
Picea abies 'Little Gem' • Norway spruce
Picea mariana 'Nana' • Blue nest spruce
Potentilla fruticosa & cultivars • Potentilla
Potentilla tridentata • Wineleaf potentilla
Rhododendron species • Azalea and rhododendron
Rhus aromatica 'Gro-low' • Fragrant sumac
Rosa cultivars • Rose
Spiraea species & cultivars • Spirea
Stephanandra incisa 'Crispa' • Stephanandra
Symphoricarpos x chenaultii & 'Hancock' • Chenault coralberry
Thuja occidentalis 'Hetz Midget' • Arborvitae
Vaccinium vitis-idaea • Cowberry
Vinca minor & cultivars • Periwinkle
Weigela 'Minuet' • Weigela
Xanthorhiza simplicissima • Yellowroot

Woody Plants for Barriers

Aralia spinosa • Hercules club
Berberis species & cultivars • Barberry
Carpinus species & cultivars • Hornbeam
Crataegus species (especially *C. crus-galli*) • Hawthorn
Eleutherococcus sessiliflorus • Tatarian aralia
Eleutherococcus sieboldianus • Five-leaved aralia
Hippophae rhamnoides • Sea buckthorn
Malus ioensis & *M. sargentii* • Crabapples
Picea species & cultivars • Spruce
Prinsepia sinensis • Cherry prinsepia
Prunus maritima • Beach plum
Robinia pseudoacacia • Black locust
Rosa species & cultivars • Rose
Smilax hispida • Bristly greenbrier
Zanthoxylum americanum • Northern prickly ash

Woody Plants Tolerant of High Levels of Air Pollution

Acer platanoides & cultivars • Norway maple
Eleutherococcus sieboldianus • Five-leaved aralia
Euonymus species & cultivars • Euonymus
Ginkgo biloba • Ginkgo
Gymnocladus dioica • Kentucky coffee tree
Pachysandra terminalis • Pachysandra
Pinus nigra • Austrian pine
Sophora japonica • Japanese pagoda tree (trial)
Vinca minor • Periwinkle

Deer Resistant Plants

Amelanchier species & cultivars • Shadbush
Berberis species & cultivars • Barberry
Betula papyrifera • Canoe birch
Clematis species & cultivars • Clematis
Cotinus species & cultivars • Smokebush
Elaeagnus angustifolia • Russian olive
Forsythia species & cultivars • Forsythia
Juniperus chinensis & cultivars • Juniper
Magnolia species & cultivars • Magnolia
Picea abies • Norway spruce
Picea pungens • Colorado spruce
Pinus nigra • Austrian pine
Pinus sylvestris • Scotch pine
Pseudotsuga menziesii glauca • Douglas fir
Pyrus species & cultivars • Pear
Robinia pseudoacacia • Black locust
Spiraea species & cultivars • Spirea
Syringa vulgaris • Lilac
Vinca minor • Periwinkle

Woody Plants with Colored Summer Foliage

Red and purple

Acer platanoides 'Crimson King', 'Crimson Sentry', 'Royal Red', 'Schwedleri' • Norway maple
Berberis thunbergii cultivars • Barberry
Betula 'Crimson Frost' • Birch
Betula pendula 'Purpurea' • European birch
Cotinus coggygria 'Nordine', 'Royal Purple' • Smokebush
Prunus 'Newport' • Ornamental plum
Prunus x cistena • Purpleleaf sandcherry
Prunus virginiana 'Schubert' • Chokecherry
Robinia pseudoacacia 'Purple Robe' • Black locust

Acer platanoides 'Royal Red' ('Royal Red' maple)

A variegated dogwood cultivar (*Cornus*).

A blueberry hybrid (Vaccinium).

Rosa glauca • Redleaf rose
Spiraea cultivars • Spirea
Weigela 'Java Red' • Weigela

Variegated

Acer platanoides 'Variegatum' • Norway maple
Actinidia kolomitka 'Arctic Beauty' • Kiwi
Ampelopsis brevipedunculata 'Elegans' • Porcelain berry
Cornus alba 'Argenteo-marginata', 'Gouchaultii', Ivory Halo®, 'Spaethii' • Tatarian dogwood
Cornus stolonifera 'Silver and Gold' • Redosier dogwood
Daphne x burkwoodii 'Carol Mackie' • Daphne
Euonymus fortunei 'Gracilis' • Wintercreeper
Populus alba • White poplar (gives variegated appearance)
Spiraea cultivars • Spirea

Yellow or golden

Acer platanoides 'Princeton Gold' • Norway maple
Alnus glutinosa 'Aurea' • European alder
Berberis thunbergii 'Aurea' • Barberry
Gleditsia triacanthos Sunburst® • Honeylocust
Physocarpus opulifolius 'Dart's Gold', 'Luteus' • Ninebark
Robinia pseudoacacia 'Frisia' • Black locust
Sambucus racemosa 'Sutherland Gold' • European red elder
Spiraea cultivars • Spirea
Thuja occidentalis 'Aurea', 'Gold Cargo' • American arborvitae

Silver or gray

A red-leaved cultivar of erry (*Berberis*) used in the ot garden, part of the Herb Garden at the Arboretum.

Artemisia abrotanum • Southernwood
Elaeagnus angustifolia • Russian olive
Elaeagnus commutata • Silverberry
Hippophae rhamnoides & 'Sprite' • Sea buckthorn
Shepherdia argentea • Silver buffaloberry

Dioecious Plants

These plants require male and female plants to bare fruit.

Acer negundo • Boxelder
Acer rubrum • Red maple
Celastrus species • Bittersweet
Cercidiphyllum japonicum • Katsura tree
Chionanthus virginicus • White fringe tree
Cotinus obovatus • American smoketree
Fraxinus americanus • White ash
Fraxinus mandshurica • Manchurian ash
Fraxinus nigra • Black ash
Fraxinus pennsylvanica • Green ash
Ginkgo biloba • Ginkgo
Gleditsia triacanthos • Honeylocust
Gymnocladus dioica • Kentucky coffee tree
Ilex verticillata • Winterberry
Juniperus chinensis • Chinese juniper
Juniperus communis • Common juniper
Morus alba tatarica • Russian mulberry
Myrica pensylvanica • Bayberry
Nemopanthus mucronatus • Mountain holly
Phellodendron species • Cork tree
Populus species • Poplar, cottonwood, aspen
Rhus species • Sumac
Ribes alpinum • Alpine currant
Salix species • Willow
Shepherdia argentea • Silver buffaloberry
Smilax hispida • Bristly greenbrier
Taxus species • Yew
Vitis riparia • Riverbank grape
Zanthoxylum americanum • Northern prickly ash

Blue spruce (*Picea pungens glauca*).

'Rosy Lights' azalea (*Rhododendron* 'Rosy Lights').

University of Minnesota-Minnesota Landscape Arboretum Introductions

There have been many introductions of fruit trees that also could be added to this list including apples, plums, apricots, blueberries and grapes. These can all be attractive features in the permanent landscape.

Acer rubrum 'Autumn Spire' • Red maple
Acer rubrum 'Northwood' • Red maple
Aesculus 'Autumn Splendor' • Buckeye
Cercis canadensis 'Northern Strain' • Redbud
Cornus stolonifera 'Cardinal' • Redosier dogwood
Cornus stolonifera 'Isanti' • Redosier dogwood
Exochorda serratifolia 'Northern Pearls' • Pearlbush
Forsythia 'Northern Sun' • Forsythia
Gymnocladus dioica 'Stately Manor' • Kentucky coffee tree
Lonicera 'Freedom' • Honeysuckle
Lonicera tatarica 'Honey Rose' • Honeysuckle
Phellodendron 'His Majesty' • Cork tree
Pinus banksiana 'Uncle Fogy' • Jack pine
Pinus resinosa 'Wissota' • Red pine
Prunus 'Newport' • Ornamental plum
Prunus nigra 'Princess Kay' • Ornamental plum
Rhododendron 'Apricot Surprise' • Azalea
Rhododendron 'Golden Lights' • Azalea
Rhododendron 'Lemon Lights' • Azalea
Rhododendron 'Mandarin Lights' • Azalea
Rhododendron 'Northern Hi-lights' • Azalea
Rhododendron 'Northern Lights' • Azalea
Rhododendron 'Orchid Lights' • Azalea
Rhododendron 'Pink Lights' • Azalea
Rhododendron 'Rosy Lights' • Azalea
Rhododendron 'Spicy Lights' • Azalea
Rhododendron 'White Lights' • Azalea
Viburnum 'Emerald Triumph' • Viburnum

'Northwood' maple (*Acer rubrum* 'Northwood').

Flowering Crabs and Apples continued from page 135

'Indian Summer'
ZONE 4
18 feet tall, 18 feet wide

Another Simpson Nursery introduction. Red-pink bloom, red persistent fruit. Some disease resistance. Broadly rounded.

'Jewelberry'　flowering crab
ZONE 4
8 feet tall, 12 feet wide

White bloom, red persistent fruit. Some disease resistance. Compact, spreading growth. Research at The Minnesota Landscape Arboretum showed some dieback of stem tissue at an extreme of -32 degrees F. on this cultivar.

'Kelsey'　flowering crab
ZONES 2 TO 4
25 feet tall, 20 feet wide

Red, semi-double bloom, dark red persistent fruit. Introduced by the Morden Research Station in Manitoba in 1969. Upright growing, becoming rounded with age.

Lancelot®　flowering crab
M. 'Lanzam'
ZONE 4
8 feet tall, 8 feet wide

Dark pink buds turning to white bloom, yellow persistent fruit. Very dwarf, upright habit.

'Liset'　flowering crab
ZONE 4
15 feet tall, 15 feet wide

Introduced in 1952 from Holland. Pinkish red bloom, dark red fruit. The leaves have a dark red hue. Good disease resistance. Broadly upright.

'Louisa'　flowering crab
ZONE 4
15 feet tall, 15 feet wide

Pink bloom, yellow fruit. Some disease resistance. Broadly weeping.

Madonna®　flowering crab
M. 'Manzam'
ZONE 4
15 feet tall, 10 feet wide

Introduced by Lake County Nursery Exchange in 1987. Double white bloom, reddish orange fruit. Upright.

'Mary Potter'　flowering crab
ZONE 4
12 feet tall, 15 feet wide

Introduced by the Arnold Arboretum in 1947. White bloom, red persistent fruit. Disease can be a problem on this cultivar. Spreading, open habit. Needs a more protected location.

Molten Lava®　flowering crab
M. 'Molazam'
ZONE 4
15 feet tall, 12 feet wide

Introduced by Lake County Nursery Exchange in 1987. It is a Father John Fiala introduction. Pink buds turning to white bloom, red persistent fruit. Good disease resistance. Needs a more protected location.

'Oekonomierat Echtermeyer'　flowering crab
ZONES 3 AND 4
15 feet tall, 15 feet wide

Introduced from Germany in 1914. Red-pink bloom, dark red fruit. Has some disease resistance. Open, weeping habit.

'Ormiston Roy'　flowering crab
ZONES 3 AND 4
20 feet tall, 20 feet wide

Introduced by Mr. Arie den Boer in 1954. Pink buds turning to white bloom, orange fruit. Good disease resistance. Rounded dense form.

'Pink Spires'　flowering crab
ZONES 2 TO 4
15 feet tall, 12 feet wide

Introduced by W.L. Kerr of Saskatchewan. Reddish pink bloom, red persistent fruit. This cultivar suffers from scab which can cause defoliation in summer. Pyramidal habit.

'Prairifire'
ZONE 4
20 feet tall, 20 feet wide

Introduced by Dr. Daniel Dayton of the U. of Illinois. Pink-red bloom, dark red persistent fruit. Good disease resistance. Rounded, upright grower. *See photographs on page 146-47.*

'Professor Sprenger'   flowering crab
ZONE 4
20 feet tall, 20 feet wide

White bloom, reddish orange persistent fruit. Good disease resistance. Upright, somewhat spreading. Planted at the entrance to the Snyder Building at The Minnesota Landscape Arboretum. *See photograph page 165.*

'Profusion'   flowering crab
ZONE 4
20 feet tall, 25 feet wide

Red-pink bloom, red fruit. Some disease resistance. Has rounded crown.

'Purple Prince'   flowering crab
ZONE 4
20 feet tall, 20 feet wide

Good disease resistance with a rounded canopy. Its foliage is dark purple in the spring fading to a reddish green. Rosy red flowers and deep maroon red fruit.

'Radiant'   flowering crab
ZONES 3 AND 4
15 feet tall, 15 feet wide

Introduced in 1958 by the University of Minnesota. Reddish pink bloom, red fruit. This cultivar suffers from scab which can cause defoliation in summer. Round-headed tree.

'Red Barron'   flowering crab
ZONE 4
18 feet tall, 8 feet wide

Introduced by Simpson Nursery in 1980. Red bloom, dark red fruit. Good disease resistance. Upright, narrow grower.

'Red Jade'   flowering crab
ZONE 4
10 feet tall, 15 feet wide

Introduced by the Brooklyn Botanic Garden in 1953. White bloom, red persistent fruit. This cultivar suffers moderate damage from apple scab. Broadly pendulous.

Red Jewel®   flowering crab
M. 'Jewelcole'
ZONE 4
15 feet tall, 12 feet wide

Introduced by American Garden Cole. White bloom, red persistent fruit. Has some disease resistance. Upright pyramidal form. Noted for its persistent fruit.

'Red Splendor'   flowering crab
ZONES 3 AND 4
20 feet tall, 20 feet wide

Introduced by Bergeson Nursery of Fertile, Minnesota in 1948. Pinkish red bloom, red persistent fruit. Good disease resistance. Open, round-headed tree.

'Robinson'   flowering crab
ZONE 4
25 feet tall, 25 feet wide

Introduced by C.M. Hobbs in Indianapolis in 1968. Pink bloom, red fruit. Good disease resistance. Upright grower, spreading with age.

'Royalty'   flowering crab
ZONES 3 AND 4
18 feet tall, 18 feet wide

Introduced by W.L. Kerr of Saskatchewan in 1962. Red bloom, few dark red fruit. It is extremely susceptible to both fire blight and apple scab. Spreading, round-headed tree. Often grown for its foliage which remains red throughout the summer.

'Selkirk'   flowering crab
ZONES 2 TO 4
20 feet tall, 25 feet wide

Introduced by the Morden Experiment Station in 1962. Reddish pink bloom, red persistent fruit. Has some disease resistance. Broadly upright.

'Sentinel'   flowering crab
ZONE 4
18 feet tall, 12 feet wide

A narrow, upright growing variety. It has reasonable disease resistance. The flowers are white pink and the fruit is a persistent bright red.

'Sinai Fire'   flowering crab
ZONE 4
15 feet tall, 15 feet wide

A semi-weeping variety with good disease resistance. It features pink buds opening to white flowers with red fall fruit.

'Snowcloud'   flowering crab
ZONE 4
20 feet tall, 15 feet wide

Introduced by the Princeton Nurserymen's Research Assoc. in 1969. Pink bud turning to white bloom, orange-red fruit. This cultivar has some disease problems. Upright grower.

'Snowdrift' flowering crab
ZONES 3 AND 4
15 feet tall, 20 feet wide

Introduced by Cole Nursery in 1965. White bloom, orange-red fruit. Some disease resistance. Upright, spreading with age.

'Sparkler' flowering crab
ZONES 3 AND 4
15 feet tall, 18 feet wide

Introduced by the University of Minnesota in 1969. Rosy red bloom, dark red fruit. This cultivar suffers from scab which can cause defoliation in summer. A flat-topped, wide-spreading tree.

'Spring Snow' flowering crab
ZONES 3 AND 4
25 feet tall, 15 feet wide

Introduced by Interstate Nursery in 1966. White bloom, no fruit. This cultivar suffers from scab which can cause defoliation in summer. A dense, upright tree. For those who want a fruitless variety.

'Strawberry Parfait' flowering crab
ZONE 4
15 feet tall, 20 feet wide

An open, spreading, vase-formed tree. Its flowers are unusually pink colored with darker margins. The fruit is yellow with red markings. It has good disease resistance.

Sugar Tyme® flowering crab
M. 'Sutyzam'
ZONE 4
18 feet tall, 15 feet wide

Pink buds turn to white bloom, red persistent fruit. Good disease resistance. Upright, spreading habit. Introduced by Milton Baron of Michigan State University.

'Thunderchild' flowering crab
ZONES 3 AND 4
15 feet tall, 15 feet wide

An introduction from Percy Wright in Saskatchewan. Pink bloom, red fruit. Good disease resistance. Upright, vase-shaped. Grown especially for its purplish red summer foliage.

'Van Eseltine' flowering crab
ZONE 4
25 feet tall, 12 feet wide

Introduced by the New York Experiment Station in 1938. Pink bloom, yellow fruit. This cultivar suffers from scab which can cause defoliation in summer. Upright, vase-shaped, unique at maturity.

'Vanguard' flowering crab
ZONES 3 AND 4
18 feet tall, 15 feet wide

Introduced by the University of Minnesota. Rose-red bloom, red fruit. This cultivar suffers from scab which can cause defoliation in summer. Vase-shaped.

Velvet Pillar® flowering crab
M. 'Velvetcole'
ZONE 4
20 feet tall, 14 feet wide

Introduced by Cole Nursery in 1981. Few pink bloom, few red fruit. Has some disease resistance. Upright, vase-shaped.

Weeping Candied Apple® flowering crab
M. 'Weepcanzam'
ZONE 4
15 feet tall, 15 feet wide

Introduced by Lake County Nursery Exchange in 1977. Pink bloom, red persistant fruit. This cultivar suffers moderately from apple scab. Weeping broad crown. Also sold as 'Candied Apple'.

'White Cascade' flowering crab
ZONE 4
15 feet tall, 15 feet wide

A semi-weeping selection featuring pink buds opening white. It has yellow fall fruit. Good disease resistance.

'Winter Gold' flowering crab
ZONE 4
25 feet tall, 20 feet wide

This broadly pyramidal selection is larger growing. Flowers are white; fruit persistent yellow. Reasonable disease resistance.

SIBERIAN CRAB
Malus baccata (L.) Borkh.
HARDY IN ZONES 2 TO 4
30 feet tall, 30 feet wide

HABIT. Roundheaded tree; there are 35 species distributed in Europe, North America and Asia.
BRANCHES. Smooth, slender when young.
LEAVES. Elliptic or ovate to ovate-oblong, acuminate, wedge-shaped or rounded at base, 1 to 3 in. long, finely serrate, slightly hairy beneath when young; petioles 0.7 to 2 in. long.

FLOWERS. 1 to 1.3 in. across, white, in May; calyx smooth, deciduous, with long-acuminate lobes; pedicels slender, 0.5 to 1.5 in. long; styles usually longer than stamens, slightly hairy at base.
FRUIT. Subglobose, 0.3 to 0.4 in. across, red or yellow, in September and October.

LANDSCAPE USE

The Siberian crabapple has been widely used in shelterbelts and in wildlife plantings. Birds also distribute the seeds, and volunteer plants can be found in open areas and in woodlands. It is native to northeastern Asia to northern China, and was introduced into North America in 1784. When it was first introduced it was used in breeding programs to produce hardier apples.

CULTURE

Siberian crab withstands drought and a wide range of soil conditions. The species has variable resistance to apple scab and also has variable resistance to fire blight. In Arboretum trials, *M. baccata* 'Jacki' showed good resistance to scab, but another cultivar was very susceptible to it.

CULTIVARS AND VARIETIES:

'Columnaris' — Siberian crab
ZONES 3 AND 4
30 feet tall, 8 feet wide

Introduced by the Arnold Arboretum in 1940. It has not flowered as profusely as the species and has been very susceptible to fire blight and scab in Arboretum plantings. A narrow, upright tree.

'Jackii' — Siberian crab
ZONES 3 AND 4
20 feet tall, 20 feet wide

A selection by the Arnold Arboretum in 1915 from Korea. White bloom, red fruit. Arboretum trees have been quite disease free. Broadly round-headed.

'Walters'
ZONES 3 AND 4
20 feet tall, 20 feet wide

This selection has good disease resistance. White flowers with yellow fruit. Advertised as a good street tree.

var. mandshurica — Manchurian crab
ZONES 3 AND 4
25 feet tall, 25 feet wide

Native from central Japan to the Amur River in central China. A compact, roundheaded tree with sturdy branches. Flowers several days earlier than the species. Also spelled *M.b. mandschurica*.

WILD SWEET CRAB
Malus coronaria (L.) Mill.
HARDY IN ZONE 4
30 feet tall, 20 feet wide

HABIT. Small tree.
BRANCHES. Spreading; branchlets hairy at first.
LEAVES. Ovate to ovate-oblong, acute, usually rounded at base, 2 to 4 in. long; irregularly serrate and usually slightly lobed.
FLOWERS. 1 to 1.5 in. across, pink.
FRUIT. Depressed-globose, about 1 in. across, green, in September.

LANDSCAPE USE AND CULTURE

Difficult to find in the nursery trade. An attractive native species, it grows from New York to Alabama and west to Missouri. Cultivated since 1724.

CULTIVAR:

'Charlottae' — flowering crab
Flowers are larger than in the species and semi-double. Only one mail order source is listed in the 4th edition of the *Andersen Horticultural Library's Source List of Plants and Seeds*.

JAPANESE FLOWERING CRAB
Malus floribunda Van Houtte.
FOR PROTECTED AREAS IN ZONE 4
25 feet tall, 30 feet wide

HABIT. Small tree.
BRANCHES. Spreading; young branchlets hairy, becoming smooth.
LEAVES. Elliptic-ovate or ovate to oblong-ovate, acuminate, usually wedge-shaped, 1.5 to 3 in. long, sharply serrate; petioles 0.5 to 1 in. long.
FLOWERS. Deep carmine in bud, changing to pale pink or nearly white, 1 to 1.2 in. across, on hairy purple pedicels 1 to 1.3 in. long; calyx hairy, purple, with pointed lobes; petals obovate-oblong; styles usually 4.
FRUIT. Globose, 0.2 to 0.3 in. across, red, in September.

LANDSCAPE USE AND CULTURE

One of the most floriferous of all crabs. As this crab many times grows wider than its height, it gives a horizontal character to the landscape. The flowers change to white as they mature, but often the plant looks pink in the distance. Yellow fruit. It was native to Japan, but is no longer found in the wild and is only known as a cultivated plant. A choice plant especially in bloom. This species shows good disease resistance. Research at The Minnesota Landscape Arboretum showed dieback of stem tissue at a -32 degree F. on this species.

PRAIRIE CRAB
Malus ioensis (Wood) Britt.
HARDY IN ZONES 2 TO 4
30 feet tall, 25 feet wide

HABIT. Open, spreading tree.
BRANCHES. Hairy.
LEAVES. Ovate-oblong or elliptic-obovate, acute or short-acuminate, broadly wedge-shaped or rounded, 2 to 4 in. long, coarsely serrate or shallowly lobed; undersurface hairy, sometimes nearly smooth at maturity except on veins; petioles stout, hairy.
FLOWERS. Pink, about 1.5 in. across, fragrant, in early June.
FRUIT. Subglobose or broad-ellipsoid, 1 to 1.2 in. across, green, in September.

LANDSCAPE USE

This crab is best suited for naturalistic planting. The birds love its fruit in late summer. Thoreau on his visit to Minnesota in 1861, as noted in the account edited by Walter Harding (1962, 17-18), searched for wild crabs near Lake Calhoun (in south Minneapolis). He "went in search of it with [Mr. J.T. Grimes] in his pasture, where I found it first myself, quite a cluster of them." They were probably *M. ioensis,* possibly *M. coronaria.* (This account makes fascinating reading as Thoreau kept reasonable notes on trees, wildflowers, birds and general natural history as he planned to write an account of his journey. He unfortunately died in May, 1862.) This crab is thorny and stiff in character.

CULTURE
This crab is susceptible to cedar-apple rust, but connoisseurs of crabs still seek out the species and its cultivars because of its beautiful bloom. Will withstand dry conditions.

CULTIVAR:

'Plena'   prairie crab
ZONE 3 AND 4
This cultivar is confused in the nursery trade and probably includes double flowered forms such as 'Bechtel's' and 'Klehm's Improved'. Differs from the species in having a more compact form and double flowers with numerous petaloid stamens. Its susceptibility to cedar-apple rust limits its usefulness. A striking tree in full bloom.

PLUM-LEAVED CRAB
Malus prunifolia (Willd.) Borkh.
HARDY IN ZONES 3 AND 4
30 feet tall, 25 feet wide

HABIT. Spreading tree.
BRANCHES. Hairy when young, becoming smooth at maturity.
LEAVES. Ovate or elliptic, 2 to 4 in. long, acute or short-acuminate, rounded or wedge-shaped at base, sharply serrate; petioles slender 0.5 to 2 in. long.
FLOWERS. White, 1.2 in. across, in May.
FRUIT. Subglobose or ovoid, about 0.7 in. across, yellow or red, in September and persisting on the tree into winter.

LANDSCAPE USE AND CULTURE
Hard to obtain in the nursery trade. This species is often used in plant breeding because its fruits are persistent. It is native to northeastern Asia, and was introduced into North America in 1750.

SARGENT CRAB
Malus sargentii Rehd.
FOR PROTECTED LOCATIONS IN ZONE 4
8 feet tall, 8 feet wide

HABIT. Low, shrub-like tree.
BRANCHES. Hairy when young; horizontally spreading.
LEAVES. Ovate, acuminate, rounded or subcordate at base, 2 to 3.2 in. long, sharply serrate, hairy when young, finally nearly smooth; petioles 0.7 to 1.2 in. long, hairy.
FLOWERS. White, 1 in. across, in mid-May; pedicels and calyx smooth; styles usually 4.
FRUIT. Subglobose, about 0.3 in. across, dark red, in September.

LANDSCAPE USE
This crab is native to Japan, it was introduced into North America in 1892.

CULTURE
Sargent crabapple needs a protected site in zone 4.

CULTIVARS:

'Candymint'
ZONE 4
10 feet tall, 15 feet wide

Much smaller than the species, it has an irregular, spreading canopy. Red flower buds open to light rose pink. Red fall fruit. It has good disease resistance.

Firebird™   Sargent crab
M. 'Select A'
ZONE 4
5 feet tall, 8 feet wide

A very dwarf growing round canopied cultivar. It was found at the Johnson's Nursery in Menomonie Falls, Wisconsin. It has white blooms with red persistent fruit. Good disease resistance. Slow growing.

'Rosea'   Sargent crab
ZONE 4
10 feet tall, 12 feet wide

Introduced by the Arnold Arboretum in 1922. Similar to the species except the flower buds are pink.

'Tina'   Sargent crab
ZONE 4
6 feet tall, 10 feet wide

Pink buds open to white flowers, red fruit. Good disease resistance. Wide spreading, short cultivar.

ZUMI CRAB
Malus x zumi (Mats.) Rehd.
FOR PROTECTED LOCATIONS IN ZONE 4
16 feet tall, 12 feet wide

HABIT. Upright, pyramidal tree.
BRANCHES. Slightly hairy when young.
LEAVES. Ovate to ovate-oblong, acuminate, 1.5 to 3.5 in. long; leaves on flowering branches entire or crenate-serrulate, those on vegetative shoots serrate or occasionally slightly lobed; undersurface of leaves hairy when young, becoming smooth.
FLOWERS. Pink in bud, becoming white, 1 to 1.2 in. across, in mid-May; calyx slightly villous, with acuminate lobes; petals elliptic.
FRUIT. Small, 0.3 in. across, red, readily eaten by birds in the fall.

LANDSCAPE USE AND CULTURE
A cross between *M. baccata* var. *mandshurica* and *M. sieboldii*. Has not been hardy in Arboretum trials. Probably zone 5 cultivars and hybrid species. Does have unique forms.

VARIETY:

var. *calocarpa* Rehd.
FOR PROTECTED LOCATIONS IN ZONE 4
16 feet tall, 12 feet wide

Similar to the species except flowers are smaller. In Arboretum trials, this cultivar had excellent fruit persistance and quality.

COMMON MOONSEED

COMMON MOONSEED
Menispermum canadense L.
FAMILY: MENISPERMACEAE
HARDY IN ZONE 4, TRIAL IN ZONE 3
6 feet long

HABIT. Suffruticose twining vine; there are 2 species distributed in North America and Asia.
BRANCHES. Herbaceous with alternate, simple leaves.
LEAVES. Long-petioled, peltate, 3- to 7-lobed.
FLOWERS. Dioecious, small, in peduncled racemes or panicles, in June; sepals 4 to 10; petals 6 to 9, suborbicular, shorter than sepals; stamens 12 to 24; anthers 4-celled; female flowers with 6 to 12 staminodes; carpels 2 to 4, with a broad subsessile stigma.
FRUIT. Drupes with compressed pits that are crescent- or kidney-shaped.

LANDSCAPE USE
This vine is native in shady areas over a large range of North America. It makes an attractive ground cover in woodland gardens. It is native from Quebec to Manitoba and south to Georgia and Arkansas. Hard to find in the nursery trade. A poisonous plant often mistaken for wild grape. If in doubt smash the berries, which in moonseed have a crescent-shaped seed.

CULTURE
It is propagated by seed and by division. It usually dies back to ground level each winter.

DAWN REDWOOD

DAWN REDWOOD
Metasequoia glyptostroboides H.H. Hu & Cheng.
FAMILY: TAXODIACEAE; TAXODIUM FAMILY
FOR PROTECTED LOCATIONS IN EASTERN PARTS OF ZONE 4
30 feet tall, 20 feet wide

HABIT. Deciduous, coniferous tree of pyramidal form; there is 1 species native to China.
BRANCHES. 2 types, persistent and deciduous; persistent branches reddish brown, shallowly ridged, bearing the deciduous branches and numerous vegetative buds.
BUDS. Nonresinous, usually produced in pairs at the base of the deciduous branchlets.
LEAVES. Needle-like, deciduous, flattened, pectinately arranged, bright green above, lighter green below with obscure lines of stomates.

FLOWERS. Monoecious, male flowers in racemes or panicles.
FRUIT. Female cones that are pendulous, on long stalks, globose or cylindrical, 0.5 to 0.7 in. across, dark brown and mature the first year.

LANDSCAPE USE AND CULTURE

The dawn redwood has not been very hardy in The Minnesota Landscape Arboretum's plantings and should only be tried by the adventurous. Of ancient origin with an interesting history, it is native to eastern Szechuan and western Hupeh, China. It famously was rediscovered and then introduced into North America in 1947. Propagated by seed and cuttings.

RUSSIAN CYPRESS

RUSSIAN CYPRESS
Microbiota decussata Komarov.
FAMILY: CUPRESSACEAE, CYPRESS FAMILY
HARDY IN ZONES 2 TO 4
1 foot tall, 4 feet wide

HABIT. Low, spreading evergreen; there is 1 species native to Siberia.
LEAVES. Opposite, resinous, scale-like, small, glandular, bright green, with acute tips.
FRUIT. Male cones terminal, ovoid; female cones berry-like, having 4 scales; seed single, shiny, dark brown.

LANDSCAPE USE

An aromatic, low-growing evergreen that has been recently introduced into the nursery trade. In the winter the bright green foliage turns bronze. It resembles juniper in habit with very lacy-like foliage. It is native to southeastern Siberia.

CULTURE

This evergreen is tolerant of many different soils but needs good drainage. It is shade tolerant; in fact, it might do better if it receives some shade.

PARTRIDGEBERRY

PARTRIDGEBERRY
Mitchella repens L.
FAMILY: RUBIACEAE, MADDER FAMILY
HARDY IN ZONES 2 TO 4
12 in. long

HABIT. Evergreen, trailing subshrub with smooth stems, rooting at nodes; there are 2 species found in North America and Japan.

LEAVES. Simple, opposite, with short petioles and minute stipules, orbicular-ovate, 0.2 to 0.8 in. long, obtuse, subcordate or rounded at base; upper leaf surface dark green and shiny; upper and lower surfaces often variegated with whitish lines.
FLOWERS. In short-peduncled pairs, their ovaries united, in June and July; corolla funnelform with 4 spreading recurved lobes, 0.3 to 0.5 in. long, white, often tinged with purple, fragrant; calyx 4-toothed; ovaries 4-celled, each with 1 ovule; stigmas 4-lobed.
FRUIT. Red berry-like globose drupes produced in pairs in September.

LANDSCAPE USE

This ground hugging, trailing plant can be attractive in the rock garden. Partridgeberry's clean, shiny foliage and showy red berries are attractive. It is native from Nova Scotia to Ontario and Minnesota and south to Florida and Texas. It has been cultivated since 1761. Purchase from a northern nursery.

CULTURE

This trailing plant requires acidic, moist, humus-rich soil and some shade. Propagated by seed and division.

MULBERRIES

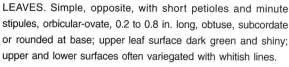

RUSSIAN MULBERRY
Morus alba var. tatarica (Pal.) Ser.
FAMILY: MORACEAE, MULBERRY FAMILY
HARDY IN ZONES 3 AND 4
30 feet tall, 25 feet wide

HABIT. Small tree with bushy heads; there are 12 species distributed worldwide.
BRANCHES. Slightly hairy at first or smooth.
LEAVES. Ovate to broad-ovate, 1.5 to 3.2 in. long, acute or short-acuminate, rounded or heart-shaped at base, coarsely toothed with obtusish teeth, often variously lobed; upper leaf surface light green and usually smooth, undersurface hairy on the veins or nearly smooth; petioles 0.3 to 1 in. long.
FLOWERS. Female catkins 0.2 to 0.4 in. long, male catkins twice as long, in May.
FRUIT. About 0.3 in. long, dark red, sweet but somewhat insipid, in July.

LANDSCAPE USE

This is the hardiest of the mulberries. It is often used in wildlife plantings to attract birds. Birds do "plant" the seeds, so this plant becomes one of the nuisance plants in our gardens and shrub borders. It is native to Russia and was introduced into North America by early settlers.

John Parkinson, in his *Paradisi in Sole* (1629, 598) states "Mulberries are not much desired to be eaten, although they be somewhat pleasant, both for that they staine their fingers and lips that eate them, and doe quickly putrefie in the stomacke...".

CULTURE
It will grow everywhere under diverse conditions.

RED MULBERRY
Morus rubra L.
FOR PROTECTED LOCATIONS IN ZONE 4
50 feet tall, 30 feet wide

HABIT. Spreading tree.
BRANCHES. Hairy at first.
BARK. Scaly, brown.
LEAVES. Broad-ovate to oblong-ovate, 2.7 to 4.7 in. long, abruptly long-acuminate, square or somewhat heart-shaped at base, rather closely and sharply serrate, lobed or unlobed, rough or sometimes nearly smooth above, soft-hairy beneath; petioles 0.7 to 1.2 in. long, hairy at first.
FLOWERS. Male catkins 0.7 to 2 in. long, female catkins 0.7 to 1 in. long, in May.
FRUIT. 0.7 to 1.2 in. long, dark purple, juicy, in July.

LANDSCAPE USE
The fruit are larger than the Russian mulberry and are better tasting. Native from Massachusetts to Florida and west to southeastern Minnesota, Kansas and Texas, it has been cultivated since 1629.

CULTURE
Of questionable hardiness in most of zone 4, it has not done well in the Twin Cities area.

BAYBERRY

BAYBERRY
Myrica pensylvanica Lois.
FAMILY: MYRICACEAE, BAYBERRY FAMILY
FOR PROTECTED LOCATIONS IN ZONE 4
6 feet tall, 3 feet wide

HABIT. Deciduous shrub; there are 35 species distributed worldwide.
BRANCHES. Gray hairy and glandular.
LEAVES. Alternate, short-petioled, obovate to oblong, 1.5 to 4 in. long, obtuse or acutish, shallowly toothed toward the apex or entire, dull green and hairy above, hairy beneath, resinous-dotted.
FLOWERS. Dioecious, small, inconspicuous in April.
FRUIT. Grayish white, covered with wax, berry-like, 0.1 to 0.2 in. in diameter in October and into the winter.

LANDSCAPE USE
Makes an attractive bank cover where it proves hardy if pruned back each spring. Native from Newfoundland to western New York and Maryland, chiefly along the seashore. It has been cultivated since 1727 and is used in making bayberry candles.

CULTURE
It is of borderline hardiness and also seems to be quite specific as to its soil requirements. It needs sandy, well-drained soil on the acidic side. It has not proven hardy at The Minnesota Landscape Arboretum.

MOUNTAIN HOLLY

MOUNTAIN HOLLY
Nemopanthus mucronatus (L.) Trel.
FAMILY: AQUIFOLIACEAE, HOLLY FAMILY
HARDY IN ZONE 4, FOR PROTECTED LOCATIONS IN ZONE 3
9 feet tall, 9 feet wide

HABIT. Deciduous shrub with slender branches; there is 1 species native to North America.
BRANCHES. Purplish when young, older ones ashy gray.
LEAVES. Elliptic to oblong, 1 to 1.2 in. long, mucronate, entire or sometimes slightly toothed, grayish green beneath; petioles 0.2 to 0.5 in. long.
FLOWERS. Less than 0.2 in. across on pedicels 1.2 in. long, polygamo-dioecious, whitish, in 1- to 4-flowered clusters, in late May or early June.
FRUIT. Dull red, 0.2 to 0.3 in. across, in September.

LANDSCAPE USE AND CULTURE
A native plant that needs more attention. Similar to winterberry, *Ilex verticillata*, it has showy red berries in the fall and similar growth habit. It needs an acidic soil. Difficult to obtain in the nursery trade.

SOUR GUM

SOUR GUM, TUPELO
Nyssa sylvatica Marsh.
FAMILY: NYSSACEAE
FOR PROTECTED LOCATIONS IN THE EASTERN PART OF ZONE 4
60 feet tall (in zone 4), 30 feet wide

HABIT. Deciduous tree with a flat-topped, nearly cylindrical head; there are 5 species found in North America and Asia.
BRANCHES. Slender, spreading, somewhat pendulous.

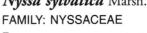

BUDS. With overlapping scales.

LEAVES. Alternate, simple, obovate or elliptic, 2 to 4.7 in. long, acute or obtusish, rarely acuminate, wedge-shaped or sometimes rounded at base, entire, rarely coarsely dentate, shiny above, glaucescent beneath, hairy on the veins or smooth at maturity; fall color bright scarlet; petioles 0.2 to 1.4 in. long, round or wing-margined.

FLOWERS. Small, polygamo-dioecious, in axillary peduncled clusters, in June; male flowers in many flowered clusters; female flowers sessile, rarely short-stalked, 1 to several, with bractlets at base, on slender or sometimes short peduncles; calyx disk- or cup-shaped on male flowers, bell-shaped on female, 5-toothed; petals 5, small, ovate to linear-oblong, inserted on margin of conspicuous disk; stamens 5 to 12, exserted; ovaries 1- to 2-celled with recurved round styles, stigmatic on inner face.

FRUIT. Oblong drupes, 0.3 to 0.5 in. long, blue-black, with a thin, bitter flesh, in October; seed stone, slightly 10- to 12-ribbed.

LANDSCAPE USE AND CULTURE

Another North American native that many wish would do better in zone 4. The Minnesota Landscape Arboretum's specimens suffer considerable dieback in most winters. It is probably a zone 4b plant. Also, the source of the seed for specimens is very important for the North. Native from Maine to Michigan and south to Florida and Texas, it has been cultivated since 1750.

IRONWOOD

IRONWOOD, AMERICAN HOP HORNBEAM

Ostrya virginiana

(Mill.) K. Koch.

FAMILY: BETULACEAE, BIRCH FAMILY

HARDY IN ZONES 3 AND 4

40 feet tall; 30 feet wide

HABIT. Deciduous tree, often growing in clumps; there are 9 species distributed throughout the northern hemisphere.

BRANCHES. Hairy when young.

BARK. Shallowly furrowed, distinctive.

BUDS. Pointed with many overlapping scales.

LEAVES. Alternate, simple, ovate to ovate-oblong, acuminate, usually somewhat heart-shaped at base, 2.2 to 4.7 in. long, dark green and sparingly hairy above and hairy on veins beneath, with 11 to 15 pairs of veins; leaves persist on tree into winter.

FLOWERS. Monoecious, in May; male catkins slender, pendulous, naked during the winter, flowers without a perianth, each bract with 3 to 14 stamens; female catkins upright, slender, with 2 flowers in the axil of each deciduous bract; ovaries enclosed in tubular involucres formed by the union of a bract and 2

bractlets and open at the apex; stigmas 2, linear.

FRUIT. Ribbed, spindle-shaped nutlets; 0.2 to 0.3 in. long, enclosed by the bladder-like involucres in August and September.

LANDSCAPE USE

A native understory tree that features fine textured twigs, hop-like fruit, persistent leaves in the winter and interesting exfoliating bark. A very good medium-sized tree for specimen plantings that also can be grown as a clump specimen. Native from Ontario to Minnesota and south to Florida and Texas, it has been cultivated since 1690.

Charles S. Sargent in volume 9 of his *Silva of North America* (1895, 35-36) describes it as owing "its common name to the clusters of fruit that hang from its branches in summer and autumn and resemble those of the Hop-vine; it is a handsome shapely tree, with its beautiful scaly bark, its dark leaves, and its broad head of slender lustrous pendulous branches presenting broad flat surfaces of yellow-green foliage, which form in the sunshine effective masses of light and shadow."

CULTURE

Ironwood has no regular insect or disease problems and will tolerate a wide range of soils. Its desired soil duplicates its woodland native habitat in being cool, moist soil, although it seems to be also drought tolerant. It is intolerant of salt and soil compaction, so does not make a good street tree. It does not transplant easily or cannot easily be grown from bareroot specimens, so is most often balled and burlapped or container grown. This tree is propagated from seed so a northern seed source is important because of its wide range. It leafs out late in the spring. Slow growing.

PACHYSANDRA

PACHYSANDRA, ALLEGHANY SPURGE

Pachysandra procumbens Michx.

FAMILY: BUXACEAE, BOX FAMILY

HARDY WITH SNOW COVER IN ZONES 2 TO 4

6 in. tall, 18 in. wide

HABIT. Half-evergreen, procumbent subshrub; there are 4 species found in North America and Asia.

BRANCHES. Slightly hairy.

LEAVES. Broadly ovate to round, 1.2 to 3.2 in. long with 5 to 10 coarse teeth toward apex, abruptly narrowed at base to a long petiole; leaves persist into winter.

FLOWERS. White to pink, in axillary spikes that are 2 to 4.7 in. tall, in May.

LANDSCAPE USE

This ground cover has grown well in protected Arboretum plantings. Native from Kentucky to Florida and Louisiana, it was been cultivated since 1800. The whorls of leaves are larger than the more often cultivated Japanese spurge. It will winter kill without snow cover.

CULTURE

Plant in semi-shade where the plants will receive good snow cover. More difficult to propagate than Japanese spurge, it is propagated by seed and softwood cuttings.

PACHYSANDRA, JAPANESE SPURGE

Pachysandra terminalis Sieb. & Zucc.

HARDY WITH SNOW COVER IN ZONE 4

10 in. tall, 18 in. wide

HABIT. Stoloniferous, evergreen subshrub.
BRANCHES. Ascending, smooth.
LEAVES. Obovate to ovate, 2 to 4 in. long, acute, wedge-shaped at base, coarsely dentate, dark green and shiny above; petioles 0.3 to 1.2 in. long.
FLOWERS. In terminal spikes that are 1.2 to 2 in. long, in May.
FRUIT. White, ovoid, 0.3 in. long, 2- to 3-horned, berry-like, in August.

LANDSCAPE USE

This pachysandra is a very good evergreen ground cover in the right location. It is native to Japan and was introduced into North America in 1882. *See photograph page 155.*

CULTURE

It must have dependable snow cover. Propagated by softwood cuttings.

CULTIVARS:

'Green Carpet'   pachysandra

Foliage develops close to the ground and is a deeper green than in the species.

'Green Sheen'   pachysandra

This cultivar features darker green, shiny leaves.

'Variegata'   pachysandra

Leaves are prominently variegated with white. Plants are not as vigorous as the species.

TREE PEONY

TREE PEONY

Paeonia suffruticosa Andr.

FAMILY: PAEONIACEAE, PEONY FAMILY

TRIAL WITH WINTER PROTECTION IN ZONE 4

6 feet tall, 4 feet wide

HABIT. Deciduous woody shrub; there are 33 species distributed throughout the northern hemisphere.
BRANCHES. Stout.
BUDS. Large with few outer scales.
LEAVES. Alternate, bipinnate, 4 to 10 in. long; leaflets broad-ovate to ovate-oblong, stalked or sessile, 3- to 5-lobed, rarely entire, glaucescent beneath and smooth or sparingly hairy; petioles 2 to 4 in. long.
FLOWERS. Perfect, solitary, 4 to 12 in. across, white, rose, or red, in early June; sepals 5, persistent, petals 5 to 10; stamens numerous; carpels 2 to 5, densely hairy, developing into dehiscent follicles, each with several large seeds.

LANDSCAPE USE AND CULTURE

It is possible to grow these borderline hardy plants in the North if one is willing to give them extra protection in the winter. They also seem to vary greatly in hardiness. One determining factor is if they are grown on their own rootstock; own root specimens seem to be much hardier.

They first must be tried in a protected location where winter snow cover is probable. They then need a structure built around them in the fall to be filled with leaves or other insulating material for good winter protection. This structure can be a wire cage or a wooden shell that completely surrounds the plants, sides and top. Enough space should be allowed so insulating material can be placed completely around each specimen. Other cultural requirements are similar to herbaceous peonies, among them being good soil drainage, full summer sun, and fertile soil. Although there are hundreds of cultivars of tree peonies, none have been tested for hardiness.

WOODBINES & IVIES

WOODBINE, THICKET CREEPER

Parthenocissus inserta (Kern.) K. Fritsch.

FAMILY: VITACEAE, GRAPE FAMILY

HARDY IN ZONES 2 TO 4

16 feet long

HABIT. Trailing or climbing vine often covering shrubs and small trees; there are 10 species distributed in North America and Asia.

BRANCHES. Green when young; tendrils with 3 to 5 long, twining branches that very rarely end in adhesive disks, and with no aerial rootlets.

LEAVES. With 5 to 7 leaflets; leaflets elliptic to oblong, 2 to 4.7 in. long, acuminate, usually wedge-shaped at base, coarsely and sharply serrate, dark green and shiny above, lighter and unusually lustrous beneath, smooth; fall color scarlet.

FLOWERS. In dichotomously branched cymes on peduncles 1.2 to 2.7 in. long, in June and July.

FRUIT. Bluish black, usually bloomy, about 0.3 in. across, 3- to 4-seeded, in August.

LANDSCAPE USE

This vine does not cling to buildings but is useful on fences, trellises and for covering rocks. It is often planted for its brilliant fall colors. Native from Quebec to Manitoba and south to Indiana and southwest to Wyoming and Texas, it has been cultivated since 1898.

CULTURE

Unlike Virginia creeper, this vine needs support similar to a trellis in order to climb. To do well it also needs more sun than the Virginia creeper.

VIRGINIA CREEPER
Parthenocissus quinquefolia
(L.) Planch.
HARDY IN ZONES 2 TO 4
30 feet long

HABIT. High-climbing vine that clings to walls.

BRANCHES. Reddish when young; tendrils with 5 to 8 branches ending in adhesive tips.

LEAVES. With 5 leaflets; leaflets stalked, elliptic to obovate-oblong, 1.5 to 4 in. long, acuminate, usually wedge-shaped at base, coarsely and often crenately serrate, dull green above, glaucescent beneath; fall color scarlet and crimson.

FLOWERS. In cymes that usually form terminal panicles in July and August.

FRUIT. Bluish black, slightly bloomy, 0.2 in. across, with 2 to 3 seeds in September and October.

LANDSCAPE USE

One of the most frequently used vines for the North because of its ability to cling to a variety of surfaces. It is used to cover walls, posts, fences, and other structures. On walls, birds often build their nests in the vines, and this can create a sanitation problem. Native from New England to Florida and west to Minnesota and Colorado, it has been cultivated since 1622. Outstanding fall color.

CULTURE

Very hardy, and tolerates a wide variety of conditions. It is one of the few vines that tolerates shaded conditions.

VARIETY:

var. *engelmannii* Rehd.   Engelmann ivy
ZONE 3 AND 4

Similar to the species except the leaflets are smaller. More often found in the nursery trade.

BOSTON IVY
Parthenocissus tricuspidata
(Sieb. & Zucc.) Planch.
HARDY IN SHELTERED LOCATIONS IN ZONE 4
30 feet long

HABIT. High-climbing vine with short, much-branched tendrils ending in sucker-like disks.

LEAVES. 3-lobed or 3-foliate with stalked leaflets; simple leaves on slender petioles, broad-ovate, 4 to 7.7 in. wide, 3-lobed with acuminate, coarsely serrate lobes; compound leaves mostly on young plants and basal shoots, 3-foliate with stalked leaflets (the middle one obovate, the lateral ones obliquely broad-ovate), coarsely serrate, smooth and shiny above, hairy on the veins beneath; fall color scarlet and orange.

FLOWERS. In cymes that are usually on short 2-leaved branches, narrow and somewhat elongated, in June and July.

FRUIT. Bluish black, 0.2 to 0.3 in. across, in September and October.

LANDSCAPE USE

This vine is useful for covering brick and stucco walls. Boston ivy clings tightly by the sucker-like tendrils. The branches make an interesting pattern on walls in winter. Native to Japan and central China, it was introduced into North America in 1862. *See photograph page 153.*

CULTURE

Occasionally the vines die back following a severe winter but new growth from the base soon vigorously grows. Unlike Virginia creeper, Boston ivy will not tolerate full shade.

ROYAL PAULOWNIA

ROYAL PAULOWNIA
Paulownia tomentosa (Thunb.) Steud.
NOT HARDY IN ZONE 4

Often advertised with glowing descriptions, often stating "hardy". It is not hardy in zone 4 and should not be attempted unless one likes to try new plants and does not worry about failure.

PAXISTIMA

CLIFF GREEN, CANBY PAXISTIMA
Paxistima canbyi A. Gray.
FAMILY: CELASTRACEAE
HARDY WITH SNOW COVER IN ZONES 2 TO 4
12 in. tall, 4 feet wide

HABIT. Low, spreading evergreen shrub; there 2 species found in North America.
BRANCHES. Root where they touch the ground.
BUDS. Ovoid with 2 pairs of outer scales.
LEAVES. Opposite, simple, broad-elliptic to oblong-obovate, 0.3 to 1.2 in. long, slightly revolute and usually serrulate above the middle.
FLOWERS. Small, green or reddish, in few flowered axillary cymes, in May; sepals 4, broad; petals 4, obovate; stamens 4, with short filaments; ovaries incompletely 2-celled, immersed in the disks; styles short, with capitate, obscurely 2-lobed stigmas.
FRUIT. Leathery capsules, opening by 2 valves, 1 to 2 seeded.

LANDSCAPE USE

Paxistima is an excellent ground cover and is also a good rock garden plant. Its growth habit and texture is more shrub-like than many ground covers. In a protected area, it could be maintained as a formal hedge. Native in the mountains of Virginia and West Virginia, it has been cultivated since 1880.

CULTURE

Needs a well-drained soil but is tolerant of a wide range of soil pH. If it does not have snow cover, it will suffer dieback in winter. Plants tolerate some shade but grow best in full sun. Propagated by cuttings. Can suffer from a leaf blight if it is under regular overhead irrigation.

The CORK TREE
Phellodendron Rupr.
FAMILY: RUTACEAE, RUE FAMILY

Cork trees feature clean, attractive foliage, and are trouble-free trees that make excellent shade or boulevard trees. If its bold fall and winter fruit are not wanted in the landscape, consider the new cultivar described below. These trees should be more widely planted in zone 4.

CULTIVAR:

'HIS MAJESTY'   cork tree

ZONE 4
40 to 60 feet tall

A fruitless male selection with an upright, vase-shaped form. It makes a good street tree. Features clean green summer foliage with yellow fall color. An introduction of Dr. Harold Pellett of The Minnesota Landscape Arboretum in 1996. It is described as being slightly hardier than the species, *P. amurense*.

AMUR CORK TREE
Phellodendron amurense Rupr.
HARDY IN ZONE 4, FOR PROTECTED LOCATIONS IN ZONE 3
40 feet tall, 30 feet wide

HABIT. Broad-headed deciduous tree; there are 10 species native to Asia.
BRANCHES. Wide-spreading, stout, orange-yellow, or yellowish gray, turning brown, with prominent lenticels; leaf scars raised, horseshoe-shaped, with the buds located in the "U" formed by the leaf scars.
BARK. Deeply ridged and furrowed on old trees, grayish black.
LEAVES. With 5 to 13 leaflets; leaflets ovate to lance-ovate, 2 to 4 in. long, long-acuminate, rounded or narrowed at base, dark green and shiny above, smooth beneath or with a few hairs along the base of the midrib.
FLOWERS. About 0.2 in. long, in minutely hairy panicles 2.2 to 3.2 in. high, in June.
FRUIT. About 0.3 in. across, with strong turpentine-like odor when crushed, in September and October.

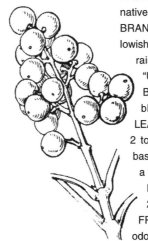

LANDSCAPE USE

An excellent shade tree with a broad, rounded canopy. The wide-spreading branches, irregular form, fall color, and interesting bark are all desirable features. Native to northern China and Manchuria, it was introduced into North America in 1856. *See photograph page 145.*

CULTURE

The Amur cork tree is generally pest and disease free. It tolerates a wide range of soil including compacted, poorly drained soils. This tree has salt tolerance and also will withstand dry soils. Some reports have been made of damage to new growth by early fall frosts. It is best to plant early in the spring from container or balled and burlapped stock so new growth hardens off before fall.

CULTIVAR:

Macho®
TRIAL IN ZONE 4
35 feet tall, 30 feet wide

A male form that does not produce seed. The leaves are thicker than the species. It has not proved to be hardy in most of zone 4.

SAKHALIN CORK TREE
Phellodendron sachalinense (F. Schmidt.) Sarg.
HARDY IN ZONE 4, FOR PROTECTED LOCATIONS IN ZONE 3
40 feet tall, 30 feet wide

HABIT. Vase-shaped tree.
BARK. Dark brown, slightly fissured and finally broken into thin plates.
LEAVES. With 7 to 11 leaflets; leaflets ovate to ovate-oblong, 2.2 to 4.7 in. long, acuminate, wedge-shaped or rounded at base, dull green above, and smooth or nearly so beneath.
FLOWERS. In nearly smooth panicles 2.2 to 3.2 in. long, in early June.
FRUIT. About 0.3 in., in September and October.

LANDSCAPE USE

Somewhat less broad and more vase-shaped than the Amur cork tree. This species also has dark brown bark as opposed to the more grayish bark of the Amur cork tree. Otherwise it is difficult to differentiate between the species. Native to Korea, northern Japan and western China it was introduced into North America in 1877.

CULTURE

Marginally hardier than *P. amurense*, it is a fast growing species.

MOCKORANGE

CULTIVARS:

(Of interspecific parentage)

'Buckley's Quill'   mockorange
ZONE 4
5 feet tall, 4 feet wide

Developed at the Ottawa Research Station, this cultivar has white double flowers that are fragrant. Good texture for a mockorange.

'Miniature Snowflake'   mockorange
ZONE 4
3 feet tall, 1 foot wide

An upright, compact grower. Double white flowers that are fragrant. Selected at Bailey Nursery of Minnesota.

'Snowgoose'   mockorange
ZONE 4
5 feet tall, 3 feet wide

Another mockorange developed at the Ottawa Research Station, this cultivar also has double white, fragrant flowers.

SWEET MOCKORANGE
Philadelphus coronarius L.
FAMILY: HYDRANGEACEAE
HYDRANGEA FAMILY
HARDY IN ZONE 4, IN SHELTERED SITES IN ZONE 3
9 feet tall, 9 feet wide

HABIT. Spreading shrub; there are 60 species distributed in North America and Asia.
BRANCHES. Arching; young branches smooth or slightly hairy.
BARK. Chestnut-brown, exfoliating.
LEAVES. Ovate to ovate-oblong, 1.5 to 3.2 in. long, remotely denticulate or dentate, smooth except bearded in the axils of the veins beneath and sometimes hairy on the veins.
FLOWERS. 1 to 1.2 in. across, creamy white, very fragrant, in 5- to 7-flowered racemes, in June; pedicels smooth or hairy, the lower ones 0.2 to 0.4 in. long; calyx smooth, rarely sparingly hairy; styles divided along half their length.

LANDSCAPE USE AND CULTURE

Often grown in the cultivar, 'Aureus', listed below. However, the species is prized for its very fragrant flowers. Native in southern Europe, it has been cultivated since 1560. It does best in full sun. It has a bold, coarse texture, so it needs to be planted at the back of a shrub border.

CULTIVAR:

'Aureus' golden mockorange

ZONE 4

4 feet tall, 4 feet wide

Commonly sold as Golden mockorange. Leaves are bright yellow when young but soon turn greenish yellow; in hot weather the leaf margins turn brown. Commonly used in foundation plantings and shrub borders for color contrast. This cultivar should be used for accent and used sparingly.

LEWIS MOCKORANGE
Philadelphus lewisii Pursh.

HARDY IN ZONE 4

6 feet tall, 6 feet wide

HABIT. Medium shrub.
BRANCHES. Smooth when young.
BARK. Red-brown or yellowish brown, with cross-cracks and slowly exfoliating.
LEAVES. Ovate to ovate-oblong, 1.2 to 2.7 in. long, acute, usually wedge-shaped at base, entire or denticulate, 3- to 5-veined with the strongest pair of veins arising above the base, usually woolly in the axils of the veins below, otherwise smooth.
FLOWERS. 1 to 1.2 in. across, scentless, in 5- to 9-flowered, dense racemes; only the lowest pair of flowers are in the leaf axils; flowers bloom from June to August; pedicels smooth, with the lower ones about 0.2 in. long; sepals lance-ovate; petals elliptic to elliptic-oblong; styles divided only at the apex or nearly to the middle.

LANDSCAPE USE AND CULTURE

Native to Alberta, Idaho, Montana, Washington and Oregon, it has been cultivated since 1823. Hardier forms and cultivars have been selected to the north of its range.

CULTIVARS:

'Blizzard' mockorange

ZONES 2 TO 4

5 feet tall, 3 feet wide

Selected in Alberta, this hardy cultivar has white, single, fragrant flowers on a medium-sized upright shrub.

'Waterton' mockorange

A hardy selection with single flowers. Planted more often than the species.

VIRGINAL MOCKORANGE
Philadelphus x virginalis Rehd.

HARDY IN SHELTERED SITES IN ZONE 4

3 to 9 feet tall, 3 to 6 feet wide

HABIT. Medium to large sized shrub.
BARK. Brown and exfoliating or gray-brown and little exfoliating.
LEAVES. Generally ovate, 1.5 to 3.2 in. long, remotely dentate or denticulate, hairy beneath.
FLOWERS. Double or semi-double, in 3- to 7-flowered racemes, in June; calyx usually densely hairy, rarely nearly smooth; styles shorter than stamens, divided along half their length.

LANDSCAPE USE AND CULTURE

This variable hybrid species probably resulted from a cross between *P. x lemoinei* and *P. x nivalis* 'Plena'. It was developed before 1910. The species and 'Minnesota Snowflake' are tall, lanky shrubs which are best used in the back of a shrub border.

CULTIVARS:

'Minnesota Snowflake' mockorange

ZONE 4

9 feet tall, 6 feet wide

Introduced by Guy D. Bush of Minneapolis and patented in 1935. Flowers double, very fragrant. Plants can grow to a height of 9 feet and also are rather leggy.

'Minnesota Snowflake Dwarf'

ZONE 4

A confused cultivar. Most often seen growing to 3 feet.

'Virginal' mockorange

FOR PROTECTED LOCATIONS IN ZONE 4

6 feet tall, 6 feet wide

Flowers double, fragrant, on plants that are 9 feet tall. This cultivar does not produce a heavy crop of flowers, which very often indicates a lack of complete hardiness.

The
NINEBARK
Physocarpus Maxim.
FAMILY: ROSACEAE, ROSE FAMILY

Ninebark species and cultivars are hard to describe. Although very useful in many differing situations they have a rather nondescript appearance. Shrubby certainly describes them. They are used as hedges and for filling in a shrub border or screen.

MOUNTAIN NINEBARK
Physocarpus monogynus (Torr.) Coult.
HARDY IN ZONE 4
3 feet tall, 3 feet wide

HABIT. Compact shrub; there are 10 species found in North America and Asia.
BRANCHES. Smooth to sparingly stellate.
LEAVES. Broad-ovate to reniform, rounded or subcordate, 0.5 to 1.2 in. long, incisely 3- to 5-lobed, with rounded, incisely serrate lobes, smooth or nearly so.
FLOWERS. 0.3 in. across, often pinkish, in few flowered umbels, in June and July; pedicels and calyx sparingly or rather densely stellate-hairy.
FRUIT. Follicles normally 2, united to about the middle, densely stellate-hairy, with spreading beaks.

LANDSCAPE USE AND CULTURE
This shrub resembles *Ribes alpinum* and should be planted more often than it is. It is useful for hedges and foundation plantings. Native from the Black Hills of South Dakota and Wyoming south to Texas and New Mexico, it has been cultivated since 1879. It is hard to find in the nursery trade.

COMMON NINEBARK
Physocarpus opulifolius (L.) Maxim.
HARDY IN ZONES 2 TO 4
9 feet tall, 9 feet wide

HABIT. Large shrub.
BRANCHES. Smooth or nearly so.
LEAVES. Roundish-ovate, 0.7 to 2.7 in. long, usually 5-lobed, with crenate-dentate obtuse or acutish lobes; undersurface smooth or nearly so.
FLOWERS. White or pinkish, about 0.3 in. across, in many flowered clusters 1.2 to 2 in. across, in June and July; pedicels and calyx smooth or sparingly hairy; stamens purplish.
FRUIT. Follicles 4 to 5, smooth, twice as long as sepals; acuminate, sometimes red, in September and October.

LANDSCAPE USE
The species is best used as a background shrub in a border. The cultivars are more often grown. Native from Quebec to Minnesota and south to Virginia and Tennessee, it has been cultivated since 1687. *See photograph page 149.*

CULTURE
Trouble-free culture with few requirements. Does better in full sun.

CULTIVARS:

'Dart's Gold'   ninebark
ZONES 3 AND 4
4 feet tall, 4 feet wide

More compact than 'Luteus' and with a better yellow color.

'Luteus'   golden ninebark
ZONES 3 AND 4
7 feet tall, 7 feet wide

Leaves bright yellow when young, becoming yellowish green as they mature. Otherwise similar to the species.

'Nanus'   dwarf ninebark
ZONES 3 AND 4
4 feet tall, 4 feet wide

A dwarf form with dark green, small leaves. Excellent for hedges.

'Nugget'   ninebark
ZONES 3 AND 4
6 feet tall, 5 feet wide

Introduced by South Dakota State University. It has good texture with light yellowish green leaves.

'Snowfall'   ninebark
ZONES 2 TO 4
6 feet tall, 6 feet wide

An introduction of Peter Dziuk from the north shore of Lake Superior. Features a more uniform, upright growth habit and good texture. Described as tolerating dry situations.

The SPRUCE

Picea A. Dietr.
FAMILY: PINACEAE, PINE FAMILY

Spruce as with other conifers add visual weight to the landscape and provide year-around interest. They are among the most adaptable conifers. The species and cultivars listed below are truly some of the most valuable ornamentals for the North. Most have a stiff character in both shape and texture.

They can be used for screening, wind breaks, and background plantings in the home landscape. They are often used as accent plants to add impact to a landscape design. Northern gardeners could not do without spruce.

NORWAY SPRUCE
Picea abies (L.) Karst.
HARDY IN ZONES 3 AND 4
90 feet tall, 40 feet wide

HABIT. Large tree; there are 35 species distributed throughout the northern hemisphere.
BRANCHES. Spreading and branchlets drooping.
BARK. Reddish brown.
BUDS. Reddish or light brown, without resin, scales at base.
LEAVES. 0.3 to 1 in. long, acute, dark green and usually shiny.
FRUIT. Cones pendulous, cylindric, 4 to 5.7 in. long, light brown, purple or green before maturity; scales thin, rhombic-ovate, with a truncate, erose-denticulate or emarginate apex.

LANDSCAPE USE
Norway spruce is the largest and fastest growing spruce for the North. It can be used in shelterbelts for a larger growing specimen. This species can thin out and loose its lower branches as it becomes mature.

It has one of the largest cones of all spruce and also has a unique pendulous branching habit. The needles are less prickly than other spruce. Native to northern and central Europe, it was introduced into North America by early settlers. This species can be used as stock for grafting any spruce species or cultivar.

CULTURE
Will withstand adverse conditions. As with most spruce, it is not tolerant of especially dry soils.

CULTIVARS:

The following cultivars should be considered only for protected sites.

'Acrocona'   Norway spruce
ZONES 3 AND 4
16 feet tall, 4 feet wide

A semi-dwarf selection that very slowly reaches its mature height. Cones produced at the tips of lateral branches. Dark green needles. Common in Europe. *See photograph page 154-55.*

'Clanbrassiliana'   Norway spruce
ZONES 3 AND 4
3 feet tall, 6 feet wide

A low, dense, flat-topped shrub. An interesting plant for a rock garden. First found in a garden in Belfast, Ireland in the 1700s.

'Little Gem'   Norway spruce
ZONE 4
1 foot tall, 1 foot wide

A very dwarf variety often found in rock gardens. It has medium green needles and is very slow growing.

'Mucronata'   Norway spruce
ZONES 3 AND 4
18 feet tall, 4 feet wide

A slow growing, upright form with sharp-pointed needles. Has an open branching habit that can be damaged by winter snows. This cultivar stays dwarf through at least the first 15 years. Introduced in France in 1835.

'Nidiformis'
ZONES 3 AND 4
3 feet tall, 4 feet wide

Similar to 'Clanbrassiliana' but with outer branches turned up, suggesting one common name, nest spruce. Vegetatively propagated from a witches'-broom.

'Pendula'   Norway spruce
ZONES 3 AND 4
Pendulous branches. Variable in the trade.

'Pumila'   Norway spruce

ZONES 3 AND 4

3 feet tall, 3 feet wide

Sold as dwarf Norway spruce. Very dense and globe-shaped. A very hardy cultivar. Light green hue.

WHITE SPRUCE

Picea glauca (Moench) Voss.

HARDY IN ZONES 2 TO 4

60 feet tall, 40 feet wide

HABIT. Large tree, pyramidal when young, becoming a narrow spire at maturity.
BARK. Grayish, scaly.
BUDS. Ovoid, obtuse, with smooth, loosely overlapping scales, rounded and bifid at the tips.
LEAVES. 0.3 to 0.7 in. long, acute or acutish, slightly curved, more or less bluish green, with a strong disagreeable odor when bruised.
FRUIT. Cones cylindric-oblong, 1.2 to 2 in. long, pale brown and glossy; scales suborbicular, with rounded and entire margins, thin and flexible; bracts spatulate, rounded at apex.

LANDSCAPE USE

White spruce is the most commonly used spruce for shelterbelts and screening. The varieties and cultivars are mainly used for ornamental purposes. Native from Labrador to Alaska and south to Montana, South Dakota, Minnesota and New York, it has been in cultivation since 1700.

CULTURE

The white spruce is more tolerant of dry conditions. The Black Hills spruce ('Densata') is one of our toughest, medium growing evergreens for adverse conditions.

CULTIVARS:

'Conica'   dwarf Alberta spruce

ZONE 4

5 feet tall, 3 feet wide

A dwarf, densely pyramidal spruce sold as dwarf Alberta spruce. It is very susceptible to winter burn and must be protected by a burlap shade during the winter. Slow growing. Found by Dr. Alfred Rehder in the Canadian Rockies in 1904.

'Densata'   Black Hills spruce

ZONES 3 AND 4

40 feet tall, 30 feet wide

Native in the Black Hills of South Dakota and usually sold as Black Hills spruce. It has a denser habit than the species. Foliage also has a more bluish cast than the species. Often

sheared in the landscape, but looks best if left more natural. It is often classified as a subspecies.

BLACK SPRUCE

Picea mariana (Mill.) BSP.

HARDY IN ZONES 2 TO 4

50 feet tall, 25 feet wide

HABIT. Conical tree.
BRANCHES. Slender, often pendulous; branchlets brown, hairy.
BARK. Red-brown, fissured.
BUDS. Ovoid, acute; hairy, pointed scales at base of terminal buds.
LEAVES. 0.2 to 0.7 in. long, obtusish, dull dark or bluish green, with stomatic bands that are broader on the upper leaf surface than on the lower surface.
FRUIT. Cones ovoid, 0.7 to 1.2 in. long, dull grayish brown, dark purple when young; scales rigid, rounded, and finely denticulate at the margin.

LANDSCAPE USE AND CULTURE

This spruce is seldom used ornamentally. It usually has irregular form as it reaches maturity. Although native to swamps it also grows in well-drained soils. Native from Labrador to Alaska and south to Minnesota, Wisconsin and Virginia, it has been in cultivation since 1700.

CULTIVAR:

'Nana'

ZONES 3 AND 4

2 feet tall, 3 feet wide

This mounded-shaped cultivar is sold as blue nest spruce. Bluish cast needles. Needs a cooler, partially shaded site. It is very slow-growing.

SERBIAN SPRUCE

Picea omorika (Pancic) Purk.

HARDY IN ZONE 4

60 feet tall, 30 feet wide

HABIT. Narrow, pyramidal tree.
BRANCHES. Short, ascending or pendulous.
BARK. Coffee-brown, scaling off in plate-like layers.
BUDS. Dark brown, not resinous; long pointed scales at base of terminal buds.
LEAVES. Compressed, 0.3 to 0.7 in. long, keeled on both sides, about less than 0.1 in. wide, obtuse and mucronulate, with 2 broad white bands above, shiny dark green beneath.
FRUIT. Cones ovoid-oblong, 1.2 to 2.2 in. long, shiny cinnamon-brown; scales suborbicular, finely denticulate.

LANDSCAPE USE AND CULTURE

A most attractive spruce suitable for sheltered locations. Some needle burn can be expected in an exposed site. Native to southeastern Europe, it was introduced into North America in 1880.

CULTIVAR:

'Nana' dwarf Serbian spruce
ZONE 4
4 to 5 feet tall, 6 feet wide

A dense shrub, broader than high, with horizontal spreading branches. Originated in the Netherlands in the 1930s. Sold as dwarf Serbian spruce.

COLORADO SPRUCE
Picea pungens Engelm.
HARDY IN ZONES 3 AND 4
60 feet tall, 30 feet wide

HABIT. Pyramindal tree.
BRANCHES. Horizontal, stout, in whorls.
BUDS. With brownish yellow, usually reflexed scales.
LEAVES. Rigid, 0.7 to 1.2 in. long, spiny-pointed, incurved, bluish green, rarely dull green.
FRUIT. Cones cyclindric-oblong, 2.2 to 4 in. long, light brown; scales thin, flexible, rhombic-oblong, narrowed and erose at apex.

LANDSCAPE USE

One of the more widely planted of the spruce. There are many cultivars which vary in form and foliage color. The species is often used for shelterbelt plantings. Native in Colorado, New Mexico, Utah and Wyoming, it has been in cultivation since 1862. The species is not grown as much as the glaucous forms.

CULTURE

In exposed or dry soils, blue spruce is shorter-lived. Cytospora canker can cause the death of lower branches as trees approach maturity at about 25 years of age. Mike Zins of the Minnesota Landscape Arboretum calls these denuded specimens, "Minnesota palms".

CULTIVARS AND VARIETIES:

f. *glauca* (Reg.) Beissn.
ZONES 3 AND 4
60 feet tall, 30 feet wide

This variety name is given to all plants whose foliage has a bluish cast. The following cultivars probably have been selected from this variety. *See photograph pages 182-82*

'Bakeri' Colorado spruce
ZONES 3 AND 4
20 feet tall, 15 feet wide

Needles are very deep blue. Selected in Connecticut in 1933.

'Fat Albert' Colorado spruce
ZONE 2 TO 4
15 feet tall, 10 feet wide

An introduction of Iseli Nursery that has done well in northern climates. It is a grafted variety that is very slow-growing. It has an outstanding blue color.

'Globosa' Colorado spruce
ZONES 3 AND 4
4 feet tall, 5 feet wide

Mound-shaped and very compact. Selected in the Netherlands in 1937. Slower maturing.

'Hoopsii' Colorado spruce
ZONES 3 AND 4
25 feet tall, 10 feet wide

A very dense, pyramidal tree. Probably the most glaucus form. Seldom seen at mature height and width.

'Moerheimii' Colorado spruce
ZONES 3 AND 4
Slow growing to 30 feet

A narrow, upright tree with short, irregularly whorled branches.

'Montgomery' Colorado spruce
ZONES 3 AND 4
3 feet tall, 3 to 4 feet wide

A dwarf, compact shrub with blue-gray foliage. Hardy, it can be used in shelterbelt plantings.

Other spruce to try:

ENGELMANN SPRUCE
P. engelmannii Parry & Engelm.
This spruce has done well at The Minnesota Landscape Arboretum but it is seldom planted in the Midwest.

The PINES
Pinus L.
FAMILY: PINACEAE, PINE FAMILY

Pine, as with spruce, are among the North's feature plants. Ranging from some of the tallest trees for the North to very dwarf conifers, this genus should be represented in everyone's landscape. Pines have many utilitarian uses in the landscape, including use in windbreaks, for screening and attracting wildlife. Ornamentally, pines add visual weight, winter interest, and attractive textures of leaf, fruit and bark. There are many which are certainly among the hardiest plants to consider for the North.

Thoreau in his *A Week on the Concord and Merrimack Rivers* (1961, 150) saw "the very uprightness of pines...asserts the ancient rectitude and vigor of nature. Our lives need the relief of such a background, where the pine flourishes and the jay still screams." Aldo Leopold in *A Sand County Almanac* (1949, 70) stated "The only conclusion I have ever reached is that I love all trees, but I am in love with pines." And again in pages 86-87, "Pines have earned the reputation of being 'evergreen' by the same device that governments use to achieve the appearance of perpetuity: overlapping terms of office. By taking on new needles on the new growth of each year, and discarding old needles at longer intervals, they have led the casual onlooker to believe that needles remain forever green."

BRISTLE-CONE PINE, HICKORY PINE
Pinus aristata Engelm.
TRIAL IN SHELTERED LOCATIONS IN ZONE 4
9 feet tall, 6 feet wide

HABIT. Irregular, bushy tree; there are 110 species distributed throughout the northern hemisphere.

BRANCHES. Smooth or minutely hairy at first, light orange.
LEAVES. 5 in a cluster, stout or slender, 0.7 to 1.5 in. long, dark green, usually with a conspicuous whitish exudate of resin.
FRUIT. Cones cylindric-ovoid, 1.5 to 3.5 in. long.

LANDSCAPE USE
An interesting novelty for the back of a rock garden. Native to California, Utah, Colorado and Arizona, it has been in cultivation since 1861. In native stands this species is reported to be the oldest of living plants. Some trees are 3000 years old.

CULTURE
Plant only in sheltered locations and protect from the winter sun. Winter burn can be a serious problem in the sunny midwest. Bristle-cone pine require a well drained soil.

JACK PINE
Pinus banksiana Lamb.
HARDY IN ZONES 2 TO 4
60 feet tall, 30 feet wide

HABIT. Open-headed tree.
BRANCHES. Slender, spreading.
BARK. Dark brown, slightly tinged with red, fissured into narrow ridges covered with thick scales.
BUDS. Oblong-ovoid, light brown, very resinous.
LEAVES. 2 in a cluster, rigid, twisted, spreading, 0.7 to 1.5 in. long, acute or obtusish, bright or dark green.
FLOWERS. Male, yellow.
FRUIT. Female cones erect, conic-ovoid, oblique and usually curved sharply, 1.2 to 2 in. long, tawny yellow, shiny.

LANDSCAPE USE AND CULTURE
Jack pine should be used more ornamentally. It has an open character that matches modern architecture. Sometimes planted to reforest sandy soils. Native from Hudson Bay to New York and Minnesota, it has been in cultivation since 1783.

CULTIVARS:

'Uncle Fogy' Jack pine
ZONES 3 AND 4
6 feet tall, 6 feet wide

Introduced by The Minnesota Landscape Arboretum in 1971. A prostrate form with ascending branching. It can also be grown as a weeping tree if grafted on a jack pine understock at the desired height.

Various other forms of witches'-broom
About half of the seedlings grown from seed collected from witches'-broom will be dwarf and the other half normal. Most dwarf plants are very compact and more or less globe-shaped. The size varies with the seed source, but plants are seldom more than 3 to 5 feet tall.

SWISS STONE PINE
Pinus cembra L.
HARDY IN ZONE 4, FOR PROTECTED LOCATIONS IN ZONE 3
50 feet tall, 20 feet wide

HABIT. Narrow-pyramidal tree.
BRANCHES. Short with densely brown-hairy branchlets.
BUDS. Globose-ovoid, acuminate.
LEAVES. In clusters of 5, straight, 2 to 4.7 in. long, serrulate, dark green.
FRUIT. Cones short-stalked, ovoid, 2 to 3.2 in. long, light brown; scales slightly reflexed at the tips.

LANDSCAPE USE AND CULTURE
A very ornamental pine with great character. It makes a great specimen tree in a more protected location. Native to the central European Alps, northeastern Russia and northern Asia, it was introduced into North America by early settlers. It seldom reaches its mature height in the North.

VARIETY:

ssp. sibirica (Du Tour) Rupr.
Taller than the species and with shorter leaves and larger cones. Possibly hardier than the species. Some authorities now treat this variety as a species, *P. sibirica*.

JAPANESE RED PINE
Pinus densiflora Sieb. & Zucc.
HARDY IN ZONE 4, SELECTED STRAINS HARDY IN ZONE 3
50 feet tall, 30 feet wide

HABIT. Picturesque tree.
BRANCHES. Horizontal, orange-yellow.
BARK. Orange-red, thin, scaly.
BUDS. Oblong-ovoid, chestnut-brown.
LEAVES. 2 in a cluster, 3.2 to 4.7 in. long, bright bluish green.
FRUIT. Cones, short-stalked, conic-ovoid to oblong, 1.2 to 2 in. long, dull tawny yellow.

LANDSCAPE USE AND CULTURE
Care should be taken in buying these pines. Specimens in the nursery trade vary greatly as far as hardiness. The hardy specimens found at the Arboretum came from seed from the Forestry Research Station at Cloquet, Minnesota. Many of the other Japanese red pine at the Arboretum have died of winter injury.

CULTIVAR:

'Umbraculifera' Japanese umbrella pine
FOR PROTECTED LOCATIONS IN ZONE 4
9 feet tall, irregular width

The Japanese umbrella pine is an interesting tree with an umbrella-like head. Winter burn has been a serious problem on this cultivar.

LIMBER PINE
Pinus flexilis James.
HARDY IN ZONES 2 TO 4
45 feet tall, 30 feet wide

HABIT. Narrow-pyramidal tree when young, becoming broad and round-topped with age.
BRANCHES. Slightly hairy at first, soon smooth.
BARK. At first smooth and silvery white to gray, becoming dark brown to nearly black and deeply fissured.
LEAVES. 5 in a cluster, slender, 1.2 to 3.5 in. long, with stomata on the back, usually entire, dark green.
FRUIT. Cones, short-stalked, ovoid to cylindric-ovoid, 2.7 to 5.7 in. long, yellow to light brown, shiny; scales rounded at apex.

LANDSCAPE USE AND CULTURE
An adaptable pine that can be used as a specimen tree or in mass plantings. It has attractive twisted needles. Winter burn can be a problem on younger trees. Native from Alberta to California and east to western North Dakota and Texas, it has been in cultivation since 1861. Needs a more moist soil than other pines, although it is used extensively in western parts of our region.

KOREAN PINE
Pinus koraiensis Sieb. & Zucc.
HARDY IN ZONES 3 AND 4
65 feet tall, 40 feet wide

HABIT. Loosely pyramidal tree spreading with age.
BARK. Gray-brown, scaly.
BRANCHLETS. With yellow-brown hairs.
BUDS. Oblong-ovoid, dark chestnut-brown.
LEAVES. Dark green, straight, 2.2 to 4.7 in. long, serrulate.
FRUIT. Cones, short-stalked, 3.5 to 5.5 in. long, conic-ovoid, or conic-oblong, yellow-brown; scales with recurved obtuse apex.

LANDSCAPE USE AND CULTURE
Korean pine is slow growing and makes a beautiful specimen tree in protected locations. Korean pine is one of the best pines for our area. Native to Japan and Korea, it was introduced into North America in 1861. It has large edible seeds.

MUGO PINE, SWISS MOUNTAIN PINE
Pinus mugo Turra.
HARDY IN ZONES 3 AND 4
35 feet tall, 30 feet wide

HABIT. Usually mounded shrub.
BRANCHES. Brown.
LEAVES. 2 in a cluster, crowded, stout, 1.2 to 3.2 in. long, bright green.
FRUIT. Cones, subsessile, ovoid or conic-ovoid, 0.7 to 2.7 in. long, tawny-yellow or dark brown, shiny.

LANDSCAPE USE
A confused plant in the nursery trade. Evergreens sold as mugo pine can range from large, if slow growing, specimens to 35 feet tall, to cultivars which can be very dwarf rock garden plants. The species makes a very handsome specimen plant or can be used in large-scale, mass plantings. The dwarf cultivars are often sheared giving them an unattractive, polka dot effect in the landscape. Native to the mountains of central and southern Europe, this pine was introduced into North America in 1779. There are many named cultivars of this species.

CULTURE
Tolerant of a wide range of conditions, they do best in a reasonably moist, protected site. In exposed locations they do less well and can suffer from scale insects and other problems.

CULTIVARS AND VARIETIES:

'Compacta'   mugo pine
ZONES 3 AND 4
3 feet tall, 4 feet wide

A dense, globe-shaped shrub, but is unfortunately difficult to obtain in the nursery trade.

var. *pumilio*   mugo pine
A variable variety up to 10 feet tall and 20 feet wide. This is probably the variety being grown by most nurseries as mugo pine. A variety found in alpine environments, naturally dwarfed through the millennia.

AUSTRIAN PINE
Pinus nigra Arnold.
HARDY IN ZONE 4, FOR PROTECTED LOCATIONS IN ZONE 3
65 feet tall, 50 feet wide

HABIT. Large tree that is pyramidal when young, becoming flat-topped with age.
BRANCHES. Light brown, horizontally spreading.
BARK. With dark brown furrows and gray or gray-brown mottled ridges.
BUDS. Ovoid or oblong-ovoid, light brown, resinous.
LEAVES. 2 in a cluster, stiff, 3.5 to 6.2 in. long, dark green.
FRUIT. Cones, subsessile, ovoid, 2 to 4.7 in. long, yellowish brown, shiny.

LANDSCAPE USE
One of the most widely used pines for ornamental purposes. It has a bold texture. Native to central and southern Europe and to Asia Minor, it was introduced into North America in 1759.

CULTURE
Austrian pine should be selected from seed sources from northern strains. These strains are variously listed as var. *nigra*, subspecies *nigra* or var. *austriaca*. This pine has shown more tolerance to salt than have most of our native pines. Winter burn can be a problem on young trees, so plant in more protected sites.

PONDEROSA PINE, WESTERN YELLOW PINE
Pinus ponderosa Dougl. & Lawson.
ssp. scopulorum (Engelm.) E. Murray.
HARDY IN ZONE 4, FOR PROTECTED LOCATION IN ZONE 3
65 feet tall, 40 feet wide

HABIT. Large tree that is pyramidal at first, becoming irregularly cylindrical with age.
BRANCHES. Horizontally spreading; branchlets orange-brown, fragrant when broken.
BARK. Deeply fissured into ridges or large plates on mature trees, dark brown to nearly black.
BUDS. Oblong to ovoid, resinous.

LEAVES. 2 to 3 in a cluster, generally rigid, 4.7 to 6.2 in. long, dark green.
FRUIT. Cones, subsessile, often in clusters, ovoid, 3.2 to 4.7 in. long, light reddish or yellowish brown, shiny.

LANDSCAPE USE AND CULTURE

This form of ponderosa pine is widely used in shelterbelts, as specimen trees, and for mass plantings. Native in western North and South Dakota, Nebraska, and eastern Wyoming, it has been in cultivation since 1827. Other forms of the species are not as hardy, so care should be taken of where the original seed source was obtained. Ponderosa pine has many disease and physiological problems and can be short-lived in our area.

RED PINE, NORWAY PINE

Pinus resinosa Ait.

HARDY IN ZONES 3 AND 4
65 feet tall, 40 feet wide

HABIT. Large tree; stout spreading, sometimes pendulous branches form a broad pyramidal crown.
BARK. Red-brown, shallowly fissured, and scaly.
BUDS. Ovoid, acuminate, light brown, resinous.
LEAVES. 2 in a cluster, flexible, 4.7 to 7 in. long.
FRUIT. Cones, subsessile, conic-ovoid, symmetrical, 1.5 to 2.2 in. long, nut-brown, falling the third year.

LANDSCAPE USE

Red pine is the state tree of Minnesota. This pine makes a handsome large growing specimen. Mature specimens have attractive fissured bark. Native from Nova Scotia to Manitoba and south to Pennsylvania and Minnesota, it has been in cultivation since 1756.

CULTURE

Grows best in sandy loam soils. Suffers salt damage if planted close to salted highways.

CULTIVAR:

'Wissota'   red pine

ZONES 3 AND 4
4 to 5 feet tall, 5 to 6 feet wide

A dwarf form introduced by The Minnesota Landscape Arboretum in 1996. This round-shaped dwarf conifer can be used in rock gardens or other sites where a slow-growing evergreen is needed.

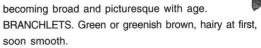

EASTERN WHITE PINE

Pinus strobus L.

HARDY IN ZONES 3 AND 4
80 feet tall, 50 feet wide

HABIT. Symmetrical, pyramidal tree when young, becoming broad and picturesque with age.
BRANCHLETS. Green or greenish brown, hairy at first, soon smooth.
BARK. Thick, deeply fissured into broad scaly ridges, dark grayish brown.
BUDS. Ovoid, acuminate, slightly resinous.
LEAVES. 5 in a cluster, slender, soft, 2.2 to 5.5 in. long, serrulate, bluish green to dark green.
FRUIT. Cones, narrow-cylindric, often curved, 3.2 to 7.7 in. long, brown.

LANDSCAPE USE

Much of the climax conifer forest of eastern North America was the white pine. Very few remnants remain of this vast forest. It must have been amazing to view these over 100 foot tall mammoths. They are very suited for use as ornamentals if their few cultural requirements are met. Native from Nova Scotia to Manitoba and south to Pennsylvania and Minnesota, white pine have been in cultivation since 1756. Relatively fast growing. "Each pine is like a great green feather stuck in the ground" as described by Thoreau in his *Journal*, vol 4 (1851, 200).

CULTURE

White pine grows best on sandy loam soils. They can suffer winter burn in extremely exposed sites, especially to the north of their range. If considering them for planting along roadways, remember they can suffer from salt injury. It is important to select specimens grown from northern seed sources.

CULTIVARS:

As with the jack and red pines, there are many dwarf, mounded selections grown from seed collected on "witches'-broom". These have not been named. Cultivars should be considered only for protected locations.

'Contorta'   Eastern white pine

ZONE 4?
An interesting novelty with twisted branches and twisted needles. Selected in Rochester, New York in the 1930s.

'Fastigiata'   Eastern white pine

ZONE 4
25 feet tall, 8 feet wide

A narrow tree with fastigiate branches that ascend at a 45° angle.

'Nana'   Eastern white pine
ZONE 4
4 feet tall, 6 feet wide

Features a compact, rounded form. Needles have a bluish-silver cast.

'Pendula'   Eastern white pine
ZONE 4
10 feet tall, 10 feet wide

A weeping form with pendulous branches. Must be staked when young in order to develop a symmetrical form. It takes many years before specimens reach mature size and form.

SCOTCH PINE
Pinus sylvestris L.
HARDY IN ZONE 4, SELECTED STRAINS
HARDY IN ZONE 3
65 feet tall, 40 feet wide

HABIT. Pyramidal tree when young but soon becoming round-topped and irregular.
BRANCHLETS. Dull grayish yellow.
BARK. Red or reddish brown, resinous.
LEAVES. 2 in a cluster, rigid, usually twisted, 1.2 to 2.7 in. long, bluish green.
FRUIT. Cones, short-stalked, reflexed, conic-oblong, symmetrical or sometimes oblique, 1.2 to 2.7 in. long, dull tawny yellow.

LANDSCAPE USE
Useful ornamental for a specimen tree. Perhaps best planted in groupings. Its reddish brown bark becomes a feature in the landscape as specimens mature and become more open. Native from Europe to Siberia, it was introduced into North America by early settlers.

CULTURE
The hardiness of the Scotch pine varies with the seed source. Make sure you plant strains known to be hardy in your area.

CULTIVARS:

Again, plant only in protected locations.

'Fastigiata'   Scotch pine
ZONE 4

A narrow, upright form often called the sentinel pine.

'Watereri'   Scotch pine
ZONE 4
10 feet tall, 7 feet wide

A slow-growing, densely pyramidal tree that develops a flat top with age. It has silvery blue needles.

HIMALAYAN PINE
Pinus wallichiana Jackson.
HARDY IN ZONE 4
40 feet tall, 40 feet wide

HABIT. Large conical, open-crowned tree.
BRANCHES. Whorled, ascending.
LEAVES. In clusters of 5, hanging, to 8 in. long, grey-green to blue-green.
FRUIT. Cones long-stalked, 6 to 10 in. long, resinous; scales keeled.

LANDSCAPE USE AND CULTURE
This handsome pine's hardiness has been rated variously from zone 8 to zone 4. Like many other pines, hardiness depends on the seed source. Specimens at The Minnesota Landscape Arboretum are growing well. In its native habitat and further south, this pine reaches over 100 feet; it remains smaller in the North. It is a stout grower so it needs room to spread. Also, if planted in a sunny location it seems to retain its lower branches. In exposed locations it is susceptible to winter burn.

PLANE TREE & SYCAMORE

LONDON PLANE TREE
Platanus x acerifolia
(Ait.) Willd.
FAMILY: PLATANACEAE
FOR PROTECTED LOCATIONS IN ZONE 4
90 feet tall, 60 feet wide

HABIT. Deciduous tree; there are 6 species native mostly in North America.
BRANCHES. Wide spreading, the lower ones drooping.
BARK. Exfoliates in large flakes.
LEAVES. With square to heart-shaped bases, 4.7 to 10 in. wide, smooth or nearly so at maturity, 3- to 5-lobed; lobes triangular-ovate or broad-triangular, not or sparingly toothed, with acute or rounded sinuses extending to about one-third the length of the blade; petioles 1.2 to 4 in. long.
FRUIT. Heads 1 to 3, usually 2, about 1 in. across, bristly; seeds nutlets ovoid or rounded at the apex and crowned by a persistent remnant of the style.

LANDSCAPE USE AND CULTURE
This large growing tree should only be tried in a very protected location. It probably is not as hardy as *P. occidentalis*, but is used throughout eastern North America as a boulevard tree. This hybrid species probably resulted from a cross between *P. occidentalis* and *P. orientalis*. It has been cultivated in North America since 1700.

SYCAMORE, BUTTONWOOD
Platanus occidentalis L.
FOR PROTECTED LOCATIONS IN ZONE 4
90 feet tall, 60 feet wide

HABIT. Large tree in favorable climates, with a tall central trunk and a round or oval crown.
BARK. Almost creamy white, exfoliating in rather small plates.
LEAVES. Square or heart-shaped (rarely wedge-shaped) at base, 4 to 9 in. wide, often broader than long, 3- or sometimes 5-lobed with shallow sinuses and broad triangular lobes, coarsely toothed or rarely entire.
FRUIT. Usually solitary, about 1.2 in. across, rather smooth at maturity; seeds nutlets with square or obtuse apex and a short style, no exserted hairs between nutlets.

LANDSCAPE USE AND CULTURE

Again, a large growing tree that should be tried in protected locations. A few trees of this species can be found growing in parks and yards from the Twin Cities southward. Native from Maine to Ontario and south to Florida and Texas, it has been in cultivation since 1640.

The POPLARS, ASPEN and COTTONWOODS
Populus L.
FAMILY: SALICACEAE, WILLOW FAMILY

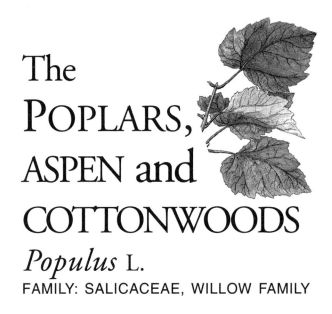

A rather weedy genus of trees, but with trees that meet specific site requirements. They are often used in shelterbelts and in locations where more desirable trees will not survive. Some are very short-lived, others live to become mammoths.

CULTIVARS:

Numerous natural and man-made hybrids are sold as fast growing trees. The following are some of the more-often found.

'Highland'   poplar
ZONES 3 AND 4
40 feet tall, 25 feet wide

'Highland' is seedless and smaller growing, so it could be considered in home landscapes. Introduced by Highland Nursery of Colorado.

'Nor'easter'   poplar
ZONE 4
70 feet tall, 45 feet wide

A sterile female form (non-fruiting) introduced by the Nebraska Experiment Station. Has disease resistance.

'Prairie Sky'   poplar
ZONES 2 TO 4
65 feet tall, 10 feet wide

One of the most hardy poplars, seedless and fast growing. Introduced by the Morden Experiment Station in Manitoba.

'Robusta'   poplar

ZONES 3 AND 4
50 feet tall, 35 feet wide

A seedless variety introduced in 1895 in France. Somewhat susceptible to cytospora canker.

'Tower'   poplar

ZONES 3 AND 4
50 feet tall, 8 to 10 feet wide

A rapidly growing columnar, seedless variety introduced by the Morden Research Station in Manitoba. Has disease resistance.

WHITE POPLAR
Populus alba L.

HARDY IN ZONES 2 TO 4
65 feet tall, 50 feet wide

HABIT. Tree with spreading crown; there are 35 species distributed throughout the northern hemisphere.
BRANCHES and BUDS. White-hairy when young.
BARK. Whitish gray, smooth, becoming rough and blackish at the base.
LEAVES. Ovate to elliptic-oblong, usually 3- to 5-lobed (with triangular, coarsely toothed lobes), acute, sub-cordate or rounded at base, 2.2 to 4.7 in. long, dark green above, white-hairy beneath; petioles hairy.
FLOWERS. Female catkins about 2 in. long, male catkins longer; scales dentate, fringed with long hairs; stigmas 4; stamens 6 to 10.

LANDSCAPE USE AND CULTURE

A weed tree that is not suited for most landscape conditions. However, many are intrigued by the white poplar's leaves which are shiny green on top and stark white-hairy on the underside. It has an invasive root system that can plug sewer lines. It also annoyingly suckers too freely with suckers appearing throughout the growing season in lawns and cultivated beds. As with many poplars its branching is also brittle, often breaking in storms. Native to central and southern Europe, western Siberia and central Asia, it was introduced into North America by early settlers.

CULTIVAR:

'Pyramidalis'   Bolleana poplar

ZONE 3 & 4
To 60 feet, 10 feet wide

The Bolleana poplar is a narrow, pyramidal form has the same objectionable features as the species and is not long-lived. It is often planted for a quick windbreak where space is limited.

COTTONWOOD
Populus deltoides

Bart. & Marsh.
HARDY IN ZONES 2 TO 4
90 feet tall, 65 feet wide

HABIT. Large tree, upright-spreading branches form a rather open, broad head.
BRANCHLETS. Slightly angled or nearly round, smooth.
BUDS. Brownish, sticky.
LEAVES. Deltoid-ovate or broad-ovate, acuminate, subcordate to square and with 2 or 3 glands at base, coarsely crenate-dentate with curved teeth, entire near base and apex, densely ciliate, 2.7 to 4.7 in. long, bright green below, smooth; fall color golden yellow.
FLOWERS. Male catkins 2.7 to 4 in. long; scales divided into filiform lobes; stamens 40 to 60; stigmas 3 to 4; female catkins 5.8 to 7.7 in. long.
FRUIT. Capsules, short-stalked, 3- to 4-valved.

LANDSCAPE USE AND CULTURE

One sees giant-sized specimens in western parts of our region in river bottoms or lake margins where other trees will not survive. Its cotton-like seeds can cause summer blizzards where the trees are prevalent. Cottonwood is generally too large growing to consider planting in home landscapes. Less objectionable are male selected varieties, which do not produce the prolific seeds.

Thoreau, on his visit to Minnesota, as found in Walter Harding's edition of his journal (1962, 18) remarked on a specimen near Lake Harriet (in south Minneapolis) Thoreau estimated as being 90 feet high and 7 feet in diameter. Native from Quebec to North Dakota and south to Florida and Texas, it has been in cultivation since 1750. One also recalls Howard Nemerov, in his poem *Above* (1981, 443.): "And puffs of seed go raining down the wind."

CULTIVARS AND VARIETIES:

ssp. *monilifera* (Ait.) Eckenw.   Sargent poplar

ZONE 4
80 feet tall, 40 feet wide

It is very similar to the species, although less hardy. Research at The Minnesota Landscape Arboretum showed considerable dieback on new shoots at an extreme -32 degrees F. on this species. Sometimes listed as *P. sargentii.*

'Siouxland'   cottonwood

ZONES 3 AND 4
90 feet tall, 40 feet wide

A male selection (no seeds) introduced by South Dakota State University. It is resistant to rust. Fast growing.

BLACK POPLAR
Populus nigra L.
HARDY IN MOST SITES IN ZONE 4
80 feet tall, 50 feet wide

HABIT. Large tree, usually with a short trunk.
BRANCHES. Stout, wide spreading; branchlets round, smooth, orange, changing to ashy gray.
BARK. Deeply furrowed, often with large burs.
BUDS. Sticky, reddish, elongated and curving outward at apex.
LEAVES. Rhombic-ovate, long-acuminate, broadly wedge-shaped at base, finely crenate-serrate, 2 to 4 in. long, smooth, light green beneath; petioles slender.
FLOWERS. Male catkins 1.5 to 2.2 in. long; scales laciniate; stamens 20 to 30; fruiting catkins 4 to 5.8 in. long.
FRUIT. Capsules, 2-valved on slender pedicels.

LANDSCAPE USE AND CULTURE
The species is not planted, but the cultivars are planted for their unique form, especially the Lombardy poplar. Cytospora canker is a major problem.

CULTIVARS AND VARIETIES:

Most cultivars are relatively short-lived, especially on droughty soils.

'Afghanica'   Theves poplar
ZONES 2 TO 4
50 feet tall, 12 feet wide

This variety, native to western Asia and northern Africa, has an upright shape but is broader than 'Italica'. More resistant to the cytospora canker.

'Italica'   Lombardy poplar
ZONES 3 AND 4
50 feet tall, 8 feet wide

This is the narrow, columnar tree, that was widely planted for its upright form. Subject to cytospora canker. The Theves poplar should be planted in its place.

QUAKING ASPEN
Populus tremuloides Michx.
HARDY IN ZONES 2 TO 4
65 feet tall, 40 feet wide

HABIT. Tree with a roundish crown and a suckering habit.
BRANCHLETS. Smooth, reddish brown, slender.
BARK. Smooth and grayish white.
BUDS. Ovoid, pointed, slightly sticky.
LEAVES. Thin, ovate to orbicular, short-acuminate, square to broadly wedge-shaped at base, finely grandular-serrate, 1.1

to 2.7 in. long, smooth and glaucescent beneath; fall color golden yellow.
FLOWERS. Male and female catkins on separate trees, 1.5 to 2.5 in. long, scales deeply lobed and fringed.

LANDSCAPE USE AND CULTURE
Can be used effectively in naturalistic plantings, although again it suckers too frequently for most landscape conditions. It will withstand wet spring soils. The clean, green-gray bark is attractive. An important pulp tree. Native from Labrador to Alaska and south to Pennsylvania and California, it has been in cultivation since 1812.

The contemporary nature writer, Ann Zwinger, in her classic *Beyond the Aspen Grove* describes the uniqueness of the aspen's leaves (1970, 184):

> The leaf stalks are longer than the leaf itself, and are flattened at right angles to the leaf, acting like pivots. The leaves quiver and catch the light in a nervous rhythm...Any whisper of air sets them sibilating, telling all they know over the back fences of the pine ridges.

CULTIVAR:

'Pikes Bay'
ZONES 2 TO 4
70 feet tall, 30 feet wide

Described as being more canker-resistant. This cultivar was found bythe University of Minnesota Department of Forestry in northern Minnesota.

Others poplars to try:

All should be considered fast-growing, and short-lived.

LANCELEAF POPLAR
P. x acuminata Rydb.
ZONES 3 AND 4
40 feet tall, 25 feet wide

Upright growing and smaller-sized.

NARROWLEAF POPLAR
P. angustifolia James.
HARDY IN ZONES 2 TO 4
60 feet tall, 40 feet wide

Has reasonable pyramidal habit, but suckers readily limiting its usefulness.

BALSAM POPLAR, TACAMAHAC
P. balsamifera L.
HARDY IN ZONES 2 TO 4
80 feet tall, 50 feet wide

This poplar could be planted in parks and large grounds. It can also be considered a pulp timber tree.

LARGE-TOOTHED ASPEN
P. grandidentata Michx.
HARDY IN ZONES 2 TO 4
65 feet tall, 50 feet wide

A native tree that is seldom planted. It is used for pulp.

JAPANESE POPLAR
P. maximowiczii Henry.
HARDY IN ZONE 4
80 feet tall, 50 feet wide

An ornamental poplar that is hard to obtain in the nursery trade. The bark is attractive. Resistant to cytospora canker.

EUROPEAN ASPEN
P. tremula L.
HARDY IN ZONES 2 TO 4
65 feet tall, 40 feet wide

The cultivar, 'Erecta', is planted more often than the species. This male selection from the forests of Sweden is a narrow, columnar tree. It is slower growing and more disease resistant than the Bolleana or Lombardy poplars.

POTENTILLA

POTENTILLA,
SHRUBBY CINQUEFOIL
Potentilla fruticosa L.
FAMILY: ROSACEAE, ROSE FAMILY
HARDY IN ZONES 2 TO 4
Variable 1 to 4 feet tall, 2 to 4 feet wide

HABIT. Compact deciduous shrub; there are 500 species distributed throughout the northern hemisphere.
BARK. Shreddy.
LEAVES. Alternate, pinnately compound, with 3 to 7 leaflets; leaflets sessile, elliptic to linear-oblong, acute, 0.3 to 1 in. long, more or less silky, with revolute margins.
FLOWERS. Usually yellow, occasionally white or pink, 0.7 to

1 in. across, solitary or few on slender stalks from June to frost; sepals triangular-ovate; bractlets unsually linear.

LANDSCAPE USE
Shrubs that are widely planted for their more or less continuous bloom of small, rose-like flowers. They can be useful in foundation plantings, as low hedges, and in the foreground of shrub borders. They do not have a bold character or texture and probably are most successful used in mass as opposed to single specimens. Also, some of the more pastel shades of flowers are more attractive than the traditional bright yellow. The many cultivars are similar except for flower color. Native throughout the northern hemisphere, they have been in cultivation since 1700.

CULTURE
Potentilla grows best in full sun. They tolerate a wide range of soil types. These cultivars should be hardy in zones 2 to 4:

CULTIVARS:

'Abbotswood'
Flowers white with a pinkish blush, on a 2 to 3 foot shrub.

'Coronation Triumph'   potentilla
A mound-shaped plant, about 3 feet tall, with abundant yellow bloom.

Dakota Goldrush™   potentilla
P.f. 'Absaraka'
Bright yellow flowers on a dwarf shrub 2 to 3 feet tall.

Dakota Sunspot™   potentilla
P.f. 'Fargo'
Golden yellow flowers on a dwarf shrub 2 to 3 feet tall.

'Farreri'   potentilla
Flowers golden yellow on a 2 foot shrub. Same plant as 'Gold Drop' in the trade.

'Goldfinger'   potentilla
A compact shrub, 3 feet tall, with bright yellow flowers.

'Jackmanii'   potentilla
A vigorous shrub to 4 feet tall with large bright yellow flowers.

'Katherine Dykes'   potentilla
A low-arching plant, seldom over 2 feet tall, with light lemon-yellow flowers.

Potentilla

'Longacre'   potentilla

One of the dwarfest varieties, seldom over 2 feet tall with medium yellow flowers.

'McKay's White'   potentilla

Creamy white flowers on a 2 to 3 feet tall shrub.

'Mount Everest'   potentilla

A vigorous shrub, to 4 feet tall, with white flowers.

'Pink Beauty'   potentilla

Clear pink flowers on a 3 foot shrub. Introduction from the Morden Experiment Station in Manitoba.

'Primrose Beauty'   potentilla

A compact shrub, to 3 feet tall, with pale cream-yellow flowers. Probably the same plant as 'Vilmoriniana'.

'Red Ace'   potentilla

Shrubs have not done well in our areas with flowers turning from reddish to yellow in warm weather.

'Snowbird'   potentilla

Semi-double white flowers on a 2 to 3 foot shrub.

'Tangerine'   potentilla

Flowers are yellow in full sun and orange only in cool weather or when plants are grown in the shade.

'Yellow Gem'   potentilla

Yellow flowers on a shorter 1 to 2 foot plant.

WINELEAF POTENTILLA
Potentilla tridentata Ait.

HARDY IN ZONES 2 TO 4

12 in. tall, 20 in. wide

HABIT. Low, suckering perennial with a woody base.
LEAVES. Semi-evergreen, palmate, with 3 leaflets; leaflets leathery, wedge-shaped to oblong, 3- to 5-toothed at the apex, nearly smooth, turning wine-red in the fall.
FLOWERS. Small, white, in flat-topped cymes in June and July; bractlets lanceolate, somewhat shorter than the acute ovate-triangular sepals; ovaries and achenes hairy, with a lateral style.

LANDSCAPE USE

This potentilla can be used as a ground cover in drier soils. It is planted also commonly in rock gardens. One reason to grow this shrub is for the attractive fall coloring. Native from Greenland to Ontario and south to Georgia and Iowa, it has been in cultivation since 1789.

CULTURE

An adaptable plant as long as it has good drainage.

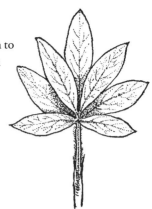

PRINSEPIA

CHERRY PRINSEPIA
Prinsepia sinensis (Oliv.) Oliv.

FAMILY: ROSACEAE, ROSE FAMILY

HARDY IN ZONES 3 AND 4

6 feet tall, 6 feet wide

HABIT. Spiny, deciduous shrub; there are 4 species found in Asia.
BRANCHES. Light gray-brown with chambered pith; spines axillary, 0.2 to 0.4 in. long.
BUDS. Small, with few hairy scales, enclosed by the stipules.
LEAVES. Alternate, simple, mostly fascicled, slender-petioled, ovate-lanceolate to lanceolate, 2 to 3 in. long, long-acuminate, entire or sparingly serrulate, finely ciliate, otherwise smooth, bright green.
FLOWERS. 1 to 4 in fascicles, white, 0.5 in. across, in early May; stamens 10.
FRUIT. Subglobose or ovoid drupes, 0.5 in. long, reddish purple, juicy, in August; seed, stone, ovoid, compressed.

LANDSCAPE USE AND CULTURE

A rarely seen and hard to obtain plant. It can be used as a barrier plant because of its spines. Showy fruit. Native to Manchuria, it was introduced into North America in 1896.

The CHERRIES, PLUMS And OTHER RELATIONS

Prunus L.

FAMILY: ROSACEAE, ROSE FAMILY

This diverse genus includes apricots, cherries, plums, nectarines, peaches and many ornamental shrubs and trees. Some are well-suited for growing in the North; others are not hardy. Many of the most ornamental flowering cherries are not for the North. Many ornamentals of this genus are also susceptable to several disease and plant pests which can shorten their lives considerably. Therefore, extreme care should be taken when ordering these plants from mail order sources. They do bloom and fruit at an early age.

Those interested in growing fruit, especially plum, in their landscapes will want to include some of the hardier fruit varieties bred especially for the North. Many fruit trees in this genus need cross pollination, so a number of varieties should be planted.

FRUIT-BEARING CULTIVARS:

APRICOTS

Two different cultivars are required for pollination.

'Moongold' apricot
HARDY IN ZONE 4; TRIAL IN ZONE 3
Size depends on rootstock

A selection introduced by the University of Minnesota Horticultural Research Center. The tree has a broad crown, nearly white flowers, and golden yellow fruit.

'Scout' apricot
HARDY IN ZONES 3 & 4
Size depends on rootstock

An upright, roundheaded tree with yellow fruit blushed with red. Introduced by the Morden Experiment Station in Manitoba.

'Sungold' apricot
HARDY IN ZONE 4; TRIAL IN ZONE 3
Size depends on rootstock

More upright than 'Moongold'; fruit with a reddish blush. Also introduced by the University of Minnesota.

CHERRIES

Some sour cherries are hardy; sweet cherries are not. These cherries are self-fertile, no pollinators required.

'Meteor' cherry
ZONE 4
8 foot on standard

Introduced by the University of Minnesota Horticultural Research Center in 1952. A vigorous tree with disease-free foliage and bright red fruit of good quality.

'North Star'
ZONE 4
Dwarfed 5 feet tall, standard 12 feet

Introduced by the University of Minnesota Horticultural Research Center in 1950. This is a small tree seldom more than 12 feet tall. Its foliage is dark green and fruit are dark red, of excellent quality.

PLUMS

'Alderman' plum
HARDY IN ZONE 4

A 1986 introduction of the University of Minnesota Horticultural Research Center. An attractive ornamental, it has red fruit. Named after W.H. Alderman, Professor of Horticulture, University of Minnesota.

'Pipestone' plum
HARDY IN ZONE 3 & 4

A 1942 introduction with red fruit.

'Superior' plum
HARDY IN ZONE 4

Red mottled fruit; a 1933 introduction.

'Toka' plum
HARDY IN ZONE 3 & 4

An excellent pollinator that also produces good tasting plums. Introduced from the South Dakota Experiment Station in 1911.

'Underwood' plum
HARDY IN ZONE 4

A 1920 red with yellow introduction.

ORNAMENTAL CULTIVARS:

'Newport' flowering plum
ZONE 4
20 feet tall, 20 feet wide

Introduced by the University of Minnesota Horticultural Research Center (now part of the Arboretum) in 1923. This cultivar resulted from a cross between *P. cerasifera* 'Atropurpurea' and the 'Omaha' plum. It has been widely planted in zones 4 and 5 for its purple foliage, pale pink flowers, and dull purple fruit. Arboretum plants have been short-lived. There are different strains of this variety in the nursery trade.

WILD PLUM
Prunus americana Marsh.
HARDY IN ZONES 3 AND 4
20 feet tall, 16 feet wide

HABIT. Small tree with rounded head, suckering freely; there are 430 species distributed worldwide
BRANCHES. Smooth when young.
LEAVES. Obovate to oblong-obo-vate, 2 to 4 in. long, acuminate, broadly wedge-shaped at base, sharply and often doubly serrate, smooth or slightly hairy along the midrib beneath; petioles without glands.
FLOWERS. 2 to 5 in clusters, white, 0.7 to 1 in. across, in early May; calyx and pedicels smooth, with entire, acuminate lobes.
FRUIT. Subglobose, 1 in. across, red or yellow, ripening in August; seed, stone compressed.

LANDSCAPE USE
This native perfumes the landscape in early spring. It can be used in naturalistic or wildlife plantings. Native from Massachusetts to Manitoba and south to Georgia and New Mexico, it has been in cultivation since 1768. It can be used for rootstock for others in the *Prunus* genus and is an excellent pollinator for hybrid plums. *See photograph page 169.*

CULTURE
Adaptable to a wide range of soils and conditions.

WESTERN SANDCHERRY
Prunus besseyi Bailey.
HARDY IN ZONES 2 TO 4
6 feet tall, 6 feet wide

HABIT. Low, suckering shrub.
LEAVES. Elliptic to elliptic-lanceolate, 0.7 to 2 in. long, acute, appressed-serrate, smooth; petioles 1.5 to 4 in. long.
FLOWERS. White, 2 to 4 in clusters, 0.5 in. across, in early May; pedicels about 0.3 in. long.
FRUIT. Subglobose, 0.5 in. across, purple-black, sweet, in July and August.

LANDSCAPE USE
The sandcherry is useful in wildlife plantings. The fruit is edible and often used for preserves. Native from Manitoba to Wyoming and south to Kansas and Colorado, it has been in cultivation since 1892.

CULTURE
Needs well-drained soil.

CISTENA SANDCHERRY
PURPLELEAF SANDCHERRY
Prunus x cistena (N.E. Hansen) Koehne.
HARDY IN ZONES 3 AND 4
8 feet tall, 6 feet wide

HABIT. Upright shrub.
BRANCHES. Bright red when young.
LEAVES. Lanceolate to obovate, 1 to 2 in. long, acuminate, reddish purple.
FLOWERS. Solitary or in 2's, white, not especially showy, in May.
FRUIT. Purplish black, in August.

LANDSCAPE USE

These ornamentals were introduced by Dr. N.E. Hansen of South Dakota State University in 1910. They are well-suited for areas where other ornamentals do not prove hardy. Their purple leaves can provide accent in the landscape. However, as with other purple-leaved plants they should be used sparingly. This sandcherry is a hybrid species resulting from a cross between *P. pumila* and *P. cerasifera* 'Atropurpurea'.

CULTURE

Some dieback can occur on sandcherry following a severe winter.

EUROPEAN DWARF CHERRY
Prunus fruticosa Pall.
HARDY IN ZONES 2 TO 4
3 feet tall, 3 feet wide

HABIT. Spreading shrub.
BRANCHLETS. Slender, smooth.
LEAVES. Elliptic-obovate to obovate-oblong, 0.7 to 2 in. long, obtuse to short-acuminate, crenate-serrulate, smooth and dark glossy green, thick; petioles 2 to 4.7 in. long.
FLOWERS. 2 to 4 in sessile umbels, with leafy bracts, white, 0.5 in. across, in May; pedicels 0.5 to 1 in. long; sepals broad, obtuse.
FRUIT. Dark red, globose, about 0.3 in. across, in July.

LANDSCAPE USE AND CULTURE

This species suckers freely, otherwise makes an attractive shrub especially when it is in bloom. The fruit is tart. Native to central and eastern Europe and east to Siberia, it was introduced into North America in 1587.

DWARF FLOWERING ALMOND
Prunus glandulosa Thunb.
HARDY IN ZONE 4
4 feet tall, 4 feet wide

HABIT. Small shrub.
BRANCHLETS. Smooth, rarely minutely hairy.
LEAVES. Ovate-oblong or oblong to oblong-lanceolate, 1 to 3.5 in. long, acute, rarely acuminate, broadly wedge-shaped at base, crenate-serrulate, smooth beneath or slightly hairy on midrib; petioles about 0.2 in. long.
FLOWERS. 1 or 2, pink or white; pedicels about 0.3 in. long.
FRUIT. Subglobose, less than 0.5 in. across, red, in August.

LANDSCAPE USE AND CULTURE

This shrub is almost always sold as one of the double-flowering varieties listed below, but it often sold in the nursery trade as a species. In bloom these plants are very attractive, otherwise they are nondescript. Native to central and northern China and Japan, it was introduced into North America in 1835.

CULTIVARS:

'Alboplena'   flowering almond
A double white flowering form that is showier than the species.

'Rosea'   flowering almond
A double pink flowering form.

'Sinensis'   flowering almond
Flowers are pink and fully double. Probably not as hardy as the species. Some dieback can be expected in most years.

AMUR CHERRY, AMUR CHOKECHERRY
Prunus maackii Rupr.
HARDY IN ZONES 3 AND 4
30 feet tall, 25 feet wide

HABIT. Upright tree.
BRANCHLETS. Hairy when young.
BARK. Reddish brown, flaky.
LEAVES. Elliptic to oblong-ovate, 2 to 4 in. long, acuminate, rounded at base, finely serrulate, gland-dotted beneath and slightly hairy on the veins; petioles less than 0.5 in. long, usually glandular.
FLOWERS. White, about 0.3 in. across, in dense hairy racemes 2 to 2.7 in. long, in mid-May; calyx tube tubular-campanulate, longer than the glandular-denticulate sepals; petals oblong-obovate; styles about as long as stamens, shorter than petals.
FRUIT. Black, 0.2 in. across, in August.

LANDSCAPE USE

Amur cherry is an excellent medium-sized ornamental tree. Although showy in bloom, this cherry is grown for its reddish brown bark which is attractive in all parts of the year. There is variation in the coloration of the Amur cherry's bark as it is sold in the nursery trade. Purchasers might want to compare bark on more mature specimens before purchasing. It is most effective when grown as a clump specimen. Native to Manchuria and Korea, it was introduced into North America in 1878.
See photograph page 155.

CULTURE

Amur cherry needs a well-drained soil but will withstand a wide pH range and will tolerate light shade. It is propagated from seeds.

    This cherry needs to be planted in a protected area as it can be damaged by strong winds.

MANCHURIAN APRICOT
Prunus mandshurica
(Maxim.) Koehne.
HARDY IN ZONES 3 AND 4
25 feet tall, 20 feet wide

HABIT. Roundheaded tree.
BRANCHES. Spreading.
LEAVES. Broad-elliptic to ovate, 2 to 4.7 in. long, acuminate, rounded or broadly wedge-shaped at base, sharply and doubly serrate, with narrow, elongated teeth; undersurface of leaves green and smooth except for axillary tufts of hairs; fall color golden yellow, sometimes with a touch of orange; petioles 1 in. long, minutely hairy.
FLOWERS. Solitary, varying from almost white to deep pink, about 1 in. across, in early May; pedicels 0.08 to 0.2 in. long.
FRUIT. Yellow, sometimes with a reddish blush, subglobose, 1 in. across with small stones, edible in July.

LANDSCAPE USE AND CULTURE
Along with the apricot cultivars discussed above, the Manchurian apricot is often cultivated. Native to Manchuria and Korea, it was introduced into North America in 1900. This apricot was classified as *P. armeniaca var. mandshurica*.

BEACH PLUM
Prunus maritima Marsh.
ZONES 3 AND 4
6 feet tall, 6 feet wide

HABIT. Informal shrub.
BRANCHES. Arching downwards; young branchlets hairy.
LEAVES. 1.5 to 3 in. long, folded in bud; ovate, acute, broadly wedge-shaped at base, smooth above, downy underside.
FLOWERS. 0.5 in across, umbels of 2 to 10, sepals toothed, petals white.
FRUIT. 0.5 in., round, red, seed ovoid stone, flattened.

LANDSCAPE USE
This native has become more used for difficult sites. The dense branching make it useful for a barrier plant. Its white flowers are noticeable in the spring and it has reasonable fall color. Its fruit can be used as other members of this genus. Native along the Atlantic Coast from Canada to Delaware.

CULTURE
Beach plum is tolerant of stress conditions. It will withstand salt and very poor soils.

CANADA PLUM
Prunus nigra Ait.
HARDY IN ZONES 3 AND 4
16 feet tall, 16 feet wide

HABIT. Small tree.
BRANCHES. Those upright form a narrow crown; young branchlets smooth or hairy.
BARK. Reddish brown.
LEAVES. Elliptic to obovate, 2 to 4 in. long, acuminate, broadly wedge-shaped to subcordate, coarsely and doubly obtuse-serrate, smooth above, hairy or nearly smooth beneath; petioles less than 1 in. long, glandular.
FLOWERS. 3 to 4, white fading to pink, 1 in. across, in early May; calyx reddish and glabrous, lobes acute becoming reflexed; petals broad-ovate.
FRUIT. Ellipsoid, 1 in. long, red or yellowish red, in August.

LANDSCAPE USE
Most often grown as the cultivar, 'Princess Kay' described below.

CULTURE
Tolerates a wide range of climatic and soil conditions. It needs good drainage.

CULTIVAR:

'Princess Kay'   Canada plum
ZONES 3 AND 4
15 feet tall, 10 feet wide

A double flowered form found by Kay and Robert Nylund near Grand Rapids, Minnesota. It was introduced by The Minnesota Landscape Arboretum in 1986. It flowers freely and is fragrant. The flowers contrast strongly with its dark, almost black, bark and twigs. *See photograph page 146-47.*

EUROPEAN BIRD CHERRY
Prunus padus L.
HARDY IN ZONES 3 AND 4
30 feet tall, 25 feet wide

HABIT. Tree with dense crown.
BRANCHLETS. Finely hairy or smooth.
LEAVES. Elliptic to obovate or oblong-ovate, 2 to 4 in. long, abruptly acuminate, rounded or subcordate at base, sharply serrate, dull green above, grayish beneath, smooth or with axillary tufts of hairs; petioles less than 0.6 in. long, smooth, glandular.
FLOWERS. White, less than 0.6 in. across, fragrant, in drooping, loose racemes with the peduncle 4 to 6 in. long and glabrous, in early May; calyx tube pubescent inside.
FRUIT. Globose, 0.2 to 0.3 in. across, black, in August.

LANDSCAPE USE AND CULTURE
This hardy cherry has been widely used for screening and as a specimen tree. It is very showy in bloom. Unfortunately,

this species suffers from the black knot disease which produces rough, swollen black growths on the twigs and branches. Many times this disease is unsightly enough to cause the trees to be cut down. Native to Europe and northern Asia, it was introduced into North America by early settlers.

VARIETY:

var. *commutata* Dipp.
ZONES 3 AND 4
20 feet tall, 20 feet wide

This is the common Mayday tree. It has the same faults as the species.

PIN CHERRY, FIRE CHERRY
Prunus pensylvanica L.f.
HARDY IN ZONES 2 TO 4
30 feet tall, 20 feet wide

HABIT. Large shrub or small tree.
BRANCHLETS. Smooth, slender, reddish and shiny.
LEAVES. Ovate to oblanceolate, 2 to 4 in. long, acuminate, finely and sharply serrulate, smooth; fall color red; petioles 0.4 to 0.7 in. long.
FLOWERS. White, 0.5 in. across, in 2- to 5-flowered umbels or short racemes, in mid-May; pedicels 1 to 0.5 in. long, smooth; sepals ovate, obtuse, entire, shorter than calyx tube.
FRUIT. Globose, 0.2 in. across, red, in July and August.

LANDSCAPE USE AND CULTURE
A native tree that can be used for naturalizing. It is attractive in bloom, in fruit, and in the fall when the leaves turn red. Native from Newfoundland to British Columbia and south to North Carolina, it has been in cultivation since 1773. Some of the forms growing West of its native range are more compact growing, about half the size of the eastern species.

CULTIVAR:

'Stockton'   pin cherry
This double flowered form was discovered near Stockton, Manitoba, by Mrs. M.N. Badhan. It was introduced by the Morden Experiment Station in 1929. It is a very compact, roundheaded tree with dark green foliage that turns brilliant red in the fall. An excellent small tree. It is difficult to find in the nursery trade.

SARGENT CHERRY
Prunus sargentii Rehd.
TRIAL IN SHELTERED LOCATIONS IN ZONE 4
30 feet tall, 25 feet wide

HABIT. Pyramidal to roundheaded tree.
BRANCHLETS. Smooth.
BARK. Smooth, chestnut-brown, with large lenticels.
LEAVES. Purplish when unfolding, elliptic-obovate to oblong-obovate, 2.7 to 4.7 in. long, acuminate, rounded or sometimes subcordate at base, sharply serrate with acuminate teeth, smooth and glaucescent beneath; petioles 1 in. long.
FLOWERS. Rose-colored, 1.2 to 1.5 in. across, in 2- to 4-flowered sessile umbels, in early May; pedicels 0.5 to 1 in. long; calyx tube tubular-campanulate with ovate-oblong lobes, entire; petals obovate, emarginate.
FRUIT. Globose-ovoid, 0.4 in. long, purplish black, in July.

LANDSCAPE USE AND CULTURE
Sargent cherry is the hardiest of the Japanese cherries. However, specimens at The Minnesota Landscape Arboretum have been vegetatively hardy but often the flower buds have been killed. Native to Japan, it was introduced into North America in 1890.

BLACK CHERRY
Prunus serotina Ehrh.
HARDY IN ZONES 3 AND 4
80 feet tall, 50 feet wide

HABIT. Large tree.
BRANCHLETS. Smooth.
BARK. Rough, dark brown; inner bark aromatic.
LEAVES. Oblong-ovate to lance-oblong, 2 to 4.7 in. long, acuminate, wedge-shaped at base, serrulate with small incurved teeth, shiny above, light green beneath and often hairy along the midrib, thickish and firm at maturity; petioles 0.2 to 1 in. long, glandular.
FLOWERS. White, 0.3 to 0.4 in. across, in cylindric glabrous racemes 4 to 5.5 in. long, in late May; pedicels 0.1 to 0.3 in. long; sepals oblong-ovate, often toothed.
FRUIT. Globose, 0.3 to 0.4 in. across, finally black in September.

LANDSCAPE USE
Black cherry can be used for attracting wildlife or in naturalistic plantings. It is a large-growing, interesting tree with its dark bark and white flowers. Native from Ontario to North Dakota and south to Florida and Texas, it has been in cultivation since 1629. Black cherry is valued for its ornamental lumber.

CULTURE
Trouble-free. Its fruit drop in late summer and into the fall and can be messy in the landscape.

Russian almond

Prunus tenella Batsch.

HARDY IN ZONES 2 TO 4

4 feet tall, 4 feet wide

HABIT. Low, suckering shrub.
BRANCHLETS. Smooth.
LEAVES. Lanceolate or oblanceolate to oblong-obovate, 1 to 2 in. long, acute, wedge-shaped at base, sharply serrate, smooth, light green and prominently veined beneath, leathery; petioles 0.1 to 0.2 in. long.
FLOWERS. 1 to 3, rosy red, 0.4 to 0.7 in. across, sessile, in early May; sepals serrate; petals oblong-obovate.
FRUIT. Ovoid, about 0.7 in. long, hairy, in July.

LANDSCAPE USE AND CULTURE

A small, suckering shrub that is very attractive in bloom. Its suckering can be a problem in the landscape. Native to southeastern Europe, western Asia and eastern Siberia, it was introduced into North America in 1683.

Nanking cherry

Prunus tomentosa Thunb.

HARDY IN ZONES 3 AND 4

9 feet tall, 9 feet wide

HABIT. Spreading shrub.
BRANCHLETS. Hairy.
LEAVES. Obovate to elliptic, 2 to 2.7 in. long, abruptly acuminate, unequally serrate, rugose, dull green and hairy above, densely hairy beneath; petioles 0.1 to 0.15 in. long.
FLOWERS. 1 to 2, white to slightly pinkish, 0.5 to 0.7 in. across, in early May; calyx tubes hairy outside; sepals serrate.
FRUIT. Subglobose, scarlet or yellow, about 0.4 in. across, smooth or slightly hairy, edible, in July.

LANDSCAPE USE AND CULTURE

Nanking cherry is widely planted for its edible fruit which make excellent jelly and juice. Birds are fond of the fruit, so unless you have several plants you will need to protect the fruit with bird nettings. It is used for hedging and as a background shrub in a border. Native to China, Japan and the Himalayas, it was introduced into North America in 1870.

Flowering plum
Flowering almond

Prunus triloba var. simplex

(Bunge.) Rehd.

HARDY IN ZONE 4, FOR PROTECTED LOCATIONS IN ZONE 3

12 feet tall, 9 feet wide

HABIT. Large shrub or small tree.
BRANCHLETS. Smooth or slightly hairy.
LEAVES. Broad-elliptic to obovate, 1.2 to 2.2 in. long, acuminate, or sometimes 3-lobed at the apex, broadly wedge-shaped at base, coarsely and doubly serrate, slightly hairy beneath; petioles about 0.2 in. long.
FLOWERS. 1 or 2, pinkish, 0.7 to 1 in. across, in early May; calyx tubes broadly bell-shaped, shorter than pedicels; sepals ovate, serrulate, smooth or hairy outside; stamens about 30.
fRUIT. Red, subglobose, 0.5 in. across, hairy.

LANDSCAPE USE AND CULTURE

Many purchase this plant when they see it in bloom, as the bloom is very striking. Unfortunately, this shrub has little character the rest of the year. It can be tucked into the shrub border where one can enjoy its bloom. Native to China, it was introduced into North America in 1855.

CULTIVAR:

'Multiplex'   flowering plum

Flowers fully double, attractive in bloom, but the plant offers little of ornamental value during the rest of the year. Position toward the back of the shrub border for an early spring accent Flower buds are often killed following a severe winter.

Chokecherry

Prunus virginiana L.

HARDY IN ZONES 2 TO 4

30 feet tall, 25 feet wide

HABIT. Suckering shrub or small tree.
BRANCHES. Smooth.
LEAVES. Broad-elliptic to obovate, 1.5 to 4.7 in. long, abruptly acuminate, broadly wedge-shaped at base, closely serrulate, dark green and somewhat shiny above, glaucescent or grayish green beneath, smooth except for axillary tufts of hair; petioles 0.4 to 0.7 in. long, glandular.
FLOWERS. White, 0.3 to 0.4 in. across, in dense glabrous racemes 2 to 6 in. long, in mid to late-May.
FRUIT. Globose, about 0.3 in. across, dark purple, edible in July and August.

LANDSCAPE USE

The species is widely planted in conservation plantings and for bird food. Some believe the jelly made from its fruit is a delicacy. Native from Newfoundland to Saskatchewan and south to North Carolina and Kansas, it has been in cultivation since 1724.

Jonathan Carver in his *Travels through the Interior Parts of North America* (1781) in the collection of Andersen Horticultural Library found, "The juice of this fruit, though not of a disagreeable flavour, is extremely tart, and leaves a roughness in the mouth and throat when eaten, that has gained it the name of choak berry."

CULTURE

Chokecherry grows on a variety of soils and is shade tolerant. It fruits best in full sun. It spreads by suckering, so care should be used in placing it in the landscape.

CULTIVARS AND VARIETIES:

var. *leucocarpa*

Similar to the species but fruit are amber colored.

var. *melanocarpa* (A. Nels.) Sarg.

ZONES 2 TO 4

15 feet tall, 15 feet wide

A dwarf form native to the Rocky Mountains.

'Schubert'   chokecherry

ZONES 3 AND 4

20 feet tall, 20 wide

Mature leaves are purplish red. This cultivar is often trained as a small tree and makes an excellent screen planting. Also sold as 'Canada Red'. There have been further selected cultivars such as 'Shubert Select'.

DOUGLAS FIR

ROCKY MOUNTAIN DOUGLAS FIR
Pseudotsuga menziesii
ssp. glauca (Beissn.) E. Murray.

FAMILY: PINACEAE, PINE FAMILY

HARDY IN ZONE 4, FOR PROTECTED LOCATIONS IN ZONE 3

65 feet tall, 40 feet wide

HABIT. A pyramidal, evergreen; there are 8 species native in North American and Asia.
BRANCHES. Whorled; branchlets hairy, rarely smooth, pale orange at first, changing to reddish brown and later to grayish brown.
BARK. Smooth at first, becoming corky, deeply fissured into scaly ridges.
BUDS. Ovate, acute, smooth with overlapping scales.
LEAVES. Spirally arranged, linear, flattened, 0.7 to 1 in. long, obtuse to acute, bluish green above with grayish or whitish stomatic bands beneath.
FLOWERS. Male, in axillary, cylindric cones; female flowers in terminal cones.

FRUIT. Pendulous cones, 2 to 4 in. long, ovoid to ovoid-oblong, with rounded concave rigid scales subtended by exserted 3-lobed bracts; 2 winged seeds under each scale.

LANDSCAPE USE

Douglas fir has selected forms that seem to be hardier in the North. Unfortunately, these forms are confused in the nursery trade. Many selections of Douglas fir are not hardy in the North, so care should be taken when buying this plant. It is often used for tall screening purposes or as an ornamental specimen. *See photograph page 180-81.*

CULTURE

Care should be taken when purchasing this plant and also where it is planted in the landscape. It will not take an exposed location in the North and sometimes is short-lived.

HOP TREE

HOP TREE, WAFER ASH
Ptelea trifoliata L.

FAMILY: RUTACEAE, RUE FAMILY

HARDY IN ZONE 4

20 feet tall, 15 feet wide

HABIT. A deciduous shrub or small, roundheaded tree; there are 11 species native in North America.
BRANCHLETS. Sparingly hairy, becoming reddish brown the second year.
BUDS. Superposed, small, hairy; no terminal buds.
LEAVES. Alternate, 3-foliate; leaflets subsessile, ovate to elliptic-oblong, 2.2 to 4.7 in. long, narrowed at ends, sometimes acuminate, entire or obscurely crenulate, dark green and shiny above, pale and usually smooth below; lateral leaflets oblique at base and smaller than other leaflets.
FLOWERS. Small, greenish white, polygamous, 4- to 5-merous, in corymbs on short lateral branchlets, in June; petals oblong, short-hairy outside, 3 to 4 times longer than sepals; stamens 4 or 5, shorter than petals, with filaments villous at the base; female flowers with 4 to 5 small staminodes and a compressed 2- to 3-celled ovary; style short.
FRUIT. Compressed samaras, usually broadly winged and suborbicular and 2-seeded, rarely 3-celled and 3-winged, in September.

LANDSCAPE USE AND CULTURE

This shrub or small tree is not familiar to many, but it should be used more. It is very ornamental in fruit and foliage. Larger growing and shade tolerant, it should be used at the back of a shrub border. Native from Ontario to Minnesota and south to Florida, it has been in cultivation since 1724.

The PEARS

Pyrus L.
FAMILY: ROSACEAE, ROSE FAMILY

Many edible pear hybrids are not hardy in zone 4. Varieties to be considered are 'Luscious', 'Summercrisp', 'Golden Spice', 'Patten' and 'Parker'. These varieties need a protected site in the landscape, although the first 3 cultivars can be tried in zone 3. Cross-pollination from more than one variety produces better fruiting.

There is work being done on the adaption and hybridization of pear to northern environments. There probably will be many more introductions, especially from the parentage of *P. ussuriensis*.

CALLERY PEAR

Pyrus calleryana Decne.
FOR PROTECTED LOCATIONS IN EASTERN PARTS OF ZONE 4
25 feet tall, 20 feet wide

HABIT. Upright tree; there are 30 species native in North America and Asia.
BRANCHLETS. Smooth.
BUDS. Hairy.
LEAVES. Broad-ovate to ovate, rarely elliptic-ovate, short-acuminate, rounded or broadly wedge-shaped at base, 1.5 to 3 in. long, crenate, usually quite smooth; petioles 0.7 to 1.5 in. long.
FLOWERS. 0.7 to 1 in. across, in early May; pedicels 0.5 to 1.2 in. long; stamens 20; styles 2, rarely 3.
FRUIT. Dotted brown, globose, 0.4 in. across, on slender pedicels.

LANDSCAPE USE AND CULTURE

There are many cultivars but most are not suited for zone 4. Widely planted in the eastern part of North America they have not done well in midwestern zone 4. Research at the Minnesota Landscape Arboretum showed considerable stem tissue mortality on three cultivars at an extreme -32° F.

USSURIAN PEAR, CHINESE SAND PEAR

Pyrus ussuriensis Maxim.
HARDY IN ZONES 3 AND 4
25 feet tall, 20 feet wide

HABIT. Small, roundheaded tree.
BRANCHLETS. Smooth or nearly so, yellow-gray to purple-brown the second year, older branches usually yellow-gray or yellowish brown.
LEAVES. Orbicular-ovate to ovate, acuminate, rounded or subcordate at base, 2 to 4 in. long, setosely serrate, smooth or nearly so; petioles 0.7 to 2 in. long; inflorescence dense, hemispherical, smooth; pedicels 0.4 to 0.7 in. long.
FLOWERS. 1.3 in. across, white, flower buds sometimes tinged with pink, in early May; petals obovate, gradually narrowed toward the base; styles pilose near the base.
FRUIT. Subglobose, short-stalked, greenish yellow, 1.3 in. across.

LANDSCAPE USE

This species is the hardiest of the pears and is useful as a lawn specimen. Work is being done on hybridizing using this species for hardiness. Native to northeastern Asia, it was introduced into North America in 1855.

CULTURE

This species is resistant to fire blight which is a major problem with this genus. This pear needs a well-drained soil.

CULTIVARS:

Mountain Frost™   Ussurian pear
P.u. 'Bailfrost'
ZONES 3 AND 4
30 feet tall, 20 feet wide

A recent Bailey Nurseries introduction which features a vigorous, upright growth habit. It has not been tested yet in Arboretum trials.

Prairie Gem®   Ussurian pear
P.u. 'Mordak'
ZONES 3 AND 4
20 feet tall, 20 feet wide

An introduction of the North Dakota State University. More compact than the species.

The OAKS

Quercus L.
FAMILY: FAGACEAE, BEECH FAMILY

Oaks are long-lived shade trees. Many have specific attributes such as drought tolerance. Although many are large growing, it is a shame if home owners cannot find space for at least one oak in their landscape. Recent advances in growing oaks include root pruning techniques and container growing. These practices have improved the transplanting success of trees up to 1.5 inch in diameter.

Oaks often are the main features of our landscapes. If one is fortunate enough to have a large oak, it can greatly increase the value of your property. John Evelyn in his *Silva* (1706) quotes the verse:

How much to Heaven her towring head ascends,
So much toward Hell her piercing Root extends.

Oaks' strong character also appealed to Thoreau in his *Journal*, vol. 4 (1852, 469): "That oak by Darbys is a grand object seen from any side——It stands like an athlete & defies the tempest in every direction. It has not a weak point. It is an agony of strength."

Oak wilt is a major disease of oak that needs to be understood. Most wilt is transferred through populations by direct contact. Most often root grafts (grafts formed naturally in adjacent oak) are the method of transmittal. The wilt also can be spread by insects interacting with wounded areas, so for this reason it is recommended not to prune or wound oaks during the period when insects are most active, generally in May and June. Not only should pruning not be done from April 15th to July 1st, but when pruning, pruning tools should be sterilized between specimens. However, oak wilt is a problem mainly of native stands of oak (especially red oak). Landscape specimens are usually isolated enough not to be at risk.

CULTIVARS:

(Of interspecific parentage)

Heritage®   oak
Q. 'Clemons'
HARDY IN ZONE 4
60 feet tall, 45 feet wide

A newer introduction that has not been tested at the Minnesota Landscape Arboretum. It is described as being a fast growing oak with glossy, tough foliage. It grows upright becoming broadly pyramidal with age. A cross between *Q. robur* and *Q. macrocarpa*.

Regal Prince®   oak
Q. 'Long'
HARDY IN ZONE 4
50 feet tall, 25 feet wide

Another untested, newer cultivar. A upright, columnar specimen. A cross between *Q. robur* 'Fastigiata' and *Q. bicolor*.

WHITE OAK
Quercus alba L.
HARDY IN ZONE 4, HARDY IN SOUTHERN
PARTS OF ZONE 3
65 feet tall, 50 feet wide

HABIT. Large tree; there are 600 species distributed throughout the northern hemisphere.
BRANCHES. Wide spreading; branchlets soon smooth, light reddish brown, often glaucous.
LEAVES. Obovate to oblong-obovate, 4 to 8 in. long, narrowed at base, with 5 to 9 oblong and obtuse, usually entire lobes; upper leaf surface bright green; undersurface glaucescent; fall color vinous red or violet-purple; petioles 0.5 to 1 in. long.
FRUIT. Acorns, ovoid-oblong, 0.7 to 1 in. long; about one-quarter of each acorn is enclosed by the cup; basal scales much thickened.

LANDSCAPE USE AND CULTURE

One of the more stately of the North's oaks, white oak should be planted more often. Disease resistant, this oak also has drought tolerance. Native from Maine to Minnesota and south to Florida and Texas, it has been in cultivation since 1724. *See photographs pages 144, 168.*

SWAMP WHITE OAK

Quercus bicolor Willd.

HARDY IN ZONE 4
65 feet tall, 65 feet wide

HABIT. Large tree.
BRANCHES. Sturdy, spreading; branchlets scurfy-hairy at first.
BARK. Grayish brown, scaly.
LEAVES. Oblong-obovate to obovate, 4 to 6 in. long, narrowed toward the base and acute or rounded at the apex, coarsely sinuate-dentate with 6 to 10 pairs of entire, usually obtuse teeth or sometimes lobed halfway to the midrib, dark green above, whitish hairy or grayish green and velvety beneath; petioles 0.4 to 0.7 in. long.
FRUIT. Acorns, ovoid-oblong, 0.7 to 1.2 in. long; about one-third of each acorn is enclosed by the cup.

LANDSCAPE USE

The canopy of this oak is open, rounded and somewhat narrow. Mature specimens sometimes have a wider spread than height. It can make a handsome specimen or shade tree. Native from Quebec to Minnesota and south to Pennsylvania and Arkansas, it has been in cultivation since 1800.

CULTURE

Will grow in both wet or dry soils. Its taproot is not as well developed as in many oaks, so it is not as difficult to transplant. One of the tougher oaks for the landscape and one of the fastest growers.

SCARLET OAK

Quercus coccinea Muench.

HARDY IN ZONE 4
65 feet tall, 50 feet wide

HABIT. Large tree with round-topped, rather open crown.
BRANCHLETS. Soon smooth and orange-red.
BARK. Gray, inner bark reddish.
BUDS. Dark reddish brown, hairy above the middle.
LEAVES. Oblong or elliptic, 3 to 6 in. long, bright green, smooth, square or rarely broadly wedge-shaped at base, sinuately pinnatifid, with 7 to 9 oblong, sparingly repand-dentate lobes; fall color a brilliant scarlet; petioles slender, 1.2 to 2.2 in. long.
FRUIT. Acorns, ovoid, 0.5 to 0.7 in. long; about one-third to one-half of each acorn is enclosed by a turbinate or hemispheric cup.

LANDSCAPE USE

Large and open growing, it makes a fine shade tree. Native from Maine to Minnesota and south to Florida and Missouri, it has been in cultivation since 1691.

CULTURE

This species prefers acid, sandy soil. It is important to plant only strains grown from northern sources. The leaves persist into the winter on this oak.

NORTHERN PIN OAK

Quercus ellipsoidalis E.J. Hill.

HARDY IN ZONES 3 AND 4
65 feet tall, 50 feet wide

HABIT. Large tree.
BRANCHLETS. Hairy at first.
BARK. Gray, close and smooth or shallowly fissured.
BUDS. Slightly hairy.
LEAVES. Elliptic, 3 to 4.7 in. long, square to broadly wedge-shaped at base, deeply sinuately 5- to 6-lobed, with oblong, coarsely repand-dentate lobes; petioles 1.2 to 2 in. long.
FRUIT. Acorns, ellipsoid to subglobose, 0.5 to 0.7 in. long; one-third to one-half of each acorn is enclosed by a turbinate cup.

LANDSCAPE USE AND CULTURE

This native oak usually grows on sandy soils. It is susceptible to the oak wilt disease and is seldom planted. It often has spectacular red fall color. Tolerates more neutral soils than pin oak. Native from southern Michigan to Manitoba and south to Indiana and Iowa, it has been in cultivation since 1902.

SHINGLE OAK
Quercus imbricaria Michx.
HARDY IN ZONE 4
65 feet tall, 50 feet wide

HABIT. Large, open crowned tree.
BRANCHLETS. Smooth and shiny, light brown.
BARK. Becomes ridged and scaly with age, dark brown.
BUDS. Ovule, pointed at tip.
LEAVES. Lance-shaped, 2 to 3 in. long, slightly wavy margined, finely hairy on undersurface; petioles 0.5 in long.
FRUIT. Acorns, solitary or paired, 0.5 to 0.7 in. long; one-third of acorn enclosed by a bowl-shaped cup.

LANDSCAPE USE AND CULTURE
Shingle oak makes a medium-sized shade tree. Tolerates dry soils; intolerant of shade. As the common name indicates, this oak was once used for making shingles. Native from Pennsylvania west to southern Iowa, south to Tennessee.

BUR OAK, MOSSYCUP OAK
Quercus macrocarpa Michx.
HARDY IN ZONES 3 AND 4
65 feet tall, 50 feet wide

HABIT. Large tree.
BRANCHES. Sturdy, wide spreading; branchlets stout, densely hairy at first, later nearly smooth, sometimes developing corky wings.
BARK. Light brown, deeply furrowed, and scaly.
LEAVES. Obovate to oblong-obovate, 4 to 9 in. long, wedge-shaped or rounded at base, lyrate-pinnatifid; the lower portion of each leaf usually has 2 to 3 pairs of lobes separated by wide and deep sinuses from the terminal lobe, which is usually very large, dark green, and lustrous above, grayish or whitish woolly beneath.
FRUIT. Acorns, broadly ovoid or ellipsoid, 0.7 to 1.3 in. long; up to one-half of each acorn is enclosed by a large mossy cup.

LANDSCAPE USE
An excellent large shade tree. Slow growing. During Thoreau's visit to Minnesota in 1861 he often remarked on this tree, noting it near Lake Calhoun, the "Minnesota University", along the Minnesota and Mississippi Rivers and elsewhere.

Aldo Leopold in this classic, *A Sand County Almanac*, (1949, 27) wrote, "Bur oaks were the shock troops sent by the invading forest to storm the prairie; fire is what they had to fight." Native from Nova Scotia to Manitoba and south to Pennsylvania and Texas, it has been in cultivation since 1811.

CULTURE
Grows in many soil types. Bur oak withstands city conditions, alkaline soil, drought and salt from highways. It is moderately difficult to transplant.

MONGOLIAN OAK
Quercus mongolica Fischer & Turcz.
HARDY IN ZONES 2 TO 4
30 feet tall, 25 feet wide

HABIT. Slow growing tree.
BRANCHLETS. Smooth.
LEAVES. With short petioles and crowded at the ends of branchlets, obovate to obovate-oblong, 4 to 8 in. long, obtuse, narrowed toward the auricled base, coarsely sinuate-dentate with 7 to 10 broad obtuse teeth, dark green above, paler beneath; leaves turn brown in the fall and stay on the trees into winter.
FRUIT. Acorns, ovoid or ellipsoid, about 0.7 in. long; about one-third of each acorn is enclosed by a thick cup.

LANDSCAPE USE AND CULTURE
The Mongolian oak is hard to obtain in the nursery trade. It is, however, a more compact ornamental that should be grown more. Native to Siberia, China, Korea and Japan, it was introduced into North America in 1879.

CHINKAPIN OAK, YELLOW CHESTNUT OAK
Quercus muehlenbergii Engelm.
TRIAL IN ZONE 4
65 feet tall, 50 feet wide

HABIT. Large tree.
BRANCHLETS. Hairy at first, soon smooth.
LEAVES. Oblong to oblong-lanceolate, 4 to 6.2 in. long, acute or acuminate, usually rounded at base, coarsely toothed, with 8 to 13 pair of acute and mucronate, often incurved teeth; dark or yellowish green above, whitish woolly beneath; petioles 0.7 to 1.3 in. long.
FRUIT. Acorns, globose-ovoid to ovoid, less than 0.7 in. long; one-half of each acorn is enclosed by a thin cup.

LANDSCAPE USE AND CULTURE
An oak that is grown more often further south, so a northern seed source is important. It is often listed as being hardy to zone 5. The fall color is not exceptional. It grows on dry, calcareous soils and might be planted where such conditions exist.

Notably, the underside of the leaves have a whitish cast. Native from Vermont to Nebraska and south to Virginia and New Mexico, it has been in cultivation since 1822.

PIN OAK
Quercus palustris Muench.
HARDY IN ZONE 4
65 feet tall, 50 feet wide

HABIT. Pyramidal tree, usually with a central stem.
BRANCHLETS. Soon smooth and dark red-brown or orange.

BUDS. Chestnut-brown, nearly smooth.

LEAVES. Elliptic or elliptic-oblong, 3 to 4.7 in. long, usually wedge-shaped at base, sinuately pinnatifid, with 5 to 7 oblong to oblong-lanceolate repand-dentate lobes; bright green above, lighter green, shiny, and smooth beneath; fall color a brilliant red; petioles slender, 0.7 to 2 in. long.

FRUIT. Acorns, nearly hemispheric, 0.5 in. across, about one-third of each acorn is enclosed by a thin, saucer-shaped cup.

LANDSCAPE USE

Pin oak is the most widely planted oak in eastern North America. It is a fine shade and boulevard tree. The broadly pyramidal form and brilliant red fall color are outstanding features. Native from Massachusetts to Wisconsin and south to Delaware and Arkansas, it has been in cultivation since 1770. *See photograph page 143.*

CULTURE

This oak often suffers from iron chlorosis in western, alkaline soils and should only be planted on soils that are slightly acid. It transplants more easily than most oaks.

ENGLISH OAK
Quercus robur L.
FOR PROTECTED LOCATIONS IN ZONE 4
65 feet tall, 50 feet wide

HABIT. Roundheaded tree.
BARK. Deeply furrowed, dark.
BRANCHLETS. Smooth.
LEAVES. Obovate to obovate-oblong, 2 to 4.7 in. long, subcordate or square at base, with 3 to 7 pairs of rounded lobes, smooth, dark green above, pale bluish green beneath; petioles 0.1 to 0.3 in. long.
FRUIT. 1 to 5 on stalks 1.2 to 3 in. long; acorns ovoid to ovoid-oblong, 0.5 to 1 in. long; one-third of each acorn is enclosed by a cup-like involucre.

LANDSCAPE USE AND CULTURE

Where hardy, this is an attractive shade tree. Native to Europe, northern Africa and western Asia, it was introduced into North America by early settlers. There are various reports of this oak being much hardier than it sometimes seems. This oak is another tree whose hardiness varies greatly upon its seed source.

RED OAK
Quercus rubra L.
HARDY IN ZONES 3 AND 4
80 feet tall, 50 feet wide

HABIT. Large tree.
BRANCHLETS. Soon smooth and dark red.
BUDS. Smooth except at the apex.

LEAVES. Oblong, 4.7 to 8.5 in long, usually wedge-shaped at base, sinuately 7- to 11-lobed about halfway to the midrib; lobes triangular-ovate or ovate-oblong, with a few irregular teeth; upper leaf surface dull green; undersurface grayish or whitish; fall color yellow to red; petioles 0.7 to 2 in. long.

FRUIT. Acorns, ovoid, 0.7 to 1 in. long; one-third of each acorn is enclosed by a turbinate cup.

LANDSCAPE USE AND CULTURE

This species is often listed as *Q. borealis*. Because it is susceptible to oak wilt, it is seldom planted. Faster growing than many oaks, it makes a great shade tree. The leaves persist into the winter. Native from Nova Scotia to Minnesota and south to Pennsylvania and Iowa, it has been in cultivation since 1800.

BLACK OAK
Quercus velutina Lam.
HARDY IN ZONE 4
65 feet tall, 50 feet wide

HABIT. Large tree with open crown.
BRANCHLETS. Scurfy-hairy, slender.
BARK. Dark brown, inner bark orange.
BUDS. Hairy.
LEAVES. Ovate to oblong, 4 to 10 in. long, wedge-shaped to square at base, sinuately lobed halfway to the middle with 7 to 9 broad, repand-dentate lobes, shiny dark green above, brown-hairy beneath at first; fall color dull red to orange-brown; petioles stout, 1.2 to 2.2 in. long, yellow.

FRUIT. Acorns, ovoid, 0.5 to 0.7 in. long, about half of each acorn is enclosed by a turbinate cup.

LANDSCAPE USE AND CULTURE

Another seldom planted but worthy oak. Native from Maine to southeastern Minnesota and south to Florida and Texas, it has been in cultivation since 1800.

BUCKTHORNS

COMMON BUCKTHORN
Rhamnus catharticus L.
FAMILY: RHAMNACEAE
HARDY IN ZONES 3 AND 4
20 feet tall, 15 feet wide

This native to Europe has escaped from cultivation and is now one of the Midwest's major pest trees. It should not be planted and should be removed from your landscape if already there.

GLOSSY BUCKTHORN, ELDER BUCKTHORN
Rhamnus frangula L.
HARDY IN ZONES 3 AND 4
20 feet tall, 15 feet wide

HABIT. Shrub or small tree; there are 150 species distributed worldwide.
BRANCHLETS. Hairy.
LEAVES. Oval or obovate to obovate-oblong, 1.2 to 2.7 in. long, acute, rounded or broadly wedge-shaped at base, entire, dark shiny green above, lighter green and often slightly hairy beneath, with 8 or 9 pairs of veins; fall color golden yellow; petioles 0.2 to 0.5 in. long.
FLOWERS. In clusters of 2 to 10, smooth, in June and July; pedicels 0.3 to 0.5 in. long.
FRUIT. Globose, 0.2 in. across, changing from red to dark purple, 2-seeded, in August and September.

LANDSCAPE USE AND CULTURE
This species and its cultivars are the most ornamental of the buckthorns. However, these buckthorns also can prove to be invasive and should not be planted. Native to Europe, western Asia and northern Africa, this buckthorn was introduced into North America in 1860.

CULTIVARS:

'Asplenifolia'   glossy buckthorn
HARDY IN ZONE 4, TRIAL IN ZONE 3
10 feet tall, 8 feet wide

This is a cut-leaf selection with fern-like foliage.

'Columnaris'   glossy buckthorn
HARDY IN ZONE 4, TRIAL IN ZONE 3
12 feet tall, 4 feet wide

A narrow, upright form that is widely planted in hedges, relatively short-lived. It is sometimes sold as 'Tallhedge' (probably confused in the nursery trade).

The AZALEAS and RHODODEN-DRONS
Rhododendron L.
FAMILY: ERICACEAE, HEATH FAMILY

Rhododendron is yet another genus that has many species and cultivars one wishes would do better in zone 4. Until recently, there were very few that plant lovers in zone 4 could rely on or even attempt to grow for their landscapes.

Introductions from The Minnesota Landscape Arboretum have given zones 3 and 4 residents the possibility of enjoying azaleas (deciduous *Rhododendron*) in their landscapes. The Northern Lights series of azaleas have great hardiness and a pleasing array of color selections. Those attempting to grow any of this genus should start with these selections.

Evaluation of the sites where these plants are to be grown is necessary. Generally, full sun is best with part shade conditions acceptible. They generally do not flower well if they receive too much shade. Full sun, however, also might mean conditions of too much summer heat. Azaleas and rhododendrons are very sensitive to extreme heat. Poorly drained soils should be avoided.

Those wanting to try azaleas and rhododendrons should keep in mind they need acidic growing conditions. Generally for most areas of the midwest this means the preparation of a special growing bed or area. Existing soil should be removed and an entire area replenished with an acidic soil mixture or a raised bed can be built. This can be done with the addition of acidic peat moss, granular sulfur, and the use of acid fertilizers such as ammonium sulfate or specially formulated azalea fertilizers. The optimum pH for these plants is from 4.0 to 5.5. Beds for this genus do not have to be prepared too deeply as most azalea

roots are within six inches of the surface. However, because of their shallow root system azaleas and rhododendrons are very susceptible to drought conditions. Mulching and irrigation during dry periods is very beneficial to these plants.

Those attempting the many non-deciduous species and cultivars of Rhododendron must also prevent winter damage to their evergreen foliage. Windswept areas should be avoided. Protecting the foliage from winter sun with burlap is often necessary.

These are woody plants that need special care.

AZALEA AND RHODODENDRON CULTIVARS:

Northern Lights Series

These azaleas introduced by The Minnesota Landscape Arboretum are hybridized from *R. x kosteranum, R. austrinum* and other existing hybrids. A number of named varieties are described below.

'Apricot Surprise'   azalea
ZONE 4
6 feet tall, 6 feet wide

A complex colored hybrid with pink, yellow and oranges. Of limited availability. A 1987 introduction.

'Golden Lights'   azalea
ZONE 4
4 feet tall, 4 feet wide

Golden yellow, open flowers. A 1986 introduction. Research at the Minnesota Landscape Arboretum showed flower bud damage on this cultivar at extremes of -32 degrees F.

'Lemon Lights'   azalea
ZONE 4
4.5 feet tall, 4 feet wide

Clear medium yellow flowers with a darker blotch. A 1996 introduction.

'Mandarin Lights'   azalea
ZONE 4
6 to 7 feet tall, 6 to 7 feet wide

Reddish orange, slightly fragrant flowers. A 1996 introduction. Research at the Minnesota Landscape Arboretum shows little flower bud damage at the extreme of -32 degrees F.

'Northern Hi-Lights'   azalea
ZONE 4
4 feet tall, 4 to 5 feet wide

Creamy white flowers with a bright yellow upper petal. A 1994 introduction. This cultivar has attractive, glossy foliage.

'Northern Lights'   azalea
ZONES 3 AND 4
8 feet tall, 8 feet wide

Introduced in 1978, this was the first of the Lights Series. It is a seed strain with variable flowers in shades of pink. Fragrant.

'Orchid Lights'   azalea
ZONES 3A AND 4
3 feet tall, 4 feet wide

Light pink or orchid flowers with darker shadings. A 1986 introduction. *See photograph on cover; p 137.*

'Pink Lights'   azalea
ZONES 3A AND 4
8 feet tall, 8 feet wide

Light pink, very fragrant flowers. Floriferous. A 1984 introduction. Not as widely available as the other cultivars in this series mainly because it is more difficult to propagate.

'Rosy Lights'   azalea
ZONES 3A AND 4
5 feet tall, 5 to 6 feet wide

Dark rosy pink flowers. A 1984 introduction. *See photograph page 183.*

'Spicy Lights'   azalea
ZONES 3B AND 4
6 feet tall, 8 feet wide

Features salmon colored fragrant flowers. A 1987 introduction.

'White Lights'   azalea
ZONES 3B AND 4
5 feet tall, 5 feet wide

Glistening white flowers with a yellow blotch. A 1984 introduction. Research at the Minnesota Landscape Arboretum showed little flower bud damage at the extreme of -32 degrees F. One of the best azaleas for reliable, heavy bloom on a compact-growing specimen.

Exbury Hybrids

This group of hybrids was developed in England and in New Zealand from crosses involving *R. caledulaceum, R.*

arborescens, R. occidentale, and *R. molle.* Over 150 cultivars have been named, with colors ranging from white to yellow to red. A number of these have been grown at the Arboretum. Some have been quite hardy, but most have lacked flower bud hardiness.

Marjatta Hybrids

A number of newer cultivars have been introduced from the University of Helsinki, Finland. They are under evaluation at The Minnesota Landscape Arboretum. They are worth being tried in zone 4.

'Elviira'   azalea
TRIAL IN ZONE 4
2 feet tall, 2 feet wide

Low growing with bright red flowers.

'Haaga'   azalea
TRIAL IN ZONE 4
5 feet tall, 5 feet wide

An upright-growing cultivar with pink flowers.

'Hellikki'   azalea
TRIAL IN ZONE 4
5 feet tall, 5 feet wide

An upright growing cultivar with red-violet flowers.

'Mikkeli'   azalea
TRIAL IN ZONE 4
5 feet tall, 5 feet wide

A compact-growing, upright cultivar with mainly white flowers.

'Peter Tigerstedt'   azalea
TRIAL IN ZONE 4
6 feet tall, 6 feet wide.

A larger-growing, upright cultivar with mainly white flowers.

Mollis Hybrids

Sometimes classified under *R. x kosterianum.* These hybrids are usually seed-propagated; after repeated generations of seed propagation, plants resemble the hardier *R. japonicum.* Hardiness varies greatly, depending on the source of the plants. A strain at the Arboretum that came from the Waltham Field Station in Massachusetts has been quite hardy. Flower buds may be injured following a severe winter. There are a number of questionably hardy cultivars.

P.J.M. Hybrids

These hybrids resulted from a cross made at the Weston Nurseries in Massachusetts between *R. minus* and *R. dauricum* var. *persistens.* Their appearance is somewhat variable, and several cultivars have been named. The cultivar, 'PJM' is most often grown and seems to be hardy with the right growing conditions into zone 3. The plants are evergreen and bloom early in May with lavender pink flowers. This is one of the hardiest of the evergreen rhododendrons. Little winter protection is required, but bloom is usually better if the plants are protected from winter sun. They can be short lived in poorly drained soil.

OTHER CULTIVARS AND SPECIES:

There are numerous other cultivars that can be attempted in the North. The purchaser should first determine that these are hardy in the North. The species described below are harder to obtain and probably should be attempted only by rhododendron enthusiasts.

'Aglo'   rhododendron
TRIAL IN ZONE 4
4 feet tall, 4 feet wide

A compact pink-flowering cultivar. The foliage turns dark in the winter in the North. Needs protection.

'Northern Starburst'   rhododendron
TRIAL IN ZONE 4
4 feet tall, 3 feet wide

Similar to 'P.J.M.' but probably hardier. Pink bloom.

SWEET AZALEA
Rhododendron arborescens Torr.
HARDY IN ZONE 4
9 feet tall, 6 feet wide

HABIT. Arborescent, deciduous shrub; there are 800 species distributed worldwide.
BRANCHLETS. Mostly smooth, rarely with a few scattered hairs, often slightly whitish.
BUDS. Smooth.
LEAVES. Obovate to elliptic or oblong-oblanceolate, 1.2 to 3.1 in. long, acute or obtuse, ciliate, smooth and bright green above, glaucous or sometimes green beneath, fragrant when dry; petioles slender.
FLOWERS. 3 to 6, opening after the leaves, very fragrant, in June; corolla white or pinkish with tubes 1 in. long, slightly dilated at the apex, longer than the ovate-oblong, acuminate lobes; stamens about twice as long as tube, purple above; styles as long as or longer than stamens, usually smooth, purple above; sepals ovate to narrow-oblong, 0.1 to 0.2 in. long.

FRUIT. Oblong-ovoid, less than 0.5 in. long.

LANDSCAPE USE AND CULTURE

There may be flower bud injury following a severe winter. It is important to purchase plants grown from a northern seed source. Native from the mountains of southern Pennsylvania to Georgia and Alabama, it has been in cultivation since 1814.

COAST AZALEA
Rhododendron atlanticum
(Asche.) Rehd.
HARDY IN ZONE 4
20 inches tall, 3 feet wide

HABIT. Suckering, deciduous shrub.
LEAVES. Obovate to oblong-obovate, rarely elliptic, 1.2 to 2.2 in. long, roundish or acutish at apex, smooth above, bright green or glaucous beneath.
FLOWERS. In clusters of 4 to 10 in mid-May; very fragrant; corolla white, usually flushed with pink; tubes cylindric, less than 1 in. long; stamens twice as long as tube, styles longer.
FRUIT. Ovoid-oblong, less than 0.7 in. long.

LANDSCAPE USE AND CULTURE

This species has been surprisingly hardy considering its native range. Native along the coast from Delaware to South Carolina, it has been in cultivation since 1916.

ROSEHILL AZALEA
Rhododendron austrinum Rehd.
HARDY IN ZONE 4
3 feet tall, 3 feet wide

HABIT. Low shrub.
BRANCHLETS. Finely hairy and usually sparingly strigilose.
BUDS. Grayish hairy.
LEAVES. Elliptic or obovate to obovate-oblong, 1.2 to 2.7 in. long, acute or short-acuminate, dull bluish green and sparingly hairy above, grayish hairy beneath.
FLOWERS. 5 to 9, very fragrant, in mid-May; corolla bright pink, rarely whitish, about 1.5 in. across; tubes gradually dilated, 0.5 to 0.7 in. long, about as long as the ovate lobes; stamens about twice as long as tube; styles longer than stamens, purple above.
FRUIT. Oblong, 0.5 to 0.7 in. long.

LANDSCAPE USE AND CULTURE

Was previously known as *R. prinophyllum* and *R. roseum*. This species has been very hardy at the Arboretum and blooms every year. However, these plants have not been very vigorous and seldom grow more than 20 inches. Native from New Hampshire and Quebec to Virginia and Missouri, it has been cultivated since 1790.

FLAME AZALEA
Rhododendron calendulaceum (Michx.) Torr.
HARDY IN ZONE 4
9 feet tall, 6 feet wide

HABIT. Large, deciduous shrub.
BRANCHLETS. Hairy.
BUDS. Smooth with ciliolate scales.
LEAVES. Broad-elliptic to elliptic-oblong or obovate-oblong, 1.5 to 3 in. long, acute and gland-tipped, broader wedge-shaped at base, finely hairy above, more densely so beneath when young.
FLOWERS. In clusters of 5 to 7 in mid-May; corolla yellow or orange to scarlet, nearly scentless, about 2 in. across, tubes gradually dilated above the middle, 0.5 to 0.7 in. long, hairy.

LANDSCAPE USE AND CULTURE

This species has done well at the Arboretum with only occasional flower bud injury. Native from Pennsylvania to Ohio, south to Georgia and Kentucky, it has been cultivated since 1800.

RHODORA
Rhododendron canadense
(L.) Torr.
HARDY IN ZONES 3 AND 4
3 feet tall, 3 feet wide

HABIT. Much-branched shrub.
BRANCHLETS. Minutely hairy when young, yellowish red or pinkish, often bloomy.
BUDS. With acute to acuminate minutely hairy and ciliolate scales.
LEAVES. Petioled, elliptic to oblong, 0.7 to 1.5 in. long, obtuse to acute, wedge-shaped at base, with ciliate and revolute margins, dull bluish green above, thinly grayish woolly beneath; usually sparingly glandular and hairy on midribs.
FLOWERS. 3 to 7, in early May; corolla 0.5 to 0.7 in. long, rose-purple, 2-lipped, the lower lip divided nearly to the base into 2 narrow-oblong lobes, the upper lip with 3 short ovate lobes; stamens 10, about as long as corolla, hairy near base; styles slightly longer, smooth or nearly so.
FRUIT. Ovoid-oblong, less than 0.5 in. long, puberulous and setose.

LANDSCAPE USE AND CULTURE

This species requires wet, acid, peaty soil. It blooms early. It is best suited for bog-like culture. Native from Newfoundland and Labrador to Pennsylvania, it has been in cultivation since 1756.

CATAWBA RHODODENDRON
Rhododendron catawbiense Michx.
HARDY WITH WINTER SHADE IN ZONE 4
6 feet tall, 6 feet wide

HABIT. Spreading, evergreen shrub.

LEAVES. Elliptic to oblong, 2.2 to 4.7 in. long, obtuse or mucronulate, rounded at base, shiny green above, whitish beneath, smooth; petioles 0.5 to 1 in. long.
FLOWERS. Many, in early June; corolla broad-campanulate, 2.2 in. across, lilac-purple, spotted olive-green, with broad roundish lobes; pedicels rusty-hairy and glandular; filaments hairy at base, whitish; styles red.
FRUIT. Rusty-hairy.

LANDSCAPE USE AND CULTURE

The leaves of this species and its many cultivars need winter shading. A burlap structure is necessary. The flowers are very ornamental but may be damaged in a severe winter. Native in the mountains from Virgina to Georgia, it has been in cultivation since 1809. There are many cultivars offered by rhododendron nurseries outside of zone 4.

DAHURIAN RHODODENDRON
Rhododendron dauricum L.
HARDY IN ZONE 4
6 feet tall, 6 feet wide

HABIT. Upright, deciduous shrub.
LEAVES. Persistent, occasionally stay green over winter; elliptic to elliptic-ovate to oblong-ovate, 0.4 to 2 in. long, obtuse, rounded or broadly wedge-shaped at base, dark green and slightly scaly above, paler and densely scaly beneath, aromatic.
FLOWERS. Solitary, formed from axillary buds at the ends of branchlets in early May; corolla rotate, bell-shaped, 0.7 to 1.3 in. across, rosy purple, with lobes longer than tubes; stamens about as long as lobes; styles longer than stamens.

LANDSCAPE USE AND CULTURE

One of the parents of the PJM series, this species is difficult to obtain. Native to Korea, Manchuria, and northern Japan, it was introduced into North America in 1790.

JAPANESE AZALEA
Rhododendron japonicum (A. Gray) Suringar.
HARDY IN ZONE 4
6 feet tall, 6 feet wide

HABIT. Deciduous shrub with stout, erect branches.
BUDS. Ovoid, acute or acutish, slightly hairy.
LEAVES. Obovate to obovate-oblong, 1.5 to 4 in. long, obtuse and mucronulate, wedge-shaped at base, ciliate, appressed-hairy above and on the veins beneath.
FLOWERS. 6 to 12, in late May; corolla campanulate-funnelform, 2 in. across, orange to salmon-red; stamens shorter than corolla, hairy below the middle, anthers brown; pedicels usually setose.

LANDSCAPE USE AND CULTURE

Flower buds can be damaged in a severe winter in zone 4. Native to Japan, introduced into North America in 1861.

MANCHURIAN RHODODENDRON
Rhododendron micranthum Turcz.
HARDY IN ZONE 4
6 feet tall, 6 feet wide

HABIT. Evergreen shrub.
LEAVES. Elliptic-oblong to oblanceolate, 0.7 to 1.3 in. long, acute, smooth above, densely rusty scaly beneath; year-old leaves turn golden yellow in the fall, with only the new leaves remaining green over the winter; petioles less than 0.1 in. long.
FLOWERS. In many flowered, dense racemes 1.3 in. across, in late June or early July; corolla bell-shaped, white, with oval, spreading lobes; lobes as long as or shorter than tube, 0.4 in. across, styles longer than corolla, shorter than stamens.
FRUIT. Oblong, 0.2 to 0.3 in. long.

LANDSCAPE USE AND CULTURE

Features very small flowers resembling *Ledum groenlandicum* (Labrador tea). Does not need winter protection. Difficult to obtain in the nursery trade.

KOREAN RHODODENDRON
Rhododendron mucronulatum Turcz.
HARDY IN ZONE 4
6 feet tall, 6 feet wide

HABIT. Upright, deciduous shrub.
BRANCHLETS. Sparingly scaly.
LEAVES. Deciduous, thin, elliptic-lanceolate to lanceolate, 1.2 to 2.7 in. long, acute, or acuminate, wedge-shaped at base, loosely scaly on both surfaces, pale green beneath; fall color golden yellow to bronzy crimson; petioles 0.1 to 0.2 in. long.
FLOWERS. 3 to 6 at the tips of branchlets in early May; pedicels short, scaly; corolla funnel-campanulate, less than 1.5 in. across, pale rosy purple, minutely hairy outside; stamens villous below the middle; styles smooth, longer than stamens.

LANDSCAPE USE AND CULTURE

This species is reliably hardy in zone 4. Also, the cultivar, 'Cornell Pink', is one of the most dependable hybrids for the North.

CULTIVAR:

'Cornell Pink'
HARDY ZONE 4, TRIAL ZONE 3
6 feet tall, 6 feet wide

Similar to the species except the flowers are clear pink. Outstanding bloom in the North.

Other rhododendrons to try:

ROSEBAY RHODODENDRON
Rhododendron maximum L.
HARDY WITH WINTER SHADE IN ZONE 4
9 feet tall, 6 feet wide

It needs reliable winter shade. Since it is so large, it is difficult in the North to provide this shade.

CAROLINA RHODODENDRON
Rhododendron minus Michx.
FOR PROTECTED LOCATIONS IN ZONE 4
6 feet tall, 6 feet wide

The flower buds often are killed overwinter. Also known as *R. carolinianum.*

PINXTERBLOOM
Rhododendron periclymenoides (Michx.)
Shinn.
FOR PROTECTED LOCATIONS IN ZONE 4
6 feet tall, 6 feet wide

Flower buds are often killed overwinter.

ROYAL AZALEA
Rhododendron schlippenbachii Maxim.
FOR PROTECTED LOCATIONS IN ZONE 4
6 feet tall, 6 feet wide

This species is vegetatively hardy, but flower buds are often killed.

PINKSHELL AZALEA
Rhododendron vaseyi A. Gray.
FOR PROTECTED LOCATIONS IN ZONE 4
6 feet tall, 6 feet wide

Again, flower buds are often killed overwinter.

SWAMP AZALEA
Rhododendron viscosum (L.) Torr.
HARDY IN ZONE 4
3 feet tall, 3 feet wide

Flowers undistinguished. Could be planted in bog gardens.

YODOGAWA AZALEA
Rhododendron yedoense var. poukhanense Nak.
HARDY IN ZONE 4
3 feet tall, 6 feet wide

Flower buds are often killed overwinter.

BLACK JETBEAD

BLACK JETBEAD
Rhodotypos scandens (Thunb.) Mak.
FAMILY: ROSACEAE, ROSE FAMILY
FOR PROTECTED LOCATIONS IN ZONE 4
3 feet tall, 3 feet wide

This shrub is of borderline hardiness and frequently kills back in zone 4. It is often described as a trouble-free, graceful shrub. Native to central China and Japan, it was introduced into North America in 1866. For trial for the adventuresome.

SUMACS

FRAGRANT SUMAC
Rhus aromatica Ait.
FAMILY: ANACARDIACEAE
HARDY IN ZONES 3 AND 4
3 feet tall, 4 feet wide

HABIT. Low, spreading shrub; there are 200 species distributed worldwide.
BRANCHES. Ascending, aromatic; branchlets hairy.
LEAFLETS. 3, subsessile, ovate, 1 to 2.7 in. long; acute or acuminate, crenulate-serrate, hairy; terminal leaflet wedge-shaped; lateral leaflets oblique and rounded at base; fall color orange to red.
FLOWERS. Yellowish, in solitary or clustered spikes 0.2 to 0.8 in. long, forming short panicles at the ends of branchlets in late April.
FRUIT. Subglobose, about 0.2 in. across, red, and hairy, in August and September.

LANDSCAPE USE
Fragrant sumac makes a useful ground cover shrub for banks. It is conspicuous in early spring with its colorful flowers. It is colorful again in the fall with orange to red foliage. Native from Vermont and Ontario to Minnesota and south to Florida and Louisiana, it has been in cultivation since 1759.

CULTURE

This sumac will grow on poor soil as long as the soil is well-drained. It spreads by underground rhizomes. Needs full sun.

CULTIVAR:

'Gro-low'   fragrant sumac

HARDY IN ZONE 4
2.5 feet tall, 6 feet wide

A dense, compact selection suited as the species for use as a ground cover.

SMOOTH SUMAC
Rhus glabra L.

HARDY IN ZONES 3 AND 4
9 feet tall, 9 feet wide

HABIT. Suckering shrub.
BRANCHLETS. Smooth and glaucous.
LEAFLETS. 11 to 31, lance-oblong, 2 to 5 in. long, acuminate, serrate, glaucous beneath.
FLOWERS. Greenish, in dense panicles 4 to 9.7 in. long, minutely hairy, in July and August.
FRUIT. Scarlet, viscid pubescent, in dense panicles, in September and October.

LANDSCAPE USE

A good ground cover for hard to cover sites. We see it along highways on gravelly soils. Great fall color. Howard Nemerov captures it in his poem *Spell Before Winter* (1981, 246): "The sumac's candelabrum darkly flames".

Thoreau in *Walden* (1852, 120) describes it carefully, as it grew up around his Walden cabin: "The sumach (*rhus glabra*) grew luxuriantly about the house pushing up through the embankment which I had made, and growing five or six feet the first season. Its broad pinnate tropical leaf was pleasant though strange to look on. The large buds, suddenly pushing out late in the spring from dry sticks which had seemed to be dead, developed themselves as by magic into graceful green and tender boughs…"

CULTURE

Grows anywhere in full sun. Suckers freely, so not for every site.

CULTIVARS AND VARIETY:

var. *cismontana* (Greene) Cockerell.

ZONES 2 TO 4
6 feet tall, 6 feet wide

A western variety with fewer and narrower leaflets, smaller flowers and fruit clusters than in the species. Even more drought-tolerant than the species.

'Laciniata'   smooth sumac

ZONES 2 TO 4
7 feet tall, 6 feet wide

A cutleaf selection with growth habit similar to the species. Powdery mildew can mar the beauty of the foliage in late summer. Tolerates poor soils.

'Morden Select'   smooth sumac

ZONES 2 TO 4
6 feet tall, 6 feet wide

Smaller-sized and slower growing than the species. An introduction of the Morden Experiment Station in Manitoba.

SKUNKBUSH SUMAC
Rhus trilobata Nutt.

HARDY IN ZONES 3 AND 4
6 feet tall, 6 feet wide

HABIT. Upright shrub, parts ill-scented when crushed.
BRANCHES. Hairy.
LEAFLETS. 3, sessile or subsessile, elliptic or obovate, 0.5 to 1 in. long, wedge-shaped at base, with few rounded teeth; terminal leaflet usually 3-lobedY
FLOWERS & FRUIT. Similar to those of *R. aromatica*.

LANDSCAPE USE AND CULTURE

Similar to *R. aromatica*, this can also be used as a ground cover for poor soils. It is susceptible to leaf spot disease which can limit its effectiveness. Native from Illinois to Washington and south to Texas and California, it has been in cultivation since 1877.

STAGHORN SUMAC
Rhus typhina L.

HARDY IN ZONE 4, TRIAL IN ZONE 3
25 feet tall, 12 feet wide

HABIT. Large, suckering shrub.
BRANCHLETS. Densely velvety-hairy.
LEAFLETS. 11 to 13, lance-oblong, 2 to 4.7 in. long, acuminate, serrate, glaucous beneath, hairy when young; fall color orange to red.
FLOWERS. Greenish, in dense, hairy panicles 4 to 7.7 in. long, in June and July.
FRUIT. Crimson, showy, densely hairy, in August and September.

LANDSCAPE USE AND CULTURE

The species is useful for a large growing ground cover for poor soils. The cultivars are used for more ornamental purposes. Native from Quebec to Minnesota and south to Georgia and Iowa, it has been cultivated since 1629. The common name describes the velvety branches.

CULTIVAR:

'Laciniata' staghorn sumac
<small>HARDY IN ZONE 4, TRIAL IN ZONE 3</small>
8 feet tall, 15 feet wide

Leaves deeply and laciniately lobed, giving a fern-like appearance. This cultivar usually colors later than the species. Often sold as the cutleaf staghorn sumac. In the right site, this shrub can be stunning. Although single specimens could be effective, it is best for mass plantings as it suckers. *See photograph page 169.*

Other sumac to try:

SHINING SUMAC
Rhus copallina L.
<small>FOR PROTECTED LOCATIONS IN ZONE 4</small>
9 feet tall, 9 feet wide

A sumac with handsome foliage that has not proved too successful at the Arboretum. Worth a trial for the adventuresome.

NOTE:

There are two native pest plants, often placed in this genus, that are described below so they can be strictly avoided.

***R. radicans* L. (Poison ivy).** (Many now classify this plant as *Toxicodendron radicans*). Hardy in zones 2 to 4; variable growth habit, usually a procumbent vining-type plant in the North. DESCRIPTION: Suberect or climbing vine clinging by aerial rootlets; branches sparingly hairy or smooth; leaflets 3, ovate or rhombic, 1 to 1.5 in. long, acute or short-acuminate, entire or sparingly and coarsely dentate or sinuate, smooth and shiny above, more or less hairy beneath; lateral leaflets short-stalked; terminal leaflets on a stalk 1 to 1.5 in. long; petioles 2 to 4 in. long; flowers greenish white, in panicles 1 to 2 in. long, in June and July; fruit subglobose, 0.2 in. across, whitish or yellowish, smooth or short-hairy, in October.

***Rhus vernix* L. (Poison sumac).** (Again, many now classify this plant as *Toxicodendron vernix*). Hardy in zone 4; 12 feet tall, 9 feet wide. As with *R. radicans* (Poison ivy), poison sumac should be learned, so contact with it in the landscape may be avoided. DESCRIPTION: Upright shrub; branchlets smooth, glaucous at first, becoming gray; leaflets 7 to 13, short-stalked, elliptic to elliptic-oblong, 1.5 to 4 in. long, acuminate, wedge-shaped, entire, slightly hairy at first, becoming smooth; fall color brilliant red; flowers greenish yellow, in slender panicles 3 to 7.7 in. long, in June; fruit subglobose, 0.2 in. across, yellowish gray, in drooping clusters, in September.

The CURRANTS
Ribes L.
FAMILY: GROSSULARIACEAE

This genus contains some commonly grown ornamental woody plants and small fruit plants. Alpine currant, *R. alpinum*, is probably the most commonly used small growing hedging plant in the North. Edible currants and gooseberries also belong to this genus and are relatively easy to grow. There are many named cultivars of these fruits available, including 'Red Lake' currant an older University of Minnesota introduction.

ALPINE CURRANT
Ribes alpinum L.
<small>HARDY IN ZONES 2 TO 4</small>
5 feet tall, 5 feet wide

HABIT. Compact shrub; there are 150 species found in North America.
BUDS. Acute.
LEAVES. Roundish or ovate, square or subcordate at base, 1.2 to 2 in. across, 3- or rarely 5-lobed, with obtuse or acute dentate lobes.
FLOWERS. Dioecious, greenish yellow, in upright racemes, in early May, male racemes 1.2 to 2.2 in. long, with 20 to 30 flowers; female racemes smaller; calyx tubes rotate; sepals ovate.
FRUIT. Subglobose, scarlet, smooth, in July and August.

LANDSCAPE USE

This attractive, mound-shaped shrub is widely used in foundation plantings and for hedges. Native to Europe, it was introduced into North America in 1588. *See photograph page 156.*

CULTURE

Although female plants are showier when in fruit, male plants are usually propagated since they are reported to be more resistant to the white pine blister rust disease. Red spiders and leaf spot disease can also be problems; the latter may be quite serious in a wet season. Various strains of the plant exhibit different degrees of susceptiblity to leaf spot disease. However, disease problems are not serious enough to limit the use of this popular plant. Withstands part shade. It tolerates heavy pruning, so makes good hedge material. Propagation is largely by softwood cuttings.

CULTIVAR:

'Green Mound'   alpine currant
ZONES 2 TO 4
3.5 feet tall, 2.5 feet wide

A male selection that is very compact. It shows good resistance to leaf spot. Its size makes it better for a small hedge.

GOLDEN CURRANT, YELLOW FLOWERING CURRANT, BUFFALO CURRANT
Ribes aureum Pursh.
HARDY IN ZONES 2 TO 4
6 feet tall, 6 feet wide

HABIT. Erect shrub.
BRANCHES. Spineless, dark brown.
LEAVES. Broadly elliptic, 1.2 to 2 in. long, toothed, 3- to 5-lobed, smooth.
FLOWERS. Yellow, in many flowered racemes, fragrant, in May; sepals spreading, petals turning red.
FRUIT. Dark purple turning black, in August.

LANDSCAPE USE AND CULTURE
Round-shaped, with clean foliage and fragrant yellow flowers. Use for a background shrub or taller hedge. Confused with *R. odoratum*.

CLOVE CURRANT, BUFFALO CURRANT
Ribes odoratum Wendl.
HARDY IN ZONES 3 AND 4
6 feet tall, 3 feet wide

HABIT. Upright shrub with few suckers.
BRANCHLETS. Hairy.
LEAVES. Ovate to orbicular-reniform, wedge-shaped or square at base, 1.2 to 3.1 in. wide, deeply 3- to 5-lobed with coarsely dentate lobes.
FLOWERS. Yellow, fragrant, in 5- to 10-flowered nodding racemes, in May; sepals scarcely half as long as calyx tube, revolute or recurved; petals reddish.
FRUIT. Globose to ellipsoid, 0.3 to 0.4 in. long, black.

LANDSCAPE USE AND CULTURE
This attractive ornamental shrub should be planted more often than it is. Its flowers are quite showy with a unique clove scent, and its fruit makes fine jelly. The species is often confused with the western species *R. aureum*, from which it can be distinguished by its longer calyx tube. Many plants sold as *R. aureum* are *R. odoratum*. Native from Minnesota to South Dakota and south to Arkansas and Texas, it has been in cultivation since 1812.

Other currants to try:

EUROPEAN BLACK CURRANT
Ribes nigrum L.
HARDY IN ZONE 4
6 feet tall, 6 feet wide

Sometimes planted, although it is hard to find in the nursery trade. It sometimes escapes from cultivation and can be found in swamps.

RED CURRANT
Ribes silvestre (Lam.) Mert. & Koch.
TRIAL IN ZONE 4
5 feet tall, 5 feet wide

A parent of the cultivated garden currants. Previously known as *R. sativum*.

ROSE ACACIA & LOCUST

ROSE ACACIA
Robinia hispida L.
FAMILY: LEGUMINOSAE, PEA FAMILY
HARDY IN ZONES 3 AND 4
6 feet tall, 6 feet wide

HABIT. Suckering shrub with stems; there are 20 species found in North America; branchlets, peduncles and petioles hispid.
LEAFLETS. 7 to 13, suborbicular to broad-oblong, 0.7 to 1.3 in. long, obtuse and mucronulate, smooth or nearly so.
FLOWERS. Rose-colored or pale purple, 1 in. long, in 3- to 5-flowered hispid racemes, in June.
FRUIT. 2 to 3.1 in. long, glandular-hispid, rarely produced, in September.

LANDSCAPE USE
A suckering ornamental with very showy flowers. Its ornamental use is restricted because of its suckering habit. Native from Virginia to Kentucky and south to Georgia and Alabama, it has been in cultivation since 1758. Those seeing this plant in bloom often want to add it to their landscape.

CULTURE
It may show some dieback in the North and requires frequent pruning of dead wood. It grows on poor soils and is sometimes used for a ground cover on banks.

BLACK LOCUST
Robinia pseudoacacia L.
HARDY IN ZONES 3 AND 4
65 feet tall, 50 feet wide

HABIT. Large tree.
BRANCHLETS. Smooth or slightly hairy at first.
BARK. Deeply furrowed, brown.
LEAFLETS. 7 to 19, elliptic or ovate, 1 to 1.7 in. long, rounded or square and mucronate at apex.
FLOWERS. White, very fragrant, 0.5 to 0.7 in. long, in dense racemes 4 to 7.7 in. long, in June; standards with yellow spots at base.
FRUIT. Linear-oblong, 2 to 4 in. long, smooth, 3- to 10-seeded.

LANDSCAPE USE

This species suckers freely and frequently escapes from cultivation, often forming thickets on highway slopes. It is native from Pennsylvania to Iowa and south to Georgia and Oklahoma.

The late Henry Mitchell, one of our best contemporary garden writers, in his *One Man's Garden* (1992, 104) describes what is memorable about locust "Coming to this tree suddenly, I was transported to the Virginia countryside that I drove through early in May years ago on the way to my wedding. As everyone knows, a perfume that is come on suddenly and without anticipation has the power to evoke not only old memories but also a particular place and a precise instant." Its fragrance is outstanding.

CULTURE

Trees are very susceptible to the locust borer, an insect that can kill young trees. The species seems to grow best in drier sites.

CULTIVARS:

'Frisia'
ZONE 4
45 feet tall, 35 feet wide

A yellow leaved form whose color lasts throughout the season. Spines on young branches have a reddish appearance.

'Inermis'   black locust
ZONE 4
20 feet tall, 20 feet wide.

A globe shaped, compact tree that does not have spines. It is denser than the species.

'Purple Robe'   black locust
ZONE 4
50 feet tall, 30 feet wide

Globe-shaped crown with dark red foliage turning greener during the summer. Probably the hardiest cultivar.

'Pyramidalis'
ZONE 4
35 feet tall, 15 feet wide

It looks similar to the Lombardy poplar in the landscape. It is also spineless. Great for narrow sites.

'Umbraculifera'
FOR PROTECTED LOCATIONS IN ZONE 4
12 feet tall, 10 feet wide

A globe-shaped cultivar that must be grafted. It seldom produces flowers and is generally short-lived. It is not as hardy as the species and is very susceptible to the borer. For a protected site.

The HARDY ROSES

Rosa L.
FAMILY: ROSACEAE, ROSE FAMILY

One of the recent developments in hardy woody plants has been the number of new cultivars of shrub roses introduced that can effectively be used as landscape plants in the North. Twenty years ago when the first edition of this text was written, there were a few shrub roses of the old-fashioned type which could be utilized in the northern landscape. There has been a lot of recent research on roses and introductions that have proven to be hardy and trouble-free in the landscape without special care.

However, these should be purchased carefully as many described as hardy and trouble-free prove to be neither for the North. One should also know which rootstock many of these roses are budded on, as some are hardier than others. Many knowledgeable gardeners look also for own-root roses (non-budded). Many of the shrub hybrids can dieback to the crown in the North, but this only requires careful pruning in the spring. They are vigorous yearly growers.

A recent Minnesota Extension Publication, *Roses for the North: Performance of Shrub and Old Garden Roses at the Minnesota Landscape Arboretum*, contains much detailed research information on these varieties. Among the hardy shrub roses recently developed include impressive series from Canada named the Explorer Series from Ottawa and the Parkland Series from Manitoba.

Roses in general need full sun to do well. They also need good air circulation to reduce the possibilites of disease problems such as black spot and powdery mildew. The soil needs to be perfectly drained. Container grown roses can be planted anytime during the first half of the growing season. Planting of bareroot roses should be done early in spring while dormant. Irrigation during dry seasons is often necessary. Mulching with organic mulches greatly benefits roses. There are reports that too much fertilizer or spraying for disease control can actually hurt many of the newer introductions, especially the Explorer Series.

Following these few cultural requirements usually gives great results. Roses are no longer just for those who devote a major part of their hobby time to them. Roses can be almost carefree.

'A. MacKenzie'   rose
ZONE 4
5 feet tall, 4 feet wide

This 1982 Canadian shrub rose has double, red blended bloom. (Explorer Series).

'Adelaide Hoodless'   rose
HARDY IN ZONE 4, FOR PROTECTED LOCATIONS IN ZONE 3
3 feet tall, 3 feet wide

This shrub-type rose was introduced by the Morden Station of Manitoba in 1972. Flowers are red and semi-double. It dies back in zone 3. Repeat bloomer. It is susceptable to black spot disease. (Parkland Series).

'Agnes' rose

ZONE 4

4.5 feet tall, 4 feet wide

This rugosa-type was introduced in 1922. It has double, fragrant, amber-yellow flowers.

'Assiniboine' rose

HARDY IN ZONE 4, FOR PROTECTED LOCATIONS IN ZONE 3

4 feet tall, 5 feet wide

Features semi-double, red flowers. Dies to crown in severe winters in zone 3. An 1962 introduction of the Morden Experiment Station.

'Belle Poitevine' rose

HARDY IN ZONES 3 AND 4

5 feet tall, 4 feet wide

This rugosa-type features pink, semi-double bloom. It was introduced in 1894.

'Blanc Double de Coubert' rose

HARDY IN ZONES 3 AND 4

5 feet tall, 5 feet wide

This rugosa-type shrub has white bloom. Repeat bloomer. Introduced in 1892.

Bonica® rose

R. 'Meidomonac'

FOR PROTECTED LOCATIONS IN ZONE 4

3 feet tall, 3 feet wide

Without some protection will die back to the crown in zone 4. Clear pink bloom. An All-American winner introduced in 1958 in France.

'Captain Samuel Holland' rose

HARDY IN ZONES 3 AND 4

5 feet tall, 5 feet wide

Repeat red blooms. A 1991 introduction. (Explorer Series).

Carefree Beauty™ rose

R. 'Bucbi'

HARDY IN ZONE 4

4 feet tall, 3 feet wide

Pink, semi-double repeat bloomer. Some dieback in zone 4. Has light-orange rose hips in fall. Introduced in 1977.

Carefree Delight™ rose

R. 'Meipotal'

HARDY IN PROTECTED LOCATIONS OF ZONE 4

5 feet tall, 5 feet wide

Pink almost single repeat bloom. Some dieback in zone 4.

Carefree Wonder™ rose

R. 'Meipitac'

FOR PROTECTED LOCATIONS IN ZONE 4

2 to 3 feet tall, 3 feet wide

Brilliant pink repeat bloom. Dieback to crown in zone 4. A 1990 introduction from France. *See photograph page 150.*

'Champlain' rose

FOR PROTECTED LOCATIONS IN ZONE 4

3 feet tall, 3 feet wide

Variable red repeat bloom. A 1982 introduction. (Explorer Series).

'Charles Albanel' rose

HARDY IN ZONES 3 AND 4

1 foot tall, 3 feet wide

Red rugosa-type, repeat bloom. Useful as a low ground cover. A 1982 introduction.

'Cuthbert Grant' rose

HARDY IN ZONE 4, FOR PROTECTED LOCATIONS IN ZONE 3

2.5 feet tall, 3 feet wide

Purple-red repeat bloom. Fragrant. It has done very well in the parking lot area of the Arboretum. A 1967 introduction. (Parkland Series).

'David Thompson' rose

HARDY IN ZONES 3 AND 4

3 feet tall, 3 feet wide

Pink repeat bloom. A 1979 introduction. (Explorer Series).

'DeMontarville' rose

HARDY IN ZONES 3 AND 4

3 feet tall, 3 feet wide

A pink repeat bloomer with upright growing habit. (Explorer Series).

'F.J. Grootendorst' rose

HARDY IN ZONE 4

5 feet tall, 5 feet wide

Striking red, rugosa-type, repeat bloom. A 1918 introduction.

'Frau Dagmar Hartopp'   rose

HARDY IN ZONE 4

4 feet tall, 4 feet wide

This rugosa-type rose was introduced in 1914. With single, fragrant, shell pink flowers with repeat bloom.

'Frontenac'   rose

HARDY IN ZONES 3 AND 4

3 feet tall, 3 feet wide

A dark pink bloomer that blooms from June to frost. Good disease resistance. (Explorer Series).

'George Vancouver'   rose

HARDY IN ZONE 4

2 feet tall, 3 feet wide

Red, repeat bloom. This smaller-sized rose can be used as a ground cover. Red hips in fall. A 1994 Canadian introduction. (Explorer Series).

'Grootendorst Supreme'   rose

HARDY IN ZONE 4

5 feet tall, 4 feet wide

This hybrid rugosa-type was introduced in 1936. Clusters of small, deep pink flowers exhibit repeat bloom.

'Hansa'   rose

HARDY IN ZONES 3 AND 4

6 feet tall, 5 feet wide

A hybrid rugosa-type introduced in 1905. Semi-double, reddish violet flowers exhibit repeat bloom. Insect galls on stems can be a problem.

'Harison's Yellow'   rose

HARDY IN ZONES 3 AND 4

6 feet tall, 5 feet wide

Shrub developed in 1830 from a cross between *R. foetida* and *R. pimpinellifolia*; similar to *R. foetida* 'Persiana' except the flowers are pale yellow and less double. It blooms in June. One of the hardiest shrub roses. Sometimes listed as *R. x harisonii*.

'Henry Hudson'   rose

HARDY IN ZONES 3 AND 4

2 feet tall, 3 feet wide

White repeat bloom opening from pink buds. More compact. A 1976 introduction. (Explorer Series).

'Henry Kelsey'   rose

HARDY IN ZONES 3 AND 4

6 feet tall, 4 feet wide

A climbing rambler with clusters of red repeat bloom. A 1984 introduction. (Explorer Series).

'Hope for Humanity'   rose

HARDY IN ZONES 3 AND 4

2 feet tall, 3 feet wide

Red bloom repeats until frost. Flowers resemble hybrid teas. Introduced by Morden Research Center (Parkland Series).

'J.P. Connell'   rose

HARDY IN ZONE 4, FOR PROTECTED LOCATIONS IN ZONE 3

4 to 5 feet tall, 4 feet wide

Light yellow repeat bloom. Dieback occurs in zone 3 in harsh winters. A 1986 introduction. (Explorer Series).

'Jens Munk'   rose

HARDY IN ZONES 3 AND 4

5 feet tall, 5 feet wide

Pink, repeat bloom. A 1974 introduction. (Explorer Series).

'John Cabot'   rose

HARDY IN ZONES 3 AND 4

6 feet tall, 4 feet wide

Pink, repeat bloom. Best treated as a climber. A 1978 introduction. (Explorer Series).

'John Davis'   rose

HARDY IN ZONES 3 AND 4

8 feet tall, 4 feet wide

Rambling rose that is best treated as a climber. Pink, fragrant, repeat bloom. Very vigorous. A 1986 introduction. (Explorer Series).

'John Franklin'   rose

HARDY IN ZONE 4, FOR PROTECTED LOCATIONS IN ZONE 3

3 feet tall, 3 feet wide

Clusters of red repeat bloom. Dieback occurs in a severe winter. A 1980 Canadian introduction. (Explorer Series).

'Lambert Closse'   rose

HARDY IN ZONE 4

2.5 feet tall, 3 feet wide

A more compact variety with pink repeat bloom. A 1994 Canadian introduction. (Explorer Series).

'Lillian Gibson'   rose

HARDY IN ZONE 4
12 feet tall, 12 feet wide

A hardy introduction from South Dakota. A very large shrub that produces large numbers of double, light pink flowers. Blooms once in June. Grow best when supported by a fence where the very large growing canes can be tied. This was one of Dr. Snyder's favorite roses. A 1936 introduction.

'Louis Jolliet'   rose

HARDY IN ZONES 3 AND 4
4 feet tall, 4 feet wide

Clusters of pink repeat bloom. Fragrant. (Explorer Series).

'Martin Frobisher'   rose

HARDY IN ZONE 4
6 feet tall, 6 feet wide

A pink repeat bloomer. A 1968 introduction. (Explorer Series).

'Morden Blush'   rose

HARDY IN ZONE 4, FOR PROTECTED LOCATIONS IN ZONE 3
2.5 feet tall, 3 feet wide

Very light pink with repeat bloom. In severe winters, dieback can occur. A 1988 introduction. (Parkland Series).

'Morden Centennial'   rose

HARDY IN ZONE 4, FOR PROTECTED LOCATIONS IN ZONE 3
4 feet tall, 4 feet wide

Clusters of pink with repeat bloom. In severe winters, dieback to the crown can occur. A 1980 introduction. (Parkland Series).

'Morden Fireglow'   rose

HARDY IN ZONE 4, FOR PROTECTED LOCATIONS IN ZONE 3
Less than 2 feet tall, 3 feet wide

Bright red with repeat bloom. In severe winters, dieback to the crown can occur. A 1989 introduction. (Parkland Series).

'Morden Ruby'   rose

HARDY IN ZONE 4, FOR PROTECTED LOCA-
TIONS IN ZONE 3
2.5 feet tall, 3 feet wide

Rich red with repeat bloom. In severe winters, dieback to the crown can occur. A 1977 introduction. (Parkland Series).

'Nearly Wild'   rose

HARDY IN ZONE 4
2 feet tall, 2 feet wide

Single, pink repeat bloom. A floribunda-type introduced in 1941.
In severe winters, dieback to the crown can occur. Perhaps some winter protection is advised. The bloom resembles a wild rose.

'Pink Grootendorst'   rose

HARDY IN ZONE 4
4 feet tall, 4 feet wide

Pink, rugosa-type, repeat bloom. A 1923 introduction.

'Prairie Dawn'   rose

HARDY IN ZONE 4, FOR PROTECTED LOCATIONS IN ZONE 3
6 feet tall, 5 feet wide

A 1959 shrub rose from Morden, Manitoba. Double, fragrant, deep pink, repeat bloom. (Parkland Series).

'Prairie Fire'   rose

FOR PROTECTED LOCATIONS IN ZONE 4
5 feet tall, 5 to 6 feet wide

Red, semi-double, repeat bloom. An introduction in 1960 by Robert Phillips of the University of Minnesota.

'Prairie Joy'   rose

HARDY IN ZONES 2 TO 4
5 feet tall, 5 feet wide

Double pink bloom in June. One of the hardiest roses from Canada often used as hedging. A 1990 introduction. (Parkland Series).

'Robusta'   rose

TRIAL IN ZONE 4
5 to 6 feet tall, 5 feet wide

A vigorous shrub rose with bright red bloom. A repeat bloomer. The Arboretum specimens show some damage after a severe winter. *See photograph page 162.*

'Rosa Mundi'   rose

FOR PROTECTED LOCATIONS IN ZONE 4
4 feet tall, 4 feet wide

Old-fashioned type that could date to before 1500. Features a striped bloom of the *R. gallica*-type. John Rea in his *Flora* of 1676 in the collection of Andersen Horticultural Library describes this rose: "The Rose of the World…[is] diversly spotted, marked and striped, throughout every leafe of the double flower." Some protection is required.

'Royal Edward'
HARDY IN ZONE 4, TRIAL IN ZONE 3
1 to 2 feet tall, 2 feet wide

Deep pink bloomer from June until frost. Good disease resistance. (Explorer Series).

'Seven Sisters'   rose
HARDY IN ZONE 4
12 feet tall, 12 feet wide

Light red bloom in June. Another rambler that needs a fence or support to contain. This rose dates from 1817 and dates in the Upper Midwest to early in its settlement. Resembles *R. multiflora.*

'Simon Fraser'   rose
HARDY IN ZONE 4
2 feet tall, 3 feet wide

Clusters of pink repeat bloom. A 1992 introduction featuring compact growing habit. (Explorer Series).

'Sir Thomas Lipton'   rose
HARDY IN ZONES 3 AND 4
8 feet tall, 8 feet wide

White, fragrant, repeat bloom. An old favorite dating from 1900.

'The Fairy'   rose
FOR PROTECTED LOCATIONS IN ZONE 4
Less than 2 feet tall, 3 feet wide

A floribunda-type rose with clusters of light pink, repeat bloom. Needs some protection in zone 4. Introduced in 1932. Very popular.

'Therese Bugnet'   rose
HARDY IN ZONES 3 AND 4
6 feet tall, 6 feet wide

Fragrant, double, lavender-pink, repeat bloom. An old favorite dating from 1950.

'Viking Queen'   rose
FOR PROTECTED LOCATIONS IN ZONE 4
6 feet tall, 6 feet wide

Introduced 1963 by Robert Phillips of the Univeristy of Minnesota. Used as a climber but needs winter protection. Light pink blooms.

'William Baffin'   rose
HARDY IN ZONES 3 AND 4
8 feet tall, 8 feet wide

Pink, repeat bloom. A pillar-type rose, best treated as a climber. A 1983 introduction. (Explorer Series). *See photograph page 174.*

'William Booth'   rose
HARDY IN ZONES 3 AND 4
4 feet tall, 6 feet wide

Red repeat blooms on a large informal shrub. (Explorer Series).

'Winnipeg Parks'   rose
HARDY IN ZONES 3 AND 4
2 feet tall, 2 feet wide

Clusters of bright red, repeat bloom. A 1990 introduction. (Parkland Series).

SMOOTH WILD ROSE, MEADOW ROSE
Rosa blanda Ait.
HARDY IN ZONES 2 TO 4
6 feet tall, 4 feet wide

HABIT. Shrub with slender, unarmed stems, or with scattered bristles when young; there are 150 species distributed throughout the northern hemisphere.
LEAFLETS. 5 to 9, elliptic to obovate-oblong, 0.7 to 2.2 in. long, usually acute, coarsely serrate, dull and smooth above, paler beneath; stipules dilated.
FLOWERS. Solitary or few, pink, 2 in. across, in June.
FRUIT. Red, subglobose, about 0.4 in. across, sometimes ellipsoid, in September and October.

LANDSCAPE USE AND CULTURE
This wild rose is common in the Midwest and very hardy. Native from Newfoundland to Manitoba and south to Pennsylvania and Missouri, it has been in cultivation since 1773. Available only from a few mail order nurseries.

AUSTRIAN BRIER ROSE
Rosa foetida Herrm.
HARDY IN ZONE 4
6 feet tall, 6 feet wide

HABIT. Spiny shrub.
STEMS. Slender, brown, with straight prickles.
LEAFLETS. 5 to 9, broad-oval or obovate, 0.5 to 1.5 in. long, usually rounded at base, doubly glandular-serrate, dark green above; stipules glandular-serrate.
FLOWERS. Solitary or several, deep yellow, 2 to 2.7 in. across, with an unpleasant odor, in June.
FRUIT. Globose, red, in September and October.

LANDSCAPE USE AND CULTURE

Grown only in the cultivars listed below. These roses are very susceptible to black spot.

CULTIVARS:

'Bicolor' rose
HARDY IN ZONE 4
8 feet tall, 8 feet wide

This is sold as the Austrian copper rose. It differs from the species in the color of its flowers, which are orange-scarlet or coppery red inside. Has been cultivated since the 1500s. Blooms in June.

'Persiana'
HARDY IN ZONE 4
6 feet tall, 6 feet wide

This rose has double flowers and is often sold as Persian yellow. Blooms in June.

REDLEAF ROSE
Rosa glauca Pourr.
HARDY IN ZONES 3 AND 4
6 feet tall, 4 feet wide

HABIT. Upright shrub.
BRANCHES. Slender, purplish, and bloomy, covered with a few, rather small bristles.
LEAFLETS. 7 to 9, elliptic to ovate-lanceolate, 0.7 to 1.3 in. long, serrate, bluish green and more or less tinged with purplish red, smooth.
FLOWERS. Few, deep red, 1.2 to 1.3 in. across, in June.
FRUIT. Subglobose, about 0.5 in. across, bright red, in August and September.

LANDSCAPE USE AND CULTURE

Sometimes listed as *R. rubrifolia*. This shrub is grown for its unique foliage. In full sun it has a purplish cast; in less sun it appears grayish red. The rose hips often remain into the winter.

SCOTCH ROSE
Rosa pimpinellifolia L.
HARDY IN ZONE 4
3 feet tall, 3 feet wide

HABIT. Medium shrub.
BRANCHES. Spreading, densely prickly and bristly.
LEAFLETS. 5 to 11, orbicular to oblong-ovate, 0.4 to 0.7 in. long, serrate, smooth.
FLOWERS. Solitary but usually very numerous on short branchlets, pink, white or yellow, 0.7 to 2 in. across, in June.

FRUIT. Subglobose, black or dark brown, in September.

LANDSCAPE USE AND CULTURE

Sometimes listed as *R. spinosissima*. Single white blooms. Very bristly and seldom planted.

RUGOSA ROSE
Rosa rugosa Thunb.
HARDY IN ZONES 3 AND 4
6 feet tall, 6 feet wide

HABIT. Upright shrub.
STEMS. Stout, densely bristly and prickly.
LEAFLETS. 5 to 9, elliptic to elliptic-obovate, 1.0 in. long, acute or obtuse, serrate, shiny and dark green, glaucescent, rough and smooth above, reticulate and hairy beneath, thick and firm.
FLOWERS. Solitary of few, 2.2 to 3.1 in. across, purple to white, from June to August.
FRUIT. Depressed-globose, smooth, brick red, less than 1 in. across, in September and October.

LANDSCAPE USE AND CULTURE

A hardy shrub rose suitable for the border or as a clump forming specimen shrub. Usually very fragrant. Many newer cultivars have some parentage from this shrub. Disease resistant, tolerant of city conditions and resistant to salt damage.

CULTIVARS:

'Alba' rugosa rose
HARDY IN ZONES 3 AND 4
6 feet tall, 6 feet wide

Flowers single, white.

'Albo-plena' rugosa rose
HARDY IN ZONES 3 AND 4
6 feet tall, 6 feet wide

Flowers double, white.

'Plena' rugosa rose
HARDY IN ZONES 3 AND 4
6 feet tall, 6 feet wide

Flowers double, purple. This may often be sold as the species.

APPLE ROSE
Rosa villosa L.
HARDY IN ZONE 4
6 feet tall, 4 feet wide

HABIT. Densely branched shrub.
STEMS. Stout, covered with straight, slender spines.

LEAFLETS. Usually 5 to 7, elliptic to elliptic-oblong, acute or obtuse, 1.2 to 2 in. long, doubly glandular-serrate, grayish green and hairy above; auricles of stipules spreading or converging.
FLOWERS. Subglobose, large, 1 in. across, hispid, with persistent upright sepals, in August and September.

LANDSCAPE USE AND CULTURE

Also classified as *R. pomifera*. This species is suitable for the back of the shrub border. Attractive orange rose hips into the winter.

FATHER HUGO'S ROSE
Rosa xanthina f. hugonis (Hemsl.) A.V. Roberts.
HARDY IN ZONE 4
6 feet tall, 6 feet wide

HABIT. Dense shrub.
BRANCHES. Arching with straight prickles intermixed with bristles.
LEAFLETS. 5 to 13, oval to obovate or elliptic; 0.3 to 0.8 in. long, obtuse, sometimes acutish, finely serrate.
FLOWERS. Solitary on short branches, light yellow, 2 in. across, in early June.
FRUIT. Depressed-globose, about 0.5 in. across, dark scarlet to blackish red, in August.

LANDSCAPE USE AND CULTURE

Incorrectly classified as *R. hugonis*. Suitable for the back of a shrub border, it features light yellow bloom. It is native to Japan, Korea and China, and was introduced into North America in 1907.

The RUBUS

Rubus L.
FAMILY: ROSACEAE, ROSE FAMILY

Raspberries, blackberries and many of the other bramble fruit belong to this genus. These fruit and others can be grown in the landscape to yield produce. Raspberries are hardiest and easiest to grow. The section of photographs *(page 164)* illustrate using raspberries as a hedge and property divider. The challenge in landscape conditions is to keep the plantings neat and tidy. Don Gordon in *Growing Fruit in the Upper Midwest*, an excellent book on fruit growing, illustrates different methods of growing raspberries attractively.

Blackberries are more of a challenge. Unprotected, most blackberry canes will winterkill above the snow line. Blackberries sprawl more, so they are difficult to make attractive in the landscape.

FLOWERING RASPBERRY
Rubus odoratus L.
HARDY IN ZONE 4
9 feet tall, 9 feet wide

HABIT. Upright shrub; there are 250 species distributed worldwide; young shoots, petioles and peduncles hairy and glandular.
LEAVES. Heart-shaped, 5-lobed, 4 to 12 in. broad, lobes broad-triangular, abruptly acuminate, irregularly dentate, green and pilose on both sides; petioles 0.7 to 3 in. long, villous.
FLOWERS. Purple, showy, fragrant, 1.2 to 2 in. across, in short, many-flowered panicles, in June and July; sepals broad-ovate, abruptly caudate, acuminate, glandular outside; petals suborbicular.
FRUIT. Red, flat, less than 1 in. broad.

LANDSCAPE USE AND CULTURE

Native from Nova Scotia to Michigan and south to Georgia and Tennessee. Best planted toward the back of the shrub border. It tolerates shade, has an open habit, needs a moist soil.

THIMBLEBERRY
Rubus parviflorus Nutt.
HARDY IN ZONES 2 TO 4
6 feet tall, 3 feet wide

HABIT. Deciduous, upright shrub; young branchlets, petioles, and inflorescence slightly hairy and more or less glandular.
LEAVES. Kidney-shaped with 3 to 5 triangular lobes, 2.2 to 7.7 in. across, short-acuminate or acute, dentate, sparingly hairy on both sides; petioles 2 to 4.7 in. long.
FLOWERS. White, 1.2 to 2.2 in. across, in 3- to 10-flowered, dense corymbs, in June; sepals broad-ovate, abruptly caudate-acuminate, densely glandular outside; petals broad-oval or ovate.
FRUIT. Convex, red, 0.5 to 0.7 in. across, in July and August.

LANDSCAPE USE AND CULTURE

Thimbleberry is a native bramble that could be used in naturalistic plantings. Common on the North Shore of Lake Superior, this species is attractive in bloom especially after a winter with good snow cover. Native from Ontario to Alaska and south to New Mexico and California, it has been cultivated since 1918.

Other Rubus to try:

HIGHBUSH BLACKBERRY
Rubus allegheniensis L.H. Bailey.
HARDY IN ZONE 4, WITH SNOW COVER IN ZONE 3
9 feet tall, 9 feet wide

This species, though native, is not very useful ornamentally.

BOULDER RASPBERRY
Rubus deliciosus Torr.
FOR PROTECTED LOCATIONS IN ZONE 4
9 feet tall, 9 feet wide

Native to Colorado, this raspberry has been in cultivation since 1870. An attractive, informal ornamental shrub, it has not been grown in our area. One of the most attractive *Rubus* in bloom.

BLACK RASPBERRY
Rubus occidentalis L.
HARDY IN ZONE 4
9 feet tall, 9 feet wide

Native from New Brunswick to Minnesota and south to George and Colorado, it has been in cultivation since 1696. The species is quite susceptible to anthracnose disease and should not be planted near red raspberries.

JAPANESE RASPBERRY
Rubus parvifolius Nutt.
HARDY IN ZONE 4
20 inches tall, 3 feet wide

Native to China and Japan, it was introduced into North America in 1818. This species forms a dense mat and is useful as a ground cover.

The WILLOW
Salix L.
FAMILY: SALICACEAE, WILLOW FAMILY

There are about 300 species native throughout the world. Of these, only a few have been selected as being suitable for ornamental purposes. They range from shrubs that are grown for their spring bloom to very large trees such as the weeping willow. Most willows prefer moist soil. They can be used as specimen trees, windbreaks, hedges and for their colored twigs in winter. Care should be taken to fit these rather coarse textured plants into the landscape.

Henry Beston in *Especially Maine* (1970, 177) wrote poetically seeing "old farms and fields with willows bordering their shores and silvering in the wind." Jonathan Carver in his *Travels through the Interior Parts of North America* (1781) in the collection of Andersen Horticultural Library describes how the "bark of this shrub supplies the beaver with its winter food; [and with the red roots] Indians tinge many of the ornamental parts of their dress."

CULTIVARS:

(Of interspecific parentage)

'Flame'
HARDY IN ZONES 3 AND 4
20 feet tall, 15 feet wide

This cultivar features an orange-red bark in the winter. It has an oval-shaped canopy. Introduced by Bergeson Nursery in Fertile, Minnesota.

'Golden Curls'
HARDY IN ZONE 4
25 feet tall, 20 feet wide

It has a semi-contorted habit somewhat resembling the corkscrew willow which is not as hardy. Somewhat pendulous. Introduced by Beardslee Nursery in 1976. Some die back has been observed on trees in the Twin Cities area.

'Prairie Cascade'   willow
HARDY IN ZONES 3 AND 4
40 feet tall, 40 feet wide

A hardier willow with golden stem color. Like many willows it relishes moist conditions. There seems to be confusion in the nursery trade over this cultivar. The specimens at The Minnesota Landscape Arboretum do not have weeping habits. An introduction of the Morden Research Station in Manitoba in 1981.

WHITE WILLOW
Salix alba L.
HARDY IN ZONES 2 TO 4
80 feet tall, 50 feet wide

HABIT. Large tree; there are 300 species distributed worldwide.
BRANCHES. Spreading; branchlets silky when young, olive-brown, spreading at an acute angle from the branches.
LEAVES. Lanceolate, 1.5 to 2.2 in. long, acuminate, wedge-shaped at base, serrulate, glaucous and silky beneath; petioles 0.2 to 0.5 in. long, with small glands; stipules lanceolate.
FLOWERS. Catkins, 1.5 to 2.2 in. long, on leafy stalks; stamens villous at base; ovaries subsessile, conic-ovoid, smooth, with a short style.

LANDSCAPE USE AND CULTURE
The species can be grown as a timber tree, but the cultivars below are used in landscapes. It is often used in the western parts of our region as a tree for shelterbelts or for problem areas. Native to Europe, central Asia and Northern Africa, it was introduced into North America by early settlers.

Thoreau again captures this willow in his *Journal*, vol 5 (1852, 430): "The salix alba has bloomed today—& fills the causeway with sweet fragrance though there are yet but few flowers. Here are boys making whistles—now no instrumental music should be heard in the streets more youthful and innocent than willow whistles——Its sound has something soft in it as the wood of the willow."

CULTIVARS AND VARIETIES:

'Britzensis'   white willow
A selection with bright red branches. It is often grown as a shrub by cutting the stems back to the ground each spring. Also sold as 'Chermesina'.

'Tristis' (Now classified as *S. x sepulcralis chrysocoma*.)

var *vitellina* (L.) Stokes.
Similar to the species except that the branches are yellow.

PUSSY WILLOW, GOAT WILLOW
Salix caprea L.
FOR PROTECTED LOCATIONS IN ZONE 4
20 feet tall, 13 feet wide

HABIT. Shrub or small tree.
BRANCHLETS. Gray-hairy when young, becoming smooth, brown, and shiny.
LEAVES. Broad-elliptic to oblong, 2.2 to 4.7 in. long, acute, rarely rounded at base, irregularly and slightly dentate or nearly entire, rough and dark green above, gray-hairy beneath; petioles 0.3 to 0.8 in. long, stipules oblique-reniform, serrate.
FLOWERS. Male catkins, oval, less than 1.3 in. long, dense and soft; female catkins to 2.2 in. long.

LANDSCAPE USE AND CULTURE
This shrub is often confused with our native *S. discolor*. It has larger flowers than other pussy willows. It is not as hardy as other shrubs grown for the early spring flowers, so it should be given a protected location. Native to Europe, northeastern Asia, and northern Persia, it was introduced into North America by early settlers.

CULTIVAR:

'Pendula'   pussy willow
FOR PROTECTED LOCATIONS IN ZONE 4
6 feet tall, 8 feet wide

A weeping form that can be used as an ornamental specimen tree. Try a protected location.

PUSSY WILLOW
Salix discolor Muhlenb.
HARDY IN ZONES 3 AND 4
20 feet tall, 15 feet wide

HABIT. Shrub or small tree.
BRANCHLETS. Hairy at first, soon smooth.
LEAVES. Elliptic-oblong to oblong-oblanceolate, 1.5 to 4 in. long, acute at ends, irregularly crenate-serrate or nearly entire, glaucous beneath; petioles 0.3 to 1 in. long; stipules semicordate, deciduous.
FLOWERS. Showy catkins, appear before the leaves.

LANDSCAPE USE AND CULTURE
This very hardy native shrub is grown to harvest the flowers in early spring. The native pussy willow blooms are not as large as in the European species. For naturalistic plantings, wet sites, or the back of shrub borders. Thoreau, in vol. 4 of his *Journal* (1852, 467), describes it: "The skunk cabbage is inclosed in its spathe but the willow catkin expands its bright yellow blossoms without fear at the end of its twigs."

PEKIN WILLOW
Salix matsudana Koidz.
TRIAL IN SHELTERED, MOIST SITES IN ZONE 4
30 feet tall, 15 feet wide

HABIT. Small tree.
BRANCHES. Upright or spreading, yellowish or olive-green and smooth when young.
LEAVES. Narrow-lanceolate, 2 to 3 in. long, long-acuminate, rounded or rarely wedge-shaped at base, sharply glandular-serrate, glaucescent or whitish beneath; silky at first, soon smooth, petioles 0.08 to 0.3 in. long; stipules lanceolate, often wanting.

LANDSCAPE USE AND CULTURE
The species is seldom planted, but the contorted 'Tortuosa' is an ornamental cultivar that needs a protected location. Native to northern China, Manchuria and Korea, the species was introduced into North America in 1903.

CULTIVAR:

'Tortuosa'   Pekin willow
FOR PROTECTED LOCATIONS IN ZONE 4
30 feet tall, 25 feet wide

A selection that is planted often. The spiral stems are used in flower arrangements. Winter dieback is frequent.

WISCONSIN WEEPING WILLOW, NIOBE WEEPING WILLOW
Salix x pendulina Wender.
HARDY IN ZONE 4
65 feet tall, 65 feet wide

HABIT. Tree with broad, rounded crown.
BRANCHES. Long, drooping; branchlets dull green or brown, brittle at base.
LEAVES. Lanceolate to narrow-lanceolate, 3 to 6.0 in. long, long-acuminate, wedge-shaped at base, serrulate, dark green above, bluish green beneath, smooth; petioles 0.2 to 0.5 in. long; stipules ovate to oblong-ovate.
FLOWERS. Catkins, slender, 1 in. long; stamens hairy at base; ovary short-stalked with a short style.

LANDSCAPE USE
Incorrectly known as *S. x blanda*. Developed from a cross between *S. babylonica* and *S. fragilis*. Widely planted as a specimen tree because of its weeping habit. Often confused with *S. x sepulcralis chrysocoma* (golden weeping willow). Often planted near water, it is a messy tree in the landscape, constantly dropping branches and twigs. It was developed in 1830.

LAUREL WILLOW
Salix pentandra L.
HARDY IN ZONES 3 AND 4
65 feet tall, 40 feet wide

HABIT. Medium-sized tree.
BRANCHLETS. Shiny, brownish green.
BARK. Gray, fissured.
BUDS. Yellow.
LEAVES. Elliptic or ovate to elliptic-lanceolate, 1.5 to 4.7 in. long, short-acuminate, rounded or subcordate at base, glandular-denticulate, shiny dark green above, lighter beneath with a yellow midrib; petioles 0.2 to 0.4 in. long, glandular; stipules oblong-ovate, small.
FLOWERS. Catkins, on leafy stalks, golden yellow.

LANDSCAPE USE AND CULTURE
This is a handsome willow with very glossy, dark green leaves. It is often planted in shelterbelts and for screening purposes. Native to Europe and the Caucasus Mountains, it was introduced into North America by early settlers.

PURPLE OSIER WILLOW
Salix purpurea L.
HARDY IN ZONES 2 TO 4
9 feet tall, 6 feet wide

HABIT. Upright shrub.
BRANCHES. Slender, tough, smooth, at first purplish, later gray.
LEAVES. Oblanceolate, rarely oblong-obovate, often subopposite, 2 to 4 in. long, acute or acuminate, wedge-shaped at base, serrulate toward apex, dull green above, pale or glaucous beneath; petioles 0.1 to 0.3 in. long; stipules small or wanting.
FLOWERS. Catkins, usually curved, less than 1 in. long, appear before the leaves.

LANDSCAPE USE
A willow that is sometimes planted as an ornamental and also used for making baskets. It is more commonly found in one of the forms listed below. Native to Europe, northern Africa, central Asia and Japan, it was introduced into North America by early settlers.

CULTIVARS:

'Gracilis'
HARDY IN ZONES 3 AND 4
5 feet tall, 7 feet wide

A selection with slender branches and narrow leaves. Hardier than 'Nana'. Makes a wider and taller hedge.

'Nana'   purple osier willow
HARDY IN ZONE 4
4 feet tall, 5 feet wide

A dwarf selection frequently used as a low hedge. It is also
used in shelterbelt plantings.

NIOBE WEEPING WILLOW, GOLDEN WEEPING WILLOW
Salix x sepulcralis var. chrysocoma
(Dode) Meikle.
HARDY IN ZONE 4
50 feet tall, 50 feet wide

HABIT. Large, weeping tree.
BRANCHES. Slender, yellow, pendent; older bark fissured.
LEAVES. Lanceolate, acuminate, 2.3 to 4.7 in. long; silky at
first, then almost hairless; green above, glaucous below, margins minutely toothed.
FLOWERS. Catkins, narrowly cylindric, 1.5 in. long, bisexual;
scales yellow.

LANDSCAPE USE AND CULTURE
Incorrectly known as *S. alba* 'Tristis'. This weeping willow
like other willows is known as a messy tree losing branches
and twigs regularly. It likes moisture, so planting next to
water is common. It has invasive roots. Suitable for large
properties.

Other Salix to try:

PEACH-LEAVED WILLOW
Salix amygdaloides Anderss.
HARDY IN ZONES 2 TO 4
65 feet tall, 50 feet wide

Hard to obtain in the nursery trade.
Sometimes used in windbreaks.

CREEPING WILLOW
Salix arenaria L.
TRIAL IN ZONE 4
2 feet tall, 6 feet wide

A creeping form that does well as a ground
cover in locations that are not too exposed.
It has silver hued foliage.

ELDER

AMERICAN ELDER
Sambucus canadensis L.
FAMILY: CAPRIFOLIACEAE, HONEYSUCKLE FAMILY
HARDY IN ZONES 2 TO 4
9 feet tall, 9 feet wide

HABIT. Suckering shrub; there are 25 species distributed
worldwide.
BRANCHLETS. Pale yellowish gray, slightly lenticellate.
LEAFLETS. Usually 7, short-stalked, elliptic to lanceolate, 2
to 6 in. long, acuminate, sharply serrate, bright green.
FLOWERS. White, in 5-rayed, slightly convex cymes, to 10 in.
across, in July; ovaries usually 4-celled.
FRUIT. Purple to black, edible, in September.

LANDSCAPE USE AND CULTURE
This suckering shrub can be used in naturalistic plantings. It
is often grown for its fruit which is used for jelly, wine and
pies. If growing elder for its fruit, plant more than one cultivar. It can be used as sumac often is as a ground cover for
banks. It will also tolerate wet soils. Native from Nova Scotia
to Manitoba and south to Florida and Texas, it has been in
cultivation since 1761. Borers can be a problem.

CULTIVARS:

'Adams'   American elder
HARDY IN ZONES 3 AND 4
9 feet tall, 9 feet wide

A cultivar selected for larger fruit.

'Aurea'   American elder
HARDY IN ZONES 3 AND 4
9 feet tall, 9 feet wide

Leaves golden yellow and fruit cherry-red.

'Johns'   American elder
HARDY IN ZONES 3 AND 4
9 feet tall, 9 feet wide

Another cultivar selected for size of fruit.

'Laciniata'   American elder
HARDY IN ZONES 3 AND 4
9 feet tall, 9 feet wide

An attractive, cutleaf cultivar.

'York'   American elder
HARDY IN ZONES 3 AND 4
9 feet tall, 9 feet wide

Another cultivar grown for its larger fruit.

SCARLET ELDER
Sambucus pubens Michx.

HARDY IN ZONES 2 TO 4
12 feet tall, 12 feet wide

HABIT. Sprawling shrub.
BRANCHLETS. Pale yellow-brown, with prominent winter buds.
LEAFLETS. 5 to 7, stalked, ovate-oblong to oblong-lanceolate, 2 to 4 in. long, serrate, hairy beneath becoming smooth.
FLOWERS. Yellowish white, in ovoid or pyramidal panicles up to 4 in. long, in early May.
FRUIT. Scarlet, about 0.2 in. across, in June and July.

LANDSCAPE USE AND CULTURE

This elder is also used for naturalistic plantings. It is shade tolerant. Native from New Brunswick to Minnesota and south to Georgia and Colorado, it has been in cultivation since 1812.

EUROPEAN RED ELDER
Sambucus racemosa L.

HARDY IN ZONES 2 TO 4
12 feet tall, 12 feet wide

HABIT. Large shrub.
BRANCHES. Smooth, light brown.
LEAFLETS. 5 to 7, subsessile, ovate or elliptic to ovate-lanceolate, 1.5 to 3 in. long, acuminate, sharply and rather coarsely serrate.
FLOWERS. Yellowish white, in dense, ovoid or oblong-ovoid panicles 1 to 2.2 in. long, in early May.
FRUIT. Scarlet, about 0.2 in. across, in June and July.

LANDSCAPE USE AND CULTURE

Used in naturalistic plantings and toward the back of a shrub border. More commonly planted than *S. pubens*. Native to Europe and western Asia, introduced to North America in 1596. Stem borer can destroy entire branches spoiling the landscape effect.

CULTIVAR:

'Sutherland Gold'

HARDY IN ZONES 3 AND 4
12 feet tall, 12 feet wide

A selection with golden yellow leaves. Introduced by the Sutherland Experiment Station in Saskatchewan.

SASSAFRAS

SASSAFRAS
Sassafras albidum (Nutt.) Nees.

FAMILY: LAURACEAE
TRIAL IN SHELTERED SITES IN EASTERN PARTS OF ZONE 4
30 feet tall, 18 feet wide

HABIT. Small deciduous tree; there are 3 species native in North America and Asia.
BRANCHLETS & BUDS. Smooth and glaucous.
BARK. Deeply furrowed.
LEAVES. Simple, alternate, ovate to elliptic, 3 to 4.7 in. long, entire or 1- to 3-lobed at apex, acute or obtuse, wedge-shaped at base, bright green above, smooth and glaucous beneath; fall color orange and scarlet; petioles 0.5 to 1 in. long.
FLOWERS. Dioecious, yellow, 0.3 in. across, in racemes 1.2 to 2 in. long, in early May; calyx 6-parted; male flowers with 9 stamens in 3 whorls; anthers 4-celled; female flowers with an ovoid ovary, slender style, and with rudimentary stamens.
FRUIT. Bluish black, ovoid drupes 0.4 in. long, on club-shaped, fleshy, and bright red pedicels; fruit ripens in September.

LANDSCAPE USE AND CULTURE

Sassafras can be tried in protected locations of eastern zone 4. They have not survived at the Arboretum. There are probably other environmental factors other than cold hardiness that can determine success with this understory tree. Native from Massachusetts to Missouri and south to South Carolina and Tennessee, it has been in cultivation since 1630.

BUFFALOBERRIES

SILVER BUFFALOBERRY
Shepherdia argentea
(Pursh.) Nutt.

FAMILY: ELAEAGNACEAE
HARDY IN ZONES 2 TO 4
18 feet tall, 18 feet wide

HABIT. Large shrub; 3 species are native to North America.
BRANCHES. Spiny, covered with silvery scales when young.
LEAVES. Oblong to oblong-lanceolate, 0.5 to 2.2 in. long, obtuse, wedge-shaped at base, silvery on both surfaces.
FLOWERS. Yellow, small, in April and May.
FRUIT. Ovoid, 0.1 to 0.2 in. long, scarlet, sour, edible, in August.

LANDSCAPE USE AND CULTURE

Buffaloberry is an excellent shrub for wildlife plantings. With its silvery foliage it is sometimes used in the shrub border to provide a color contrast. The fruit were important in the diet of Native Americans. Native from Manitoba to Saskatchewan and south to Kansas and Nevada, it has been in cultivation since 1818.

RUSSET BUFFALOBERRY
Shepherdia canadensis
(L.) Nutt.

HARDY IN ZONES 2 TO 4
6 feet tall, 6 feet wide

HABIT. Spreading, unarmed shrub.
BRANCHLETS. Brown, scurfy.
LEAVES. Elliptic to ovate, 0.7 to 2 in. long, obtuse, green and sparingly scurfy above, silvery mixed with brown scales beneath.
FLOWERS. Yellow, 0.1 in. across, in April.
FRUIT. Ovoid, 0.1 to 0.2 in. long, yellowish red, insipid, in June and July.

LANDSCAPE USE AND CULTURE

Less ornamental than *S. argentea*, this buffaloberry has little landscape value, but can be planted in poor soils and for erosion control purposes. Native from Newfoundland to Alaska and south to Ohio and New Mexico, it has been in cultivation since 1759.

SMILAX

BRISTLY GREENBRIER
Smilax hispida Muhlenb.
FAMILY: LILIACEAE; LILY FAMILY
HARDY IN ZONES 2 TO 4
50 feet long

HABIT. Deciduous, spiny vine; there 200 species native in North America and Asia.
BRANCHES. Long, with prickles that are straight, slender, blackish.
LEAVES. Ovate or broad ovate, 2.7 to 4.7 in. long, pointed, 5- to 9-veined, with tendrils near the base of the petioles.
FLOWERS. Dioecious, small, greenish, in axillary umbels, in June; perianth segments 6, deciduous; stamens usually 6; ovaries 3-celled.
FRUIT. Small, black berries, in September and October.

LANDSCAPE USE AND CULTURE

Smilax is seldom planted but might be used where a barrier plant is needed because of its spines. It is native in deciduous woods. Native from Connecticut to Ontario and south to North Carolina and Texas, it has been in cultivation since 1688. Propagated by seed. Difficult to find in the nursery trade.

JAPANESE PAGODA TREE

JAPANESE PAGODA TREE
Sophora japonica L.
FAMILY: LEGUMINOSAE; PEA FAMILY
TRIAL IN SHELTERED SITES IN ZONE 4
50 feet tall, 30 feet wide

HABIT. Small- to medium-sized deciduous tree; there are 52 species distributed worldwide.

BRANCHLETS. Smooth or nearly so, green.
LEAVES. Odd-pinnate, alternate, with 7 to 17 leaflets; leaflets stalked, ovate to lance-ovate, 1 to 2 in. long, acute, broadly wedge-shaped to rounded at base, dark green and shiny above, glaucous and appressed-hairy beneath.
FLOWERS. Creamy white, mildly fragrant, in loose terminal panicles 6 to 12 in. long.
FRUIT. Dry legumes, 2 to 3 in. long and round in cross section.

LANDSCAPE USE

The pagoda tree is used as a specimen ornamental and occasionally as a street tree. Both its leaves and flowers are unique. As there are few summer blooming trees, it can be especially useful. Native to China and Korea, it was introduced into North America in 1747.

CULTURE

As the bark of this tree is prone to winter sunscald damage, it should be wrapped or protected overwinter. It tolerates high pH levels and air pollution. The Japanese pagoda tree is of questionable hardiness.

URAL FALSE SPIREA

URAL FALSE SPIREA
Sorbaria sorbifolia (L.) A. Braun.
FAMILY: ROSACEAE, ROSE FAMILY
HARDY IN ZONES 2 TO 4
6 feet tall, 4 feet wide

HABIT. Upright, suckering shrub; there are 4 species native in Asia.
LEAVES. Alternate, odd-pinnate, with 13 to 23 leaflets; leaflets lanceolate or ovate-lanceolate, long-acuminate, 2 to 4 in. long, doubly serrate, usually smooth or nearly so beneath.
FLOWERS. Small, white, in upright panicles 4 to 10 in. long, in June and July; cup-shaped calyx tubes with 5 reflexed sepals; petals 5, oval to orbicular, 0.3 in. across; stamens 20 to 50, twice as long as petals.
FRUIT. Dry, dehiscent follicles.

LANDSCAPE USE

This suckering shrub is often used as a high-growing ground cover. Most successful when grown in an area by itself. The panicled flowers are very showy but after flowering turn brown. Native to northern Asia in the Ural Mountains and to Japan, it was introduced into North America about 1900. *See photograph page 178.*

CULTURE

Trouble-free in most locations and soil types. Especially tolerant of shade. Easily propagated by softwood cuttings.

The MOUNTAIN ASH

Sorbus L.

FAMILY: ROSACEAE, ROSE FAMILY

Mountain ash are on many gardeners favorite tree listings because of their very ornamental fruiting characteristics. Unfortunately, this member of the rose family suffers from fire blight and also sunscald. Exposed locations should be avoided. Also, some species and cultivars do better in our area. In the right location these trees can add much to our landscapes.

KOREAN MOUNTAIN ASH
Sorbus alnifolia (Sieb. & Zucc.) K. Koch.
HARDY IN ZONE 4
50 feet tall, 25 feet wide

HABIT. Dense tree; there are 100 species distributed throughout the northern hemisphere.
BRANCHES. Speckled with prominent lenticels; branchlets smooth or slightly hairy.
LEAVES. Ovate to elliptic ovate, simple, short-acuminate, rounded at base, 2 to 4 in. long, unequally serrate, smooth or slightly hairy beneath, with 6 to 10 pairs of veins.
FLOWERS. 0.4 in. across, in loose, 6- to 10-flowered corymbs, in May.
FRUIT. Subglobose, 0.3 in. across, red or yellow, in September and October.

LANDSCAPE USE

Korean mountain ash has done well at the Arboretum. Unlike other mountain ash, this species leaves are not compound but simple. The bark is also smooth and gray unlike other species which are rough and brown. It is rather pyramidal when young but the canopy broadens with age. Native from central China, Korea and Japan, it was introduced into North America in 1892. *See photograph page 179.*

CULTURE

Trees have not suffered from sunscald and fire blight as have other species. This species can suffer from stress in street plantings.

AMERICAN MOUNTAIN ASH
Sorbus americana Marsh.
HARDY IN ZONES 2 TO 4
30 feet tall, 25 feet wide

HABIT. Small tree, sometimes shrubby with multiple stems.
LEAVES. Odd-pinnate with 11 to 17 leaflets; leaflets lance-oblong to lanceolate, acuminate, 1.5 to 4 in. long, sharply serrate, light green above, paler green beneath.
FLOWERS. 0.2 in. across, in dense, smooth inflorescences 2.7 to 5.5 in. across, in May and early June.
FRUIT. Globose, 0.2 in. across, bright red, in September and October.

LANDSCAPE USE AND CULTURE

This native tree can be attractive in the landscape where the birds will enjoy the fruit in the fall. It is unique in that it often naturally forms a clump specimen from a single plant.

Lower-growing than *S. aucuparia* and more shrub-like. Native from Newfoundland to Manitoba and south to North Carolina and Minnesota, it has been in cultivation since 1811.

EUROPEAN MOUNTAIN ASH, ROWAN TREE
Sorbus aucuparia L.
HARDY IN ZONES 3 AND 4
50 feet tall, 30 feet wide

HABIT. Medium-sized tree.
BUDS. Hairy.
LEAVES. Odd-pinnate with 9 to 15 leaflets; leaflets oblong to oblong-lanceolate, acute or obtusish, 0.7 to 4 in. long, serrate near tip, dull green above.
FLOWERS. 0.3 to 0.4 in. across, in inflorescences 4 to 6 in. across, in May and early June; stamens about as long as petals.
FRUIT. Globose, about 0.3 in. across, bright red, in September, lasting sometimes well into winter.

LANDSCAPE USE AND CULTURE

European mountain ash is the most widely planted of this genus. It is commonly used as an ornamental lawn specimen. This species needs good drainage. It is susceptible to fire blight. After the fruit has been subjected to freezing and thawing, it appears to be more palatable to birds. Native to Europe, western Asia and Siberia, it was introduced into North America by early settlers.

CULTIVAR:

Cardinal Royal® European mountain ash
S.a. 'Michred'
HARDY IN ZONES 2 TO 4
25 feet tall, 20 feet wide

Introduced in 1972 by the J. Frank Schmidt Nursery. It grows symmetrically upright and its fruits are cardinal red.

SHOWY MOUNTAIN ASH
Sorbus decora (Sarg.) Schneid.
HARDY IN ZONES 2 TO 4
30 feet tall, 25 feet wide

HABIT. Small to medium tree.
LEAVES. Odd-pinnate with 11 to 17 leaflets; leaflets elliptic to oblong, obtuse to abruptly short-acuminate, 1.2 to 2.7 in. long, serrate with spreading teeth, smooth and dark green above, paler and usually hairy beneath; slightly hairy.
FLOWERS. 0.3 to 0.4 in. across, in loose inflorescences 2 to 4 in. across, in May and early June.
FRUIT. Globose-ovoid, 0.3 to 0.4 in. across, bright red, in September and October.

LANDSCAPE USE AND CULTURE
Similar to *S. americana*, this native has larger-sized fruit. Birds are fond of the ripe fruit and the trees are usually stripped long before winter starts, except on the North Shore of Lake Superior where the ratio of trees to birds is greater. Native from Labrador to Minnesota and south to New York, it has been in cultivation since 1636.

OAK-LEAVED MOUNTAIN ASH
Sorbus x hybrida L.
HARDY IN ZONES 2 TO 4
30 feet tall, 20 feet wide

HABIT. Upright tree.
BRANCHES. Ascending; young branches flocose-hairy.
LEAVES. Ovate to oblong-ovate or oblong, 2.7 to 4.7 in. long, with 7 to 10 pairs of veins, often with 1 to 4 pairs of basal leaflets that are acute or acutish and serrate toward the apex; upper portion of each leaf is lobed; petioles flocose-hairy, 0.5 to 1 in. long.
FLOWERS. 0.4 in. across, in hairy inflorescences 2.2 to 4 in. across, in May.
FRUIT. Subglobose, 0.5 in. wide, red, in September and October.

LANDSCAPE USE AND CULTURE
A naturally occurring cross between *S. intermedia* and *S. aucuparia*. Introduced from Scandinavia into North America in 1779. The foliage of this species is more distinctive than other mountain ash.

The
SPIREA
Spiraea L.
FAMILY: ROSACEAE, ROSE FAMILY

There are over 80 species of spirea worldwide. Many of these and the many newly developed cultivars are important shrubs in the landscape. Many of the new cultivars have interesting foliage color. Spirea bloom over a long period in the summer garden. They are also trouble-free and require a minimum of maintenance. These shrubs range in size from large sprawly specimens to very compact growers.

CULTIVAR:

(Of interspecific parentage)

'Goldmound'　　　　　　　　spirea
HARDY IN ZONE 4
18 inches tall, 2.5 feet wide

'Goldmound' has light yellow leaves with pink early summer flowers. An accent shrub.

GARLAND SPIREA
Spiraea x arguta Zab.
HARDY IN ZONE 4, FOR PROTECTED LOCATIONS IN ZONE 3
6 feet tall, 4 feet wide

HABIT. Upright shrub; there are 80 species distributed throughout the northern hemisphere.
LEAVES. Oblong-obovate to oblong oblanceolate, acute, 0.7 to 1.5 in. long, sharply and sometimes doubly serrate.
FLOWERS. Pure white, 0.3 in. across, in many flowered umbels, in May; petals nearly twice as long as stamens.

LANDSCAPE USE AND CULTURE
A cross between *S. thunbergii* and *S. x multiflora*. This free-flowering hybrid is more vigorous than *S. thunbergii* but less tolerant of alkali chlorosis than *S. x multiflora*. It is early-flowering with white bloom and features good foliage texture. Often used in shrub borders.

CULTIVAR:

'Compacta'   garland spirea

HARDY IN ZONE 4

4 feet tall, 3 feet wide

A compact form sold as dwarf garland spirea.

BILLARD SPIREA

Spiraea x billardii Herincq.

HARDY IN ZONES 3 AND 4

6 feet tall, 4 feet wide

HABIT. Upright sometimes suckering shrub.
BRANCHLETS. Hairy, brown.
LEAVES. Short-petioled, oblong to oblong-lanceolate, acute at ends, 2 to 4 in. long, sharply and often doubly serrate except for the lower one-third (which is untoothed), usually grayish beneath when young.
FLOWERS. Rose-colored in upright, narrow, and dense panicles 4 to 8 in. long, from June to August; stamens nearly twice as long as petals.
FRUIT. Follicles, glabrous, parallel, with spreading styles.

LANDSCAPE USE AND CULTURE

A cross between *S. douglasii* and *S. salicifolia*. This spirea is useful in the shrub border where its rather strong character can fit in with other shrubs. The spent flower heads must be removed as they remain on the shrub into the next blooming year. It is very susceptible to iron chlorosis. Hard to obtain in the landscape trade.

JAPANESE SPIREA

Spiraea japonica L.f.

HARDY IN ZONE 4

4 feet tall, 3 feet wide

HABIT. Upright shrub.
BRANCHES. Smooth or slightly hairy when young, striped, nearly round.
BUDS. Ovoid, acute.
LEAVES. Ovate to ovate-oblong, acute, wedge-shaped, 0.7 to 3 in. long, doubly serrate, pale beneath and usually hairy on the veins; petioles less than 0.1 in. long.
FLOWERS. Pale to deep pink, rarely white, 0.1 to 0.2 in. across, in compound, loose, slightly hairy corymbs, in July; stamens much longer than petals.
FRUIT. Follicles, smooth, spreading, with ascending styles.

LANDSCAPE USE AND CULTURE

This attractive summer-flowering shrub has many cultivars. It is one of the most frequently planted of summer-flowering shrubs. The species is native to Japan and was introduced into North America in 1870. The colored leaved forms do best in full sun while the more green-leaved varieties withstand part shade.

CULTIVARS:

'Albiflora'

HARDY IN ZONES 3 AND 4

20 inches tall, 3 feet wide

Was incorrectly classified as *S. albiflora.* An attractive shrub for foundation of border plantings. Since this plant blooms on new wood, it is best to prune it back in early spring. *See photograph page 175.*

'Alpina'   spirea

HARDY IN ZONE 4

10 inches tall, 2.5 feet wide

A dwarf selection that makes an excellent ground cover. Space plants about 12 inches apart. A choice plant for the North, it features light pink bloom.

'Anthony Waterer'   spirea

HARDY IN ZONE 4

2 feet tall, 3 feet wide

A compact, broad, rounded-shaped selection with deep pink flowers. New growth is reddish purple.

'Bumalda'   spirea

HARDY IN ZONES 2 TO 4

30 inches tall, 3 feet wide

Formerly *S. x bumalda*, this low shrub forms a low, mound-shape with deep pink flowers. Confused in the nursery trade.

'Coccinea'   spirea

HARDY IN ZONE 4

2.5 feet tall, 3 feet wide

This mutation of 'Anthony Waterer' has dark red flowers.

'Crispa'   spirea

HARDY IN ZONE 4

2 feet tall, 3 feet wide

Burgundy leaves are somewhat curled. Pink flowers.

Dakota Goldcharm™   spirea

S.j. 'MERTYANN'

HARDY IN ZONES 3 AND 4

12 inches tall, 2 feet wide

An introduction of North Dakota State University that forms a low, mounded shrub. The leaves darken to a yellow-gold hue. Light pink flowers.

'Dart's Red'   spirea

HARDY IN ZONE 4

2.5 feet tall, 4 feet wide

Another sport of 'Anthony Waterer' with deep red flowers.

'Froebelii'   spirea

HARDY IN ZONE 4

3 feet tall, 4 feet wide

More vigorous than 'Anthony Waterer'. Features pink bloom. *See photograph page 156.*

Golden Princess®   spirea

S.j. 'Lisp'

HARDY IN ZONES 3 AND 4

3 feet tall, 4 feet wide

New leaves are bronze and fade to yellow-gold in summer.

'Goldflame'   spirea

HARDY IN ZONE 4

3 feet tall, 4 feet wide

New growth mottled with red, copper, and gold. Colors repeated in the fall. Bright red flowers.

'Gumball'   spirea

HARDY IN ZONES 3 AND 4

2 feet tall, 3 feet wide

A rounded form with leaves with dark purple tips. Pink flowers.

'Limemound'   spirea

HARDY IN ZONE 4

2 feet tall, 3.5 feet wide

This cultivar features light green foliage.

'Little Princess'   spirea

HARDY IN ZONE 4

2 feet tall, 3 feet wide

A cultivar that is often used as a ground cover. It has light green foliage with pink summer flowers. This cultivar will do well in light shade.

'Magic Carpet'

HARDY IN ZONES 3 AND 4

20 inches tall, 20 inches wide

The foliage on this cultivar is variable, from dark red in spring to multicolored bronze in the summer. For full sun.

'Norman'   spirea

HARDY IN ZONE 4

2 feet tall, 3.5 feet wide

A mound-shaped shrub with light green foliage. Very striking pink summer flowers. Good fall color.

'Shirobana'   spirea

FOR PROTECTED LOCATIONS IN ZONE 4

3.5 feet tall, 4 feet wide

A unique plant in the landscape having white, pink and red flowers on the same plant.

NIPPON SPIREA
Spiraea nipponica Maxim.

HARDY IN ZONES 3 AND 4

7 feet tall, 6 feet wide

HABIT. Vigorous shrub.
BRANCHES. Upright, spreading.
BRANCHLETS. Angled, smooth.
BUDS. Small, with 2 exposed scales.
LEAVES. Obovate to oval, broadly wedge-shaped, 0.5 to 1 in. long, crenate at the rounded apex, rarely entire, dark green above, bluish green beneath.
FLOWERS. White, 0.3 in. across, in many-flowered umbel-like racemes; petals orbicular longer than stamens, in early June.
FRUIT. Follicles, upright, slightly hairy, with spreading styles.

LANDSCAPE USE AND CULTURE

The species is seldom seen, but the cultivars below are grown. Native to Japan, it was introduced into North America in 1882.

CULTIVARS:

'Halward's Silver'   spirea

HARDY IN ZONE 4

3 feet tall, 3 feet wide

White flowers with dark green foliage. Described as being hardier than 'Snowmound'.

'Snowmound'   spirea

HARDY IN ZONE 4

3 feet tall, 3 feet wide

More compact and floriferous than the species.

THUNBERG SPIREA
Spiraea thunbergii Sieb. & Bl.
HARDY IN ZONE 4

7 feet tall, 6 feet wide

HABIT. Spreading shrub.
BRANCHES. Slender, spreading; branchlets angled.
LEAVES. Linear-lanceolate, acuminate, 0.7 to 1.5 in. long, sharply serrate, smooth, bright green.
FLOWERS. White, about 0.3 in. across, in 3- to 5-flowered umbels, in May; petals obovate, much longer than stamens.
FRUIT. Follicles divergent, with spreading styles.

LANDSCAPE USE AND CULTURE
This species suffers tip dieback necessitating pruning in the spring. However, there are newer cultivars in the trade that can be considered. This spirea is native to northern China, Siberia, and Turkestan and was introduced into North America in 1801.

CULTIVARS:

'Fujino'   spirea
HARDY IN ZONE 4

6 feet tall, 6 feet wide

A newer cultivar that features very light pink bloom in the spring.

Mellow Yellow®   spirea
S.t. 'Ogon'
HARDY IN ZONE 4

4 feet tall, 4 feet wide

Another spring blooming cultivar with white bloom. The foliage is yellowish green throughout the season. An upright informal habit.

THREELOBE SPIREA
Spiraea trilobata L.
HARDY IN ZONES 3 AND 4

4 feet tall, 3 feet wide

HABIT. Medium shrub.
BRANCHES. Spreading or arching.
BUDS. Ovoid, blunt.
LEAVES. Suborbicular, rounded or sometimes subcordate at base, 0.5 to 1 in. long, crenate-dentate, usually 3-lobed and palmately veined, pale bluish green beneath; petioles 0.2 to 0.3 in. long.
FLOWERS. White, in many flowered umbels, in May; petals longer than stamens.
FRUIT. Follicles, slightly divergent.

LANDSCAPE USE AND CULTURE
The cultivar below is most often grown. The species is native to northern China, Siberia and Turkestan and was introduced into North America in 1801.

CULTIVAR:

'Fairy Queen'   spirea
HARDY IN ZONES 3 AND 4

3 feet tall, 3 feet wide

Early-flowering variety with white bloom and dark green foliage.

VANHOUTTE SPIREA
Spiraea x vanhouttei (Briot) Zab.
HARDY IN ZONES 3 AND 4

6 feet tall, 6 feet wide

HABIT. Small shrub.
BRANCHES. Arching.
LEAVES. Rhombic-ovate to rhombic-obovate, acute, rounded or wedge-shaped at base, 0.7 to 1.2 in. long, serrate with mucronate teeth, usually 3- to 5-lobed, dark green above, pale bluish green beneath.
FLOWERS. White, 0.3 in. across, in many flowered umbels, in early June; petals orbicular, twice as long as stamens.
FRUIT. Follicles, slightly divergent.

LANDSCAPE USE AND CULTURE
A cross between *S. cantoniensis* and *S. trilobata*, this old-fashioned shrub was a favorite in Victorian times. One still sees it around foundations where it probably has lived for generations.

CULTIVAR:

'Renaissance'   spirea
ZONES 3 AND 4

5 feet tall, 7 feet wide

An introduction of Bailey Nurseries, this more compact grower has good disease resistance.

Other spirea to try:

SNOW GARLAND SPIREA
Spiraea x multiflora Zab.
HARDY IN ZONE 4

6 feet tall, 4 feet wide

An old-fashioned variety which is no longer in the nursery trade. Similar to *S. x arguta*.

BRIDALWREATH SPIREA

Spiraea prunifolia Sieb. & Zucc.

HARDY IN SHELTERED SITES IN ZONE 4

9 feet tall, 6 feet wide

This large-growing spirea is only for protected locations in zone 4. Native to Korea, China and Formosa, introduced into North America in 1864.

AMERICAN BLADDERNUT

AMERICAN BLADDERNUT

Staphylea trifolia L.

FAMILY: STAPHYLEACEAE

HARDY IN ZONES 3 AND 4

15 feet tall, 9 feet wide

HABIT. Upright, deciduous shrub or small tree; there are 11 species distributed throughout the northern hemisphere.
BARK. Smooth, striped.
BUDS. Ovoid, with 2 to 4 scales.
LEAVES. Opposite with 3 leaflets; leaflets elliptic to ovate, 1.2 to 3 in. long, acuminate, sharply and unequally serrulate, hairy beneath when young.
FLOWERS. Perfect, about 0.3 in. long, in nodding panicles or umbel-like racemes, in May or June; sepals 5, greenish white; petals 5, white, upright and longer than sepals; styles exserted.
FRUIT. 3-lobed, inflated capsules with few bony, yellow seeds.

LANDSCAPE USE

Bladdernut can be used as a border shrub or trained as a small tree. When trained as a tree it has a compact vase-shape. It also is grown for its attractive striped bark. Native from Quebec andOntario to Minnesota and south to Georgia, it has been in cultivation since 1640. It should be grown more often as it has many unique qualities that make it valuable in the North.

CULTURE

This small tree is tolerant of dry soils and a higher pH. Propagated by seed.

CUTLEAF STEPHANANDRA

CUTLEAF STEPHANANDRA

Stephanandra incisa (Thunb.) Zab.

FAMILY: ROSACEAE, ROSE FAMILY

HARDY IN SHELTERED SITES IN ZONE 4

6 feet tall, 6 feet wide

HABIT. Deciduous shrub; there are 4 species native in Asia.

BRANCHES. Slender and spreading, with lower branches distinctively zigzag and round.
BUDS. Superposed, small, with 4 exposed scales.
LEAVES. Alternate, simple, ovate, long-acuminate, heart-shaped to square at base, 0.7 to 1.5 in. long, incisely lobed and serrate; petioles 0.1 to 0.4 in. long; stipules conspicuous, ovate-oblong to lanceolate, sparingly toothed.
FLOWERS. Perfect, small, greenish white, in loose, terminal panicles 0.7 to 2.2 in. long, in June.
FRUIT. Small oblique follicles.

LANDSCAPE USE AND CULTURE

Stephanandra is best used for mass plantings. Its fine leaf texture is a valuable addition to the landscape. Its zigzag branching is unique. This shrub will withstand some shade. Some dieback can be expected following a severe winter. It is available in the nursery trade in the cultivar listed below. Propagated by cuttings. Native to Japan and Korea, it was introduced into North America in 1872.

CULTIVAR:

'Crispa'   cutleaf stephanandra

FOR PROTECTED LOCATIONS IN ZONE 4

2 feet tall, 5 feet wide

A compact selection that makes an attractive ground cover.

SNOWBERRY & CORALBERRIES

SNOWBERRY

Symphoricarpos albus

(L.) Blake.

FAMILY: CAPRIFOLIACEAE, HONEYSUCKLE FAMILY

HARDY IN ZONES 2 TO 4

3 feet tall, 3 feet wide

HABIT. Small shrub; there are 17 species native in North America and Asia.
BRANCHES. Upright, slender.
LEAVES. Oval to elliptic-oblong, 0.7 to 2 in. long, obtuse, often sinuately lobed on shoots.
FLOWERS. In terminal spikes or clusters, from June to September; corolla pinkish, about 0.2 in. long.
FRUIT. Globose or ovoid, 0.3 to 0.5 in. long, white, from September to November.

LANDSCAPE USE AND CULTURE

An undistinguished shrub that can be used as a ground cover for troublesome areas. Snowberry grows best in moist, partly shaded locations. It is redeemed in the fall by its prominent white fruit. Native from Nova Scotia to Alberta and south to Virginia and Minnesota, it has been in cultivation since 1879.

VARIETY:

var. laevigatus (Fern.) Blake.
HARDY IN ZONES 2 TO 4
5 feet tall, 4 feet wide

Taller than the species and with larger berries. Perhaps confused in the nursery trade.

CHENAULT CORALBERRY
Symphoricarpos x chenaultii Rehd.
TRIAL IN SHELTERED SITES IN ZONE 4
2 feet tall, 3 feet wide

HABIT. Low, mound-shaped shrub.
LEAVES. Elliptic or ovate, 0.5 to 1.2 in. long, obtuse, rounded at base, dull green.
FLOWERS. Pink, in June and July.
FRUIT. Globose, pink or white tinged with pink in small clusters.

LANDSCAPE USE AND CULTURE
A cross between *S. microphyllus* and *S. orbiculatus*. Of borderline hardiness, this should only be tried in protected locations. Its pinkish red fruit is attractive.

CULTIVAR:

'Hancock'
FOR PROTECTED LOCATIONS IN ZONE 4
2 feet tall, 5 feet wide

A very compact form suitable for use as a ground cover. Only for the most protected site.

CORALBERRY, INDIAN CURRANT
Symphoricarpos orbiculatus Moench.
HARDY IN ZONES 3 AND 4
3 feet tall, 3 feet wide

HABIT. Spreading, arching shrub.
BRANCHES. Slender.
LEAVES. Elliptic or ovate, 0.5 to 1.3 in. long, obtuse or acutish, rounded at base, dull green above, glaucescent beneath; fall color crimson.
FLOWERS. In dense and short axillary clusters and terminal spikes, in July; corolla campanulate, 0.1 in. long, yellowish white, flushed rose; stamens and hairy styles included within the corolla.
FRUIT. Subglobose, 0.1 to 0.2 in. across, purplish red, in October and November.

LANDSCAPE USE AND CULTURE
Coralberry is often used as a ground cover for banks, many times by roadways. It is grown for its colorful fruit and crimson fall color.

Other Symphoricarpos to try:

WOLFBERRY
Symphoricarpos occidentalis Hook.
HARDY IN ZONES 2 TO 4
3 feet tall, 3 feet wide

Seldom planted and difficult to obtain.

The LILACS

Syringa L.
FAMILY: OLEACEAE, OLIVE FAMILY

If there is one genus of plants that should be featured in the North it is *Syringa*. It is the group of plants that those further to the South wish they can grow but many times cannot.

Lilacs range in size from small ornamental trees to shrubs that can be large-sized or very compact. They are generally plants with strong character and textures. Their bloom often can be overwhelming with color and fragrance. They also are quite trouble-free in the landscape, often outlasting even the buildings in the landscape. They can provide screening and visual weight to the landscape.

Cultivars should not only be judged by flower color and height, but also to their resistance to mildew, other foliage diseases and foliage discoloration due to physiological stresses. Dr. Harold Pellett and Ken Vogel of The Minnesota Landscape Arboretum evaluated the performance of lilacs by late summer. Those looking for lilacs with good foliage characteristics should consider these findings, which are given for many species and cultivars.

Lilacs need full sun to flower well in the landscape. Although they will survive in part shade they will not flower profusely. A good gardening soil is necessary, but they can tolerate more alkaline conditions. For clump-forming and suckering shrubs, pruning is necessary to keep them vigorous. To rejuvenate old plantings, one-third of the older canes can be removed each year, cutting them clear to the ground. Following this pruning regime over a three-year period can result in a renewal of a lilac planting. Lilacs used as screening should not be sheared as they are too coarse twigged for use as a formal hedge. A side-dressing of fertilizer in early spring is beneficial.

SYRINGA HYBRIDS:

Many cultivars are selections of *S. x hyacinthiflora, S. x prestoniae,* and *S. vulgaris*, but there are also many that are crosses between other species which belong here.

'Aladdin'   lilac
HARDY IN ZONES 3 AND 4
9 feet tall, 9 feet wide

Lavender-pink bloom.

'Minuet'   lilac
HARDY IN ZONES 2 TO 4
6 feet tall, 5 feet wide

Compact, dense grower with single, pinkish purple bloom.

'Miss Canada'   lilac
HARDY IN ZONES 2 TO 4
7 feet tall, 6 feet wide

Flowers single, bright pink. This cultivar had excellent resistance to mildew with acceptable summer foliage in Arboretum trials.

Tinkerbelle ™   lilac
S. 'Bailbelle'
HARDY IN ZONES 3 & 4
5 feet tall, 5 feet wide

An exciting new introduction that has not been tested at The Minnesota Landscape Arboretum. This cultivar is from a cross between *S. meyerei* 'Palibin' and *S. microphylla* 'Superba'. It has single, deep pink bloom. Of great size for a multitude of uses. Developed by Sheyenne Gardens in North Dakota.

CHINESE LILAC
Syringa x chinensis Willd.
HARDY IN ZONES 3 AND 4
12 feet tall, 12 feet wide

HABIT. Large shrub; there are 20 species native to Europe and Asia.
BRANCHES. Slender, spreading, and often arching.
LEAVES. Ovate-lanceolate, 1.5 to 3 in. long, acuminate, wedge-shaped at base, dark green; petioles about 0.5 in. long.
FLOWERS. Purple-lilac, in large and rather loose panicles, in May; corolla tubes 0.3 in. long, with 4 ovate lobes.

LANDSCAPE USE AND CULTURE

A cross between *S. x laciniata (not S. persica)* and *S. vulgaris*. This lilac is nonsuckering and so is very useful in shrub borders and in informal, tall hedges. They can have an enormous quantity of bloom each year. One of the most useful screening shrubs having graceful form and dense foliage. The cross for this byspecific hybrid was first described in 1777. *S. rothomagensis* is a former name.

CULTIVARS:

'Alba'   Chinese lilac
HARDY IN ZONE 4
7 feet tall, 8 feet wide

'Alba' means white. A more compact shrub.

'Saugeana'   Chinese lilac
HARDY IN ZONE 4
9 feet tall, 7 feet wide

The flower color on this cultivar is a medium red, otherwise quite similar to its parent.

HYACINTH LILAC
Syringa x hyacinthiflora (Lemoine) Rehd.
HARDY IN ZONES 2 TO 4
12 feet tall, 12 feet wide

HABIT. Tall shrub.
LEAVES. Broad-ovate, turning purplish in the autumn.
FLOWERS. Variable (see cultivars).

LANDSCAPE USE AND CULTURE

All crosses are between *S. oblata* and *S. vulgaris*. Numerous cultivars have been developed by Dr. Frank Skinner of Dropmore, Manitoba and Elizabeth Preston at the Dominion Experiment Station in Ottawa.

These cultivars are very hardy and bloom before the French hybrid lilacs (*S. vulgaris*). They bloom earlier than the common lilac and can be slightly taller. Many cultivars are highly resistant to mildew and are rated highly in summer foliage characteristics.

CULTIVARS:

These cultivars are very hardy and bloom before the French hybrid lilacs derived from *S. vulgaris*.

'Asessippi'   lilac
HARDY IN ZONES 2 TO 4
9 feet tall, 9 feet wide

Flowers single, lilac. Developed by Dr. Frank Skinner in 1935. This cultivar was rated highly resistant to mildew and having very good summer foliage in Arboretum trials. The International Lilac Registrar spells it 'Asessippi' (spelled 'Assessippi' in the trade). *See photograph page 163.*

'Blanche Sweet'   lilac
HARDY IN ZONES 2 TO 4
8 feet tall, 8 feet wide

Flowers single, light blue. A Father John Fiala introduction.

'Evangeline'   lilac
HARDY ZONE 3 & 4
8 feet tall, 8 feet wide

This cultivar was rated highly resistant to mildew with very good summer foliage in Arboretum trials. Double magenta bloom.

'Excel'
HARDY IN ZONES 2 TO 4
9 feet tall, 8 feet wide

Another Skinner introduction with single, pink bloom. This cultivar was rated highly resistant to mildew with very good summer foliage in Arboretum trials.

'Gertrude Leslie'   lilac
HARDY IN ZONES 2 TO 4
8 feet tall, 8 feet wide

Flowers double, white. This cultivar was rated good in resistance to mildew with good summer foliage in Arboretum trials.

'Maiden's Blush'   lilac
HARDY IN ZONES 2 TO 4
9 feet tall, 9 feet wide

Flowers single, pink.

'Mount Baker' lilac
HARDY IN ZONES 2 TO 4
9 feet tall, 9 feet wide

A Skinner introduction with single, white bloom. This cultivar was rated excellent in resistance to mildew with excellent summer foliage in Arboretum trials.

'Pocahontas' lilac
HARDY IN ZONES 2 TO 4
9 feet tall, 9 feet wide

A Skinner introduction with purple-blue bloom. This cultivar was rated excellent in resistance to mildew with excellent summer foliage in Arboretum trials. *See photograph page 180-81.*

MEYER LILAC
Syringa meyeri Schneid.
HARDY IN ZONES 3 AND 4
4 feet tall, 5 feet wide

HABIT. Low, dense shrub that suckers freely.
BRANCHLETS. Quadrangular.
LEAVES. Elliptic-ovate to sometimes elliptic-obovate, 0.7 to 1.5 in. long, acute or obtuse, broadly wedge-shaped at base, dark green and smooth above, paler beneath; slightly crinkled; petioles 0.2 to 0.4 in. long.
FLOWERS. Violet, in dense, minutely hairy panicles 0.1 to 0.3 in. long, usually with several pairs of flowers at the ends of branches, in late May and early June; calyx dark violet, smooth; corolla tubes very slender, about 0.5 in. long, scarcely dilated at apex, with spreading, acute lobes 0.1 in. long; anthers inserted below the mouth.
FRUIT. Warty.

LANDSCAPE USE AND CULTURE
A small, compact shrub that can be used in foundation plantings or the shrub border. This lilac requires well-drained soil. Found in gardens in northern China, it was introduced into North America in 1908. It is now found only as a cultivated plant. It sometimes has chance repeat bloom in the fall. Often found under the incorrect name, *S. palibiniana.*

CULTIVAR:

'Palibin' Meyer lilac
HARDY IN ZONES 3 AND 4
4 feet tall, 5 feet wide

Sold often in the trade under the name dwarf Korean lilac, it is a shrub with compact, uniform habit. It is also sometimes sold as a small tree standard of about 5 feet with very compact shape for use as accent in the landscape. Pale lilac blooms open darker purple. Fragrant. It has shown little damage from mildew in Arboretum trials.

EARLY LILAC
Syringa oblata Lindl.
HARDY IN ZONES 2 TO 4
12 feet tall, 12 feet wide

HABIT. Large shrub or small tree.
BRANCHLETS. Stout.
LEAVES. Orbicular-ovate or reniform, often broader than long, 1.5 to 4 in. broad, abruptly acuminate, heart-shaped to sub-cordate at base; petioles 0.3 to 0.7 in. long.
FLOWERS. Pale lilac to purple-lilac, in dense, rather broad panicles 2.2 to 4.7 in. long, in early May; corolla tubes 0.4 to 0.5 in. long, with spreading, obtuse lobes.
FRUIT. Compressed, 0.3 to 0.7 in. long, acuminate, smooth.

LANDSCAPE USE AND CULTURE
The coarse texture of this lilac limits its use in the landscape. Native to northern China, it was introduced into North America in 1856.

CULTIVAR AND VARIETY:

'Cheyenne' early lilac
HARDY IN ZONES 3 AND 4
8 feet tall, 8 feet wide

Flowers, light blue on a compact, dense shrub.

var. *dilatata* (Nak.) Rehd. Korean early lilac
ZONES 3 AND 4
Leaves longer and corolla longer and more slender than in the species. Native to Korea. This variety is a good landscape shrub but is most valuable as a parent in breeding. It has shown good resistance to mildew in Arboretum trials with good clean foliage throughout the summer.

MANCHURIAN LILAC
Syringa patula (Palib.) Nakai.
HARDY IN ZONES 2 TO 4
9 feet tall, 9 feet wide

HABIT. Large shrub.
LEAVES. Elliptic to ovate-oblong, acuminate, broadly wedge-shaped or rounded at base; petioles 0.2 to 0.4 in. long.
FLOWERS. Lilac, in hairy panicles 2.2 to 7.7 in. long, in May; corolla tubes slender, 0.3 to 0.4 in. long, with short, obtuse or acute lobes; anthers violet, not reaching the mouth.
FRUIT. Oblong, 0.3 in. long, warty, acute.

LANDSCAPE USE AND CULTURE
The cultivar, 'Miss Kim', is most often planted. Native to northern China and Korea, the species was introduced in 1902.

CULTIVAR:

'Miss Kim'   lilac
HARDY IN ZONES 3 AND 4
6 feet tall, 6 feet wide

Denser than the species. This is one of the few lilacs turning purplish red in the fall. A dense shrub that is sometimes grown as a small standard tree grafted on *S. reticulata* rootstock. Developed in New Hampshire and very hardy. 'Miss Kim' is often featured in foundation and border plantings. This cultivar has shown good resistance to mildew in Arboretum trials with clean foliage throughout the summer. *See photograph page 180.*

PEKIN LILAC
Syringa pekinensis Rupr.
HARDY IN ZONE 4
18 feet tall, 15 feet wide

HABIT. Large shrub or small tree.
BRANCHES. Slender, spreading, brownish red when young.
LEAVES. Ovate to ovate-lanceolate, 2 to 4 in. long, acuminate, wedge-shaped at base, dark green above, grayish green beneath; petioles 0.5 to 1 in. long.
FLOWERS. Yellowish white, in large smooth panicles 3 to 6 in. long, in late June and early July; corolla 0.2 in. across; stamens as long as limb.
FRUIT. Oblong, acute, 0.5 to 0.7 in. long, brown.

LANDSCAPE USE AND CULTURE
Not as hardy as Japanese tree lilac (*S. reticulata*), this smaller-sized tree can also be used as an ornamental. Native to northern China, it was introduced into North America in 1881. This species has shown good resistance to mildew in Arboretum trials with good clean foliage throughout the growing season.

PERSIAN LILAC
Syringa x persica L.
HARDY IN ZONE 4
6 feet tall, 6 feet wide

HABIT. Medium-sized shrub.
BRANCHES. Upright or arching.
LEAVES. Lanceolate, 1.2 to 2.2 in. long, acuminate, wedge-shaped at base, sometimes 3-lobed or pinnatifid; petioles 0.2 to 0.5 in. long.
FLOWERS. Pale lilac, fragrant, in loose, broad, smooth panicles 2 to 3 in. long, in mid-May; corolla tubes slender, about 0.3 in. long, with ovate, acute lobes.
FRUIT. 4-angled, 0.3 to 0.4 in. long, obtuse, smooth.

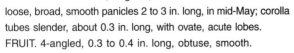

LANDSCAPE USE AND CULTURE
A cross between *S. vulgaris* and *S. x laciniata*. This plant is confused in the trade; plants sold as this hybrid species are often *S. x chinensis*. Introduced about 1614.

PRESTON LILAC
Syringa x prestoniae McKelvey.
HARDY IN ZONES 3 AND 4
9 feet tall, 9 feet wide

HABIT. Large shrub.
LEAVES. Broad-elliptic to oblong, 2 to 7 in. long, acute at ends, green above, grayish green beneath.
FLOWERS. Variable in color in late May or early June; corolla tubes slender, funnel-form.

LANDSCAPE USE AND CULTURE
A cross between *S. villosa* and *S. reflexa*. Much work on these byspecific hybrids were done by Isabella Preston in Ottawa in the early 1900s. They are medium growing shrubs suited for the back of a shrub border.

CULTIVARS:

Several named cultivars are commonly planted. The following cultivars have done well in Arboretum plantings.

'Agnes Smith'   lilac
HARDY IN ZONES 2 TO 4
6 feet tall, 6 feet wide

A single, white selection made by Dr. Rogers of the University of New Hampshire. A late bloomer.

'Coral'   lilac
HARDY IN ZONES 3 AND 4
8 feet tall, 7 feet wide

Flowers single, light pink. This cultivar had excellent resistance to mildew but was rated rather poorly in summer foliage in Arboretum trials.

'Donald Wyman'   lilac
HARDY IN ZONES 2 TO 4
8 feet tall, 7 feet wide

Flowers single, purple.

'Isabella'   lilac
HARDY IN ZONES 2 TO 4
Flowers single, lilac. This cultivar had excellent resistance to mildew with very good summer foliage in Arboretum trials.

'James Macfarlane' lilac
HARDY IN ZONES 3 AND 4
7 feet tall, 6 feet wide

Flowers single, pink. Introduction of the University of New Hampshire. This cultivar had excellent resistance to mildew but was rated poor in summer foliage in Arboretum trials.

JAPANESE TREE LILAC
Syringa reticulata
(Blume) Hara.
HARDY IN ZONES 3 AND 4
20 feet tall, 20 feet wide

HABIT. Small tree.
BRANCHES. Upright or spreading, stout, and stiff.
LEAVES. Broad-ovate to ovate, 2 to 4.7 in. long, abruptly or gradually acuminate, usually rounded or square at base, bright green above, grayish green and netted beneath; petioles 0.3 to 0.7 in. long.
FLOWERS. Creamy white, in large, loose panicles 4 to 6 in. long, in late June and early July; stamens almost twice as long as limb of corolla.
FRUIT. Oblong, 0.5 in. long, obtuse, smooth or slightly warty.

LANDSCAPE USE AND CULTURE
One of the most useful smaller ornamental trees. Especially useful as they blossom creamy white in early summer when few other trees are blossoming. They seem to blossom most heavily in alternate years. They can be grown as a single trunked or clump specimen.

Native to Manchuria and northern China, it was introduced into North America about 1855. Sometimes found incorrectly as *S. amurensis*. The Japanese tree lilac has shown good resistance to mildew and features clean foliage throughout the summer as reported in Arboretum trials. It is tolerant of alkaline soils.

CULTIVARS:

'Ivory Silk' Japanese tree lilac
HARDY IN ZONE 4
25 feet tall, 15 feet wide

Selected for its superior bloom and foliage. A compact grower. Introduced by Sheridan Nursery of Ontario in 1973.

'Summer Snow' Japanese tree lilac
HARDY IN ZONE 4
20 feet tall, 15 feet wide

This cultiavar is described as somewhat smaller than the species. Introduced by Schichtel's Nursery.

LATE LILAC
Syringa villosa Vahl.
HARDY IN ZONES 2 TO 4
12 feet tall, 12 feet wide

HABIT. Large, dense shrub.
BRANCHES. Stout.
LEAVES. Broad-elliptic to oblong, 2 to 7 in. long, acute at the ends, dull dark green above, usually hairy; petioles 0.3 to 0.7 in. long.
FLOWERS. Rosy lilac to white, short-stalked, in rather dense, pyramidal panicles 3 to 7 in. long, in late May and early June; corolla tubes about 0.4 in. long, with spreading, obtuse lobes; anthers inserted near the mouth.
FRUIT. 0.3 to 0.5 in. long, obtuse or acute.

LANDSCAPE USE AND CULTURE
It blooms later than the common lilac, closer to the blooming time of *S. x prestoniae* cultivars. Native to northern China, it was introduced into North America in 1882. Has shown good resistance to mildew in Arboretum trials.

COMMON LILAC, FRENCH LILAC
Syringa vulgaris L.
HARDY IN ZONES 3 AND 4
20 feet tall, 12 feet wide

HABIT. Upright shrub or small tree.
BRANCHES. Stout.
BUDS. Large.
LEAVES. Ovate or broad-ovate, 2 to 4.7 in. long, acuminate, square or subcordate to broad-cuneate at base, smooth, leathery; petioles 0.5 to 1.2 in. long.
FLOWERS. Lilac in the species, very fragrant, in panicles 4 to 8 in. long, in mid-May; corolla tubes slender, about 0.3 in. long, with spreading, ovate lobes.
FRUIT. 0.3 to 0.5 in. long, smooth.

LANDSCAPE USE
Thoreau in *Walden* (1852, 266) wrote this oft-quoted passage:
"Still grows the vivacious lilac a generation after the door and lintel and sill are gone, unfolding its sweet-scented flowers each spring, to be plucked by the musing traveller; planted and tended once by children's hands, in front-yard plots-now standing by wall-sides in retired pastures, and giving place to new-rising forests; the last of the stirp, sole survivor of that family. Little did the dusky children think that the puny slip with its two eyes only, which they stuck in the ground in the shadow of the house and daily watered, would root itself so, and outlive them, and house itself...and tell their story faintly to the lone wanderer a half century after they had grown up and died..."

John Rea, describing seventeenth century England in his *Flora: Seu de Florum Cultura* (1676, 226) states this lilac "is so common, that it needeth no description, especially the ordinary kind with blew flowers…".

CULTURE

This is the most popular grouping of lilacs. There are hundreds of cultivars. The named cultivars do not sucker as much as the species and are preferred in landscape plantings. Native to southeastern Europe, it was introduced into North America by early settlers. The resistance to mildew in Arboretum trials is given for each cultivar below that was evaluated.

CULTIVARS:

The following cultivars should all be hardy in zones 3 and 4 unless noted.

'Adelaide Dunbar' lilac
HARDY IN ZONE 3 & 4
12 feet tall, 9 feet wide

Flowers semi-double, reddish purple. This cultivar had very good resistance to mildew in Arboretum trials with good summer foliage.

'Alba' lilac
HARDY IN ZONES 2 TO 4
14 feet tall, 12 feet wide

Flowers single, white.

'Albert F. Holden' lilac
ZONES 2 TO 4
6 feet tall, 8 feet wide

A compact cultivar with single, dark violet bloom. A Father John Fiala introduction.

'Alphonse Lavelle' lilac
12 feet tall, 10 feet wide

Flowers double, lilac. This cultivar had some resistance to mildew and acceptable summer foliage in Arboretum trials.

'Andenken an Ludwig Spaeth/ Ludwig Spaeth'
10 feet tall, 8 feet wide

More of an upright grower with flowers single, purple. This cultivar had some resistance to mildew in Arboretum trials with acceptable summer foliage.

'Arch McKean'
8 feet tall, 8 feet wide

Flowers single, dark purple. A Father John Fiala introduction.

'Avalanche'
8 feet tall, 8 feet wide

Flowers single, white. A Father John Fiala introduction.

'Belle de Nancy' lilac
12 feet tall, 10 feet wide

Flowers double, pink. Vigorous.

'Charles Joly'
9 feet tall, 8 feet wide

Flowers double, purple. This cultivar had very good resistance to mildew and had clean foliage throughout the growing season in Arboretum trials.

'Charles X' lilac
12 feet tall, 10 feet wide

Flowers single, magenta. This cultivar had very good resistance to mildew in Arboretum trials with good summer foliage.

'Charm' lilac
8 feet tall, 7 feet wide

Flowers single, pink on rounded form.

'Congo' lilac
8 feet tall, 6 feet wide

Flowers single, magenta.

'Edith Cavell' lilac
9 feet tall, 8 feet wide

Flowers double, white. This cultivar had some resistance to mildew in Arboretum trials with acceptable summer foliage.

'Katherine Havemeyer' lilac
10 feet tall, 9 feet wide

Flowers double, pink. This cultivar had very good resistance to mildew in Arboretum trials with good summer foliage.

'Krasavitsa Muskovy/Beauty of Moscow'
9 feet tall, 8 feet wide

A newly introduced cultivar that has double pink flowers. This upright grower is becoming very popular.

'Lucie Baltet'　　　lilac

6 to 8 feet tall, 6 feet wide

Flowers single, pinkish. This cultivar had some resistance to mildew in Arboretum trials although its foliage was rated lower in appearance throughout the summer season.

'Macrostachya'　　　lilac

8 feet tall, 8 feet wide

Flowers single, pinkish. This cultivar had some resistance to mildew and was rated having good foliage during the summer.

'Marechal Lannes'　　　lilac

12 feet tall, 10 feet wide

Flowers double, bluish.

'Marie Frances'　　　lilac

8 feet tall, 7 feet wide.

Single, pink. A Father John Fiala introduction.

'Marie Legraye'　　　lilac

8 to 10 feet tall, 8 feet wide

Flowers single, white. This cultivar had some resistance to mildew in Arboretum trials with its summer foliage rated good.

'Michel Buchner'　　　lilac

8 feet tall, 8 feet wide

Flowers double, purple.

'Miss Ellen Willmott'

9 feet tall, 9 feet wide

Flowers double, white. This cultivar had some resistance to mildew in Arboretum trials, but its foliage was rated low in summer appearance.

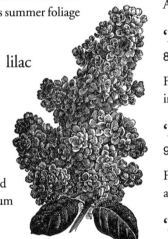

'Mme Lemoine'　　　lilac

9 feet tall, 9 feet wide

Flowers double, white. This cultivar was rated moderate in resistance to mildew and just acceptable summer foliage in Arboretum trials.

'Monge'　　　lilac

9 feet tall, 9 feet wide

Flowers single, purple. This cultivar was susceptible to mildew and its summer foliage was rated just acceptable in Arboretum trials.

'Montaigne'　　　lilac

9 feet tall, 9 feet wide

Flowers double, pink. This cultivar was somewhat resistant to mildew and judged having acceptable summer foliage in Arboretum trials.

'Mrs Edward Harding'　　　lilac

9 feet tall, 9 feet wide

Flowers double, magenta. This cultivar was rated somewhat resistant to mildew with acceptable summer foliage in Arboretum trials.

'Mrs W.E. Marshall'　　　lilac

8 feet tall, 7 feet wide

Flowers single, purple. This cultivar was rated acceptable in mildew resistance and summer foliage in Arboretum trials. It is a slow growing cultivar.

'Night'　　　lilac

8 feet tall, 7 feet wide

Flowers single, purple. This cultivar was rated acceptable in mildew resistance but just acceptable for summer foliage in Arboretum trials.

'Paul Thirion'　　　lilac

8 to 10 feet tall, 8 feet wide

Flowers double, magenta. This cultivar was rated acceptable in mildew resistance and summer foliage in Arboretum trials.

'President Grevy'　　　lilac

9 feet tall, 8 feet wide

Flowers double, blue. Rated acceptable in mildew resistance and having good summer foliage in Arboretum trials.

'President Lincoln'　　　lilac

9 feet tall, 9 feet wide

Flowers single, blue. This cultivar was rated acceptable in mildrew resistance and having good summer foliage in Arboretum trials.

'President Poincare'　　　lilac

12 feet tall, 10 feet wide

Flowers double, magenta. Rated exceptional in mildew resistance and having good summer foliage in Arboretum trials.

'Primrose'   lilac
9 feet tall, 9 feet wide

Flowers single, light yellow. This cultivar was rated acceptable in mildew resistance and summer foliage in Arboretum trials.

'Sarah Sands'   lilac
9 feet tall, 9 feet wide

Flowers single, purple.

'Sensation'   lilac
9 feet tall, 9 feet wide

Flowers single, purple.

'Vestale'
Flowers single, white.

'Victor Lemoine'
8 to 10 feet tall, 7 feet wide

Flowers double, lilac. This cultivar was rated acceptable in mildew resistance and summer foliage in Arboretum trials.

'Wedgwood Blue'   lilac
6 feet tall, 6 feet wide

A more compact grower with flowers single, blue. A Father Fiala introduction.

'Wonderblue'   lilac
5 feet tall, 5 feet wide

Compact. Flowers single, blue.

'Yankee Doodle'   lilac
HARDY IN ZONES 2 TO 4
8 feet tall, 8 feet wide

Flowers single, dark purple. A Father Fiala introduction.

Another lilac to try:

LITTLELEAF LILAC
Syringa microphylla Diels.
FOR PROTECTED LOCATIONS IN ZONE 4
4 feet tall, 6 feet wide

There has been a lot of dieback on plantings at the Arboretum making it an unsuccessful shrub for zone 4. There are other smaller-growing lilacs that will perform the same tasks as this species in the North.

TAMARISK

TAMARISK
Tamarix ramosissima Ledeb.
FAMILY: TAMARICACEAE
HARDY IN ZONES 3 AND 4
15 feet tall, 12 feet wide

HABIT. Deciduous shrub or small tree; there are 54 species native in Europe and Asia.
BRANCHES. Purple; terminal small branchlets fall with the leaves.
LEAVES. Small, scale-like, alternate lance-ovate, acute, glaucous or pale green.
FLOWERS. Small, showy, rosy pink, in dense, slender racemes 1.2 to 3 in. long, forming large terminal panicles, in July and August; sepals and petals 4 or 5; stamens 4 or 5.
FRUIT. Dehiscent capsules with 3 to 5 valves.

LANDSCAPE USE
This rangy shrub is grown for its attractive foliage and summer flowers. It is useful at the back of a shrub border where its height and spread is acceptable. This is the only species of this genus that has been hardy in trials at The Minnesota Landscape Arboretum. Native from southeastern Europe to central Asia, it was introduced into North America in 1883.

CULTURE
Tamarisk should be planted in full sun in a well-drained soil.

CULTIVAR:

'Summer Glow'
HARDY IN ZONES 3 AND 4
9 feet tall, 7 feet wide

Flowers are deeper pink than in the species. It blooms over a long period. Also sold as 'Rubra'.

BALD CYPRESS

BALD CYPRESS
Taxodium distichum (L.) Rich.
FAMILY: CUPRESSACEAE, CYPRESS FAMILY
FOR PROTECTED LOCATIONS IN ZONE 4
65 feet tall, 30 feet wide

HABIT. Deciduous tree with tapering trunks that are buttressed at the base, pyramidal when young, becoming open and spreading with age; there are 3 species native in North America.
BRANCHLETS. Green, becoming brown the first winter.
LEAVES. 2-ranked, linear-lanceolate, pointed, 0.3 to 0.5 in. long, soft bright green above, yellowish green or whitish beneath, turning dull orange in the fall.
FLOWERS. Male in panicles 4 to 4.7 in. long, female flowers produced near the ends of branches formed the previous year.
FRUIT. Globose cones composed of numerous peltate scales, each 4-sided; seeds winged, produced 2 per scale.

LANDSCAPE USE AND CULTURE

When in a younger state, this can be a handsome tree with feathery, light green foliage. It is of borderline hardiness, so it needs a very protected location. Bald cypress does best in a bog-like environment, but also seems to tolerate dry soils. Only trees grown from northern seed strains should be used.

Current evelation at The Minnesota Landscape Arboretum is being done on specimens grown from two fairly large trees growing in North Minneapolis. Native from Delaware to Illinois and south to Florida and Louisiana, it has been in cultivation since 1640.

YEWS

CANADIAN YEW, AMERICAN YEW
Taxus canadensis Marsh.
FAMILY: TAXACEAE
HARDY IN ZONES 2 TO 4
6 feet tall, 9 feet wide

HABIT. Low, spreading shrub; there are 10 species distributed throughout the northern hemisphere.
BRANCHES. Ascending; branchlets green at first, becoming reddish brown.
BUD. Scales pointed.
LEAVES. Abruptly narrowed to a fine point, 0.4 to 0.7 in. long, short-stalked, dark green above, with pale green bands beneath, assuming a purplish tint in winter.

LANDSCAPE USE AND CULTURE

Although this is the hardiest yew, it must be planted where it will receive winter shade or dependable snow cover. Canadian yew can be used as a large, sprawly ground cover but is more often found in shrub borders. It suffers winter burn in exposed locations. Native from Newfoundland to Manitoba and south to Virginia and Iowa, it has been in cultivation since about 1800.

JAPANESE YEW
Taxus cuspidata Sieb. & Zucc.
SOME STRAINS HARDY IN SHADED SITES IN ZONE 4
30 feet tall, 15 feet wide

HABIT. A variable species with upright forms and low, spreading forms.
BRANCHLETS. Green, becoming reddish brown.
LEAVES. Irregularly 2-ranked, 0.5 to 1 in. long, abruptly constricted at base to form a distinct yellowish stalk, dark and dull green above, with 2 tawny yellow bands beneath.

LANDSCAPE USE AND CULTURE

Widely planted south of zone 4, it develops winter burn in our region. Native to Japan, Korea and Manchuria, it was introduced into North America in 1855.

CULTIVARS:

Only a few have shown resistance to winter burn. Those with the greatest resistance include those below.

'Capitata'   Japanese yew
FOR PROTECTED LOCATIONS IN ZONE 4
25 feet tall, 10 feet wide

An upright, pyramidal selection. Likely to develop winter burn when small. As plants grow taller, their needles are less affected by the light reflected from the snow and consequently there is less winter burn.

'Cross Spreading'   Japanese yew
FOR PROTECTED LOCATIONS IN ZONE 4
3 feet tall, 9 feet wide

This selection, grown by Cross Nurseries of Lakeville, Minnesota is highly resistant to winter burn. Unfortunately, it is difficult to find in the trade.

'Nana'   Japanese yew
FOR PROTECTED LOCATIONS IN ZONE 4
6 feet tall, 6 feet wide

A dense, mound-shaped shrub that shows some resistance to winter burn.

Taxus x media Rehd.

SOME STRAINS HARDY IN ZONE 4
9 feet tall, 6 feet wide

HABIT. Typically broad-pyramidal in form.
BRANCHLETS. Olive-green, often reddish above.
LEAVES. Distinctly 2-ranked and horizontally spreading, 0.5 to 1 in. long, dark green above, light green below.

LANDSCAPE USE AND CULTURE

A cross between *T. cuspidata* and *T. baccata*. This spreading shrub can be planted in protected locations in shrub borders or foundation planting. It should be protected from winter sun.

CULTIVARS:

There are many cultivars, but most are susceptible to winter burn.

'Dark Green'   yew

FOR PROTECTED LOCATIONS IN ZONE 4
6 feet tall, 6 feet wide

This cultivar has good foliage color. It needs winter shade.

'Nigra'   yew

FOR PROTECTED LOCATIONS IN ZONE 4
5 feet tall, 5 feet wide

Introduced in 1951 by Cottage Garden Nursery in New York, this cultivar is rather widespreading with dark green needles. Reportedly more resistant to diseases and insect problems.

'Taunton'   yew

FOR PROTECTED LOCATIONS IN ZONE 4
3 feet tall, 4 feet wide

This is the only cultivar that has shown resistance to winter burn. It is a spreading plant that still should be planted in a protected location. *See photograph page 173.*

The
ARBORVITAE
Thuja L.
FAMILY: CUPRESSACEAE, CYPRESS FAMILY

There are few evergreens that tolerate shade, but arborvitae is one to consider. Arborvitae will also withstand zones 2 to 4 winter conditions. They have cultivars with many shapes and sizes to fulfill many specific tasks in the landscape. While many find this plant used in too many locations in the North's landscape, no one can fault its many virtues and uses. It is the most commonly planted evergreen for hedging, small to medium-sized screening, and foundation plantings.

However, even these hardy northern natives will not do well in exposed locations. Hot, dry, windswept locations are not suited for arborvitae. Those planning to use arborvitae should look carefully at the diverse landscape forms.

John Rea in his *Flora: Seu de Florum Cultura* (1676, 228) describes arborvitae thus: "The Tree of Life by long standing groweth as big as a mans leg, with many branches hanging downwards, and set with winged leaves, something like those of Savin [juniper], but flatter, and platted like a Lace, of a fair green colour in Somer, but dark and brown in Winter, of a strong resinous scent...".

AMERICAN ARBORVITAE
Thuja occidentalis L.

HARDY IN ZONES 3 AND 4
65 feet tall, 30 feet wide

HABIT. Upright tree with stout, buttressed trunks; there are 5 species native in North America and Asia.
BRANCHES. Short, spreading; branchlets flattened in one plane.
BARK. Reddish brown, fissured into narrow ridges.
LEAVES. Opposite, scale-like, abruptly pointed, dark green.
FLOWERS. Monoecious; male catkins globose, with 3 pairs of stamens.
FRUIT. Small, light brown cones 0.3 in. long, with 8 to 10 scales; seeds about 0.1 in. long.

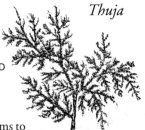

Thuja

LANDSCAPE USE

The species is sometimes used for screens. The cultivars are also used for specimen shrubs, foundation plantings, and formal hedges. Native from Nova Scotia to Manitoba and south to North Carolina and Minnesota, it has been in cultivation since 1536.

CULTURE

Winter burn can be a problem if planted in an exposed location. For foundation plantings, an east or northern exposure (if not entirely shaded) will do well. Winter winds can also be a problem, so planting areas should not be windswept. Propagated from winter cuttings. Deer relish arborvitae, so where deer are found extreme measures must be taken to protect plantings in the winter.

CULTIVARS:

There are many cultivars. The following are most resistant to winter burn or are commonly found in the trade.

'Aurea'   arborvitae
HARDY IN ZONE 4
6 feet tall, 7 feet wide

A broad-pyramidal form with golden foliage. It often suffers from winter burn.

'Brandon'   arborvitae
HARDY IN ZONES 3 AND 4
18 feet tall, 8 feet wide

A naturally spire-like grower that requires little pruning. It has done reasonably well in the western part of our region.

'Gold Cargo'   arborvitae
HARDY IN ZONE 4
12 feet tall, 6 feet wide

A golden foliaged form introduced by Cross Nurseries of Minnesota. It seems to be more resistant to winter burn than 'Aurea'.

'Hetz Midget'
HARDY IN ZONES 3 AND 4
2 feet tall, 3 feet wide

A very dense, globe-shaped selection that is often used in rock gardens or as accent plants in a perennial border. It also makes an excellent low hedge.

'Holmstrup'
HARDY IN ZONE 4, FOR PROTECTED LOCATIONS IN ZONE 3
4 feet tall, 3 to 4 feet wide

A smaller, upright grower that seems to do well in adverse conditions, such as poor drainage and some shade.

'Little Gem'   arborvitae
HARDY IN ZONES 3 AND 4
3 feet tall, 5 feet wide

Smaller, globe forming, although broader than it is tall.

'Little Giant'   arborvitae
HARDY IN ZONE 4, FOR PROTECTED LOCATIONS IN ZONE 3
6 feet tall, 6 feet wide

A globe-shaped selection that one often sees sheared into a perfect ball in the landscape (a gardening cliche that should be avoided). Slower-growing.

'Nigra'   arborvitae
HARDY IN ZONES 3 AND 4
15 feet tall, 15 feet wide

Compact when young, with dark green foliage. Also sold as 'Dark Green'.

'Pygmy Globe'   arborvitae
HARDY IN ZONES 3 AND 4
3 feet tall, 3 feet wide

'Pygmy Globe' is very slow growing and forms a very compact, globe shaped dwarf evergreen.

'Pyramidalis'   arborvitae
HARDY IN ZONES 3 AND 4
20 feet tall, 8 feet wide

A narrow, columnar form; has been susceptible to winter burn in Arboretum trials. Often sheared.

'Sherman'   arborvitae
HARDY IN ZONE 4, FOR PROTECTED LOCATIONS IN ZONE 3
25 feet tall, 12 feet wide

A newer introduction described as having a broad, pyramidal form. Dense foliage.

Thuja

'Techny'
HARDY IN ZONES 3 AND 4
15 feet tall, 15 feet wide

A dense, pyramidal form with dark green foliage. This is one of the best cultivars that can be chosen as shown by the mature specimens in front of the Snyder Building at The Minnesota Landscape Arboretum. Probably the most resistant to winter burn.

'Wareana'   arborvitae
HARDY IN ZONES 3 AND 4
15 feet tall, 10 feet wide

A broad-pyramidal plant that grows slowly to maturity. Very hardy and quite resistant to winter burn. Also sold under the name of Siberian arborvitae.

'Woodwardii'   arborvitae
HARDY IN ZONES 3 AND 4
6 feet tall, 8 feet wide

A large, globe-shaped shrub, broader than tall. It can develop winter burn, but it is often planted in zone 3. Plant where it will receive winter shade.

The LINDENS
Tilia L.
FAMILY: TILIACEAE

Lindens are among the most important trees in the North. Relatively trouble-free, these are among our hardiest shade and specimen trees. They are also used many times in street plantings. They range in size from the very tall (90 feet), to medium-sized (35 feet) trees. They generally have a dense summer texture. Many, such as littleleaf linden, offer fragrant summer bloom.

Leaf gall can sometimes be a problem on specimens grown in stress situations. Some newer cultivars are resistant to this damage. Sunscald on newly planted specimens can be a problem, so winter wrapping of newer plantings is recommended.

CULTIVAR:

(Of interspecific parentage)

'Glenleven'   linden
HARDY IN ZONE 4, FOR PROTECTED LOCATIONS IN ZONE 3
40 feet tall, 35 feet wide

Introduced by Sheridan Nurseries of Ontario in 1963. A fast growing, pyramidal selection with a straight trunk. Has a more open texture than *T. cordata*. Sometimes listed under *T. x flavescens* which is a hybrid species between *T. americana* and *T. cordata*.

'Harvest Gold'   linden
HARDY IN ZONES 3 AND 4
30 feet tall, 25 feet wide

A hybrid between *T. cordata* and *T. mongolica*. It features exfoliating bark and good hardiness. Introduced in Canada and advertised as a good street tree.

BASSWOOD, AMERICAN LINDEN
Tilia americana L.
HARDY IN ZONES 3 AND 4, FOR PROTECTED LOCATIONS IN ZONE 2
90 feet tall (occasionally taller), 50 feet wide

HABIT. Large tree; there are 45 species distributed throughout the northern hemisphere.

BRANCHLETS. Smooth, green.
LEAVES. Broad-ovate, 4 to 8 in. long, abruptly acuminate, heart-shaped to square at base, coarsely serrate with long-pointed teeth, light green beneath with tufts of hair in the axils of lateral veins; petioles 1.2 to 2 in. long.
FLOWERS. About 0.5 in. across, in drooping, 6- to 15-flowered cymes, in June and July; floral bracts usually stalked, tapering toward the base; stamens shorter than petals.
FRUIT. Ellipsoid to subglobose, thick-shelled, without ribs.

LANDSCAPE USE

One of the best large-scaled shade trees for the far North especially in one of the cultivars described below. Its large growing size limits where the species can be planted. The cultivars generally are of smaller scale. Native from Nova Scotia to Manitoba and south to Virginia and Texas, it has been in cultivation since 1752. It grows in the wild in the company of maples.

Thoreau in his *A Week on the Concord and Merrimack Rivers* (1961, 139-40) lists the many uses parts of this tree was considered to have: fisherman's matting, ropes, peasant's shows, nets, coarse cloth, paper, roofs, baskets, wood for carving, sounding boards of pianofortes, medicinal tea, and bees use its pollen for one of the best honeys. Thoreau probably confused some of the usages to that of other lindens.

CULTURE

Basswood grows best in moist soils, but will tolerate drier conditions. The sprouts that develop at the base of the trunk can routinely be pruned out.

CULTIVARS:

'Boulevard'   American basswood
HARDY IN ZONE 4, FOR PROTECTED LOCATIONS IN ZONE 3
60 feet tall, 35 feet wide

A selection chosen because it has a unique columnar shape. An important tree where width but not height is important.

'Fastigiata'   American basswood
HARDY IN ZONE 4, FOR PROTECTED LOCATIONS IN ZONE 3
50 feet tall, 35 feet wide

A selection that is distinctly pyramidal, especially when young. Selected from a tree found in Rochester, New York in the 1920s.

Frontyard®
T.a. 'Bailyard'
HARDY IN ZONES 3 AND 4
70 feet tall, 40 feet wide

A cultivar with a broadly pyramidal canopy. Yellow fall color. Introduced by Bailey Nurseries of Minnesota.

Legend®
T.a. 'DTR123'
FOR PROTECTED LOCATIONS IN ZONE 4
40 feet tall, 30 feet wide

Another pyramidal form of smaller size. Has not been tested in our area.

'Redmond'   American basswood
HARDY IN ZONE 4, PROTECTED LOCATIONS IN ZONE 3
50 feet tall, 35 feet wide

Introduced by Plumfield Nurseries of Fremont, Nebraska in 1927. Densely pyramidal when young. Unique red younger branches and buds are very noticeable in early spring. An outstanding cultivar, tolerant of a wide range of soil and climatic conditions. Some list this cultivar under *T. x euchlora.*

'Sentry'   American basswood
HARDY IN ZONES 3 AND 4
60 feet tall, 35 feet wide

A cultivar with upright branching habit.

LITTLELEAF LINDEN
Tilia cordata Mill.
HARDY IN ZONE 4, FOR PROTECTED LOCATIONS IN ZONE 3
65 feet tall, 50 feet wide

HABIT. Roundheaded tree.
LEAVES. Suborbicular, 1.2 to 2.2 in. long, abruptly acuminate, heart-shaped at base, sharply and rather finely serrate; upper leaf surface dark green; undersurface glaucous and smooth except for axillary tufts of hair; petioles slender, 0.5 to 1 in. long.
FLOWERS. Yellowish white, fragrant, 5 to 7 in pendent or nearly upright cymes, in July; stamens about as long as petals; floral bracts 1.3 to 3 in. long.
FRUIT. Globose, slightly ribbed, thin-shelled.

LANDSCAPE USE

Somewhat smaller growing than *T. americana*, this tree and its many cultivars are often used as a shade or street tree. Because of its smaller scale, it is better suited for modern landscapes. Native to Europe, it was introduced into North America by early settlers. It has very fragrant early summer bloom. Linden tea is made from the blossoms.

CULTURE

Littleleaf linden do well under city conditions. Grown from seed, the populations of this linden can be variable. It is tolerant of a wide range of soil conditions, is easily transplanted and has fairly rapid growth.

CULTIVARS:

Greenspire®

HARDY IN ZONE 4
60 feet tall, 35 feet wide

A pyramidal form with a central leader. This is one of the most common cultivars in the midwest. It was introduced in New Jersey in 1961.

Norlin™   linden

T.c. 'Ronald'
ZONES 3 AND 4
45 feet tall, 30 feet wide

An introduction of Jeffries Nursery in Manitoba. It has darker branching than the species. Described as having resistance to damage from leaf gall.

'Olympic'   linden

HARDY IN ZONE 4
40 feet tall, 30 feet wide

A symmetrical, pyramidal selection with vigorous growth. Introduced by J. Frank Schmidt Nursery in 1970.

Shamrock®   linden

T.c. 'Baileyi'
HARDY IN ZONE 4
50 feet tall, 30 feet wide

A 1988 introduction of Bailey Nurseries of Minnesota, which is similar to 'Greenspire' but having a more open canopy.

MONGOLIAN LINDEN
Tilia mongolica Maxim.

HARDY IN ZONES 2 TO 4
30 feet tall, 20 feet wide

HABIT. Small tree.
BRANCHLETS. Smooth, reddish.
LEAVES. Reddish when unfolding, suborbicular to ovate, 1.5 to 2.7 in. long, coarsely serrate and often 3-lobed, dark green and lustrous above, glaucescent and smooth beneath; petioles reddish, 0.7 to 1.2 in. long.
FLOWERS. 10 to 20 in cymes, in July; floral bracts stalked.
FRUIT. Subglobose, thick-walled.

LANDSCAPE USE AND CULTURE

A graceful, small tree, hardy in zones 2 to 4. Native to Mongolia and China it was introduced into North America in 1820. Relatively rare, it is well worth seeking out in the nursery trade.

CANADIAN HEMLOCK

CANADIAN HEMLOCK; EASTERN HEMLOCK
Tsuga canadensis (L.) Carriere.

FAMILY: PINACEAE, PINE FAMILY
HARDY IN ZONES 3 AND 4
65 to 90 feet tall (many times shorter in the North), 50 feet wide

HABIT. Evergreen tree; there are 10 species native in North America and Asia.
BRANCHES. Are long, slender, often drooping, forming a broad pyramidal head at maturity; branchlets yellow-brown, hairy.
BARK. Cinnamon red, furrowed.
BUDS. Acute, slightly hairy.
LEAVES. Linear, 2-ranked, 0.3 to 0.7 in. long, rounded, shiny dark green and slightly grooved above, with narrow white bands beneath.
FLOWERS. Solitary, monoecious, male flowers globose, axillary; female flowers terminal on lateral branches.
FRUIT. Cones, short-stalked, ovoid, 0.5 to 0.7 in. long, with roundish, obovate scales.

LANDSCAPE USE

The species is commonly planted for screens and clipped hedges in eastern North America. Native from Nova Scotia to Minnesota and south to northern Georgia and Alabama, it has been in cultivation since 1736. Specimens at the Arboretum are grown from seed collected from a small native population near Mille Lacs Lake and have grown well on slopes with a northeastern exposure.

CULTURE

Most commercially available cultivars are susceptible to winter burn in our area. Hemlock needs a protected site, in a woodland and protected from drying winter winds. It is cold hardy to zone 3 but in the midwestern parts of North America it suffers from winter injury. On the East Coast the woolly adelgid, an insect pest, has caused widespread death in native populations of hemlock. It should not be planted in those areas.

CULTIVAR:

'Pendula'   Canadian hemlock

FOR PROTECTED LOCATIONS IN ZONE 4
A low, weeping form that is very slow growing. It takes many years before it reaches 4 to 5 feet. Grows broader than tall. Must be planted in sheltered locations or where snow cover is assured.

ELMS

AMERICAN ELM
Ulmus americana L.
HARDY IN ZONES 2 TO 4
FAMILY: ULMACEAE
80 feet tall, 65 feet wide

HABIT. Large tree; there are 45 species native in North America and Asia.
BRANCHES. Arching; branchlets hairy when young.
BARK. Gray, scaly, and deeply fissured.
BUDS. Ovoid, obtuse or acute.
LEAVES. Ovate-oblong, 2.7 to 6 in. long, acuminate, unequal at base, doubly serrate, smooth or rough above, hairy or nearly smooth beneath; petioles 0.2 to 0.3 in. long.
FLOWERS. On pedicels 0.3 to 0.7 in. long; stamens 7 to 8, exserted; stigmas white.
FRUIT. Elliptic, about 0.3 in. long, deeply notched at apex with the incision reaching the nutlet, ciliate.

LANDSCAPE USE AND CULTURE
Before the outbreak of the Dutch elm disease, this was the most widely planted shade and street tree in the northern U.S. and in Canada. Thoreau in his *Journal* , vol 3 (1850, 102) comments on this:: "There was reason enough for the first settlers selecting the elm out of all the trees of the forest with which to ornament his villages...It is almost become a villageous tree..." Now it is not planted or recommended.

Many replacements for American elm have been proposed and much research has been done trying to find resistant strains. Dr. George Ware of the Morton Arboretum and researchers at the University of Wisconsin, Madison are actively working on new elm cultivars. Some of these have been planted in test plots at the Minnesota Landscape Arboretum, but have not matured enough to be fully evaluated. Among these are cultivars Accolade™ 'Cathedral', and 'Discovery'.

Other elms to try:

DAVID ELM
Ulmus davidiana Schneid.
FOR PROTECTED LOCATIONS IN ZONE 4
35 feet tall, 25 feet wide

This elm has an upright, vase-shaped form which is useful in the landscape. It does not grow as large as its native height of 50 feet in the North. The David elm is native to northern China. It is difficult to obtain in the nursery trade.

WYCH ELM
Ulmus glabra Huds.
FOR PROTECTED LOCATIONS IN ZONE 4
80 feet tall, 35 feet wide

The pendulus cultivar 'Camperdownii' is a novelty that is sometimes planted. Its height is much smaller and depends on where the graft is placed.

JAPANESE ELM
Ulmus japonica (Rehd.) Sarg.
HARDY IN ZONES 2 TO 4
65 feet tall, 50 feet wide

This species is reported to be highly resistant to the Dutch elm disease. It is being used in many breeding programs. Native to Japan and northeastern Asia, it was introduced in 1895. Also listed as *U. davidiana japonica*.

SIBERIAN ELM
Ulmus pumila L.
NORTHERN STRAINS HARDY IN ZONES 2 TO 4
65 feet tall, 50 feet wide

This rather weed-like tree is widely planted in the Dakotas in shelterbelts. It is a fast-growing tree but is relatively short-lived and often damaged in winds and ice storms. It is very invasive in parts of our area.

SLIPPERY ELM, RED ELM
Ulmus rubra Muhlenb.
HARDY IN ZONES 2 TO 4
65 feet tall, 50 feet wide

Native from Quebec to North Dakota and south to Florida and Texas, it is sometimes planted.

ROCK ELM
Ulmus thomasii Sarg.
HARDY IN ZONES 2 TO 4
65 feet tall, 40 feet wide

Another native seldom planted although it has interesting corky bark on its branches.

The BLUEBERRIES and RELATED PLANTS

Vaccinium L.
FAMILY: ERICACEAE, HEATH FAMILY

Modern hybrid blueberries can be used ornamentally in the landscape. Cultivars which were bred between highbush and lowbush blueberries can be very successful. The Horticultural Research Center of the Arboretum has introduced 'Northblue', 'Northsky', 'Northcountry', 'St Cloud', 'Chippewa', and 'Polaris' which do well in zone 4. They need full sun.

They do need special soil requirements, however. The soil has to be well drained, such as a sandy loam. The pH has to be in the 4.5 to 5.5 range. Soils can be acidified by adding spaghnum peat. Fertilizing with iron sulfate (not aluminum sulfate), ammonium sulfate or other acid fertilizer is recommended. Cross-pollination is beneficial so two or more varieties should be planted. There are also low-growing natives in this genus that can be very ornamental in the landscape. *See photograph pages 182-83.*

COWBERRY
Vaccinium vitis-idaea L.
HARDY WITH SNOW COVER IN ZONES 2 TO 4
12 inches tall, 3 feet wide

HABIT. Low, evergreen shrub with creeping rootstocks; there are 450 species distributed worldwide.
STEMS. Upright.
LEAVES. Oval to obovate, 0.3 to 1 in. long, obtuse or emarginate, dark green and shiny above, pale and black-dotted beneath; leathery.
FLOWERS. In short subterminal racemes, nodding, in May and June; corollas bell-shaped, 4-lobed, 0.2 in. long, white or pink.
FRUIT. Dark red, acid and bitter, 0.3 in. across, from August to October.

LANDSCAPE USE AND CULTURE
This species and its cultivars are sometimes planted in rock gardens or more widely as ground covers in acid soils. This plant does not do well in hot, dry situations. Native in Europe, northern Asia, Canada, Alaska, and south to Massachusetts and Minnesota, it has been in cultivation since 1789.

VARIETY:

MOUNTAIN CRANBERRY, LINGENBERRY, LINGONBERRY
var. *minus* Lodd.
HARDY WITH SNOW COVER IN ZONES 2 TO 4
4 inches tall, mat-forming

A ground hugging novelty. The berries are a delicacy to Scandinavians. In rock gardens it is attractive in bloom and fruit. It needs acidic soil and partial shade in summer.

Other Vaccinium to try:

LOWBUSH BLUEBERRY
Vaccinium angustifolium Ait.
HARDY IN ZONES 2 TO 4
20 inches tall, 20 inches wide

Our native blueberry can be planted for an ornamental ground cover. It does not bear heavily, so it is not grown for its fruit.

HIGHBUSH BLUEBERRY
Vaccinium corymbosum L.
FOR PROTECTED LOCATIONS IN ZONE 4
9 feet tall, 6 feet wide

Because it is of borderline hardiness in zone 4, the cultivars listed above are planted.

LARGE CRANBERRY
Vaccinium macrocarpon Ait.
HARDY WITH SNOW COVER IN ZONES 2 TO 4
3 feet long

Needs acid, bog-like conditions to do well. They are commercially grown in specially constructed large fields that can be flooded to protect the plants from frost injury.

The VIBURNUM

Viburnum L.

FAMILY: CAPRIFOLIACEAE, HONEYSUCKLE FAMILY

Viburnum include some of the most ornamental and useful shrubs for the North. They have a wide range of height, textures, and flowering and fruiting characteristics. They can be feature shrubs in our landscape or add to a shrub border. Some of the large growing viburnum are sometimes pruned and trained to form a small specimen tree. Some of the more dwarf varieties make very good specimens for hedges.

Charles Sprague Sargent in vol 5 of his *The Silva of North America* (1893, 94) wrote of *Viburnum.*

"The leaves and fruit of some of the species are astringent, and those of the European *Viburnum lantana* are used in dyeing and for making ink. The bark of the North American arborescent *Viburnum prunifolium* is used in medicine; and the bark and leaves of several of the American species are said to have been employed by the Indians and in early dometic practice in the treatment of various diseases. The wood of *Viburnum opulus* produces charcoal valued in the manufacture of gunpowder; and in America the bark is sometimes employed as a tonic and antispasmodic, and the fruit is occasionally eaten. Many of the species produce beautiful flowers and fruit, and are prized in gardens..."

CULTIVAR:

(Of interspecific parentage)

'Emerald Triumph'   viburnum
HARDY IN ZONE 4
6 feet tall, 6 feet wide

A Minnesota Landscape Arboretum 1994 introduction featuring very glossy foliage and a compact, rounded habit.

This cultivar features creamy white, flat flower clusters in May followed by orange-red fruit that slowly turns black. It can be a feature of the shrub border. It originated from a cross between *V. lantana* and *V. rhytidophyllum.*

MAPLELEAF VIBURNUM
Viburnum acerifolium L.
HARDY IN ZONES 3 AND 4
6 feet tall, 6 feet wide

HABIT. Upright shrub; 150 species are distributed worldwide.
BRANCHLETS. Hairy.
LEAVES. Suborbicular to ovate, 3-lobed, 2.2 to 4 in. long, rounded or heart-shaped at base, lobes acute to acuminate, coarsely dentate; fall color bright crimson; petioles 0.3 to 1 in. long.
FLOWERS. Yellowish white, in long, stalked cymes 1 to 3 in. wide, in June.
FRUIT. Ellipsoid, 0.2 to 0.3 in. long, black, in September.

LANDSCAPE USE AND CULTURE

This low to medium shrub is useful for naturalizing. Native from New Brunswick to Minnesota and south to North Carolina, it has been in cultivation since 1736. Mapleleaf viburnum is very shade tolerant.

WITHEROD
Viburnum cassinoides L.
HARDY IN ZONES 2 TO 4
6 feet tall, 6 feet wide

HABIT. Upright shrub.
LEAVES. Elliptic or ovate to oblong, 1.2 to 4 in. long, acute or bluntly acuminate, obscurely dentate, dull green above, nearly smooth.
FLOWERS. All perfect, in flat-toped cymes 2.2 to 4.7 in. across, in June.
FRUIT. Ovoid to subglobose, 0.3 to 0.4 in. across, blue-black, in September.

LANDSCAPE USE AND CULTURE

This medium-sized viburnum should be planted more often. The showy fruit attracts birds to the landscape. Native from Newfoundland to Manitoba and south to North Carolina and Minnesota, it has been in cultivation since 1761.

ARROWWOOD
Viburnum dentatum L.
HARDY IN ZONES 3 AND 4
9 feet tall, 9 feet wide

HABIT. Dense shrub.
BRANCHLETS. Smooth, becoming gray.
LEAVES. Suborbicular to ovate, 1.2 to 3 in. long, acute, short-acuminate, rounded or subcordate at base, coarsely dentate, smooth or nearly so above, stellate-hairy beneath; fall color russet red; petioles 0.3 to 0.7 in. long, hairy.
FLOWERS. White, in slender-stalked cymes that are 2.2 to 4.7 in. across, slightly hairy; in late May or early June.
FRUIT. Globose-ovoid, 0.2 in. long, blue-black, in October.

LANDSCAPE USE

Arrowwood is commonly used as an informal hedge and in the back of shrub borders. Flat cymed, white flowers are followed by blue-black berries. The contrast between fruit and leaf texture in late summer is outstanding. It is noted for its good fall color. As with many viburnum, birds enjoy the berries. Native from New Brunswick to Minnesota and south to Georgia, it has been in cultivation since 1736.

Humphry Marshall, in his *Arbustrum Americanum* (1785), states "The young shoots of this tree are generally used by the natives for arrows; whence it is know by the name of Arrowwood." It can be a feature shrub in any landscape.

CULTURE

Although it inhabits wet, lowland areas in its native populations, arrowwood is also drought tolerant. It also withstands salt injury. This viburnum is resistant to leaf spot diseases and stem cankers that can be a problem with others of this genus.

CULTIVAR:

Northern Burgundy®   viburnum
V.d. 'Morton'
HARDY IN ZONE 4
9 feet tall, 9 feet wide

This cultivar has very attractive, glossy green foliage with white flowers in June followed by blue-black fruit. The foliage has good dark red fall color. A Chicagoland Grows introduction.

WAYFARINGBUSH
Viburnum lantana L.
HARDY IN ZONES 3 AND 4
12 feet tall, 12 feet wide

HABIT. Upright shrub.
BRANCHLETS. Scurfy-hairy.
LEAVES. Ovate to oblong-ovate, 2 to 4.7 in. long; acute or obtuse, rounded or heart-shaped at base, closely denticulate, sparingly stellate-hairy above, stellate-hairy beneath; fall color red; petioles 0.3 to 1 in. long.
FLOWERS. Cream-colored, showy, in flat-topped cymes 2.2 to 4 in. across, in early June.
FRUIT. Ovoid-oblong, 0.3 in. long, changing from green to red to black in August.

LANDSCAPE USE

With its showy flowers, attractive fruit, and vivid dark red fall color, this species is an attractive medium- to tall-growing shrub for the shrub border. It can also be used as an informal hedge or for screening. This viburnum is noted for its textured foliage. Birds are fond of the fruit which starts yellow, changes to red and appears blue-black towards fall. Native to Europe and western Asia, it was introduced into North America by early settlers.

CULTURE

Tolerant of western soils, easy to transplant and maintain, it is one of the choice shrubs for the Midwest. It will withstand some shade.

CULTIVAR:

'Mohican'
HARDY IN ZONES 3 AND 4
6 feet tall, 7 feet wide

A more compact form with showy red fruit in August. The fruit turns dark in the fall.

HOBBLEBUSH
Viburnum lantanoides Michx.
HARDY IN ZONES 2 TO 4
9 feet tall, 9 feet wide

HABIT. Open shrub that is sometimes decumbent and rooting.
BRANCHES. Forked; branchlets scurfy-hairy.
LEAVES. Broad-ovate or suborbicular, 4 to 8 in. long, short-acuminate, heart-shaped at base, irregularly denticulate; upper leaf surface stellate-hairy at first, becoming smooth; under surface more densely hairy; fall color deep claret red; petioles 1 to 2.2 in. long, scurfy.
FLOWERS. White, in sessile, stellate-hairy cymes 3 to 4.7

in. across; sterile flowers 0.7 to 1 in. wide, in June; stamens as long as corolla lobes.
FRUIT. Broad-ellipsoid, 0.3 in. long, first red, then purple-black, in September.

LANDSCAPE USE

This medium-sized shrub is useful for naturalizing. It was known as *V. alnifolium.* Native from New Brunswick to Michigan and south to North Carolina, it has been in cultivation since 1820. Difficult to find in the nursery trade.

CULTURE

Hobblebush grows best in moist soil in semi-shade.

NANNYBERRY
Viburnum lentago L.
HARDY IN ZONES 3 AND 4
25 feet tall, 12 feet wide

HABIT. Large shrub or small tree.
BRANCHES. Slender; branchlets scurfy.
BUDS. Elongated, valvate, 1 in. long.
LEAVES. Ovate to elliptic-obovate, 2 to 4 in. long, acuminate, broadly wedge-shaped to rounded at base, finely toothed, glabrous or scurfy on veins beneath; fall color red; petioles 0.3 to 1 in. long, mostly winged with a wavy margin.
FLOWERS. Creamy white, in cymes 2.2 to 4.7 in. across, in June.
FRUIT. Ellipsoid, 0.3 in. long, blue-black, in September and October.

LANDSCAPE USE

This large, native shrub is excellent for the back of a shrub border. With proper pruning, nannyberry also can make an attractive small ornamental tree. The blue-black fruit have a sweet, date-like flavor after a frost. Native from Hudson Bay to Manitoba and south to Georgia and Mississippi, it has been in cultivation since 1761.

CULTURE

Nannyberry will tolerate moist or dry soil conditions and also grows in sun or part shade.

EUROPEAN HIGHBUSH CRANBERRY
Viburnum opulus L.
HARDY IN ZONES 2 TO 4
12 feet tall, 12 feet wide

HABIT. Large shrub.
BRANCHES. Smooth, light gray.
LEAVES. Broad-ovate, 2 to 4.7 in. long, 3-lobed, the lobes acuminate and coarsely dentate, square at base; petioles 0.3 to 1 in. long, with a narrow groove and a few disk-like glands.

FLOWERS. White, in flat-topped cymes, in June; marginal flowers sterile and showy.
FRUIT. Subglobose, 0.3 in. across, red, from August through most of the winter.

LANDSCAPE USE

The European highbush cranberry is a very popular shrub for shrub borders and for use as screening. Its single, white flowers in June are followed by showy red fruit from August through the winter. Native to Europe, northern Africa, and northern Asia, it was introduced into North America by early settlers.

CULTURE

Somewhat tolerant of differing moisture levels and lightly shaded conditions. Aphids frequently cause the leaves to curl early in the season.

CULTIVARS:

'Compactum'   Eur. highbush cranberry
HARDY IN ZONES 3 AND 4
6 feet tall, 6 feet wide

A compact, mound-shaped shrub with flowers and fruit that are similar to those of the species. It is wider than its look-alike, *V. trilobum* 'Compactum'.

'Nanum'   Eur. highbush cranberry
HARDY IN ZONE 4
3 feet tall, 4 feet wide

A very dwarf form that seldom has flowers or fruit. An excellent shrub that needs little pruning for a low hedge or in foundation plantings. It also makes a good bank ground cover.

'Roseum'   Common snowball viburnum
HARDY IN ZONES 3 AND 4
12 feet tall, 12 feet wide

All flowers are sterile and form a round ball. It is also sold as the cultivar 'Sterile'. This is the old-fashioned snowball bush. Aphids can be a problem.

'Xanthocarpum'
HARDY IN ZONE 4
6 feet tall, 6 feet wide

Grown for its golden fruit in the fall which can stay on the shrub into winter. It has white flowers in the beginning of June.

BLACKHAW
Viburnum prunifolium L.
HARDY IN ZONE 4
12 feet tall, 12 feet wide

HABIT. Large shrub or small tree.
BRANCHES. Rigid, spreading.
BUDS. Pointed, valvate, 0.3 in. long, reddish hairy.
LEAVES. Broad-elliptic to ovate, 1.2 to 3 in. long, acute or obtuse, rounded at base or broadly wedge-shaped, serrulate, smooth or nearly so; fall color red; petioles not or narrowly winged, 0.3 to 0.6 in. long.
FLOWERS. Pure white, showy, in sessile cymes 2 to 4 in. across, in May.
FRUIT. Short-ellipsoid to subglobose, 0.3 to 0.5 in. long, blue-black, bloomy, in September and October.

LANDSCAPE USE
This large-growing shrub is useful for shrub borders or for screening. Although somewhat coarse textured it can be sheared for formal hedges. Its growth habit is informal when young but can mature into a interestingly shaped small tree as it matures. It has good fall color. Native from Connecticut to Michigan and south to Florida and Texas, it has been in cultivation since 1727.

CULTURE
It should be grown from a northern seed source. Blackhaw will withstand poor soils and drought but unlike other viburnum, it will not tolerate shade.

DOWNY ARROWWOOD
Viburnum rafinesquianum Schult.
HARDY IN ZONES 2 TO 4
6 feet tall, 6 feet wide

HABIT. Dense, mound-shaped shrub.
BRANCHLETS. Smooth, grayish brown.
LEAVES. Ovate to nearly elliptic, 1 to 2 in. long, acute or acuminate, rounded or subcordate at base, coarsely dentate, smooth or slightly hairy above, densely soft-hairy beneath; petioles less than 0.2 in. long.
FLOWERS. White, in dense cymes 1 to 2.2 in. across, in June.
FRUIT. Ellipsoid, 0.3 in. long, bluish black, in September.

LANDSCAPE USE AND CULTURE
This is an excellent shrub for a larger, informal hedge or for a shrub border. Native from Quebec to Manitoba and south to Georgia and Minnesota, it has been in cultivation since 1830.

SARGENT HIGHBUSH CRANBERRY
Viburnum sargentii Koehne.
HARDY IN ZONES 2 TO 4
12 feet tall, 12 feet wide

HABIT. Large shrub.
BARK. Dark gray, fissured, and somewhat corky.
LEAVES. Broad-ovate, 3-lobed, 2 to 4.7 in. long, lobes acuminate, rounded or square at base, coarsely dentate, thick; petioles 0.7 to 1.3 in. long, with large disk-like glands.
FLOWERS. White, showy, in flat-topped cymes 4 to 6 in. across, in June; marginal flowers sterile and larger than those of *V. opulus*, up to 1 in. across; stamens with purple anthers.
FRUIT. Subglobose, 0.3 to 0.4 in. across, scarlet, from August to early winter.

LANDSCAPE USE
This viburnum of the highbush cranberry-type makes an excellent shrub for the shrub border or for screening purposes. Native to northeastern Asia, it was introduced into North America in 1904.

CULTURE
Sargent highbush cranberry seems more resistant to aphids than the more common *V. opulus*.

CULTIVAR:

'Onondaga'   viburnum
HARDY IN ZONE 4
8 feet tall, 8 feet wide

The leaves open dark red but change to dark green by midsummer. The flowers also have a slight shading of red.

AMERICAN HIGHBUSH CRANBERRY
Viburnum trilobum Marsh.
HARDY IN ZONES 2 TO 4
12 feet tall, 12 feet wide

HABIT. Large shrub.
BRANCHES. Gray, smooth.
LEAVES. Broad-ovate, 2 to 4.7 in. long, rounded or square at base, 3-lobed with acuminate lobes, coarsely dentate; petioles 0.3 to 1 in. long, with a shallow groove and small, usually stalked glands.
FLOWERS. White, in flat-topped cymes 2.7 to 4 in. wide; stamens about 2 times as long as petals, in June; marginal flowers sterile.
FRUIT. Ellipsoid, 0.3 to 0.4 in. long, scarlet, from August to late winter.

LANDSCAPE USE

A widely planted species that is a feature of the landscape over a long period of time. Its flowers in June are attractive and the fruit which starts in August and persists into the winter is outstanding. In the fall with its fruit and fall color it can be a highlight of the landscape.

Highbush cranberry can be used as a specimen plant, towards the back of the shrub border, or as screening. The dwarf cultivars of this species are often used as hedging. The fruit are edible and can be used for jelly. It is native from New Brunswick to British Columbia and south to New York and Oregon. *See photographs pages 148, 158, 164.*

CULTURE

Tolerates a wide range of soils and conditions. It will not fruit as well if grown in part shade.

CULTIVAR:

'Alfredo'   highbush cranberry

HARDY IN ZONES 2 TO 4
6 feet tall, 6 feet wide

A compact form introduced by Bailey Nursery of Minnesota. It is described as being denser and slightly broader than other compact forms.

'Compactum'   highbush cranberry

HARDY IN ZONES 2 TO 4
6 feet tall, 6 feet wide

A compact form growing to about 6 feet tall. Two different selections are sold under this cultivar name; the selection 'Bailey Compact' grown by Bailey Nursery of Minnesota produced better fall color than the selection from the eastern United States.

'Wentworth'

HARDY IN ZONES 2 TO 4
12 feet tall, 12 feet wide

Growing to the same size as the species, this cultivar was selected because of its heavy fruiting characteristics.

Other Viburnum to try:

BURKWOOD VIBURNUM

Viburnum x burkwoodii Burkwood & Skipw.
FOR PROTECTED LOCATIONS IN ZONE 4
9 feet tall, 6 feet wide

Often attempted but really not hardy in zone 4.

KOREANSPICE VIBURNUM

Viburnum carlesii Hemsl.
TRIAL INPROTECTED LOCATIONS
IN ZONE 4
4 feet tall, 4 feet wide

Another choice viburnum that is not hardy in most of zone 4. It is desired because it perfumes the landscape in very early spring.

VINCA

VINCA, PERIWINKLE, MYRTLE

Vinca minor L.
FAMILY: APOCYNACEAE,
DOGBANE FAMILY
HARDY WITH SNOW COVER IN ZONE 4
8 inches tall, 3 feet wide

HABIT. Evergreen, trailing vine; there are 6 species distributed worldwide.
LEAVES. Simple, opposite, elliptic-ovate to elliptic-lanceolate, 0.7 to 1.5 in. long, acutish or obtuse, shiny dark green above; petioles 0.7 to 1.5 in. long.
FLOWERS. Lilac-blue, about 1 in. across, on erect stems, from May to frost; calyx small, 5-parted, with narrow-acuminate teeth; corolla salverform, the lobes twisted to the left; stamens adnate to the middle of the tube, anthers free; carpels with 6 to 8 ovules; stigmas large, with 5 tufts of hair.
FRUIT. Cylindric follicles, 3 in. long.

LANDSCAPE USE

This ground cover will grow in zone 4 where there is reliable snow cover. Otherwise, it will often die out over winter. Native to Europe and western Asia, it was introduced into North America by early settlers. It is an invasive plant in zone 5 southward. Because it is of borderline hardiness, planting the species rather than cultivars is advised.

CULTURE

If it will not receive snow cover, mulching with straw overwinter will help protect it. Propagated by cuttings.

The GRAPES
Vitis L.
FAMILY: VITACEAE

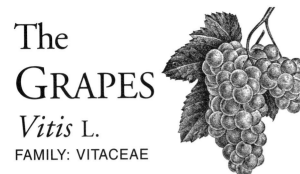

Breeding of more winter hardy grapes have enabled many to grow these desired vines in the landscape. If grown under controlled conditions (using cultural intensive methods such as espalier) they can be very ornamental.

The planting, cultivation and care of grapes is rather complex, so those interested should consult works giving detailed cultural instructions. Many European and wine grapes are not hardy but could be considered if one is willing to bury them overwinter. However, newer cultivars such as 'Edelweiss', 'Swenson Red', 'Frontenac' and many others can be successful without major winter protection. The native grapes can be used for more informal, naturalistic purposes.

RIVERBANK GRAPE
Vitis riparia Michx.
HARDY IN ZONES 2 TO 4
30 feet long

HABIT. Vigorous, high-climbing vine; there are 65 species distributed throughout the northern hemisphere.
LEAVES. Broad-ovate to ovate, 3 to 7 in. long, with a broad open basal sinus, usually 3-lobed, with short acuminate lobes, unequally and coarsely toothed with triangular acuminate teeth, shiny, bright green beneath.
FLOWERS. In panicles 3 to 7 in. long, fragrant, in June; male flowers with long, erect stamens; female flowers with shorter, recurved stamens.
FRUIT. Globose, 0.3 in. across, purple-black, densely bloomy.

LANDSCAPE USE AND CULTURE
This native is often used for screening. A substantial support structure is needed. The fruit is small but can be harvested for jellies. Native from Nova Scotia to Manitoba and south to Texas, it has been in cultivation since 1656.

THE WEIGELA
FAMILY: CAPRIFOLIACEAE,
HONEYSUCKLE FAMILY

WEIGELA CULTIVARS:
Some of the newer developed garden hybrids have been hardy in zone 4. Some of the cultivars listed below might be progeny just of the species, *W. florida*.

'Centennial'   weigela
HARDY IN ZONE 4; TRIAL IN ZONE 3
7 feet tall, 6 feet wide

One of the hardiest of the weigela. Red flowers.

'Java Red'   weigela
HARDY IN ZONE 4
4 feet tall, 5 feet wide

A compact selection with reddish foliage. The flower buds are red opening to a reddish pink blossom.

'Minuet'   weigela
HARDY IN ZONE 4; TRIAL IN ZONE 3
2 feet tall, 3 feet wide

A compact variety introduced from Ottawa. Red blooms. Perhaps the hardiest of the lower growing weigela.

'Pink Delight'   weigela
HARDY IN ZONE 4
5 feet tall, 5 feet wide

Introduced by Mission Gardens in Illinois. Pink bloom.

'Pink Princess'   weigela
HARDY IN ZONE 4
5 feet tall, 5 feet wide

A hardy selection from Iowa State University, with pink flowers.

'Polka'   weigela
HARDY IN ZONE 4; TRIAL IN ZONE 3
4 feet tall, 5 feet wide

Another selection introduced from Ottawa with pink flowers.

'Red Prince'
PROTECTED LOCATION IN ZONE 4
6 feet tall, 6 feet wide

Another introduction from Iowa State University with clear red bloom.

'Rumba'   weigela

HARDY IN ZONE 4; TRIAL IN ZONE 3
3 feet tall, 3 feet wide

An introduction from the Ottawa Research Station. The flowers are red with a yellow center. A compact grower.

WEIGELA
Weigela florida
(Bunge) A. DC.
HARDY IN ZONE 4
9 feet tall, 6 feet wide

HABIT. Open shrub; there are 10 species native in Asia.
BRANCHLETS. With 2 rows of hairs.
LEAVES. Short-petioled to subsessile, elliptic to ovate-oblong, or obovate, 2 to 4 in. long, acuminate, rounded to wedge-shaped at base, serrate.
FLOWERS. About 1.2 in. long, rosy pink outside, paler within, in early June; calyx smooth, united for one-half its length; corolla funnelform to bell-shaped, abruptly narrowed below the middle, with spreading lobes; stigmas 2-lobed.
FRUIT. Glabrous capsules.

LANDSCAPE USE AND CULTURE

This is the hardiest species, but it is not planted as often as the variably hardy cultivars. Native to northern China and Korea, it was introduced into North America in 1845. To do well in zone 4, these shrubs need a relatively protected site. Pruning out the frequent dead wood in the spring keeps these shrubs looking their best. They bloom best in full sun.

The WISTERIA
Wisteria Nutt.
FAMILY: LEGUMINOSAE, PEA FAMILY

Wisteria is one of the staples in the landscape farther south. Recent introductions have made this vine possible to grow in our hardiness zones. In the North, care must be taken to obtain the hardiest strains and also in their placement in the landscape. It is, however, possible to grow wisteria in zone 4 if the exacting cultural conditions are met.

KENTUCKY WISTERIA
Wisteria macrostachya (Torr. & A. Gray) Nutt.
FOR PROTECTED LOCATIONS OF ZONE 4
20 feet long

HABIT. Vigorous climber; there are 10 species native in North America and Asia.
BRANCHES. Hairless, climbing counter clockwise.
LEAVES. Alternate, 6 to 8 in. long, leaflets usually 9, 1 to 2 in. long, hairy beneath when young.
FLOWERS. Dense racemes, lilac-purple,7 to 12 in. long.
FRUIT. Pod, hairless, constricted between seeds.

LANDSCAPE USE

W. macrostachya has been the hardiest of the wisteria attempted in the North. It needs sturdy support, full sun and good drainage. Dead wood should be pruned out early in the spring. Only for protected locations.

CULTIVAR:

'Aunt Dee'
PROTECTED LOCATIONS IN ZONE 4
20 feet long

This cultivar has done well in protected sites.

Other wisteria to try:

JAPANESE WISTERIA
Wisteria floribunda (Willd.) DC.
FOR PROTECTED LOCATIONS IN ZONE 4

25 feet long

There are few plantings of Japanese wisteria that have been successful in zone 4. However, there are those who relish challenges....

YELLOWHORN

YELLOWHORN
Xanthoceras sorbifolium Bunge.
FAMILY: SAPINDACEAE

HARDY IN ZONE 4

15 feet tall, 20 feet wide

HABIT. Deciduous small tree or large shrub, only one species is found.
BRANCHES. Dark brown, coarse.
LEAVES. Stalkless, alternate, compound pinnate, 9 to 17 serrate leaflets, 1 to 2.5 in. long, with terminal leaflet.
FLOWERS. Showing with the leaves, terminal racemes usually female, with lateral racemes male, sometimes female; fragrant, white with basal yellowish red blotch, in late May.
FRUIT. Capsule, opening 3 flaps, with pea-like seeds.

LANDSCAPE USE

A small tree or large shrub not often found in the Midwest. It is very ornamental and could be featured in a large shrub border. A great plant to seek out. It is native to northern China.

CULTURE

Yellowhorn needs a well-drained, acidic soil. It needs full sun to flower well.

YELLOWROOT

YELLOWROOT
Xanthorhiza simplicissima
Marsh.
FAMILY: RANUNCULACEAE, BUTTERCUP FAMILY

HARDY IN ZONES 3 AND 4

24 inches tall, 20 inches wide

HABIT. Deciduous shrub; there is 1 species native in North America.
BRANCHES. Sparse.

LEAVES. Alternate, pinnately compound with 5 leaflets; leaflets ovate to ovate-oblong, 1 to 2 in. long, incisely toothed.
FLOWERS. Polygamous, brownish purple, in racemes 2 to 4 in. long, in May; sepals 5; petals 5, reduced to small 2-lobed nectaries; stamens 5 to 10; carpels 10, developing into fruit.
FRUIT. 1-seeded follicles.

LANDSCAPE USE AND CULTURE

This informal grower can be used as a ground cover. Yellowroot prefers moist soil in which it spreads by rhizomes. It has a rather sparse growth habit. Its fall color of mainly yellows can give interest to the late autumn landscape. Native from New York to Kentucky and Florida, it has been cultivated since 1776.

YUCCA

SPANISH BAYONETTE, ADAMS NEEDLE
Yucca filamentosa L.
FAMILY: AGAVACEAE

HARDY IN ZONES 3 AND 4

9 feet tall, 3 feet wide

HABIT. Stemless shrub, spreading by short stolons; there are 40 species native in North America.
LEAVES. Erect and spreading, linear-lanceolate, acute, 10 to 30 in. long with numerous curly threads at the margins.
FLOWERS. In erect panicles 3 to 9 feet tall, in July, pendulous, yellowish white, 2 to 2.7 in. across.
FRUIT. 2 in. long, in September.

LANDSCAPE USE AND CULTURE

Many are surprised to find yucca in a book on woody plants. However, they do have evergreen leaves and are classed as a stemless shrub. *Y. filamentosa* is of variable hardiness for zones 3 and 4. Plant in a protected site. Also, mulching the leaves during winter with a protective mulch of straw is advised. This yucca will withstand dry conditions. This species is the showiest of the semi-hardy yuccas.

SOAPWEED
Yucca glauca Nutt. & J. Fraser.
HARDY IN ZONES 3 AND 4

3 feet tall, 3 feet wide

HABIT. Shrub with a short prostrate stem.
LEAVES. Narrow-linear, 12 to 30 in. long and 0.2 to 0.5 in. wide, grayish or glaucous beneath with a narrow white margin.
FLOWERS. Pendulous, greenish white, 2.5 in. long, in narrow, rarely branched racemes 3 to 6 feet tall, in July; styles swollen, green.
FRUIT. Brown capsules, 2 in. long, in September.

LANDSCAPE USE AND CULTURE

This is the hardiest of the yuccas. It is slow to flower when grown from seed. Native from South Dakota to New Mexico, it has been in cultivation since 1656. Used as an accent plant in the flower or shrub border.

NORTHERN PRICKLY ASH

NORTHERN PRICKLY ASH
Zanthoxylum americanum Mill.
FAMILY: RUTACEAE, RUE FAMILY
HARDY IN ZONES 3 AND 4
20 feet tall, 9 feet wide

HABIT. Large, suckering deciduous shrub or small tree, often forming thickets; there are 250 species distributed worldwide.
BRANCHES. With prickles about 0.3 in. long.
LEAVES. Alternate, odd-pinnate with 5 to 11 leaflets; leaflets ovate to elliptic, 1 to 2 in. long, acuminate, entire or crenulate, dark green above, lighter and hairy beneath.
FLOWERS. Dioecious, small, yellowish green, in axillary clusters on branchlets from the past season, in early May.
FRUIT. Dehiscent follicles about 0.2 in. long, red brown; seeds black.

LANDSCAPE USE AND CULTURE

This prickly shrub can be used for naturalizing, for a barrier shrub and for wildlife plantings. It is rarely planted because of its suckering habit and unfriendly nature. Henry David Thoreau's manuscript written on his visit to Minnesota (1861, 5) stated he found *Zanthoxylum* on Nicollet Island (close to downtown Minneapolis) and also sugar maple, hackberry, and bur oak. Jonathan Carver in his *Travels through the Interior Parts of North America* (1781) states, "The decoction of it will expeditiously and radically remove all impurities of the blood."

BASIC WOODY PLANT INFORMATION

How Plants Get Their Names

All plants regardless of size or importance have a scientific name and sometimes one or more common names. The scientific name always consists of the genus and the species and is the same in all countries of the world. The common name of a plant, however, can be different in various parts of the country, and even in the same area a plant may be known by several common names. Let us consider the example of the red maple. The scientific name for this tree is *Acer rubrum* (*Acer* is the genus, *rubrum* is the species), and its common names are red maple, swamp maple, scarlet maple, and soft maple. In this book only the most frequently used common names are given. The first name listed, when more than one common name is included, is the preferred name.

The authors of the scientific names are cited in abbreviated form following the names. Parentheses are used to indicate the original author whenever the scientific name has been changed. For example, *Berberis koreana* Palib., the correct scientific name for Korean barberry, was named by Ivan Vladimirovich Palabin; *Calluna vulgaris* (L.) Hull, the scientific name for Scotch heather, was named by John H. Hull, who changed the original name *Erica vulgaris* L. (named by Carl von Linnaeus), to *Calluna vulgaris* (hence the "L." in parentheses).

Some plants also have variety names. A botanical variety is a group of individuals that differ noticeably from the species. The Colorado blue spruce has a bluer foliage cast than the Colorado spruce, *Picea pungens*, and its scientific name is, not surprisingly, *Picea pungens* var. *glauca*.

Sometimes a single plant differs from all other individuals in a seedling population. If this plant possesses desirable characteristics and can be propagated vegetatively, it may be given a cultivar (or cultivated variety) name. Occasionally cultivars of woody plants can be reproduced by seeds, but this is rare. The difference between a botanical variety and a cultivar is that the botanical variety reproduces itself in nature from seeds whereas a cultivar must be increased by humans.

The cultivar name follows the scientific or common name. Two methods for indicating a cultivar are used. The name can be enclosed by single quotes (most common) or preceded by "cv." For example, the cutleaf weeping European birch would be either *Betula pendula* 'Gracilis' or *Betula pendula* cv. Gracilis. In this book single quotes are used to indicate all cultivar names.

In efforts to create new and better cultivars, humans have often crossed two or more species of the same genus. The seedling population from a cross between two species is often given a third? new? species name. To distinguish this interspecific hybrid from a natural species, an "x" is used between the genus and the species names. *Syringa* x *prestoniae* is a hybrid species resulting from a cross between *Syringa villosa* and *Syringa reflexa*. Usually the seedlings from an interspecific cross will vary. Individual plants within the seedling population can be selected and given a cultivar name. *Syringa* x *prestoniae* 'Donald Wyman' is such a cultivar.

When more than two species are used in a breeding program, it is not practical to use a specific name to designate the progeny. This has happened with our modern roses, crabapples, clematis and so on. For these plants, the cultivar name is preceded by either the genus or the common name. *Malus* 'Sparkler' or *Rosa* 'Lillian Gibson' are proper designations.

To prevent a cultivar name from being used more than once in the same genus, registering authorities have been established for all woody ornamentals. Usually the national or international organization that promotes a certain genus of plants is the designated registering authority. It is important that all names be cleared by the proper registering authority before being used. The registering authority requires a description of the plant and usually a color photograph or herbarium specimen.

Plant nomenclature has been complicated by the patenting and trademarking processes in the introduction of new plants. Both patents and trademarks are strictly regulated by the Patent and Trademark Office of the U.S. Department of Commerce. Plant patenting a cultivar name gives the applicant the right to exclude others from propagating a plant for 20 years. This patent is non-renewable and once it has expired, it allows anyone the right to propagate the plant.

Trademarks can be symbols, designs, or words or a combination of any. It protects a plant's trade name rather than the actual plant material itself and is renewable. No one, thus, has the right to use a trademark designation without the permission of the owner. However, owners of trademarks may not exclude others from propagation of plant material. The trademark designation is ™, and also a name that has also been registered with the Patent and Trademark Office is designated as ®.

In the nursery trade the trademark name is frequently associated with a single cultivar. This causes much confusion. The cultivar name is often a nonsensical, unmarketable name while the trademarked name is the name everyone soon associates with a plant. By the use of trademarks, introducers of new plants can extend the exclusive period during which they may receive royalties from others.

Bud Morphology

Characteristics of the stems and buds used in identification include bud placement, bud size and shape, the number of bud scales, leaf scars, color and nature of the bark, lenticels, and pith. Bud placement is the same as leaf placement: alternate, opposite, or whorled. Alternate arrangement is the most common, occurring in plants like birch, elm, and oak. In opposite arrangement, two buds occur at each node on opposite sides of the stem. Ash, buckeye, and maple are familiar examples. The catalpa is an example of whorled arrangement, win which three or more buds occur at each node.

The size of buds differs greatly and ranges from minute buds that are barely visible to large, prominent buds. Most buds are sessile but a few are stalked. Most are covered with overlapping scales, although some are naked with no protective scales. In the willow the buds are protected by a single scale. Normally the buds are single, one being formed in each leaf axil. In some plants, like honeysuckle, the buds are superposed, with one or more buds above the axillary bud. Different types of buds develop into different plant structures. A vegetative bud develops into a leafy branch, a flower bud into a flower cluster. A mixed bud develops both a leafy branch and flowers. In the stone fruits the flower buds often develop on either side of the vegetative bud.

Terminal buds are usually larger than lateral buds. When the bud scales on the terminal buds drop, a ring is left around the stem. This ring is known as the terminal bud scar. On some trees the age of a branch can be determined by counting the number of these rings.

Leaf Scars

Leaf scars are left on the stems when the leaves drop in the fall. They are often triangular and smooth, with vascular bundles clearly visible. The size, shape, and arrangement of these leaf scars and vascular bundles are useful characteristics in identifying trees and shrubs in winter.

Bark

The color of the bark is an easily observed characteristic. Twig color is most noticeable in early spring. Minnesota's native redosier dogwood and golden willow are easily recognized in late March.

Determining the nature of the bark is also helpful in identification. The bark of most birch, for example, peels off in papery layers. A young aspen has a fairly smooth bark, whereas the cork tree has a thick corky bark. In shrubs like the ninebark, the outer bark peels off in long narrow strips. On most trees the bark becomes quite thick. As trees continue to grow in diameter, the bark must stretch and usually breaks to form ridges and furrows on the surface. These marks occur in patterns that are characteristic for the species.

Lenticels are usually visible on young stems. They are openings in the bark for gas exchange and are usually elongated. The shape and arrangement of the lenticels are used in identification.

Pith

A less obvious characteristic used in the identification of certain plants is the pith, located in the center of the stem. It is normally a center core of thin-walled cells. The pith is usually white or brown and may be solid, hollow, or chambered.

Leaf Morphology

A typical leaf is made up of a flat expanded portion (the blade) and a stalk portion (the petiole). In some leaves a pair of leaflike bracts (stipules) is found at the base of the petiole.

Leaf arrangement, like bud arrangement, may be alternate, opposite, or whorled. A slight modification occurs in buckthorn and a few other plants where the leaves are subopposite. That is, instead of being opposite each other, one leaf is slightly above the other, but on the opposite side of the stem.

Leaf Venation

Leaf venation refers to the arrangement of the main veins. In pinnate venation there is a central midrib, and the lateral veins spread out from this midrib very much like a feather. In palmate venation 3 or more prominent veins radiate from near the attachment of the petiole. Lateral veins spread out from these main veins. In parallel venation the veins run parallel to each other. This type of venation is common to the grass family but rather rare in woody plants. The yucca is a familiar example.

There is also a type of venation called dichotomous in which the veins fork into two equal parts. Ginkgo is an example.

Leaf Shape

Leaves may be simple or compound. A simple leaf has the blade in one piece. Such a leaf may be pinnately, palmately, parallel, or dichotomously veined. In a compound leaf, the leaf blade is divided into separate leaflets. Pinnately compound leaves have been derived from pinnately lobed leaves, and palmately compound leaves have been derived from palmately lobed ones.

The leaves of conifers may be awl-shaped, scalelike, or elongated narrow needles. Awl-shaped leaves are found on certain juniper and typically occur in whorls of 3. Scale-like leaves are usually opposite, with each pair alternating with the pair above. Arborvitae, false cypress, and certain juniper have scale-like leaves. Needles are found on the pine, spruce, and fir.

The leaves of broad-leaved plants, both evergreen and deciduous, take a variety of shapes. These shapes are quite uniform for each species. Leaf margins are also fairly uniform for a given species. They vary from entire to deeply lobed. Leaf apexes and leaf bases are also characteristic for each species and are useful in plant identification.

Flower Morphology

The flower is the least variable of the morphological characteristics and is used in most identification keys. The typical flower consists of four sets of modified leaves that are arranged spirally or in whorls. These are attached to a short terminal stem swelling called the receptacle. The four sets of modified leaves are as follows:

- Sepal. Lowest leaves, usually green. Collectively called the calyx.
- Petal. Attached above the sepals, usually colored. Collectively called the corolla.
- Stamen. Located above the corolla. Each stamen consists of a stalk or filament attached to the pollen-producing anthers. The number of stamens per flower varies from a few to a hundred or more. Collectively called the androecium.
- Carpel. Produced in the center of the flower. May be separate from or fused to a compound pistil. The pistil is made up of the swollen base (ovary), the neck portion (style), and the terminal portion (stigma). Carpels in a single flower are collectively called the gynoecium.

The stamens and carpels are the reproductive organs of the flower. Pollen grains alight on the stigma and germinate to form a pollen tube that digests its way down through the style into the ovary chamber. Each pollen tube finds its way into an ovule where sperm are discharged to fertilize the egg and endosperm nuclei. The ovule then develops into a seed, and the fertilized egg becomes the embryo.

The floral parts may remain separate or they may fuse. The fused calyx and corolla may be tubular or funnel-like with spreading lobes. Fused stamens are less common, but in the pea family the filaments are often fused.

Types of Flowers

- Regular flower. Has radial symmetry. That is any line cut vertically through the flower will divide it into two symmetrical halves.
- Irregular flower. Asymmetrical in structure, so there is only one precisely placed vertical line which will divide the flower into symmetrical halves.
- Incomplete flower. Lacks one or more floral parts. For example, in the willow, calyx and corolla are lacking and the flower consists of only stamens and carpels.

- Perfect flower. Has both stamens and carpels; may or may not have a calyx or corolla.
- Imperfect flower. Has either stamens or carpels but not both in the same flower. Calyx and corolla may or may not be present. If staminate and pistillate flowers occur on the same plant, it is said to be monoecious; if on separate plants, it is dioecious.
- Hypogynous flower. The ovary (gynoeium) is above (hypo) the attachment of the other flower parts. Thus the ovary is said to be superior.
- Perigynous flower. The calyx cup, called the hypanthium, grows up around the ovary but is not attached to it. Sepal lobes, petals, and stamens are attached to the rim of the hypanthium.
- Epigynous flower. The hypanthium fuses with the ovary, and sepal lobes, petals, and stamens appear to arise above the ovary, which is said to be inferior.

An inflorescence is the grouping of the flowers in a flower cluster.

Fruit Morphology

A typical fruit develops from the ovary. In some fruit, like the apple, accessory flower parts, like the hypanthium, become part of the fruit and, in a few, like the mulberry, several flowers are involved in fruit development. Fruit are classified as either dry or fleshy.

Dry Fruit

DEHISCENT DRY FRUIT
(split open at maturity to shed seeds)

- Legume (pod). Composed of one carpel that opens along two sutures, with seeds attached in a single row. Examples: black locust, honey locust, Kentucky coffee tree.
- Follicle. Has one carpel that opens along one suture. A many-seeded fruit. Examples: ninebark, spirea.
- Capsule. Composed of more than one carpel,

opening near the tip either by pores or by longitudinal splitting. A many-seeded fruit. Examples: lilac, mockorange.

- Cone. Formed in the pine family. Made up of overlapping scales that separate at maturity to discharge the seeds. Examples: arborvitae, pine, spruce.

INDEHISCENT DRY FRUIT

(does not split open at maturity)

- Achene. A one-seeded fruit with the thin ovary wall separate from the seed. Examples: clematis, potentilla.
- Samara. Usually has one seed. A winged portion of the fruit aids in seed dispersal. Examples: ash, elm, maple.
- Nut. A one-seeded fruit with a hard bony shell. Examples: chestnut, hazelnut, oak.
- Nutlet. A small nut. Examples: birch, hornbeam.

Fleshy Fruit

- Berry. A many-seeded fruit with a thin exocarp and a fleshy mesocarp. Examples: blueberry, honeysuckle.
- Drupe. Has a thin exocarp, fleshy mesocarp, and a stony endocarp. Usually one-seeded. Examples: plum, viburnum.
- Pome. An accessory fruit in which the fleshy portion develops from the hypanthium that surrounds the many-seeded ovary (core). Examples: apple, hawthorn.
- Aggregate. Fruit consists of several pistils from separate flowers. Example: mulberry.

GLOSSARY

Acaulescent. Apparently without a stem; the leaves and flowers arise near the surface of the ground.

Achene. A dry, indehiscent fruit with a thin wall and seed.

Acicular. Needle-shaped.

Acuminate. Tapering to a slender point.

Acute. Ending in an acute angle or point.

Adnate. Two unlike organs that are joined, as when the filament of a stamen is fused with the corolla tube.

Alternate. Situated singly at each node, as leaves or flowers along an axis.

Anastomosing. Forming a network.

Andro-monoecious. Bearing male flowers and perfect flowers on the same plant.

Andro-polygamus. Bearing male, female, and perfect flowers on the same plant.

Anther. The pollen-bearing portion of the stamen.

Anthesis. Period when a flower is open and receptive to pollen.

Apetalous. Without petals.

Apical. At the apex or tip of an organ.

Apiculate. Ending abruptly in a small, usually sharp tip.

Appressed. Lying close and flat against.

Aril. An appendage on some seeds, developed as an outgrowth from the point of attachment and covering the seed partly or completely.

Ascending. Rising somewhat obliquely and curving upward.

Auriculate. Furnished with ear-shaped appendages.

Axil. The upper angle formed by a leaf or a branch and the stem.

Axillary. Situated in an axil.

Berry. A fleshy fruit developed from a single ovary and usually containing several seeds embedded in a fleshy pulp.

Bifid. Two-cleft at the apex.

Bipinnate. Twice pinnate.

Bloom. Covered with a fine, waxy powder.

Bract. A modified leaf from the axil of which a flower or flower cluster arises.

Bracteolate. Having small bracts.

Branchlet. A small branch grown during the current or preceding year.

Budding. A form of propagation or grafting in which the scion is a bud.

Bullate. Blistered or puckered.

Caducous. Falling off very early.

Calcareous. Soil high in lime.

Calyx. The outer whorl of modified leaves in a flower, usually green.

Campanulate. Bell-shaped.

Capitate. Headlike; in a head.

Capsule. A dry, dehiscent fruit formed from a multi-carpelled ovary and usually producing many seeds.

Carpel. A modified floral leaf that forms a simple pistil or part of a compound pistil.

Cartilagenous. Hardened, tough, resembling cartilage.

Catkin. A scaly-bracted spike of usually unisexual flowers.

Caudate. Having a taillike terminal appendage.

Ciliate. Having marginal hairs.

Ciliolate. Minutely ciliate.

Clavate. Club-shaped, gradually enlarging toward the upper end.

Coherent. Two or more similar parts or organs that are joined.

Connate. United; joined into one organ.

Convulate. Rolled up lengthwise.

Cordate. Heart-shaped.

Corolla. The second whorl of flower leaves called petals; usually large and showy; petals may be fused or separate.

Corymb. A modified raceme with a short axis and rather long lower pedicels, forming a flattopped flower cluster with the outer flowers opening first.

Cotyledon. Leaves of the embryonic plant with the seed.

Crenate. Toothed with rounded, shallow teeth.

Crenulate. Finely crenate.

Cultivar. A cultivated variety as distinguished from a botanical variety.

Cuneate. Wedge-shaped.

Cuspidate. Ending in a sharp, abrupt, and often rigid point.

Cutting. A form of propagation in which a portion of a stem, leaf, or root is used.

Cyme. A convex or flattopped flower cluster in which the central flower opens first.

Deciduous. Falling off at the end of the growing season; not persistent.

Decumbent. Prostrate at base, erect or ascending elsewhere.

Decurrent. Extending downward, as when the blade of a leaf is projected downward as two wings along the petiole or the stem.

Dehiscent. Opening to emit the contents, as in capsules or anthers.

Deltoid. Broadly triangular.

Dentate. Toothed, with teeth pointing outward.

Denticulate. Diminutive of *dentate*.

Depressed. Flattened, compressed.

Dichotomous. Forked regularly in pairs.

Dioecious. Bearing male and femal flowers of separate plants.

Disk. An enlargement of or an outgrowth from the receptacle, appearing in the center of a flower; in composites the disk refers to the central tubular flowers.

Drupe. A fruit with a fleshy exocarp and a hard or bony endocarp that enclosed the seed or seeds.

Drupelet. A small drupe.

Echinate. Covered with prickles.

Ellipsoid. Shaped like a football.

Elliptic. Shaped like an ellipse and about two times as long as wide.

Emarginate. With a shallow notch at the apex.

Entire. With a continuous unbroken margin.

Erose. Irregularly cut or toothed along the margin.

Evergreen. Leaves persistent, green all year.

Exfoliating. Peeling off in thin layers.

Exsert. Extending beyond surrounding organs; often refers to stamens or styles that project beyond the perianth.

Extrorse. Facing outward.

Fasciated. Abnormally flattened and malformed.

Fascicle. A small bundle or cluster.

Fastigiate. With branches erect and nearly parallel.

Ferrugineous. Rust colored.

Filament. The basal, stalklike portion of a stamen.

Filiform. Threadlike; very thin and round.

Floccose. Clothed with soft hair or wool.

Foliaceous. Leaflike texture and appearance.

Follicle. A dry, dehiscent fruit developed from a simple ovary and splitting along one suture.

Frond. The leaf of a fern.

Funnelform. The gradual widening of a tube.

Gall. An abnormal growth or swelling caused by an insect or a disease.

Gamo-. A prefex meaning united.

Gibbous. Swollen on one side and usually toward the base.

Glabrate. Nearly glabrous or becoming glabrous with age.

Glabrous. Without hairs.

Glandular. Bearing glands or glandlike appendages.

Glaucescent. Somewhat glaucous.

Glaucous (*glauca*). Covered with a powdery bloom that is bluish white or bluish gray.

Globose. Spherical.

Glutinous. Gluey or sticky.

Head. A dense flower cluster of sessile or nearly sessile flowers.

Herb. A plant in which the stem dies back to the ground each fall.

Herbaceous. Dying back to the ground each fall.

Hirsute. With rather coarse or stiff hairs.

Hispid. Covered with stiff hairs.

Hybrid. A cross between two parents that are unlike.

Hypanthium. A cup-shaped or tubular receptacle that grows up around the ovary.

Imbricate. Overlapping like shingles.

Incised. Deeply and irregularly cut.

Incurved. Curved inward.

Indehiscent. Not opening at maturity.

Inferior. Beneath or below, as when the ovary is below the perianth.

Inflorescence. A flower cluster.

Involucre. A set of floral bracts that surround a flower cluster.

Involute. Rolled inward so the lower side of the organ is exposed.

Irregular. A flower in which the members of one or more sets of organs (usually the corolla) differ in size, shape, or structure.

Keel. A longitudinal ridge; two united lower petals in members of the pea family.

Laciniate. Deeply cut into narrow lobes.

Lamellate. Chambered; refers to pith with thin transverse plates.

Lanceolate. Lance-shaped, about 4 times as long as wide, and broadest at or below the center.

Layering. A form of propagation in which a portion of the plant is rooted while attached to the parent plant.

Leaflet. A single segment of a compound leaf.

Legume. A dry, dehiscent fruit that opens along two sutures.

Lenticel. A small, corky dot or spot on the bark of young branches.

Lepidote. Covered with scales.

Ligulate. Having a ligule.

Ligule. A small, usually flat outgrowth from an organ.

Limb. The upper, more or less widened or spreading part of a united corolla or calyx.

Linear. Long and narrow, with nearly parallel margins.

Lobulate. Divided into small, shallow lobes.

Locule. A cavity within an ovary or anther.

Lyrate. Pinnately lobed, with the terminal lobe larger than the lateral lobes.

-merous. A suffix referring to the parts in each circle of the floral organs.

Monoecious. With unisexual flowers of both sexes on the same plant.

Mucro. A short, sharp, slender point.

Mucronate. Tipped with a mucro.

Mucronulate. With a minute mucro.

Naturalizing. Refers to a type of landscaping or planting that duplicates nature or appears natural.

Nectariferous. With nectar glands.

Nectary. A gland that secretes nectar or sugar.

Nut. A hard, dry, indehiscent fruit or part of a fruit with 1 seed.

Nutlet. A small nut.

Obconical. Inversely cone-shaped.

Oblanceolate. Lance-shaped and broadest above the center.

Oblique. With unequal sides.

Oblong. About three times as long as wide and with parallel sides.

Obovate. Inversely ovate.

Obovoid. Inversely egg-shaped.

Obtuse. Blunt, ending in an angle greater than 90 degrees.

Odd-pinnate. Pinnately compound, with a terminal leaflet.

Opposite. Place directly across from each other at the same node.

Orbicular. Circular.

Oval. Broadly elliptic, about 1.5 times as long as wide.

Ovary. The basal portion of the pistil in which the ovules are produced.

Ovate. A flat structure with the outline of a hen's egg, broadest below the center.

Ovoid. Same as *ovate*.

Ovule. The body within the ovary that becomes the seed after fertilization occurs.

Palmate. With three or more lobes, veins, leaflets, or branches arising from one point.

Panicle. A compound or branched flower cluster that is longer than wide.

Parietal. Located on the inner surface of the outer wall of the ovary.

Pectinate. Comblike; lobes pinnately arranged, with narrow, closely set segments.

Pedicel. The stalk of a single flower.

Peduncle. The stalk of a flower cluster.

Pellucid. Transparent.

Peltate. Shield-shaped, attached by a stalk on the undersurface near the center.

Pendulous. Hanging or drooping.

Perennial. Living for several years.

Perfect. A flower having both stamens and pistil.

Perianth. The floral envelope, a term usually used when there is no clear distinction between the sepals and petals.

Pericarp. The wall of the ripened ovary.

Perigynous. Borne around the ovary, as the attachment of sepals, petals, and stamens on a cup-shaped hypanthium.

Petal. A separate segment of the corolla.

Petaloid. Having the appearance of petals.

Petiole. Stalk of a leaf.

Pilose. With long, soft hairs.

Pinnate. Compound leaf with leaflets on either side of central axis.

Pinnatifid. With lobes pinnately arranged.

Pistil. The central organ of a flower, consisting of ovary, style, and stigma.

Pistillate. Having pistils but no stamens.

Pith. Central core of spongy cells in a stem.

Placenta. The point or place of attachment of seeds in the fruit.

Plumose. Feathery.

Pod. A dry, dehiscent fruit; same as *legume*.

Pollination. The transfer of pollen from the anthers to the stigma.

Polygamo-dioecious. Part of the flowers are perfect and part are unisexual with male and female flowers on separate plants.

Polygamous. Bearing perfect and unisexual flowers on the same plant.

Pome. A fleshy fruit like the apple and the pear in which the fleshy portion is developed from the hypanthium.

Prickle. A spinelike outgrowth from the bark or epidermis.

Procumbent. Trailing; lying on the ground.

Prostrate. Lying flat on the ground.

Puberulent. Minutely pubescent.

Puberulous. Same as *puberulent.*

Pubescent. Covered with hairs.

Punctate. Covered with glandular dots.

Pyriform. Pear-shaped.

Quadrate. A square (usually 1 mile) of vegetation.

Raceme. An elongated simple inflorescence of stalked flowers borne along the axis, with the oldest flowers at the base.

Rachis. An axis bearing flowers or leaflets.

Ranked. Refers to the number of longitudinal rows of leaves or other structures along an axis.

Recurved. Curved backward or downward.

Reflexed. Abruptly bent backward.

Reniform. Kidney-shaped; rounded in outline, longer than wide, with a sinus on one side.

Repand. With a slightly wavy margin.

Resiniferous. Sticky with resin.

Reticulate. Netted.

Retuse. Slightly notched at the rounded apex.

Revolute. Rolled backward.

Rhizome. An underground creeping stem.

Rootlets. Little roots; often refers to holdfast roots of climbing plants.

Rotate. Wheel-shaped.

Rufous. Reddish brown.

Rugose. A wrinkled surface.

Rugulose. Diminutive of *rugose.*

Sagittate. Shaped like an arrowhead, with the basal lobes directed downward.

Salverform. With a slender tube abruptly expanding into a flat limb.

Samara. A dry indehiscent, 1-seeded fruit with a well-developed wing.

Sarmentose. Producing long runners that root, as in the strawberry.

Scabrous. Rough to the touch.

Scale. Any small, flat structure that is dry and bractlike.

Scarious. Thin, dry, and membranous, not green.

Scurfy. Covered with dry scales.

Sepal. A separate segment of the calyx.

Septicidal. Applied to a capsule that dehisces along or through the septa which separate its cells.

Serrate. Toothed along the margin, with the sharp teeth pointing forward.

Serrulate. Diminutive of *serrate.*

Sessile. Without a stalk.

Setose. Covered with stiff bristles.

Shrub. A woody plant that is branched from the base and usually not more than 20 feet tall.

Simple. With the leaf blade in one piece and the pistil made up of a single carpel.

Sinuate. With a wavy margin.

Sinus. The space between lobes.

Spatulate. Shaped like a spatula; rounded at the apex and gradually tapering downward.

Spike. A simple flower cluster with flowers sessile along the axis.

Spine. A sharp-pointed woody outgrowth along the stem.

Spinescent. Becoming spiny; with short, spinelike branches.

Spinulose. Having small spines.

Spur. A saclike or tubular projection on a sepal or petal.

Stamen. The pollen-producing organs in a flower, consisting of a filament and anther.

Staminate. Bearing stamens; usually refers to a unisexual flower that lacks pistils.

Staminode. A sterile stamen that produces no pollen.

Standard. The uppermost petal in the flowers of members of the pea family.

Stellate. Star-shaped.

Stigma. Terminal portion of the pistil adapted for the reception of pollen.

Stipe. The stalk of a pistil or similar organ.

Stipitate. Having a stipe.

Stipular. Belonging to the stipules.

Stipulate. With stipules.

Stipules. A pair of small leaflike structures at the base of the petioles of certain leaves that may be persistent or fall off early.

Stolon. A horizontal stem that creeps along the ground and that roots and produces new plants at the nodes.

Stoloniferous. Producing stolons.

Stomate. An opening in the epidermis of a leaf for the exchange of gases.

Stomatic. Bearing stomates.

Stomatiferous. Same as *stomatic.*

Stratification. The necessary treatment of seeds with a cold period before they germinate.

Strigilose. Dimuntive of *strigose.*

Strigose. Hairy surface with the hairs appressed close to the surface and pointing in one direction.

Strobile. A small cone.

Style. The narrow portion of the pistil between the ovary and the stigma.

Sub-. A prefix meaning more or less.

Subcoriaceous. More or less leathery.

Subglobose. Not quite spherical.

Subshrub. An herbaceous plant that is woody at the base.

Subulate. Awl-shaped.

Suffruticose. A perennial plant with only the base woody and persistent.

Sunscald. A type of winter injury in which the bark on the southwest side of the trunk is killed.

Superposed. Place one above another.

Syncarp. A compound fruit made up of several fused carpels.

Tendril. A portion of a stem or leaf modified for climbing, usually slender and coiled.

Terete. Round in cross section.

Ternate. Borne in 3's.

Tomentose. Woolly, with matted hairs.

Tomentulose. Diminutive of *tomentose*.

Tomentum. A dense covering of matted hairs.

Torus. The receptacle of the flower-bearing ovaries.

Truncate. Ending abruptly as if cut off.

Tubercle. A minute, tuberlike structure on an organ.

Tuberculate. Bearing tubercles.

Turbinate. Top-shaped.

Umbel. A flower cluster with numerous elongated pedicels arising from a common point.

Urceolate. Urn-shaped.

Valvate. Meeting along the margins but not overlapping.

Ventricose. Swelling on one side.

Verrucose. Warty.

Verticillium. A plant disease caused by a fungus.

Villous. Bearing long and soft, usually curly hairs.

Viscid. Sticky.

Whorled. A circle of 3 or more organs.

Works Cited

Beston, Henry. 1970. *Especially Maine.* Stephen Greene Press, Brattleboro VT.

Borland, Hal. 1983. *A Countryman's Woods.* Knopf, New York.

Botanical Register. 1815-1847. vol 1-33. James Ridgway, London.

Carver, Jonathan. 1781. *Travels Through the Interior Parts of North America.* 3rd. edition. C. Dilly, London.

Coles, William. 1657. *Adam in Eden.* J. Streater, London.

Curtis's Botanical Magazine. 1787-. vol 1- [various firms & institutions], London.

Evelyn, John. 1706. *Silva and Terra.* 4th edition. Robert Scott, London.

Fairchild, David. 1938. *The World Was My Garden; Travels of a Plant Explorer.* C. Scribner, London.

Fry, Marion M. 1992. *A Space of One's Own.* Andersen Horticultural Library, Chanhassen, MN.

Garden and Forest; a Journal of Horticulture, Landscape Art and Forestry. 1888-97. Edited by Charles S. Sargent. Garden and Forest Publ. Co., New York.

Gerard, John. 1597-98. *The Herball or Generall Historie of Plantes.* J. Norton, London.

Green, Samuel B. 1898. *The Forestry in Minnesota.* The Minnesota Forestry Assoc., Delano, MN.

Leopold, Aldo. 1949. *A Sand County Almanac, and Sketches Here and There.* Oxford U. Press, New York.

Loudon, J.C. 1838. *Arboretum et Fruticetum Britannicum; Or, The Trees and Shrubs of Britain.* 8 vol. Longman, Orme, Brown, Green & Longmans, London.

--------- 1842. *Encyclopaedia of Trees and Shrubs.* Author, London.

Marshall, Humphrey. 1785. *Arbustrum Americanum.* J. Crukshank, Philadelphia.

Mitchell, Henry. 1992. *One Man's Garden.* Houghton Mifflin, Boston.

Nemerov, Howard. 1977. *The Collected Poems of Howard Nemerov.* U. of Chicago Press, Chicago.

Nuese, Josephine. 1970. *The Country Garden.* Scribner, New York.

Orloff, H. Stuart and Henry B. Raymore. 1959. *The Book of Landscape Design.* M. Barrows, New York.

Parkinson, John. 1629. *Paradisi in Sole.* H. Lownes and R. Young, London.

Peattie, Donald. 1950. *A Natural History of Trees of Eastern and Central North America.* Houghton Mifflin, Boston.

Rea, John. 1676. *Flora: Seu de Florum Cultura.* G. Marriott, London.

Sackville-West, Vita. 1939. *Country Notes.* Michael Joseph, London.

---------- 1951. *In Your Garden.* Michael Joseph, London.

---------- 1953. *In Your Garden Again.* Michael Joseph, London.

Sargent, Charles Sprague. 1891-1902. *The Silva of North America; a Description of the Trees Which Grow Naturally in North America Exclusive of Mexico.* 14 vol. Houghton Mifflin, Boston.

Sowerby, James. 1790-1814, 1902. *English Botany; or, Coloured Figures of British Plants...3rd edition.* 13 vol. G. Bell, London.

Thoreau, Henry David. 1841- 1981- . *Journal.* Edited by John C. Broderick. vol 1-5. Princeton U. Press, Princeton, New Jersey.

------------ 1962. *Thoreau's Minnesota Journey: Two Documents.* Edited by Walter Roy Harding. Thoreau Society, Genesco, New York.

----------1854, 1939. *Walden, or, Life in the Woods.* Heritage Press, New York.

----------1849, 1961. *A Week on the Concord and Merrimack Rivers.* Houghton Mifflin, Boston.

Wilson, Ernest Henry. 1926. *Aristocrats of the Garden.* The Stratford Co., Boston.

-------- 1929. *China Mother of Gardens.* The Stratford Co., Boston.

-------- 1931. *If I Were to Make a Garden.* The Stratford Co., Boston.

Wyman, Donald. 1990. *Trees for American Gardens.* 3rd edition. Macmillan, New York.

Zwinger, Ann. 1970. *Beyond the Aspen Grove.* Random House, New York.

--------- 1972. *Land Above the Trees; a Guide to American Alpine Tundra.* Harper & Row, New York.

--------- 1998. *The Nearsighted Naturalist.* U. of Arizona Press, Tucson.

ILLUSTRATION CREDITS

(Page numbers refer to pages in the text)

Botanical Register: Consisting of Coloured Figures of Exotic Plants... 1815-1847. vol 1-33. James Ridgway, London. (page 120, 125, 260)

Browne, D.J. 1832. *The Sylva Americana; Or, A Description of the Forest Trees Indigenous to the United States...* William Hyde, Boston. (page 95, 98, 99, 104, 112, 115, 129, 188, 190, 192, 201, 206, 209, 217, 221, 222, 223, 224, 234, 245, 267, 269)

Catalogs.

    Bushberg Vineyards and Grape Nursery. 1883. St. Louis, Missouri. (page 276)

    Currie Brothers Co. 1899. Milwaukee, Wisconsin. (page 76, 276)

    ------------ 1903. Milwaukee, Wisconsin. (page 73, 198)

    ------------ 1904. Milwaukee, Wisconsin. (page 218, 239)

    ------------ 1905. Milwaukee, Wisconsin. (page 237)

    ------------ 1906. Milwaukee, Wisconsin. (page 261)

    ------------ 1908. Milwaukee, Wisconsin. (page 238)

    M.H. Harman Nursery. 1910. Geneva, New York. (page 125)

    James Vick Seedsman. 1884. Catalog. Rochester, New York. (page 61, 88, 195, 253)

    ------------------ 1891. Catalog. Rochester, New York. (page 61)

Curtis's Botanical Magazine. 1787-. [published by various firms & institutions], London. (pages 50, 65, 92, 96, 121, 128, 130, 131, 193, 278)

Duhamel du Monceau, Henri Louis. 1755. *Traité des Arbres et Arbustes.* 2 vol. H.L. Guérin & L.F. Delatour, Paris. (page 13, 80, 85, 91, 94, 106, 117, 131, 135, 250, 256, 257, 262)

Evelyn, John. 1812. *Silva: Or, A Discourse of Forest-Trees.* 2 vol. T. Wilson for Longman, Hurst, Rees, Orme, and Brown, London. (page 82, 85, 98, 99, 191, 200, 221, 243, 249, 263, 266)

Garden and Forest: A Journal of Horticulture, Landscape Art and Forestry. 1888-97. Edited by Charles S. Sargent. 10 vol. Garden and Forest Publ. Co., New York. (pages 46, 50, 54, 56, 67, 69, 70, 74, 75, 94, 99, 100, 108, 110, 122, 124, 126, 127, 197, 215, 228, 229, 230, 232, 235, 245, 247, 249, 253, 268)

Gerard, John. 1597-98. *The Herball.* J. Norton, London. (page 59)

    -------1633. *The Herball.* Enlarged and revised by T. Johnson. A. Islip, J. Norton & R. Whitakers, London. (page 32)

Hooker, William Jackson. 1829-40. *Flora Boreali-Americana; Or, The Botany of the Northern Parts of British America.* 2 vol. Henry G. Bohn, London. (page 219, 241, 246)

The Illustrated Dictionary of Gardening: A Practical and Scientific Encyclopaedia of Horticulture for Gardeners and Botanists. 1887-89. Edited by George Nicholson. 9 vol. L. Upcott Gill, London. (pages 49, 70, 74, 77, 96, 107, 109, 114, 115, 127, 194, 197, 198, 225, 226, 227, 228, 232, 242, 251, 255, 256, 257, 259, 264, 268, 270, 275)

Kennion, Edward. 1815. *An Essay on Trees in Landscape.* T. Bensley for C.J. Kennion, London. (page 27)

Lamarck, Jean Baptise Antoine Pierre Monnet de. 1783-1817. *Encyclopédie Méthodique. Botanique...*Chez Panckoucke, Paris. (page 66, 72, 77, 81, 82, 89, 90, 95, 101, 103, 106, 107, 123, 124, 128, 132, 191, 219, 220, 251, 262, 275, 278)

Linnaeus, Carl. 1737-38. *Hortus Cliffortianus.* Amsterdam. (page 48, 89)

Loudon, J.C. 1838. *Arboretum et Fruticetum Britannnicum; Or, The Trees and Shrubs of Britain.* 8 vol. Longman, Orme, Brown, Green & Longmans, London. (pages 33, 35, 36, 38, 49, 51, 68, 69, 83, 84, 87, 93, 98, 102, 103, 104, 105, 111, 121, 129, 130, 135, 185, 186, 187, 188, 189, 204, 207, 208, 209, 210, 213, 214, 215, 216, 219, 223, 224, 231, 234, 240, 242, 243, 244, 246, 247, 248, 263)

---------- 1842. *An Encyclopedia of Trees and Shrubs.* Longman, Brown, Green and Longmans, London. (pages 43, 52-53, 60, 62, 63, 67, 75, 79, 81, 88, 89, 101, 114, 116, 123, 131, 192, 211, 229, 233, 252, 253, 258, 265, 266, 272, 273, 277, 278)

Michaux, André. 1801. *Histoire des Chênes de l'Amérique.* ed. by F.A. Michaux. Crapelet Press, London. (page 1)

Millspaugh, Charles F. 1892. *Medicinal Plants; An Illustrated and Descriptive Guide to Plants...* J.C. Yorston, Philadelphia. (page 111)

MacMillan, Conway. 1899. *Minnesota Plant Life.* St Paul, Mn. (*Report of the Survey, Botanical Series III).* (page 275)

Newhall, Charles S. 1897. *The Vines of Northeastern America.* G.P. Putnam, New York. (page 92, 124)

Passe, Crispijn van de, the younger. 1614-1617. *Hortus Floridus.* C. van de Passe, Utrecht. (page 113, 222)

Paxton's Magazine of Botany. 1841-49. 16 vol. William Orr, London. (page 277)

Rosendahl, Carl Otto. 1955. *Trees and Shrubs of the Upper Midwest.* University of Minnesota Press, Minneapolis. (pages 31-38, 44, 47, 52, 54, 61, 62-63, 64, 67, 68, 77, 78, 79, 82, 84, 91, 101, 102, 112, 120, 126, 193, 194, 195, 199, 203, 210, 211, 212, 232, 241, 245, 246, 247, 252, 254, 276, 279)

Sargent, Charles Sprague. 1891-1902. *The Silva of North America; a Description of the Trees Which Grow Naturally in North America Exclusive of Mexico.* 14 vol. Houghton Mifflin, Boston. (pages 29-30, 41-42, 45, 50, 55, 57-58, 63, 65, 66, 72, 80, 83, 86, 87, 97, 105, 117, 133, 134, 193, 202, 203, 204, 205, 206, 214, 218, 248, 264, 265, 267, 268, 271, 274)

Ventenat, Etienne P. 1803-08. *Choix de Plantes Dont la Plupart Sont Cultivées dans le Jardin de Cels.* Crapelet, Paris. (page 7)

Willmott, Ellen. 1914. *The Genus Rosa.* 2 vol. John Murray, London. (page 240)

CLASSIFIED BIBLIOGRAPHY

PLANNING AND LANDSCAPE DESIGN

(Not listed are the many "idea" books giving design examples and uses of woody plants. These range from Sunset or Ortho paperbacks to elaborate, glossy, coffee-table books.)

Booth, Norman K. and James E. Hiss. 1991. *Residential Landscape Architecture: Design Process for the Private Residence.* Prentice Hall, Englewood Cliffs.

Eckbo, Garrett. 1978. *Home Landscaping: The Art of Home Landscaping.* Rev. and Enl. Edition. McGraw-Hill, New York.

Fry, Marion M. 1992. *A Space of One's Own.* Andersen Horticultural Library, Chanhassen, MN.

Garden Design. 1982- Meigher Communications, New York.

Hannebaum, Leroy. 1981, 1990. *Landscape Design: A Practical Approach.* Second edition. Prentice Hall, Englewood Cliffs, NJ.

PLANTING AND MAINTENANCE OF WOODY PLANTS

Journal of Arboriculture. 1975- International Society of Arboriculture, Champaign, IL.

Pirone, P. P. 1988. *Tree Maintenance.* Sixth edition. Oxford U. Press, New York.

Shigo, Alex L. 1991. *Modern Arboriculture: a Systems Approach to the Care of Trees and Their Associates.* Shigo and Trees Associates, Durham, NH.

RESOURCES ON WOODY PLANTS

(Also very useful are the many nursery catalogs from northern nurseries.)

Andersen Horticultural Library's Source List of Plants and Seeds. 2000. Fifth edition. Andersen Horticultural Library, Chanhassen, MN. (also online at plantinfo.umn.edu).

Dirr, Michael. 1997. *Dirr's Hardy Trees and Shrubs: An Illustrated Encyclopedia.* Timber Press, Portland, OR.

------------ 1998. *Manual of Wood Landscape Plants: Their Identification, Ornamental Characteristics, Culture, Propagation and Uses.* Fifth edition. Stipes Pub. Co., Champaign, IL.

Flint, Harrison L. 1997. *Landscape Plants for Eastern North America.* Second edition. John Wiley, New York.

Gordon, Don. 1991. *Growing Fruit in the Upper Midwest.* University of Minnesota Press, Minneapolis.

Hightshoe, Gary L. and Harlen D. Groe. 1998. *North American Plantfile: a Visual Guide to Plant Selection for Use in Landscape Design.* McGraw-Hill, New York.

Right Tree Handbook: Tree Selections for Plants Under and Near Power Lines and Other Locations. 1991. Harold Pellett, Nancy Rose and Mervin Eisel. University of Minnesota, Minneapolis.

Snyder, Leon C. 1991. *Native Plants for Northern Gardens.* Andersen Horticultural Library, Chanhassen, MN.

PLANT NAMES

Griffiths, Mark. 1994. *Index of Garden Plants.* Timber Press, Portland, OR.

Index

Page numbers appear in roman type. Photographs are given in italics.

Abelialeaf 29
Abeliophyllum
  distichum 29
Abies
  balsamea 29-30, **166-67**
    'Nana' 30
  concolor 30
  fraseri 30
  homolepis 30
  koreana 30
  lasiocarpa arizonica 31
    'Green Globe' 31
  nordmanniana 31
  veitchii 31
Acacia
  rose 233
Acanthopanax see
  Eleutherococcus
Acer 31-39
    Autumn Blaze™ 32
    Celebration® 32
    'Marmo' 32
    Norwegian Sunset® 32
    Pacific Sunset™ 32
    Scarlet Sentinel™ 32
  campestre 32-33
  x freemanii 32
  glabrum 39
  griseum 39
  mandschuricum 39
  miyabei 39
  negundo 33, 37
    'Sensation' 33
    'Variegatum' 33
  palmatum 31
  pensylvanicum 39
  platanoides 33-35
    'Columnare' 34
    'Crimson King' 34
    'Crimson Sentry' 34
    'Deborah' 34
    Emerald Lustre® 34
    'Emerald Queen' 34
    'Fairview' 34
    'Globosum' 34
    Parkway® 34
    'Princeton Gold' 34
    'Royal Red' 34, **182-83**
    'Schwedleri' 34
    'Superform' 35
    'Variegatum' 35

  pseudoplatanus 39
  rubrum 35-36, **138-39**
    'Armstrong' 35
    Autumn Flame® 35
    'Autumn Spire' 35
    Karpick® 35
    Northfire® 36
    'Northwood' 36, **183**
    October Glory® 36
    Red Sunset® 36
  saccharinum 36
    'McKay's Seedless' 36
    'Silver Queen' 36
    'Skinneri' 36
  saccharum 37, **142-43, 158**
    'Commemoration' 37
    Fall Fiesta™ 37
    'Flax Mill Majesty' 37
    'Globosum' 37
    Green Mountain® 37
    'Legacy' 37
  leucoderme 37
  spicatum 38
  tataricum 38
    ginnala 38-39
      'Bailey Compact' 38
      'Embers' 39
      'Emerald Elf' 39
      'Flame' 39
  triflorum 39
  truncatum 39
Acidic soil
  selection list 168
Actinidia
  arguta 40
    'Ananasnaja' 40
    'Issai' 40
  kolomitka 40
    'Arctic Beauty' 40
Adams Nursery 134
Adam's needle 278
Aesculus
    'Autumn Splendor'
    41,**140, 178**
  carnea 42
  flava 42
  glabra 41-42
    arguta 42
  hippocastanum 42
    'Alba' 42
    'Baumannii' 42
    'Umbraculifera' 42
  parviflora 42
  sylvatica 42
Ailanthus
  altissima 43
Air pollution tolerant
  selection list 182

Akebia
  fiveleaf 43
Akebia
  quinata 43
Alder
  black 43-44, 111
  European 43-44
  gray 44
  hazel 44
  mountain 44
  smooth 44
  Sitka 44
  speckled 44
  white 44
Alderman, W.H. 214
Alkaline soil
  selection list 174
Allspice
  Carolina 60-61
Almond
  dwarf flowering 215
  flowering 218
  Russian 218
Alnus
  glutinosa 43-44
    'Aurea' 44
    'Imperialis' 44
    'Laciniata' 44
    'Pyramidalis' 44
  incana 44
    'Laciniata' 44
  rugosa 44
  serrulata 44
  sinuata 44
  tenuifolia 44
Amelanchier 45-46, **170-71**
  alnifolia 45-46
    'Northline' 45
    'Pembina' 45
    'Regent' 45
    'Smokey' 46
    'Thiessen' 46
  arborea 46
  canadensis 46, **180-81**
    'Prince William' 46
  x grandiflora 46-47
    Autumn Brilliance® 46
    'Ballerina' 46
    'Coles Select' 46
    'Princess Diana' 47
    'Robin Hill' 47
    'Strata' 47
  laevis 47, **168**
    'Cumulus' 47
    'Snowcloud' 47
  lamarckii 47
  ovalis 47
  stolonifera 47

American Chestnut
  Foundation 65
American Garden Cole 186
Amorpha
  canescens 47-48
  fruticosa 48
  nana 48
Ampelopsis
  brevipedunculata 48-49
    'Elegans' 49
Andersen Horticultural
  Library 4-5
Andorra Nurseries 115
Andromeda
  polifolia 49
    'Nana' 49
Angelica, Japanese 49
Apples 132-90
Apricot 213
  Manchurian 216
Aralia
  five-leaved 91-92
  Tatarian 91
Aralia
  elata 49
  hispida 49-50
  spinosa 50
Arborvitae
  American 264-66
Arbutus
  trailing 92
Arctostaphylos
  uva-ursi 50-51
    'Massachusetts' 51
Aristolochia
  durior see *A. macrophylla*
  macrophylla 51
Arnold Arboretum 96, 129,
  130,134, 135, 185, 188, 190
Aronia
  arbutifolia 51-52
    'Brilliantissima' 52
  melanocarpa 52, **169**
    elata 52
    'Autumn Magic' 52
  x prunifolia 52
Arrowwood 272
Artemisia
  abrotanum 52
  frigida 53
Ash 97-100
  black 99
  blue 100
  European 98
  green 99-100
  Manchurian 98-99
  mountain see Mountain ash

Ash *(continued)*
prickly 279
red 99-100
wafer 219
white 97-98
Asjes, Evert, Jr. 98
Aspen
large-toothed 211
European 211
quaking 210
Azalea 225-30
flame 228
Japanese 229
pinkshell 230
Rosehill 228
royal 230
swamp 230
sweet 227-28
Yodogawa 230

Badhan, Mrs M.N. 217
Bailey Nurseries 34, 37, 53,
79, 197, 220, 252, 267,
268, 275
Bakker Nursery 116
Barberry
Japanese 54-55
Korean 54
Bark
selection list 159
Baron, Milton 187
Barrier plantings
selection list 182
Bartram, John 42
Bayberry 192
Bayonette
Spanish 278
Bean tree
Indian 66
Bearberry 50-51
Beardslee Nursery 242
Beauty bush 120-21
Beech
American 95
blue 63-64
European 95
water 63-64
Berberis **182-83**
Emerald Carousel® 53
Golden Carousel® 53
koreana 54, **165**
thunbergii 54-55
'Atropurpurea' 54
'Atropurpurea Nana' 54
'Aurea' 54
Burgundy Carousel® 55
'Crimson Pygmy' see *B.t.*
'Atropurpurea Nana'
Jade Carousel™ 55
'Kobold' 55
'Rose Glow' 55
Ruby Carousel® 55
'Sparkle' 55
'Thornless' 55

Berg, C.V. 119
Bergeson, Melvin 99
Bergeson Nursery Co. 99,
186, 242
Beston, Henry *Especially Maine*
29-30, 242
Betula
'Crimson Frost' 56
alleghaniensis 56
fontinalis 56
lenta 56-57
lutea see *B. alleghaniensis*
nana 59
nigra 57, **159, 172-73**
Heritage® 57
occidentalis see *B. fontinalis*
papyrifera 57
pendula 57-58
'Dalecarlica' 58
'Fastigiata' 58
'Gracilis' 58
'Purpurea' 58
'Youngii' 58
platyphylla
japonica 58
'Whitespire' 58
populifolia 59
pumila 59
x sandbergii 59
utilis
jacquemontii 59
Birch 55-59
bog 59
canoe 57
cherry 56-57
dwarf 59
European 57-58
gray 59
Japanese white 58
paper 57
red 56
river 57
Sandberg 59
swamp 59
sweet 56-57
water 56
whitebark Himalayan 59
yellow 56
Bittersweet
American 67-68
Chinese 67
oriental 67
Blackberry
highbush 242
Blackhaw 274
Bladdernut
American 253
Blueberry 270
highbush 270
lowbush 270
Borders
selection list 150-51

Borland, Hal *A Countryman's*
Woods 33
Botanical Register 125
Boughen Nurseries 79
Boxelder 33, 37
Boxwood
American 60
Korean 59-60
Brooklyn Botanic Garden 186
Broom
hairy 71
Buckeye
bottlebrush 42
Ohio 41-42
painted 42
sweet 42
Texas 42
yellow 42
Buckthorn
common 225
elder 225
glossy 225
sea 107
Buffaloberry
russet 246-47
silver 246
Bush, Guy D. 198
Butternut 111-12
Buttonbush 68
Buttonwood 208
Buxus
microphylla
koreana 59-60
'Wintergreen' 60
sempervirens 60

Calluna
vulgaris 60
Calycanthus
floridus 60-61
Campsis
radicans 61, **152**
Caragana
arborescens 61-62, **157**
'Lorbergii' 62
'Pendula' 62
'Walker' 62
brevifolia 62
frutex 62
'Globosa' 62
microphylla 62-63
pygmaea 63
Carpinus
betulus 63
'Columnaris' 63
'Fastigiata' 63
caroliniana 63-64
Carver, Jonathan *Travels*
Through the Interior Parts
of N.A. 97, 218-19, 242, 279
Carya
cordiformis 64
glabra 64

laciniosa 64
ovata 64-65
Caryopteris
x clandonensis 65
'Blue Mist' 65
'Dark Knight' 65
Castanea
dentata 65
mollissima 65-66
Catalpa
common 66
northern 66
southern 66
western 66
Catalpa
bignonioides 66
speciosa 66
Ceanothus
inland 67
Ceanothus
americanus 66-67
ovatus 67
Cedar
red 119-20
Celastrus
orbiculatus 67
rosthornianus 67
scandens 67-68
Celtis
occidentalis 68, **139**
Cephalanthus
occidentalis 68
Cercidiphyllum
japonicum 69
Cercis
canadensis 69
'Northern Strain' **cover,**
69, **137, 146-47, 180-81**
Chaenomeles
speciosa 69
Chamaebatiaria
millefolium 70
Chamaecyparis **178-79**
obtusa 70
'Nana' 70
pisifera 70
'Boulevard' 70
'Filifera' 71
'Filifera Aurea' 71
'Filifera Nana' 71
'Squarrosa' 71
thyoides 71
Chamaecytisus
hirsutus 71
Chamaedaphne
calyculata 71
Checkerberry 101
Cherry 213
Amur 215
black 217
Cornelian 81
European bird 216-17
European dwarf 215

fire 217
Nanking 218
pin 217
sand 214-15
Sargent 217
Chestnut
American 65
Chinese 65-66
Chicagoland Grows 272
Chionanthus
virginicus 72
Chokeberry
black 52
purple 52
red 51-52
Chokecherry 218-19
Amur 215
Cinquefoil
shrubby 211
Cladrastis
lutea 72, **169**
Clarke's Nursery 114
Clematis 73-77
curly 75
fragrant tube 75-76
golden 77
ground 77
Jackman 76
oriental 76
scarlet 77
solitary 76
sweet autumn 77
Clematis
'Ascotiensis' 73
'Barbara Dibley' 73
'Bees Jubilee' 74
'Belle of Woking' 74
'Blue Bird' 74
'Comtesse de Bouchaud' 74
'Daniel Deronda' 74
'Dr Ruppel' 74, **162**
'Duchess of Edinburgh' 74
'Elsa Spaeth' 74
'Ernest Markham' 74
'Gipsy Queen' 74
'Hagley Hybrid' 74
'Henryi' 74
'Huldine' 74, **152-53**
'Hybrida Sieboldiana' see
C. 'Ramona'
'Jan Pawl II/John Paul II' 74
'Lady Betty Balfour' 74
'Lady Northcliffe' 74
'Lasurstern' 74, **174-75**
'Lincoln Star' 75
'Madame Baron Veillard' 75
'Madame Edouard Andre' 75
'Mrs Cholmondeley' 75
'Multi Blue' 75
'Nelly Moser' 75
'Niobe' 75
'Ramona' 75

'Rouge Cardinal/Red
Cardinal' 75
'Star of India' 75
'The President' 75
'Ville de Lyon' 75
'Will Goodwin' 75
'Xerxes' see *C.* 'Elsa Spaeth'
crispa 75
henryi see *C.* 'Henryi'
heracleifolia
davidiana 75-76
integrifolia 76
x *jackmanii* 76
'Alba' 76
macropetala 76
'Markham's Pink' 75
mandshurica 76
maximowicziana see *C.*
terniflora
orientalis 76
paniculata see *C. terniflora*
recta 77
mandshurica see
C. mandshurica
tangutica 77
terniflora 77
texensis 77
'Duchess of Albany' 74
virginiana 77
viticella
Etoile Violette' 74
Clethra
alnifolia 77-78, **163**
'Hummingbird' 78
'Paniculata' 78
'Rosea' 78
'Ruby Spice' 78
Cliff green 196
Clover
shrub bush 122
Coffee tree
Kentucky 104-05
Cole Nursery 104, 187
Coles, William *Adam in Eden* 97
Collinson, Peter 42, 125
Columnar habit
selection list 153
Comptonia
peregrina 78
Conifers
selection list 152
Connor, Sheila 106
Container plantings 4
Coralberry 254
Chenault 254
Cork tree
Amur 196-97
Sakhalin 197
Cornus 79-82, **182-83**
alba 79
'Argenteo-marginata' 79
'Bud's Yellow' 79

'Elegantissima' see *C. a.*
'Argenteo-marginata'
'Gouchaultii' 79
Ivory Halo® 79
'Sibirica' 79
'Spaethii' 79
'Variegata' see *C.a.*
Argenteo-marginata'
alternifolia 80, **180-81**
baileyi see
C. stolonifera 'Baileyi'
florida 81
mas 81
obliqua 80
purpusii see *C. obliqua*
racemosa 80, **180**
rugosa 80-81
sanguinea 82
sericea see *C. stolonifera*
stolonifera 81
'Baileyi' 81
'Cardinal' 81
coloradensis 81
'Flaviramea' 81
'Isanti' 81
'Kelseyi' 81
'Silver and Gold' 81
Corylus
americana 82
avellana 82
'Contorta' 82
colurna 82
cornuta 82-83
Cotinus
coggygria 83
'Nordine' 83
'Royal Purple' 83
obovatus 83
Cotoneaster 83-85
cranberry 84
creeping 83-84
European 84
hedge 84
many-flowered 84-85
spreading 85
Cotoneaster 83-85
adpressus 83-84
apiculatus 84
divaricatus 85
integerrimus 84
lucidus 84
multiflorus 84-85
Cottage Garden Nursery 264
Cottonwood 209
Cowberry 270
Crab
flowering 132-90
Japanese flowering 188-89
Mancherian 188
plum-leaved 189
prairie 189
Sargent 189-90
Siberian 187-88

wild sweet 188
Zumi 190
Cranberry
American highbush 274-75
European highbush 273
large 270
mountain 270
Crataegus 85-88,
ambigua 85
crus-galli 86, **165**
Crusader® 86
'Inermis' 86, **151**
laevigata 86
'Paul's Scarlet' 86
'Superba' 86
mollis 86
x *mordenensis* 87
'Snowbird' 87
'Toba' 87
phaenopyrum 87
punctata 87
viridis 87-88
'Winter King' 88
Creeper
thicket 194-95
Virginia 195
Cross Nursery 263, 265
Cully, Earl 57
Cultivars 4, 281-82
Currant
alpine 232
buffalo 233
clove 233
European black 233
golden 233
Indian 254
red 233
yellow flowering 233
Curtis's Botanical Magazine 48,
50, 92, 105-06
Cypress
bald 263
false 70-71
Hinoki false 70
Russian 191
Sawara false 70-71
white cedar false 71

Daphne
Burkwood 88
February 88-89
rose 88
Daphne
x *burkwoodii* 88
'Carol Mackie' 88
'Somerset' 88
cneorum 88
mezereum 88-89
Dayton, Daniel 185
Deer resistant
selection list 182
den Boer, Aire 134, 135, 185
Desert sweet 70

Deutzia
  Lemoine 89
  slender 89
Deutzia
  gracilis 89
  x lemoinei 89
    'Compacta' 89
Devil's walking stick 50
Diervilla 89-90
Diervilla
  lonicera 89-90
  sessilifolia 90
Dioecious plants
  selection list 183
Dirca
  palustris 90, **168**
Disease control 23
Disturbed sites
  selection list 175
Dogwood 79-82
  bloodtwig 82
  flowering 81
  gray 80
  pagoda 80
  redosier 81
  round-leaved 80-81
  silky 80
  Tatarian 79
Douglas Nursery 115
Drainage 11
Dry soil
  selection list 169
Dumbarton Oaks 64
Dundee-Hill Nursery 117, 118
Dutchman's pipe 51
Dziuk, Peter 199

Edible landscaping
  selection list 163
Elaeagnus
  angustifolia 90-91
  commutata 91
  umbellata 91
Elder
  American 245
  European red 246
  scarlet 246
Eleutherococcus
  sessiliflorus 91
  sieboldianus 91-92
Elm
  Americana 269
  David 269
  Japanese 269
  red 269
  rock 269
  Siberian 269
  slippery 269
  Wych 269
Epigaea
  repens 92
Erosion control
  selection list 175

Espalier 132, **164**
Euonymus 92-95
  dwarf 94
  Hamilton 94
  running 94-95
  winged 92-93
  winterberry 93
Euonymus
  alatus 92-93
    'Compactus' 93
    'Nordine' 93
  atropurpureus 93
  bungeanus 93
  europaeus 93
    'Aldenhamensis' 93
  fortunei 93-94
    'Coloratus' 94
    'Gracilis' 94
    'Minimus' 94
  hamiltonianus 94
  maackii 94
  nanus 94
    'Turkestanicus' 94
  obovatus 94-95
Evelyn, John *Silva* 43, 221
Evergreen Nursery 56
Exochorda
  serratifolia 95
    'Northern Pearls' 95

Fagus
  grandifolia 95
  sylvatica 95
Fairchild, David *The World Was My Garden* 62
Fairview Evergreen Nursery 114
Fall color
  selection list 158
Ferguson, Al 99
Fern, sweet 78
Fernbush 70
Fertilizing 16, 21-22
Fiala, John 185, 256, 260, 262
Fir, Arizona corkbark 31
  balsam 29-30
  concolor 30
  Douglas 219
  Fraser 30
  Korean 30
  Nikko 30
  Nordmann 31
  Veitch 31
  white 30
Flax Mill Nursery 37
Flowering crab see Crab
Flowers 283-84
  shrub & vine selection list 162
  tree selection list 161
Foliage
  colored summer list 182-83
Forsythia 96
  white 29

Forsythia
  'Arnold Dwarf' 96
  'Beatrix Farrand' 96
  'Lynwood Gold' 96
  'Meadowlark' 96
  'Northern Gold' 96
  'Northern Sun' 96, **157**
  'Spring Glory' 96
  'Sunrise' 96
  ovata 96
Foundation plantings
  selection list 149
Fragrance
  selection list 163
Fraxinus 97-100
  'Northern Gem' 97
  'Northern Treasure' 97
  americana 97-98, **178**
    Autumn Applause® 98
    'Autumn Blaze' 98
    Autumn Purple® 98
    Northern Blaze™ 98
    'Rosehill' 98
    Skyline® 98
  excelsior 98
  mandshurica 98-99
    'Mancana' 99
  nigra 99
    'Fallgold' 99
  pennsylvanica 99-100, **159**
    'Bergeson' 99
    Centerpoint™ 99
    Dakota Centennial™ 99-100
    'Foothills' 100
    'Kindred' 100
    Leprechaun™ 100
    'Marshall's Seedless' 100
    'Patmore' 100
    Prairie Dome® 100
    Prairie Spire® 100
    'Summit' 100
  quadrangulata 100, **143**
Fringe tree, white 72
Fruit 284-85
  woody plants with selection list 164
Fry, Marion *A Space of One's Own* 5, 9

Garland flower 88
Gaultheria 101
Gaultheria
  hispidula 101
  procumbens 101
Gaylussacia
  brachycera 101
Genista
  tinctoria 101-02
    'Royal Gold' 102
Genus 281
Gerard, John *Herball* 31-32, 52, 113
Gideon, Peter 64

Gilbertson, Ben 100
Ginkgo 102-03
Ginkgo
  biloba 102-03, **178-79**
    Autumn Gold™ 102
    'Fairmount' 102
    'Fastigiata' 103
    'Magyar' 103
    Princeton Sentry® 103
    Shangri-la® 103
Gleditsia
  triacanthos 103-04, **138**
    inermis 104
    Imperial® 104
    Shademaster® 10
    Skyline® 104
    Sunburst® 104
Globular habit
  selection list 154
Gordon, Don *Growing Fruit in the Upper Midwest* 241
Grape 276
  Oregon 131
  riverbank 276
Green, Samuel B. *Forestry in Minnesota* 30, 46
Greenbrier
  bristly 247
Greenweed
  dyer's 101
Ground covers
  selection list 155
Gum
  sour 192-93
Gymnocladus
  dioica 104-05
    'Stately Manor' 105, **145**

Hackberry 68
Halesia
  monticoola 105
  tetraptera 105
Halimodendron
  halodendron 105-06
d'Hamale, Canaert 119
Hamamelis
  vernalis 106
  virginiana 106
Hamilton, William 33
Hansen, N.E. 135, 215
Hardiness 4, 11-12
  zone maps 11, 19-20
Harry Lauder's walking stick 82
Hasselkus, Ed 32, 47, 58
Hawthorn 85-88
  cockspur 86
  Crimson Cloud 86
  dotted 87
  downy 86-87
  English 86
  green 87-88
  Russian 85
  Washington 87

Hazel
American 82
beaked 82-83
European 82
Turkish 82
Heather
Scotch 60
Hedera
helix 107
'Baltica' 107
'Bulgaria' 107
Hedges
selection list 156
Height, growing
selection lists 178-82
Hemlock
Canadian 268
Eastern 268
Hercules club 50
Hickory
bitternut 64
pignut 64
shagbark 64-65
shellbark 64
Highland Nursery 208
Hill, Arthur 117
Hill Nursery, D. 116, 117
Hillside Gardens 119
Hippophae
rhamnoides 107
'Sprite' 107
Hobblebush 272-73
Hobbs, C.M. 186
Holly
mountain 192
Holmason, Martin 34
Holmlund Nursery 34
Honeylocust 103-04
thornless 104
Honeysuckle
Alps 127
Amur 125-26
Belle 127
Brown's 124-25
bush 89-90
Donald 127
European fly 127
hairy 127
limber 125
Morrow 127
Sakhalin 126
scarlet trumpet 124-25
southern bush 90
sweetberry 125
Tatarian 126
Trumpet 127
Vienna 126-27
Hop tree 219
Horizontal habit
selection list 152
Hornbeam
American 63-64
American hop 193
European 63

Horsechestnut
common 42
red 42
Huckleberry
box 101
Hydrangea
bigleaf 109
climbing 110
French 109
hills-of-snow 108-09
oakleaf 108
panicle 109-10
peegee 109-10
Hydrangea
anomala petiolaris see
H. petiolaris
arborescens 108-09
'Annabelle' 108, **148-49, 162**
'Grandiflora' 108
radiata 109
macrophylla 109
'Nikko Blue' 109
paniculata 109-10
'Compacta' 109
'Grandiflora' 109-10
'Kyushu' 110
'Praecox' 110
'Tardiva' 110
'Unique' 110
petiolaris 110
quercifolia 108
Hypericum
kalmianum 110
prolificum 110

Ilex
'Sparkleberry' 111
verticillata 111
'Afterglow' 111
'Red Sprite' 111
'Shaver' 111
'Winter Red'
Indigo bush 48
Indigo
false 48
fragrant false 48
Insect control 23
Interstate Nursery 187
Iowa State U. 96, 113, 276
Ironwood 63-64, 193
Irrigation 17
Iseli Nursery 202
Ivy
Boston 195
Engelmann 195
English 107
poison 232

Jackman, George 73, 74
Jeffers, Glenn 32
Jeffries Nursery 98, 268
Jetbead
black 230

Johnson's Nursery 190
Juglans
cinerea 111-12
nigra 112
'Thomas' 112
'Weschcke' 112
regia 112
Juniper 113-20
Chinese 113-14
common 114-15
creeping 115-16
Japanese garden 117
red cedar 119-20
Rocky Mountain 118-19
Sargent 118
Savin 117-18
single seed 119
Waukegan 115
Juniperus 113-20, **156, 178-79**
chinensis 113-14
'Ames' 113
'Blaauw' 114
'Hetzii' 114
'Iowa' 114
'Maney' 114
'Mountbatten' 114
'Robusta Green' 114
'San Jose' 114
communis 114-15
Blueberry Delight™ 114
'Depressa Aurea' 114
'Effusa' 114
'Repanda' 115
saxatilis 115
horizontalis 115-16
'Andorra Compacta' 115
'Bar Harbor' 115
'Blue Chip' 115
'Blue Prince' 115
'Douglasii' 115
'Dunvegan Blue' 115
'Hughes' 115
'Plumosa' 115
Prairie Elegance™ 116
'Prince of Wales' 116
'Webberi' 116
'Wiltonii' 116
x media 116
Gold Star® 116
'Mint Julep' 116
'Old Gold' 116
'Pfitzeriana' 116
'Pfitzeriana Aurea' 116
'Pfitzeriana Glauca' 116
'Ramlosa' 116
procumbens 117
'Nana' 117
sabina 117-18
'Arcadia' 117
'Blaue Donau/Blue
Danube' 117
'Blue Forest' 117
'Broadmoor' 117

'Buffalo' 117
Calgary Carpet™ 118
'Mini Arcade' 118
'Pepin' 118
'Skandia' 118
'Tamariscifolia' 118
'Von Ehren' 118
sargenii 118
'Glauca' 118
'Viridis' 118
scopulorum 118-19
'Blue Haven' 118-19
'Blue Trail' 119
'Medora' 119
'Moonglow' 119
'Sutherland' 119
'Welchii' 119
'Wichita Blue' 119
'Winter Blue' 119
squamata 119
'Blue Star' 119
virginiana 119-20
'Canaertii' 119
Emerald Sentinel™ 120
'Grey Owl' 120
'Manhattan Blue' 120

Kalmia
latifolia 120
polifolia 120
Katsura tree 69
Kerr, W.L. 185, 186
Kerria
Japanese 120
Kerria
japonica 120
Kiwi 40
arctic 40
Kolomitka 40
Kolkwitzia
amabilis 120-21

Labrador tea 122
Lake Country Nursery 86,
134-35, 185, 187
Landsburg, Roger 36
Landscape design 9-12
Landscape Plant Development
Center 99
Larch
American 121-22
European 121
Japanese 121
Larix
decidua 121
'Pendula' 121, **154**
kaempferi 121, **159**
leptolepis see *L. kaempferi*
laricina 121-22
Laurel
bog 120
Lead plant 47-48

Leather
flower 75
Leatherleaf 71
Leatherwood 90
Leaves 282-83
Ledum
groenlandicum 122
Leopold, Aldo *A Sand County
Almanac* 203, 223
Lespedeza
bicolor 122
Ligustrum
amurense 123
obtusifolium
regelianum 123
x vicaryi 123
vulgare 123
'Cheyenne' 123
'Lodense' 123
Lilac 255-62
Chinese 256
common 259-62
early 257
dwarf Korean 257
French 259-62
hyacinth 256-57
Japanese tree 259
Korean early 257
late 259
littleleaf 262
Manchurian 257-58
Meyer 257
Pekin 258
Persian 258
Preston 258-59
Linden 266-68
American 266-67
littleleaf 267-68
Mongolian 268
Lingenberry 270
Lingonberry 270
Linnaea
borealis 124
Liriodendron
tulipifera 124
Locust
black 234
Lonicera
'Freedom' 124
alpigena 127
x bella 127
x brownii 124-25
'Dropmore Scarlet' 125, **163**
caerulea
edulis 125
dioica 125
glaucescens 127
hirsuta 127
maackii 125-26
podocarpa 126
maximowiczii
sachalinensis 126
morrowii 127

sempervirens 127
tatarica 126
'Arnold Red' 126
'Honey Rose' 126
'Rosea' 126
'Zabelii' 126
x xylosteoides 126-27
'Clavey's Dwarf' 127
'Miniglobe' 127
xylosteum 127
'Emerald Mound' 127
Loudon, J.C. *Arboretum et
Fruticetum Britannicum* 38;
*Encyclopaedia of Trees and
Shrubs* 103
Lycium
barbarum 127-28
chinense 128
halimiifolium see *L. barbarum*

Maackia
Amur 128
Chinese 128
Maackia
amurensis 128, **147**
chinensis 128
McGill & Son Nursery 34, 35
McKay Nursery 36, 98
Mackie, Carol 88
Maclura
pomifera 128
Magnolia 129-31
anise 131
Kobus 131
Loebner 129
saucer 131
star 130
umbrella 130-31
Magnolia 129-31
acuminata 129
kobus 131
x loebneri 129
'Leonard Messel' 129
'Merrill' 129, **161**
salicifolia 131
x soulangiana 131
stellata 130, **146**
'Centennial' 130
'Royal Star' 130
'Waterlily' 130
tripetala 130-31
Mahonia
creeping 131
Mahonia
aquifolium 131
repens 131
Maidenhair tree 102-03
Malus 132-90, **140-41, 164**
'Adams' 134
'Adirondack' 134, **160-61**
'Beacon' 132
'Beverly' 134
'Bob White' 134

Brandywine® 134
'Callaway' 134
Camelot® 134
'Cardinal' 134
Centurion® 134-35
'Coral Cascade' 135
Coralburst® 135
'David' 135
'Dolgo' 135
'Donald Wyman' 135
'Doubloons' 135
'Flame' 135
Golden Raindrops® 135
Guinevere® 135
'Haralson' 132
Harvest Gold® 135
'Honeycrisp' 132
'Hopa' 135
'Indian Magic' 135
'Indian Summer' 185
'Jewelberry' 185
'Kelsey' 185
Lancelot® 185
'Liset' 185
'Louisa' 185
Madonna® 185
'Mary Potter' 185
'Molten Lava® 185
'Oekonomierat
Echtermeyer' 185
'Ormiston Roy' 185
'Pink Spires' 185
'Prairifire' **146-47**, 185
'Professor Sprenger' **165**, 186
'Profusion' 186
'Purple Prince' 186
'Radiant' 186
'Red Barron' 186
'Red Jade' 186
Red Jewel® 186
'Red Splendor' 186
'Robinson' 186
'Royalty' 186
'Selkirk' 186
'Sentinel' 186
'Sinai Fire' 186
'Snowcloud' 186
'Snowdrift' 187
'Sparkler' 187
'Spring Snow' 132, 187
'Strawberry Parfait' 187
Sugar Tyme® 187
'Thunderchild' 187
'Van Eseltine' 187
'Vanguard' 187
Velvet Pillar® 187
Weeping Candy Apple® 187
'White Cascade' 187
'Winter Gold' 187
Zestar™ 132
baccata 187-88
'Columnaris' 188
'Jackii' 188

mandshurica 188
'Walters' 188
coronaria 188
'Charlottae' 188
floribunda 188-89
ioensis 189
'Plena' 189
prunifolia 189
sargentii 189-90
'Candymint' 189
Firebird™ 190
'Rosea' 190
'Tina' 190
x zumi 190
calocarpa 190
Maney T.J. 113
Maple 31-39
Amur 38-39
boxelder 33, 37
hard 37
hedge 32-33
Japanese 31
Manchurian 39
Miyabe 39
mountain 38
Norway 33-35
red 35-36
paperbark 39
Rocky Mountain 39
scarlet 35-36
silver 36
striped 39
sugar 37
sycamore 39
Tatarian 38
three-leaved 39
whitebark 37
Marshall, Humphrey *Arbustrum
Americanum* 37, 129, 272
Matrimony vine
Chinese 128
common 127-28
Mayday tree 217
Menispermum
canadense 190
Metasequoia
glyptostroboides 190-91
Michigan State University 187
Microbiota
decussata 191
Microclimates 4, 11-12
Milton Nursery 35
Minnesota Landscape
Arboretum 4
Home Demonstration
Garden 31, 38
Introductions list 183
Mission Gardens 276
Missouri Botanical Garden 107
Mitchell, Henry *One Man's
Garden* 53, 54, 234
Mitchella
repens 191

Monrovia Nursery 114, 116, 119
Moonseed
    common 190
Morden Experiment Station 87,
    97, 98, 99, 116, 127, 185,
    186, 208, 209, 212, 213,
    231, 235, 236, 237, 243
Morphology
    bark 283
    bud 282
    flower 283-84
    fruit 284-85
    leaf 282-83
    pith 283
Morton Arboretum 32, 83,
    93, 269
Morus
    alba
        tatarica 191-92
    rubra 192
Mt. Cuba Center 81
Mountain ash
    European 248-49
    Korean 248
    oak-leaved 249
    showy 249
Mulberry
    red 192
    Russian 191-92
Multi-trunked
    selection list 154
Musclewood 63-64
Myrica
    pensylvanica 192
Myrtle 275

Nannyberry 273
National Arboretum 111
Native plants
    selection list 165-68
Native Americans 45, 50, 57
Nebraska Experiment Sta. 208
Nemerov, Howard *Above* 209;
    The Consent 102; *Spell*
    Before Winter 231; *Trees* 5
Nemopanthus
    mucronatus 192
New York Exp. Sta. 187
Ninebark
    common 199
    mountain 199
Nomenclature 281-82
North Dakota Agricultural
    Exp. Sta. 96
North Dakota State U. 100,
    114, 116, 220, 250
Nylund, Kay 216
Nylund, Robert 216
Nyssa
    sylvatica 192-93

Oak 221-24
    black 224

bur 223
Chinkapin 223
English 224
Mongolian 223
mossycup 223
northern pin 222
pin 223-24
red 224
scarlet 222
shingle 223
swamp white 222
white 221-22
yellow chestnut 223
Olive
    autumn 91
    Russian 90-91
Orange
    Osage 128
Ornamental trees
    selection list 146-47
Ortloff, H. Stuart *The Book of*
    Landscape Design 136
Ostrya
    virginiana 193
Ottawa Research Sta. 197, 277

Pachysandra 193-94
Pachysandra
    procumbens 193-94
    terminalis **155**, 194
        'Green Carpet' 194
        'Green Sheen' 194
        'Variegata' 194
Paeonia
    suffruticosa 194
Pagoda tree
    Japanese 247
Parkling lot
    selection list 174-75
Parkinson, John *Paradisi in*
    Sole 60, 191-92
Parthenocissus
    inserta 194-95
    quinquefolia 195
        engelmannii 195
    tricuspidata **153**, 195
Partridgeberry 191
Patmore, Richard 100
Paulownia
    royal 195
Paulownia
    tomentosa 195
Paxistima
    Canby 196
Paxistima
    canbyi 196
Peony
    tree 194
Pear 220
    Callery 220
    Chinese sand 220
    Ussurian 220

Pearlbush
    Korean 95
Peashrub
    littleleaf 62-63
    pygmy 63
    Russian 62
    shortleaf 62
    Siberian 61-62
Peattie, Donald *A Natural*
    History of Trees 35, 57,
    72, 105, 122
Pellett, Harold 35, 81, 255
Pemmican 45
Perennials
    woody plants considered as 152
Periwinkle 275
Pests 23
Phellodendron
    'His Majesty' 196
    amurense **145**, 196-97
        Macho® 197
    sachalinense 197
Philadelphus
    'Buckley's Quill' 197
    'Miniature Snowflake' 197
    'Snowgoose' 197
    coronarius 197-98
        'Aureus' 198
    lewisii 198
        'Blizzard' 198
        'Waterton' 198
    x *virginalis* 198
        'Minnesota Snowflake' 198
        'Minnesota Snowflake
Dwarf' 198
        'Virginal' 198
Phillips, Robert 238, 239
Physocarpus
    monogynus 199
    opulifolius **149**, 199
        'Dart's Gold' 199
        'Luteus' 199
        'Nanus' 199
        'Nugget' 199
        'Snowfall' 199
Picea
    abies 200-01
        'Acrocona' **154-55**, 200
        'Clanbrassiliana' 200
        'Little Gem' 200
        'Mucronata' 200
        'Nidiformis' 200
        'Pendula' 200
        'Pumila' 201
    engelmannii 202
    glauca 201
        'Conica' 201
        'Densata' 201
    mariana 201
        'Nana' 201
    omorika 201-02
        'Nana' 202

pungens 202
    'Bakeri' 202
    'Fat Albert' 202
    glauca 202, **182-83**
    'Globosa' 202
    'Hoopsii' 202
    'Moerheimii' 202
    'Montgomery' 202
Pine 203-07
    Austrian 205
    bristle-cone 203
    eastern white 206-07
    hickory 203
    Himalayan 207
    Jack 203-04
    Japanese red 204
    Japanese umbrella 204
    Korean 205
    limber 204
    Mugo 205
    Norway 206
    Ponderosa 205-06
    red 206
    Scotch 207
    Swiss mountain 205
    Swiss stone 204
    western yellow 205-06
    white 206-07
Pinus 203-07
    aristata 203
    banksiana 203-04
        'Uncle Fogy' 204
    cembra 204
        sibirica 204
    densiflora 204
        'Umbraculifera' 204
    flexilis 204
    koraiensis 205
    mugo 205
        'Compacta' 205
        pumilio 205
    nigra 205
    ponderosa
        scopulorum 205-06
    resinosa 206
        'Wissota' 206
    strobus 206-07
        'Contorta' 206
        'Fastigiata' 206
        'Nana' 207
        'Pendula' 207
    sylvestris 207
        'Fastigiata' 207
        'Watereri' 207
    wallichiana 207
Pinxterbloom 230
Plane tree
    London 207
Plant names 3
Platanus
    x *acerifolia* 207
    occidentalis 208

Plum 214
  beach 216
  Canada 216
  flowering 214, 218
  wild 214
Plumfield Nursery 118-19, 267
Pollution
  air pollution tolerant list 182
Poplar 208-11
  balsam 211
  black 210
  Bolleana 209
  Japanese 211
  lanceleaf 210
  Lombardy 210
  narrowleaf 210
  Sargent 209
  Theves 210
  white 209
Populus 208-11
  'Highland' 208
  'Nor'easter' 208
  'Prairie Sky' 208
  'Robusta' 209
  'Tower' 209
  x acuminata 210
  alba 209
    'Pyramidalis' 209
  angustifolia 210
  balsamifera 211
  deltoides 209
    monilifera 209
    'Siouxland' 209
  grandidentata 211
  maximowiczii 211
  nigra 210
    'Afghanica' 210
    'Italica' 210
  tremula 211
  tremuloides 210
    'Pikes Bay' 210
Porcelain berry 48-49
Porter-Walton Co. 100
Potentilla 211-12
  wineleaf 212
Potentilla
  fruticosa 211-12
    'Abbotswood' 211
    'Coronation Triumph' 211
    Dakota Goldrush™ 211
    Dakota Sunspot™ 211
    'Farreri' 211
    'Gold Drop' see *P.f.* 'Farreri'
    'Goldfinger' 211
    'Jackmanii' 211
    'Katherine Dykes' 211
    'Longacre' 212
    'McKay's White' 212
    'Mount Everest' 212
    'Pink Beauty' 212
    'Primrose Beauty' 212
    'Red Ace' 212
    'Snowbird' 212

'Tangerine' 212
'Yellow Gem' 212
tridentata 212
Preston, Elizabeth 256, 258
Princeton Nurseryman's
  Research Assoc. 37, 47, 86,
  103, 104, 186
Prinsepia
  cherry 212
Prinsepia
  sinensis 212
Privet
  Amur 123
  common 123
  Regel 123
Protected locations 4
Pruning 23-25
Prunus 213-219
  'Alderman' 214
  'Meteor' 213
  'Moongold' 213
  'Newport' 214
  'North Star' 213
  'Pipestone' 214
  'Scout' 213
  'Sungold' 213
  'Superior' 214
  'Toka' 214
  'Underwood' 214
  americana **169**, 214
  armeniaca mandshurica see
    P. mandshurica
  besseyi 214
  x cistena 214-15
  fruticosa 215
  glandulosa 215
    'Alboplena' 215
    'Rosea' 215
    'Sinensis' 215
  maackii **155**, 215
  mandshurica 216
  maritima 216
  nigra 216
    'Princess Kay' **146-47**, 216
  padus 216-17
    commutata 217
    pensylvanica 217
    'Stockton' 217
  sargentii 217
  serotina 217
  tenella 218
  tomentosa 218
  triloba 218
    simplex 218
    'Multiplex' 218
  virginiana 218-19
    'Canada Red' see *P. v.*
      'Schubert'
    leucocarpa 219
    melanocarpa 219
    'Schubert' 219
Pseudotsuga
  menziesii

glauca **180-81**, 219
Ptelea
  trifoliata 219
Pyrus
  'Golden Spice' 220
  'Luscious' 220
  'Parker' 220
  'Patten' 220
  'Summercrisp' 220
  calleryana 220
  ussuriensis 220
  Mountain Frost™ 220
  Prairie Gem® 220

Quercus 221-24
  Heritage® 221
  Regal Prince® 221
  alba **144, 168**, 221-22
  bicolor 222
  borealis see *Q. rubra*
  coccinea 222
  ellipsoidalis 222
  imbricaria 223
  macrocarpa 223
  mongolica 223
  muehlenbergii 223
  palustris **143**, 223-24
  robur 224
  rubra 224
  velutina 224
Quince
  flowering 69

Raspberry
  black 242
  boulder 242
  flowering 241
  Japanese 242
Raulston, J.C. 69
Raymore, Henry B. *The Book of
  landscape Design* 136
Rea, John *Flora* 42, 238,
  260, 264
Redbud
  eastern 69
Redwood
  dawn 190-91
Registered 282
Rehder, Alfred 201
Rhamnus
  catharticus 225
  frangula 225
    'Asplenifolia' 225
    'Columnaris' 225
    'Tallhedge' see *R.f.*
      'Columnaris'
Rhododendron 225-30
  Carolina 230
  Catawba 228-29
  Dahurian 229
  Korean 229
  Manchurian 229
  rosebay 230

Rhododendron 225-30
  'Aglo' 227
  'Apricot Surprise' 226
  'Elviira' 227
  Exbury Hybrids 226-27
  'Golden Lights' 226
  'Haaga' 227
  'Hellikki' 227
  'Lemon Lights' 226
  'Mandarin Lights' 226
  Marjatta Hybrids 227
  'Mikkeli' 227
  Mollis Hybrids 227
  'Northern Hi-lights' 226
  'Northern Lights' 226
  Northern Lights Series 226
  'Northern Starburst' 227
  'Orchid Lights' **cover**,
    137, 226
  P.J.M. Hybrids 227
  'Peter Tigerstedt' 227
  'Pink Lights' 226
  'Rosy Lights' **183**, 226
  'Spicy Lights' 226
  'White Lights' 226
  arborescens 227-28
  atlanticum 228
  austrinum 228
  calendulaceum 228
  canadense 228
  catawbiense 228-29
  dauricum 229
  japonicum 229
  maximum 230
  minus 230
  micranthum 229
  mucronulatum 229
    'Cornell Pink' 229
  periclymenoides 230
  prinophyllum see *R. austrinum*
  roseum see *R. austrinum*
  schlippenbachii 230
  vaseyi 230
  viscosum 230
  yedoense
    poukhanense 230
Rhodora 228
Rhodotypos
  scandens 230
Rhus
  aromatica 230-31
    'Gro-low' 231
  copallina 232
  glabra 231
    cismontana 231
    'Laciniata' 231
    'Morden Select' 231
  radicans 232
  trilobata 231
  typhina 231-32
    'Laciniata' **169**, 232
  vernix 232

Ribes
  'Red Lake' 232
  alpinum **156**, 232-33
    'Green Mound' 233
  aureum 233
  nigrum 233
  odoratum 233
  sativum see *R. silvestre*
  silvestre 233
Robinia
  hispida 233
  pseudoacacia 234
    'Frisia' 234
    'Inermis' 234
    'Purple Robe' 234
    'Pyramidalis' 234
    'Umbraculifera' 234
Rosa 235-41
  'A. MacKenzie 235
  'Adelaide Hoodless' 235
  'Agnes' 236
  'Assiniboine' 236
  'Belle Poitevine' 236
  'Blanc Double de
    Coubert' 236
  Bonica® 236
  'Captain Samuel Holland' 236
  Carefree Beauty™ 236
  Carefree Delight™ 236
  Carefree Wonder™ **150**, 236
  'Champlain' 236
  'Charles Albanel' 236
  'Cuthbert Grant' 236
  'David Thompson' 236
  'DeMontarville' 236
  'F.J. Grootendorst' 236
  'Frau Dagmar Hartropp' 237
  'Frontenac' 237
  'George Vancouver' 237
  'Grootendorst Supreme' 237
  'Hansa' 237
  'Harison's Yellow' 237
  'Henry Hudson' 237
  'Henry Kelsey' 237
  'Hope for Humanity' 237
  'J.P. Connell' 237
  'Jens Munk' 237
  'John Cabot' 237
  'John Davis' 237
  'John Franklin' 237
  'Lambert Closse' 237
  'Lillian Gibson' 238
  'Louis Jolliet' 238
  'Martin Frobisher' 238
  'Morden Blush' 238
  'Morden Centennial' 238
  'Morden Fireglow' 238
  'Morden Ruby' 238
  'Nearly Wild' 238
  'Pink Grootendorst' 238
  'Prairie Dawn' 238
  'Prairie Fire' 238
  'Prairie Joy' 238

'Robusta' **162**, 238
'Rosa Mundi' 238
'Royal Edward' 239
'Seven Sisters' 239
'Simon Fraser' 239
'Sir Thomas Lipton' 239
'The Fairy' 239
'Therese Bugnet' 239
'Viking Queen' 239
'William Baffin' **174**, 239
'William Booth' 239
'Winnipeg Parks' 239
blanda 239
foetida 239-40
  'Bicolor' 240
  'Persiana' 240
glauca 240
x harisonii see
  R. 'Harison's Yellow'
hugonis see
  R. xanthina hugonis
pimpinellifolia 240
pomifera see *R. villosa*
rubrifolia see *R. glauca*
rugosa 240
  'Alba' 240
  'Albo-plena' 240
  'Plena' 240
spinosissima see
  R. pimpinellifolia
villosa 240-41
xanthina
  hugonis 241
Rose, Nancy 49
Rosemary, bog 49
Roses 235-41
  apple 240-41
  Austrian brier 239-40
  Austrian copper 240
  Father Hugo's 241
  Persian yellow 240
  redleaf 240
  rugosa 240
  Scotch 240
Ross, Henry 135
Rowan tree 248-49
Rubus **164**
  allegheniensis 242
  deliciosus 242
  occidentalis 242
  odoratus 241
  parviflorus 241-42
  parvifolius 242

Sackville-West, Vita *Country
  Notes* 106; *In Your
  Garden* 109; *In Your
  Garden Again* 79
Sage
  mountain 53
Sagebrush 52
  fringed 53

St. John's-Wort
  Kalm's 110
  shrubby 110
Salix 242-45
  'Flame' 242
  'Golden Curls' 242
  'Prairie Cascade' 243
  alba 243
    'Britzensis' 243
    'Tristis' see *S. x sepulcralis
      chrysocoma*
    vitellina 243
  amygdaloides 245
  arenaria 245
  x blanda see *S. pendulina*
  caprea 243
    'Pendula' 243
  discolor 243
  matsudana 244
    'Tortuosa' 244
  x pendulina 244
  pentandra 244
  purpurea 244-45
    'Gracilis' 244
    'Nana' 245
  *x sepulcralis
    chrysocoma*
Salt tree
  Siberian 105-06
Sambucus
  canadensis 245
    'Adams' 245
    'Aurea' 245
    'Johns' 245
    'Laciniata' 245
    'York' 245
  pubens 246
  racemosa 246
    'Sutherland Gold' 246
Sampson, D.R. 96
Sandcherry
  Cistena 214-15
  purpleleaf 214-15
  western 214
Saratoga Horticultural
  Foundation 102
Sargent, Charles Sprague 118;
  Garden & Forest 36;
  Silva of North America 30,
  45, 55, 86, 104, 193, 271
Sarsaparilla
  bristly 49-50
Sassafras 246
Sassafras
  albidum 246
Schichtel's Nursery 259
Schmidt, J. Frank Nursery 32,
  34, 36, 135, 248-49, 268
Scientific names 281
Screening
  selection list 156

Serviceberry, Alleghany 47
  apple 46-47
  downy 46
  running 47
  Saskatoon 45-46
  shadblow 46
Shadblow 46
Shade trees
  selection list 143-45
Shade tolerant
  selection list 173
Shakespeare, William 130
Shannon, Jerry 4
Shannon, Lee 4
Shelterbelts
  selection list 157
Shepherdia
  argentea 246
  canadensis 246-47
Sheridan Nursery 114, 259, 266
Sherwood Nursery 116
Sheyenne Gardens 255
Shrubs *see* Woody plants &
  specific shrubs
Silverbell
  Carolina 105
  mountain 105
Silverberry 91
Simpson Nursery 88, 111, 135,
  185, 186
Skinner, Frank 125, 256, 257
Skinner Nursery 36, 74
Smilax 247
Smilax
  hispida 247
Smokebush 83
Smoketree
  American 83
Snowberry 253-54
  creeping 101
Soapweed 278-79
Soils 10-11
  selection list for acidic 168
  selection list for alkaline 174
  selection list for dry 169
  selection list for stabilization 175
  selection list for wet 171
  improvement 15-16
Sophora
  japonica 247
Sorbaria
  sorbifolia **178**, 247
Sorbus
  alnifolia **179**, 248
  americana 248
  aucuparia 248-49
    Cardinal Royal® 248-49
  decora 249
  x hybrida 249
South Dakota Agricultural
  Exp.Sta. 96, 214
South Dakota State University
  135, 199, 209, 215

South Wilton Nurseries 116
Southernwood 52
Sowerby, James
    English Botany 32-33
Species 281
Spindle tree
  Chinese 94
  European 93
Spiraea
    'Goldmound' 249
  albiflora see *S.j.* 'Albiflora'
  x *arguta* 249-50
    'Compacta' 250
  x *billardii* 250
  bumalda see *S.j.* 'Bumalda'
  japonica 250-51
    'Albiflora' **175**, 250
    'Alpina' 250
    'Anthony Waterer' 250
    'Bumalda' 250
    'Coccinea' 250
    'Crispa' 250
    Dakota Goldcharm™ 250
    'Dart's Red' 251
    'Froebelii' **156**, 251
    Golden Princess® 251
    'Goldflame' 251
    'Gumball' 251
    'Limemound' 251
    'Little Princess' 251
    'Magic Carpet' 251
    'Norman' 251
    'Shirobana' 251
  x *multiflora* 252
  nipponica 251
    'Halward's Silver' 251
    'Snowmound' 251
  prunifolia 253
  thunbergii 252
    'Fujino' 252
    Mellow Yellow® 252
  trilobata 252
    'Fairy Queen' 252
  x *vanhouttei* 252
    'Renaissance' 252
Spirea
  Billard 250
  blue 65
  bridalwreath 253
  garland 249-50
  Japanese 250
  Nippon 251
  snow garland 252
  threelobe 252
  Thunberg 252
  Ural false 247
  Vanhoutte 252
Spruce
  black 201
  Black Hills 201
  Colorado 202
  dwarf Alberta 201
  dwarf Serbian 202

Engelmann 202
Norway 200-01
Serbian 201-02
white 201
Spurge
Alleghany 193-94
Japanese 194
Staphylea
  trifolia 253
Stephanandra
  cutleaf 253
Stephanandra
  incisa 253
    'Crispa' 253
Street trees
  selection lists 138-41
Sumac
  fragrant 230-31
  poison 232
  shining 232
  skunkbush 231
  smooth 231
  staghorn 231-32
Summersweet 77-78, **163**
Summit Nurseries 100
Sutherland Exp. Sta. 246
Sutherland Nurseries 119
Sweet fern 78
Sweetshrub 60-61
Sycamore 208
Symphoricarpos
  albus 253-54
    laevigatus 254
  x *chenaultii* 254
    'Hancock' 254
  occidentalis 254
  orbiculatus 254
Syringa 255-62
    'Aladdin' 255
    'Minuet' 255
    'Miss Canada' 255
    Tinkerbelle™ 255
  amurensis see *S. reticulata*
  x *chinensis* 256
    'Alba' 256
    'Saugeana' 256
  x *hyacinthiflora* 256
    'Asessippi' **163**, 256
    'Blanche Sweet' 256
    'Evangeline' 256
    'Excel' 256
    'Gertrude Leslie' 256
    'Maiden's Blush' 256
    'Mount Baker' 257
    'Pocahontas' **180-81**, 257
  meyeri 257
    'Palibin' 257
  microphylla 262
  oblata 257
    'Cheyenne' 257
    dilatata 257
  palibiniana see *S. meyeri*

patula 257-58
  'Miss Kim' **180**, 258
pekinensis 258
x *persica* 258
x *prestoniae* 258-59
  'Agnes Smith' 258
  'Coral' 258
  'Donald Wyman' 258
  'Isabella' 258
  'James Macfarlane' 258
reticulata 259
  'Ivory Silk' 259
  'Summer Snow' 259
rothomagensis see *S.* x *chinensis*
villosa 259
vulgaris 259-62
  'Adelaide Dunbar' 260
  'Alba' 260
  'Albert F. Holden' 260
  'Alphonse Lavelle' 260
  'Andenken an Ludwig
    Spaeth/Ludwig
    Spaeth' 260
  'Arch McKean' 260
  'Avalanche' 260
  'Belle de Nancy' 260
  'Charles Joly' 260
  'Charles X' 260
  'Charm' 260
  'Congo' 260
  'Edith Cavell' 260
  'Katherine Havemeyer' 260
  'Krasavitsa Muskovy/Beauty
    of Moscow' 260
  'Lucie Baltet' 261
  'Macrostachya' 261
  'Marechal Lannes' 261
  'Marie Frances' 261
  'Marie Legraye' 261
  'Michel Buchner' 261
  'Miss Ellen Willmott' 261
  'Mme Lemoine' 261
  'Monge' 261
  'Montaigne' 261
  'Mrs Edward Harding' 261
  'Mrs W.E. Marshall' 261
  'Night' 261
  'Paul Thirion' 261
  'President Grevy' 261
  'President Lincoln' 261
  'President Poincare' 261
  'Primrose' 261
  'Sarah Sands' 261
  'Sensation' 261
  'Vestale' 261
  'Victor Lemoine' 261
  'Wedgwood Blue' 261
  'Wonderblue' 261
  'Yankee Doodle' 261

Tacamahac 211
Tamarack 121-22

Tamarisk 262
Tamarix
  ramosissima 262
    'Summer Glow' 262
Taxodium
  distichum 263
Taxus
  canadensis 263
  cuspidata 263
    'Capitata' 263
    'Cross Spreading' 263
    'Nana' 263
  x *media* 264
    'Dark Green' 264
    'Nigra' 264
    'Taunton' **173**, 264
Tea
  Labrador 122
  New Jersey 66-67
Texas Nursery 116
Thimbleberry 241-42
Thoreau, Henry David *Journal*
  43, 65, 132, 206, 221, 243,
  269; *A Week on the Concord
  and Merrimack Rivers* 203,
  267; *Thoreau's Minnesota
  Journey* 189, 209, 223,
  279; *Walden* 231, 259
Thuja
  occidentalis 264-66
    'Aurea' 265
    'Brandon' 265
    'Dark Green' see *T.o.* 'Nigra'
    'Gold Cargo' 265
    'Hetz Midget' 265
    'Holmstrup' 265
    'Little Gem' 265
    'Little Giant' 265
    'Nigra' 265
    'Pygmy Globe' 265
    'Pyramidalis' 265
    'Sherman' 265
    'Techny' 266
    'Wareana' 266
    'Woodwardii' 266
Tichner, Robert 51
Tilia
    'Glenleven' 266
    'Harvest Gold' 266
  americana 266-67
    'Boulevard' 267
    'Fastigiata' 267
    Frontyard® 267
    Legend® 267
    'Redmond' 267
    'Sentry' 267
  cordata 267-68
    Greenspire® 268
    Norlin™ 268
    'Olympic' 268
    Shamrock® 268
  mongolica 268

Toxicodendron
  radicans 232
  vernix 232
Trademark 282
Tradescant, John 35
Tree of heaven 43
Trees *see* Woody Plants &
      specific trees
Trumpet vine 61
Tsuga
  canadensis 268
    'Pendula' 268
Tulip tree 124
Tupelo 192-93
Twinflower 124

Ulmus
  americana 269
  davidiana 269
    japonica see *U. japonica*
  glabra 269
  japonica 269
  pumila 269
  rubra 269
  thomasii 269
United States Department of
    Agriculture 39
University of British Columbia 52
University of Helsinki 227
University of Illinois 108, 185
University of Minnesota
    introductions list 183
University of New Hampshire
    258, 259
University of Wisconsin 269

Vaccinium **182-83**
    'Chippewa' 270
    'Northblue' 270
    'Northcountry' 270
    'Northsky' 270
    'Polaris' 270
    'St Cloud' 270
  angustifolium 270
  corymbosum 270
  macrocarpon 270
  vitis-idaea 270
    minus 270
Van Vloten Nursery 115
Viburnum 271-75
  Burkwood 275
  common snowball 273
  downy 274
  Koreanspice 275
  mapleleaf 271
  Sargent highbush 274
Viburnum 271-75
    'Emerald Triumph' 271
  acerifolium 271
  alnifolium see *V. lantanoides*
  x *burkwoodii* 275
  carlesii 275
  cassinoides 271-72

  dentatum 272
    Northern Burgundy® 272
  lantana 272
    'Mohican' 272
  lantanoides 272-73
  lentago 273
  opulus 273
    'Compactum' 273
    'Nanum' 273
    'Roseum' 273
    'Xanthocarpum' 273
  prunifolium 274
  rafinesquianum 274
  sargentii 274
    'Onondaga' 274
  trilobum **148, 158, 164**, 274-75
    'Alfredo' 275
    'Compactum' 275
    'Wentworth' 275
Vinca 275
Vinca
  minor 275
Vines
  selection lists 152
Virgin's bower 77
Vitis
    'Edelweiss' 276
    'Frontenac' 276
    'Swenson Red' 276
  riparia 276
Vogel, Ken 255

Wahoo 93
Walnut
  black 112
  English 112
  Persian 112
Waltham Field Sta. 227
Wandell, Willet 37, 46, 98, 103
Ware, George 269
Watering 17
Wayfaringbush 272
Weeping habit
  selection list 154
Weigela 276-77
Weigela
    'Centennial' 276
    'Java Red' 276
    'Minuet' 276
    'Pink Delight' 276
    'Pink Princess' 276
    'Polka' 276
    'Red Prince' 276
    'Rumba' 277
  florida 277
Weston Nurseries 227
Wet soil
  selection list 171
Willow 242-45
  creeping 245
  goat 243
  golden weeping 245
  laurel 244

  Niobe weeping 244-45
  peach-leaved 245
  Pekin 244
  purple osier 244-45
  pussy 243
  white 243
  Wisconsin weeping 244
Wilson, E.H. *Aristocrats of the*
      Garden 102; *China*
      Mother of Gardens 128;
      If I Were to Make a
      Garden 67-68, 77
Winter protection 22-23
Winterberry 111
Wintercreeper 93-94
Wintergreen 101
Wisteria 277-78
  Japanese 278
  Kentucky 277
Wisteria
  floribunda 278
  macrostachya 277
    'Aunt Dee' 277
Witchhazel
  common 106
  vernal 106
Witherod 271-72
Woadwaxen
  common 101-02
Wolfberry 254
Woodbine 194-95
Woody plants
  maintenance 21-25
  planting 15-17
  selection 12
  value to landscape 3, 9
Wright, Percy 187
Wyman, Donald *Trees for*
      American Gardens 68

Xanthoceras
  sorbifolium 278
Xanthorhiza
  simplicissima 278

Yellowhorn 278
Yellowroot 278
Yellowwood 72
Yew
  American 263
  Canadian 263
  Japanese 263
Yucca 278-79
Yucca
  filamentosa 278
  glauca 278-79

Zanthoxylum
  americanum 279
Zins, Mike 202
Zwinger, Ann *Land Above the*
      Trees 122; *Beyond the Aspen*
      Grove 210; *The Nearsighted*
      Naturalist 5